Signed
au

CW00794265

Le dea-mhéin an údair,
James O'Shea 9 December 1999.

PRINCE OF
SWINDLERS

JOHN SADLEIR M.P. 1813 – 1856

JAMES O'SHEA

GEOGRAPHY PUBLICATIONS

Published in Ireland by
Geography Publications,
Kennington Road,
Templeogue, Dublin 6W

ISBN 0 906602 56 4

Design and typesetting by Phototype-Set, Lee Road, Dublin Industrial Estate, Dublin 11.
Printed by the Leinster Leader, Naas, Co. Kildare.

FOR
FRANCES, BREDA, DEIRDRE, BILL
AND
CATHAL

Contents

List of Plates

PLATES BETWEEN PAGES 278 AND 279

Sadleir family tree
Kilnahalagh Castle
Shronell House
Sopwell Hall
Old James Scully of Kilfeacle
James Scully of Shanballymore
James Scully of Athassel
Frank Scully MP
Clongowes College entrance
Clongowes College
Memorial of Nicholas Sadleir
Great Denmark Street, Dublin location of John Sadleir's Dublin office
Emo Court, one of Sadleir's purchases under the Encumbered Estates
    Act
Mitchelstown Castle, one of John Sadleir's purchases under the
    Encumbered Estates Act
Parliament of 1847 in which John Sadleir sat as MP for Carlow
Jack Straw's Castle, Hampstead Heath behind which John Sadleir was
    found dead

Abbreviations

A.S.	*Athlone Sentinel.*
B.H.	*Buck's Herald, Uxbridge Advertiser, Windsor and Eton Journal.*
B.M.	*Bankers' Magazine.*
B. N.	*Belfast Newsletter.*
B.U.	*Banner of Ulster.*
C.C.	*Clonmel Chronicle.*
C.P.	*Carlow Post.*
C.R.	*Clongowes Record.*
C.S.	*Carlow Sentinel.*
C.S.N.	*Champion or Sligo News.*
C.T.	*Catholic Telegraph and Irish Sun.*
D.D.A., C.P.	Dublin Diocesan Archives, Papers of Archbishop Paul Cullen.
D.D.A., M.P.	Dublin Diocesan Archives, Papers of Archbishop Patrick Murray.
D.E.M.	*Dublin Evening Mail.*
D.E.P.	*Dublin Evening Post.*
D.N.B., e.v.	*Dictionary of National Biography, electronic version.*
F.J.	*Freeman's Journal.*
G.V.	*Galway Vindicator and Connaught Advertiser.*
I.C.D.	*Irish Catholic Directory.*
I.C.L.R.	*Irish Common Law Reports.*
I.C.R.	*Irish Chancery Reports.*
I.G.	*Irish Genealogist.*
K.D.A., H.P.	Kildare and Leighlin Archives, Bishop Haly Papers.
L.E.	*Leinster Express.*
L.R.	*Limerick Reporter.*
M.G.	*Manchester Guardian.*
N.A. , C.S.O., R.P.	National Archives, Chief Secretary's Office, Registered Papers
N.G.	*Nenagh Guardian.*
N.L.I.	National Library Ireland.
P.R.O.I.	Public Record Office of Ireland.
P.R.O.N.I.	Public Record Office of Northern Ireland.
R.T.	*Railway Times .*
S.C.	*Sligo Chronicle.*
S.J.	*Sligo Journal.*
S.N.	*Saunders Newsletter.*
T.F.P.	*Tipperary Free Press.*
T.L.	*Tipperary Leader.*
W.C.	*Waterford Chronicle.*
W.M.	*Waterford Mail.*
W.N.	*Waterford News and General Advertiser.*
W.T.	*Weekly Telegraph.*

Foreword

John Sadleir is an appropriate subject for a book. He was a member of parliament, a prominent businessman, a banker, one of the world's greatest swindlers and a suicide. Ingredients for a novel, one might think, and fiction possibilities have been explored by nineteenth century novelists like Dickens, Lever, or Bradden, who modelled some of their villains on him.

Historians have consigned him to a few articles in journals and newspapers or brief references in major works. Political analysts may view him as a minor hiccup on the stormy seas of mid-nineteenth century politics, and economic historians see his swindles as part of the financial instability of the time. Yet he is part of the mid-Victorian middle-class dynamic; an Irishman from an obscure rural parish in west Tipperary whose wealthy connections, ruthlessness, ambition and speculative nature made him dream of vast wealth and high political office. For a time it seemed as if these would materialise but his eventual resorting to corruption and fraud ended the dream on a cold winter's evening on Hampstead Heath, and brought misery to thousands of people, not least his family and relatives who bore the shame of his infamy and who were subjected to years of litigation in the courts.

Because Sadleir's career was so brief there is no collection of private papers for the historian to draw on. Presumably, too, his family had no desire to preserve the material of one who caused them so much shame. I am, therefore, very grateful to all who assisted me in my research. Much of this was done in London and I appreciate the kindness of the staffs in the British Library, the Newspaper Library in Colindale and the Public Record Office in Kew. My thanks also to Ms. Eileen Robinson of the Victoria and Albert Museum, Mrs C.S. Scott, Librarian in the Reform Club, Mr H.S. Cobb, Clerk of the Records, House of Lords and Mr George Charteris, Librarian of the Irish Genealogical Research Society. I also thank Mr Brian MacDermot of Suffolk, an expert on the Scully family, Sadleir's maternal relatives. I very much appreciate the invaluable assistance of Mr Peter Dougherty of the London Metropolitan Police in tracing Sadleir's unmarked grave, bringing me to Standon to see Sadlier tombs. I must also thank Mr Trevor Parkhill of the Public Record Office Northern Ireland and Ms. Mary L. Robinson, Curator of manuscripts in the Huntington Library, San Marino, California. A special word of appreciation to Dr Noel

Kissane, Mr Martin Ryan, Mr Jim O'Shea and the staff in the National Library of Ireland for their unfailing courtesy and professionalism. I am grateful to Fr. Kevin Kennedy, archivist in Holy Cross College, Clonliffe, Mrs V. Cremin and Ms. Mary B. Higgins in Trinity College, Ms. Anne Neary of the State Paper Office, Dublin Castle, Mr K. Hannigan, archivist in the Public Record Office of Ireland, Mr Eddie Mackey of the Law Society of Ireland Library, Ms. Sinéad O'Gorman of King's Inns Library, Mr Roderick Tierney, O'Hagans solicitors, Harcourt Street , Fr. Stephen Redmond S.J., archivist of the Society of Jesus in Ireland, Fr. F.J. Turner, Stonyhurst College, and the Dr John B. O'Brien, University College, Cork. I owe a special words of thanks to those who aided me nearer home. The encouragement of Mr Martin Maher, County Librarian, Thurles, was always forthcoming, and Ms. Norma McDermott of that same library and now Director of an Comhairle Leabharlanna, was most helpful. Ms.Mary Guinan Darmody, her successor as archivist, was equally kind and efficient. I will always be indebted to the late Archbishop Thomas Morris, Fr. Christopher O'Dwyer and Dr Maurice Dooley, St. Patrick's College, Thurles, Dom Mark Tierney of Glenstal Abbey, Fr Fearghus Ó Fearghail, St. Kieran's College, Kilkenny, Mr Michael O'Dwyer B.A., Kilkenny, Ms. Carmel Flahavan, Carlow County Library, and Br Linus Walker, Archivist in Bishop's House, Carlow. I would like to record my appreciation of assistance by Mr William Corbett B.A., Mr Déaglán Breathnach B.A., H.D.E, Mr John O'Grady B.A., H.D.E., Mr Patrick J. O'Meara, solicitor, the late Dean David Woodward, the Doctors Knightly, who now live in Shronell House, where John Sadleir was born, Mr Michael Ramsden of Sopwell Hall, once owned by the Sadleirs of north Tipperary, and Mr Anthony McCan, who supplied the Scully photographs reproduced in this book. A particular word of thanks to Mr John Devane and the board of the Tipperary Leader Group who grant-aided its publication. Finally, I must express my thanks to its publisher, Dr William Nolan, for his kindness, understanding and patience.

Return my brother his letters to me and all other papers. The prayers of one so wicked could not avail or I would seek to pray for those I leave after me, and who will have to suffer such agony. and all owing to my criminal acts.

Oh that I had never quitted Ireland – Oh that I had resisted the first attempts to launch me into speculations.

If I had had less talents of a worthless kind and more firmness I might have remained as I once was, honest and truthful – and I would have lived to see my dear father and mother in their old age – I weep and weep now but what can that avail.

Extract from letter of John Sadleir, on the eve of his suicide, to his cousin Robert Keating.

Chapter 1

Origins and early career

Contemporary reports that John Sadleir came from humble tenant farming stock did little justice to a genealogy traceable to Henry Sadeleyer of Hackney, Middlesex, in the fifteenth century.[1] It is difficult to precisely define his social background, but for a time he was accountant to Sir Edward Belcamp, Chief Butler to Henry VIII, and had the means to rent a house for forty pounds a year in Hackney.[2] Nothing is known of his family apart from two sons, one of whom became a prominent member of the English ruling classes during the reigns of the four Tudor monarchs. These were Sir Ralph Sadleir of Standon in Hertfordshire and John Sadleir of Hackney, from whom descended the two principal Irish branches, the Sadleirs of Sopwell Hall, Cloughjordan in north Tipperary and the Sadleirs of west Tipperary.[3]

The Sopwell Hall line through Sir Ralph had the most distinguished ancestry. He was born in 1507, and at an early stage was received into the family of Thomas Cromwell, whose influence with Henry VIII advanced his career.[4] He prospered under the four Tudor monarchs although as a confirmed Protestant he retired from political involvement during the reign of Queen Mary. He survived until 1587 by which time he had been granted a vast acreage of land in seven counties stretching from Standon to Yorkshire and from Bristol to Cambridgeshire.[5] Throughout the centuries his descendants married into the English aristocracy and gentry.

Sir Ralph's second son, Edward of Temple Dinsley, Hertfordshire, married Anne Lee, the daughter and co-heiress of Sir Richard Lee, the famous military engineer, of Sopwell, Hertfordshire.[6] Edward's son, Richard, inherited Sopwell from his mother, and the North Tipperary connection was made through Richard's fourth son, Colonel Thomas Sadleir, whose career illustrates the Sadleir facility of forging advantageous links with the ruling powers, monarchic or otherwise.[7]

Thomas Sadleir joined the Parliamentary army in 1643, and came to Ireland in 1649 as Commander of an infantry regiment.[8] He then served as Adjutant General under Cromwell, and captured Poulkerry Castle, near Clonmel, where he executed more than thirty of the garrison and incinerated those who refused to surrender.[9] He also captured Ballydine, between Carrick-on-Suir and Clonmel, and went on to take Dunhill castle near Waterford City.[10] He was awarded a gold medal and chain in recognition of his services.

Sadleir was one of those intimately involved in the consolidation of the Cromwellian victory in Ireland. Following the defeat of the Irish forces in 1650, the English parliament appointed four commissioners to govern the country. When they arrived in 1651 they found administrative chaos, plague, famine and crime following a span of almost continuous warfare since the outbreak of the 1641 rebellion. They instituted a system of local government by appointing twelve military governors each in charge of a precinct. Colonel Thomas was appointed Governor and High Sheriff of the Wexford area. As Governor he was responsible, among other things, for assessing its wealth, identifying artisans or craftsmen, deciding the fate of Catholics, receiving petitions, certifying the competency of ministers to preach the puritan doctrine, clearing overcrowded jails.[11]

He was an able administrator, and was rewarded with the representation of Wexford, Carlow and Kilkenny in the parliaments of 1654 to 1655 and 1656 to 1658. He was sent as Governor to Galway in 1658, when the Cromwellian confiscation was nearing completion, following the mapping of the country through Sir William Petty's *Down Survey*.[12] He acquired land in Galway and sat as M.P. for Mayo and Galway in the Parliament of 1658 and 1659.

His career suffered a temporary reverse with the restoration of Charles 11 in 1660, when Lord Broghill[13] had him arrested on suspicion of being involved in an anti-royalist plot.[14] Broghill, however, was anxious to have the Cromwellian land settlement maintained and legalised under the monarchy, and he found Sadleir's explanation sufficiently plausible to release him.

It was through this land settlement that Sadleir established his connection with County Tipperary. His acquisition of land was typical of other Cromwellian officers, who received debentures instead of cash salaries. These debentures were redeemed by land grants equal to the value of salary arrears. Sadleir held debentures for £2,396 arrears, and for an additional £2,308 purchased those held by 146 soldiers, who did not wish to exchange them for land.[15] He exchanged £2,747 of these for the confiscated lands of the McEgan families in the Kilnahalagh area, and refurbished the derelict Kilnahalagh Castle, which he renamed Sopwell Hall.[16]

He subsequently became M.P. for County Tipperary from 1661, when he was appointed High Sheriff of the county. During that period he married his second wife, Mary Salmon, widow of Vincent Gookin, who had been Surveyor General of Ireland.[17] This is an indication of former intimacy with Gookin, an influential figure in the distribution of land to Cromwellian officers.

The Sadleirs of Sopwell Hall were among the leading landowners and gentry of County Tipperary, and intermarried with equally influential families throughout Ireland during the eighteenth and nineteenth centuries. They acquired the Castletown estate in Tipperary through such intermarriage, and in 1766 Colonel Thomas Sadleir's great, great granddaughter, Catherine, married Henry Prittie M.P. of Kilboy, near Silvermines, who became First Baron Dunally. The Dunally's accumulated over 21,000 acres, which made them one of the most extensive landowners in the county and the centre of Conservative politics there at various times during the nineteenth century.

Another interesting connection was made when Colonel Francis Sadleir of Sopwell Hall, the great grandson of Colonel Thomas, married Catherine Wall, daughter of William Wall M.P. owner of the Coolnamuck estate in County Waterford.[18] In an ironic twist of fate John Sadleir was involved in the acquisition of this estate in 1855.[19]

He could, therefore, legitimately claim a connection with the Sadleirs of Sopwell Hall, and one of his cousins, Henry Sadleir of Scalaheen, who emigrated to Kingston, Ontario, named his residence there Sopwell Hall. Sadleir was incorrect, however, in claiming a direct line from Sir Ralph.[20] He was, instead, directly descended from Sir Ralph's brother, John Sadleir of Hackney.[21] These Sadleirs may not have been as distinguished as those of Sopwell, but they were, nonetheless, influential. Like his brother, John of Hackney was an officer in the army of Henry V111, and commanded a company at the siege of Boulogne in 1544. His eldest son, John acquired property in Stratford-on-Avon, where he was an alderman and High Sheriff from 1570 to 1571. The Sadleirs and Shakespeares became close friends and William Shakespeare's twin children, Hamnet and Judith, were named after their godparents, Hamnet and Judith Sadleir.[22] The Shakespeares and Sadleirs were also related in marriage through the Quiney family, who were political and business associates of the Sadleirs. John Sadleir, great grandson of John of Hackney, married Elizabeth Quiney,[23] and in 1654 drew lots in the Irish adventure, when they were given land grants in Kilkenny, Queen's County (now Laois), and Tipperary. He died before taking possession but his son, John Sadleir of London, came to Ireland and in 1669 registered under the act of settlement of Charles 11. He settled in Ballintemple, but the hearth money records for 1665-67 show a John Sadleir as having one hearth in the civil parish of Ballygraine, and two hearths and a kiln in 'Sallohode-More Towne', both of which are not far removed from Ballintemple.[24]

Throughout the seventeenth, eighteenth and nineteenth centuries the Sadleirs spread, in a relatively confined geographical circle, to Tipperary Town, Scalaheen, Ardfinnan, Brookville, Shronell and Holycross. They were not in the same category as the great landlord class, but were well off, and as befitted their status lived in large country houses such as Kingswell House, Scalaheen House or Shronell House. Many of them became Justices of the Peace, and intermarried with families of a similar, and sometimes higher, social rank. Richard Sadleir of Sadlers Wells and Nelson Street, Tipperary, married Francis Matilda Cooper, fourth daughter of the Honourable Eyre Massy of Altavilla, Queen's County. During the seventeenth, eighteenth and nineteenth centuries the Sadleirs intermarried with the Chadwicks of Ballinard, one of the three principal inhabitants of Shronell, the other two being the Sadleirs themselves and the Chadwicks of Damerville.[25] Sadleir's grandfather, William, married Grace Ryan of Ballyvistea, County Limerick. In 1796 the Ryans moved to Scarteen House, near Knocklong, about six miles from Shronell. This family were as well known then as they are to-day for their famous hounds.[26]

The Sadleir influence was not diluted as they multiplied in the late eighteenth and early nineteenth centuries. At that stage not all were landowners, but some were army officers or had entered the legal profession. A few emerged as entrepreneurs. A 1788 directory of Irish towns, compiled by Richard Lucas, recorded a Clement Sadleir as the proprietor of a Cotton factory in Tipperary.[27] It was a large concern with a four hundred feet frontage, an adjoining premises for sixteen apprentice weavers, an extensive bleach green and a mill dam. The same source lists a Richard Sadleir as a woollen manufacturer in the town.[28]

Pigot's Directory of 1824 listed the Sadleirs among the nobility, gentry and clergy of Tipperary.[29] These included John and William Sadleir of Nelson Street, William and Richard Sadleir of Sadler's Wells, James Sadleir of Oakfield and Richard Sadleir of Scalaheen. In the late 1820s and early 1830s William Sadleir J.P. was one of the commissioners who compiled the tithe applotment books for the civil parish of Bruis contiguous to Shronell.

If John Sadleir could claim a prestigious Protestant pedigree on his father's side, his maternal forebears were the Scullys, a Catholic family, who settled near Cashel after the restoration, and spread chiefly to neighbouring Kilfeacle, Athassel, Shanballymore and Mantle Hill, a short distance to the east of the Sadleir enclave. They could not boast a similar ancestral status, but by a combination of agricultural expertise and prudent marriages became extremely wealthy, and could afford to send their sons to Stonyhurst, Clongowes, Trinity and Oxford.[30]

The earliest genealogical trace on the family is about 1665, when, according to family tradition, two brothers, Darby[31] and Roger came from either Kings County (now Offaly) or Longford.[32] In his 1806 *Gleanings Concerning Our Family History*, John Sadlier's uncle, Denys Scully, opined that they might have been expelled from their holdings during the years of confiscation. Neither Scully nor Bourke's *Landed Gentry* provide much information about Roger except the date of his death. It was through Darby that Sadleir's maternal line came. He was born on 18 September 1645, and according to *Gleanings* his eldest son, Thady,[33] Sadleir's great great grandfather, was an 'industrious, intelligent and honest' individual, who 'considerably augmented the portion he received from his father, extended himself in business with various success, but eventually to great advantage'.[34] Thady Scully bequeathed a 'handsome property' to each of his children, but gave a 'very large fortune in money, stock and farms' to his eldest son, Darby, also known as Jeremiah, who lived at Shanbally near Thurles.

While conceding that Darby, his grand-uncle, was a person of 'very superior talents and powers of mind and conversation', Denys Scully portrayed him as a vain individual more concerned with spending his inheritance upon 'acts of expense and ostentation', than developing his farm.[35] The result was that Darby depleted his fortune, and left a 'numerous family of children, not much edified by such an example, or instructed by his precepts'.[36]

Denys Scully was not born during Darby's lifetime, but he was ten years old when Thady Scully's second son, Roger, died. He was Denys's grandfather, and was recalled by him with respect, if not affection, as 'industrious, persevering, methodical, grave and silent, kind in his family, warmly true to his friends, grateful to his benefactors, and upright in his dealings'.[37]

Roger Scully's natural shrewdness was also evident in his choice of wife. In January 1734 he married Mary Maher, daughter of a 'reputable farmer' from Tullowmacjames in the civil parish of Templetuohy. She bought him 'a good fortune' plus 'great quickness of thought, sagacity and activity'.[38] They lived on a rented farm at Ballysheehan until mid-century, and then moved to nearby Dualla until about 1774, when they changed to Kilfeacle. When she died in 1780 Roger came to Cashel, and died there in 1783.[39] During his lifetime he accumulated a great deal of property and money. At various times he handed out £8,000 in marriage settlements, and at his death distributed another £8,000 among his family.

His eldest son, James, epitomised the enterprising spirit of previous generations of Scullys, and other Catholic families, who had survived unscathed the conflict between James 11 and William of Orange. He subsequently went on to rent and sublet large tracts of land during the penal laws' era, when the Protestant ascendancy tightened its grip on eighteenth century Ireland. He was born on 9 November 1737, and had an arduous upbringing, receiving little formal education, but was employed from a young age in what might be called a farming apprenticeship. At thirteen he was sent to Ballinasloe fair by his father and at seventeen was entrusted with buying stock upon his own judgement. In 1760 he married Kitty Lyons of Croom House, who proved as prudent and steady as his mother had been. She was given a dowry of £1,000 to augment the £1,500 from his father. This gave them a solid financial foundation on which they built in the years ahead.

He spent the first two years of married life at his father-in-law's house in Croom before moving to Cashel, and in 1765 rented a large farm in Garnacanty near Tipperary. In 1770 he sub-let this and other farms, and relocated to a substantial farm at Ballyvouden near Kilteely, County Limerick. His growing family, by then eight daughters,[40] was a considerable burden on his income, which had been affected by a decline in agricultural prices in the 1760s, and the loss of a large part of his cattle herd through the murrain.[41]

But, in August 1780 his prospects were greatly enhanced when his father gave him Kilfeacle, which henceforth became his permanent home. By then his property was worth almost £8,000, and with the relaxation of the penal laws from the late 1770s he was able to buy farms in Castlemore, Shronell, Ballycohey and Shanballymore, and take longer leases on Ballyvouden, Kilfeacle, Garnacanty, Ballynaclogh and Rathmacon. With a £14,000 inheritance in land and money from his father in 1783, he invested in more land, and by 1792 was worth almost £40,000. He invested some of this in bonds, and for the first time loaned £3,000 as a short term mortgage on a County Waterford estate.[42]

This is not only an example of a middleman securing a grip on the estate of a head landlord, but it also provides insight into how wealthy individuals may have become attracted to the idea of money lending *per se*. In James Scully's case, his loan was repaid within two years, but he saw lending as a lucrative addendum to land speculation. By 1802 he was considering the possibility of establishing a bank. His daughter-in-law, Mary Huddleston,[43] informed her mother in April of that year that 'Mr. S. is going to set up a bank at Tipperary, which will most likely be no small addition to his riches'.[44]

By the turn of the nineteenth century private banks were beginning to proliferate throughout Ireland. This was a recent phenomenon considering that the first Irish banking act had been passed almost a century earlier in 1709, to facilitate the transfer of bank notes, and meet the daily currency needs of the country.[45] The 1782 Act establishing the

Bank of Ireland gave it a monopoly, effectively preventing the development of a sound banking system.[46] It made no effort to create its own network and remained in Dublin for forty years after its foundation, thereby severely curtailing the supply of money throughout the country. The arrival of small private banks was a response to this banking vacuum. Their effectiveness, however, was weakened, because the 1782 Act specifically excluded the wealthy merchant sector from banking.[47] This was a strong inducement to rich graziers or land owners like Scully to become bankers, and between 1797 and 1804 the number of private banks increased from nine to fifty.[48]

In 1803 he went into partnership with his son, James Scully of Shanballymore, and established a bank. It became known locally as the Tipperary Bank,[49] and he confined its operation to Tipperary town, refusing in 1813 to open a discount office in Clonmel.[50] This was to protect himself from over extending the bank's resources, and while it limited his profits it also controlled potential liabilities. Such liabilities were always a possibility because his clientele were farmers and small merchants depending upon the agricultural sector, which was subject to economic depression especially following the Napoleonic wars.

Scully's bank withstood this, although many private banks failed in the banking crises of 1804, 1810 and 1814.[51] After his death in 1816 Denys assisted his brother in running it. They managed to come through the more severe banking crisis during the economic downturn of 1820.[52] The crises itself was sparked by the closure of Roche's Bank in Cork, and the subsequent chain reaction saw seven of the fourteen private banks in Munster fail.[53] Among those who closed was that belonging to old Scully's son-in-law, Richard Sausse, in Carrick-on-Suir.[54]

Although Scully's bank survived this crisis, the age of private banking was coming to a conclusion. General public confidence in such banks waned after 1820 and the increased demand for currency called for a more extensive and stable network. The banking legislation of 1821, 1824 and 1825 confined the Bank of Ireland's monopoly to a fifty mile radius of Dublin[55] and promoted the spread of joint stock banks with rights of issue.[56] The Scully brothers bowed to the inevitable and closed in 1827.

Their bank had the almost unique distinction of ceasing trading in a state of solvency thereby enhancing the Scully reputation for integrity. Its solvency was due not only to sound management, but to the great wealth of old James from land investment. This wealth was detailed by him in his diary covering the period from 1773 until his death in 1816. It recorded his justifiable pride as a purchaser of land, cattle and sheep, the marriage settlements of some of his children, his frequent travels to the Ballinasloe fair and to Cork, where his cattle were slaughtered for export.[57] An entry for 1777 referred to his 450 bullocks and 1,658 sheep in Garnacanty and Kilfeacle, while another for 1781 records a total of 607 bullocks and 95 cows. In December 1784 he slaughtered 668 bullocks in Cork at £6. 17. 6 (£6.87) each, and in 1792 he sheared 3,165 sheep. By 1812 his bank balance, nourished by the profits of prime Golden Vale lands, had reached £24,486. This significant sum, nevertheless, was dwarfed by the £60,000 left by his brother, Darby, five years earlier.[58]

Still, by the end of the century, James, the unlettered[59] descendant of Darby Scully held over 9,000 acres[60] and was regarded as the principal Catholic in County Tipperary. His diary records a visit by Lord Donoughmore and an overnight stay by the Catholic Archbishop, Thomas Bray.[61] This status was officially recognised, when he became one of the first Catholic magistrates appointed after the abatement of the Penal Laws, and in 1774 was 'very highly instrumental in quietning some commotions and risings against tythes etc.', in his district.[62] Scully was inclined to view local disturbances in Tipperary four years later as quasi-sectarian, when his diary recorded two visits to his house by what he termed Defenders, who were looking for weapons. On the second visit in the early hours of the morning a shot was fired, and some of his windows were broken.

Tipperary, however, was relatively untouched by the 1798 rebellion,[63] and although Scully lost some favour in the public mind by his stand against popular demonstrations, he was, unlike his famous grandson, Billy Scully of Ballinaclogh,[64] liked by his tenants. This was due in part to the generosity and kindness of his wife to the less well off.[65] Not only, however, was her husband opposed as a magistrate and a property owner to local disturbances, but he had little sympathy with the 1798 uprising. His diary records satisfaction at the reverses suffered on 5 June by the United Irishmen at New Ross – 'Tuesday the 5th the King's army fought the rebels at New Ross – the rebels lost 2,000 and our army about 200 – very bad accounts now but I believe we will soon hear of the rebels being defeated with great slaughter'.[66] His loyalty to the crown was also reflected in his diary comments on the Anglo-French conflict of that year. An August entry refers to 'an account of a most glorious battle gained by Admiral Nelson, now Lord Nelson over the French fleet near Alexandria at the mouth of the Nile'.[67]

Scully was not content, however, to confine himself to private anglophilic sentiments. He offered to raise a troop of horse to put down the Irish rebellion or to fight against the French.[68] Such loyalty by middle-class Catholics, combined with the critical demands of the time, was part of the reason for relaxing the penal laws. The subsequent opening up of career vistas to Catholics meant that some of the descendants of wealthy loyalists like Scully received a superior education, and moved into the higher professions, especially the legal one. This was encapsulated in the career of his son, Denys, author of the notes on the family pedigree. Over six hundred of his letters and his London diary for part of March 1805 have survived, and give a fascinating insight into the official rehabilitation and growing confidence of monied Catholics, who met and corresponded with English and Irish nobility.[69]

Denys Scully received his early education in the Kilkenny Academy,[70] where he distinguished himself in 1785 and 1786.[71] In 1791 he was apprenticed to a Dublin merchant, but following the Relief Act of 1792 he abandoned this to pursue a legal career. He was admitted to the Middle Temple in 1793 and the following year entered Cambridge as a pensioner.[72] It appears that he was the first Catholic in living memory to attend Cambridge.[73] In 1794 he was called to the Irish bar and having returned to London for further studies he joined the Leinster Circuit in 1796, but on the advice of John Scott, the 1st Earl of Clonmell and Chief Justice of the Kings Bench, did not commence practice for a further two years. It is more than likely that Clonmell, popularly known as Copper-faced Jack, knew the Scully family well, having married Catherine Mathew of Thomastown, near Kilfeacle.[74] Apart, however, from any possible ties of friendship, Clonmell sometimes offered such personal attention to promising young barristers, who were likely to benefit from a lucrative career. He had no doubt that Scully would 'make some money by it, especially as the country grows richer; and indeed it will be the case whether the country became richer or poorer – the law must thrive in either case'.[75] He had urged Scully to spend the two extra years in the offices of an English law firm because he was unimpressed at the training by Irish barristers,

> Here a man after 3 years in London, half amusing and half instructing himself between elegant literature, poetry, the classics and Belles Lettres comes to the bar unacquainted with practice; he is frightened at the 1st brief he gets; afterwards during his first years which are years of leisure, he gets into knots and clubs of barristers and young men, who pass their evenings not unpleasantly, (I will add, not very improvingly) over a bottle and gay conversation, now and then regaled by a good song; from this way of life he rarely emerges. Those are the men that overstock and croud the profession – I see acres of their wigs daily before me in court; but talents, good conduct, good sense and assiduity never fail to attain eminence and distinction.

Scully finally began to practise in 1798, and joined the lawyers' corps of yeomanry, which was called out on 24 August when news broke of the French landing in Killalla.[76] This type of loyalism, however, did not signify sympathy with plans to bring about a union between the two countries. Scully imbibed ideas hostile to the Act of Union from his intimate involvement with the Moira House circle.[77] But like many others, including his father,[78] he ultimately supported the Act in the expectation that the remaining Catholic disabilities would be removed.

He judged that the exodus of nobility to England after the Act was more beneficial than damaging to Irish interests. Writing to his brother-in-law, Major Richard Huddleston, on 5 March 1801 he noted that,

> few of them were useful or estimable public or private characters, and the gaudy splendour of their style of living, their pernicious habits, and the scandal of their example only served to provoke public discontent and to exhibit to us the vanity and worthlessness of those who draw immense sums from the country, who enjoy all public emoluments and who, to secure that monopoly, would depress the rest of the country and would involve all things in confusion and ruin, rather than consent to the emancipation of the Catholics.[79]

Catholic emancipation was to become the great cause of Scully's political life. He had pretensions to sit for Tipperary County,[80] and when emancipation failed to materialise he became one of the pivotal figures in the early restricted campaign, and drafted the 1805 petition rejected by the Prime Minister, William Pitt.[81] Daniel O'Connell collaborated with Scully on the Catholic Committee,[82] and while he went on to lead the later more widespread movement, Scully was regarded by contemporaries as the real, if more hidden, leader in the early years.[83] He continued his involvement for several years, and in 1813 won popular acclaim for his book, *Statement of the Penal Laws*,[84] which was condemned by the Irish Chief Secretary, and led to the imprisonment of its publisher, Hugh Fitzpatrick.[85]

It was a detailed and substantial work,[86] whose philosophical aim was to 'expose the nature and extent' of the penal code and 'to develop its severe operation upon the people of Ireland.'[87] Its practical purpose was to provide a reference work for lawyers, philosophers and legislators on the 'rights, liberties, properties and lives of the Catholic population.'[88] Its thesis centred on the anomalous existence of a penal code against a people, who not only formed the great majority of the population, but were also the main bulwark of agriculture, trade and manufacture.[89] Their crime lay in their adherence to the Catholic religion, and for this 'the Catholics of Ireland are the prostrate victims, of a teazing, intolerant code of laws; rendering them, in effect, almost "Aliens" in their native land.'[90]

By 1815 Scully was still committed to the cause of Catholic

emancipation, but was less optimistic of its success following the end of the Napoleonic wars. He endorsed the motto that England's difficulty was Ireland's opportunity, and the threat of insurrection kept alive by the war was seen by him as a valuable adjunct to the movement's dynamic. He expressed this in a letter of 13 January 1815 to Thomas Cloney, a '98 rebel, whose death sentence had been commuted.[91] The removal of the revolution threat meant that 'our enemies, tho not more strong are less placable than before – our friends, so called, are dropping off one after another'. In this private letter, wisely never posted, Scully displayed a sectarianism that could never have been publicly voiced. He proposed exclusive dealing among Catholics, amounting to a boycott of Protestants 'by marking and avoiding those trading or professional Protestants who have acted hostilely towards us'. He was also pleased that many Protestants would be commercially damaged by the peace, and 'they and their families must speedily choose between indigence and emigration, and at all events we and the country will get rid of them'.

Scully largely withdrew from political activity the following year[92] when his father died, and he was distracted by his mother's prolonged legal proceedings to contest her husband's will, which, she successfully pleaded, breached her marriage agreement.[93] The flouting of this agreement by old James Scully was not an indication that he undervalued such settlements. On the contrary he saw the forging of appropriate family connections through marriage as an important ingredient in the dynamic of status and wealth. He exercised a strong influence on his children in this respect. He had reservations about the 1801 marriage of Denys to his first wife, Mary Huddleston of Sawston Hall near Cambridge. He was concerned because her dowry was not secured by the usual land assignment.[94] By then the Huddlestones had lost most of their wealth. Nevertheless, they were an old Catholic family and blood relatives of the Plantagenets. Their near neighbour was the Third Earl of Hardwicke, the new Lord Lieutenant of Ireland. In Dublin the Scullys were visited by Lady Hardwicke, and Denys attended Vice-regal levees.[95]

Old James was more pleased with Catherine Eyre, Denys's second wife. She came from a wealthy Sheffield family, and brought a dowry of £13,000 to her marriage, which nicely augmented the £14,000 fortune given to Denys by James.[96] Similarly, his diary for 1806 described Margaret Wyse, the new wife of his son, James of Shanballymore, as 'a very fine tall young woman' and a 'good bargain'.[97] He might have had mixed feelings had he known that her nephew, Thomas Wyse, would marry Letitia Bonaparte, niece of Napoleon.[98] He was ruthless in his opposition to any prospective daughter-in-law lacking the required connections. His diary of 20 February 1798 recorded his fury that his son, William, had secretly married Anna Sophia Roe, 'the widow Row's daughter, an old girl without a fortune, he will and she will repent as I will give him but £50 a year'.[99] He disowned William, never forgave him and forbade him to come to Kilfeacle ever again, relenting only to increase his annuity.[100] He was less successful with his second son, Edward, known to the family as Mun, who overcame his initial intransigence, and married Mary Anne O'Brien of Nenagh in January 1806. Mun's letter of 15 April 1805 to Denys outlines his grievance against old James,

> You recollect when I first fixed my affections on Miss O'B., I took the liberty thro' you of consulting my father's inclinations, which I then found so averse to my Desires, that I was determined to proceed no further. I accordingly gave up to the Will of a Father, an object, I thought no Consideration whatever should induce me to. I must tell you I first stated my father's aversion to Miss O'B. and had her full consent to act the part I did. When I afterwards thought of Miss N. his objections to her were still greater, as soon as she was married he thought proper to mention thro' a friend to me, that if I acted an affectionate & dutiful part to him, till James would be married, that he would then fully agree to allow me to marry Miss O'B. or any other girl I thought proper. With this declaration I was fully satisfied, till we were at Castle Connell, when James was kind enough to ask my father's permission to allow me to go to Nenagh for a Day to see Miss O'B. This he refused in the most absolute manner, and said tho' he did once promise his Consent 'twas merely that time may alter my affections, and concluded by saying if I proceeded further, he would act to me as he had done to William and abused her and her family in such a manner as I feel ashamed to mention.[101]

If James Scully exercised such pressure on his sons, he wielded total control over the marital fate of his daughters. The outcome, however, was not always financially successful; for example his daughter, Nancy, married Thomas Mahon, a Dublin banker and businessman, who went bankrupt despite the efforts of his father-in-law to save him.[102] The others were more satisfactory. In 1780 his daughter, Lucy,[103] married Leonard Keating of Garranlea, near Cashel,[104] whose father leased 22,000 acres.[105] Old James also conducted the negotiations leading to the marriage of his daughter Joanna, or Johanna, which established the Sadleir connection.

From November 1804 until July 1805 he bargained with both John Harney of Somerville, County Limerick, father of Joanna's suitor, Charles, and with Clement William Sadleir, a well off Protestant tenant farmer from nearby Shronell.[106] Catherine Scully wrote to Denys on 3

November that a match had been made with Sadleir, which seemed to please her daughter if only because of the proximity of Shronell House,

> I wou'd have reply'd to your affectionate letter before now but wait'd to know the result of Joanna's match with Mr. Sadleir. It was agreed on the day before yesterday but is not to take place ontill your Father returns from Cork to which place he went this day and I believe will not return for three weeks ontill he will finish his cattle. I find Joanna was more partial to Sadleir as being near home than to Harney tho the later has much a larger fortune and that for ever.[107]

The larger fortune prevailed however, and Scully concluded the marriage settlement with Harney on 19 January 1805. He recorded that he gave her a dowry of £3,500,[108] and on the same day the compliant Joanna hoped that Denys would like his 'intended brother. He seems a sensible, steady very well tempered man. At least he is a great cheat from his countenance if he proves otherwise'.[109] Her mother also liked Charles Harney,[110] and was anxious that the wedding should take place before Lent.[111] She was to be disappointed. His father baulked at the final details of the settlement, much to the annoyance of old James, whose irritation was relayed to Denys on 2 April by his younger brother, Jerry,

> Joannah's nuptials with Charles Harney are not so near taking place as we all expected. There are produced by him some objections to the articles stiled "Objections on the part of Mr. Harney" (the old Gentleman). These are drawn up by a Mr. Westrop and Mr. Harney, father to the Bachelor. Mr. Westrop is a neighbour of Harneys – a young man just retired from the Co. Limerick Militia. I am confident if you saw those objections you would be much amused at the idea of their setting their opinion in competition with that of the Lawyers who drew them up. The objections are highly disagreeable to my father. One of them is a reduction of £30 a year on the jointure of Joannah.[112]

Catherine Scully hoped that Harney's objections would be overcome, but her husband refused to alter the settlement, and resumed negotiations with Sadleir. These were finally completed in July.[113] Despite a provision in his 1803 will for a dowry of £4,000,[114] he gave her £2,500 with a further £1,000 on his death. Sadleir settled £2,000 on her if they had children, and £5,000 on their children, otherwise £3,000.[115]

Clement William Sadleir and the twenty-nine year old Joanna Scully were married on 19 September 1805 and their first child, a daughter who died in infancy, was born, as James Scully noted, nine months and one week later.[116] Their eldest son, William, arrived on 7 August 1807, and was followed by five others, James, Clement, who died in infancy, John, another Clement and Kate.

John was born 17 November 1813,[117] a year when his father sold 179 cattle[118] and had almost £3,000 on deposit in the Tipperary Bank.[119] Nothing is known of his early childhood, but it is certain that he grew up in comfortable surroundings. Clement William Sadleir held almost 700 acres on the Damer estate,[120] and lived in a fine bow fronted residence set against the backdrop of Slievenamuck and the Galtee mountains.[121] The long row of stables at the rear was a symbol of the family's status, and fostered a lifelong love of horses in John.[122]

The Sadleir residence contrasted with the majority of dwellings in west Tipperary. As late as 1841 almost ninety per cent of these were either mud cottages or mud huts.[123] The quality of the schoolhouses in the area was equally poor, ranging from mud cabins and sections of cowhouses to thatched or slated houses, the latter being in the minority.[124] Sadleir did not attend any of these, but, like his younger brother, Clement, was educated at home by private tutors.[125]

Shronell itself was an unremarkable place containing few visible features to arouse the interests of visiting topographers like Samuel Lewis, who briefly described it as a small parish of 2,747 acres of pastoral land.[126] But, it was this lush and fertile pasture that was coveted by wealthy graziers. Despite its uninspiring topography Shronell was not without some interesting historical facets. John Wesley visited and preached there, and the grandparents of the essayist, William Hazlitt, worked a small farm on the Damer estate in the eighteenth century.[127] They were buried in Shronell. The locality was, perhaps, best known for its connection with the poet Liam Dall Ó hIfearnáin,[128] who came from neighbouring Lattin, but spent much of his time in Shronell, where he taught the classics.[129]

Ó hIfearnáin was a typical eighteenth century Gaelic poet, an anglophobe who lamented the supplanting of the Irish by the English invader. He sometimes digressed from his usual condemnatory sweep of the English planters in general, to pillory the local aristocracy in the person of John Damer, nephew of the Cromwellian Joseph Damer. In his 1780 poem Mo Mhíle Brón-Chreach, Ó hIfearnáin exulted at the death of Damer[130] and the destruction of his splendid mansion, Damer's Court,

> I rejoice that Shronell Court is down
> walls and groves razed to the ground,
> I rejoice that the boor is dead
> And the low tribe forever fled,

14

I rejoice that the bright gold is spent
By that buck aged and grey[131]
And a farthing I would not give the priest
To come and save him from the grave.[132]

These sentiments would not have found favour with the Sadleirs, who, as landlords or middlemen, were occasionally the targets of violence. This was particularly true in times of agricultural depression. A combination of economic downturn, poor harvests, land hunger and a change from village to pasture at a time of population increase, spawned several periods of serious unrest coinciding with Sadleir's childhood and adolescence.

Modern research has pinpointed the years 1814 to 1816 and 1821 to 1823 as times of agrarian violence in the Barony of Clanwilliam, where the Sadleir and Scully lands largely lay.[133] It is unlikely that Sadleir would have been aware of the earlier period which resulted in Tipperary being proclaimed under the 1814 Insurrection Act, permitting the suspension of habeas corpus. In August 1816 several men were executed for the murder of William Baker, a magistrate who owned the Lismacre estate near Bansha. As a warning to others their bodies were left hanging in the village of Golden for several years.[134]

The young Sadleir would have heard this grisly story from his parents when he was old enough to understand its significance, but would have been more aware of the violence that occurred during the later period of unrest, when Clanwilliam was proclaimed from 15 April 1822 until 5 June 1825.[135] In 1822 memorials were sent to Dublin Castle requesting that some Tipperary baronies be placed under the Insurrection Act.[136] A memorial of 13 March was sent by magistrates from Tipperary town district to the Under-Secretary, requesting the deployment of extra troops to enforce the Act.[137] William Sadleir, of Sadleir's Wells, was one of the signatories of this memorial demanding 'decisive action to preserve the lives of the people'. This was supported by a list of incidents, which indicated that labourers and small farmers were the main culprits.

It reported an episode of 27 January, when a group of men visited Bansha, Cullen and Emly administering illegal oaths to recruits for a secret organisation, and posting threatening notices signed by the ubiquitous 'Captain Rock.' On 9 February a 'very large body of men' assembled on the mote of Donohill sounding horns and firing shots. Some days later two houses were burned in Coolnagun near Tipperary, and the Hibernian Society School there was reduced to ashes. On 24 February a house in Garnacanty belonging to Sadleir's uncle, James Scully, was burned. This pattern continued in March with the burning of two houses in Donaskeagh belonging to the Protestant minister, William Massy, and a house in nearby Drishane owned by one of the Scullys was also destroyed.[138] The attack on Massy was inspired by the tithes' grievance. The Protestant curate in Bansha was spared this fate, but received a notice warning him to lower his demand.

There was a decrease in the level of violence during 1823, although Sadleir's relatives were again victims when a dwelling in more distant Holycross was burned down.[139] This probably belonged to Richard Sadleir of Scalaheen, whose father had moved from Holycross when he purchased Scalaheen House. Finally, a military communique of November reported that eight men were arrested and imprisoned in Tipperary jail for 'an improper meeting' in the village of Cullen.[140]

Agrarian violence declined considerably in 1824 and 1825 with an increase in the price of corn and a plentiful potato crop.[141] The type of incidents reported were sporadic mail coach robberies, faction fights and drunken riots at fairs.[142] These were regarded as the norm, and magistrates meeting in Cashel on 1 June 1825 agreed that the baronies of Middlethird and Clanwilliam, 'being now restored to apparent tranquillity', should no longer be subject to the Insurrection Act.[143] A memorial was accordingly sent to the Lord Lieutenant, who complied with their wishes.

Despite this, however, there was a resurgence of agrarian violence in the Spring of 1826, when Sadleir's relatives were subject to further attacks. Edward Wilson, the Chief Magistrate of Tipperary, reported on 10 April that a house belonging to Edmund Scully of Ballyneill, in Donohill, was burned by 'unknown persons'.[144] He again reported on 24 April that a house containing nine calves, the property of William Sadleir of Sandymount, was burned,[145] and a dairy house with thirty cows, owned by his brother Richard of Scalaheen, was similarly destroyed.[146]

The thirteen year old John Sadleir may have felt some relief that September, when he departed for the more peaceful atmosphere of Clongowes Wood College to begin five years of second level education under the guidance of the Jesuits.[147] This college was only a year younger than Sadleir, having been founded in 1814. But, already he was well acquainted with life there. His older brothers, William and James had attended from 1821 to 1825 and 1823 to 1824, respectively.[148] He was joined by Clement in 1828, and many of his Scully relatives were Clongownians. These included Billy Scully of Ballinaclough, who entered in 1831, the year Sadleir left.

The Scully connection with Clongowes went back to 1813, when Peter Kenney, the Jesuit Vice-President of Maynooth, was instructed by the order in Stonyhurst to found a school in Ireland for the education of the Catholic middle-classes.[149] He was impressed by the publication of Denys Scully on the penal laws, and saw him as an ideal adviser on the pitfalls facing a religious order in purchasing a property for conversion to a school. The type of politico-legal expertise Scully had was important, since the Jesuits, who were about to be formally restored by the Pope, were viewed with more than usual suspicion by Protestants in general, and by the British establishment in particular.

In 1813 the imposing Castle Browne mansion and part of the demesne near Clane, County Kildare, came on the market. The vendor was Lieutenant General Michael Wogan Browne, a Catholic in the service of the King of Saxony. He had inherited the property in 1812 from his brother Thomas, who had conformed to the Established Church, and wished to dispose of it partly for the benefit of his widowed sister-in-law.[150] Kenney purchased the freehold of the mansion and demesne of 137 acres for £16,000. He also acquired a further 131 acres through a combination of purchase and lease.[151]

This was the easiest part of Kenney's task. Its legal conversion to a school was more difficult. Scully provided him with contacts[152] to counteract the influence of powerful English opponents, especially Sir John Coxe Hippisley, member of parliament for Sudbury, and one time agent of the British government in Rome.[153] When Kenney was called for interview by Sir Robert Peel, the Chief Secretary and future Prime Minister, he followed Scully's advice and said that the purchase money was his private property, that the school was not a Jesuit one and would accept Protestants as students.[154]

A further hurdle was the securing of a teaching licence from the Protestant Consistorial court. This required a recommendation from the local parson. Scully tried to use his influence with the Protestant bishop of Kildare, Charles Lindsay, a brother-in-law of Lord Hardwicke, one time Lord Lieutenant and neighbour of his in-laws the Huddleston. The bishop diplomatically responded that the granting of the licence was a matter of course.[155] Scully sent this letter by return to Kenney with the comment that it was 'as courteous and liberal as we could wish'.[156] In reality Lindsay was unwilling to pressurise the local minister, whose recommendation was not forthcoming,[157] and Scully advised Kenney to proceed with the school, which without the licence was subject to an annual tax. He also supplied him with a list of families, most of them his relatives, whose children were prospective applicants. These included the Scullys, Keatings, Sausses and Lyonses of Croom.

These families were impressed by the new school, and by the time Samuel Lewis visited it in 1837 the enrolment was 120 students.[158] Kenney, the first Rector, made some additions to the original building, and Lewis was struck by its imposing presence in an attractive setting,

The building, to which large additions have been made for the accommodation of the students, is a spacious quadrangular structure, flanked at the angles by four lofty towers, and is pleasantly situated in the centre of an ample and richly wooded demesne. The principal corridor is more than 300 feet in length; the hall for study is above 80 feet long and 38 feet wide, and is lighted by a double range of windows on each side; the refectory is of the same dimensions, and the apartments of the students are spacious and lofty. The college chapel is 80 feet in length, and is divided into a nave and aisles by two ranges of Ionic columns; it has a fine organ, and the tabernacle on the high altar is wholly of marble and agate. The college contains an extensive library and museum, with a theatre for lectures in natural philosophy and experiments in chemistry, for public exercises in declamation, and musical concerts of the pupils. The institution is under the direction of a president, a minister or dean of the college, a procurator or bursar, and a prefect or general director of studies; there are six professors in the classical department, a professor of mathematics, and a professor of natural philosophy and chemistry. There are also three prefects, whose duty is to superintend the conduct of the pupils during the hours of study and recreation.[159]

The 1817 prospectus, which remained unchanged during Sadleir's period there, indicated a disciplined system of formation that did not acknowledge any need for parental support in the psychological development of the students. Holistic formation was considered best delivered by their Jesuit mentors to the extent that home visits were forbidden throughout the school year, and not encouraged even during the brief Summer break,

Absence from school cannot be allowed at any time during the academical year, which commences in the first week of September, and ends on the 1st of August. Parents are most earnestly requested to consider this stipulation before they send their children, and to adhere to it with the greatest exactness. Indeed the progress and happiness of the young student, not less than the discipline of collegiate life, require that he should not be removed even at the time of vacation, which begins on 1st August, and ends on the 7th of September. Should parents, however, wish to take their children home at that time, they will be pleased to give a month's notice of their determination.[160]

The daily time table during Sadleir's years in the college lived up to the discipline promised in this prospectus.[161] From 1 April to 31 July the students rose at 5 a.m. Following morning prayers, Mass and almost two hours study, they were allowed fifteen minutes for breakfast at 8 a.m. before embarking on three and a half hours classes and study.

Altogether, study and classes accounted for nine hours, while the three recreational periods amounted to three and a half hours. They finally retired at 8.45, having closed a sixteen hour day with night prayers.

Behind this testing regime, however, lay a varied curriculum, which inculcated a spirit of self-confidence in the students. Central to it was a 'progressive plan for religious instruction',[162] conforming to the order's centuries old aim of inculcating Catholic principles in their wealthy students, who paid a minimum of fifty guineas per annum for their education.[163] The Jesuit historian of Clongowes concluded that 'the creation of Catholic boarding schools, with a sound tradition of thorough and positive Catholic training, moral and intellectual, was thus a plain need in Ireland'.[164]

The aims and programme of religious instruction in these schools were based on the 1599 Jesuit *Ratio Studiorum,* reproduced in the Clongowes 'Masters' Rules'. The introduction to these left no doubt about the central duty of those who taught there,

> A Master in the Society of Jesus is a person to whom Jesus Christ has entrusted a number of children, purchased with His own Precious Blood, not merely for the purpose of being taught secular knowledge, but above all for the purpose of being made good Christians.
>
> Therefore, the principal and first duty of a master, a duty of the strictest and gravest obligation, to which all others are subordinate, is to instruct his scholars in the doctrine and morality of our holy religion; to teach them to avoid and to have a horror of vice; to make them know, love, and practise piety and virtue. As children pay but little heed to the instructions of those whom they do not respect, a Master must in his own person be an example of the virtue and piety which he teaches, actuated by reason and justice, free from caprice, levity, and passion; polite, honourable, impartial; zealous in the performance of duty; in a word, what the Society and his pupils expect from him.
>
> But example alone is not sufficient. He will consider it a conscientious obligation faithfully to employ in the religious instruction of his class the whole time appointed for that purpose, never permitting any part of that sacred time to be otherwise occupied.
>
> He will exact from all a correct knowledge of the Catechism; he will explain its meaning, and give practical Instructions, particularly on the Sacrament of Penance and on the Commandments; teaching them how to assist at Mass with profit, and to perform the other duties of Religion, adding such words of exhortation as are suited to their age and needs.[165]

In practice, life in the college followed a regular pattern of religious observance with more extensive content at particular times. One and a quarter hours were spent at prayer, including the Mass, each day. Extra efforts were made in the month of May and during Lent.[166] An 1834 diary noted that 'we abstain two days a week more than usual' at Lent[167]. The sodality of Our Lady Immaculate, whose rules were based upon the Jesuit Dublin Sodality of 1628, was considered important by the college authorities. Although confined in numbers, it apparently sowed the seeds of a Jesuit vocation in many students.[168] New sodalists were admitted during the annual three day retreat for the older boys. The 'great festivals' were also celebrated with special care, particularly those of the Jesuit saints such as the order's founder, St. Ignatius, St. Francis Xavier and St. Aloysius, the patron of the college.[169] While they enjoyed a six day break at Christmas, the students having celebrated midnight Mass, as local people peered through the windows of the chapel, were obliged to rise again for Mass at 6.15 on Christmas morning. The Christmas records for 1819 and 1823 noted that there was 'no feasting for the children' on Christmas evening.[170]

This practical promotion of spirituality was supported by a programme of religious education, with a written examination at the end of each term.[171] Each year the students also had to produce six essays on ecclesiastical history and religious knowledge, making religious education a major subject on the curriculum.

There is no certainty that the delivery of this curriculum lived up to the expectations of those who designed it, but it was remarkably broad. The *Ratio Studiorum* laid out a detailed and precise system of study, teaching organisation and examinations. Careful planning combined with adaptability was central to this. It bore a European imprint, and parents sent their sons to Clongowes knowing that they would be educated in preparation for the professions and high office. The Jesuits consulted the parents on their vocational aspirations for their sons, so that individual attention could be given to them in that regard. Daniel O'Connell wrote to Kenney on 14 January 1815 of his wish that his sons Maurice, Daniel and Morgan John should pursue a legal career, following their education in Clongowes.[172]

The core of this education was the Classics, Philosophy, (delivered through Latin), and the Sciences. This was enriched by courses in History, Geography, English, Maths and French. But, the Classics were seen as pivotal in pursuing the cultural, utilitarian and civic aspirations of the Jesuits for the students. Their aim was to turn out cultivated young men, who would be useful and valuable members of society. The Classics, therefore, were studied as much for the beauty and form of the language, as for the virtues extolled by the great Classical writers. A wide array of these was studied, and at the end of each term the students underwent written and oral examinations.[173] In addition, teachers were required to present the board of examiners with a weekly record of marks for compositions and exercises.[174] Trinity

College Fellows came to conduct oral examinations, and were impressed by the standard reached by the students. The learning process and competitive spirit were also sharpened by the Jesuit practice of dividing classes[175] to compete for awards and prizes.[176] The Rector then reviewed the overall progress of each class at the end of term. This took the form of a long report, read in public, on the success or failure of the various classes to imbibe the style or ideas of the classical writers.

One interesting facet of a Clongowes education was the apparent success of some teachers in cross-curricular teaching. Maurice Daniel O'Connell, writing to a friend in October 1816, casually remarked that 'Cicero himself was a bit of a botanist, as Chapter 15 of the *De Senectute* shows. Be so kind as to tell my father to get me Linnaeus's botanical works'.[177]

The well-defined academic courses at Clongowes were enhanced by an admirable social and cultural curriculum, provided at extra cost. Tuition on the flute, flageolet, piano, violin, oboe, French Horn and clarinet was availed of by many students.[178] Fencing and dancing were also popular, and appear to have been seen as complementary.[179] In 1820 the acting Rector, Bartholomew Esmonde, advertised for a teacher to give tuition in fencing and broadsword exercises to '60 young gentlemen' one day a week.[180]

For many, such classes were a form of recreation. Periods of informal recreation and free time were also part of the daily routine. Games were not compulsory, but those available included handball, rounders, football, marbles and a primitive form of cricket with a hurley-like bat.[181] Some students liked to fish in the nearby Liffey, but walking was the most popular outdoor pastime because the surrounding countryside, with its wooded areas, was peaceful and attractive. Coursing was one of the more unusual pursuits, and the older students were allowed keep greyhounds. Indoor recreation mainly consisted of cards and backgammon with surprisingly high stakes.[182]

There is no evidence of Sadleir's recreational taste in Clongowes, or that he distinguished himself in any subject area. But, when he left in August 1831, the influence of such an elitist education in a society of functional literacy enabled him to face the future with confidence. His wealthy background and influential connections were a guarantee of success. One of these was his forty-one year old cousin, Nicholas Sadleir, an attorney[183] and solicitor with practices in Dublin and Tipperary.[184] He accumulated considerable wealth from his profession, his land and his first marriage to Mary O'Brien Butler, daughter of Pierce O'Brien Butler of Dunboyne Castle, County Meath,[185] which he inherited.[186]

Various directories for the 1830s show that he changed his Dublin address with some frequency, all situated, however, in Lower Gardiner Street, whose 121 premises were almost all inhabited by solicitors.[187] This was probably to avail of lower rents, and betrays the Sadleir interest in money.[188] He was a member of the Law Club, a society established in 1791 for the better regulation of practising solicitors, whose club house was in Dame Street.[189]

John began his apprenticeship in April 1832, and may have divided his training between his cousin's Dublin and Tipperary practices.[190] A five year apprenticeship was the only qualifying requirement for solicitors, prior to the introduction of an examination system in 1860.[191] He was admitted a solicitor in 1837, when he was twenty-four years old, and practised in Tipperary for more than a year. As a member of the legal profession he joined a privileged sector, with tentacles stretching into the political and commercial arenas. Money, inherited and professionally acquired, and contacts through their social circle and clientele, gave lawyers an opportunity to invest in profitable areas like real estate, railways or banking.[192]

Sadleir's entry into the profession coincided with a period of exceptional expansion in the Irish banking system, beginning in the early 1830s. The legislation of the 1820s, promoting the spread of joint stock banking, was supplemented by the banking Act of 1830, which allowed banks with more than six partners to pay notes through their agents within the fifty mile radius of Dublin.[193] It was the first step in undermining the Bank of Ireland's monopoly, and resulted in the foundation of the Provincial, Hibernian and Belfast banks. The Act was a response to the demand for increased money circulation by a mushrooming population, and kick-started a wave of joint stock bank expansion from 1833. Within three years the number of branches increased from thirty nine to one hundred and seventy five.[194]

One of the difficulties facing Irish banking institutions in the 1830s was a lack of expertise, which resulted in the arrival of more experienced Scots to work in them.[195] But the Scullys and the Sadleirs had such expertise, and began to plan a venture in 1837, at the end of a banking crisis which saw the collapse of the Agricultural Bank.[196] Their timing was influenced by an expectation that the privileges of the Bank of Ireland would end the following year. The government was free to do this under the 1821 legislation, but chose not to, although in 1840 it passed an enabling bill to end the monopoly at its pleasure.[197]

It is not possible to precisely define the role of Sadleir in the establishment of the new bank. His first cousin, Vincent Scully, son of Denys and Catherine Eyre, maintained that he was the 'moving spring of the whole concern'.[198] His almost free access to its funds at a later stage,[199] and his subsequent career as a banker in England seems to substantiate this, although by his own admission Sadleir was never a director. He was, however, a shareholder, and acted as its solicitor until 1846.[200] He was also a secretive individual, exerting an influence behind the scenes rather than in a public or ostentatious manner.

It is unlikely, however, that his early authority was over extensive, although his younger brother, Clement, was the bank's accountant and secretary.[201] Sadleir's power gradually evolved until it eventually came under his total control, whereby James, his elder brother, did his bidding. Initially, however, his uncle, James Scully, was the inspiration behind the bank. He had the experience of running the old Tipperary bank until its closure ten years earlier. James Sadleir was also a key figure because of his banking knowledge. He had been the manager of the National Bank in Tipperary, and may have brought some of its customers to the new establishment.[202] When the deed of partnership was drawn up he was appointed Managing Director and either his cousin, Richard Sadleir, or his uncle, became the first chairman.[203]

The Scully connection was an obvious advantage, signifying a combination of business acumen, wealth and integrity. This connection was signalled by its local title, the Tipperary bank, after its predecessor, although its official one was the Tipperary Joint Stock bank. It opened in Tipperary in August 1838[204] under the *6 Geo.1V Cap 42 (Irl.)* Act, and in October public confidence was increased by its special arrangement with the Bank of Ireland. This entitled the Tipperary to issue Bank of Ireland notes only, in return for which its approved bills were discounted there at one per cent under the current rate. It was also allowed draw letters of credit within agreed limits on the bank's agencies.[205]

This almost gave it the status of a Bank of Ireland branch, and had the added benefit of greatly increasing the circulation of its notes in the rural areas of the county.[206] It also enabled the Sadleirs and Scullys to entice fifty shareholders by 1840.[207] But, there was a less desirable dimension to the connection between the two banks. The influence exerted by the Bank of Ireland circumscribed to some extent the expansion of the Tipperary; for example in 1841 it thwarted efforts to open a branch in Gorey, County Wexford, and prevented attempts to discount through an agent in Belfast.[208] Nevertheless, by that year branches were operating in Carrick-on-Suir, Nenagh, Thurles, and Thomastown.[209]

Sadleir's part in this expansion is not known. It is more likely that he concentrated in gaining wider experience in his profession, rather than any central involvement in the bank. A small town like Tipperary did not provide the range of experience he desired, and the year the bank opened he set out for Dublin and more lucrative prospects. He joined his cousin Nicholas, his brother William, a barrister since 1837, and his second cousin Leonard Morrogh, an apprentice,[210] in 88 Lower Gardiner Street.[211] Within two years he took on Clement as an apprentice.[212]

The little family of lawyers remained in Gardiner Street until 1843, when they moved to nearby 5 Great Denmark Street adjoining Belvedere House,[213] which the Jesuits bought in December 1840, and converted into a school.[214] The premises occupied by the Sadleirs was Killeen House, once the town residence of the Earls of Fingal, and subsequently subsumed into Belvedere College in 1880.[215] It was one of the most comfortable buildings in Great Denmark Street, itself superior to Gardiner Street. The rateable valuation of number 5 was £120 per annum, compared with the £70 valuation of their previous premises.[216]

Dublin lost much of its social glamour following the Act of Union and the accompanying migration of aristocratic families like the Belvederes and the Fingals from the area. In the late eighteenth century the Gardiner Street-Great Denmark Street sector, situated on an elevated site overlooking Sackville Street, the widest boulevard in Europe, was one of the most select areas north of the Liffey,[217] being 'built for the occupation of persons of acknowledged position on the social scale.'[218] In Sadleir's time these houses were colonised by a middle-class of barristers, solicitors, merchants and doctors and in the early twentieth century were to degenerate into slums and tenements, a tangible symbol of social neglect following the Act of Union.

Modern research, largely through statistical evidence, has examined Dublin's social decline,[219] while contemporary observations were more graphic and emotional. In April 1850 the Government's proposal to abolish the Viceroyalty provoked a nostalgic recalling of Dublin's pre-union status. A.R. Stritch, a Dublin barrister and Repealer, who had been a fellow student of Thomas Davis,[220] commented that the departure of the aristocracy had 'placed a pauper middle-class into the position of a mock aristocracy'.[221] At a protest meeting in the Round Room of the Rotundo, William Long J.P. drew upon an old report of the building committee of the Room which had proudly referred to the presence of the nobility and gentry 'when places of public interest and entertainment' formed a 'rational connection of polished manners and society'.[222] The upper classes had paid ten guineas a year to promote balls in Dublin Castle and the Rotundo,

> We had families of the highest rank and fashion then resident in Dublin, and teaching by their example decorum and propriety of every kind. At that period Paris was the gayest and most profligate metropolis in the world, while the gayest, the most refined, and virtuous society in the

world existed in Dublin. The subscribers to these rooms included one duke, ten earls, ten viscounts, four barons, thirteen right honourables, five baronets, and thirty-nine esquires; and then of lady subscribers, there were two duchesses, seven countesses, five viscountesses, six baronesses, fourteen right honourables, and thirty-two ladies of rank and high distinction.

Thirteen years earlier Samuel Lewis had noted Dublin as a city where 'the places of public amusements are few. The drama is little encouraged by the fashionable and the wealthy, the theatre is thinly attended except on the appearance of some first rate performances from London...'[223] Sadleir was as unmoved by Dublin's loss of prestige as his uncle Denys, who had been a witness to its decline.[224] If his subsequent social life in London was a reflection of that in Dublin, it was very modest indeed.[225] He would not have been attracted by most of the clubs and public houses, and others were of a specialised nature with members chosen by ballot.[226] Some of these were confined to music lovers and included the Beefsteak Club, the Hibernian Catch Club, the Anacreontic and the Dublin Philharmonic Society. The legal circle had their own distinctive group of clubs such as the Law Club frequented by Nicholas, the Law Debating Society and the Law Society of Ireland, a type of legal quasi-trade union. The published lists do not show Sadleir as a member of any of these, although William was a committee member of the Debating Society, where barristers honed their adversarial skills.[227]

While there is little concrete evidence of Sadleir's social activities in Dublin, extant records give an insight into his legal transactions and show an interconnection between his profession, banking and investment in land, ultimately leading to speculation in commercial enterprises in England and abroad. As a lawyer he was largely concerned with conveyancing, trusteeships and receiverships, some of which he used to advance both his own prospects and that of the Tipperary bank. Shortly after his arrival in Dublin, for example, he administered the dowries of Godfrey Taylors' four daughters. Taylor held an estate in Noan in the parish of Killenaule, County Tipperary. He had died by 1840 but made provision for his daughters in a will of September 1794. On 4 March 1840 Richard Moore, a Senior Counsel in Fitzwilliam Square, complied with Sadleir's request to forward the £800 joint dowry.[228] Such control of dowries was an integral part of solicitors' portfolios, another example being Sadleir's management of Charlotte Goold's annuity from July 1843. Her husband, Henry R. Goold of Old Court Cork, also entrusted him with the sale of his estate some years later.[229]

A more profitable source of income for solicitors was their role as receivers over heavily mortgaged estates. The rents of these went directly to the receivers, supposedly for the benefit of the embarrassed owners, but were open to abuse. For other reasons lawyers were not always considered the most suitable choice for land agencies or receiverships. In his evidence to the Devon Commission, Edward Dalton, who farmed 500 acres near Golden, condemned them as 'the worst description of agents', quick to initiate legal proceedings for rent arrears, indifferent to the question of improvements and confined to their office and their quill.[230] The evidence of Michael Doheny followed a similar vein. He attributed the 'miserable' state of the tenants on the Glengall estate in Cahir to the strict exactions of the landlord's law agent.[231]

In November 1842 Sadleir was appointed receiver and agent to the Newtown House estates in County Louth.[232] Some of these lands were situated in Armagh and Tyrone. The immensely wealthy Thomas Joseph Eyre of Bath was listed on the indenture as a mortgagee. He was Vincent Scully's sixty two year old bachelor uncle, and invested large sums as mortgages on different estates through the advice of Sadleir, and often involving Sadleir himself.[233] Some of these agreements were complicated by various addenda over the years, making them difficult to unravel, not least for Eyre. One concerned the purchase of the Coolnamuck estate in County Waterford. In 1845 Eyre,who had loaned the owner, James William Wall, £28,000 as a mortgage on the estate four years earlier, authorised Sadleir to proceed with the purchase and to hold it in trust for him, in effect making Sadleir the legal and himself the equitable owner of the property. The mortgage was executed in October but Sadleir did not register it, and entered the trust in James Sadleir's name thereby causing much confusion years later.[234]

Such confusion was minor, however, compared with what happened in the case of the Mitchelstown estate owned by Robert Henry King, the mentally unstable Earl of Kingston.[235] This estate stretched into Cork, Limerick and Tipperary overlooked by the Galtee mountains and centred around Mitchelstown Castle, a magnificent eighty bedroom mansion set in extensive gardens and grapevines.[236] There was stabling for twenty-four horses.

Because of mismanagement and extravagance, the Earl was in serious financial difficulties by 1845. Nicholas Sadleir made his acquaintance the previous year, when he had been sued for a debt of £17,000, and offered him an apparently attractive solution.[237] He convinced the Earl that his cousin, John, could relieve his financial pressure by means of a loan from the Tipperary bank. By then rent arrears were £17,000 and the Earl agreed to allow John Sadleir manage his affairs. Sadleir recovered over £8,000 of these arrears from the previous receiver, and in an agreement of 22 February 1845 Kingston vested the estate in Eyre and James Scully, when he took out a mortgage of £50,000 from the Tipperary bank, citing James Sadleir as its representative.[238]

The bank did not pay this, and a few months later Kingston was forced to execute another deed vesting his plate, furniture and other goods to secure the advance. He only received £16,755, and was forced to take out a policy from the Albion Insurance Company at 6% interest. In return he was promised an annuity of £4,000 by the Sadleirs, which did not materialise.[239] The £50,000 was paid by the Albion to the bank to enable it make the advance to Kingston, but John Sadleir kept it and issued a forged receipt.[240] The Albion later took an action against Sadleir because the security he had given was defective.

Sadleir, however, persuaded Eyre to advance £40,000 to Kingston. This was paid in two instalments in June and July 1845 to the credit of Vincent Scully's account in the Tipperary bank, but only £7,000 was passed on to Kingston. Eyre became a trustee of the estate although the trusts were not explained to him. This mortgage was executed by a deed of 17 July 1846, which cited Vincent Scully and Sylvester Young as trustee for Eyre.[241] By this deed John and Nicholas Sadleir were appointed agents to the Cork estates, with the ostensible aim of collecting the rents to repay the interest on Kingston's loan.[242]

During the Famine Sadleir also established a tentative connection with the Glengall estate in Cahir, which he eventually bought.[243] He made this connection through Eyre's great nephew, Anthony Norris.[244] From 1845 onwards Norris loaned money to the Earl of Glengall using either Sadleir's funds or those of the bank. In April 1847 he advanced £10,500 of the bank's money. As the solicitor for the Tipperary, Sadleir also prepared the securities of the estate for Norris.[245]

His influence there was crucial in exploiting the difficulties of Glengall and Kingston. The licence he exercised over its funds was the clearest proof of control over its operation at the beginning of the Famine period. By then the bank had undergone significant legal and structural changes. As solicitor, Sadleir was closely involved in the reconstitution completed on 5 July 1842, when a new deed of partnership was drawn up to facilitate further expansion.[246] Fragments of this have survived. They chiefly concern the holding and disposing of shares, maintaining the shareholders' register, creation of new rules, the filling and vacating of directorships and the remuneration of directors.[247]

The deed was signed by James Scully, James B. Kennedy, who had joined the law firm in Great Denmark Street, and Sadleir's cousin, John Ryan of Scarteen, on the one hand, and Sadleir himself with individuals named Hartwick and Cook on the other.[248] The court of directors was James Scully, James Sadleir and Wilson Kennedy, a Clonmel solicitor and member of the Presbyterian community there.[249] Scully was appointed chairman and James Sadleir managing director with a salary of £1,000 per annum, and an entitlement to twenty per cent of the net profits.[250]

The bank operated under the umbrella of the *6 Geo.IV Cap.42* banking Act, and had a nominal capital of £500,000, made up of 10,000 shares at fifty pounds each. The paid up capital was ten pounds per share.[251] The deed of partnership sanctioned the usual banking powers of lending on cash accounts, bills of exchange, promissory notes, letters of credit, property or pledges of any type of goods, and of accepting deposits from individuals, corporations or political bodies. It was also permitted to deal in bullion and currency of all countries.

With the legal technicalities complete, the bank continued its expansion. It immediately opened branches in Roscrea and Clonmel. The move to Clonmel was initially resisted by the Bank of Ireland, which had an agency there, but eventually capitulated to public demand. It proved a significant step for the smaller bank. As the largest town in the county, with a population of 13,000, it was an attractive prospect, and the branch became the head office under James Sadleir's management. This removed the bank further from the direct influence of the Scullys in Tipperary town, and brought it more under John Sadleir's control. Within a short time it became known locally as Sadleir's bank, and a judge later declared that James exercised 'uncontrolled authority' in its management,

> without the slightest attempt at interference on the part of the directors and of the shareholders at large ... even in such matters as discounting bills, permitting customers to overdraw their accounts to any extent, Mr. James Sadleir acted according to his own unlimited discretion.[252]

Vincent Scully became increasingly alarmed at such control, and the failure to carry out an annual audit.[253] Initially, however, he did not have any reservations and supported the expansion plans. Some months prior to the restructuring he was easily persuaded by the Sadleirs to buy 400 shares at a premium.

The satisfaction of the Scully and Sadleir families at the bank's success in 1842 was marred by the assassination of Vincent's thirty one year old bachelor brother, James Vincent, in November of that year. He managed the Kilfeacle estate, and received death threats following evictions in the Winter of 1841. An assassination attempt on him in his house in April 1842 did not deter him, and the hatred of his victims hardened into a determination to exact a more fatal retribution.[254]

Their opportunity came when he and his brother Billy spent Saturday 26 November duck shooting. The latter returned home that evening but James remained at the lakeside, and, concealed by the gathering dusk, his assassins did not fail in their second attempt. An anonymous local landowner and fellow magistrate expressed little surprise that Scully had met such a bloody fate,

> About twelve o'clock that same night his body was found, near the lough to which I have referred, having had three shots fired into it, and the head broken by strokes of a gun, a dead duck at his side, and his gun carried off. Up to this time (Tuesday) no clue has been had to the operators in this dreadful murder. And you will ask, had he no notice of that which seems to have been anticipated by every body in the county? He had; he had notice from every friend and relation, in every form and shape; he had notices and warnings from all the clergy around him, far and near, and from the police authorities. In short, no course by which it was thought his feelings or caution would be acted on was left untried; but so much did he rely on his muscular strength, and such his wrongheadedness in his undertakings, that nothing would induce him to give up those practices which have been in this instance, as well as in others, and ever will be attended in every country with a similar result.[255]

The Tipperary magistracy did not share this diagnosis.[256] They were more concerned at the murder of a colleague, and within a week met in Cashel to discuss it.[257] Glengall, an inveterate complainer to Dublin Castle, convened the meeting, and condemned the murder as particularly diabolical in the consistency of the perpetrators' resolve. The Scully family had already offered £1,000 reward for information on these, and Glengall proposed that other landowners should augment this. He highlighted the availability of arms to 'the lower orders' as a major contribution to serious crime and the magistrates sent a memorial to Earl de Grey, the Lord Lieutenant, requesting a change in the law enabling firearms, even if legally registered, to be confiscated from 'those not duly qualified'.[258] This was signed by Sadleir's brother-in-law, Nicholas Biddulph Greene, married to his sister Kate,[259] his uncle-in-law Leonard Keating,[260] and his cousins Richard Sadleir of Scalaheen and Edward Scully.

Glengall was also offended by press comments citing landlords as the root cause of agrarian outrages. Papers like the *Freeman's Journal* were the 'aiders and abettors' of assassination. Its editorial of 3 December had condemned the murder as cruel rather than wanton.

Agrarian outrages were a response to injustice and the failure of the 'landlord legislature' to alleviate the conditions of the peasantry,

> It is time the landlords should be made to look to their own best interests, and coerced by the legislature into a sense of their duties. It is time, too, the Irish tenant should be no longer as the beast of the field, bred for the use of another – fed that he might labour for another – and at length cast out to make room for the sleek ox or the fatted sheep, which lives but that it may in turn die for the use of that other. It is time there should be an end on this system. There has been a rueful harvest gathered from it these centuries past, in the wailings of the houseless and homeless – in the ditch-side deaths of the evicted – in the murders of the murderers of thousands, and in the counter-murders of their assassins! Again, we repeat it, the legislature is responsible for the agrarian crimes that disgrace the land:

John Gray, co-owner and editor of the *Freeman's,* further reacted against Glengall's remarks. His editorial of 9 December accused the Tipperary magistrates of presenting only one side of the picture, and observed that while they 'may consider it a duty to override the tenantry – the latter may consider it equally a duty to resist', Gray saw the offer of a reward as insidious and contrary to the Irish dislike of informing. Such a reward was 'a bribe to the vile and worthless to destroy the innocent and helpless'.

This defence of Irish tenantry was followed by another editorial on 12 December labelling the motivation of the magistrates not as justice, but as revenge for the death of Scully, 'a bold and uncompromising assertor of landlord rights'. His accusation of bias was more graphic in this,

> while vengeance on the peasantry, the purchase by a 'heavy reward' of an adequate informer, and the calling in of arms, that will not answer to the call, have been largely dwelt upon, not one word has been said of the crimes, the 'diabolical crimes', to use his lordship's phrase, that have disgraced many of the landlords of Tipperary. The suffering of the peasantry – the ejectment of tenants – the burning of villages – the wanderings of the families – the destitution – the want of money – the heartburnings – the deaths caused by landlord oppression, was not once mentioned. These – these are to be continued – and yet peace is to be reaped as the fruit thereof!

The editor of the *Freeman's* was unable to resist publishing an article from the *Times,* an unlikely ally, which also commented on the 'systematic neglect and abuse of the duties of the landlord to his tenants'.[261] Gray finally concluded his attacks on landlordism with an editorial of 17 December advocating repeal as the ultimate solution to the land question in Ireland, where 'an Irish parliament elected by the Irish people and composed of the friends of the people will alone do justice to the cottier, the trader and the merchant'.

This closed the controversy, but he was proven wrong in his belief that the offer of a reward would result in the conviction of an innocent victim. Arrests were made, but insufficient evidence resulted in the release of the suspects and the murderers were never brought to justice.[262]

The publicity about the murder died down, the large unencumbered property of the murdered Scully reverted to Vincent,[263] who had a good practice at the bar and had been made a Queens Counsel in 1840. He further added to his wealth by the accumulation of 700 shares of the Tipperary Bank, by means of bonus shares at par. Supported by the Bank of Ireland the Tipperary continued to prosper under James Sadleir, whose own fortunes were enhanced by his marriage to Emma Wheatley in November 1843, almost exactly a year after his cousin's murder. She was the daughter of Joseph Wheatley, a Leicester industrialist, who set up a trust of £10,000 for her. Clement William Sadleir in turn assigned 461 acres of land in the Barony of Coonagh, County Limerick, as the settlement for James,[264] under whose administration the bank was then flourishing.

He published an optimistic annual report for 1844 which concentrated upon its stability underpinned by the agreement with the Bank of Ireland,

> The success of the Tipperary Bank conducted on this principle, seems to show that it is not unadapted to Ireland, where the existing banks of issue have all, in the early years of their existence, been subjected to several severe and general runs on their branches, by which they must have suffered great losses. The general failure of the old private country banks in Ireland (all but two or three) before 1822 or 1823, produced a want of confidence in any notes but those of the Bank of Ireland, which, however, the stability of the Joint Stock Banks since established, notwithstanding these runs has pretty well done away with.[265]

This was issued on 4 February 1845, immediately prior to the onset of the Famine, and reported a steady increase in profits 'notwithstanding the diminished value of money'. These were sufficient to pay an eight per cent dividend. The Report for the following year, however, announced a drop to six per cent.[266] It set aside £115 for famine relief and summarised the initial impact of the Famine on banking,

Since the last annual meeting a most important change has taken place in the business of banking in Ireland; the loss of the potato crop, and consequent reduction of the export of agricultural produce, having caused almost a total cessation of the greatest branch of business in this country, namely, the discount of bills drawn against the shipment of such produce. Hence the want of a profitable investment of funds formerly so employed, and until the calamity alluded to shall have passed away, it is to be feared that the business of banking in Ireland cannot be so remunerating as hitherto.[267]

While the Famine curtailed the further expansion of banking,[268] the Tipperary opened its final branches at Athy and Carlow in 1845 bringing its total network to nine, and mirroring the stabilisation of the Irish banking network at 173 branches in ninety towns. The Athy and Carlow branches were a direct response to Peel's Irish Banking Act, of 1845.[269] The Act, which received the royal assent on 21 July, applied the principles of the 1844 Bank Charter Act to Ireland. It was designed to maintain public confidence in bank notes, by specifying the ratio between bullion and notes. This was to regulate issue and it forbade the establishment of new banks of issue, confining this right to those banks already possessing it. Such a step automatically made the Bank of Ireland's monopoly irrelevant, and it was formally abolished. Henceforth existing banks with more than six partners could operate and issue in any location, irrespective of distance from Dublin. But, section 31 of the Act required the Bank of Ireland to continue its non-issue agreement with the Tipperary until January 1856.[270] Because the Tipperary had voluntarily surrendered its right to issue, and was the only bank in Ireland to make such a choice, the Act provided for compensation if the Bank of Ireland terminated the agreement within the ten years.[271]

This was unlikely to happen, and John Sadleir could view with satisfaction the stability of the bank in 1845 and 1846 as the Famine showed no signs of abating. In contrast to a large segment of Irish people struggling to survive in a harsh environment, he could also contemplate his own fortunes with some optimism. He had seen how useful the bank was in securing a hold on a valuable estate and had not hesitated to use it. The move to Clonmel gave him greater, if unseen, power over its operation. His Dublin practice provided a greater insight into land purchase, extended his contacts and deepened his legal experience. But, he was by then contemplating a move away from the practice of law to take advantage of more abundant business opportunities in England. Such a plan required research, and it is certain that he visited London on several occasions to assess the level of opportunity for an aspiring entrepreneur. One of his Scully cousins, who was living there and had married into a wealthy family, was an important conduit of information in this regard.[272] Contemporary sources do not name him, but it may have been his first cousin, Rodolph Scully, who lived in Rickmansworth, Middlesex in 1846.[273]

References

1. The *Times* quoted in *T.L.* 15 March 1856 and *D.E.P.* 11 March 1856.
2. H. Drummond, *Our Man in Scotland. Sir Ralph Sadleir 1507 – 1587*, (London, 1961), pp 9 – 10 on Henry Sadlier.
3. For Genealogical details see under Trench in *Burke's Irish Family Records*, (London, 1976), pp 1138 et. seq.
4. Career of Sir Ralph in Drummond, *Our Man in Scotland*, passim. See also T.U. Sadleir, *A Brief Memoir of the Right Hon. Sir Ralph Sadleir, Knight Banneret P.C. M.P.*, (Hertford, 1907), *passim,* and R. Wetherall, *Standon*, (Standon, 1988), p26. See also *D.N.B.*, e.v. under Sadler, Sadleir, Sadeyeler Sir Ralph.
5. Drummond, *Our Man in Scotland*, p151 indicates that as early as 1546 it took twenty five closely written sheets to record his lands.
6. Edward's grandson Edwin Sadleir became the First Baronet of Temple Dinsley, Hertfordshire which was created in 1661. Sir Edwin's son, also Sir Edwin, married Mary Croune, foundress of the Sadleirian Lectures in Mathematics in Cambridge. When he died without issue in 1719 the baronetcy became extinct.
7. Sir Ralph's great grandson.
8. References in Burke's, *The Landed Gentry of Ireland*, (London,1958), p. 622; *Burke's Irish Family Records*, (1976), p. 1143; John p. Prendergast, *The Cromwellian Settlement in Ireland*, (Dublin, 1875 2nd ed.), pp 119,, l30, et. seq; Edward Walford, *The County Families of the United Kingdom* , (London, 1865 3rd ed.) p. 874; *Hansard's Parliamentary History*, vol.111, 1642-1660, pp 1433, 1483, 1538; Dermot F. Gleeson; 'An Unpublished Cromwellian Document' in *North Munster Antiquarian Journal*, vol.1 (1936-39), pp 78-81; John T. Gilbert (ed.) *A Contemporary History of Affairs in Ireland from 1641 to 1652*, vol.11, part 11, (Dublin 1880),p.386, vol.3, pt.1, p. 164, vol.3, pt.2, pp 262, 311,324, et.seq. H. Gordon, *Reminiscences of an Irish Land Agent,* (London 1904), p. 4.
9. Gleeson, 'An Unpublished Cromwellian'. p. 78. Gleeson's source is a paper found among the uncalendared manuscripts in Kilkenny Castle and is considered a contemporary copy of a Cromwellian document.
10. See Gilbert, *A Contemporary History of Affairs*, vol.11 pt.11, p. 386 for a letter from Cromwell 2 April 1650 on Sadleir's victories in Tipperary, Kilkenny and Waterford; Ibid. vol.111 pt.11. pp 262,311,324 locate Sadleir in Waterford, Clare and other places accepting the surrender of garrisons.
11. Prendergast, *The Cromwellian Settlement*, pp 119, 130, l32.
12. As Governor of Galway, Sadleir received £100 to help priests build cabins on Inis Buffin – see Prendergast, *The Cromwellian Settlement*, pp 145, 163, 325.
13. Broghill was one of three commissioners appointed by the 'Rump Parliament' in 1659 to govern Ireland. An ex-Royalist, he was closely involved in negotiating the restoration of the monarchy. See J.C. Beckett, *The Making of Modern Ireland 1603-1923*, (London, 1966),pp.116-117, 129-130, 134 on Broghill's role.
14. Gleeson, 'An Unpublished Cromwellian'., p. 78.
15. Ibid., pp 79-80 lists three soldiers and the amount of individual debentures.
16. Ibid., p. 78. See *The Civil Survey A.D.1654-1656, County of Tipperary, vol.11*

Western and Northern Baronies, (Dublin, 1934), p. 329 and Ibid., pp 281-350 for details of McEgan lands in the Barony of Lower Ormond. Kilnahalagh (Kinelagh, Killnalahagh) is near the modern town of Borrisokane. It was in the ancient parish of Uskean.

17.   His first wife was Anne Goadridge of St. Albans, who was the widow of John Shadd. The last will and testament of his only son, Thomas, by this marriage may be seen in R.D., vol.15, p. 477, mem. no.8230, will dated 28 October 1715. For other references in the Registry of Deeds to the Sadleirs of Sopwell Hall in the early eighteenth century see R.D., vol. 34, p. 413, mem.22132, lease 8 October 1711 by the same Thomas Sadleir, and R.D., vol.28, p. 178, mem.17100, lease by Thomas Sadleir 11 November 1715 and R.D., vol.36, p. 403, mem.23200, lease 30 January 1722.

18.   For a history of the Wall family see H. Gallwey, *The Wall Family in Ireland 1170 – 1970,* (Naas, 1970), *passim.*

19.   pp 100, 456, 458-9 below.

20.   Sadleir contributed to a self portrait in the *London Illustrated News* in 1850 and claimed a direct line from Sir Ralph Sadleir, no doubt to enhance his own status as an M.P.

21.   *Burke's Irish Family Records,* (1976),.pp.1138.

22.   S. Schoenbaum, *William Shakespeare, a Compact Documentary Life,* (Oxford, 1975), p. 76. Judith and Hamnet Sadleir lived in a house at the corner of High Street and Sheep Street near the Corn market. Hamnet Sadleir was one of the five witnesses of Shakespeares will, (ibid. p. 250).

23.   Eleanor Sadleir married Elizabeth's brother, Richard. Another brother, Thomas Quiney, married Judith, William Shakespeare's daughter.

24.   T. Laffan, *Tipperary's Families, being the Hearth-Money Records for 1665-6-7,* (Dublin 1911), pp 62,ll5.

25.   *Burke's Irish Family Records,* (1976), pp 1138 et. seq. See also R.D., Bk.264, p. 575, abs. 179439, articles of intermarriage, 16 Feb. 1728, Bk.133, p. 201, abs.90319, article of agreement 25 April 1748, Bk. 393, p. 482, abs. 261012, marriage settlement 11 June 1765; Bk.241, p. 624, abs.161496, lease and release 10-11 June 1765; Bk.247, p. 560, abs.163976, articles of agreement 29 Jan 1767, Bk.346, p. 549, abs. 234688, deed 27 Aug. 1782, Vol. l, 1842, abs. 184, deed of release, 20 Dec. 1841, reciting an indenture of 18 Jan. 1818, Vol.1, 1834, abs. 230, marriage settlement 2 Dec. 1834, Vol.25, 1852, abs. 104, assignment 3 May 1849.

26.   See Michael MacEwan.*The Ryan family and the Scarteen Hounds,* (Labourer Press, 1990), p. 36. (The Ryans were relatives of Daniel O' Connell).

27.   R. Lucas, 'Irish Provincial Directories 1788 – Directory of the six towns in Tipperary' in *The Irish Genealogist,* 3 (H), October 1966, p. 476 .

28.   Ibid.

29.   *Pigot's Directory, 1824,* (London, 1824), p. 312.

30.   For Scully genealogy see Burke's, *The Landed Gentry of Ireland,* p. 632, B.C. MacDermot, 'Letters of John Scully to James Duff Coughlan 1923-1927,' in *The Irish Genealogist,* vol. 6, no 1, November 1980, pp 59-76, no.2, November 1981, pp 227-246, no.3, November 1982, pp 353-369, (henceforth referred to as *I.G.*vol.6), D. Scully, *Gleanings Concerning our Family History,* (1806), (this typescript is in the Scully papers, N.L.I., MS.27577), D. G. Marnane, *Land and Violence. A History of West Tipperary from 1660,* (Tipperary, 1985), pp 95 et. seq.

31.   Darby was used by the family and was the more common name for Jeremiah used by Burke.

32.   Now County Offaly.

33. Thady was the more common name for Timothy or Teigue used in Burke.
34. Scully, *Gleanings* , p. 2.
35. Ibid., pp 2-3.
36. Ibid., p. 3.
37. Ibid.
38. Ibid., Mary Meagher, (Maher), was an aunt of Nicholas Maher whose family purchased the Nicholson estate in Thurles. The Maher mansion is now the club house of Thurles golf club.
39. Ibid., p. 4.
40. The Scullys had twelve children in sixteen years.
41. A cattle plague especially foot and mouth.
42. Scully, *Gleanings*, p. 6. The owner of the estate was J. Power.
43. p. 11 above.
44. Mary Scully (nee Huddleston) to her mother Mary Huddleston, 29 April 1802 in B.C. MacDermot, (ed.), *The Catholic Question in Ireland and England 1798-1827, The Papers of Denys Scully* , (Dublin, 1988), p. 59.
45. 'The Banking and Currency System' in *Saorstát Éireann, Official Handbook*, (Dublin, 1932), p. 101.
46. 21 and 22 Geo.111. C.16 (Irl).
47. For details of the 1782 Act and its effect upon banking in general see G.L. Barrow, *The Emergence of the Irish Banking System 1820-1845*, (Dublin, 1975) pp 2,12.
48. J.F. McCarthy, 'The Story of Sadleir's Bank', in *Clonmel Historical and Archaeological Society* , vol. 1, no.3, 1954-55, p. 3.
49. A ledger and a letter book of the bank survive and are in N.L.I., Scully Papers, MSS. 27492 and 27495.
50. Dan O'Brien, a Clonmel shopkeeper to Denys Scully, 27 September 1813 in Scully, *The Catholic Question*, p. 473.
51. See *The Irish Almanac and official Directories for the year 1847*, (Dublin, MDCCCXLV11), p. 213 for statistics from 1804 onwards.
52. Barrow, *The Emergence of the Irish Banking.*, p. 53, see also Marnane, *Land and Violence*, p. 74, T*he Banking and Currency System*, p. 74. C. Ó Gráda, *Ireland a New Economic History 1780 – 1939*, (Oxford, 1994), pp 52 – 55, T.K. Whitaker, 'Origins and Consolidation' in F.S.L. Lyons, *Bicentenary essays. Bank of Ireland 1783 – 1983*, (Dublin, 1983), p. 17, O. MacDonagh, 'The Victorian Bank, 1824 – 1914' in ibid., p. 31. See *F.J.* 16 June 1820 on the strength of Scully's bank during the crisis.
53. Barrow, *The Emergence of the Irish Banking.*, p. 18, Ó Gráda, *Ireland a New Economic*, pp 56 – 57, Whitaker, *Origins.*, p. 26. See *F.J.* 2 June 1820 on the difficulties of Leslie's Bank Cork, the suspension of trading by Bruce's Bank Limerick, the run on Riall's Bank, Clonmel, and Roche's Bank in Cork. See ibid., 3 June 1820 for reference to the difficulties of Maunsell and Kennedy's Bank in Limerick. The *Freeman's Journal* reported the panic in some areas of the south particularly in Kerry where Bank of Ireland notes only were in circulation because of public unwillingness to use those of other banks. The fair of Molahiffe was severely curtailed because farmers refused to accept paper money.
54. It finally went into liquidation in 1823 or 1824. Sausse was married to Catherine Scully.
55. i.e. fifty Irish miles or sixty-five statute miles.
56. Barrow,*The Emergence of the Irish Banking.*, pp 56,63-65. – The acts were 1821 – 1&2 Geo. IV c.72; 1824 – 5 Geo.IV.c.73; 1825 – 6 Geo.IV. c.42.

57. N.L.I., Scully Papers, MS. 27479. See also MS. 17579 for a typescript of this diary by Denys. The latter is used in this work and henceforth is sourced as *Diary*.

58. *Diary*, p. 276.

59. The diary is an almost illegible scrawl.

60. Marnane, *Land and Violence*, p. 96.

61. *Diary*, pp 223, 288.

62. Scully, *Gleanings*, p. 6.

63. Marnane, *Land and Violence.*, p. 34. For a detailed commentary on Tipperary see W. J. Hayes, *Tipperary in the Year of Rebellion 1798*, (Roscrea, 1998), *passim*. Thomas Judkin Fitzgerald, High Sheriff of Tipperary and arch enemy of the rebels lived in Lisheen House, Golden, near the Scullys. In 1804 he quarrelled with Denys Scully's brother, Jerry, who physically chastised him. The nature of the quarrel is not known – see Edward Scully to Denys 21 July 1804 in MacDermot, *The Catholic Question*, p. 75.

64. The career of Billy Scully (1821-1906) lies outside the scope of this book but was sufficiently adventurous to merit a separate study. He became infamous for his harshness as a landlord which resulted first in his prosecution by the state and then in an unsuccessful attempt to assassinate him during an eviction process at Ballycohey in August 1868. He is also remembered as an immensely wealthy individual who became one of the largest landowners in the United States. In 1888 his holdings, purchased in four states for almost half a million pounds, totalled 224,738 acres. He died a multi-millionaire in London in October 1906. See H.E. Socolofsky, *Landlord William Scully*, (Kansas, 1979), *passim* see also Marnane, *Land and Violence*, pp 96-99, see also G. Moran, 'William Scully and Ballycohey, a Fresh Look' in *Tipperary Historical Journal*, (Thurles, 1992), pp 63 – 74.

65. Scully, *Gleanings*, p. 5.

66. *Diary*, pp 216-217.

67. Ibid., p. 219. This refers to Nelson's destruction of the French fleet anchored at Aboukir on 1 August 1798.

68. *1.G.*,vol.6, pp 239,241. See B.C. MacDermot, (ed.). *The Diary of Denys Scully, The Irish Catholic Petition of 1805* (Dublin 1992), p. XX on Scully's offer to raise a regiment in 1803.

69. The correspondence of Denys Scully from 1798 to 1830 recorded by MacDermot runs to almost 700 pages. His diary chronicled his close association with Lord Fingall and Sir Thomas French. While in London he met Lord Castlereagh, Lord Southwell, Sir Evan Nepean, The Earl of Dorchester, Sir John Throck Morton, The Marquis of Sligo and Lord Trimelston. His daughter, Catherine, was baptised by Daniel Murray, Coadjutor to Archbishop Troy of Dublin. Murray later succeeded Troy.

70. Now St. Kieran's College.

71. In 1785 he came first in the Greek, Latin and French examinations and excelled in Greek and Latin in the 1786 examinations. In later life he was President of the Kilkenny Academic Society, a type of past pupils' union – see MacDermot, *The Catholic Question*, p. 150; F. Ó Fearghail, *St. Kieran's College, Kilkenny, 1782 – 1982*, (Kilkenny, 1982), p. 21.

72. A Cambridge pensioner was the equivalent of an Oxford commoner i.e. a student who paid for his room and board in the college.

73. MacDermot, *The Catholic Question*, p. X1.

74. Catherine Mathew was the widow of Philip Roe and sister of 1st Earl of Llandaff. When she died Clonmell remarried in 1779. For an amusing biographical sketch

of Clonmell see *D.N.B.*, E.V under Scott John. For an extract from his diary see M. Lenox – Conyngham, *Diaries of Ireland. An Anthology 1590 – 1987*, (Dublin 1998), pp 57-60.

75. MacDermot, *The Catholic Question*, p. 7n.5.

76. Ibid., p. 69.n.1. The Corps was also put on permanent duty after Emmet's Rising.

77. Here he met Lady Elizabeth Hastings, daughter of the 9th Earl of Huntingdon and Third wife of the 1st Earl of Moira. Her son, Lord Francis Rawdon-Hastings, 2nd Earl of Moira, was a friend of the Prince of Wales.

78. James Scully signed a requisition on 3 August 1799 in favour of the Union – MacDermot, *The Catholic Question*, p. 41.

79. Scully to Huddleston, 5 March 1801 in ibid., pp 48-49.

80. Ibid., p. 398 n.4.

81. For full details of the Catholic Committee which discussed the petition, its text and Scully's diary see Mac Dermot, *The Catholic Question*, letters 68, 84 to 111; MacDermot, *The Diary of Denys Scully, passim,* (see pp 80-86 for the meeting with Pitt).

82. MacDermot, *The Catholic Question, passim,* contains a great deal of correspondence, some of it personal, between O'Connell and Scully, who loaned him money. O'Connell referred to him as the 'great brute of brutes', because of his physical size in later years – MacDermot, *The Catholic Question*, p. XX1.

83. In 1806 he was described by Robert Marshall, used by Lord Castlereagh to liaise with the Catholics, as the 'son of an eminent grazier in Tipperary who has very much influence in all the southern counties – strongly Catholic feelings, anxious for emancipation – attentive to his religious duties and, therefore, much respected by bishops and clergy – of great weight at public meetings, where he has generally carried all his points – by far the more intelligent than any other Catholic upon the Penal Laws and their consequences' – MacDermot, *The Diary of Denys Scully*, p. 155.

84. D. Scully, *Statement of the Penal Laws* , (Dublin, 1812), *passim*. The ideas in the book had been germinating at least since 1805 when Lord Fingall had asked him to draw up a statement of the penal laws still in force. He was also encouraged by others to publish such a work. See Fingall to Scully 20 March 1805 in MacDermot, *The Catholic Question*, p. 98. The Earl of Donoughmore to Scully 7 October 1810 in Ibid., p. 244. Edward Marnane the Parish Priest of Tipperary recommended some minor changes in a section of the book which Scully adopted, Marnane to Scully 21 October 1810 in ibid., p. 246.

85. The offending section was a footnote in part one which was an implied indictment of the Irish government by its statement that a Catholic named Barry was executed in Kilkenny in 1810 although his innocence had already been shown. There is ample evidence that Scully had been advised by several friendly sources that the inclusion of this reference could lead to prosecution, see e.g. letter of a barrister, Thomas Wallace to Scully in May 1811 in MacDermot, *The Catholic Question*, pp 271-272, see also William Tighe M.P, (who was married to Hannah Bunbury of Kilfeacle) to Scully 15 April 1812 and 13 June 1812 in ibid., pp 341,355. The facts of the Barry case were outlined by Scully in a letter to Tighe on 28 May 1812 in ibid., pp 348-350. Fitzpatrick decided to include the footnote and the Lord Lieutenant advised the Home Secretary to submit it to the law offices. When Fitzpatrick was prosecuted Scully sent the summons to Sir Charles Grey with a threat that a prosecution would exasperate the Irish people: he described the attorney general and the solicitor general as 'crafty and intriguing men' – Scully to Grey 5 July 1812 in ibid., pp 361-363. The prosecution

proceeded and O'Connell defended Fitzpatrick whose premises in 4 Capel Street were for a long time used as the meeting place of the Catholic Committee. He was sentenced to eighteen months imprisonment and a £200 fine. He began his term of imprisonment on 28 April 1813. Scully used his influential contacts in a vain effort to secure his release, see e.g. his letter 24 April 1814 to Lord Henry Holland asking him to intercede with the intransigent Duke of Richmond, who as Lord Lieutenant had been greatly angered by the reference, ibid., pp 497-498. Fitzpatrick, himself, apologised to the Duke in a petition but Richmond refused to interfere on the basis that 'the licentiousness of the press had increased so much that it was his duty to correct it as far as the laws allowed', see ibid.. p. 500 and p. 500 n.2. (The Catholic Board paid Fitzpatrick's expenses and Scully generally subscribed to a collection).

86. It was a two part, 370 page work. Its call number in the Royal Irish Academy is RR61H2.
87. Scully, *Statement*, p. 142.
88. Ibid., p. 145.
89. Ibid., p. 141.
90. Ibid., p. 142.
91. MacDermot, *The Catholic Question*, p. 530.
92. He continued to have an interest in the political direction of the Repeal movement under O'Connell but by 1824 their views had considerably diverged. Scully's last political statement was a strong attack on O'Connell's petition to parliament that year in a public letter from 'A Munster Farmer'. This letter, published as a thirty-three page pamphlet expressed suspicion of how the public subscriptions (Catholic rent) to maintain the newly founded Catholic Association, would be applied (p.3). It attacked the apparent lack of focus of the petition – 'why construct your petition like the multifarious recipes of quack physicians, in which one or two effective remedies are sometimes combined with, and perhaps frequently neutralised by, their many nauseous and unnecessary accompaniments' (p.11). Scully condemned the petition's hostility to the Protestant Establishment and the tithes, which to him were extraneous to the Catholic cause. He also objected to the language in the petition and to O'Connell's 'harangues' in general, which not only showed disrespect for parliament but were an incitement to violence, the suppression of which would only bring further suffering to Catholics. See A Munster Farmer, *A Letter to Daniel O'Connell, Esq., occasioned by the petition adopted at the late aggregate meeting of the Catholics of Ireland,* (Dublin, 1824), Passim. (R.I.A. Haliday Pamphlets 1314.5).
93. Denys and his younger brother, James of Shanballymore were the executors and main beneficiaries of the will and were reputed to have lost £30,000 by their mother's legal victory. The case was only resolved when it was decided by the House of Lords in 1825 – see MacDermot, *I.G.*, vol. 6, pp 69,74 and MacDermot, *The Catholic Question* , p. 577 n2.
94. MacDermot, *The Catholic Question*, p. 53n1.
95. Ibid., p. XII.
96. Ibid., pp 74, 170-171.
97. *Diary*, p. 261. Margaret Wyse was the daughter of John Wyse of the Manor of St. John, Waterford.
98. MacDermot, *I.G.*, vol. 6, op.cit p. 66. Sir Thomas Wyse later became a Lord of the Treasury in Melbourne's Government. His marriage failed. The Bonaparte Wyse connection is explored in J. J. Auchmuty, *Sir Thomas Wyse 1791 1862. The Life and Career of an Educator and Diploma*t, (London,1939) passim, and Olga

Bonaparte – Wyse, *The Spurious Brood, Princess Letitia Bonaparte and her children*, (London, 1969), passim.

99. *Diary*, pp 215,169. William married Anna Roe when he was under eighteen and his parents were convinced that her mother had exploited his youth and inveigled him into marriage; see e.g. letter 3 November 1804 from his mother, Kitty Scully, to his brother Denys in MacDermot, *The Catholic Question*, pp 78-79.

100. William (Thady) Scully was educated in Trinity College and studied medicine in Edinburgh. He practised as a doctor first in Totnes and then in Torquay where he died in 1842.

101. MacDermot, *The Catholic Question* , pp 102-105.

102. MacDermot, *I.G.*, vol. 6, pp 242-243. Nancy received a dowry of £1,500 with a further £500 to follow after the birth of a son. Scully was especially fond of his Mahon grandchildren, made generous provision for them in his will and provided them with employment. See also MacDermot, *The Catholic Question*, letters 17,121,140,193,215.

103. Lucinda. (Linny was the family name for her.)

104. In the Civil Parish of Knockgraffon, near Rockwell College.

105. For a brief pedigree of the Keatings who were dispossessed during the Cromwellian Confiscations see MacDermot, *I.G.*, vol. 6, p. 361, n92. See A. Young, *A Tour of Ireland 1776-79*, (London, 1892) p. 391, and Marnane,*Land and Violence*, p. 96.

106. MacDermot, *The Catholic Question*, p. 710 shows Sadleir as a Protestant. See also *The Gentleman's Magazine* ,1 May 1856, p. 530.

107. Letter in MacDermot, *The Catholic Question*, pp 78-79.

108. *Diary,* p. 256.

109. MacDermot, *The Catholic Question*, p. 83. Only one other letter from Joanna Scully is extant. This was written to her brother Denys on 30 January 1799 in which she indicated that her main opposition to the proposed Union stemmed from her fear that, if passed, Denys like other lawyers would be forced to live in England. The letter also referred to a visit to Kilfeacle by Nicholas Maher and his son, Val (Valentine). (Her father was a first cousin of Nicholas Maher, who was a grand-nephew of her grandmother, Mary Maher). Letter in MacDermot, *The Catholic Question* , p. 23.

110. See Catherine's letter to Denys 29 December 1804 referring to a prolonged visit by the Harneys to Kilfeacle, in which she described Charles Harney as 'a steady proper gentleman like young man' – MacDermot, *The Catholic Question* , p. 82. Joanna's brother, Jeremiah, described him as 'about 20 years of age, corpulent and rather inactive. He has not the smallest taste for business of any kind, nor can I say what his favourite amusement is. He is a very good humoured man and good tempered' – MacDermot, *I.G.*, vol. 6, p. 358.

111. Catherine Scully to Denys Scully 9 February 1805 in MacDermot, *The Catholic Question*, p. 85.

112. Ibid., p. 100.

113. Catherine Scully to Denys Scully 3 April 1805 in ibid., pp 100-101.

114. MacDermot,*I.G.*, vol. 6, p. 358.

115. *Diary* p. 258. Scully was to get back £1,250 if Joanna died with issue within two years.

116. MacDermot, *I.G.*, vol. 6, p. 358.

117. Ibid., p. 359, *Diary* p. 351, see also R.D., 1827, vol.835, p. 7, abs.560843, lease 14 September 1827 citing his age.

118. *Diary* , p. 349.
119. N.L.I., Scully Papers, MS. 27492, ledger of the Tipperary Bank.
120. See Marnane, *Land and Violence* , p. 73.
121. The house survives to-day minus the rear section and is the residence of the Knightly family.
122. p. 52 below.
123. Marnane, *Land and Violence*, p. 162.
124. Ibid., pp,164 et. seq.
125. See King's Inns Society, Petition of Clement Sadleir N.D. to be admitted as an apprentice solicitor: This gives details of Clement's education.
126. S. Lewis, *A Topographical Dictionary of Ireland*, vol. 2, (London, 1837), p. 554.
127. Marnane, *Land and Violence*, p. 25.
128. c.1720-1803.
129. See R. Ó Foghludha, Ar Bruach na Coille Muaire, Liam Dall Ó hIfearnáin, (Dublin 1939), pp 16-17. Lattin was only a mile and a half from Shronell where his mother was born.
130. He had died in 1768.
131. Joseph Damer, John Damer's brother.
132. See Ó Foghludha, *Ar Bruach*, p. 82 for the poem in Irish. A far more bitter satire, *Ar Bhás Dhawson*, was attributed to Ó hIfearnáin, but was written by his friend Seán Clárach MacDomhnaill, another minor poet of the time. For an account of the Damer family see Marnane, *Land and Violence*, pp 25-26.
133. See Marnane, *Land and Violence*, pp 41-47.
134. Ibid., pp 44,180 n.19.
135. N. A., S.O.C. 1827,2834/59.
136. N. A., S.O.C. 1822, 2355/39A.
137. N. A., S.O.C. 1822, 2355/55.
138. It is not possible to decipher the Christian name; see N.A., S.O.C., 1822, 2355/85 for disturbances near Cashel where farmers houses were raided for guns. The house of the Smithwick family near Golden was also raided. See also N.A., S.O.C., 1822, 2355/45 for incidents in other areas. See Military Report, 14 October 1822 on the burning of two dairy houses belonging to Peter Smithwick of Cullen in N.A., S.O.C., 1822, 2356/65. In a letter of 5 October 1822 James Roe of Roesborough wrote that this was the first outrage of its kind in the locality – N.A., S.O.C., 1822, 2356/60.
139. N.A., S.O.C., 1823, 2518/14, Report from Thurles 1 April 1823.
140. N. A., S.O.C., 1823, 2518/65, Report 27 November 1823.
141. N. A., S.O.C., 1824, 2621/11, Military Report 30 January 1824.
142. N.A., S.O.C., 1824, 1822/23/24, S.O.C. 1825 2729/9. See however the alarmist letter 1 November 1825 from Joseph Gubbins, Golden about the lawlessness of his neighbourhood – murder, assassinations, and unlicensed whiskey houses.
143. N. A., S.O.C., 1825, 2729/12.
144. N. A., Private Index Papers, 1826, W4, Report 10 April 1826. Edmund was the brother of Denys and the Ballyneill lands eventually passed to Vincent Scully, grandson of Denys, who sold it in 1905. This Ballyneill property should not be confused with the 1000 acre Ballyneale estate near Clonmel which Denys Scully inherited from his father. The head landlord of this was the Corporation of Yarmouth. He tried in vain to purchase it for £4000 in 1824 – Denys Scully to Richard Huddleston, (his brother-in-law), 8 February 1824 in MacDermot, *The Catholic Question*, pp 660-661. This letter complains of extensive sub-letting on his lands.

145. N. A., Private Index Papers, 1826, W4, Report 24 April 1826. (This file contains accounts of other outrages).
146. N. A., S.O.C. 1827, 2834/37 for a letter 11 June 1827 from Richard Sadleir in his capacity as magistrate querying whether an individual who had attacked a house should be granted bail. Some unusual incidents occurred in Tipperary Town in 1827. One of these which involved attacks on flour cars indicated a degree of localised famine. Another was a sectarian attack by a mob upon a group of soldiers who wore orange emblems on 12 July. See N.A., S.O.C., 1827, 2834/41, Military Report 16 July 1827.
147. See T. Corcoran S.J., *The Clongowes Record 1814-1932*, (Dublin,1932), p. 165.
148. Ibid., for the Sadleirs and Scullys who were students in Clongowes.
149. Some of Sadleir's Scully cousins attended Stonyhurst, e.g.. Edmund from 1826 to 1830, Jeremiah from 1829 to 1833, William from 1837 to 1838. – letter to writer 26 May 1998 from F.J. Turner S.J., Archivist. Fr. Turner also forwarded the Stonyhurst prospective for 1827 and an academy programme of 1830.
150. Ibid., p. 45.
151. Ibid. See Peter Costello, *A History of Clongowes Wood College 1814-1989*, (Dublin, 1989), p. 20 putting the total area purchased and leased at 315 acres.
152. e.g. he advised Kenney to send prospectuses to Lords Holland, Lansdowne, Grenville, Grey and the Duke of Norfolk. He also advised him to contact Sir Henry Parnell, General Montagu, Mathew and George Ponsonby, with the freedom to 'freely use my name to those persons' – Scully to Kenney 22 March 1814 in MacDermot, *The Catholic Question*, pp 496-497.
153. See Kenney to Scully 29 May 1814 and 19 June 1814 in ibid., pp 512-513, 522-523. See also Corcoran, *The Clongowes Record*, pp 52, 56. Costello has little to say about Scully's involvement and mistakenly refers to him as Kenney's solicitor – (Costello, *A History of Clongowes*, p. 22) A very good account of Scully's central role as legal adviser is contained in Thomas Morrissey, *As One Sent: Peter Kenney S.J. 1779-1841*, (Dublin,1996), pp 99,100,108,110.
154. Scully to Kenney 19 December 1813 and 22 March 1814 in MacDermot, *The Catholic Question*, pp 493-497 and 497 n4. For subsequent difficulties encountered by Kenney see Corcoran, *The Clongowes Record*, p. 55.
155. Lindsay to Scully 13 May 1814 in MacDermot, *The Catholic Question* , p. 510.
156. Scully to Kenney 13 May 1814 in ibid.
157. Kenney to Scully 19 June 1814 in ibid., pp 523-523.
158. Lewis, *A Topographical Dictionary*, vol.2 p. 337.
159. Ibid., vol.1, p. 328.
160. Corcoran, *The Clongowes Record*, p. 63.
161. Ibid., p. 66 for timetable. Students arose at 6 A.M. for the rest of the year and morning study was cut by an hour.
162. Ibid., p. 82.
163. Ibid., p. 62. Students who wished to study Chemistry, 'or other branches of experimental philosophy', were charged an extra five guineas.
164. Ibid., p. 71.
165. Ibid., p. 82.
166. Ibid., pp 73-74, 77,79.
167. Ibid., p. 77.
168. Ibid., pp 72-73.
169. Ibid., p. 76.
170. Ibid.
171. Ibid., p. 82.

172. Ibid., p. 86.

173. Throughout his stay at Clongowes the student could expect to study Demosthenes, Homer, Horace, Cicero, Levy, Virgil, Lucan, Quintilian, Tacitus, Xenophon and Ovid – see Corcoran, *The Clongowes Record*, pp 94-95. For a well balanced account of Clongowes education see Morrissey, *As One Sent*, pp 118 *et seq.*

174. Corcoran, *The Clongowes Record*, p. 100.

175. These were known as Scholae Geminae.

176. Motivated by this, many students rose earlier than normal to avail of an extra period of voluntary study.

177. Corcoran, *The Clongowes Record*, p. 115.

178. Ibid., p. 118.

179. Ibid., p. 117.

180. Ibid.

181. Ibid., pp 113-116.

182. Ibid., p. 116.

183. Attorneys were not permitted to practice in Chancery but could practice in the Courts of Kings/Queen's Bench, Exchequer and Exchequer. Solicitors were entitled to practice in Chancery. Attorneys were regarded as having inferior social status to solicitors. See D. Hogan, *The Legal Profession in Ireland 1789-1922*, (Naas, 1986), pp 1,6.

184. Obituary notes on John Sadleir mistakenly refer to Nicholas as his uncle. He died in 1858 and not 1855 as shown in *Burke's Family Records*. Nicholas Sadleir was the son of Richard Sadleir of Nelson Street, Tipperary and Grace Sadleir (her maiden name was also Sadleir). He was apprenticed to the Solicitor Edward Shadwell Hickman on 31 March 1807 when he was sixteen years old. He was educated at the school of the Rev. Marshall Clarke, Tipperary. See Society of King's Inns, Memorial of Edward Shadwell Hickman to be permitted to take Nicholas Sadleir as an apprentice, 31 March 1807.

185. Mary O'Brien Butler's granddaughter, Catherine, was sister to John Butler, one time Catholic Bishop of Cork who renounced Catholicism and married to secure the Dunboyne line. The marriage, however, did not secure the desired result.

186. See his will of 31 July 1858 in p. R.O.I., T.12016. This will lists his considerable property. See Marnane, *Land and Violence*, p. 170 for the family tree of the O'Brien Butlers, who had an estate in Bansha, Co. Tipperary. See *Irish Independent* 26 February 1999 for the impending sale of Dunboyne Castle by the Keating family, owners of Kepak Ltd.

187. In 1830 he lived in 2 Lr. Gardiner Street. The following year he moved to number 33 and in 1835 he was in number 45. By 1836 he was practising from no.103. See *Wilson's Dublin Directory for the year 1830, The Treble Almanac for the year 1830* , (Dublin,1830), p. 172, Ibid., 1831, p. 175. ibid., 1832, p. 280, ibid.,1835, p. 327, ibid., 1836 p. 343, *The Post Office Annual Directory for 1832*, (Dublin, 1832), and ibid. for 1836 p. 343.

188. e.g. the valuation in 103 Gardiner Street was only £35 p. A., while that for the other addresses occupied by him ranged from £70 to 72 p. A. – *Thoms Directory for 1878*, pp 707-708.

189. *Wilson's Dublin Directory 1830*, p. 152.

190. See King's Inns Society, Memorial of Nicholas Sadleir April 1832 requesting permission to take John as an apprentice. Attached was a petition from John verifying his years at Clongowes and his instruction in Latin and an affidavit of his father Clement William. The biographical notes on Sadleir following his death

mistakenly show him as an attorney rather than a solicitor and 1831 as the year he began his apprenticeship. (It was a strict requirement that masters of apprentices attended the courts in Dublin and so it is probable that John Sadleir spent some period of training in the Dublin office). For lists of attorney, solicitor and barrister apprentices see E. Keane, p. B. Phair, T.U. Sadleir (eds.), *King's Inns Admission Papers, 1607 – 1867*, (Dublin, 1982), passim. Details of the Sadleirs and Scullys are listed in ibid., pp 435-436, 441-442.

191. See Hogan, *The Legal Profession*, p. 7 on the training requirements for admission to the profession of attorney and solicitor.

192. Unlike solicitors, barristers were not permitted to become involved in commercial enterprises or to become land agents or moneylenders. A legal education was considered extremely suitable for appointments as land agents. See Hogan, *The Legal Profession*, p. 9.

193. 11 Geo.IV and 1 Will. IV C.32.

194. Barrow, *The Emergence of the Irish Banking*, p. 137. See ibid pp 108 et.seq for the establishment and collapse of the Agricultural and Commercial Bank of Ireland and pp 120 *et. seq* for the setting up of the National Bank under the aegis of Daniel O'Connell. See Ó Gráda, *Ireland a New Economic*, pp 139 – 146, Whitaker, 'Origins and Consolidation', p. 27 MacDonagh, 'The Victorian Bank'., pp 32 *et. seq.*, See also *A Return of the Joint Stock Banks existing in England and Wales in each of the three years ending with the 5th day of January 1839; specifying the Date of the establishment of each bank, the number and situation of its branches (if it had any) and the number of partners in each bank during each of the above mentioned years. Similar returns for Scotland and Ireland*, H.C. 1839 (530) XXX. 215, and *Accounts of the number of Private and Joint Stock Banks registered in Ireland in each year from 1820 to 1844, both inclusive and of all Joint Stock Banks existing in Ireland on the 1st day of January 1840, distinguishing those Banks that issued and those that did not issue notes*, H.C. 1844 (232) XXX11.445, (henceforth *Private and Joint Stock Banks Ireland 1840*).

195. Barrow, *The Emergence of the Irish Banking*, p. 113.

196. Ibid., p. 142 for this crisis which resulted not from a commercial cause but because of overextension.

197. Ibid., p. 169.

198. His affidavit in *L.E.* 3 May 1856.

199. See pp 64, 99, 395-96 below.

200. See *Full Report of the Trial of the issues directed by the Court of Exchequer in Ireland in the case of Edward Dowling V Edward Lawlor*, (Dublin,1854), (henceforth referred to as *Dowling*), p. 60, see also evidence of Leonard Morrogh in *W.T.* 5 April 1856.

201. See King's Inns Society, Petition of Clement Sadleir 1839 to be admitted an apprentice solicitor.

202. *Times* 3 March 1856.

203. There is some conflict of evidence about this. The original sources for the bank's collapse cited James Scully as the first Chairman but they may have confused this with his chairmanship of the reconstituted bank in 1842 – see e.g. *W.T.* 5 April 1856, *F.J.* 7 December 1858, *C.P.* 5 April 1856, *L.E.* 3 May 1856, *I.C.R.* 1856 and 1857 vol. 6 p. 121. *B.M.* 1846-47 p. 415. But Barrow, *The Emergence of the Irish Banking*, p. 161 cites Richard Sadleir as chairman. While he does not offer any source as proof his work is a detailed well sourced study of banking. The individual in question was probably Richard Sadleir of Scalaheen, brother of Nicholas, John's solicitor cousin.

204. Barrow, *The Emergence of the Irish Banking*, p. 162 points out that the bank was registered although this was not necessary for a non-issuing institution, but it gave the bank the right to conduct its affairs under a public officer.

205. *T.L.* 15 March 1856, *C.S.* 4 October 1856. It was reported that Lamie Murray, the founder of the National Bank advised the Sadleirs not to issue their own notes but to enter into an arrangement with the Bank of Ireland.

206. *L.E.* 23 February 1856.

207. *Private and Joint Stock Banks Ireland, 1840.* (Not paginated).

208. Barrow, *The Emergence of the Irish Banking*, p. 163.

209. See appendix 1 for statistics of branches.

210. Leonard Morrogh was the great grandson of old James Scully and the nephew of Robert Keating (Sadleir's first cousin and future M.P. for Waterford). Morrogh's mother was Catherine Keating who had received £750 from old James, her maternal grandfather, on her marriage. Morrogh's paternal grandfather was Leonard Keating, Garranlea – MacDermot, *I.G.*, vol. 6, p. 361. When Sadleir went to Dublin in 1838, Morrogh was only a teenager.

211. *The Post Office Annual Directory, 1838* in *Almanac Registry Directory*, (Dublin,1838) p. 318. See King's Inns Society, Memorial of William Sadleir to be admitted a student, 1833, (verified by Richard Lalor Shiel), and Memorial of William Sadleir to be admitted a barrister 1837. The second memorial had attached a certificate that William had fulfilled the requirement of keeping eight terms commons in the Dining Hall of Grays Inns, London. (This meant no more than attending dinners there for a number of days each term. The requirement to attend one of the inns of court in London was abolished in 1870 – see Hogan, *The Legal Profession*, p. 5.

212. See Society of King's Inns, Memorial of John Sadleir, n.d.. Attached was an affidavit 28 October 1839 of his father Clement William, and a petition of Clement himself to be admitted as apprentice.

213. *Post Office Annual Directory*, (Dublin 1843), p. 459, and ibid.,1844 p. 213, *Thoms Directory 1844*, pp 707-708. They were later joined by another solicitor James B. Kennedy – See *Thoms Directory 1848*, p. 689.

214. Morrissey, *As One Sent*, p. 430. The house was purchased from one of Lady Belvedere's sons who had inherited it.

215. Killeen House took its name from Killeen Castle, the seat of the Fingals in County Meath. They were the Catholic branch of the Plunketts. See *The Belvederian* vol. 1, no.1 p. 19. See S.A.O. Fitzpatrick, *Dublin, A Historical and Topographical account of the City*, (London, 1907), p. 313, M. Craig, *Dublin 1660-1860*, (Dublin, 1980), pp 229-231,319.

216. *Thoms Directory 1848*, pp 689,707-708 for comparisons. J.H. Martin, 'Aspects of the Social Geography of Dublin City in the Mid Nineteenth Century', M.A. thesis, (N.U.I.,1973), pp 52 refers to the colonisation of the Mountjoy Square area, including Great Denmark Street, by lawyers and doctors. Ibid., p. 85 shows Great Denmark Street classified as a first class private street in the 1851 census, while Gardiner Street was shown as second class.

217. G.N. Wright, *An Historical Guide to the City of Dublin*, (London, 1825 republished by the Four Courts Press, 1980), p. XXVII. Craig, *Dublin 1660 – 1860*, p. 265, D. Clarke, *Dublin*, (London, 1977), p. 81.

218. Fitzpatrick, *Dublin A Historical and Topographical*, p. 31

219. Martin, 'Aspects of the Social Geography', Passim.

220. See R.Davis, *The Young Ireland Movement*, (Dublin, 1987), p. 157 on Stritch.

221. *Nation* 6 April 1850.

222. Ibid.,13 April 1850.
223. S. Lewis, *A History and Topography of Dublin City and County*, (Dublin, 1837, reprinted by Mercier Press, 1980), p. 96. See also Wright, *An Historical Guide*, pp 147-148, Clarke, *Dublin*, pp 150-153.
224. p. 10 above.
225. p. 52 below.
226. For information on the clubs of Dublin see Lewis, *A History*, p. 97, *Thom's Directory, 1839* , p. 174, ibid., 1846 pp 189-190. Clarke, *Dublin*, p. 102.
227. *Thoms Directory, 1839*, p. 169.
228. R.D., 1840, vol. 12, Memorial 119, Deed of assignment 4 June 1840. This deed outlined the will and instructions that the estate in Noan be mortgaged or some of it sold to raise the dowries.
229. See R.D., 1843 Vol.12 Memorial 237, Indented deed of assignment 29 July 1843, R.D.,1846, vol. 7, Memorial 236, R.D., 1848, vol.13, Memorial no.43, indented deed of release, R.D., 1849, vol.6, Memorial 77. These records also detail the dowry.
230. *Evidence taken before her Majesty's Commissioners of Inquiry into the state of the Law and Practice in respect to the occupation of land in Ireland*, Part II, *H.C.* 1845 (XXI) iii pp 264 – 265 (Henceforth cited as the *Devon Commission*).
231. ibid., p. 300.
232. R.D., 1843, vol.2, Memorial 166, an indenture in seven parts dated 25 November 1842.
233. There was also a Thomas Eyre who was Vincent Scully's brother-in-law and he too was occasionally involved in Sadleir's land deals. See MacDermot, *I.G.*, vol.6 op. cit p. 355 n.83. For Eyre's genealogy see under Eyre of Lindley Hall in Ashworth p. Burke, *History of the Landed Gentry of Great Britain and Ireland*, (London, 1900), p. 513.
234. See appendix 2, see pp 100, 456, 458-9 below, see Gallwey, *The Wall Family*, p. 172.
235. This property had come into the hands of Viscount Kingsborough in the eighteenth century through his wife, the daughter and heir of Richard Fitzgerald, County Kildare – see H.A. Doubleday and Lord Howard de Walden, *The Complete Peerage*, vol. Vll, (London, 1929), p. 300.
236. See A.M. Sullivan, *New Ireland*, vol.1, (London, 1877), pp 271 *et. seq.* for a description.
237. *L.R.* 8 July 1856.
238. R.D., 1845, vol.5 Memorial 282, Indenture 22 February 1845. The Honourable William Stourton was also a party to the conveyance. This source lists the many townlands in the Mitchelstown estate.
239. *L.R.* 8 July 1856 – He only received £8,000 over the next eleven years.
240. Ibid., The date of this forged receipt is not given and it may not have been issued as early as 1845.
241. *C.T.* 12 July 1856. Since Eyre was already a trustee he could not advance the money to himself and hence the need to have Young act as trustee.
242. *C.T.* 5 July, 1856 Kingston v Eyre.
243. p. 385 below.
244. Norris was married to Julia Eyre; he was Vincent Scully's first cousin once removed and a great nephew of Thomas Eyre – see MacDermot, *I.G.* ,Vol. 6 pp 355 – 356 on Norris.
245. Evidence of Leonard Morrogh to the Master of Chancery in *W.T.* 5 April 1856.)
246. *I.C.R.*, 1856 and 1857, vol. 6, pp 350-352.

247. *Irish Chancery Reports* 1855, 1856 and 1857, vol. 5, pp 175-8 and ibid., 1856 and 1857, vol. 6. pp 74-6, 181-6.

248. *Times* 6 March 1856. Neither Hartwick nor Cook were listed on the shareholding from 1853 to 1856.

249. *C.R.* 1856 and 1856 vol.6 p. 121.

250. *I.C.R. 1858 and 1859* ,vol.9 p. 51.

251. *I.C.R. 1855, 1856 and 1857*, vol., 5, p. 185. *Times* 8 March 1856.

252. Judge Longfield in *I.C.R. 1858 and 1859*, vol.9, p. 44.

253. *L.E.* 3 May 1856.

254. See MacDermot, *I.G.*, vol. 6, p. 74 and p. 74n6. See Marnane, *Land and Violence*, p. 56 on the assassination. See *F.J.* 29 November 1842.

255. *F.J.* 1 December 1842. This paper also quoted details from the *Limerick Reporter*. Billy had fallen into a pool of water and went home to change his clothes. When James Vincent failed to return for dinner a messenger was sent for Jeremiah, the victim's uncle, who lived at Golden, 'lights were obtained and the neighbourhood of the lake searched, when after some time, the mutilated remains of Mr. Scully presented themselves – the back part of the skull being literally broken in pieces and the body as if it had been riddled with shot! A mallard lay by his side – his watch, rings etc. were untouched; but a double-barrelled gun which he had been using was carried off by his assassins'.

256. Evidence to the Devon Commission in 1843 on the murder was also contradictory. The evidence of Edward Dalton, Golden, was that Scully had evicted the tenant to secure the land for his own use. Dalton had little sympathy for Scully although his death resulted in many people losing their jobs on his estate. Michael Doheny, who had publicly disagreed with Scully politically and had been engaged by the Griffith family who were arrested for the murder, described Scully as a harsh landlord whose immediate 'act of oppression' prior to the murder was to dig up a large quantity of potatoes, which had been grown on con – acre at £14 an acre, and dump them on the road. He described an extended state of warfare between Scully and his tenants. Vincent Scully, however, emphatically denied that his brother had interfered with the potatoes and refused the suggestion that £14 was an exorbitant rent because the land had been let to potato jobbers who made large profits from their speculation despite the heavy rent. Both Scully and Dalton agreed that the potato incident had nothing to do with the murder. Scully denied that his brother intended to evict the Griffiths but had resolved to remove one of them who was in considerable arrears with his rent and who had neglected his farm. He was seriously wounded by an assassin although on 16 April 1842 because of this threat, was determined to proceed with his plan. Vincent Scully also rejected any suggestion that James was generally a harsh landlord but was a direct and outspoken individual whose reputation had been maligned by a group of tenants. See *Devon Commission* , pp 265, 294 – 296, 898 – 904.

257. *F.J.* 8 December 1842.

258. Text of the memorial in *F.J.* 12 December 1842.

259. Greene married Kate in 1838. See R.D., 1838, Vol. 13, abs. 138, marriage settlement May 1838.

260. He was married to Sadleir's aunt, Lucy Scully.

261. *F.J.* 14 December 1842.

262. See Marnane, *Land and Violence*, p. 57.

263. *F.J.* 29 November 1842, MacDermot, *I.G.* vol. 6, p. 361.

264. For details of the marriage settlement 25 November 1843 see R.D., 1844, vol. 28,

memorial 275, deed 14 November 1865 and R.D., 1883, vol. 5, memorial 95 deed 26 January 1883 which cited this marriage settlement.

265. *B.M.* 1845, vol.lll, p. 41.

266. *B.M.* 1846-47, vol.Vl, pp 414-415.

267. See J. O'Shea 'Thurles Savings Bank 1829-71', in *Thurles: The Cathedral Town,* (Dublin,1989), pp 109 *et. seq.* for the impact of the Famine on a small bank.

268. Barrow, *The Emergence of the Irish Banking,* p. 181.

269. For an account of the Act see ibid., pp 177-183.

270. Clause xxxi from the 1845 Bank Act.

271. It would be obliged to pay the Tipperary l% of the average amount of Bank of Ireland notes it kept in circulation provided it continued to exclusively issue these.

272. *N.G.* 3 March 1856. This source, citing *The Press,* reported that Sadleir, as receiver over several estates, had established other contacts in London.

273. His son, James Rodolph (1853-19ll) lived there. *Burkes Landed Gentry,* p. 632.

Carlow College.

Chapter 2

Beginning in politics

In 1846 as Dublin was experiencing harrowing cholera scenes,[1] brought about by poor housing, sanitation and hunger, the thirty three year old Sadleir gave up his practice to his partners, Morrogh and Kennedy.[2] He sailed on one of the steampackets to London, a rapidly growing metropolis with a population of over two million[3] compared with a quarter of a million in Dublin.[4] Like Dublin, however, it was a city of two faces, one of great wealth, the other extreme poverty.

Dickens, who loosely based one of his characters on Sadleir,[5] wrote about its 'melancholy streets; in their 'penitential garb of soot'.[6] He drew upon the poverty, crime and brutality in the disease-ridden slums of the East End, in places like Devil's Acre, Clerkenwell, Cheapside and Southwark. The *London Illustrated News,*whose proprietor, Herbert Ingram, became a friend of Sadleir,[7] reported on 12 February 1848 that 1,478 people had died in one week, many from contagious diseases.

Most mid-century commentators, however, did not dwell upon this more sordid aspect of London life. As the Great Exhibition was launched various publications and tour guides boasted of its power and wealth. One typical example, published in 1851, was *London as it is to-day: Where to go and what to see during the Great Exhibition,*

> London, 'Busy, Glamorous, Crowded, Imperial London', may be considered not merely as the capital of England, or of the British Empire, but as the metropolis of the civilised world – not merely as the seat of Government, which extends its connections and exercises its influence to the remotest point of the earth's surface – not merely as containing the wealth and the machinery by which the freedom and the slavery of nations are bought and sold – not merely as possessing a freedom of opinion, and a hardihood in the expression of that opinion, unknown to every other city – not merely in taking the lead in every informing science, and in every useful and embellishing art – but as being foremost, and without a rival, in every means of aggrandisement, and enjoyment of everything that can render life sweet and man happy ...
>
> Indeed London is now not merely the largest city in the known world, but it exceeds in opulence, splendour, and luxury (perhaps in misery),

all that ever was recorded of any city. Indeed, it may be safely affirmed to be the largest congregate mass of human life, arts, science, wealth, power, and architectural splendour, that exists; or in almost all these particulars that ever have existed within the known annals of mankind ... It has been called the Modern Babylon; but Babylon resembled it only in the oriental imaginations of ancient writers; and Thebes, Nineveh, and Rome, merely in the appendages of despotism. London is equal in extent to any three or four other European capitals united; and superior to thirty of the largest towns in the United Kingdom, if brought together. It would require sixty cities as large as Exeter, or 534 towns as large as Huntingdon, to make another metropolis; and it is computed that a population equal to that of Salisbury is added to London every three months.[8]

Sadleir was in a position to exploit what London had to offer in terms of opportunities and recreation. On arrival he settled at 171 Regent Street[9] in the heart of the West End, then colonised by the wealthy.[10] It is not clear if he rented the entire house or merely an apartment there. Furnished apartments in the Regent Street area cost from three to ten guineas a week, depending on size.[11] It was situated close to the great parks such as St. James's Park, Green Park, Hyde Park and Kensington Gardens, collectively known as the 'lungs of London.'[12]

The West End was the London of comfortable clubs, mostly situated in the Pall Mall area, fashionable cigar divans, coffee houses, high class taverns, chop houses and oyster rooms, the best of which were close to the theatres.[13] Chop houses were 'a class of houses much frequented by lawyers and men of business, at which only steaks, chops, kidneys and sausages, with potatoes were dressed'.[14] It advised that the higher grade coffee houses were equal to hotels and clubhouses 'for respectability, comforts and even luxuries.' Some of these coffee houses had facilities for business men to meet and discuss their affairs. The cigar divans were essentially coffee houses, but of a more 'distingue character, expensive in their charges, and more studied, elegant and luxurious in their appointments and conveniences'.[15] One of the most popular with the middle-class was Kilpack's Cigar Divan near Covent Garden. The Oyster Rooms were invariably located near the theatres.[16]

One theatre reminded him of home. This was the famous Sadler's Wells Theatre so called after its founder of 1683, and the mineral wells close by. The name Sadleirswells near Tipperary Town, where his cousins lived, was almost certainly inspired by this. When Richard Sadleir of Golden Garden bought Kingswell, where there was a well called Tobar na Righ, from which Tipperary was supposed to have taken its name,[17] he renamed it Sadleirswells.[18]

Whether curiosity drew Sadleir to this theatre or not remains unknown, but he sometimes attended Her Majesty's Theatre in Haymarket, which was

> originally established for the performance of Italian operas, to which ballets and divertisements are now always added, and is now one of the most fashionable places of amusement in the metropolis, its only rival being the Royal Italian Opera, Covent Garden, which has recently been established to gratify the increasing taste of the public for exquisite music and dancing.[19]

During his early years in London singers such as Cruvelli, Giulani and Bordas featured prominently in the Operas of this theatre, which was almost as large as the La Scala opera house in Milan. It had an eighty foot stage, and an overall capacity to hold an audience of two and a half thousand. The five tiered section of over two hundred boxes held a thousand people, all of them wealthy. The first three tiers were the property of the nobility and wealthy commoners, and were let at rates varying from 150 guineas to 400 guineas per season, depending on their size and situation.[20] Some of the double boxes on the grand tier had been sold for sums of up to £8,000. The usual charge per night for a box in the other tiers was a guinea. All patrons except those who inhabited the gallery were obliged to wear evening costume, and those who ventured in frock coats, coloured trousers and cravats were turned away.

Sadleir's interest in Her Majesty's was not entirely inspired by a love of opera. He was attracted to Clara Morton, one of the performers there, and for some time courted her.[21] Little is known of the affair. She was reputed to have been a well known beauty, but the theatre's archives do not contain any record of her. She was not a leading ballerina of Her Majesty's such as Carlotta Grisi Marie Taglioni,[22] but more than likely belonged to one of the dancing troupes.[23]

This is a rare glimpse into the romantic side of his life. He showed no inclination to marry, and at one stage formed a liaison with the widow or grass widow of a member of parliament.[24] This type of secretive alliance was in keeping with his character, and while his enemies were later to write about his physical characteristics in an unflattering way, Sadleir was not unattractive to women. He was described by John Francis Maguire of the *Cork Examiner* as being above medium height with black hair, dark eyes and a sallow complexion.[25] Another source described him as of handsome appearance and dignified manners.[26] He had certainly not inherited the frame of his uncle, Denys Scully, nicknamed Bullstag because of his great bulk, 'being fully as broad as he is long', and referred to as 'our fat friend' by Lady Granard in a letter to her brother in January 1800.[27]

According to the *Annual Register* Sadleir's dress and deportment were modest,

> a person of very good appearance and address, but by no means showy. His dress was habitually neat, but not smart, nor did he affect any style of manners; he appeared a clear-headed active man of business, without pretensions to high-breeding, but not deficient in proper courtesy. His habits were very moderate.[28]

These habits appear to have included gambling at White's Club in St. James's Street.[29] The source for his gambling is not particularly accurate, but his subsequent career as a speculator reflected the gamblers' instincts. He was a member of the Erectheum Club, an establishment noted for its good food and connection with the swindler, John Dean Paul.[30]

One of the pastimes most enjoyed by Sadleir was hunting, and he bought three hunters which he kept at Leighton Buzzard for riding with the Gunnersbury Hounds.[31] He also had the opportunity of attending some of the major race meetings of the time. The Newmarket course was not far away and he almost certainly attended the Leamington Grand Steeplechase there.[32] It is likely, too, that he went to the Epson Derby.

These were modest interests in the context of mid-Victorian middle-class pastimes, and Sadleir indulged without any show of ostentation. He was a reserved individual[33] from whom, according to a business acquaintance, 'it was extremely difficult to get any information beyond what he chose to impart'.[34] The *Observer* reported after his death that he 'lived plainly and entertained sparingly, if he entertained at all'.[35] James, who was to live with him for eighteen months in London, saw him as a 'very temperate man' who only drank 'one glass of sherry or perhaps two, but nothing after.'[36] The *Spectator* recalled him as 'gentlemanly, cool and collected in manners; was at home in the House, the field, in the drawing room, in the general meeting of shareholders'.[37]

If Sadleir was identified as a person of sober habits and reserved lifestyle, he quickly became noted for his commercial acumen, which in turn led to political involvement. The nature of his social life enabled him to meet others of similar background and tastes, who provided further contacts with the world of business and politics. From the commercial standpoint his introduction into the London business world in 1846 was well timed. This was a period of extensive private investment in railway expansion, offering the prospect of large returns.[38]

England experienced a railway boom between 1844 and 1846, and by mid-century private companies had invested £250,000,000.[39] By then London was the terminus of a national network. The first terminal at Euston was opened in 1838, and by 1840 links were constructed at London Bridge, Paddington, Waterloo, Kingscross, St. Pancras, Victoria, Charing Cross, Cannon Street, Liverpool Street and Marlebone.[40] Between June 1847 and December 1850 the rail network for Great Britain and Ireland almost doubled from 3,500 miles to 6,600 miles. This was reflected by an increase in passenger travel from 44,000,000 for the year ending 30 June 1846 to 73,000,000 for the year ending 31 December 1850. Receipts from passenger and freight for the earlier period came to £7,500,000, and that for the later period was £13,000,000.[41]

Sadleir, whose relatives in Ireland were cognisant of the advantages of railways to their locality,[42] initially became involved in railway enterprises in a legal capacity as a parliamentary agent for wealthy investors. As such he was their legal adviser drafting and protecting bills through Parliament on their behalf. Although he would later compare the relative simplicity of railway legislation with the more complex legal issues of land purchase, the *Drummond Report* gave an indication of the legal technicalities involved,[43] and Sadleir not only befriended influential and wealthy individuals, but impressed them by his efficiency .

The Railway Times was sometimes critical of early railway enterprises, but reserved its most severe criticism for lawyers whose fees were always certain, irrespective of the success or failure of the railways they promoted. An editorial of 8 June 1850 was heavily laced with irony,

> But if there be no other gainers by railways, looking to them as *entities*, there were plenty who gained by them as *possibilities*, of this 'legion' are the lawyers. These *Jack Horners*, little and big, picked out the plums and other sweetmeats with laudable discernment and assiduity, whether the schemes to which they lent their professional aid were as solid as the pudding of the nursery self-encomiast, or vanishing as the object of search of his experimental contemporary ... In some Companies the confidence of the Directors has been unlimited, and the solicitors' accounts have passed, without a question; in other instances the solicitor has been 'too much' for inquiring aspirants at financial reform.. Certainly professional skill never had a more glorious field for its exercise. The novelty, the variety, the magnitude of the undertaking was each a mine of wealth. Get us our Act was the watchword, the battlecry – vociferated

with the same disregard of cost as the Exquisite manifested in his demand for a glass of water and a toothpick – sometimes the Act was gotten, sometimes lost; but always the legal adviser's bill was at hand.

The editorial cited several cases where bills of costs from solicitors were £2,116 and £23,900, very significant sums in the currency value of the time. It is not known how much Sadleir gained as parliamentary agent, but he was regarded with satisfaction by investors, and as his reputation grew he was to advance from agent to active participator in the ownership and management of railway companies such as the East Kent.[44] Because of expertise acquired at home and the availability of capital there, entrepreneurs like Sadleir also invested in European railways, some of which had an English as well as a European board of directors. He became a shareholder and chairman of the Royal Swedish Railway Company, the Rome and Frascati Railway, a short line of thirty kilometres, and the Grand Junction Railway in France[45]

One of the factors enabling him to invest in railways was his connection with the banking fraternity, which gave him added status and inspired confidence in him as a successful businessman. In 1848, only two years after his arrival in England, he became chairman of the London and County Joint Stock Banking Company.[46] Clearly, he was already a shareholder in this sizeable concern of sixty branches stretching from Dover and Hastings on the south east coast to Banbury, not far from Stratford-on-Avon, where his ancestral roots lay.[47] Apart from head office, the branches had over 20,000 accounts. Robert Keating became a director through his influence, and Sadleir also secured the Royal Swedish Railway as a client.[48]

The real key to his commercial success was political power. By the 1840s the business sector had established a strong foothold in Westminster beside the wealthy landowning classes, the real masters of political office. In Sadleir's case there was the added bonus of experience as parliamentary agent, which made him familiar with the workings of Westminster. His opportunity came in 1847, but he had not yet achieved a reputation sufficiently great to ensure his success in any of the English urban constituencies. So he turned to Ireland, where wheels were set in motion to find him a seat.

The borough of Carlow was chosen. The small urban electorate, numbering less than 300, were well informed of Sadleir's rising reputation as a businessman.[49] The presence of the Tipperary bank in the town, and its willingness to grant liberal lending terms at election times[50] was no small advantage either. This policy was promoted by its manager, Thaddeus O'Shea, a relative of Sadleir.[51] The borough was also ripe for exploitation due to the political vulnerability of its sitting member, Major Brownlow Villiers Layard, son of the Rector of Effington in Lincolnshire and grandson of the Dean of Bristol, who had held the seat since 1841.[52] He was a Liberal, whose pedigree and status might have earlier recommended him to an Irish electorate, but the Famine fostered a dislike of English politicians among the electorate, who equated them with the Whig party, the scapegoat for this unparalleled calamity.

Layard's election address was sketchy, and, apart from mentioning the subject closest to his heart, army reform, it lacked focus. Its vagueness reflected the confidence of a candidate who was assured by his local contacts that he would be returned unopposed. It was greeted with a mixture of respect and skepticism by the *Carlow Sentinel* ,

> To major Layard personally we have no objection; but as we do not approve of the principles he generally maintained since his election, and as he must have by this period acquired some knowledge of the condition of Ireland, it is to be regretted that the honourable member was not more explicit in his views, by expounding to some extent that course of policy which he intends to pursue if returned to the next parliament. A pledge to support every measure conducive to 'civil and religious liberty' is one which may be taken without risque by a member of any party. It is a line of policy so indefinite as to afford him full scope to support a Whig Cabinet, *per fas aut ne fas.*[53]

This newspaper, owned by Thomas H. Carroll, was Conservative, but in this election did not troop its colours due to the absence of a Conservative candidate. Instead, it reflected the ethos of urban middle-class voters, and demanded that Layard explicitly articulate measures of industrial and commercial development to create employment. It highlighted investment in railways and drainage as pertinent examples, and castigated the Government for failing to promote this – 'had justice been rendered this country, less than one half the amount freely granted to the West Indian Planters would enable us to employ and to feed our population'.

Layard would have easily countered the criticism in the absence of an opposing candidate, but he was soon confronted with a well-planned and well executed campaign by the Sadleirites. Initially Sadleir did not issue any address, the usual recourse of would-be candidates in testing opinion in a constituency. This had already been done behind the scenes, and a formal invitation was forwarded to him by a number of electors through O'Shea.[54] This prompted another address to Layard to stand down, almost amounting to a *fait accompli.*[55] He angrily rejected it in several statements, alleging that he had been stabbed in the back and treacherously abandoned, especially as 'the Bishop informed me that he would support me even if his own brother were to enter the field'.[56] There is some evidence that Layard was telling the truth, because in January Pierce Mahony, a would-be candidate, abandoned his plans to contest the seat in the face of Bishop Haly's insistence that Layard had 'faithfully discharged his duty' and should not be disturbed.[57] Mahony, however, indicated that a previous conversation with Haly had indicated the possibility of a compromise to avoid an election conflict.

Layard was further disgruntled because his expectations had led him to maintain the Liberal electorate register at his own expense, and no doubt for his own benefit, as well as donating money to the needy during the Famine.[58] This was an important consideration in the minds of the Catholic clergy, who had witnessed harrowing scenes during the Famine[59] and who were a powerful force in electioneering politics.[60] But the bank neutralised Layard's advantage by playing a similar benevolent role,[61] and despite the bishop's earlier assurances to the Englishman, the priests solidly supported Sadleir when news of his candidature leaked and canvassing intensified.

He was especially fortunate in getting the backing of the respected parish priest of Carlow, James Maher, uncle of Paul Cullen, then rector of the Irish College Rome and later Cardinal Archbishop of Dublin. Maher was pleased at the arrival of a strong Liberal candidate,[62] and his support of Sadleir continued throughout much of his political career. As well as canvassing he took the unusual step of issuing addresses to the electorate, which were closely studied in the borough.

His lengthy address of 22 July 1847 was exactly the type of introduction the would-be politician dreamed of, and reflected the shrewdness of Maher in hitting the precise note needed in a small borough.[63] He praised Sadleir's personal integrity, his standing in the community, business acumen, knowledge of Irish affairs, connections with the town and interest in its commercial prosperity. The Tipperaryman was one whose,

> pretensions are of the fairest and most legitimate character; his thorough knowledge, as an Irishman, of our country, of its wants and underdeveloped resources; his connection with our town, and his interest in its commercial prosperity; his business-like habits, and that capability which a clear and well informed mind confers in giving effect to his views, his high character in every relation of life; his stake and standing in the country; his principles identical with those of the majority of the electors; all combine to announce him to be a very formidable rival.

Maher dismissed Layard's claims of betrayal, particularly by the clergy who had promised him vital support,

Major Layard has still to learn that Ireland is not a seminary of Raw Recruits, nor the clergy of the people, puppets in his hands. Their object has always been to save the constituency from the evil of disunion, from all corrupt influence and to give effect to the will of the majority.

Apart from such an unequivocal, if disingenuous, indictment of the traditional practice of wealthy candidates in purchasing the votes of those more than willing to sell,[64] the parish priest ridiculed the major's election manifesto and his emphasis upon army reform, a theme in which the Carlow electorate had little interest,

> There is certainly in this document something to amuse the military fancy of dreaming imbecility, to please the old fogies of the Royal Hospital; but the man who put it forward nakedly in an address to an Irish constituency must have thought, if indeed his vanity has left any power of thinking, that any garbage would go down with the mere Irish. I confess that I felt not only disgusted, but insulted, on reading this foolish twaddle of the mess room, the silly vapourings and boasting of the belted knight fresh from the Horse Guards to the electors of Carlow.[65]

Sadleir himself was one of the most courteous politicians, and seldom indulged in the frequently abusive public oratory of the nineteenth century. Apart from an innate politeness there was little need for him to do so, because there were many, like Maher, who did it splendidly on his behalf.

In his own address he introduced himself as a Liberal in politics, who would, however, enter Parliament 'unfettered and independent of all Government control'.[66] Unlike some candidates, he highlighted the commercial element of the Irish economy, and with the Famine in mind advised that the 'rigid rules of political economy' were inapplicable to prevailing Irish circumstances.[67] Only 'the protection of good government' would encourage investment in manufacture and the development of industrial resources.

These principles were equally important to agricultural development. Legislation was required to address tenant right, compensation for permanent improvements and the granting of leases. On the question of land ownership he advocated a mechanism to dispose quickly of encumbered estates, and a tax on the income of absentee landlords 'for the support of our suffering people'.[68] These proposals had the main aim of raising 'our country from the low condition in which she has continued during a lengthened period of bad legislation and misrule'.

As a Liberal he wished to see the 'great principles of civil and religious liberty firmly established in every country'. He pledged support for a wider franchise, and ended the address with a declaration of his 'deep and personal interest in the welfare of Carlow', and a promise to use 'every possible means to promote the local improvement of the town'.

Sadleir reached Carlow in late July accompanied by the Earl of Portarlington, over whose estates he was receiver. The Earl was en route to Emo Court, his summer residence in Queen's County.[69] Sadleir used this as his local address, but stayed in Morrison's hotel. His election headquarters were set up in Burren Street, probably in the bank's premises, and his campaign took the normal course of methodical canvassing and public speeches. In these his emphasis remained on the development of Irish manufacture and the promotion of free trade,[70] policies which would appeal to the urban electorate of all political persuasions. It was also a policy he believed in, and continued to press in later years. To him free trade was 'the great principle of commercial policy which gave to the poor man his food untaxed'.[71] Underdevelopment in Irish industry concerned him in the light of the opposite trend in England, whose government was supposed to be looking after Irish interests.

At one meeting in his committee room he summarised this dimension of his political ethic,

we are bound as Irishmen to look to the present condition of every class and interest in the country, and in uniting and bringing them together it is the sacred duty of every Irish constituency at this political crisis to prefer the national interests of their native land to the predilections or purposes of party. As Irishmen we cannot approve or become reconciled to the present state and condition of this country. No class in Ireland can prosper under our present Irish system of internal legislation; no individual exertion, no resolutions to prefer Irish manufactures, no desire to awaken a spirit of self reliance amongst our people will be found sufficient to remove the evils which press so severely and so suddenly upon all classes in the community from the peer to the peasant. The disposition so general and so sincere... to lay aside and to forget the bitterness of party and to unite the country as one man in the pursuit and encouragement of every good and practical measure for the employment of our people, should control our political actions at this moment. Without full and permanent employment for our industrious people we are without the first element of national prosperity; and without decided, direct and liberal protection and aid from the legislature, we cannot see our national capabilities developed. Without manufactures our people must continue depressed and idle and become the wretched objects of an expensive and demanding system of relief, and without parliamentary aid the successful establishment of manufactures in Ireland becomes impossible.[72]

In the atmosphere of the time it was not difficult to convince the public that an Englishman would be unable or unwilling to either understand such Irish issues, or have the will to do anything about them. He forecast that the next parliamentary session would see English and Irish interests polarised. His question to the electors was direct and effective even if it lacked Maher's satirical bite – 'can we expect an English gentleman to become the informed, the practical and the warm advocate of Irish interests and Irish rights opposed to the continuance of an English system of commercial protection and of trade monopoly?'.[73]

Layard failed to respond in kind and proceeded to his political demise. His speeches during the election campaign were mainly devoted to his previous voting pattern in Westminster, and to castigating his 'treacherous friends'.[74] Nomination day, when a show of hands was taken, was the most accurate pre-voting barometer of electoral support, and on that Tuesday Sadleir proceeded to the Courthouse accompanied by his brothers, Clement and James, and a number of friends.[75] To prevent the rowdy scenes so common on such occasions, the High Sheriff, Hugh Faulkner, ordered a troop of cavalry and a large body of police to be stationed near the courthouse. Forty policemen were positioned inside the building.

These precautions prevented physical violence, but despite Sadleirs pleas, Layard's speech was frequently interrupted by the much larger Sadleirite faction. According to the local newspaper the 'uproar was for a time indescribable', but it failed to shake Layard's determination to proceed irrespective of any loss of support,

> many told me the game was up. I said no; when you wanted a cock to fight your battles before I placed myself in the front of the battle. The cock is here again and he will fight too – well my old friends gone what was I to do? I told a few people who cheered me that I would fight the battle over again. I drew the sword, cast the scabbard to the winds and here I am once more.

Layard's military imagery provoked greater uproar, which eventually subsided, allowing Sadleir to make his address. Much of this was spent undermining Layard as removed from the interests and welfare of his constituents,

> one would imagine that a gentleman seeking the suffrage of an Irish constituency would advert to those measures that are calculated to perpetrate friends and dissensions and keep your country in all the bitterness of bondage. His days and nights were spent not in the removal of that mass of misery which hangs over this afflicted country and

threatens to overwhelm all, from peer to peasant – no, his time was more profitably occupied in striking off the shackles of the soldier, without exhibiting that local knowledge, broad grasp of mind or experience to qualify him to represent an Irish Commercial Constituency. His position is surely an anomalous one, and after his exhibition today, I am at a loss to know upon what section of the electors he pretends to have a claim. He tells you that he instituted mighty reform in the army for the benefit of 120,000 men, but he has overlooked the claims of millions of Irishmen whose numbers were thinned by Famine and pestilence. No gentlemen, my opponent has confined himself to the indulgence of a pique, and of that personal vituperation in which he appears to be proficient .

Following brief statements by some of Layard's erstwhile supporters defending their change of allegiance to the Sadleir camp, the show of hands was taken. This favoured Sadleir and was confirmed two days later at the polls, when he won by 164 votes to 101, the largest majority he would ever receive.[76] He was then only aged 34 and his success was enhanced by the election of his first cousins Robert Keating for Waterford city and Frank Scully for Tipperary County. The circumstances of Keating's return were remarkable. The principal planks in the election platforms for both Waterford city and county were the Repeal and land issues, in that order. The election committees for both constituencies were dissatisfied with the performance of sitting members as Repealers.[77] The county committee was unable, however, to find suitable local candidates and approached Keating in Garranlea. He did not publish any address,[78] but was proposed on nomination day by Sir Richard Musgrave and seconded by Nicholas Cantwell, the parish priest of Tramore.[79] Musgrave introduced him as a Catholic of 'Repeal opinions', while Cantwell hastened to clarify that Repeal did not signify separaratism, but a wish 'to see the Queen of England, the Queen also of Ireland, and that is our hope and pleasure'.

Keating's response was brief. He was 'an old Repealer', who had espoused the cause 'since first the association was founded'. Although a landlord himself, he pointed to his own class as neglecting their proprietorial duty and thereby being the cause of tenant distress. He was returned unopposed and published an address of thanks to the electors, which mentioned Repeal, constitutional agitation and the tenant question as his prime policies.[80] He did not elaborate on any of these on the basis that he had already enlightened the nomination meeting of his views.

Unlike Keating, Frank Scully was an early candidate in the Tipperary election campaign. Keating's family, however, played a prominent role in Scully's return. The first election meeting took place in Cashel towards the end of June.[81] It was chaired by Archdeacon Michael Laffan, parish priest of Fethard and Killusty,[82] and was attended by such influential individuals as the sitting M.P. Nicholas V. Maher of Turtulla near Thurles, a relative of the Scullys,[83] Charles Bianconi, proprietor of an extensive road transport network based in Clonmel,[84] Maurice Lenihan of the the *Tipperary Vindicator and Limerick Reporter* in Nenagh, John Hackett, an alderman of Clonmel Corporation and proprietor of the *Tipperary Free Press*, Michael Doheny, Keating's father, Leonard, Edward and Rodolph Scully, and a dozen priests.

The meeting passed a resolution to withold support from any candidate who was not 'in a position to act independently of any government opposed to Repeal and tenurial reform'. Scully was not present, but his candidature was proposed by Bianconi, who was authorised by James Scully of Shanballymore to say that his brother was ready 'to stand for the county on Repeal principles and no mistake'.

Scully arrived in Garranlea a week later, and conducted his canvass of the Clonmel and Cashel areas from there. His uncle-in-law, Leonard Keating, accompanied him to Clonmel, where he was described by the *Tipperary Free Press* as a member of the English bar, who was 'young, healthy and vigorous' with 'all the advantages of a handsome person, gentlemanly exterior, winning manners and address'.[85] More relevantly, he had been a convinced Repealer since the launch of the association.[86]

He was formally introduced at a campaign meeting in Ryall's Hotel, Cashel, on 6 July, which was attended by the same electors present at the June meeting.[87] Archdeacon Laffan praised Scully's father, James, chairman of the Tipperary Bank, who had died the previous year, for his adherence to the Repeal movement. Laffan also drew attention to the connection between O'Connell and Denys Scully as part of the family tradition. The Archdeacon, one of the most influential political figures in Tipperary, promised Scully the support of the priests, a decisive factor in the county's electoral politics.

Scully outlined his principles, which were similar to Keating's, but more emphatic. He pronounced himself 'a thorough Repealer of the obnoxious measure of the union.' He judged that addressing the question of improvements was crucial to solving the land question. Fixity of tenure was a basic requirement, and, to loud applause, he pledged to grant all his tenants generous leases of three lives plus thirty one years. He closed his introductory statement with a condemnation of tithes as an insulting and degrading tax. In his written address to the constituency some days later he added that he would advocate the appropriation of surplus revenues of the established Church to support the poor and lighten the rates burden.[88]

Although Scully had covered all the relevant issues, Michael Doheny was not fully satisfied with this address and in a letter of 6 July challenged Scully to state approval for the principle of remaining independent of all English governments refusing to espouse his election principles, especially that of Repeal.[89] This was in accord with the Cashel resolution, but Doheny maintained that such opposition presupposed 'keeping yourself free from personal obligations' to the government including soliciting favours for any friends. He was in no doubt that Repeal could only be achieved by such a stance and foreshadowed the policy of independent opposition, which caused serious political and personal disharmony in the following decade when Repeal had vanished as an election issue, but when this core creed of Young Ireland policy was carried on by Charles Gavan Duffy and others.[90]

Scully's response two days later confirmed the principle of opposition to any government hostile to the Cashel resolutions, but regarded personal obligations to any government as a private matter. Doheny's threat to publish their correspondence, if he was not satisfied with Scully's response, materialised, and he issued a longer letter rebutting the argument of the Tipperary candidate. As far as Doheny was concerned the issues in dispute were of public interest. Every representative should remain 'completely independent of the English government and especially so in reference to personal obligations of the kind referred to in my note'. With some justification he felt that personal favours compromised a representative and rendered all pledges useless. To him the issue was 'as clear as light,' and he signalled his determination not to vote for any candidate who held otherwise.

Scully ignored this threat and his election campaign proceeded smoothly. It was well organised, with his relatives as central figures. Leonard Keating was appointed permanent chairman of the election committee of fifty five members covering the twelve baronies of Tipperary.[91] Each barony had its own sub-committee of five.[92] The sub-committee for Middlethird included Keating, James Keating and Jeremiah Scully of Silverfort. Edward Scully was on the Clanwilliam Committee and Carbery Scully, Frank's first cousin, was a member of the Owney and Arra group. Sadleir's brother, Clement, was present at the nomination of candidates in early August when Archdeacon Laffan formally proposed Scully, who easily secured his seat following an election seen as a triumph for Repeal.[93]

The shade of old James Scully surely smiled at the political success of his three grandsons, which would open up many advantageous avenues to them. He would have been less cheered, however, at the further weakening of the Scully influence at the Tipperary bank on the death of its Chairman, James Scully of Shanballymore in December 1846. He had been an active participant, but the Sadleirs now turned to his nephew Vincent to take up the vacant directorship. He only agreed with great reluctance and never attended any meetings. He was a nominal director, which was permitted by the deed of partnership and designed to create confidence in the bank. The Sadleirs were well pleased with this, but Scully, although a distant director, was a constant thorn in their side and immediately expressed earlier reservations about the absence of an annual external audit.[94] When he failed to get a response from James Sadleir in September 1847 he contacted John Sadleir, whom he then realised was the real power in the bank. Sadleir's response from 171 Regent Street on 15 September promised that the audit would be carried out, and agreed to arrange it with James when he came to Ireland the following month.

This was never done, more than likely on Sadleir's instructions, because he saw the bank as a valuable vehicle to finance in particular his land purchase schemes.[95] The annual reports of 1847 and 1848 were carefully tailored to portray an institution coping well with the continuing economic downturn, but not altogether immune to it. The 1847 report declared a dividend of 6% and highlighted the bank's ability to survive the commercial impact of the Famine,[96]

> It need hardly be mentioned that the past year has been one of unexampled difficulty, and it can scarcely be supposed that in passing through the late panic, any bank would be expected to escape without loss. The directors, however, are happy in being able to say that, without withdrawing from their customers any reasonable facility required for the conducting of their business, not a single loss has been sustained by the failure of any of the large mercantile firms connected with the trade of this country. The directors deem the Bank peculiarly fortunate in this respect, and feel assured the shareholders will concur therein, when they are made aware that an amount of mercantile bills drawn on English and Scotch houses or Dublin factors has been discounted by the Bank during the year exceeding a million sterling, without a single bill remaining unpaid.

The 1848 report was pessimistic about the profitability of banking institutions, and advised as a matter of prudence that the Doubtful Debt Fund be doubled.[97] Yet the 6% dividend was maintained without drawing on the Reserve Fund. It was also considered important to increase publicity to attract funds, and the shareholders were reminded of the 'importance of their co-operation in forwarding the interests and promoting the extension of the business of the bank'.

Sadleir's input into these reports is not known, but he continued to exercise close control over its affairs through James, who trusted him implicitly. It was the latter who responded to Vincent Scully's anxious enquiries about the state of the bank in February 1849. He wrote to Scully on 7 February to re-assure him about its relative strength compared with other banks experiencing difficulties -'We do not find our deposits etc. reducing, but we find everywhere we are, we have the best business such as it is, which is much reduced for want of solvent persons to do business with.'[98] Scully had always maintained that small depositors should be accommodated as a matter of policy, but James Sadleir did not consider it worthwhile trying to attract any depositors under ten pounds, because most of these intended emigrating to America.

His brothers amenability to his wishes enabled Sadleir to concentrate upon his business and political careers. He was determined to feature regularly in Westminster debates, but his impact on the House was not particularly striking. Rarely an impassioned speaker, he was rather courteous, cool and logical, qualities which commanded respect rather than admiration. Perhaps because of the nature of some debates, several of his parliamentary speeches were long winded, clogged with legal terminology and sprinkled with examples to prove his point. He sometimes tended to stray from his central theme and range over the entire spectrum of Irish problems. On one occasion in 1849, having treated his colleagues to one such presentation, the irritated Solicitor General casually dismissed his remarks on the presumption that Sadleir was more interested in making his speech than in convincing the House of the subject under debate.[99]

Sadleir's political classification between 1847 and the general election of 1852 could be called independent Liberal, the term he used in his introduction to the electorate in 1847. This label was to distinguish him from the Tories and the Whigs, and he was at pains to stress the independent aspect at a time when a large sector of the non-Conservative section of the audience frowned upon any liaison with the Whigs.[100] Neither did he share the Repeal sentiments of Scully or Keating. The Repeal movement had been a powerful one, but internal divisions and the death of O'Connell in May 1847 sapped its strength, although the election in that year saw thirty eight Repealers as against twenty five Liberals returned.[101] The commitment of many to the policy, however, was doubtful. But, Sadleir's name is not listed for any of the Repeal meetings, even when it attracted a large number of solicitors and barristers in the early 1840s,[102] nor did he show any inclination to come under the banner of John O'Connell, the eldest son and self-styled political successor of the Liberator. Despite the emotive appeal of Repeal in the election so soon after O'Connell's death[103] he rarely mentioned it in any of his political addresses or speeches. His motto 'Ireland for the Irish' during his election campaign was not an endorsement of it, but a statement that Irishmen rather than Englishmen should be the preferred choice of the voters. His election address briefly mentioned self-government as a solution to Irish ills, if the Government failed to help Ireland in her hour of need, but this was a sop to the handful of Repealers among the borough voters, and cannot be taken seriously.

Considering his lack of sympathy with Repeal, it is not surprising that he was less than friendly towards the revolutionary tenets of the Young Irelanders, who had split from the movement, partly because of their disillusionment and frustration at the failure of the constitutional agitation to achieve worthwhile results. After 1843 they took a stand against O'Connell's inclination to abandon Repeal and ally himself with the Whigs. In 1846 they set up the Irish Confederation and ultimately became convinced that the answer was a violent severing of the connection with England and the establishment of an Irish republic.[104]

This was alien to Sadleir whose family tradition, reflected in his grandfather's diary, was strongly loyalist. Such loyalism was reinforced by a mid-Victorian business ethic, whereby his commercial pursuits and contacts made him feel more at ease in the presence of an English merchant than an advanced Irish nationalist. His opposition to rebellion was uncompromising, but because of the government's handling of famine relief his loyalism sometimes seemed ambivalent. Nonetheless, he consistently supported legislation to bring revolutionary nationalism to heel, and was evident, for example, in his contribution to the debate on the Crown and Government Security Bill in the Spring of 1848. On 7 April, Sir George Grey, the Home Secretary, sought leave to bring in this measure.[105] Grey was acting at the request of Clarendon, the Lord Lieutenant, who considered the existing criminal law inadequate to deal with the seditious speeches and inflammatory articles of Young Irelanders like Charles Gavan Duffy and John Mitchel.

The problem outlined by the Lord Lieutenant was two-fold. Firstly, sedition was a bailable offence and gave the perpetrators further time to influence public opinion. Secondly, the only statutes on treason available to him were those of Edward 111, harsh and out of tune with the comparatively more lenient criminal law of the mid-nineteenth century. Amending legislation in the reign of George 111 had not been extended to Ireland,[106] and the Home Secretary sought to have this adapted and applied there. He proposed that the sections laying down the death penalty for offences against the person of the Sovereign be made permanent. But, other acts, such as speeches and articles breaching public order, would come within the legal definition of felony, carry a minimum sentence of seven years transportation, and would not be bailable.

While Irish representatives had reservations about the Bill in the midst of famine, few opposed it. A defiant Smith O'Brien was one of the minority.[107] He spoke in contradictory terms of his loyalty to the Sovereign and his threat of a republic if Repeal was refused. He denied suggestions that he had gone to France to seek military aid since he had 'no wish to impose upon my country one description of servitude in place of another'. William Sharman Crawford, an Ulsterman representing the English constituency of Rochdale, condemned the bill as too all-embracing and harsh, because it would render those attending public meetings liable to transportation.[108] This view was shared by other English M.Ps.[109] John O'Connell, had reservations, but supported it because of his 'abhorrence' at attempts to drive the Irish people 'into the most criminal acts of rebellion', and his belief that the Young Irelanders 'were to the cause of Repeal what the United Irishmen of 1798 were to the progress of liberty in Ireland'.[110]

Henry Drummond, Conservative M.P. for West Surrey, saw the bill in a wider social context, and applauded the government's intention of applying it to quell social unrest in England under the Chartist movement.[111] Sadleir's views coincided with these, but went further in asserting that it was more applicable to England than to Ireland.[112] Neither was he under any illusion that it would cure the underlying ills of Ireland, but justified supporting it for several reasons. He took it as a matter of justice that the word of an informer or an accomplice would no longer be sufficient to secure a conviction. He upheld the distinction the bill made between mere bravado and seriously subversive intention, by meeting the case of 'juvenile persons...constantly uttering open and scandalous sedition', with a charge of felony rather than treason. He underestimated the resolve of the Young Irelanders in his hope that the practical results of the bill 'would be to save from perdition and dishonourable exile some of those unhappily deluded men who were at present the erring victims of a great political disease'.

By the Summer it was clear that the Crown and Government Probation Act, as it was finally titled,[113] was not sufficient to deal with the deteriorating political situation in Ireland. The Confederation clubs, with their avowed policy of republicanism through armed force, were quickly spreading, especially during the month of July. The Government decided to suspend the *Habeas Corpus* Act to ensure the speedy arrest and detention of those suspected of conspiracy, particularly the clubs' leaders. On 22 July, a short time before the

Ballingarry rising, Lord John Russell rose to propose this.[114] It was the ultimate restriction of civil liberty and the Prime Minister presented a detailed argument of its necessity. He painted the Confederation as a formidable organisation possessing adequate means to pursue its republican objective, and inflict great injury in the process. He listed facts which were 'patent, notorious and flagrant', and quoted reports of various club meetings throughout Ireland including Tipperary, Cork and Waterford. These indicated seditious intent, and only the suspension of the constitution could stem the tide of revolution. Any other legislation would be successfully evaded by lawyer members of the Confederation. Russell's strong presentation was accompanied by an appeal for unanimous support from all parties.

He was not to be disappointed as the full weight of the British political establishment rowed in behind him. Sir Robert Peel, Tamworth, called for the destruction of the 'conspiracy of political traitors', and Disraeli, on behalf of the Conservative Party, classed the Confederate ideals as Jacobinism, a 'system of universal plunder and unmitigated violence.'[115] Only eight members, all of them Irish, opposed the bill. Unsurprisingly one was Feargus O'Connor, the Chartist leader representing Nottingham.[116] As he declared his own separatist principles,[117] O'Connor dismissed the gesture of the Prime Minister who passed a copy of the Oath of Allegiance to him. Frank Scully, whose antagonism to Michael Doheny lingered after their election confrontation, did not share O'Connor's political ideals, and made it clear that when the Young Irelander had visited Tipperary Doheny had been 'scouted' from there.[118] But, he viewed the suspension of the constitution as counter-productive, and pointed to Mitchel's arrest as a serious cause of disaffection. Like the other opponents of the bill Scully contended that it should at least be accompanied by remedial measures.

Sadleir, however, saw the source of disaffection differently. He identified two areas, one social, the other political.[119] It was in the misery, poverty and unemployment of millions of Irishmen that revolutionary leaders found their power. The country was on the brink of civil war, because Ireland had lost confidence in the will of various Governments to convert their good intentions into concrete action. Such social neglect was compounded by political degradation, through the exclusion of most Irish people from the franchise. He dismissed Pitt's 1844 assertion that the political franchise would not give bread to the hungry or employment to the idle. Sadleir rightly saw the power of the franchise as the key to real prosperity. The threat of defeat at the hands of the electorate was a persuasive weapon, and he understood the conservatism of English statesmen in this regard. Nevertheless, unlike, Scully, he accepted that the current crisis, irrespective of its causes, demanded an immediate and decisive response, and Russell's proposal was the most appropriate. He put the political options in a simple question,

> were they prepared to suspend the constitution for a brief period, or to expose the people of Ireland to misery and carnage? The more incapable – the more unfit – the present advisers of the Crown were to wield the power of the executive, the greater was the necessity to give to the people of this realm the only security that could at present be offered to them – the safeguard and protection of a military despotism. As to the intentions of the leaders of the present movement in Ireland he apprehended that respecting those there could be no possible mistake... It was to be a struggle between the enemies and the supporters of law and order, and it remained to be seen which of the two principles were to triumph; for the population of Ireland was now clearly divided into those who supported and those who had arrayed themselves against the constitution of the empire.

He repeated that his approval of this measure was as much a desire to save the lives of 'the apostles of sedition', as it was to uphold the rule of law. He did not, however, support a policy of long term repression. He showed this in February 1849 when Sir William Somerville, the Chief Secretary, sought a renewal of the Act.[120] By that stage the political situation had changed with the suppression of the uprising in Ballingarry and the arrest of 120 Irish Confederation supporters. Sadleir was not present on 6 February when Sir George Grey explained government thinking behind its policy of renewing the bill for a further six months. Grey relied heavily upon two sources, a letter from Thomas Darcy McGee[121] to the New York *Morning Herald*, and a report from Clarendon. McGee,[122] who had fled to the United States after the rising, assured New Yorkers that a strong nucleus of armed Irish revolutionaries remained in readiness, and, appropriately, Clarendon dwelt upon the lack of remorse within the revolutionary movement for the Ballingarry disturbance. To Grey both letters were proof that Irish national security was not yet fully guaranteed.

The Home Secretary was met by the opposition of the Irish Liberal M.Ps. and a small number of English M.Ps. Some of the Irish representatives, including John O'Connell, betrayed a genuine lack of confidence in Clarendon as an individual, and a reluctance to vest too much power in one person. He did not let the opportunity pass to express surprise that Grey would use a letter of McGee, a 'mere underling' of the Young Ireland party.[123] Others, such as Frank Scully, argued that the measure would increase discontent, and add to the stature of republicans.[124]

Sadleir spoke at length during the second reading of the bill on 9 February, and opposed the measure as no longer justified, because 'the people of Ireland were not in a spirit which would dispose them to receive the poison that might be spread among them by political firebrands'.[125] He drew upon his own contacts in Ireland as proof,

> He felt bound from his acquaintance with the rural population of some of the proclaimed districts in Ireland to state his convictions that they were attached to the constitution of this country – that they were devoted to the person and Crown of Her Majesty – and that if there were discontent and dissatisfaction among them, that discontent and dissatisfaction arose solely from the policy and the conduct pursued by the existing cabinet.

On a political level he shared the prejudices of his Irish colleagues against Clarendon, but also worried that a renewal of the Act would damage industrial progress. Sadleir reminded the Prime Minister of the inconsistency of his views in power as against his period in opposition, when he had highlighted Irish grievances,

> the Irish people were not a nation of barbarians – they were not a set of unmitigated boors – the light of education had been extended to them; and they were not therefore, likely so soon to forget the time when the noble lord at the head of the Government had carried his opposition to the coercion system, so far as to spend the greater part of a night in protesting against the payment of 25,000 men who had been employed in enforcing the Queen's authority in Ireland.

There was no inconsistency between his admonition of the government and his antipathy to violent revolution, nor between this antipathy and his consciousness of the conditions which drove people to armed rebellion. His stance on the suspension of the *Habeas Corpus* Act showed this awareness of the link between the folly of insurrection and desperation born from extensive famine. He attacked the government for ignoring the plight of Ireland for so long and bringing her to the verge of civil war.

He became increasingly critical as the administration seemed to bungle indecisively ahead, showing 'either a want of disposition, or a want of legislative capacity, or a want of that political knowledge and acquaintance with the affairs of Ireland, which would enable them to grapple with the difficulties of the country'.[126] He attributed the discontent which pervaded Irish society to uncertain land tenure among tenants, widespread wretchedness and poverty among the labouring classes, unemployment, the prospect of a stay in the workhouse, and lack of industrial development in the country. He condemned the English view of the Irish as a disloyal and lawless race – 'what people', he asked in April 1849, 'had exhibited greater patience under suffering, and what nation had been more submissive under her accumulating evils, embittered by the sense of neglect on the part of the legislature?'.[127]

Sadleir's linking of neglect, starvation and sedition was legitimate in the context of a famine, which in six years was to leave Ireland mourning the loss of 2,000,000 people through death and emigration. The urgent task was to arrest its onslaught. His own affluent lifestyle did not insulate him from experiencing its effects on others during his visits to Ireland during the recess, or through the many harrowing accounts sent to him as a parliamentary representative.

In his condemnation of the government Sadleir was, on the other hand, conscious of the efforts of Irish landlords to aid victims. Layard may not have been a landlord, but Sadleir was willing to use the racial label during his election campaign, when he described him as an Englishman unsympathetic to the plight of the Irish,

> when the Irish gentry worked both by day and night to rescue the people from famine and pestilence and risked their own lives to preserve those of their neighbours, and when they were calumniated by the Government and their supporters, where was Major Layard? He was listening in servile silence behind the Minister, and never uttered a word in defence of that much calumniated body![128]

This was an electioneering tactic, but it was also an honest recognition of Irish landlords as major contributors to famine relief. He identified himself as one who had helped to alleviate distress, and there is some evidence to support his statement. In March 1852, 144 tenants published an address to him as receiver over the Portarlington estates during the Famine years,

> We, the Tenants of the Earl of Portarlington on the Emo, Caron and Morette Estates in Ireland, are unwilling to allow your connections with us as Receiver under the control of the Courts of Chancery in England and Ireland, to terminate without rendering to you the expression of our grateful sense of the just and admirable spirit in which you have during the entire time of your agency, discharged the difficult duties of your position.
>
>   You have constantly endeavoured to diminish the difficulties against which we have had to struggle during years of great calamity and

distress. We can never forget your efforts in the years 1846 and 1847 to afford relief and employment to the poor of this district.

It has been our fortune to witness your acts not only as the Receiver over those estates, but also as a country gentleman and extensive employer of the poor. We most sincerely thank you for the spirit which you have always manifested towards us and we thank you too, on behalf of the several labourers to whom you have since 1845 afforded constant and remunerative employment.[129]

Personal benevolence was augmented by the bank's famine aid. At the beginning of the Famine the Clonmel branch gave a modest ten pounds to the local fund and James Sadleir added five from his own pocket. Clement could only find two pounds for the Carrickbeg fund.[130] Dr Toomey, Sadleir's proposer on the Carlow hustings in August 1847, introduced him as an Irish gentleman 'who has given an earnest of what he could do for our local advantage by the establishment of a bank in the town. How many industrious men would have been this day walking the streets or hanging on relief works but for that establishment?'.[131]

While he earned political kudos for his actions his first cousin, James Scully of Athassel and Shanballymore, was treated differently by a section of his tenantry, who disliked his method of assistance.[132] In April 1847 a group, with faces blackened, seriously assaulted his steward. Scully found this incomprehensible because the steward was in the process of distributing free seed oats to those who had the ground prepared.[133] Clearly, the culprits were those who refused, or were unable, to comply with this stipulation. Scully also intended giving them free turnip seeds, and was offended that his benevolence should be rewarded in such a fashion. With typical Scully determination he made it known

that the tenantry on this property have experienced the greatest indulgence during these last ten years. Every allowance that could be reasonably expected has been granted – many hundreds of pounds have been expended, without any remuneration whatsoever to me and the thanks I now receive is the reception that my confidential steward has met with. Property has its duties attached to it, but it certainly ought to have its rights. If a different course shall be henceforth pursued, from that hitherto used, with respect to those on that property they have only to blame themselves.

While his cousin was engaged in public controversy with his tenants, Sadleir continued his exertions to highlight the plight of the Irish. In March 1848 he put down a loaded question to Somerville demanding statistics for the previous year on famine deaths in Ireland brought about by 'an insufficient supply of the bare necessities of life, and if not, whether he can state the probable number of those persons who have died during that period in the counties of Galway, Mayo, Cork and Clare, and the steps taken by the Government, through the aid of the Coroners, Police, poor-law guardians and Clergy of Ireland, or by other means, to ascertain the probable number of persons who may so die in Ireland during the present year?'.[134] He received a one sentence reply from the Chief Secretary that such information was not available. Sadleir knew that no other answer was possible, but he used it as proof of Government indifference to Irish suffering and mortality', of which so many of his countrymen had, during the past twelve months, been the unprotected and unpitied victims; the bodies in many instances remaining uncovered, unshrouded and uncoffined'.[135]

On the other hand in February 1849 he more realistically agreed that book knowledge and statistics alone were not sufficient to appreciate the extent of Irish poverty. He suggested, nevertheless, that M.P.s with an intimate knowledge of Ireland, particularly the west, should be involved in any attempts to gather information.[136] To ensure that a full and meaningful picture was available 'he would have returns not merely of the cattle, the poultry, and the pigs that were in Ireland, but in order that their knowledge might be more comprehensive as to the state of the country, he would have them avail themselves of the assistance of the clergy of Ireland, the sheriffs, the coroners and the police of Ireland, whereby the House would be no longer left in ignorance of the great and disgraceful mortality prevailing in that country'.[137]

He had experienced this mortality himself early in 1849,

> In consequence of the failure of the potato crop the diet of the people had been changed, but it had not been changed from potatoes to corn, but from potatoes to turnips. He himself was acquainted with the cases of farmers who held from twenty to twenty-two acres of land and who were obliged to restrict themselves to a turnip diet, and who had died in consequence. Now he believed it took about six or eight weeks on a turnip diet to kill an able-bodied man, and he knew that many died from dysentery superinduced by turnip diet.[138]

He also relied on correspondence from acquaintances about the desperate conditions in Ireland. One letter was from a mining agent in Kilkenny which stated that while

> 160,000 barrels of coal had been sold at his mines in the year 1845, the sales of last year were only 24,000; and this great falling-off was

attributed to the poverty, apathy and despair of the small farmers, who, instead of burning their lime with colm and small coal, and so preparing their land for wheat crops, were merely ploughing up the lea land, evidently with the intention of removing in Autumn.[139]

He quantified the drop in lime sales from the quarries in Kilkenny as 110,223 barrels in 1845 to 24,793 barrels in 1848,[140] and used pawnbroker reports to Poor Law Inspectors as an indication of the destitution level.[141] These came from Waterford, Tipperary, Kilkenny and Queens County, and all referred to a decline in pawnbroking business, contrary to what might be expected during a period of distress. The pawnbrokers attributed this to a decimation of small farmers, cottiers and artisans either by death, eviction, emigration or entry to the workhouse. A large portion of the survivors were too destitute to use the pawn offices. The report from a Kilkenny pawnbroker showed that although pledges had increased since 1846, a big percentage was left unredeemed.

Sadleir used these accounts to refute the apparent delusion of his English colleagues that there was comparatively little distress in the provinces of Leinster and Munster. He took Tipperary, a 'notoriously rich county' in the heart of the golden vein, as an example, and quoted from a report on the impact of the Famine there,

> There were various establishments that afforded the people an opportunity of renewing their clothes, such as loan offices; and woollen drapers were in the habit of giving out materials for clothes to the people on their joint security from one to four pounds' worth, payable at one shilling per week for each pound. These resources were immediately discontinued after the potato failure, and the people's clothes became so bad that no pawnbroker could receive them as pledges, and such as were pledged remain forfeited, and when brought to a sale scarcely or never realised the original sum lent an each article. Therefore pawnbrokers had to limit their business; and the class of person I understand who resort to the establishments latterly, are the small farmers, who were in comparative comfort sometime since.

Such evidence by Sadleir and others in 1849 suggests an increasing sense of worry that the Famine was not seriously abating, and anxiety at the government's response. A disorganised amalgam of inadequate loans, soup kitchens, public works, foreign donations and voluntary organisations may have saved hundreds of thousands of lives, but ultimately over a million died from starvation or disease, and many more lived in unimaginable deprivation and hunger.[142] It was a chastening lesson that the Whig policy of *laissez faire*, which was supposed to provide cheap bread for the poor, had such a sting in its tail in a famine situation, when the law of supply and demand continued to operate, and, in any event, when bread could never be cheap enough for the starving population. Its inherent philosophy of survival of the fittest was a recipe for death, because it militated against early government interference.

When the Government acted, it was within this framework, which meant that Ireland would have to raise its own relief finance, and repay government aid through the increasing reliance upon a poor law system which was never designed to cope with such a disaster. Sadleir joined the chorus of Irish M.P.s critical of this system. He was very familiar with the circumstances in the Tipperary Union, where his father and other relatives were Guardians.[143] They were forced to establish auxiliary workhouses to cope with the influx of starving people. Both landlords and tenants were quick to exploit the famine there by offering labourers a weekly wage of one shilling, which was incapable of sustaining a family. They were less inclined, however, to meet the increase in rates necessary to fund the overstretched poor law system. The level of destitution around Tipperary in February 1848 was reflected not only in the workhouse population of 1,100 paupers, but in the 15,000 individuals on outdoor relief.[144]

Sadleir put considerable thought into the poor law system in general,[145] and offered his parliamentary colleagues an analysis of it during the Parliamentary debates of 1848 and 1849.[146] He pinpointed the structure of the unions as part of the problem, rightly placing it in a racial context. He saw the disparity between the size of union in Ireland and England as indicative of the second class status of the former. In April 1849, during the debate on the Rate-in-Aid Bill, which proposed a grant of £100,000 chargeable on the rates of all unions to relieve the most distressed ones, he saw this disparity as a contributor to the social differences between the two countries,

> In this country there was a cultivable area of about 25,000,000 acres, whilst in Ireland the cultivable area was something above 13,000,000 acres. In England there were 533 unions and union houses; but in Ireland the law was expected to work successfully with about 132 unions and union houses. Of those 533 in England, only 42 exceeded 100,000 acres in extent, whilst in Ireland there were 107 with an area exceeding 100,000 acres and of those no less than 25 exceeded 200,000 acres. The average population of the English unions did not exceed 23,400, but the average of the Irish unions was something above 62,000. This showed the great social differences of the country, and he wanted to know from the Government how they proposed to dispose of the surplus agricultural population.[147]

Apart from the size of Irish unions and their large populations, Sadleir was puzzled by the area anomalies within the Irish system itself. The population of some electoral divisions in the Tralee Union, for example, was less than 1,300, but in others there it exceeded 23,000. He pressed for a greater degree of uniformity and a doubling of the number of unions. Grey, who was responsible for the administration of the system, praised Sadleirs analysis. He promised that the first report of a boundary commission, given to the Government a short time earlier, would be shortly released.

Clearly, a large pauper population placed a heavy burden on rate payers. This became intolerable during the Famine, and, while Sadleir's perspective was balanced by sympathy for the ratepayers, he was critical of inefficiency in rate collecting.[148] By then, however, the amount of rates collected had increased enormously and the Guardians of many unions, including Tipperary, had been dismissed as inefficient and replaced by officials. But he persisted in treating his colleagues to a derisive reconstruction of what he considered the typical procedure,

> The guardians met and discovered that the sum say of £5,000 was necessary to carry out the purposes of the Act. They consulted their clerk and inquired what rate would be necessary in order to realise that sum. He would respond, perhaps 1/= in the pound. That rate would be accordingly struck and the collectors would go forth to collect it. In seven or eight weeks the collectors would return, but instead of having received £5,000 they would probably not get in more than £3,000. What was then to be done? Another rate must be struck, perhaps of 4d in the pound. Again the collectors go forth, and after another lengthened absence they return with £1,500, and the second sum has been collected almost entirely from the very person who paid the first rate; whilst those who evaded the first rate evaded the second also. This was a direct encouragement to a certain set of miserable landlords, whom he need not further particularise, to have upon their estates a class of tenants who were able to pay rack rents, but could not pay the poor rates.[149]

Sadleirs indictment of recalcitrant landlords not alone showed a lack of sympathy with those whose estates were in debt, but he also advocated a ruthlessness in collecting rates' arrears. In May 1849 he was

> entirely in favour of giving the most summary power for the recovery of arrears of poor rates from the landlords... The landlords had no reason to complain, perhaps, when it was recollected that the most stringent and extensive powers were conferred upon poor law guardians to have the rates collected where the annual value was over £4... There was the

greatest anxiety to meet the demand shown by the tenantry in Ireland and he though it was only justice to see that that portion which was payable by the landlords was enforced and that every facility should be given for its recovery.[150]

Justice demanded that such statements be tempered by the admission that not all landlords were evading their share of the burden. While he acknowledged the necessity of the poor law system, Sadleir also argued that landed property should not be saddled with it, without some parallel remedial measures.[151] He was particularly conscious of the impact of the Rate in Aid upon his own class.[152] Its principle was to shift relief from a local to a national forum in yet another effort to confront the Famine at a time when Ireland had already paid a terrible price for official reliance on prevailing economic theory and a government partially paralysed by ideological differences at cabinet level on the question of famine relief.[153] The Rate in Aid signalled the dominance of the Treasury within a ministry which was also sensitive to a changing outlook among the English electorate, where donor fatigue was accompanied by a perception of Irish ingratitude symbolised by the Ballingarry uprising.

Russell had little difficulty in getting the Rate in Aid bill through parliament, but it was strongly resisted by the Irish M.P.s. Sadleir dismissed as clap-trap his assertion that the opposition of Irish M.P.s to the Rate-in-Aid Bill was tantamount to passing a death sentence on their fellow countrymen.[154] He did not consider it a remedial initiative. It was basically unjust, because it would fall more heavily on some areas, delusive since it would not be adequate to cope with distress, and retrograde because it would diminish employment as well as weaken the principle of self-reliance. A letter to him from a landlord in Roundwood, Queen's County, upheld this view,

> The poor rate estimated for the present year was three shillings and sixpence in the pound, not for the sustainment of a single able bodied labourer, but for the weak and helpless poor in the workhouse. He states that, in addition to this three shillings and sixpence they would have sixpence as a general rate and one and sixpence as union rate in and, making in the whole, five shillings and 6d in the pound for poor rates. He further remarks that if the rate-in-aid passes, he must of necessity cease giving employment that he had hitherto contrived to give – that he had saddled himself with a debt of £196 a year as rent – charged to the Board of Works, which was equal to an additional rate of eight shillings and nine pence per acre on his land for twenty two years.

Sadleir could not accept that Irish rates were sufficiently moderate to sustain increases of this order. While he was ready to use unfavourable comparisons between Irish and English units, he rejected Russell's own contrast between the small amount of poor rates levied on prosperous areas in Ireland with those of 'the worst districts in England'. The landlords had kept the rates at a tolerable rate in Ireland, but the bill would give a 'stimulus to the most destructive and exhaustive system of emigration in the country'. Neither would he accept that some Irish unions had repudiated part of their liabilities to the imperial exchequer, by refusing to pay their instalments towards the erection of workhouses. His research showed that the appeal of some Guardians for extra time had gone unheeded but,

> when the tenant farmers in Kent applied for a little indulgence in reference to their hop duty, they were not told that their resources were exhausted, and that they must pay; but the Chancellor of the Exchequer – and very properly – gave them that extension of time for payment of the duty which circumstances entitled them to expect. But the appeal of the poor law guardians in Ireland for a short breathing space, till the next harvest, to pay up their instalments, was met by the stern response 'your resources are not utterly exhausted, and your request cannot be listened to'.[155]

Part of the debate on the Rate-in-Aid Bill concerned the possibility of extending the income tax to Ireland as a means of raising revenue. Sadleir opposed it, quoting at length from a March 1848 speech by the Chancellor of the Exchequer on a motion to do so. The tenor of the speech was its inexpediency and folly at any time, and especially in the circumstances of the famine. The Chancellor then believed that the imposition of income tax would discourage landlords from creating employment.[156] But, the Prime Minister saw the income tax as a compromise, and invited the Irish representatives to Downing Street for a discussion.[157] A delegation of fifty went and heard his offer to abandon the rate-in-aid if they supported the income tax proposal. Sadleir was among these, but his contribution was not recorded. John O'Connell appears to have been the most vocal. On 19 April thirty-two of them met under Sir Lucius O'Brien to consider Russell's Proposition. By then they had been inundated with petitions from Ireland and they decided against it.[158]

References
1. Clarke, *Dublin*, p. 172. For reference to the increase in typhus on a national level see *Disease Ireland. Abstracts of the most serious representations made by the several medical superintendents of the Public Institutions, (Fever Hospitals,*

    Infirmaries, Dispensaries, etc.) in the Provinces of Ulster, Munster, Leinster and Connaught H.C. 1846 (20) XXX VII, (I.U.P. reprint), *passim.*

2. He periodically gave money to Morrogh to advance his career, for which he received 5% interest, but henceforth he received no profits from the law firm – *Dowling* , p. 64.

3. Briggs, *Victorian Cities*, p. 59.

4. *The Census of Ireland for the Year 1851, part 1, vol.2, Province of Leinster*, pp 44-45.

5. Appendix 8.

6. C. Dickens, *Little Dorrit*, (London, n.d.), p. 48.

7. Ingram Herbert 1811-1860, was born in Boston Lincolnshire and was educated at the Boston Free School. From 1832 to 1834 he worked as a journeyman printer in London, and then settled in Nottingham as a printer, bookseller and newsagent, with his brother-in-law Nathaniel Cooke. He moved back to London in 1842 to promote a vegetable pill. That year he published the first issue of the *Illustrated London News*, which quickly reached a circulation of 66,000 copies. In 1848 he founded the *London Telegraph,* which proved unprofitable. In 1860 when on a tour of Canada he was drowned when the vessel in which he was travelling sank after a collision. *D.N.B.*, e.v.

8. pp.1,7.

9. *C.E.* 3 May 1856.

10. See *Victorian London*, (London Transport Publication, n.d.), p. 4 *et. seq.* for a sketch of the West End.

11. *London as it is to-day*, p. 398.

12. Ibid., pp 9-10.

13. Ibid., pp 395, 399-400. See also *London at Table or How When Where to dine and order a Dinner and Where to avoid dining*, (London, 1851), pp 1, 5-7, 9-10.

14. *London as it is to-day*, p. 399.

15. Ibid.

16. The theatres listed on pp 206-217 were Her Majesty's Royal Italian Opera (Covent Garden), Drury Lane, The Haymarket, Royal Lyceum, Adelphi, St. James's, Royal Princess's, Olympic, Strand and Sadlers Wells.

17. Tiobraid Árann.

18. *Burke's Irish Family Records*, p. 1139. For a historical sketch of the founding of Sadler's Wells Theatre see D. Arundel,*The story of Sadler's Wells 1683-1964*, (London, 1965), pp 1 et. seq. Dick Sadler, the owner of the Music House was a Surveyor of the Highways and owned a gravel pit from which he supplied gravel for the Highways. The discovery of a well when excavating this pit added to his income as a confectioner and wine merchant when the enterprising Sadler sold the water, which allegedly had curative properties, to patrons of his nearby Music Hall. Soon crowds flocked to avail of the water and for a short time Sadler benefited financially until the novelty wore off. The Music Hall, which became known as Sadler's Wells was known for its debauchery in the early eighteenth century. By the mid nineteenth century, however operatic performances had long replaced the earlier more earthy offerings.

19. *London as it is to-day*, pp 206-207, see *London Illustrated News* 11 March1848 for the opening of the season. Prices ranged from a half-crown to a guinea.

20. *London as it is to-day*, p. 207.

21. M. Hynes, 'Sadleir M.P. Banker', in *My Clonmel Scrapbook,* (Dundalk, N.D.), pp 229-230.

22. See *London Illustrated News* 21 April 1849 for reference to Taglioni's performance in Her Majesty's.

23. Letter 8 July 1891 from Ms. Eileen Robinson, Archivist of the Victorian and Albert Museum, which houses the theatre's archives, to the author.

24. MacDermot, *I.G.*, vol.6, p. 325.

25. *C.E.* 8 March 1856.

26. Hynes, 'Sadleir M.P'., p. 229.

27. MacDermot, *The Catholic Question*, p. XXI.

28. *Annual Register*, 1856, p. 38.

29. Hynes' article is the only source for this, but it contains several basic inaccuracies and is not supported by sources e.g. it claims that Sadleir was President of the Tipperary Bank and was the son of a 'respectable trader'. Whites Club still exists but have not responded to the writer's request to confirm Sadleir's membership.

30. *N.G.* 3 March 1856; See D. Morier Evans, *Facts, Failures and Frauds*, (London, 1859, Reprinted New York, 1968) pp 106-153 on Paul. See also *D.N.B.*, e.v. under Paul.

31. *W.T.* 23 February 1856.

32. See *Illustrated London News* 12 February 1848. See p. below on his involvement with Carlow race meetings.

33. See *T.L* 1 March 1856, *W.T.* 23 February 1856, *Times* 26 February 1856 for comments by his friends.

34. Evidence of Josiah Wilkinson in *Times* 26 February 1856.

35. Quoted in *W.C.* 1 March 1856.

36. *W.T* . 23 February 1856, *T.L* 23 February 1856.

37. Quoted in *T.L.* 1 March 1856.

38. See C. Cook and J. Stevenson, *Longman's Atlas of Modern British History, a Visual guide to British Society and Politics 1700-1970*, (London, 1978), pp 60-61.

39. Ibid., p. 60. (Despite such progress the *Railway Times* of 24 January 1852 felt that the government had not promoted railways with sufficient determination and had yielded to the objection of some landowners to railways being constructed on their property. It compared the more significant progress of railroad expansion in the United States, although it conceded that land costs were considerably cheaper there and the American system was comprised of single track whereas double track was the norm in the U.K.

40. Ibid., p. 61.

41. When analysing the statistics for the returns below the researcher should note that some returns cover a full year and others a half year – see *Return of the passenger and Goods traffic on each railway in Great Britain and Ireland for the years ending 30 June 1846 and 30 June 1847 ; together with a summary for each year showing the number of passengers, divided into classes, the receipts from each class and from goods*, H.C. 1847-48 (937) LXIII. 53 pp,102,104. See also *Return of the number of passengers conveyed on all railways in the United Kingdom during the year ending 30 June 1848, showing the different classes, the receipts from each class and from goods etc., also the number of miles of railway open on 1 July 1847 and on 30 June 1848*, H.C. 1849 LI (6) pp 6-7. see also the return for the half year ending 31 December 1848 in *H.C.* 1849 L.I.(418) p. 6 ; the half year ending 30 June 1850 in *H.C.* 1851. LI (12) pp 6-10; the half year ending 31 December 1850 in *H.C.* 1851. LI (313) p. 12, half year ending 30 June 1852 in *H.C.* 1852-53 . XCVII (252) pp 12-13; half year ending 31 December 1852 in *H.C.* 1852-53 XCVII (906) pp 14-15.

42. A memorial from sixty six landowners in Tipperary, including James Scully senior and junior, John Scully, Richard Scully, James Sadleir, Richard Sadleir and Thomas Sadleir in *Railways Ireland. Copy of all Resolutions and Memorials*

presented to the Chancellor of Ireland, or to the Chancellor of the Exchequer, respecting Railroads in that Country. H.C. 1839 (154) XCVI.7

43. *First Report of the Commissioners appointed to enquire into the manner in which Railway Communication can be most advantageously promoted in Ireland,* H.C.1837 (75) XXXiii.283 p. 9.

44. pp 332-33, 383-85, 419-20 below.

45. *C.P.* 8 March 1856, *Gentleman's Magazine* 1 May 1856 p. 530. See pp

46. *Gentleman's Magazine* 1 May 1856. *Newcastle Chronicle* 22 February 1856.

47. *W.N.* 13 July 1852.

48. *R.T.* 20 December 1856. Keating was also a member of the 'Daily Committee' – *I.C.R.* 1858 and 1859, vol. 6, p. 65.

49. C.R. Dod, *Electoral facts from 1832 to 1853*, (London, 2nd ed. 1853), p. 52. Sadleir did not later favour such a limited franchise, seeing it as promoting corruption, especially in boroughs. He supported the 1850 policy of the government to extend the franchise – his speech in *Parl. Deb.*,series 3. 1850, vol. 108, pp 1313-14,1339, and vol.109, pp 327-328.

50. See pp 267-8 below.

51. O'Shea was also a relative of the wealthy Henry O'Shea of Limerick see R.D. 1856, vol. 35, memorial 171. For other reference to him in the Registry of Deeds see R.D., 1852, vol. 16, mem. 116, deed 30 June 1852, R.D., 1852, vol. 21, mem. 242, deed of assignment 21 July 1856.

52. R. Malcolmson, *The Carlow Parliamentary Roll*, (Dublin, 1872), pp 86-87. (Layard committed suicide in the early 1850s – *Times* 26 February 1856, *B.H.* 1 March 1856).

53. *C.S.* 26 June 1847.

54. *Illustrated London News* 9 March 1850. (O'Shea had been manager of the National Bank in Nenagh in the 1830's – see *Dublin Almanac and General Register 1838,* p. 179.

55. *C.S.* 27 July 1847.

56. Ibid., 31 July and 7 August 1847.

57. Pierce Mahony to Haly 31 January 1847, K.D.A., H.P., FH/1847/02, Carton Bp 10.

58. *C.S.* 27July 1847.

59. For priestly activity during the Famine see D.A. Kerr, *The Catholic Church and the Famine,* (Dublin, 1996), pp 8 *et seq.,* pp 41 et seq., p. 70 *et seq.* D.A. Kerr, *A Nation of Beggars? Priests People and Politics in Famine Ireland (1846 -1852),* (Oxford, 1994), pp 30-65.

60. For an insight into this see J. O'Shea, *Priest, Politics and Society in Post-Famine Ireland,* (Dublin, 1983).

61. *C.S.* 31 July 1847.

62. For reference to Maher's public disputations with Protestants in Carlow during the 1820s see T. McGrath, *Politics, Interdenominational Relations and Education in the Public Ministry of Bishop James Doyle of Kildare and Leighlin, 1786-1834,* (Dublin, 1999), pp 126 to 127, see ibid., pp 136, 140. For Maher's generosity during the Famine when he sold personal possessions to raise money for poor relief, see Kerr, *The Catholic Church* , p. 30, Kerr, *A Nation of Beggars,* pp 62,99. For ref. to Maher's anti-eviction campaign in the 1830s and the tithe agitation see T. McGrath, *Religious Renewal and Reform in the Pastoral Ministry of Bishop James Doyle of Kildare and Leighlin, 1786-1834,* (Dublin, 1999), pp 198-199.

63. *C.S.* 24 July 1847.

64. See O'Shea, *Priest, Politics,* p. 47-48 on bribery and corruption at election times.

65. *C.S.* 24 July 1847.

66. Address in *C.S.* 10 July 1847, *T.F.P.* 14 July 1847.
67. Scully's address referred to the decline in manufacturing because of the Act of Union.
68. Nicholas V. Maher's address contained a similar statement.
69. *C.S.* 10 July 1847, *T.F.P.* 14 July 1847. (See D. G. Marnane, 'The Famine in South Tipperary, Part Four' in *Tipperary Historical Journal*, (Thurles, 1999), p. 13 on Portarlington's visit to his Tipperary estates in 1846 when he was accompanied by Sadleir).
70. *C.S.* 7 August 1847.
71. *Telegraph* 24 March 1852.
72. *C.S.* 31 July 1847.
73. Ibid., and see his statements in *C.S.* 7 August 1847.
74. Ibid., 24 and 31 July 1847.
75. Ibid., 7 August 1847.
76. Dod, *Electoral Facts* , p. 52, *Tablet* 14 August 1847.
77. See e.g. *W.M* . 23 June 1847 for an election meeting on 21 July 1847.
78. The author could only locate one Waterford newspaper, the *Waterford Mail*, which, however, carried the addresses of all other candidates (*W.M.* 31 July 1847).
79. *W.M* 14 August 1847.
80. Ibid., Keating became a friend of Lord Palmerston who frequently employed him to purchase Irish hunters, MacDermot, *I.G.*, vol. 6, op. cit. at p. 356.
81. *T.F.P.* 30 June 1847.
82. Laffan was a native of kilkurkee, Castleiney, near Templemore. One of his brothers was director of the National Bank in Thurles.
83. Se p. 39 n. 109 above on the Maher-Scully connection.
84. For biographical details see M.J. O'Connell, *Charles Bianconi, a Biography, 1786-1875*, (London,1878), passim.
85. *T.F.P.* 7 July 1847.
86. Scully attended some of the repeal meetings in Dublin after his election see e.g.. *T.F.P.* 23 October 1847 for one such meeting at which Scully expressed regret at the split in the repeal movement.
87. *T.F.P.* 7 July 1847.
88. Ibid., 10 July 1847.
89. Ibid., 2 July 1847 for their exchange of letters.
90. See Davis, *The Young Ireland*, pp 89, 93, 122, 133.
91. *T.F.P.* 21 July 1847.
92. The same committee dealt with the baronies of Kilnemanagh Upper and Kilnemanagh Lower.
93. *T.F.P.* 14 August 1847.
94. The death of James Scully, Vincent Scully's appointment and his contact with the Sadleirs on an annual audit in *L.E.* 3 May 1856.
95. Scully continued to protest in vain over the years. he raised the issue at the annual general meeting in February 1850 but was seen by those present as a troublemaker. They expressed satisfaction at how the bank was being managed – *L.E.* 3 May 1856.
96. *B.M.*, Vol VIII, 1848, p. 195.
97. Ibid., vol. IX, 1859 pp 182-183. The Doubtful Debt fund was increased from £2,500 to £5,013.
98. *L.E.* 3 May 1856. James further reassured Scully in December 1849, January 1850 and January 1851 about the bank's soundness. His letter of January 1850

however expressed anger that the publicity about Sadleirs role in the Kingston estate was designed to injure the bank. Reference to those letters in *L.E.* 3 May 1856, *W.T.* 3 May 1856.

99.   *Parl. Deb.*, series 3, 1849, vol.4 col.397.

100. Sadleir's speech in *C.S.* 7 August 1847. Maher's address in ibid., 24 July 1847. See also a letter from a 'Protestant Elector' in ibid., 17 July 1847.

101. See S.J. Connelly, 'The Great Irish Famine and Irish Politics' in C. Poirtéir (ed.), *The Great Irish Famine*, (Cork, 1995), pp 36, 42.

102. See *Nation* 3,10 June 1843 for some lists which included Sir Colmen O' Loghlen and Thomas O' Hagan, eminent lawyers as members. See ibid., 19 August 1843 for the great Tara meeting and ibid., 23 September 1843 for a long list of Leinster inhabitants who signed a requisition for the holding of a Repeal meeting at Mullaghmast, County Kildare. See *Nation* 29 July 1847 for a repeal dinner in Cashel at which Sadleir's in-law, John Grene, Cappamurra gave an enthusiastic address in favour of repeal.

103. For reference to O'Connell's death as a powerful electioneering weapon see Davis, *The Young Ireland*, pp 131 et. seq.

104. See Connolly, 'The Great Irish Famine, p. 43, W. Nolan, 'The Irish Confederation in County Tipperary in 1848' in *Tipperary Historical Journal 1998*, (Thurles, 1998), pp 2-18, Davis, *The Young Ireland*, passim.

105. Grey's opening speech in *Parl. Deb.*, series 3, vol. 98, 1848, cols.20 et.seq. (7 April 1848).

106. 'If any person or persons whatsoever, after the day of the passing of that Act, during the natural life of His Majesty, and until the end of the next Session of Parliament after the demise of the Crown, should within the realm or without compass, imagine, invent, devise or intend death or destruction, or any bodily harm tending to death or destruction, maiming or wounding, imprisonment or restraint of the person of the King, his heirs or successors, or to deprive or depose him or them from the style, honour, or kingly name of the Imperial Crown of this realm, or of any other of the King's dominions or countries or to levy war against the King, his heirs and successors, within this realm, in order by force or constraint to compel him or them to change their measures or counsels, or in order to put any force or constraint upon or to intimidate or over-awe either House, or both Houses of Parliament, or to move or stir any foreigner or stranger with force to invade this realm, or any other of the King's dominions or countries, and such compassings, imaginations, inventions, devices or intentions, or any of them should express, utter, or declare by publishing any printing or writing, or by any overt act or deed, legally convicted thereof, on the oaths of two credible witnesses, in due course of law, should be deemed and adjudged traitors, and suffer the pains of death, and also forfeiture, as in the case of high treason'.

107. *Parl. Deb.*, series 3, vol. 98, 1848, cols. 74, et.seq. (10 April 1848).

108. Ibid., cols. 119-120.

109. e.g. Thompson, Muntz, Bright, and Wakley – ibid., cols. 85-112, 112, 117-119, 120-122 respectively.

110. Ibid., cols. 34 *et. seq.*

111. Ibid.,cols. 112-117. (Henry Drummond was born in 1786 in Hampshire and was raised by his grandfather, Lord Melville, who was a close friend of Pitt. He was educated at Harrow and Oxford before becoming a partner in a bank at Charing Cross. He married Lady Henrietta Hay, eldest daughter of the ninth earl of Kinnoull. He entered parliament in 1810. He travelled widely to such places as

Russia, the Holy Land and Geneva where he became involved in a religious movement. In 1825 he founded the chair of political economy at Oxford and helped to found the Irvingite church where he held the rank of apostle, evangelist and prophet. He was not entirely stable and professed to hearing supernatural voices and believing that the end of the world was nigh. He wrote numerous articles and pamphlets, many of them on religious topics. *D.N.B.*, e.v.

112. Sadleir's speech in ibid., cols. 161-163 (11 April 1848).

113. Commonly called the Felon's Act.

114. Russell's speech in *Parl. Deb.*, series 3, vol.100,1848, cols. 697-713 (22 July 1848).

115. Peel's speech in ibid., cols. 716-719, Disraeli's speech in ibid., cols. 728-731.

116. O'Connor's speech in ibid., cols. 713-716. O'Connor was born in 1794 and was educated in the Portarlington Grammar School and Trinity College. He was called to the Irish bar. In the general election of 1832 he was returned as a Repealer for County Cork. He founded the London Democratic Association in 1837 and established the Northern Star newspaper that same year. He was the recognised leader of the Chartist Movement which arose from the consolidation of various radical movements in 1838. He was identified with the more violent wing of the movement and in 1840 was sentenced to eighteen months imprisonment for seditious libels in the *Northern Star*. O'Connor was the co-founder of the Chartist Co-operative Land Company, later named the National Land Company whose purpose was to purchase estates, divide them into small farms and let them to subscribers by ballot. He was elected M.P. for Nottingham in 1847. In 1852 he was pronounced insane and spent two years in an asylum in Chiswick. He died on 30 August 1855. *D.N.B.* ,e.v.

117. See Davis, *The Young Ireland Movement*, p. 19 on Chartist violence, see also J.A. Moloney, *A Soul came into Ireland. Thomas Davis 1814-1845, A Biography*, (Dublin, 1995), p. 97.

118. Speech in *Parl. Deb.*, series 3, vol.100, 1848, cols. 742-743 (22 April 1848). See Davis, *The Young Ireland*, p. 133 for reference to a physical assault on Doheny during the Tipperary 1847 election.

119. *Parl. Deb.*, series 3, vol.100, 1848, cols. 721-725, (22 July 1848).

120. *A Bill to continue for a limited time an act of the last session for empowering the Lord Lieutenant or other Chief Governor or Governors of Ireland to apprehend and detain such persons as he or they shall suspect of conspiring against Her Majesty's Person and Government.*, H.C. 1849 (9) 111.167.

121. Thomas D'Arcy McGee was born in Carlingford, Co. Louth in 1825. His maternal grandfather was imprisoned as a United Irishman. In 1842 McGee emigrated to the United States, and for a time worked as a clerk in the *Boston Pilot*. Within a short time he became its editor. He later became parliamentary correspondent of the *Freeman's Journal* and then the *Nation*. In 1847 he was appointed secretary to the Committee of the Irish Confederation, and returned to Ireland to take charge of its publicity. He also worked for the Confederation cause in Scotland, but after the suppression of the 1848 rising he fled to the United States, where he quickly established the *New York Nation* and found himself in conflict with the priests there. He then went to Boston and founded the American Celt. He later turned against revolution as a political philosophy and was ostracised by his erstwhile supporters. In 1857 he settled in Montreal and established the *New Era*. He was elected to the Legislative Assembly and became President of the Council in 1862 and 1864. His opposition to the threatened Fenian 'invasion' of Canada led to his assassination in 1868. *D.N.B.*, e.v.

122. Grey's introductory speech in *Parl. Deb.*, series 3, vol 102, 1849, cols. 306-317, (6 February 1849)

123. O' Connell's speech in ibid., cols.317 et. seq, Crawford's speech in col. 511, (6,9 February 1849 respectively).

124. Scully's speech in ibid., cols. 367-368, see also comments of Sir Henry W. Barron, M.P. Waterford City, in cols. 508-511, (6,9 February 1849, respectively).

125. Ibid., vol.102, 1849, col. 502, (9 February 1849). See also his speech in vol.104, 1849, col.396, (17 April 1849).

126. Ibid., vol.102, 1849, cols. 502,504, (February 1849).

127. Ibid., vol.104, 1849, col 551, (20 April 1849).

128. *C.S.* 7 August 1847.

129. *Telegraph* 19 April 1852.

130. *T.F.P.* 6 February 1847. Clement gave £2 to the Carrickbeg fund.

131. *C.S.* 7 August 1847.

132. He was the son of James Scully of Shanballymore, founder and chairman of the Tipperary Bank.

133. *T.F.P.* 21 April 1847. Ibid., 24 April 1847 condemned the attack and praised Scully as a benevolent landlord.

134. *Parl. Deb.*, series 3, Vol. 97, 1848, cols. 1355-1356, (22 March 1848).

135. Ibid., Vol.98, 1848, col. 162, (11 April 1848). (This was during the debate on the Crown and Government Security Bill).

136. Ibid., vol. 102, 1849, col. 453, (8 February 1849), *Tablet* 10 February 1849.

137. Ibid., Vol.104, 1849, Col.551, (20 April 1849).

138. Ibid., Col. 545, (20 April 1849).

139. Ibid., col.550, (20 April 1849).

140. Ibid., col. 538, (20 April 1849).

141. Ibid., cols. 542 and 543, (20 April 1849). For details of these reports see *Relief of Distress and Union Workhouses Ireland. Papers relating to the Proceedings for the relief of the distress and state of Unions and Workhouses in Ireland. Part 11. Distress indicated in the Clothing of the Peasantry and Pawnbrokers Returns.* H.C. 1849 (1042) xlvii (221).

142. In recent years a great deal has been written on the Famine, the government's response and the reasons underlying this response. See e.g. M.E. Daly, 'The Operations of Famine Relief' 1845-1847' in Poirtéir, *The Great Irish Famine*, pp 123-134, C. Kinealy, *The Great Calamity, The Irish Famine 1845-1852*, (Dublin, 1994), passim, J. O'Connor, The Workhouses of Ireland. The Fate of Ireland's Poor, (Dublin, 1995), pp 113 et. seq., D.A. Kerr, *The Catholic Church*. pp 28, 78, 80, C. Ó Gráda ed.), *Famine 150 Commemorative Lecture Series*, (Dublin, 1997), passim, Ó Gráda, *Ireland a New Economic* , pp 178-236, C. Ó Grada, *Ireland before and after the Famine. Explorations in Economic History 1800-1925*, (Manchester, 1988), esp. pp 110-116. Many local studies have also been written. The most comprehensive on Tipperary are D. G. Marnane, 'South Tipperary on the Eve of the Great Famine' in *Tipperary Historical Journal 1995*, (Thurles, 1995), pp 1-53, D. G. Marnane, The Famine in South Tipperary, parts one, two and three in *Tipperary Historical Journal*, (Thurles 1996, 1997 and 1998), pp 1-42, 131-150 and 56-75, respectively.

143. The Sadleir-Scully Guardians were – Clement William Sadleir, William Sadleir, Nicholas Sadleir, Richard Sadleir, James Scully, Thomas Scully, Frank Scully and Vincent Scully. Tipperary County Library, Tipperary Union Poor Law Minute Books 1845 to 1851. A roll of Guardian attendance was noted on the opening page of each book.

144. Information on the Tipperary Poor Law Union whose nucleus was Tipperary Town in Marnane, *Land and Violence*, pp 62 et.seq. see also *Accounts and Papers 1848. Relief of Distress and Union Workhouses (Ireland)*, H.C. 1847-48 (955) LVI, (I.U.P. Reprint 1970) pp609-620.

145. The Poor Law system has been dealt with in the recent Famine historiography referred to above. O'Connor's book on the workhouses is a well researched and lucid account of the system.

146. His references in *Parl. Deb.*, series 3, vol. 97, 1848, col 890, (22 March 1848), vol. 102, 1849, cols. 294-295, (4 April 1849).

147. Ibid., vol.102, 1849, cols. 295-296, (4 April, 1849).

148. See Kinealy, *The Great Calamity*, pp 115, 186-192.

149. *Parl. Deb.*, series 3, vol. 102, 1849, col.293, (4 April 1849).

150. Ibid., vol. 105, 1849, cols. 349-350, (11 May 1849).

151. Ibid., vol.102, col. 294, (4 April 1849).

152. For reference to the Rate in Aid see Kinealy, *The Great Calamity*, pp 242 et. seq.

153. See p. Gray, 'Ideology and the Famine', in Poirtéir, *The Great Irish Famine*, pp 88, 92, 94-95, 99,101

154. *Parl. Deb.*, series 3, vol. 104, 1849, cols. 540-544, (20 April 1849) for his speech.

155. Ibid., cols. 546-547, (20 April 1849).

156. Ibid., cols. 552-553, (20 April 1849).

157. *F.J* 20 April 1849, *Tablet* 21 April 1849.

158. *F.J* 21 April 1849. (Income Tax was finally introduced into Ireland in 1853 as the best method of recouping British expenditure in Ireland – see O'Connor, *The Workhouses of Ireland*, p. 278.

'Gog and Magog giving Paddy a lift out of the mire' (*Punch*, vol. 17 (1849), p. 37).

Chapter 3

Agrarian politics 1849-1851

Sadleir's refutation of the rate-in-aid or income tax as a means of funding relief was accompanied by a suggestion that the government should confer 'great and extraordinary powers' on a commission to recover rates and deal with landed property in Ireland. The inference was that efficient land management would carry the rates' burden. This was only one facet of the land question, which was subject to detailed parliamentary discussion during the late 1840s. In April 1849 he warned of its centrality to the well being of Ireland,

> So long as they hesitated to deal with the land question all their measures for the alleviation and improvement of the poor law, all their plans for the extension of the suffrage, all their proposals for the extension of the same municipal system to Ireland which existed in England, all their exertions to place a limit to the amount of the poor rate, and to exempt estates from being overwhelmed by the arrears of rates – would fail.[1]

Unlike many Irish representatives he regarded ownership as the core of the land question, and the crucial issue was the legal obstacles surrounding it. As a landlord, tenant, and attorney, Sadleir was familiar with the legal complexities of ownership and the long delays in Chancery because of these. He had first hand knowledge of the web of encumbrances and mortgages which bedevilled ownership, and which were exacerbated in the wake of the Famine. He treated the House to several long and sometimes tedious lectures on it, supported by quotations from pamphlets and judgments of leading conveyance attorneys and judges of the early nineteenth century. State interference with ownership was risky for any government, but Russell saw it as a possibility of introducing a larger element of a Catholic proprietary class to improve relations between the two countries. The government was also convinced that Irish land ownership needed revitalising, and responded with a series of acts to facilitate the prompt and cheap transfer of encumbered property on the application of a creditor. The principal one was the Incumbered Estates Act, whose conveyances would be good title to property, obviating the necessity of going through Chancery to examine existing deeds, which were complicated by all types of encumbrances requiring searches and verification.

By the time the *Incumbered Estates (Ireland) Bill* was introduced in 1848, Sadleir was already receiver or agent over estates with an annual rental of £60,000.[2] The Commons acknowledged his expertise on Irish land law, and on 11 July 1848 he opened the adjourned debate on the Bill, whose principle he supported, although he objected to its 'machinery'.[3] He refuted the arguments of the Conservative M.P., Joseph Napier, later Irish Attorney General and architect of several land bills,[4] that the bill as it stood would either end the system of Chancery suits or facilitate the drawing up of 'fresh and clear' titles. In what was to be supreme irony, one of his concerns was the absence of provisions to lessen the possibility of fraud, by giving judges more discretion to serve notices directly to would-be purchasers of estates. Instead the bill stipulated that such notices be published in newspapers and in the *Dublin Gazette*, and posted in places of public worship in the districts where the properties lay.

One flaw in the bill was the failure to reduce legal expenses by shortening the legal process. The silence of lawyers was a sure sign of this,

> There had been no remonstrance from the Irish bar with reference to the anticipated diminution of expense under this bill – no murmur had come from the attorneys and solicitors of Ireland on that head; and he returned to predict that no attorney or solicitor in that country would object to this bill on any personal ground, such as that it was calculated to curtail the emoluments of his profession.

The Peelite, Sir James Graham,[5] who, as Home Secretary, had been responsible for the administration of Famine relief in 1845, responded positively to some of Sadleir's points, but picked him up on his tendency to delve into all the 'technicalities and legal niceties' of the bill at such an early stage,

> my dread has always been that with respect to this measure it would be too much left to the professional prejudices and legal scruples of conveyers, who would consider it only with reference to the law of real property, and not sufficiently in regard to the peculiar circumstances existing in Ireland.

Graham promoted the legislation as an opportunity to help 'reunite' the Catholics of Ireland with the soil by allowing people 'of small capital' to invest in land. He chided Sadleir on his 'timidity' because the

Carlow M.P. in opening the debate strongly opposed the creation of a peasant proprietary. When it resumed a week later the Solicitor General restated the government's policy of increasing the number of small proprietors in Ireland.[6]

The 1848 Incumbered Estates Act failed to significantly simplify the procedure for selling land, and by the Spring of 1849 amending legislation was ready for its second reading. But, Sadleir felt that the legal impediments to selling land were so complex that a special committee should be established to examine them. He formally moved the appointment of such a committee, and supported his motion on 17 April with a long technical contribution, beginning with the assertion that the poor state of Irish agriculture stemmed from these, because they hindered both capital investment in agriculture and the application of agricultural science to foster development.[7] He drew attention to the finding of an 1846 Committee that the legal expenses of land transfer in England lowered the marketable value of land. This was much more damaging in Ireland 'where land was so much encumbered, and where a different law prevailed with regard to its transfer'.

The expenses stemming from the complex devolution of Irish titles were a 'flagrant and crying evil'. Every encumbrance 'however old' must be kept alive. Every individual who had a 'remote or indirect interest' in a property had to be brought before the court of Chancery. Every fact might become the separate subject of a small equity suit. Because of this a purchaser was obliged to trace all encumbrances, a costly exercise of searches, sometimes covering a span of twenty years, and lengthy litigation often involving several equity suits.

Part of the problem lay in the 'vital want of the registration of incumbrances and of judgment debts'. This was due to the Judgement Debtors Act which was so legally obscure that it tested the ability of even the finest barristers. The procedures for the sale of land in Chancery 'were directly opposite to those which any prudent or sensible auctioneer would recommend'. It insisted that the sale of a property must take place on the specified hour advertised, and so thwarted the best efforts of a purchaser to reliably trace the integrity of the title, and was akin to buying 'a pig in a poke'. The system required simplification so that properties not sold at the appointed time could be privately disposed of by the master of Chancery. Not only did the Incumbered Estates Act fail to remedy this, but was itself a disincentive to safely invest in land. Sadleir quoted the opinion of the Irish Attorney General that under it landowners wishing to transfer mortgages were bound to furnish proof to the purchasers that there were no judgment debts against them. He saw this stipulation as irrelevant to the transfer of ownership, and advocated the setting up of a commission of two or three people to quickly identify title and encumberances, thus avoiding years of Chancery investigation,

> When this was done they might confer on purchasers a primitive and perfect title; and that in the most simple form. They might make as clear a title to land as if it were the first acre of land saved from the waters of the deluge. The purchaser would want no title deeds; for all that would be requisite would be a transfer from the commissioners – duly registered by them.

With the Court of Chancery in his sights Sadleir gave several detailed examples of cases, containing a large number of litigants, dragging on over a long number of years. One of those was the Goldsmith V Glengall suit involving 180 defendants. The Master of the Rolls was unable to deal effectively with this case because of the restrictions imposed by the Incumbered Estates Act, whereby 'the suggestions of practical men were disregarded and set aside and the opinions of English Conveyancers relied upon instead, which threw the whole of the proceedings into confusion'.

He showed the House the written opinion of a member of both the Irish and the English Bar, possibly Vincent Scully, stating that the provisions of the Incumbered Estates Act

> were dogged with so many safeguards against possible frauds, and so many formalities to complete a title, as to be inoperative, and that a sale was much more complex under those provisions than under the authority of the court; that under the operation of the Incumbered Estates Bill, before an encumbrancer could proceed he was bound to pay off prior encumbrancers not only what was due to them, but what they said was due; that as matters now stood, it was better to proceed under the old and known law than incur the hazard and risk of acting under the measure of last sessions; and, finally, that that Act, unless greatly modified, would become a dead letter as regarded by those for whose benefit it was passed, and those who would seek to put it in motion.

After several digressions into other related themes Sadleir finally ended a lengthy speech and his motion[8] was seconded by John O'Connell. Sir John Romilly, the Solicitor General, refused to traverse the complex legal arguments about Chancery and conveyancing, but paid the Carlow M.P. the compliment of acknowledging his expertise on the legal dimensions of landed property in Ireland.[9] Romilly saw the unravelling of these legalities as a formidable task, and conceded that the government's intention was not a single comprehensive measure, but a series of amending and additional acts over a period of time until the law of Irish land tenure and ownership underpinned a prosperous economy. Judicial reform, however, would have to be accompanied by a new system of real property law.

Predictably, Sadleir's motion was lost, but within three weeks he had the opportunity to further air his views when Romilly moved the second reading of the Incumbered Estates (Ireland) Bill on 11 May. Sadleir again sought to prove the negative effect of Chancery with a comparison between the large number of suits for the sale of incumbered estates there, and the small number actually sold from March 1847 until April 1849.[10] Consequently, he hoped that the bill would repeal its predecessor and retain 'only those two or three valuable provisions contained in it'. He reacted favourably to the section whereby 'purchases of land should require a parliamentary title, and it would be idle to suppose that any sales of estates could be affected except under the operation of that principle, and therefore through the Commission'.

As the bill entered its third reading in June 1849 he made a wide-ranging critique, but was more satisfied with its thrust. Nevertheless, there were still clauses causing him difficulty. Chancery was not fully removed from the equation because of the difficulty in bringing estates already there under the control of the Incumbered Estates Commissioners.[11] Neither did he feel that the system had been sufficiently simplified to entice English wealth to Ireland, a view which ran contrary to that of some representatives, who feared the creation of a new body of English landlords.[12] He was concerned, also, that the Act could be circumvented by bankrupt landlords, anxious to hold onto their estates, coming to a fraudulent agreement with their creditors.[13] He disliked the exclusion of those with a life interest only in property, and indicated that a majority of encumbered estates in Ireland contained these.[14] Considering his own penchant for speculation, it was logical that he should condemn the bill as militating against landlords wishing to sell an encumbered estate in one part of the country to purchase another in a different area.[15] Considering his own role, his condemnation of the Bill's failure to limit the involvement of receivers in the sale of property was less rational.

The debates in the Spring and Summer of 1849 showed that many M.P.s viewed it almost as promoting confiscation, and depriving landlords of the chance to redeem themselves either by clearing surplus tenants or reaping the rewards of more efficient management in future. Unlike Sadleir, some were concerned at the powers given to the Commissioners. Colonel Francis Dunne, Portarlington, Queen's County, was one who 'did not think it wise or prudent to send into the country a board of Commissions with inquisitorial powers to search into the condition of any man upon whose property a debt might be secured, and whose creditors came before the board to demand a sale'.

Others were fearful that the extent of some landlords' mortgages would devour most of the profits from sales under the Act. This fear was increased by the conviction that land prices would drop as a result of dumping land onto the market. But Sadleir had no such fears and was unsympathetic to the plight of some landlords. He was under no illusion that they would suffer a great deal, but he saw their interests as less important than the welfare of the country as a whole. There were two types of landowners that attracted his attention, irrespective of whether their estates were in debt or not. These were absentee landlords and middlemen.

Evidence to the Devon Commission pinpointed middlemen in particular as the source of many ills underlying Irish tenancy. Two of Sadleir's relatives endorsed this. Nicholas V. Maher, who had been agent to his cousin Valentine Maher's 19,000 acre estate near Thurles, could not find the words 'in the English language sufficiently to describe their cruelty and barbarity as they ought to be described'.[16] He condemned them for charging high rents for conacre and ordinary tenancy. A more distant relative, Christopher Gallwey, agent to the Earl of Kenmare's Killarney estates, saw the middleman system as responsible for widespread poverty.[17]

Sadleir reserved his most severe criticism for middlemen despite the status of his own family in that respect. On 7 April 1848 when debating a land bill he divided landlords into three classes and defined middlemen as 'the worst class', most of whom were highly objectionable, and ... their example was such as could not, with safety or propriety be followed'.[18]

The following week, in a discussion on the legal obstacles to selling land, he targeted the management of the estates of Trinity College, the Ecclesiastical Commissioners, Sir Erasmus Smith and Sir Patrick Dunn as adhering 'to the pernicious system of sanctioning and encouraging the growth and spread of middlemen'. He lambasted Trinity College for granting rent terms to middlemen, of whom he claimed personal knowledge, which were less than those offered by tenants directly to the College. There was a traditional official unwillingness to interfere in the internal workings of estates, but Sadleir saw it as a matter of duty for the government to 'interpose and insist upon the due and rational management of the college lands, to confer upon the board the power of granting agricultural leases for fixed terms of years, and to prevent the practice of establishing a middle interest'.[19]

Two years later in 1850 he was afforded another opportunity to condemn Trinity during the debate on a motion concerning the Reform of Oxford, Cambridge and Trinity,

> In referring to the statements made before Committees of both Houses of Parliament with reference to the management of the college estates in Ireland, he must say that nothing could be more lamentable than the extent to which wretchedness, poverty, and immorality, existed upon those properties. Men upon whose evidence the utmost reliance could be safely placed, had been examined upon those points, and the testimony of one and all of them amounted to this, that there was no system more calculated to repress industry and prevent the cultivation of the land, than that pursued with reference to the collegiate estates by the provost and fellows of the Dublin College. Those facts were deposed to by Mr. Griffith, Mr. Collis, Sir. M. Barrington, Mr. Pierce Mahony, and many other practical men well acquainted with the system and the general condition of the country. The college received nothing like the value of their lands, but no benefit accrued to the country. The system was most detrimental to the well-being of the tenantry. The land was let at a rent equal to half its value, and a fine equal to the other half was paid by the tenant. Instead of making any effort, or holding out any inducement for the cultivation and improvement of the soil, the course pursued was one which no reasonable or sane man would adopt in the management of his estate. Every offer made by an occupier was uniformly refused, the provost and fellows preferring some half-sirs or squireens who as middlemen obtained all the advantages that should belong to the occupying tenant.[20]

The Trinity authorities did not need Sadleir to remind them that their rent income was seriously deficient. Most of the tenants on its 200,000 acre estates were indeed middlemen. The majority of them such as Daniel O'Connell or Lord Leitrim were extensive landholders.[21] In the 1830s O'Connell paid an annual rent of £900 for lands which he sub-let for £1,500. In 1851 the government finally overcame its reluctance to interfere in property relations and passed the Trinity College Dublin Leasing Powers Act, which increased its rents and made provision for ten year reviews.[22]

The second reading of the Incumbered Estates Bill on 1 May 1849 offered another platform to attack middlemen. Sadleir saw it as a vehicle to remove them, but first they would have to be brought within its remit. He believed that their exclusion was a serious flaw and an injustice,

> They did not consider themselves proprietors or landlords of the land, although they discharged many of the fiscal duties of landlords. He believed they were anxious to be denuded of the outward ostentation of

being landlords, which in reality they were not, and that they felt that the tenant occupiers were getting more desirous every day of becoming the direct tenants of the owners. He thought, therefore, that some clause might be successfully introduced to enable the Commissioners, where the owner in fee, and the parties holding the intermediate interests, were assenting parties, to extinguish those intermediate interests and offer the property for sale in such a form as would be most likely to attract the English capitalist.[23]

But it was most likely that such capitalists, while investing in Ireland, would remain living in England, and this throws up a contradiction in Sadleir's dislike of absentee landlords.[24] Neither did absenteeism necessarily signify poorly managed estates since efficient agents were key elements in proper estate management. Nevertheless, he was partly and justifiably motivated in his dislike of absentees by their ability to more easily escape paying the poor rates.[25] He saw them as the major culprits in this, and urged that the Commissioners should have the 'most extensive and summary powers, so as to enable them to enforce their orders with readiness, not only in Ireland, but in England and Scotland, where so many of the mortgagees resided'.[26] This meant bringing proceedings in the English courts and having judgments transferred to Ireland. He had no solution to the problem of dealing with landlords who resided in Europe.[27]

He was not only concerned with those in debt, but saw absenteeism *per se* as an evil, and would have liked to see the Bill contain an inducement for such landlords 'to divest themselves of their estates'.[28] He referred to a speech made in the House decades earlier condemning absenteeism, not only for depriving the country of wealth, but for producing 'great mischief in the whole frame of society'. Kerry was an example of extensive absenteeism, where in one barony alone 92,000 of the 100,000 acres belonged to four absentee landlords. One proprietor there was the Marquis of Lansdowne, who also had land in Meath and Queen's County. Sadleir, however, was careful to describe him as the 'most kind and spirited' and benevolent absentee proprietor, whose estates were carefully managed.[29] His complaint was about the extent of his land, and he reckoned that

> if that noble Lord were to consult his own interest, the interest of the tenant occupiers upon his estate, the public interest and the welfare and tranquillity of Ireland, he would denude himself by every prudent means of a portion of his landed possessions in that country.

It is difficult to avoid the suspicion that Sadleir was casting his own speculative eye on such lands if they came under the new legislation.

Over-extensive estates like Lansdowne's, absenteeism and protracted legal processes were all difficult areas unlikely to be solved by any single act. Auxiliary legislation was required to make it workable, and Sadleir made a significant contribution to the debates on some of these. The most important were the Judgements (Ireland) Bill and the Securities for Advances (Ireland) Bill. The former, whose second reading began on 13 July 1849, was a laudable though limited attempt to simplify titles and preserve them as such by forbidding the transferring of future judgments, preventing such judgments becoming a charge on the land, and curtailing the rights of those holding judgments to appoint receiverships over estates. Romilly, on behalf of the government, described the extraordinary situation of one hundred year old judgements still valid against some landholders, irrespective of when they had purchased the property, so that

> when the possessor wished to sell his estate to pay off the encumbrances it was not only necessary to hunt out all those who had any collateral right of heirship to the property, but also all the holders of judgments; and the expense of doing this, which was enormous, fell wholly to the landowner, besides which, the difficulty attending the search for claimants operated as a bar to a transfer of the land and prevented its sale.[30]

But, the Bill did not affect these judgements. It had the limited aim of ending the system of borrowing on judgments under £100 with land as security. The Solicitor General, however, saw the bill as a first step to ending the practice altogether, irrespective of the size of the judgment. His views were influenced by the recommendations of a committee on the appointment of Irish receiverships. Napier, who was a member of this committee, explained the importance of distinguishing between two classes of creditors; moneylenders and creditors who had obtained judgments on a *bona fide* demand.[31] The latter should have their rights protected as far as possible.

Sadleir's contribution to this debate was confined to 'a few cursory remarks', condemning the bill as an 'isolated and puny' measure, when 'others of a massive and general nature with respect to real property' were required.[32] Its aim was laudable, but its machinery a retrograde step, which would make it difficult to obtain money for land purchase,

> By the operation of this Bill, the owner of the land confessed his judgment was hemmed in between two evils, in the shape of the Incumbered Estates Bill and the Judgement Security Bill. If he wanted to sell the estate, the Incumbered Estates Bill would operate to prevent him, and if on the other hand he wished to dispose of the judgment, the

Judgement Security Bill would not permit of his doing so, though a capitalist were at hand to advance the money.

Nine months later on 9 April 1850, when Romilly introduced the Security for Advances (Ireland) Bill, Sadleir's attitude was different. It was one of the most important addenda to the Incumbered Estates Act. The government realised that clear titles alone were insufficient to dispose of the insolvent estates in Ireland. The immediate problem was finance, and Romilly hoped to coax wealthy Englishmen to loan money to Irish buyers.[33] He denied that the bill would create a large class of English landlords,[34] since 'English purchasers of land, like all other purchasers of that commodity, bought it partly for purposes of enjoyment; they wished, generally speaking, to see what they bought, and that it should be easy for them to frequently visit it'. Romilly may not have realised it but the proposal was a direct encouragement of speculation. It provided simpler and better securities for lenders and would by its very nature regulate the number of estates going on the market at any one time, thereby keeping the value of land buoyant. The securities would be certificates of the Incumbered Estates Commission, which could be circulated like bills of exchange and constitute a first charge upon the land.[35] Most important, the holders of certificates were not entitled to put an estate into receivership, thus removing the future spectre of Chancery becoming involved.[36] Equally valuable, the bill contained provisions to simplify titles because

> the estates would be conveyed to the new purchasers subject to the charges which it was proposed to create under the present measure, and therefore the lenders would have all the advantages of a Parliamentary title.

Sadleir, who had previously pleaded for such a measure,[37] was so enthusiastic at its prospect, that prior to the debate in parliament he wrote a public letter expressing certainty that it would be valued and supported in Ireland.[38] His own experience showed that the main difficulty for any investor was to raise money. This problem stemmed not from a lack of confidence in the borrower, the Famine, the poor law, or political agitation, but from the current state of the law,

> By our existing law the mortgagee obtains his security through abstracts of titles, lengthy deeds, counsel's opinions, volumes of searches, stamps and bills of costs. He remains for months in a state of uncertainty as to whether the mortgagee loan can be completed or not – and if he should have, at a future period, to enforce his legal rights in default of payment of his debt, he must encounter the risks, defeats, delays and all the other

adventures which fall to the lot of the plaintiff in a creditors suit in the Irish Court of Chancery. We see daily that bankers, insurance companies and private capitalists freely advance large sums of money to railway companies and similar undertakings, whilst they avoid the broad and green acres of the landed proprietor – and why is this preference given? Because, in exercise of a Parliamentary power to borrow, the railway companies can give, without abstracts of title, long opinions, searches or bills of costs, a short and simple debenture of bond, easily transferable without the intervention of a lawyer.

In Westminster he renewed his argument that the 'simplification' of borrowing, which, ironically, was to have serious implications for his own financial problems at a later stage, would go a long way to solving the problem of buying and selling encumbered land.[39] Part of this, he hoped, would be to give the Bank of Ireland or insurance companies the power to make advances on the certificates proposed in the bill. He did not believe that this would encourage undue borrowing, but would limit such by promoting fair competition. He supported this view from his own experience the previous Saturday at the sale of a Galway estate by the Commissioners. Nine 'resident gentry' competed for this estate, which had a Griffith's valuation of £287, and was sold for £6,200, which Sadleir considered a very fair price. Despite his strong approval, however, he did not feel that the Bill fully dealt with the problem of title. He saw it as a possible precedent to a more specific measure creating a second commission, empowering landholders to purge their titles of the 'legal obscurities that had accumulated upon them', and enabling the Commissioners to give parliamentary titles.

Two other bills were debated in the Spring of 1850 which, while not directly related to the Incumbered Estates Act, were of some relevance to it. These were the Court of Chancery (Ireland) Bill and the Stamp Duties Bill. The purpose of the Chancery bill was to simplify and improve the proceedings of that court, and Romilly told the House that the Irish Lord Chancellor and Master of the Rolls had given general approval of its provisions.[40] It proposed to replace lengthy Chancery petitions with a short statement of facts supported by a verifying affidavit. This would stop the practice of filing pleas and demurrers, which often led to long delays in processing leases. Sadleir agreed that the legislation 'would be attended with most important and beneficial effects'.[41] He drew upon his experience with Chancery, and welcomed the discretion that judges would have to substitute verbal for written depositions, the latter being 'the very best that could be devised for clouding the truth with exaggeration and fiction, and he was satisfied that it frequently led to the defeat of justice'.

The Stamp Duties Bill, introduced in April 1850, was a more substantial measure, and applied to the U.K. as a whole. It proposed to secure a more equitable distribution of taxation by decreasing duties on mortgages and bonds of £1,000 and under, while increasing them on larger sums on a progressive *ad valorem* scale. One of the benefits, according to the Solicitor General, would be to encourage the sale of land in smaller quantities,[42] and so dovetail with the aims of the Incumbered Estates Act.

Sadleir strongly reacted against the 'objectionable provisions' of this Bill.[43] He was disappointed that the government had not made a proper attempt to consolidate the Stamp Acts, 'which were at present so scattered'. No laws were 'so systematically evaded as the Stamp laws', partly because they were so onerous that their enforcement would destroy commerce and trade. The Bill would make matters even worse and encourage people not to register deeds at all to avoid payment of prohibitive taxes. He knew from his business activities that large companies in London evaded the law, 'if evasion it could be called', with 'transactions of vast amounts being carried out on plain paper by parties who knew very well that that paper ought to be stamped, but who dared the Government to enforce an absurd law'.

As far as land ownership was concerned, the proposal 'would be peculiarly injurious to Ireland' and would not facilitate the sale of small parcels there, because 'there was no part of the kingdom where land was concentrated in the hands of so small a number of persons'. Some estates before the Incumbered Estates Commissioners ranged from 100,000 acres to 300,000, and 'however such estates might be broken up, it was clear that they were not likely to be reduced to sufficiently small divisions to come under the advantages held out by this bill'. It would also militate against those selling encumbered estates and their creditors, since purchasers would calculate the new duty and deduct it from the purchase money. His final plea against the alleged retrospection of the bill was met by the soft rebuff of the Chancellor of the Exchequer – 'if that honourable member had taken the trouble of referring to the act he would have found that the case of existing deeds was provided for'.[44] Sadleir, however, asked that all mortgages signed before July 5 1850 should be exempt, and the Attorney General acceded to this.[45]

By the Summer of 1850, therefore, a great deal of important legislation had been enacted, which strongly impacted upon the circumstances of Irish landlords. The full impact of the Incumbered Estates Act and its subsidiary bills brought about a mini-revolution in land ownership by offering a way out to those ruined either by the Famine, extravagance or poor management of their estates. It paved the way for new proprietors less likely to make the same mistakes, and operating in a different economic climate in a post-Famine Ireland[46] of higher agricultural prices and larger farms capable of meeting rent charges. Over five million acres changed hands and Sadleir was one of the major beneficiaries. His experience as an agent and receiver enabled him to accurately judge the value of land and fully exploit the new opportunities. He established the Manchester Land Company and the Irish Land Development Society, which, for example, purchased John Lane's Lanespark estate in County Tipperary.[47] According to James B. Kennedy, he used the Incumbered Estates Court as a source of speculation much like the Stock Exchange,[48] and normally acquired land at from seven to ten years purchase with the intention of re-selling at from eighteen to twenty years.[49]

Between 1849 and 1855 he purchased ten estates worth £233,000 in Tipperary, Cork, Waterford, Mayo, Galway, Kerry, Limerick and Roscommon, some of which were parts of larger estates.[50] Abstracts in the Registry of Deeds show that he accumulated 30,000 acres prior to his death, although some of these were held in trust by him for Thomas J. Eyre.

One of Sadleir's acquisitions under the Act was the Kingston estate, over which he had secured an increasingly tight stranglehold during the Famine years.[51] By the time the Act was passed Kingston was deeply in debt to the Tipperary bank. But this debt was partly engineered by Sadleir, who issued fraudulent or understated receipts for rents lodged by his cousin, Nicholas, in the Clonmel branch. The latter was unaware that some of this money was being used by his cousin for land speculation. In the Spring of 1849 the bank foreclosed on Kingston for an alleged debt of £82,000 due on mortgage repayments and rent arrears.[52] Leonard Morrogh, acting for the bank, successfully lodged a petition for the sale of the unsettled estates in the Incumbered Estates Court. Sadleir hoped to raise £90,000 by means of a loan from ten individuals including Herbert Ingram. He eventually purchased lots for £63,000, which, however, was only a fraction of their value.

The following year he tried to get the settled estates, and pressurised Kingston to agree on a sale lest another hostile creditor force him to sell. This was unethical because the estate's encumbrances were less than half its value, placing it outside the power of the Court. Kingston was fortunate in securing the legal services of the Young Irelander, John McNamara Cantwell, who henceforth harboured a strong dislike of Sadleir that eventually cost the Carlow M.P. his political career. John and James Sadleir were in the process of selling the Earl's furniture and plate when Cantwell successfully secured an injunction against them.[53]

Kingston, however, was forced to sell a portion of the estates for £25,000 and incurred heavy costs in the Court.

The Mitchelstown affair was the most striking example of Sadleir's lack of scruples in exploiting the financial difficulties of landowners by unsavoury practices and duping his Eyre relative in the process. Eyre, however, was himself a speculator who used Sadleir as a consultant and conduit to make purchases on his behalf. He was not only to regret his involvement with Sadleir in the Kingston purchases, but found himself less than satisfied with other transactions in the Incumbered Estates Court, such as the sale of the Coolnamuck estate,[54] William de Montmorency's Uppercourt estate in Freshford, County Kilkenny, and John Hyde's Castlehyde estate in County Cork.

When the Coolnamuck estate was put on the market in 1852 Eyre and his brother, Francis William, instructed Sadleir to bid for it.[55] He spent £50,000 of their money on eleven lots, but because of prior encumbrances they were only credited with £32,000. By what was described as 'some arrangement', James Sadleir purchased the demesne section for £8,500.[56] The Eyres were so aggrieved by this that Sadleir pledged to find a purchaser for their lots at a price sufficient to cover their securities. They refused to sell at such an early stage, but several years later decided to offload the property.

As with the Coolnamuck and Mitchelstown estates Eyre also held mortgages on the Uppercourt estate since the Famine era, and when it was offered for sale in 1850 he gave Sadleir £30,000 to purchase it for him. The latter only handed over half the money, and unknown to Eyre made an arrangement with one mortgagee that the rest would remain outstanding.[57] Sadleir wished to use this money for his own speculation and Eyre was later forced to pay the remaining £15,000 into the Incumbered Estates Court to secure title.

Eyre was also marginally involved in the purchase of the Castlehyde Estate, but it was his nephew, Vincent Scully, who fell foul of Sadleir, although ultimately he made a profit from the estate. It came on the market in December 1851 when Scully had £10,000 ready money, and was owed £9,000 by Sadleir. By coincidence it was sold for £19,000. Sadleir was asked by Scully to act as his solicitor and conduct the bidding. But he purchased it in his own name in trust for Eyre without the latter's knowledge, having persuaded Scully that it would 'resell better in the market if it appeared that the purchaser was an English gentleman'. Scully expected Sadleir to repay his debt of £9,000 immediately to complete the sale. Sadleir was unable to do so, and mortgaged the estate first to the Albion Insurance Company to secure Kingston's debt, and then to the Backhouse Banking Company of Darlington for £89,000.[58] When pressed by Scully to resell, Sadleir approached Herbert Ingram in August 1852 to buy it, but annoyed Scully by citing him as a member of the Manchester Land Company, to which Ingram also belonged. Scully suspected that Sadleir and Ingram were in collusion to deprive him of his property, although Ingram was later cleared of any conspiracy to defraud. Yet it is unclear if Ingram's eventual purchase of the estate was *bona fide*. In either case Scully did not receive the purchase money from Sadleir.

While Hyde, Kingston, Wall or Montmorency and others may have been forced to sell cheaply in the Incumbered Estates Court, not all landowners were willing to part with their property. Many took remedial action to make their estates profitable. Consolidation, sometimes achieved by widespread eviction of tenants for non-payment of rent, was the principal method used by them. This in turn provoked a reaction from the tenants, which eventually led to a network of tenant protection societies. An abortive attempt was made in 1847 to form such a movement in County Tipperary when James Fintan Lalor of Tennakill, Queens County, organised a meeting which assembled on the Fair Green in Holycross on 19 September.[59] Lalor was a maverick Young Irelander who placed the land question as first priority and whose socialism did not appeal to the other leaders such as Smith O'Brien. Tipperary priests and tenant leaders resented this intrusion by the radical Lalor, and even his father, Patrick, condemned the initiative. Despite careful planning it proved difficult to persuade any of the organising committee to chair the meeting which went ahead in torrential rain. Michael Doheny was one of the main speakers and addressed the theme of securing for the south the Ulster Custom, whereby outgoing tenants were entitled to compensation for their stake in the land.[60] This was a good will payment by the incoming tenant and was popularly known as tenant right. It had no standing in law, but had almost a quasi-legal existence in Ulster, and tenant right payments were prevalent in the rest of the country also.

Despite its troubled antecedents all eleven motions were passed by the meeting and it seemed that progress might be made on the formation of a tenant organisation. But as the proceedings were coming to a close Lalor was challenged by William Conner, a relative of the Chartist leader, Feargus O'Connor, for his alleged failure to clearly outline his principles. The sensitive Lalor became enraged and physically launched himself at his critic. The platform collapsed in the ensuing melee and the meeting broke up in disorder.

Sadleir was in London, but would not have attended at Holycross, since he had no affinity with the republican Lalor, or with Doheny, a Repealer now supporting the Young Ireland position. Neither did the Carlow M.P. attend a meeting at the racecourse in Cashel on 14

November.[61] This, however, was a Catholic gentry initiative. It was chaired by Nicholas V. Maher and attended by John O'Connell, Frank Scully, Leonard Keating and a large number of priests. Scully and Keating were two of the main contributors, and regretted that other landlords had not turned up. Legal recognition of the Ulster Custom for the whole island was the main theme of this meeting also, and Scully acknowledged that the improving tenant had as good a right to the land as the landlord. Keating saw himself as a benevolent landlord, who did not interfere with the sale of tenant right, and consequently had no difficulty in securing his rents. He called for a lowering of rents in general, and the introduction of a fixed valuation of the land.

These two meetings failed to establish an organisation in the county. By 1849, however, prior to the post-Famine recovery of the agricultural economy and with evictions reaching unprecedented levels,[62] a more extensive wave of unrest spread across Ireland, and tenant protection societies were formed in many areas. Between October 1849 and May 1850 eight major land meetings to establish such societies took place in Sadleir's native Tipperary.[63] By the middle of the year twenty societies existed in ten different counties throughout Ireland.[64]

With the Repeal movement in decline a vacuum existed in mass political movements, and the growth of a large number of unconnected tenant societies offered the possibility of a new national organisation to seek justice for tenant farmers. A number of erstwhile repealers now turned their attention to this possibility, and from April 1850 onwards laid plans to establish such an umbrella body.[65] Three of the prime movers were newspaper proprietors. Gray was one of these. He was a Protestant, who had been imprisoned in 1844 for his repeal activities. Charles Gavan Duffy was the second. He abandoned revolution after the failure in Ballingarry and espoused the path of constitutional agitation, but continued to periodically eulogise the Young Irelanders in the columns of the *Nation*.[66] The third was Frederick Lucas, a convert from Quakerism to Catholicism and owner of the *Tablet*, a weekly newspaper which was transferred from London to Dublin in 1850.[67]

All of these would strongly impact upon Sadleir's political career. He had little affinity with them partly because of his dislike of Repeal, and partly because he did not attach the same importance to tenancy as to ownership. He made little reference to the tenant question on the hustings in his election campaign, when it had not yet become a dominant issue in Irish politics. When he did refer to it he was careful to juxtapose the rights of both owners and tenants. Speaking to a large crowd on the Carlow hustings in August 1847 he maintained that his

opinions on the subject of *Tenant Right* are known by those who have a personal interest in their soundness and I am happy to tell you we have no difference upon the subject. I wish to see the industrious occupier of the sale encouraged and secured in the application of his capital to the improvement of his land, and entitled to compensation – to a just, fair and liberal compensation for those improvements. I have had more than ordinary experience of the present defective management of landed property in Ireland, and I am desirous of securing the rights and protecting the interests of the landlord and the tenant, and I believe every measure calculated to advance the interests of the one must secure and improve those of the other.[68]

This was an accurate enough reflection of his outlook, and its underlying principles were shared by leading exponents of tenurial reform like Sharman Crawford,who had unsuccessfully brought a tenant right bill before Parliament in 1847 prior to Sadleir's election.[69] It also contained a sense of proportion due to the tradition of land owning as well as tenancy in his family, which was sometimes lacking in the angry anti-landlord sentiments of some popular tenant righters.

Sadleir reiterated this perspective in his nomination speech and pledged that he would be a 'steady advocate' of tenant right and 'such comprehensive measures as are calculated to maintain the rights of property, to improve the relations between landlord and tenant and to unite them by more friendly ties'.[70] His first opportunity to honour this pledge came in March 1848 when Crawford, for the fourth time since 1835, introduced his Outgoing Tenants (Ireland) Bill. This was an attempt to enshrine the Ulster Custom in legislation and extend it to the rest of Ireland. Crawford, however, also saw occupancy alone as a criterion for tenant right payment, a view which was regarded by some M.P.s as a serious interference with ownership rights. When moving the second reading on 22 March Crawford was forced to admit that the custom had been abused, but he warned that rejection of the bill would be tantamount to 'a declaration of war against the rights of the people of Ireland'.[71]

Sympathetic members like Dr. Maurice Power, Cork County, or Joseph Hume, Montrose, agreed that settlement of the tenancy issue was a priority.[72] Hume, however, realised that Crawford's bill would fall, but he saw the debate as an opportunity to air Ireland's agrarian difficulties and inform the government of what needed addressing. He presented it as a question of legislative neglect keeping Ireland in 'a state of degradation' for centuries. The Act of Union itself was a useless piece of paper. Hume asked Crawford to withdraw his bill so that the government could properly consider what legislation was appropriate for Ireland.

Somerville, the Chief Secretary, who had introduced his own Landlord and Tenant (Ireland) Bill on 15 February,[73] denied neglect by the government, and insisted that Crawford's measure would turn Ireland into 'one great field of litigation' because of different definitions of tenant right and the difficulty of putting a value on improvements.[74] Sir Benjamin Hall, Marlebone, agreed with Somerville on this, but classed the land issue as a social one, requiring a social rather than a legislative remedy.[75] While condemning the call for tenant right as a substitute for Repeal by 'the same incorrigible agitators' he, nonetheless, blamed the landlords for the 'entirely deranged' social conditions in Ireland. This contrasted with the more harmonious balance in England. Hall defined landlord dereliction of duty as a failure to instruct their tenantry in proper husbandry methods. He painted a dismal scene of widespread ignorance, poverty, slovenliness and general degradation among the Irish populace. Drawing on official investigations such as the Devon Commission, he cited Tipperary as mirroring the worst excesses of social malaise. The county was portrayed as

> the very focus of crime; remarkable not only for the extent of its outrages, but for the ferocity of their nature. It was often said that Ireland was one vast anomaly, but he would undertake to say that the County of Tipperary represented such an anomaly as never was imagined by the mind of man.[76]

The language may have been extreme but the reality was that at various times Tipperary was statistically the most significant county for agrarian outrages,[77] but Sadleir immediately rose to repudiate Hall's examples as irrelevant and irritating.[78] Nevertheless, he admitted that tenant right had not been properly defined by any of the participants in the debate, but made no attempt to define it himself. As a lawyer with expertise in land transactions, he knew it was beyond the scope of any single definition because of variations of the custom throughout Ulster itself. While reaching Somerville's conclusion that the bill contained 'the seeds of interminable legislation', Sadleir voted for the second reading. Not for the first time he betrayed a different priority by attempting to deviate into a detailed discussion of the poor law, and was called to order by Viscount Castlereagh for wasting valuable time and hindering others from contributing to the discussion. The measure was defeated, but Sadleir had a further opportunity to air his views during the second reading of Somerville's Bill on 7 April.[79] Its importance lay in a recognition by the government that legislative interference in landlord tenant relations was justified in the prevailing state of Irish agriculture.

Members in general concurred with its preamble on the expediency of amending the law, and facilitating compensation for permanent improvements. Few, however, including the Irish representatives, supported its details, which were considered too complicated, over-restrictive and undermining of the Ulster Custom.[80] By the time of the second reading on 7 April, Somerville had conceded that it should be referred to a select committee, as a better forum for examining Irish land law. Sadleir's comment was correspondingly brief, and merely asked that existing legislation governing the relationship between landlord and tenant would be replaced by a 'speedy simple and economical system, whereby the right of the landlord to the possession of the land and the contracted rent should be declared and secured'.

This relationship was governed by the types of individual tenancy agreements, and it was here that Sadleir's real interest lay. As with ownership, he was concerned with legal complexities. He saw the nature of Irish leases as a major grievance, something that was not of crucial importance to those later involved in organising tenant societies. When debating his motion about the sale of land in April 1849, he deviated momentarily to enlighten his colleagues about Irish tenancies.[81] He had examined such tenures 'in many countries' and found that 'in no other country could so absurd a system be found'.[82] The 'moral buttresses' of the tenants in England were either leases for fixed terms, or yearly tenancies supported by local usage, 'by a spirit of confidence on the part of the landlord and fidelity on the part of the tenant'. He contrasted this with the Irish system of leases 'for lives renewable forever in every possible variety' which were calculated to create 'litigation, heart burnings, neglect' and disincentive. He continued,

> Hon Gentlemen were under the impression that all leases for lives in Ireland were renewable for ever, as in England, upon payment of a fine generally equal to half a years rent, the delivery of a pair of roast fowls, or a peppercorn; but he had one in his possession renewable upon the fall of each life on the condition that the tenant deliver to the landlord as much "parliamentary whiskey" as would make one hundred and seventy-two glasses of strong Irish punch.[83]

Sadleir did not seem as concerned about the awkwardness of calculating the volume of whiskey, as the scandal of such leases in a civilised country, where there had been a great temperance movement, 'peculiarly honourable to the Irish people'. Irrespective of the absurdity of such stipulations, leases guaranteed a measure of security for the tenant, although Sadleir devoted little time to the emotive and much discussed question of evictions, which were increasingly provoking violence not least in his native country.[84] Evictions drew severe condemnation of landlords even from the priests, who were, however, emphatic that only non-violent manifestations of tenant anger would be condoned. A meeting of over 30,000 people on St Patrick's Day 1850 at Donohill, seven miles from Shronell, gave vent to an angry rhetoric.[85] The setting was a historic one symbolising the once dominant Celtic civilisation,

> The immediate locality for the meeting was particularly romantic. Donohill is one of the ancient mounts or raths which are scattered over the face of the country. It is about two hundred feet high with a table land about the centre of the mound, with a hill rising abruptly from the table, giving the entire appearance, if not the reality of the amphitheatre. The platform was placed on the table land; the immense crowds were ranged on the sides of the hill, and presented a truly imposing appearance, rising tier above tier. The hill was literally alive with human beings.[86]

The tone of the meeting was set by the local parish priest, William Mullally, who was scathing in his denunciation of some landlords – 'if you say the likeness between child and parent proves against the father of the bastard, why then no doubt the persecuting landlord, the slave slasher is the father of all calamities and ruin which have desolated our poor country'.[87]

Mullally however, was careful not to condemn all landlords, an example followed by other speakers. The more morally conscious land reformers, like his relative, Michael Mullally of the Mullinahone Tenant Protection Society, who was at Donohill, saw eviction as a necessary evil in certain circumstances. Idle and lazy tenants should have no sympathy from the tenant right societies.[88] This view, however, was generally overshadowed by severe castigation of landlords, and it is unlikely that Sadleir's own views on evictions would have found favour on local tenant platforms. Only a few weeks previous to the Donohill meeting, during the debate on the Process and Practice (Ireland) Bill, he wondered if that measure would simplify eviction procedures in the case of non-payment of rent.[89] He grumbled that the current procedure was vexatious, tedious and 'inconsistent with plain justice', and remarked that its simplification would be advantageous to both landlords and tenants. Considering the scale of evictions it is difficult to see the validity of his argument. But, he sought to prove his point with specific examples, and during one debate on the Incumbered Estates Bill he amused the Commons' stenographer when

> he exhibited to the house an immense sheet of paper, which appeared

to be closely printed, and which the hon. member observed, could be compared to nothing but a double supplement of the *Times* . This he begged to assure the House, was a genuine document in a recent ejectment case; and not withstanding its inordinate length, the pleader who drew it said that some forty or forty five demises had been omitted, which, in strictness, ought to have been inserted.[90]

Sadleir's comments upon leases and evictions were in the context of debates involving legal technicalities, which he found absorbing. Nonetheless, on the few occasions when he addressed rents, he did not apply legal criteria although they were *per se* bound by the law of contract. They were immediate, and in the context of the Famine were seen as excessive extortions by uncaring landlords from struggling tenants. Hence evictions were normally judged as unjust on the land platforms during the late 1840s and early 1850s.

Speakers at land meetings in Cashel and Killenaule in February 1850 stressed that rent reduction was a priority.[91] Matthew O'Keefe one of the curates from Callan in County Kilkenny, who were prime movers in organising tenants at local and national level, was in Killenaule, and condemned the 'landlords' parliament' which would not 'even in a fourth year of famine show the slightest inclination to relieve the tenant farmers of Ireland'. At the Donohill meeting the parish priest of Kilcommon, John Moloney, condemned 'the reckless and persecuting landlords' who 'persist in their wicked and unholy course', and who hunted the people 'like beasts of prey to America, the workhouse, or the grave'.

These individuals had witnessed scenes during the Famine, which excited their antipathy to landlords.[92] Sadleir took a more detached view, seeing the problem as a conflict between the inability of landlords to reduce rents in times of economic depression and a corresponding inability of tenants to pay them.[93] Unlike the thousands of speakers on public platforms throughout Ireland, he perceived the surrender to demands for rent reductions as economically catastrophic for some landlords. This was clear from his statement on the Rate-in-Aid Bill,

> In Ireland if a tenant should go to the mansion of the middleman, or to the house of the incumbered proprietor, and appeal to him for a reduction of his rent, to enable him to meet the difficulties of last year, such an appeal for a reduction of 20 per cent, or even ten per cent, considering the present condition of landlords in that country would amount to a sentence of expatriation, it would be a virtual intimation that he must abandon his position as a landlord in that country.[94]

Considering this attitude, it is no surprise that he remained aloof from the tenant societies and the plans to merge them into a national movement. During the summer of 1850 they continued to spread throughout Ireland,[95] and a Dublin Committee of Lucas, Gray, Duffy and Samuel Greer, a Coleraine barrister,[96] met every Tuesday, Wednesday and Saturday in the Northumberland Hotel to plan the launch of a new national organisation through a major land conference.[97]

This three day conference began on Tuesday, 6 August, in the City Assembly House, William Street.[98] Priests, Presbyterian ministers, newspaper editors from the north and south, and a large number of laity attended. The agrarian ecumenism of the movement was reflected by the appointment of a priest , a minister and a layman as joint secretaries. This was articulated by the Rev. John L Renteul, from Ballymoney, in the opening statement,

> I, a Presbyterian Minister, have come from the far north to shake hands with the Roman Catholic priests from the south and west as my brethren, and to unite our hearty energies in our Country's cause against oppression and wrong, having for our motto 'union not division', for our common rights and liberties, and the future prosperity of Ireland.

James Redmond, the Parish Priest of Arklow, Co Wicklow, responded that he had asked for an introduction to the first Presbyterian clergyman he met,

> and that was the Rev. Mr Bell – and I tendered him my hand not as a matter of simple courtesy, but as significant of the deepest sympathy, respect and feeling; and I now tell the Rev. Gentleman that that tendered hand had a heart within it.

He had been a Repealer and warned that anyone who introduced the distinctions of old Ireland and young Ireland or any religious or political differences would be a 'disgrace to his country.

The debate produced a large number of resolutions on the principles of fair rent, fixity of tenure, provided that a fair rent was paid, and freedom to sell the tenant right of a holding. The question of compensation for improvements was also emphasised. Thomas O'Shea, the other Callan curate, spoke on the importance of excluding improvements from the valuation, arguing that if a tenant

> took a mountain tract and converted it into a blooming harvest, that increased value belonged to the tenant who created it wholly and entirely and in all its integrity, and if he made land originally worth only 2/6 an acre worth £1, it would be a greater robbery to deprive him of

the 17/6 than it would be to deprive the landlord of his 2/6, because the landlord enjoyed that only as the trustee of the state for the public good.

There was much discussion on the question of valuation, which was central to fixing rent. The underlying problem was interference with the rights of property, and compulsory valuation could be interpreted as serious interference. Some of the delegates, including those from Ulster, while strongly upholding property rights, were equally in favour of compulsory valuation. M. Wilson Gray, a Dubin delegate, advised that they must decide 'whether they should interfere with those rights to an extent that was necessary or to an unnecessary extent', and James Godkin, editor of the *Londonderry Standard* asked 'what good would even fixity of tenure be if the landlord could screw up the rents as he pleased?'. Such statements implied that ownership was limited and qualified, a stand which was morally and theologically supported by priests on other land platforms.[99] It was finally agreed that valuation should take place, that it should be permanent and be carried out by local tribunals.

The Irish Tenant League was launched by this conference with enthusiasm and an impressive sense of purpose. The Rev. Renteul defined the League in moral terms – 'his idea was that there was nothing political in it. On the contrary, he regarded the question which the League was formed to carry out, a social and moral object connected with the life and death of the country'. Andrew R Stritch agreed that the league 'would be a moral and not a political association'.

Moral rhetoric was used to gain wider support in Ulster, but the politics could not be excluded. One of the conference's objectives was to have the League's principles passed into law, which presupposed the commitment of Irish parliamentary representatives. Only two, William Keogh, Athlone and James Fagan, Wexford, were present. Others, including Frank Scully, explained that their presence in Westminster was vital to oppose bills which were detrimental to the interests of Irish tenants.[100] Crawford sent a similar excuse, and listed those bills as the Small Tenants' Recovery Bill, Landlord and Tenant Bill (No 2), Distress for Rent Bill and the Crime and Outrage Act Renewal Bill.[101]

The first public meeting of the new League took place in the Music Hall the following evening, Friday 9 August,and was attended by most of the conference delegates and a large number of farmers and 'country gentlemen'. The tiered back seats were occupied by Dublin tradesmen, and 'the galleries were occupied by ladies and other spectators'.[102] Speaker after speaker condemned Irish landlords with a vigour that exceeded even the fiery language of local platforms. The Rev. John Rogers of Comber, County Down, amused the meeting with his assertion that

> In Italy they paid the rent in kind. He should like to see an Irish Landlord basking in an Italian vale, or in the black eyes of the Parisian beauties, paid in rotten potatoes – even after Sir R. Kane and Co. had saved them with turf mould and bog water ... As Indian *nonchalance* apologised for infanticide, by saying they were only females; so in this country, their apology was – they were only Irish.

The demonising of Irish landlords, however, was not the most important facet of this first meeting, but rather an unequivocal emphasis on the parliamentary process as a vehicle to promote its aims,

> That feeling convinced that any effort of the people, however, wise, vigorous, or united, outside the walls of Parliament, will be ineffectual unless men of known honesty be selected as representatives, who will give a written pledge that they will support – in and out of Parliament – tenant law, based upon, and carrying into effect, the principles adopted by the Irish Tenant League, and that they will withold all support from any cabinet that will not advance those principles, and that when called upon, in writing, because of any distinct departure from his pledge, by one half of those electors who voted for them, they will immediately resign.

This resolution was carried without much debate, and it is unlikely that those who framed it could have foreseen the divisiveness and bitterness it would introduce into Irish politics during the 1850s. It made sense that parliamentary support was vital to promote change in the relationship between landlord and tenant, but the obvious threat contained in the resolution was not good tactics at that time, because its inherent policy was not acceptable to many M.P.s until the Parnellite era.

When the Council of the League held its first meeting in 21 Upper Sackville Street the following Monday, the necessity of parliamentary support was further discussed.[103] The increasing number of evictions and crop seizures in lieu of rent was seen as an emergency situation demanding an immediate response. A committee of five was established to draw up details of a short bill to prevent landlords taking such steps. An agent was to be sent to London that evening 'to prepare the Irish Members and urge upon the Ministry the necessity of such a measure'. John Shea Lalor, a barrister from Bantry and Council member, who had been a friend of Smith O'Brien and a member of the Confederation Council, was chosen.[104] There was no time to brief him fully before his departure on the mail boat that night, but the following day the Committee forwarded a detailed letter with instructions to 'protest with all your energy against Parliament separating until they have devised some better means of meeting the evil than the renewal of a coercion act'.[105] It contained the reminder that the Law of God and of 'immutable justice' gave the subsistence of the tenant farmer the prime claim upon the produce of his farm, and the threat that farmers denied such a right 'may be tempted, by the extremity of their misery, to break the law, and add new horrors to those which already overwhelm the land'.

While the Council stressed that it was the government's responsibility to frame an appropriate bill, it took upon itself the task of outlining what this should contain. It proposed that a tenant should be empowered to serve a notice on his landlord to appoint an arbitrator, who would meet that tenant's arbitrator to value the crops of that year. They would then estimate the income necessary to sustain the tenant's family, pay production costs, labourers' wages and taxes, and award the remainder as rent.

Shea Lalor was told to give these details to Irish MPs, to Russell, and to other government members. Appended to this letter was a public address on the establishment of a national network. The most relevant section was that ordering League members to contact their MPs for 'a most explicit understanding', and to inform the council 'who are, and who are not, firm friends to the principles of the league and what vacancies or contested elections will have to be provided for in the event of a dissolution of Parliament'. They were 'to be content with no half explanations – with nothing less than a clear and unmistakable approval of our principles and an undertaking to urge those principles on the Government and Parliament'.[106]

This was clearly intended as a warning to Irish representatives, but taken in conjunction with the demand for a written pledge could only add to Shea Lalor's difficulties. When he arrived in London he discovered that parliament was about to be prorogued earlier than expected, and many Irish MPs had already left London. He circularised those who were available, and a group of them, including Scully, met him on two different occasions in one of the committee rooms in Westminster.[107] He did not find them receptive to extra-parliamentary interference, and diplomatically explained that his mission was not to embarrass them nor to discuss the general question of land reform, but merely to highlight the immediate problem of protecting tenants in the existing situation where the potato and cereal crops were at risk. Shea

Lalor's diplomacy did not sit easily beside the Council's instructions and public address.

Nevertheless, he pressed them on their obligation to inform the government about the tenants' difficulties, and, unrealistically, to request the Prime Minister not to prorogue Parliament. They refused, and he put a proposition in writing that they should go as a deputation to Russell to enlighten him about the position in Ireland. They also refused to do this, and demanded an outline of the League's proposal. At their first meeting Shea Lalor had not yet received the Councils final instructions, but his scheme closely resembled the details of its bill. He reported back to Dublin that 'the plan suggested in the memorandum met with no support from the Irish members; on the contrary they altogether and absolutely disapproved of it and distinctly declined in any way to be parties to pressing the same upon the Government'. At the second meeting, when he had received the final instructions, they were equally strong in their opposition. However E.B. Roche, prompted by the fact that Shea Lalor lived in his Cork constituency, promised that they would get him an interview with Russell on the understanding that they would be at liberty, in the Prime Minister's presence, to express their opposition to the League's demands. Shea Lalor's reminder of their constituents' expectations only increased their intransigence, and Roche introduced him to Russell by begging

> His Lordship to understand that their presence there was not to be construed into an adoption of or into an approval of, the matters about to be laid before him by me, and which I was about to read from a written paper previously laid before them.

Russell patiently listened to this long statement. His brief response was appropriately sympathetic, and expressed regret that he had not been approached earlier in the term. The congratulations which Shea Lalor earned from the group of M.P.s because of this polite response aroused the Council's anger. Lucas condemned their caution and deference with a warning that 'before very long each of the gentlemen in question will have an account to settle with his constituents of which these facts will form a most important item'.[108]

Sadleir had departed on a business trip as soon as the parliamentary session closed, and was not involved in any of those negotiations. But, sooner or later he would have to explain his views, and kept a close eye on the treacherous currents of public opinion. Throughout the Autumn of 1850 the League, supported by massive publicity, continued to consolidate itself. Bye-Laws and rules tested by legal counsel were drawn up, various committees, such as the Finance Committee, were established, and through a series of county meetings pledges of adherence to the League secured.[109]

By January 1851 a statement from Sadleir became unavoidable as plans were afoot to establish a branch in Carlow. Although the borough representative, he was locally regarded as the expert on the land question, and was invited to chair the first county meeting. He pleaded inability to do so. He was then in Leicester and on 3 January wrote that he could not abandon pressing business engagements there, 'the neglect of which would be of serious injury to others'.[110] He promised that he would 'not fail to give a constant support in Parliament to every measure calculated to improve and simplify the laws of land to place the dealings between landlord and tenant upon a just footing, and to secure, in a large and liberal sense, to the cultivator of the soil, the full fruits of his enterprising industry'.

This did not commit him to supporting the principles of the league, and merely re-echoed the outlook of other Irish MPs, some of whom were hostile to these principles. Neither did it differ significantly from that of Crawford, who also tendered his excuses while supporting the 'necessity of a combined effort for redress through the medium of associations constitutionally formed, by means of which public opinion can be concentrated and brought to act upon the legislature'. This statement may have been somewhat stronger than Sadleir's, but did not indicate approval of League principles, which Crawford later pronounced too extreme.[111]

Sadleir's stance, however, was sufficient to avoid condemnation at local level, where James Maher backed the proposal and exhorted those present to contribute to the £300 pledged to League funds. There was resentment, nonetheless, at the failure of the two county M.P.s to attend. Patrick Lalor, Fintan Lalor's father and ex-member of parliament, told the meeting that the secretary had written to them, but 'so little regard did they pay the people that one of them did not think it worth his while to answer, and the other replied in a contumacious manner'. As far as Lalor and Lucas were concerned the only response to these was a determination to elect only candidates pledged to tenant rights.

Sadleir would have felt uncomfortable at the tone of some speakers, especially the abrasive attack by Lucas on local landlords. A previous speaker had praised one of those, Thomas Butler of Ballintemple, considered a fair individual, but Lucas targeted him as a 'public robber' who had been forced to lower his rents because of pressure from League. 'The fact was', said Lucas, 'a new light had broken in on him; for the greater part of his life he had been under the impression that his tenantry were as much his property as the horses and cows and asses which he had for his own use'. Several people left the meeting in protest at such an indictment.

Their gesture reflected a crucial factor, which would also have influenced Sadleir's public stand, – an apathy, if not hostility, towards the League in Carlow, which never became a stronghold of the movement in the same way as counties like Kilkenny, Meath, Tipperary Westmeath or Wexford seen as 'advanced' by the Council.[112] The *Sentinel*, reported that the meeting was a failure and remarked upon the absence of 'respectable farmers' and most of the clergy. It speculated that the reason for the small crowd was due to the 'visionary' creed of the League, a phrase borrowed from a letter from W. Duckett, of Russellstown Park, a local landlord who declined to attend.[113] It also reported the disappointment of local organisers at the absence of national leaders like Rentoul and Rogers,

> none of the metropolitan "stars" appeared but Mr Lucas, and judging from his dismal appearance, and the absence of the great body of the farmers, he felt anything but comfortable or gratified. As the "organ of the League", however, wrapped up in a fine frieze coat, which gave him the appearance of a substantial farmer; he appeared to look upon the scene with the same gloomy thoughts and uneasiness of mind, that the lonely traveller surveys towards the close of day.

References

1. *Parl Deb.*, series 3, vol 104, 1849, col. 386, (17 April 1849)
2. Statement of Judge Longfield in the Landed Estates Court, (which succeeded the Encumbered Estates Court) – see *I.C.R. 1858 and 1859*, vol 9, p.44.
3. *Parl. Deb.*, series 3, vol. 100. 1848. cols. 385-389, (11 July 1848). See *Incumbered Estates (Ireland): Bill further to facilitate the sale of Incumbered Estates in Ireland,* H.C. 1849 (235) III.2II. and do. as amended by the Committee H.C. 1849 (284) III.233 and do. as amended by the Committee and on recommitment H.C. 1849 (309) III.257 and do. as amended by the Lords H.C. 1849 (444) III.283.
4. J.H. Whyte, *The Independent Irish Party 1850-9* , (Oxford, 1958), pp.94 et.seq.
5. Sir James Graham was born in 1792 in Netherby, son of Sir James Graham and Lady Catherine Stewart, daughter of the seventh Earl of Galloway. His political career varied with his brands of politics, and he represented six different constituencies during his lifetime – Hull, St. Ives, Carlisle, Cumberland, Pembroke and Dorchester. He was a Whig, Liberal, Reformer and Conservative at different times, but eventually attached himself to Sir Robert Peel in whose 1841 administration he was Home Secretary. He was responsible for administering the Irish poor law system and Famine relief in 1845. He was subjected to severe criticism for the imprisonment of O'Connell. He resigned with Peel and refused to join the Russell administration in 1847, but remained with the small group of Peelites. He became First Lord of the Admiralty in the 1853 Aberdeen administration, a post he had previously held in 1830. He was considered a distant, supercilious personality. He died in October 1861. *D.N.B.*, e.v.

6. *Parl. Deb*, series 3, vol.100, 1848, col.586, (20 July 1848)
7. Ibid., vol.104, 1849, col.382, (17 April 1849)
8. Sir John Romilly was born in 1802. He graduated with an M.A. from Cambridge in 1826, and was called to the bar in 1827. He was elected Liberal M.P. for Bridport in 1832 and Devonport in 1847. He became a Queen's Counsel in 1843, Solicitor General in 1848 and Attorney General in 1850. In 1851 he was appointed Master of the Rolls on the death of Lord Langdale. He lost his seat in 1852 and was the last Master of the Rolls to sit in the House of Commons. In 1865 he was raised to the peerage with the title Lord Romilly of Barry in Glamorganshire. He died in London in 1874. *D.N.B.*, e.v.
9. Romilly's reply in *Parl. Deb.*, series 3, vol. 104, 1849, cols 397-403, (17 April 1849).
10. Ibid., vol.105, 1849, col.348, (11 May 1849)
11. Ibid., cols. 775, (21 May 1849) and 1102, (4 June 1849)
12. Ibid., col.1103, (4 June 1849, and vol.110, 1850, cols. 101-102, (15 April 1850).
13. Ibid., Vol.105, 1849, col.349, (11 May 1849)
14. Ibid., col.1100, (4 June 1849)
15. Ibid., col.1101, (4 June 1849)
16. *Devon Commission*, pp 103, 105 – 106 for Maher's evidence on middlemen.
17. Ibid., pp.735 et seq. The Gallwey connection to Sadleir did not begin until October 1847 when Christopher's daughter, Catherine, married Sadleir's first cousin, James Scully of Shanballymore. This was Scully's second marriage – R.D., 1847, vol. 17, mem. 259, marriage settlement 27 October 1847.
18. Ibid., vol. 98 1848 col.61 (7 April 1848)
19. Ibid., vol.104, 1849, col 394, (17 April 1849), (see also vol.102, 1849, col.507, (9 February 1849) and vol 107, 1849, col.324, (13 July 1849)).
20. Sadleir's reference to the management of the estates in *Parl. Deb.*, series 3, vol 110, 1850, cols 744-745, (23 April 1850).
21. W.E. Vaughan, *Landlords and Tenants in Mid-Victorian Ireland*, (Oxford, 1994), p.50, Ó Gráda, *Ireland a New Economic*, p.126.
22. Vaughan,*Landlords and Tenants*, pp 50, 54, 256.
23. *Parl. Deb.*, series 3, vol.105, 1849, cols.348-49, (1 May 1849).
24. For reference to absenteeism see Ibid., pp.3, Ó Gráda, *Ireland a New Economic*, pp.124 – 125.
25. See Kinealy,*The Great Calamity*, pp 52,84 on the greater ability of absentees to avoid relief appeals.
26. *Parl. Deb.*, series 3, vol. 105, 1849, col.349, (1 May 1849). See ibid., vol.104, 1849, col.298, (4 April 1849) and *Tablet* 9 February and 9 June 1849 on the question of absentee landlords.
27. *Parl. Deb.*, series 3, vol.105, 1849, col.350 ,(11 May 1849)
28. Ibid., cols. 1102-1103, (4 June 1849)
29. Ibid., vol.104, 1849, col.395, (17 April 1849)
30. His speech in ibid., vol 107, 1849, cols. 325 et seq, (13 July 1849)
31. Ibid., col. 329, (13 July 1849).
32. Sadleir's speech in ibid., cols. 330-331, (13 July 1849).
33. His speech in ibid., vol.110, 1850, cols. 100-107, (9 April 1850).
34. F.S.L. Lyons, *Ireland since the Famine*, (Fontana ed.,1974), p.26 shows that most of the purchasers were Irish. The source of their money is not specified.
35. This system applied only to loans below half the purchase money.
36. *Parl. Deb.*, Series 3, vol.110, 1850, cols. 103-104, (9 April 1850).
37. Ibid., vol. 104, 1849, cols. 392-393, (17 April 1849).

38. Letter in *Tablet* 6 April 1850.
39. His two speeches in *Parl. Deb.*, series 3, vol 110, 1850, cols. 113, (9 April 1850), 835-837, (25 April 1850).
40. Ibid., vol.108, 1850, cols. 402-404, (6 February 1850).
41. Ibid., col.406, (6 February 1850).
42. Ibid., vol.110, 1850, col. 322, (15 April 1850).
43. His two speeches in ibid., cols. 307 et. seq. and cols. 322 et. seq., (15 April 1850).
44. Ibid., col.313, (15 April 1850).
45. Ibid., col.330, (15 April 1850).
46. Vaughan, *Landlords and Tenants*, p.218 cautions against overstating the extent of post-Famine consolidation.
47. *C.T.* 2 May 1857. Thomas Joseph Eyre was involved in this purchase.
48. *W.T.* 5 April 1856.
49. *W.C.* 1 March 1856. James Sadleir saw such speculation as a sound investment for the bank – *I.C.R. 1858 and 1859*, vol 9, p.45.
50. See appendix 2.
51. pp 26-7 above. For details of the Mitchelstown affair from 1848 to 1852 see *I.C.R. 1860 and 1861*, vol 11, pp.1-14, *L.R.* 8 July 1856, *C.T.* 5, 12 July 1856, *F.J.* 11 December 1858.
52. Evidence at a Rolls Court hearing showed that the bank claimed £77,000 in rent arrears and James Sadleir claimed £133,000 against the estate – *C.T.* 5 July 1856.
53. Cantwell examined the accounts of the estate but was unable to trace what happened to the rents which amounted to £19,000 per annum. He estimated that the income from the estates 2000 tenants was worth a quarter of a million pounds during Sadleir's receivership – his letter in *F.J.* 13 October 1856.
54. See p. 26 above.
55. The Coolnamuck case in *I.C.R. 1862 and 1863* and 1864 vol 14, p.119. See also *I.C.R. 1857, 1858 and 1859*, vol. 8 pp.326 et. seq., *W.T.* 5 April 1858.
56. James Sadleir also paid £800 for part of White's estate near Tipperary Town.
57. Castle Hyde details in *F.J.* 10,11 December 1858.
58. The Backhouse family of Darlington had banking and colliery interests in Darlington. See chapter 12 n. 81 below.
59. T. Ó Néill, *Fiontan Ó Leathlobhar*, (Áth Cliath, 1962), pp.64 – 68, see also *T.F.P.* 22 September 1847 for details,
60. The *Devon Commission* contains several references to the existence of payment for the tenant right of farms outside Ulster. See also O'Shea, *Priest, Politics* for details in County Tipperary. See Vaughan, *Landlords and Tenants*, pp.67 et. seq. for an analysis of tenant right.
61. Ibid., 17 November 1847
62. *Returns by Provinces and Counties (compiled from returns made to the Inspector General, Royal Irish Constabulary) of cases of evictions, which have come to the knowledge of the constabulary in each of the years 1849 to 1880 inclusive*, H.C. 1881 (185), LXXVll. 725.
63. See J. O'Shea, 'The Priest and Politics in County Tipperary, 1850-1891', (Ph.D. Thesis, N.U.I. 1979), Vol.2 ,Table 22, p.51.
64. White,*The Independent Irish Party*, p.6.
65. *Nation* 11 May 1850.
66. See C.G. Duffy, *The League of North and South*, (London,1886), and *Young Ireland*, (Dublin 1883). See editorial in *Nation* 23 March 1850 listing the seceders who had 'followed in the path of Tone and Fitzgerald'.
67. See E. Lucas, *The Life of Frederick Lucas M.P.*, (Dublin, 1887).

68. *C.S.* 31 July 1847.
69. *Parl Deb.*, series 3, vol.93, 1847, col.645, (16 June 1847)
70. *C.S.* 7 August 1847. Later that month more extreme tenant protestations provoked him to remind his audience that landlords had also suffered during the Famine (*F.J.* 22 August 1847)
71. Crawford's speech in *Parl. Deb.*, series 3, vol.97, 848, cols. 863-867, (22 March 1848).
72. Power's speech in ibid., cols. 868-872 and Hume's speech cols. 872-874, (22 March 1848).
73. Somerville's introductory motion in *Parl. Deb.*, series 3, vol 96,1848, cols 673 – 680 (15 February 1848).
74. Somerville's speech in ibid.,cols. 874-877 (22 March 1848)
75. Hall's speech in ibid., cols. 879-890, (22 March 1848)
76. For reference to outrages in the Golden area see *Devon Commission* , p.263. For reference to landlords failure to effect improvements see evidence of Nicholas Maher in ibid., pp.100 – 101.
77. See Vaughan, *Landlords and Tenants*, pp.142,156 – 157.
78. *Parl. Deb.*, series 3, vol. 96, 1848, col.890, (22 March 1848), for his short speech.
79. Ibid., vol.98, col.61, (7 April 1848).
80. The details of the Bill outlined in Somerville's introductory motion.
81. p. 87 above.
82. *Parl. Deb.*, series 3, vol.104, 1848, col. 393, (17 April 1849)
83. Ibid., col.394. See ibid., col.920. (27 April 1848) for his approval of the Estates Leasing (Ireland) Bill, which proposed to enable those with a limited interest in land, (e.g. tenants for life), to grant leases for a term of years to facilitate the carrying out of improvements.
84. See e.g. *N.G.* 2 January, 13 March, 5 June 1850.
85. Meeting reported in *T.F.P.* 20 March 1850, *Tablet* 23 March 1850 and *L.R.* 19 March 1850.
86. *Tablet* 23 March 1850
87. *L.R.* 19 March 1850
88. See O'Shea, *Priest, Politics and Society*, p.58 for similar references.
89. *Parl. Deb.*, series 3, vol.108, 1850, col. 402, (6 February 1850)
90. Ibid., vol.104, 1849, col.388, (17 April 1849).
91. *T.F.P.* 27 February 1850.
92. e.g. details in statement of John Moloney at a meeting in Kilcommon, County Tipperary in April 1850 – *L.R.* 16 April 1850
93. These were reported in detail in the *Freeman's Journal, Tablet* and local newspapers.
94. *Parl. Deb.*, series 3, vol.104, 1849, col.549, (20 April 1849).
95. The *Tablet* recorded many of these.
96. Although he remained a supporter of the movement Greer never joined the Tenant League.
97. *Tablet* 11 May 1850.
98. Report in ibid.,10 August 1850.
99. See e.g. *Tablet* 2 March, 20 April 1850, *L.R.* 16 April 1850, 21 March 1851.
100. *Tablet* 10 August 1850.
101. These bills were defeated.
102. *Tablet* 17 August 1850, *F.J.* 10 August 1850.
103. *Tablet* 17 August 1850.
104. See Davis,*The Young Irelanders*, pp 109, 117, 120 on Shea Lalor.

105. Ibid.
106. Ibid., 24 August 1850.
107. His Report in ibid., 31 August 1850. The members who came to the first meeting were Frank Scully, Torrens McCullagh (Dundalk), E.B. Roche (Cork County), Chisolm Anstey (Youghal), G.H Moore (Mayo), Maurice J. O'Connell (Kerry), Ouseley Higgins (Mayo), J.P. Somers (Sligo Borough), Major S.W. Blackall (Longford). John Bright and Richard Cobden also attended the first meeting. The second meeting was attended by the O'Gorman Mahon (Ennis), Higgins, Scully, O'Connell, Somers, J.T. Devereux (Wexford Borough), McCullagh, Roche and Blackall.
108. *Tablet* 31 August 1850.
109. These were detailed in all the Autumn editions of the *Tablet*.
110. His letter in *C.S.* 11 January 1851. See also *Tablet* 11 January 1851. (The meeting was reported in both of these).
111. See Whyte, *The Independent Irish Party*, p.32 on Crawford's views in August 1851.
112. See e.g. *Tablet* 24 August 1850.
113. *C.S.* 11 January 1851.

Chapter 4

Religion and sectarianism 1847-1851

Carlow apathy towards the Tenant League in February 1851 eased pressure on Sadleir to make a detailed statement on its principles, but, any contemporary observer of his parliamentary speeches would have realised that the question of tenancy was only marginal to him. With the exception of his brief references to the difficulty of evicting tenants his statements were few, brief and vague. As a representative of a borough constituency he did not feel any undue urgency to emphasise tenancy issues. His concentration upon ownership would also have been endorsed by his urban constituents. In any event by February Sadleir's attention was focussed upon the great religious controversy of the time, culminating in the Ecclesiastical Titles Bill, which ran in tandem with the land movement.

An examination of Sadleir's record from 1847 shows that there are few traits which stand out so clearly and so consistently in his career as his dislike of anything which savoured of sectarianism in religious or quasi-religious matters. He was as opposed to it as he was to racial discrimination in the allocation of official legal patronage, bias against the poor, or any type of bigotry and he set the tone of his political life immediately prior to his election in 1847 – 'in my public career I am resolved that no act of mine shall be discoloured by sectarianism or the blot of bigotry'.[1]

Sadleir's philosophy was moulded by a combination of factors. The influence of Clongowes Wood College was strengthened by the strong Catholic tradition of his mother's family and the memory of his uncle, Denys Scully, whose pamphlet on the Penal Laws was widely read. These formative factors were tempered by others. The existence of many Protestant relatives was a constant reminder of that family tradition going back for centuries. As he advanced in his professional and social life following his arrival in London, motives of self interest would also ensure that he did not depart from his inherited liberal convictions. As an increasingly wealthy businessman and as an ambitious politician he came into daily contact with influential Protestant business associates, who would have hesitated to become involved with an Irish Catholic chauvinist. Neither would such an individual advance in political rank. As he represented a borough constituency of limited franchise with a large sector of Protestant electors, an over-strident Catholicism would have endangered his political life.

An indication of his non-sectarian outlook was the fact that he was one of the members of Parliament the Presbyterian church turned to when its interests were threatened. This church was divided into four sects – the Synod of Ulster; the Presbytery of Antrim and the Remonstrant Synod of Ulster; the United Synod or Presbytery of Munster and the Secession Synod; the Presbytery of Munster. The Synod of Ulster and the Secession Synod constituted the General Assembly.

In the late 1840s and early 1850s two distinct but interconnected disputes arose between the Presbyterian Church and the administration in Dublin castle, which caused severe embarrassment to the Government and was the subject of a debate in the House of Commons. Sadlier was only indirectly involved in the Dill Case. This stemmed from the withholding of the *Regium Donum* from the Minister John Dill of the Clonmel congregation. It escalated into a major dispute between the general assembly and the government as both sides stood firm on matters of principle.[2]

The *Regium Donum* was an annual public grant, originating in 1690, to Presbyterian congregations for the maintenance of their clergy. The grant stood at £37,000 for the year 1849-1850. The formalities for receiving it were clearcut. Each congregation was obliged to submit an annual certificate stating that the congregation in question had a regular meeting-house in which worship had taken place throughout the previous year. It also had to show that a minister was attached to the congregation and had received a specified income from it. Finally it had to confirm that the congregation consisted of at least twelve resident Presbyterian families or more than fifty resident individuals.[3]

In 1847 the Clonmel congregation complied with these regulations as usual and were certified by the Cork Presbytery, under whose jurisdiction it fell, as having paid the correct stipend. But the Government agent for the fund, Dr Cooke, refused to allocate the grant on the grounds that the congregation did not reply to a letter from George Matthews, the Dublin Castle clerk, who administered it. This letter outlined an additional demand of the Government for 1847 that the certificate should state precisely the number of families in the congregation. The Clonmel congregation refused to do this and the grant was withheld.

Initially its case was fought by Wilson Kennedy, director of Sadleir's bank, who bombarded Dublin Castle with letters and led a deputation to Thomas Redington, the Under Secretary.[4] The row escalated when succeeding Moderators of the General Assembly appealed to Clarendon, the Lord Lieutenant, and Somerville, the Chief Secretary.[5] The Latter relented only so far as to intimate that all future instructions on the *Regium Donum* would be issued by the Chief or Under Secretaries rather than by Matthews. Somerville continued to insist, however, that the congregation comply with the Castle requirements.[6]

Sadleir himself did not become involved in this case except to support his cousin Frank Scully in the Commons debate on the matter in July 1850, when the dispute was still unresolved and when several speakers began to question the wisdom of the grant. John Reynolds, a Repealer with a background in banking,[7] was a more extreme exponent of this view when he described the Presbyterians as

> Little better than a set of political ecclesiastical serviles, betraying those in communion with them and betraying the Government which paid them. If they withdrew the grant, the Presbyterians would be no longer spies on the one hand, or dictators on the other.[8]

Sadleir was a central figure in the second parallel dispute which also involved George Matthews. The Carlow M.P.'s correspondence with the Lord Lieutenant in February and March 1849 differed greatly from the approach of those involved in the *Regium Donum* affair because it contained a direct onslaught on Matthews.[9] Writing on 13 February from his rooms in the Albany Club, which became his home from 1848 until he moved to 11 Gloucester Square in 1853,[10] he stated his conviction that Matthews was a 'notorious defaulter' whose real name was Duncan Chisolm, who had fled from Inverness in Scotland some years earlier. Sadleir outlined his case in some detail,

> I believe that he has been raised to a very confidential position in Dublin Castle, and that he has been placed in direct communication as the organ of the Government with the Presbyterian body in Ireland, to a considerable portion of whom his conduct has become most obnoxious. I believe he has been allowed to carry on with the heads and ministers of the Presbyterian congregation in Ireland a correspondence which, from its character and import, might perhaps have been more properly conducted by the Chief or Under Secretary of Ireland.
>
> I believe that a fund of about £4,500, referred to in the enclosed paper, has been suffered to fall under the sole management and control of this person, and I confess I have been unable to learn whether he has faithfully applied the interest of that fund, or preserved the principal unimpaired.

The paper referred to in Sadleir's letter outlined the founding rules of the Munster Presbytery and showed that Matthews was its chairman and one of its four trustees. It also explained that the smaller congregations of Trinitarian Presbyterians[11] were partly supported by an annual grant called the Royal Bounty.[12] From 1840 onwards this £210 grant was replaced by a capital sum of £4,200 referred to in Sadleirs letter.[13] One of the important rules of the Presbytery was that

> No money shall be paid by the Treasurer except upon the order of a half yearly meeting of trustees, and that the accounts of the charity shall be audited at such meetings, and an abstract of such accounts be transmitted to the Moderator of the Trinitarian Presbytery of Munster, and to every non-subscribing Trinitarian Presbyterian congregation in the Provinces of Leinster, Munster and Connaught[14] who may desire the same; and a certified copy of the entire minutes of every meeting shall be transmitted by the chairman to each trustee within two days after the meeting has been held, in order that all, whether present or absent, may be kept fully informed of the management of the trust.

Sadleir enclosed a memorandum stating his belief that Matthews had never given an account of the annual expenditure of the fund. The obvious implication was that some misappropriation was possible although Sadleir covered himself by stating that if an investigation proved his innocence 'I should feel it to be my duty to use every means within my power to have ample justice rendered to him by those who have communicated with me on the subject of his present position and past conduct'.

He did, however, enclose an advertisement from J. MacDonnell of Ness Castle in Inverness, which indicated previous wrongdoing on Matthew's part as far back as 1826, when he was declared bankrupt. MacDonnell was unable to gain legal possession to some of Chisolm's property without the presence of Chisolm, who had absconded, and he offered a reward of fifty guineas to

> Any person who will furnish me with such information as will lead to the immediate apprehension and conviction of said Duncan Chisolm, who wore, when he absconded, a blue surtout, black waistcoat, pantaloons and hat; he seems about 30 years of age, slender in person, about five feet nine inches in height, high shoulders, sallow complexion, and seldom looks one in the face.

The Under-Secretary's reply to Sadleir denied all the allegations.[15] It stated that a Board of Enquiry in 1842, had concluded that Matthews 'was a public servant of unimpeachable integrity' who had been 'completely and honourably acquitted of every charge affecting his character' by the Lord Lieutenant. Redington assured Sadleir that the Royal Bounty fund was well safeguarded by the necessary securities and provisions of the trustee agreement. The Carlow M.P. was far from satisfied with this answer. His long letter of 22 March 1849 to the Lord Lieutenant insisted that Matthews and Chisolm were one and the same person.[16] He queried the propriety of giving a position of trust in Dublin Castle to such an individual whom he further labelled a bigamist. He enclosed a marriage certificate showing that Chisolm had married under the name of Matthews and had given his fathers name as Matthews. The certificate described Matthews as a widower. He also submitted an extract from a letter written to him by an individual named Frazer, who stated that Matthews had not only prevented control of the fund by the Presbytery, but had never given an account of how the money was dispensed despite the fact that 'the Presbytery as a body, remonstrated with the Government.'

Sadleir concluded his correspondence with a series of specific demands as to

> Whether the person referred to in the Under-Secretary's letter of the 3rd instant as 'Mr George Matthews, now and for some time a clerk in the Chief Secretary's office' is the identical Duncan Chisolm who absconded from Inverness several years ago, and who subsequently assumed the name of George Matthews; and if so whether he absconded owing monies to some of the poor inhabitants of that town whose debts are still unpaid, and who till recently were led to believe he was dead. Whether he is an uncertified or undischarged bankrupt, according to the law of Scotland. If he enlisted in the 53rd regiment, was promoted to be a Sergeant and afterwards reduced to the ranks. Whether his creditors at Inverness were made acquainted with his existence in 1842, and of the Board of Inquiry of that year, and had an opportunity given to them of substantiating their charges and claims against him before that Board. Whether he is the identical George Matthews named in the enclosed officially certified copy of marriage, and whether his father's name was not William Chisolm. Whether the trust fund of about £4,000 is quite safe, and whether the interest it should yield has been duly applied, and if the covenants and conditions of the trust-deed have been observed. Whether the Moderator has received the yearly abstract of expenditure from the trustees, and if the statements contained in the extract from Mr Fraser's letter, which I beg to enclose, are without foundation.

The Under-Secretary, replying on behalf of the Lord Lieutenant, assured Sadleir that further investigation had been made in response to his queries and that the Lord Lieutenant was satisfied with Matthews recent letter of explanation.[17] This explanation was just about tenable and Redington would have accepted it partly because he would have found it difficult to believe that the Irish Government in Dublin Castle could have been duped. But such was the case. Within months of Sadleir's letters Matthews or Chisolm had fled and a report of a Treasury commission of enquiry revealed a story of deceit, manipulation and fraud by him both as regards the *Regium Donum* and the Recession Synod Fund or Royal Bounty.[18]

The Commission's work was impeded by the absence of detailed records of money dispensed under *Regium Donum* , and it complained that those available were kept in a 'slovenly and loose manner' by Matthews.[19] Despite the paucity of records they discovered that he had misappropriated £900 from the Synod of Ulster funds for the years 1846 to 1848. As an elder of the Ulster Synod, Matthews had been implicitly trusted until the Clonmel case, and the various agents never submitted accounts to Dublin Castle showing changes in their congregations, but dealt directly with Matthews who exercised total control on all information.

His manipulation of the Munster Presbytery was admitted by the Commissioners to be ingenious. Matthews had in fact set up this Presbytery in 1840 which the report described as

> A medium through which he contemplated appropriating to his own management and trust sundry funds belonging both to the government and the Presbyterian church, as well as to carry out other fraudulent intentions.[20]

This vindicated Sadleir's assertions and the Under-Secretary was embarrassed by his own declarations of confidence in Matthew's integrity. Redington's final letter to Sadleir was in May 1849, but within a month the latter was defending the rights of another religious denomination. This time it was the Jews. Although they had access to Civil and Municipal offices since 1847, Jews were not permitted to sit in Westminster unless they took the required oaths, one of which contained the words 'on the true faith of a Christian'. Between 1830 and 1847 the House of Commons had passed five bills permitting them to take a conscientiously acceptable form of this oath.[21] Each of these bills was in turn rejected by the House of Lords. The 1847 return of the benevolent and popular Baron Lionel Nathan de Rothschild[22] as running mate of Lord John Russell for the City of London made resolution of this issue urgent.[23]

Apart from his conviction of the injustice being done to Jews as British citizens, Russell was personally embarrassed at the predicament he found himself in following Rothschild's return. He endorsed a sixth bill in January 1848 which was passed in the Commons, but rejected by the Lords.[24] Russell persisted and tried to find a solution a year later by moving that the the House carry out a general review of all parliamentary oaths excluding those taken by Catholics.[25] By June 1849 the Parliamentary oaths bill had emerged. Officially it was called *A Bill to alter the oaths to be taken by members of the two Houses of Parliament not professing the Roman Catholic Religion.*[26]

The debate on this revealed a blend of bigotry, enlightenment and misguided Protestant zeal. To its opponents like Henry Drummond it was 'nothing but the old Jew bill of last session revived.' Several English members opposed it on the grounds that it would 'unchristianise the House'. Raphael pronounced that as the Jews had called Christ a 'blasphemer and an imposter' they had drawn upon themselves the anathema 'His blood be upon us and upon our children'.[27] Henry Goulborn, Member for Cambridge University, wondered how Jews would participate in the prayers recited as the Commons assembled each day, and he visualised the 'humiliating sight' of the Jewish Rabbi and the Protestant Bishop discussing ecclesiastical affairs in the Lords.[28] Others saw a financial purpose behind the bill through the connection of the Jews with the money markets.[29] Conveniently ignoring the presence of many businessmen in parliament they condemned the measure as paying homage to mammon and introducing the stock exchange ethic into the House.

Irish M.P.s, conscious of traditional Catholic disabilities and Rothschild's benevolence to Ireland during the Famine, supported the bill. Richard Lalor Sheil, M.P. for Dungarvan, questioned the illogical reality whereby 'a Jew can vote for the worst Christian, and a Christian cannot vote for the best Jew'.[30] Sadleir shared this view and despite the 'peculiar religious tenets' of Jews, he argued that many of the rules and maxims of their code were similar to those of Christianity; both deriving from the old Testament.[31] He refuted the suggestion that the oath taken by members contained any profession of faith,

> If an Englishman took an oath in China with a saucer on his head, it could not be contended that by that act he placed himself to the faith of Confucius. It was idle to pretend that the admission of the Jew would unchristianise that assembly. There were in this empire no less than 40,000 Jews; and was there any one who would be so rash as to assert that their residence in this country deprived the land of its Christian character?

Like other Irish representatives, Sadleir had a historical sympathy with the Jews' case, stemming from the struggle for Catholic emancipation. To him it was a question of recognising free citizenship and the right of a particular sector of society to parliamentary representation by one of its own kind, if it so desired. He confidently assured the House that 'notwithstanding their present prostate condition', the Irish people felt a deep interest in the maintenance of the principles that were contained in the Parliamentary Oaths Bill. Apart from such principles, however, Sadlier reiterated Irish recognition of Rothschild's significant contribution to Famine relief, and their gratification at the hoped for success of the bill

> would be the greater from the reflection that in the day of their tribulation they had no more munificent benefactor than the very gentleman who now sought admission within its walls. That noble effort of voluntary charity, which eventuated in the institution of the British Association, was promoted and indeed originated, by the man who now stood at the portals of the House; which by an accident he was precluded from entering...'

A majority of the Commons supported the measure but were once more thwarted by the Lords. It took until 1858 and another four bills before the relevant parliamentary oath was altered enabling Jews to take their seats.[32]

This was the only debate on Jewish disabilities during Sadleir's parliamentary tenure and his role in it was marginal, but in February 1850 he figured prominently in a debate about injustice against Catholics in the selection of juries, one of the recurring Irish grievances in the nineteenth century. It is difficult to evaluate the overall seriousness of this, but miscarriage of justice against Catholics was not unknown because of manipulation of jury lists. Although Catholics were on the lists they were not always picked for particular trials, sometimes with fatal consequences, as in the case of the Cormack brothers in County Tipperary, which was tried in 1858 by Sadleir's friend, William Keogh, who earned the sobriquet 'Hanging Judge' as a result.[33]

On 12 February 1850 Sadleir took the step of requesting Parliament to appoint a committee to investigate the raising of a special jury in the case of Callanan *versus* Cameron.[34] This case arose when Patrick Callanan, a shopkeeper and boat owner in Carrick-On-Suir, sued the State as a result of damage done to two of his houses by Major Cameron of the 3rd Buffs,[35] when he and a number of soldiers had forcibly occupied the houses during the 1848 disturbances. Callanan, however, refused to bring the issue to trial because of his dissatisfaction with the jury, which was partly selected by Kemmis, the Crown

Prosecutor, who represented Cameron.[36] Because this was a civil case a special jury was chosen and the method of selecting such juries, especially when the state was the defendant, was regarded with suspicion in Ireland. In civil cases forty eight numbers were drawn from a box by ballot and matched to names on the special jurors' list. The Attorneys from both sides attended privately in chamber and crossed off twelve jurors each to whom they objected.[37]

Sadleir disliked this system for its secrecy and the latitude given to attorneys, who did not have to explain why specific individuals were removed. His opening statement was a condemnation of a procedure

> Which every man who had a stake in the country was interested in putting an end to; and he would maintain that while religious sectarianism was allowed to defile the jury-box, it could not be supposed that the Irish people would cease to have those prejudices which, he admitted, his Catholic fellow countrymen entertained, as regarded the spirit and principles of Protestantism. They had no just idea of the true and liberal principles of Protestantism; they considered it as Orangeism – as something intolerant- as bigotry under another name.

He saw it as the duty of Government to ease religious dissensions and to cement the union between the two countries by reforming the method of jury selection. The Callanan case was placed in a historical context so that it would be considered on what he called 'broad constitutional grounds'. He drew the attention of the House to a report compiled by 'Protestant and Catholic gentlemen' on the system in County Tipperary which showed that out of a panel of 300 people 118 were Catholics of which sixteen were among the first fifty; whereas in 1843 the panel was reduced to 201 containing 37 Catholics of whom only four were in the first fifty. He recalled a meeting in Ireland in 1844 to protest against the exclusion of Catholics from the jury of the trials held in that year. Sadleir also referred to a statement on the question of juries by Keogh in the previous session and objected to the replies of the Home secretary and the Prime Minister at that time. He agreed with Russel that republicans should not serve on juries in state trials involving the question of separation, but felt that there was an insinuation in the Prime Minister's statement 'calculated to wound and irritate the Roman Catholic gentlemen of Ireland seeming, he thought, to imply that there were those upon the list who sympathised with rebellion'.

On the specifics of the Callanan case, Sadleir showed that Kemmis had struck nine of the ten Catholics from the list and 'the tenth probably escaped the insult merely by the accident that he was supposed to be a Protestant'. He explained that the nine names were not in consecutive order but were picked from various parts of the list. What annoyed him further was the fact that he was acquainted with those struck off and could vouch for their 'unblemished reputations and undeniable respectability'. Some of these had served on Grand Juries; one being Charles Bianconi and another a Scully relative.

Sadleir drew a distinction between Kemmis in his private capacity as a 'perfect gentleman, and of great amiability of character' and in his professional capacity as lawyer. He did not doubt that the discretionary power given to Kemmis in the selection of special jury lists 'would be exercised so as to operate as a practical insult to every Roman Catholic'. He provoked the opposition of other M.P.s with the assertion that the Crown Prosecutor 'had been cradled in bigotry and intolerance, and that he was the son of Mr Thomas Kemmis, who had been the official of one of the most rampant Orange men that ever filled the position of first law officer of the Crown'.

As proof of this he showed to the House an 1812 Jury list which bore the remarks of Kemmis's father opposite some names describing them as 'proper loyal men'. Sadleir could only conclude that such words meant 'that proper and loyal men were pliable men – men on whom the Government of the day might rely for support in the jury box'.

He was supported by Frank Scully who drew attention to the tiny percentage of Catholics on the Jury list for the trial of William Smith O'Brien in September 1848.[38] Such a system weakened respect for the law in Ireland, 'where a man, even although he might have been fairly convicted of murder, was looked upon as a martyr if he had been tried by a sectarian jury'. William Fagan, Cork City, concurred and pointed to the obvious fact that 'there were more than nineteen Catholics in the County of Tipperary who were entitled to be put on the special jury list'.[39]

Only thirty eight members were present for this debate and Fagan and Scully were the only ones who supported Sadleir's motion. John Hatchell, the Irish Attorney General, retorted that the jury in question was competent to 'try this trumpery case about taking possession of two old houses in Carrick-on-Suir'.[40] He chided Sadleir for 'seeking to arraign the son for the conduct of the deceased father' and was satisfied that the proper legal formalities had been adhered to in selecting the jury. His defence of Kemmis was supported by a letter of 24 August 1849 from the latter to the then Attorney General, James Henry Monahan, denying that any juror had been struck from the list because of his religion and asserting that he had merely exercised his judgement in the best interests of his client, as 'any respectable solicitor would have done'. Romilly agreed with his Irish counterpart and was unable to see how the House could act as a court of appeal in such cases.[41] In an unusual allusion, which showed that he understood Sadleir's frame of mind, Romilly remarked that interference by Parliament in jury trials 'on the mere assertion of parties' would undermine the confidence of English proprietors, who were about to invest in land in Ireland. Sadleir withdrew the motion ostensibly because of 'the thin state of the House', but was aggrieved that he had not been shown the letter from Kemmis. He reluctantly accepted statements in it with the avowal that they would not be believed in Ireland.

A fortnight later he had another opportunity to target sectarianism, when the second reading of the Parliamentary Voters (Ireland) Bill was being debated. It was the culmination of several years debate on extending the franchise in Ireland and the Government was determined to see it accomplished in 1850. The main component of this bill was the abolition of the franchise resting on occupation and its replacement by a simple rating qualification of £8.[42] Somerville, who introduced the bill on 11 February, defended the disconnecting of the franchise from Irish land tenure which was 'of a most disastrous character.'[43] The stipulation, however, that the payment of rates was a precondition to registration as a voter was a shrewd one by the Chief Secretary. This did not deflect the support of Irish Liberal M.P.s like Frank Scully who, nonetheless, thought that the £8 valuation was too high.[44] Joseph Hume, Montrose, supported his Irish colleagues and held that an £8 valuation for Ireland was equivalent to a £30 valuation for England.[45] As far as Hume was concerned it was symptomatic of the traditional English governments' disrespect for Irish people, who were 'treated worse than cattle'. Conservatives like Sir J.B. Walsh, however, refused to concede any electoral reform to Ireland. He saw such a 'democratic innovation' as a danger to civilisation itself, and almost a return to the forty shilling freehold system which had been abolished in 1829.[46]

As part of a blocking strategy some M.P.s tried to postpone the bill because several Irish representatives had returned home for the assizes. Sadleir was alarmed at the threat of postponement and warned that any 'threat' of a general election would be met by 'scenes of violence and riot' in Ireland because the Irish people felt that the constitution was virtually suspended and that 'the franchise was a farce'.[47] He took his native county as an example and showed that only a small proportion of its population had the franchise, most of those being clergymen of the Established Church and rent chargers.[48] He might have added that statesmen like Russell saw the franchise as a mechanism to preserve state institutions such as the Established Church.[49] Sadleir was also conscious of the perception that existed, especially among Conservatives, that the Catholic clergy exercised an unhealthy political influence over their flocks. He connected this with the exclusion of the priests from the franchise,

> It should be remembered, that while the clergymen of the Established Church possessed the franchise, the Roman Catholic and Presbyterian clergy were excluded from it. He implored the House to proceed in a true spirit of religious equality, and extend the franchise equally to all, and then there would be no complaints of unhealthy influence being exercised by any one particular class of clergymen in Ireland.

Sadleir must have known that he was wrong in his declaration that the concession of the franchise would reduce clerical involvement in politics. Parish priests, some of whom owned farms as well as enjoying their priestly income, were entitled to vote and this did not hinder their active involvement in political organisations. Similarly, the right of Protestant ministers to vote was based not on their status as ministers, but on the value of their property, a factor which he chose to ignore.

The following month he returned to the attack on the question of discrimination in appointments to India, although his concern was then more about racial than religious discrimination. On 16 April he moved for a return of all persons in India 'receiving salaries, pensions etc, by virtue of any recommendation or appointment by the President of the Board of Control'.[50] He proposed that under statutes of George III Irish barristers had a right to a share in the judicial patronage of the Indian Empire, but had in reality been excluded from such patronage. He recalled that one of the arguments in favour of the Act of Union had been that it would 'bring forward the just claim of the Irish bar to a share in that patronage', which in turn would 'unite England more closely to Ireland by a bond of common interest and identity'. He supplied statistics showing that only three out of twenty six judges appointed to the Indian bar between 1801 and 1826 were Irish, and of the twenty-two appointments from 1825 to 1850 not one Irish barrister had been appointed. He conceded that the Recordership of Penang had been offered to Baron Richards, who in 1850 presided over the Incumbered Estates Court. The opportunity to work in a penal colony did not appeal to Richards, who refused the offer.

Sir J. C. Hobhouse, Secretary of the Board of Control, was unwilling to carry out a search for the information required by Sadleir. He explained both the difficulty of compiling such a vast amount of material for the period 1832 to 1850 and questioned the benefit of doing so.[51] But, Sadleir was soon able to air his views on yet another area of sectarianism. On 23 April James Heywood, North Lancashire, proposed a motion for an address to the Queen for a Royal Commission of enquiry into Oxford, Cambridge and Dublin Universities. Heywood, a graduate of Cambridge, deplored the insulation of universities from reform by ancient collegiate statutes.[52] He outlined a long litany of complaints including financial incompetence, mismanagement of property, neglect of modern literature and outmoded thinking. His citing of Trinity's illiberal admission system drew the fire of Joseph Napier, who represented the college.[53] Trinity was a Protestant college and had been established following the Reformation, 'whether that was right or wrong was another matter'. Educating Catholics and Protestants together would 'soften some of the asperities that would otherwise embitter society', but the exclusion of Catholics from fellowships and scholarships was necessary for the preservation of the college ethic. [54] Napier quoted O'Connell's statement to the 1825 Parliamentary Committee that Catholics should not be granted scholarships to Trinity.

Sadleir looked at the *bona fides* of Napier's religious equality principles with an ironic hope that the Trinity M.P. had

> recanted the opinions for which he had been before somewhat notorious, and that he had forgotten the political tendencies which marked him out as the secretary of a Brunswick Club, created in 1829 to oppose the will of both Houses of Parliament, and to resist the inclinations and predilections of the Sovereign. He at one time thought that the hon. and learned Gentleman was about to demonstrate that Trinity College was a seat of great liberality, and open to every class of the Irish public; and that he had become at least as liberal as Claudius Beresford, a kinsman of the hon. Member for North Essex, who in 1794 brought forward a proposition that Trinity College should be thrown open to the Roman Catholics of Ireland;[55]

In a historical sketch Sadleir dwelt upon the funding of the college through the Elizabethan confiscation of the Catholic Desmond's property and its location on the site of the Catholic All Hallows Cathedral. This was a debt to Catholicism as yet unpaid and compounded by the departure of the college authorities from the founding charter, which enshrined the promotion of 'learning, knowledge and civility' among the Irish and especially the poorer sector, who constituted a majority of the population. He quoted a 1591 letter from the Lord Deputy enunciating the principles which were incorporated into the charter and rested his case upon the disproportionate intake of Catholics and Protestants, – the average annual intake of Catholics being thirty as against 350 Protestants. The exclusion of this minority from scholarships and fellowships was a further breach of the founding principles, an example of anti-Catholic discrimination and an extension of Protestant supremacy.

Yet Sadleir and his Catholic colleagues would hardly have been surprised at the unapologetic defence of Protestantism by such individuals as Napier. The generally polite exchanges in Westminster, however, masked a virulent dislike of Catholicism by a section of M.P.s and a fear that concessions to Catholics would be at the expense of the Established Church. Some were almost paranoid about the nature of papal authority over Catholics in Britain. Sadleir was well aware of this and would not have forgotten the challenge to his stand on the Parliamentary Oaths Bill the previous Summer when Richard Spooner, North Warwickshire, said that 'the Pope could not by any legal proceedings enforce his authority over Roman Catholics in this country'.[56] This was what seemed to be happening on 24 September 1850 when Pope Pius IX issued an encyclical which provoked Protestant outrage, and resulted in public controversy for almost a year.[57] The Pope abolished the vicarates – apostolic, the prevailing ecclesiastical structure in England and Wales and re-established episcopal government, dividing England and Wales into the Archdiocese of Westminster and twelve dioceses.

From a Protestant point of view there were several provocative factors about this encyclical. The Pope, for example, might have consulted the British Government before issuing it, especially since rumours of change had been in the air for the previous two years and the possibility had been broached in behind the scenes discussions between the Vatican and Russell's father-in-law, Lord Minto. Protocol would have demanded such consultation, as it did in Europe. Moreover, the language of the document, as Sadleir later conceded,[58] was somewhat belligerent displaying a lack of sensitivity peculiar to nineteenth century religious pronouncements in general. This was based upon opposing and entrenched perspectives.

The encyclical may not have been intended for publication, but the Catholic authorities could not realistically have expected it to remain secret. Lucas published it in the *Tablet* of 26 October under the signature of Cardinal Louis Lambruschini.[59] It opened with a majestic statement of papal responsibility,

> The power of governing the universal church, entrusted by our Lord Jesus Christ to the Roman Pontiff, in the person of Peter, Prince of the Apostles, hath maintained in every age in the Apostolic See, that admirable solicitude wherewith it watches over the good of the Catholic religion throughout all the world and provides with zeal for its progress.

And this answers the design of its Divine Founder, who in establishing a chief, hath, with singular wisdom, provided for the security of the church until the consummation of the world. The effect of this Pontifical solicitude hath been felt as in other nations; so in the noble kingdom of England.

It continued with a sketch of the establishment and maintenance of Christianity in England by various Popes until the 'Anglican schism' when the Catholic faith was exposed 'to the greatest dangers, and a prey to the fury of its enemies' and when 'a furious and cruel tempest had deprived Catholics of the care of their bishops'. It outlined various apostolic letters appointing vicars apostolic in England during the seventeenth, eighteenth and nineteenth centuries, each one increasing the number of vicarates apostolic to cope with a growing Catholic population.[60] This continued to expand in the nineteenth century and both clergy and laity appealed to Pius to regularise the administrative structure of the catholic church there. The encyclical was a response to this with Pius continuing the work of his predecessors and resolving 'daily to favour the development of the church in that Kingdom'.

When the contents of the encyclical became known, Protestant response was rapid, angry and sometimes violent, with extensive protests against what was seen as an act of aggression and an interference in English affairs, where there was psychological room for Anglican dioceses only. Since the Anglican Church was closely associated with the civil authority the restructuring was also viewed as interference of a temporal kind. Controversy continued throughout November and December of 1850 and January of 1851 with addresses, pastorals, pamphlets, letters, speeches and meetings on both sides.

Several meetings of Protestants in Britain reveal an interesting variety of opinion, mainly due to the presence of Dissenting Protestants who not only opposed Catholicism but advocated the separation of Church and State, meaning in effect the disestablishment of the Protestant Church. A gathering in Stowmarket, Suffolkshire, in January 1851 was typical of this type of dynamic.[61] In some areas Dissenters held their own meetings. One of these in London discussed the expunging of a resolution previously passed denouncing the Pope's action.[62] Not every Dissenter present agreed however, feeling that the question had a political dimension as well as a spiritual one. A meeting of Dissenters who met in the City Hall in Perth were more unified in their outlook.[63] While expressing sympathy with Catholics who were defending their rights and who had to pay for the upkeep of the Established Church, they had little regard for either churches seeing both the Queen and the Pope as usurpers of the headship of Christ. The Pope's action was categorised as 'the last convulsive effort of that once mighty monster' and one which should inspire the overthrow of the Antichrist. This did not mean a lack of toleration or ridicule of the religious beliefs of Catholics, a distinction made at many meetings. Neither did the Perth Dissenters manifest any fear of the establishment of the Catholic hierarchy *per se*, and one clergyman was contemptuous of the perceived threat,

> A man with a strange-looking red hat and red stockings, and answering to a long name, had been set down in the midst of them by a silly old man in Rome, and hence they were all afraid, and cried they were insulted. But why were they put so much about by this man's red hat and stockings? If he (Dr. Young) were to take a fancy to cut a figure in a red hat and red stockings, he had money to purchase them, and what did it signify? He might wear them, he thought, without frightening anyone, although his congregation might not like to see him so strangely equipped.

The Anglican attacks, however, were more severe and the initial onslaught was spearheaded by its clergy. The hierarchy published an address to the Queen, which Sadleir later mocked as 'the irritating declaration of the meek and moderate prelates of England'.[64] It denounced the Pope's view of England as 'a heathen land' restored after 300 years 'to a place among the churches of Christendom'.[65] It appealed to the Queen to discountenance by all constitutional means the claims of Rome and condemned the encyclical as

> Part of the same arrogant assumption that in defiance of the law which declares that no "foreign prelate or potentate shall use and exercise any manner of power, authority or jurisdiction, spiritual or ecclesiastical within this realm", the Bishop of Rome has pretended to exercise spiritual dominion over the people of this country; and in nominating certain Romish ecclesiastics to particular places or sees in England, has reasserted his claim of supremacy over the kingdom, and has interfered with the prerogative constitutionally belonging to your Majesty alone.

The Protestant clergy of Westminster particularly objected to Cardinal Wiseman's title of Archbishop of Westminster and sent an address of protest to the Protestant Bishop of London,[66] who advised that they petition the legislature to take appropriate action against the 'open assault upon our reformed church'.[67] In the prevailing state of public opinion the legislature was amenable to such action. The Prime Minister himself had launched the first attack on the encyclical in a response of 4 November to a letter from the Protestant Bishop of

Durham.[68] Sadleir condemned this letter as giving 'the religious excitement of the country a character, form, and spurious dignity it never could have attained otherwise'.[69]

Russell re-echoed Durham's own denunciation of the 'late aggression of the Pope upon our Protestantism' as 'insolent and insidious'. He was personally aggrieved because, according to himself, he had promoted Catholic civil rights and had seen the Catholic Church in England as an important means of instructing Irish immigrants. He summarised his views on Papal government of the Catholic Church,

> There is an assumption of power in all the documents which have come from Rome – a pretention to supremacy over the realm of England, and a claim to sole and undivided sway, which is inconsistent with the Queen's supremacy, with the rights of our Bishops and clergy, and with the spiritual independence of the nation, as asserted even in Roman Catholic times.

Russell was confident that the country could withstand such 'outward attacks' and promised to examine the law and apply it against 'the recent assumptions of power'. He was more worried, he wrote, by the favourable view that some Anglican clergymen had of certain practices within the Catholic church such as the honour paid to the saints, infallibility, 'the superstitious use' of the sign of the cross, 'the muttering of the liturgy', auricular confession and the giving of penance and absolution. He concluded with the hope that English people would resist such 'mummeries of superstition'.

The Prime Minister's feelings were endorsed by Protestants at their public meetings. A gathering in Llandilo in Carmarthenshire, Wales, praised him as a politician of integrity who would redeem his pledge to take specific measures against the 'Papal aggression.'[70] One speaker from Kilymaenllwyd denounced Roman Catholicism as 'dangerous and corrupt', but denied that he was motivated by any uncharitable spirit towards Catholics. He managed to suggest that they would not be excluded from salvation. This contemporary brand of toleration, however, was governed by the principle that as long as Catholics

> follow their religion in quietness, without seeking to proselytise this kingdom, or obtain an undue ascendancy in it, so long let them enjoy toleration and that emancipation which an enlightened age and liberal policy have accorded to them; but when they depart from this course, when they do seek to proselytise this country, and to establish their religion, as it were, with a strong hand, then I maintain that it becomes the duty of every Protestant strongly to oppose their progress.

Predictably, reaction in Ireland was considerably different. Lucas did not delay in relaying Russell's opinions to the Irish public. The *Tablet* rejoiced that 'Lord Titus Oates' had written such a letter and shown himself in his true colours'.[71] Russell was vilified as a 'man of unbounded conceit, of mean ambition, of intense bigotry, of all kinds of small cunning', who was threatening to interfere by law with purely ecclesiastical arrangements for England, which had long been tolerated in the United States. Lucas, however, retained his most detailed criticism for Russell's political colleagues, and gave a foretaste of how he would later deal with politicians such as Sadleir, who disagreed with his parliamentary tactics and political philosophy.[72] He censured those Catholics who had

> sold themselves whether for gold, for partisanship, for whig favour, or for the name of social and political respectability – to the present government, have now their just reward in the contempt of the puppet they have so ignominiously worshipped. In return for their base cringing he buffets them on the mouth; voids his rheum upon their garments; spurns them with his foot; makes proclamation of the just contempt he entertains for their servility; and shows his belief that neither insult nor injury can alienate from him their corrupt and ill-placed affections".

This reflected popular opinion in Ireland, where the priests fulminated against the Whig administration. In Clonmel the influential parish priest and Vicar General of the Waterford and Lismore Diocese, Michael Burke, publicly challenged Richard Lalor Sheil, who had been appointed Tuscan ambassador, if he would 'snugly keep his place and contentedly pocket the insult so wantonly flung upon his faith by the head of the ministry with which he is associated'.[73] James Redmond, whose letters regularly appeared in *The Tablet*, castigated Russell's intent to legislate against the new Catholic structures.[74] He emphasised the purely spiritual nature of the changes and saw Russell's stand as an invasion of the rights of conscience

> We don't want to cram our faith down any man's throat, nor to interfere with any man's religious belief or practice; but we demand the same liberty for ourselves, and if we are refused it, we will laugh to scorn the braggart boast of British freedom of conscience.

In November Archbishop Cullen issued a Pastoral which was predominantly concerned with the education question, but concluded with a reference to the controversy.[75] It mirrored the imagery of the rescript in confidently upholding the Papal 'plenitude of power over all the churches in the universe' and rejoicing in the Church triumphant,

What a noble spectacle does she not present in our own days! But a few months ago the venerable Pontiff was an exile from Rome; he is now seated more firmly on his throne than ever, and exercises a wider jurisdiction than any of his predecessors. Under his benign and paternal rule, the Holy Roman Catholic Church is breaking her chains in every country, asserting all her rights, and displaying all the vitality that was given to her by her Divine Founder, when he promised to be with her through all ages and constituted her the pillar and ground of truth.

On Tuesday 28 January Cullen chaired a gathering of the Armagh clergy in St. Patrick's Church, Dundalk to deal specifically with the religious question.[76] It was attended by Dr. McNally, Bishop of Clogher and seventy priests of the Archdiocese. The main purpose of the meeting was to congratulate Cardinal Wiseman,[77] and to identify with the English Catholics who were part of the universality of Catholicism in the Mystical Body,

> ... do we not belong to the same fold, under the one Shepherd? Are we not members of the same mystic vine? Are we not all members of Him whose law fuses into the same body every national and political difference – every social or party prejudice? Why then do we hear some persons say that our interests are not at stake – that Irish Catholics are not concerned?... We shall consider it our duty to aid them and to encourage them, and if necessary, we shall not refuse to suffer with them.

The centrality of Rome to all Catholics and the exercise of papal jurisdiction to preserve their church was a phenomenon that Cullen felt should have been apparent to English Protestants. Neither Cullen nor Thomas Loughran, parish priest of Kilsaran, Co. Louth, pretended to understand how Protestant clergy in particular could display such anti-Catholic feelings and give such bad example to their people. Loughran demonised English Protestant reaction in biblical terms, while Cullen articulated his own distaste,

> Who could describe the revolting and sacrilegious pantomimes that were performed in which not only all the decencies of social existence, but all that is sacred in religious rites, was outraged and caricatured? Who will believe that in a Christian country the image of the Most Holy Mother of God was paraded through the streets and ignominiously committed to the flames. Such scenes cannot but fill the mind with bitter affliction, and make us weep over the degradation of the country where their enactment has been not only tolerated, but encouraged by those who should have been guided by nobler motives.

Cullen could not resist the thought that ultimately such prejudice would rebound upon the Protestant Church and would make 'reflecting men' consider the folly of upholding an Establishment which threatened the harmony of a country.

But the public outcry in England, which triggered such reactions in Ireland, was about to meet a favourable legislative response, which further inflamed Irish public opinion. After the Christmas recess Parliament reassembled on Tuesday 4 February 1851. Over two hundred members were present and adjourned to the House of Lords to listen to the Queen's speech, which was cautiously balanced by the promise that she would maintain the rights of the Crown from encroachments while at the same time maintaining 'unimpaired' the religious liberty of the English people.[78]

Following the address W.G. Hayter, member for Wells and Joint Lord of the Treasury, informed Commons that on 7 February the Prime Minister would move for leave to bring in a bill 'to prevent the assumption of certain ecclesiastical titles in respect of places in the United Kingdom'.[79] John Arthur Roebuck, Sheffield, promptly delivered a well reasoned argument against the absurdity of legislating against a purely spiritual act, remarking that he himself 'might parcel out England if so inclined, and call himself D.D. or A.S.S., or any other Reverend title he chose'.

The Government was unmoved by such arguments and a large crowd attended to hear Russell's introductory speech on 7 February.[80] The speech betrayed a consciousness of the strength of Roebuck's arguments and the Prime Minister responded by putting his proposal in a European context showing civil strictures upon the introduction of papal bills in France, Belgium, Sardinia, Austria, Portugal, Prussia and the Netherlands. It was obvious, too, that he had been influenced by the great number of petitions protesting against the Pope's decision. He portrayed the Government's intentions as purely defensive. The legislation would not be comprehensive, regulating the relationship between Rome and Britain, but would confine itself to forbidding the assumption of episcopal titles by Catholic clergy residing in Britain and Ireland. Such titles were already forbidden by the spirit of the Emancipation Act and were seen as the sole prerogative of the Established Church. Not only did Russell resolve to render such titles invalid, but, equally ominously from an episcopal standpoint, he indicated his intention of including a clause which would ensure that all gifts to 'persons under those titles shall be null and void, that any act done by them with those titles shall be null and void and that property bequeathed or given for such purposes shall pass at once to the crown'.

He supported this by upholding the state's duty to resist the natural tendency of ecclesiastical bodies, both Protestant and Catholic, to intrude in purely secular matters. He viewed the direct appointment by Rome of Cardinal Cullen as an example of this, because it ignored the usual method of requesting nominations for a vacant see from the Irish clergy. The recent address under Cullen's name of the national synod was another case in point. Its condemnation of the Government's proposals to provide three non-denominational university colleges and its reference to the plight of evicted tenants were purely civil matters in Russell's eyes.

The Prime Minister's forthright introduction, not all of it on solid foundations, began five months of acrimonious debate in which the Government was opposed by a large group of Irish Liberal M.P.s, including Sadleir. It culminated in the Ecclesiastical Titles Act and absorbed much of the Governments time and energy until the Summer of 1851.[81] The irony was that, despite Russell's apparent vehemence, the initial bill was a feeble enough measure[82] and absurd in an Irish context where Catholic structures and titles already existed despite the Emancipation Act clause, and, as Sadleir later said, were publicly used and acknowledged.[83] The bill stipulated that all briefs, rescripts and letters apostolical from Rome, establishing sees, dioceses or provinces and conferring episcopal titles or that of Dean were illegal and void. The fine for each offence in assuming such titles was £100. By May 1851 David Urquhart, Staffordshire, combined wit with truth when he declared that some of his colleagues held the measure to be a nullity, others a persecution; while some could not tell whether it was one or the other.[84]

The real irony of the protracted debate was the thwarting by the Conservative opposition of a government decision to water down the original bill. Sir Frederick Thesiger, Abingdon, succeeded in having amendments passed which made it illegal to publish Roman rescripts on ecclesiastical titles or jurisdiction and empowered any individual to sue a Catholic cleric for breach of the Act. Another amendment by Spencer Walpole, Midhurst, widened the scope of the bill from the 1850 rescript to cover all such rescripts. But, from its introduction, and minus these amendments, Catholics in England were taken aback both by the prospect of legislation and by accusations of disloyalty to the Queen. This was encapsulated in an address of 'unimpaired and unalterable fidelity' to the Queen on 11 February, signed by a great number of Catholics and presented by Lords Vaux, Dormer and Lovat.[85] The address underlined the teaching of the Catholic Church to give to Caesar the things that were of Caesar and to God the things that were of God and assured the Queen that the rescript did not encroach upon her jurisdiction.

W.B. Ullathorne, the new Catholic Bishop of Bermingham, wrote a public letter in the *Times* to Lord John Russell on 10 February in less servile terms.[86] He outlined his own detailed knowledge of the events leading up to the Papal pronouncement, revealing that the rescript would have been issued in 1848, but for the outbreak of revolution in Rome. Ullathorne's letter shows that Pius was under the impression from discussions with Lord Minto that there would not be any official opposition to the establishment of a hierarchy in England. The bishop had in his possession the minutes of sixteen conversations with the Vatican authorities in Propaganda in 1848 on the subject of the proposed hierarchy. He also had seven memorials which he had presented to the Holy See, that were largely the basis upon which the hierarchy was reconstituted in England. Ullathorne was clear that the Vatican was sensitive to the feelings of the English Government and had even refused his recommendation to appoint an Archbishop of London and a Bishop of York. In his conclusion he threw down the gauntlet to Russell that the Hierarchy was established and could not be abolished by any state power, which was inferior to the Divine,

> Is it wise and in the spirit of profound legislation to put the religious teachers of a large body of Her Majesty's subjects in conscientious opposition to the law – to force them to put the principle of Divine law in opposition to a human enactment – to make their very bishops the incorporation of such a fact?... We are compelled to count for nothing enactments which we can only consider as assaults upon the cause of Heaven and of our souls – enactments which, in fact, come from no Divine fountain of justice, but are the offspring of party contests and sectarian dislikes.

Writing from the Athenaeum Club on 6 February, Charles Langdale[87] confronted Russell with the fact that an address had been presented to Cardinal Wiseman by the higher echelons of English society including twelve Catholic peers, fourteen Catholic baronets and 600 Catholic gentlemen, expressing gratitude to the Pope.[88] The Earl of Arundel and Surrey was one of these and he left Russell in no doubt of English Catholic determination to protect their religious rights,

> whatever may be said by others, no Minister of the Crown will on any occasion again attempt to stigmatise with disloyalty any portion of Her Majesty's Catholic subjects for accepting – as I hold it to be their bounden duty to do – the purely spiritual organisation given to them by the head of their Church.

Early in March a meeting of London Catholics was convened to organise petitions to parliament against the bill.[89] Sadleir was not there, but others Irish M.P.s including Frank Scully, George Henry Moore, M.P. for Mayo and John Reynolds, M.P. for Dublin attended. The meeting was mistakenly optimistic that the bill would be defeated within a month, and speakers articulated the constant theme of the consistency of allegiance to the Queen with spiritual obedience to the Catholic Church.

The *Times* scoffed at the absence of influential English Catholics and ridiculed the contribution of Sergeant William Shee,[90] Reynolds and Moore – 'Shee wandered for two hours amid the dreary masses of repealed statutes' and 'nothing redeemed the meeting from absolute and abject insipidity but the Hibernian raciness of Mr. Reynolds and the still more Hibernian metaphors of Mr. Moore.' But despite such sarcasm and an earlier editorial on the government's failure to reflect the anger of Protestant England in an appropriately penal measure allegedly due to its reliance on Irish votes,[91] the *Times'* writer was stung by Moore's reference to Protestant fanaticism. The initial irony of the article yielded to a threat,

> All this talk about toleration by the professors of a religion which is synonymous with intolerance, is an indirect homage paid to her adversary and a pointed censure upon herself. We warn these gentlemen, however, that their confidence in the tolerant nature of our institutions may lead them a little too far. Our national independence and the prerogatives of our Crown we hold to be as inviolable as the rights of conscience themselves; and it is a dangerous calculation which induces them so triumphantly to conclude that our implicit respect for the second will render us callous to every insult and outrage on the first.

At Westminster thirty nine of the sixty four Irish Liberals opposed the first reading of the Bill and forty-eight opposed the second.[92] While there was no general philosophical unity between them their opposition to the bill and to every other measure introduced by the Government made them conspicuous and earned them the title the Irish Brigade from their friends and the more derisive Popes Brass Band from their opponents.

The most outstanding members of this group were Moore, Reynolds, Keogh and Sadleir. Keogh, a close friend of Sadleir, was the most flamboyant and regarded by his contemporaries as the leader. Moore, however, saw himself in this role and as the architect of a policy of opposition to the Government on all matters while the bill was being debated. His letters to his confidante, the celebrated Lion of the West, Archbishop John McHale of Tuam, oscillated between jubilation and alarm and on 17 February he wrote,

I hope it is no more than the indulgence of an honest pride in me to say that the confederation of Irish members who voted against the Ministers on Thursday night was from first to last my handiwork. Slowly, patiently, unremittingly, I forged and united together every link of the chain on which all our hopes now hang.[93]

One method used by Moore to forge this political chain was by pressurising electors to insist on their representatives being present in the House to oppose the government. This originated at a meeting of Irish M.P.s in London early in March, which was chaired by him.[94] The list of members present was not published but Sadleir was probably present. The meeting unanimously agreed to issue an appeal to Irish voters, which was published in the national and local newspapers. It was as much a reprimand as an appeal and labelled any representatives absent from Westminster as deserters and any constituency that tolerated such desertion as unworthy of the franchise,

> It was the constituencies of Ireland that won the battle of Catholic Emancipation; it is the constituencies of Ireland that we now invite to the rescue. It becomes our duty to remind them that on a late division, involving their religious rights and liberties, a fourth part of their representatives were absent altogether; it is the duty of Irish constituencies to ensure the attendance of every man upon the division that is about to ensue. Neither business, nor partial indisposition, nor personal circumstances should be allowed as an excuse. If their own personal fortunes, liberties, or interests were endangered, they would be in London; and those, whose rights, liberties, and hopes are now at stake, should not permit them to be elsewhere.

Moore signed this address on behalf of the other M.P.s and more than likely was its author. Sadleir was less colourful in his written and oral contribution than either Moore, Reynolds or Keogh, but was regarded by the *Dublin Evening Post* as 'the brains of the Brigade'.[95] His attention to detail and his patient teasing out of the religious, legal and political consequences of the bill and his courtesy earned him the respect of the House. He may legitimately be seen as the hidden leader of the Brigadiers; he inspired confidence as a wealthy man with powerful business and banking interests. These interests prevented him from taking part in the Ecclesiastical Titles Bill debate on 7 February. The previous day he chaired the half yearly meeting of the London and County, where he congratulated the directors for correcting 'past errors' and putting the bank on a sound footing, so that customers balances then stood at two million pounds.[96]

Heartened by an increase of £1,000 in the directors' salaries, Sadleir once more turned to the great religious debate in Westminster on 14 February.[97] At that stage the parameters of the long debate were being laid and he was careful to compliment Irish Protestants and Presbyterians, who, 'with calm disdain', had refrained from involvement in the controversy. He reminded 'English gentlemen' that the No Popery slogan was one which aroused feelings of intolerance and prejudice against Catholics,

> At all times the illiterate, ignorant and scum of this country, were lashed into frenzy by the force and action of that senseless cry. The greatest men, lay and clerical, of the Protestant Church, had constantly warned us against the danger of raising such a cry – a cry which caused the active agents of infidelity to point the finger of scorn against Christianity itself.

Sadleir viewed the Prime Minister as fuelling such invective and evoked the common bond of Christianity between the churches evident in the admiration of some Protestant clergymen for the missionary work of a Catholic Church 'in every clime scaling the steepest ramparts of infidelity and planting upon its highest citadel the triumphal banner of their faith'.

When Russell maintained that much public patronage had been conferred on Catholics since the Emancipation Act, Sadleir warmed to one of his favourite themes and produced detailed statistics to prove discrimination against Catholics and Irishmen in this area. He showed that the head of every public department in Ireland was Protestant, that of twelve Common Law Judges in the Four Courts only three were Catholics; all the judges in the Queens Bench were Protestant and only one of the seven Chancery Judges was Catholic. All but sixteen of the seventy-three officers in the Chancery staff were Protestants, while all twenty two officers in the Law Exchequer were Protestant.

Sadleir concluded his case with a reminder that in the past, religious intolerance had been overcome by constitutional methods and fortitude guided by the genius, constitutional knowledge, and legal acumen of O'Connell,

> Faithful, firm, unmoved, unshaken, unterrified, unsubdued, our loyalty – our love – our zeal have always been the same. This was not the language of empty exultation – it was the practical soothing of the political soul – it was a dignified retrospect of the triumphs they had achieved.

The implication was that similar qualities were essential in combating what was seen as a fresh attack on the Catholic Church. These were in evidence and within a matter of days the Government was in crisis, having been defeated on a minor question of parliamentary reform, when Irish and some English Liberals sided with the Conservatives against it. Russell was unwilling to risk defeat on the forthcoming budget and on 22 February the Government resigned. He resumed office, however, because Lord Stanley, the leader of the Conservatives, was unable to form an administration, and the Peelite Aberdeen, who opposed Russell's policy on the Ecclesiastical Titles refused to form an administration which would contain Russell.[98] The ministerial crisis, as it was called, was debated very much in the context of the Ecclesiastical Titles Bill, which Irish members now optimistically felt was moribund.[99] Sadleir, however, worried that Russell would replace some of its clauses and proceed with legislation. While making it clear that he had no desire to oppose the Government on all issues he warned that any attempt to coerce Irish members into submission would be met by further opposition and they 'would take such a step as would compel the Government to afford them ample time to consider the probable consequences of the Bill'.[100]

Although shaken by the Government defeat, Russell was determined to proceed in the knowledge that the Conservatives would ultimately support the measure. He made the embarrassing admission, however, that legal counsel had advised him that the titles conferred by Rome were neither contrary to Common or Statute Law, which left him with no option but to modify his original proposals.[101] On 11 March the Government suffered a narrow defeat on another minor issue involving the management of Woods and Forests. The *Tablet* immediately exulted in the role played by Irish members in achieving this, but drew attention to absentees and accused them of shirking their responsibility of opposing Russell, because the question involved some measure of free trade, a policy automatically favoured by Liberal Politicians. Lucas published the list with the observation that

> Some names in the following list are — the names of honest men, whose absence may be accidental; but the whole list *cannot* be accidental; the list as a whole, we hesitate not to say is a corrupt list; and contains the names of men who stayed away out of consideration for a friend, a patron and a paymaster.[102]

Sadleir, Keating and Keogh were cited, but the Carlow M.P. chose to ignore the barb. Shortly afterwards he interrupted the debate on the Ecclesiastical Titles' Bill, when he insisted on bringing forward a motion of his own on the tithe rent charge in Ireland. His decision to raise it at that time could easily have been misinterpreted as retaliation against the Bill, but he explained that he had put down his motion during the last session.[103] When he rose to bring it forward on 18 March he prefaced his remarks with the assurance that 'it was not his intention to discuss the subject in any other spirit than that which became the consideration of a practical subject in which the rights of property were intimately involved'. He was as good as his word and never mentioned the bill in his speech.[104]

The motion, seconded by Sharman Crawford, proposed that the method of computing the tithe rent in Ireland should correspond to that of England and Wales. Sadleir relished the complexity of the question and explained that in England the tithe charge varied annually according to the average septennial value of wheat, barley and oats as published on the Thursday before Christmas Day in the *London Gazette*. The average price was taken for 150 towns. In Ireland, where only wheat and oats could be taken, the average price was according to that on the Dublin market which could be considerably higher than that for rural areas.

Tithes had ceased to be a major grievance in Ireland when they were reduced by 25% and effectively hidden by incorporating them into the rent. Despite this, the truth remained that a largely Catholic population supported a minority Protestant clergy. Sadleir, however, was not advocating their abolition. Not only that but he deplored the imposition of the poor rate onPprotestant ministers' income derived from the tithes. Few Catholic M.P.s would have been as solicitous about the plight of Protestant clergymen. Sadleir went even further, however, by expressing his concern about the unequal distribution of income among those clergymen.

He demonstrated a further unusual way of thinking when he put the issue of tithes in the context of the Incumbered Estates Courts by proposing that they should not be a charge on an entire estate, but rather an 'acreable charge which would facilitate the transfer and sale of land into divisions suitable to the wants and requirements of the community'. Neither would he have endeared himself to the tenant farmers by his parallel idea of making tithe charges redeemable. He argued that Quakers, who objected upon religious ground to purchase land which was liable to the tithe rent, would do so if the lessee was liable for such payments.

Sir George Grey, the Home Secretary, responding on behalf of the Government, sensibly refused to be drawn into the debate because the question of computing tithes was too complex to be considered on the basis of a mere motion. He promised, however, that if Sadleir brought a bill, 'carefully framed', before the House, its provisions would be considered. On that basis and on the advice of his colleagues Sadleir withdrew the motion and the House immediately proceeded to continue the debate on the Ecclesiastical Tithes Assumption Bill for the third night.

The most rancorous episode of its parliamentary path arose the next night and seemed to confirm Sadleir's worst fears about sectarian rabble-rousing. This occurred when, Henry Drummond, was in the process of analysing the nature of Papal authority and the strict obedience to Church teaching contained in the Spiritual Exercises of St. Ignatius of Loyola. Drummond's conclusion was that

> Priests that inculcate such principles as these are the Thugs of Christendom. For what are Thugs?-murderers: yes, but all murderers are not Thugs. Thugs are not only murderers, but they commit murder as an act of worship: so these priests inculcate lying as an act of worship of the God of truth, inculcate the saying that black is white, when they know it to be black, as a thing well-pleasing to God: this is what constitutes Thuggee. Never was degradation of the laity who submit to them so low as this: the negro slave was not so oppressed; in all the debates in this House, in all the evidence of cruelty committed upon him, it never yet was said that he was obliged to say sugar was sour, and lime juice was sweet.[105]

This was received in barely restrained silence by the Irish M.P.s but when the West Surrey M.P. went on to denigrate the Catholic Church and its 'cargo of blinking statues, of bleeding pictures, of liquefying blood and of the Virgin Mary's milk,' the debate degenerated into disorder for some time. The sense of outrage was sharpened because a bill was also before the House proposing biannual domiciliary inspection of convents by six J.P.s to facilitate the removal of nuns allegedly detained against their wishes.[106] Drummond was unable to resist drawing the convent question into the debate using the most objectionable imagery.

> Do idiots and insane persons ask for protection? How can a poor young lady who is locked up, where she may be either starved or whipped to death, that the priests may clutch her money, ask for protection?... I assert that nunneries are prisons and I have seen them so used... They have ever been either prisons or brothels.

This was compatible with the rhetoric of the hustings, but it was unusual in parliamentary proceedings and Graham, one of the most influential opponents of the Ecclesiastical Titles Bill, was scandalised.[107]

Sadleir did not make any response to this, but waited until 24 March for the second reading of the bill to make a detailed statement, which substantially differed in theme from his previous one and which

146

addressed some of the points emerging from the debates.[108] His diplomatic praise for fair-minded Protestants, who eschewed 'the whole of the hubbub', was laced with condemnation of 'the dismal, dark religious fanaticism which had always prevailed in England above all the nations of the world', and which prevented enlightened legislation for a multi-religious state. Sadleir played upon the Prime Minister's stated apprehension that some Protestant pastors were partial to certain aspects of Catholic practice.[109] He speculated that other Protestants might also fear a meeting of the clergy of both communions 'in a sacred and holy rivalry', in which the Protestant clergy would come off second best. Such individuals could have little confidence in the principles of their own religion. His speculation was endorsed later that night by Henry Berkeley, one of the Protestant members, who placed the issue in the context of 'Puseyite Parsons going by droves over to the faith of Rome' and the introduction of Catholic rites and ceremonies into Protestant churches. The English people 'looked upon Puseyism as occupying the same position to Popery as the grub to the butterfly. They considered it to be the chrysalis of Popery, which had nothing to do but to cast off its skin, expand its wings, and become Popery complete'.[110]

Sadleir was aware that the publication of the rescript as much as its contents had contributed to Protestant unease, and he denied that Cardinal Wiseman had anything to do with this. He almost gave the impression that it had been published by the 'promoters of religious discord', presumably Protestants. With unintended irony he went on to argue that Parliament was not the proper forum to discuss either controverted theology, nice points of international law or the construction of common or statute law – 'all the requisite paraphernalia were wanting; they had no big wigs, no minor wigs, and more than all no fees'.

In re-iterating the loyalty of Catholics to the Crown, he dismissed as a 'hackneyed and battered' calumny Russell's opinion that they gave a blind obedience to the Pope in all matters. He drew upon the statement of the deceased Bishop of Kildare and Leighlin, James Doyle, that the Catholic clergy would instruct their flocks to oppose the Pope if he interfered in the temporal rights of their sovereign. One wonders if he was aware of this Bishop's proposal twenty seven years earlier, that Anglican and the Roman Catholic communions should reunite because of the closeness of their teachings.[111]

Sadleir exposed one of the interesting ironies of the Pope's action in replacing a system over which he had extensive control with one where his power was more limited. Again, he quoted from the evidence of Doyle before a Parliamentary Committee of inquiry that the office and faculties of a vicar apostolic depended solely upon the will of the Pope and could be removed at the Pope's pleasure, but,

> It is not so with us bishops; we cannot be removed; we have a title to our place, our rights are defined from the Gospel and the common laws – defined as well as those of the Pope himself. We could not be obliged to do anything by the mere good-will or pleasure of Rome.

The Carlow M.P. characterised the vicars apostolic as the 'mere creatures and nominees' of the Pope and then turned his attention to the point made by the Conservative, Richard M. Milnes, Pontefract, that the proportionally small number of Catholics in England did not warrant a hierarchy.[112] Sadleir reminded him of Russell's allusion to the great number of Irish immigrants which swelled the Catholic population there. He revealed that he had received letters from workers employed at remote railway stations who complained that they sometimes spent from twelve to fifteen weeks without being able to go to church and requesting him to do something on their behalf. Some of those men had offered to take a large cut in their wages to be relocated near a Catholic church.

Irish Liberal M.P.s had been stung by criticism of Cullen and a large portion of Sadleirs contribution was devoted to his nomination as Archbishop of Armagh and role in the Synod of Thurles. He denied that Cullen had been foisted upon the Irish clergy against their wishes, and in a dramatic gesture showed the House documents which contained instructions on the appointment of bishops in Ireland. He emphasised that only recommendations and not nominations could be forwarded to Rome by the clergy in a vacant diocese, and that there was no obligation on the Pope to accept such recommendations. He explained Cullen's appointment as a compromise to prevent dissension in the Archdiocese following the failure of the Armagh clergy to agree on a candidate. Sadleir's eulogy of Cullen must have secured him at least the good opinion of the latter,

> In selecting Dr Cullen to fill the primatial chair, the Holy See had chosen one distinguished for great learning, great abilities and an extraordinary aptitude for the administration of ecclesiastical affairs – one universally respected and beloved by the members of the Church over which he presides, and admired for the moderation and the firmness which he has displayed.

Cullen had been labelled an 'Italian Monk' by some speakers and Sadleir objected to this, considering it improbable that the Irish hierarchy would accept such an individual to defend their interests and protect the independence of 'their national Church'. He portrayed this hierarchy as having always 'evinced a justifiable jealousy of anything approaching to ecclesiastical aggression on the part of the Court of Rome'. While this portrayal may have been melodramatic and geared towards English ears, Sadleir was correct insofar as the nationalistic John McHale was one of the bishops who had strongly urged his nomination for Armagh. Cullen had also cultivated friendships among a large number of Irish clergy.[113]

The attack on the National Synod by Russell, Gladstone and other M.P.s was resented by Sadleir, who showed that its agenda covering thirty main headings was focussed on upholding 'the true faith' and promoting 'uniformity of discipline'.[114] He denied that the rejection of the Queen's colleges was interference in temporal matters, because it was 'a mixed question and it was the duty of the Synod to consider it in its spiritual bearings'. He told the House that the bishops had failed to agree on these colleges and an appeal to Rome resulted in a decision by the Holy See to reject them. Sadleir's comments, however, betrayed a degree of regret that Catholics did not have university facilities of their own, but he blamed the Government rather than the Catholic Church for this.

He also took Russell to task for criticising the Synod's reference to the plight of the evicted in Ireland. The priests, who mainly came from a farming background, closely identified with this interest, and to Sadleir it was an essential part of the bishops' pastoral role to publicly highlight the 'wretchedness and sufferings of the poor of Christ'. Moreover, it would have been a 'disgrace in the eyes of the people' if the synod had dispersed without referring to this social evil.

Sadleir concluded one of his best statements in Westminster with a warning about the consequences of trying to enforce the proposed law in Ireland,where it would be severely tested and would

> spread the flames of religious discord throughout Ireland, and paralyse the best efforts of the best men to regenerate and disenthrall that ill-fated land. Whether it became of practical effect, or was left a dead letter, it would equally excite the contempt of the people for the Laws of Parliament; it would oppress the Roman Catholics, who from their rapidly increasing political and social influence ought to be conciliated; it would drive into the arms of America and of other foreign states the most valuable of the Irish population still left in the country, and he would resist it, because he believed if it were placed upon the statute-book it would but tend to prolong, in 1851, that state which had been described by a great living historian, when he said "that Ireland was cursed by the domination of race over race, and of religion over religion, remaining, indeed, a member of the empire, but still a withered and distorted member...

References

1. *C.S.* 3 July 1847.
2. See *Copies of any Correspondence between John Sadleir Esq., M.P. and His Excellency, the Lord Lieutenant, relative to a Fund of about £4,500 placed under the control of Duncan Chisolm, alias George Mathews, lately absconded from the Office of the Chief Secretary in Ireland*, H.C. 1851 (279) L. passim, (henceforth *Duncan Chisolm*).
3. See *Copies of the order to the Government agent in Ireland, Dr. Cooke, to withold the Regium Donum from the congregation of Clonmel in connexion with the general assembly of the Presbyterian Church, and of any correspondence between the Irish government and Dr. Cooke on the subject*, H.C.1847-48 (448) XLIX.235,pp.7-8, (henceforth *Regium Donum*).
4. Ibid., p. 1, (see pp 2-4 for Redington's response).
5. *Copy of any correspondence between the Moderator of the general assembly of the Presbyterian Church in Ireland and the Irish Government relative to the stoppage of the Regium Donum of the Minister of Clonmel, on the order of George Mathews, alias Duncan Chisolm*, H.C. 1850 (631) LI.555 pp 1-3, (henceforth *Moderator Presbyterian Church*).
6. Letter 27 September 1849 in ibid., p. 6.
7. Reynolds was secretary of the National Bank and agent for its Irish operations. When he left the National he became involved in the Dublin Banking Company which was of dubious integrity. It is not known if it ever operated and after court cases beginning in 1844 it was finally wound up in 1856. – see Barrow, *The Emergence of the Irish Banking*, pp 3-4.
8. *Parl. Deb.*, series 3, vol.113, 1850,col.263, (25 July 1850).
9. Letter 13 February 1849 in *Duncan Chisolm*, p. 3 (MS.p.927). This file contains 290 pages of evidence and letters on the Chisolm affair.
10. See *Watkins Commercial and General London Directory, 1854, p1743, Post Office London Directory 1855*, p. 346. Some of his neighbours in Gloucester Square were Sir Charles Chad, Sir Walter Minto Farquahar, Sir James p. Kay Shuttleworth and John Samual Moorat, whose daughter would marry Frank Scully. Scully lived in 94 Pall Mall near William Keogh – *Post office London Directory 1851*, pp 1740, 1744.
11. While professing belief in the doctrines of the shorter catechism of the Westminster Assembly the Trinitarians 'expressly rejected subscription' to it.
12. These congregations did not qualify for the Regium Donum.
13. The discrepancy between the figure in the letter and the official grant lay in the accumulation of interest.
14. The Royal Bounty was confined to Trinitarians in those three provinces.
15. Letter 3 March 1849 in *Duncan Chisolm, pp* 6-7 (ms. p. 931).
16. Ibid., pp 7-11.
17. Letter 12 May 1849 in ibid., pp 11-13.
18. Ibid., pp 43 et.seq.
19. Ibid., p. 44.
20. Ibid., p. 45.
21. See M.C.N. Salbstein, *The Emancipation of the Jews in Britain. An Essay on the Preconditions*, (Brighton, 1977), p. 7 and passim.
22. Rothschild, Lionel Nathan de 1808-1879, the eldest son of Nathan Meyer Rothschild was born in St. Swithin's Lane London. He was educated in Gottingen and on his father's death in 1836 he became chief manager of the Rothschild banking establishment in England. In 1838 he assumed the title baron of the

Austrian Empire. In 1847 he negotiated the Irish famine loan, and formed the British Relief Association for famine relief in Ireland. In 1856 he raised £16,000,000 for the government to defray the expenses of the Crimean War. He played a prominent role in the funding of the U.S. national debt. He co-operated with continental branches of the family in financial ventures and was a director of the Great Northern Railway of France. Rothschild had houses in Piccadilly and Gunnersbury and in 1872 he purchased Tring Park estate in Hertfordshire as well as property in Buckinghamshire. He owned several racehorses and one of these, Sir Berys, won the Derby in 1879. He died at his house, 148 Piccadilly on 3 June 1879 and was buried at Willesden. *D.N.B.* ,e.v., see also Kerr, *Catholic Church*, p. 28.

23. See *Times* 6 July 1847 for reference to the selection of Rothschild as one of the four Liberal candidates.
24. See ibid., 5 January 1848.
25. His introductory speech in *Parl. Deb.*, series 3, vol 102, 1849, cols 906 *et. seq.*, (19 February 1849).
26. Ibid., 20 February 1849. See *A Bill to alter the oaths to be taken by the members of the Houses of Parliament not professing the Roman Catholic Religion.* H.C. 1849 (65) IV.419.
27. *Parl. Deb.*, series 3, vol 105, 1849, col. 1386, (11 June 1849).
28. *Tablet* 16 June 1849.
29. See e.g. speeches of Law, Raphael and Newdegate in *Parl. Deb.*, series 3, vol. 105, 1849, cols. 1373-1385, 1385-1386, 1388-1395 respectively, (11 June 1849).
30. *Parl. Deb.*, series 3, vol.105, 1849, col.1407, (11 June 1849).
31. His speech in ibid., cols. 1398-1402.
32. The relevant bills were passed by the Commons in 1851, 1853, and 1857. The 1858 bill was only accepted by the Lords after an amendment rejecting the Jewish clause. This provoked a potentially serious conflict between the two Houses and the Prime Minister Lord Derby, accepted a bill drawn up by Lord Lucan enabling each House to determine the form of oath to be taken by its members. This was passed and Rothschild finally took his seat. His return at successive elections ensured that the matter would have to be resolved sooner rather than later. In July 1850 he presented himself at the bar of the house and demanded to be sworn on the Old Testament but the House had no option but to forbid him taking his seat without taking the usual oath. He was re-elected in 1854, and twice in 1857 after resigning and being returned again. Following the 1858 bill Rothschild was returned by the City of London in 1859 and 1865. He was defeated in the general election of 1868 but was successful in the by-election of February 1870. He lost his seat in 1874. See *D.N.B.*, e.v. under Rothschild. See also *Times* 26 July 1850 for a meeting at the London Tavern convened by Rothschild where he expressed his disappointment at Russell's decision not to proceed with a parliamentary oaths bill that session. Sharman Crawford attended the meeting. See also *Nation* 3 August 1850 for the row when Rothschild requested to swear on the Old Testament. See *Times* 26 February 1853 and 14 March 1853 on the continuing saga. A similar fate was suffered by Sir David Salomons, a member of an old London Jewish family and one of the founders of the London and Westminster Bank. In 1835 a special act of Parliament was passed to enable him, as a Jew, to accept one of the Shrievalties of London and Middlesex. In June 1851 Salomons was elected Liberal M.P. for Greenwich Borough but refused to take the oath and was not permitted to take his seat. He finally sat in Westminster in 1858 – see *D.N.B.*, e.v. under Salomons,

Sir David 1797-1873. See *Parl. Deb.*, series 3, vol 118 1851 cols 1144 *et. seq.*, 21 July 1851.

33. For insight into this see N. Murphy, *Guilty or innocent, the Cormack Brothers – trial execution and exhumation*, (Nenagh, 1997), pp 109-110,see also N.A., C.S.O., R.P., 1858, 17060, newscuttings in County Library, Thurles, *N.G.* 1 September 1858, *L.R.* 31 August 1858, *T.F.P.* 3,20,24, and 28 August 1858, N.L.I., Larcom Papers, MS. 7636, and William Smith O'Brien Papers, MS. 446.

34. His opening speech in *Parl. Deb.*, series 3, vol.108, 1850, cols.713-718, (12 February 1850).

35. See ibid., cols.719-720.

36. Ibid., col.723.

37. Procedure outlined in ibid., cols.718 and 722.

38. Scully's speech in ibid., col.721.

39. Ibid., col.723.

40. Ibid., cols. 718-721.

41. Speech in ibid., cols. 723-724.

42. Tenants for life of fee simple valued at £5 would also have the vote.

43. Somerville's introduction of the bill in *Parl. Deb.*, series 3, vol.108, 1850, cols. 699 *et.seq.* (11 February 1850).

44. Scully's statement in ibid., cols. 702 et. seq.

45. Ibid., cols. 1290 et. seq., (22 February 1850).

46. Ibid., col.1296 (22 February 1850).

47. Ibid., vol.108, 1850, col.1339, (25 February 1850).

48. His speech in ibid., cols.1313-14, (22 February 1850).

49. During the ministerial crisis of February 1851 when defending his record on electoral reform Russell would display such conservatism. He conceded that a wider franchise would increase the interest of its beneficiaries in preserving law and order, but still held the traditional view that property rather than numbers was the best basis to underpin the right to elect Members of Parliament. Such caution permeated his view that the franchise should not deprive the House 'of those conservative elements which ought to belong to it'. Over extension would endanger the cherished English institutions of the Monarchy, a hereditary House of Lords or the Established Church and would "hazard the spirit and frame of our constitution" – *Parl. Deb.*, series 3, vol.114, 1851, cols.1037 et. seq., (28 February 1851).

50. *Parl. Deb.*, series 3, vol.110, 1850, cols. 426-428, (16 April 1850).

51. His reply in ibid., cols. 428 et. seq.

52. Ibid., cols. 691-697, (23 April 1850).

53. Reply in ibid., cols. 735-741.

54. See D. A. Kerr, Peel, *Priests and Politics*, (Oxford, 1982), pp 290-291.

55. Sadleirs statement in *Parl. Deb.*, series 3, vol 110, 1850, cols 7410745, (23 April 1850).

56. *Parl. Deb.*, series 3, vol.105, 1849, col.1404, (11 June 1849).

57. Text in *Tablet* 26 October 1850. For an informative account of the circumstances leading to the rescript see Kerr, *A Nation of Beggars*, pp 241 *et. seq.*

58. *Parl. Deb.*, series 3, vol 115, 1851, col.458, (24 March 1851).

59. Career biography of Lambruschini in *Irish Catholic Directory*, 1852, p. 229.

60. See Whyte, *Independent Irish party*, pp 20-21. (Vicars Apostolic had been appointed as far back as 1685 by Pope Innocent XI).

61. *Tablet* 25 January 1851.

62. Ibid., 11 January 1851.

63. Ibid.
64. *Parl. Deb.*, series 3, vol.115, 1851, col.457, (24 March 1851).
65. Address in *Tablet* 7 December 1850.
66. Ibid., 2 November 1850.
67. Ibid.
68. Letter in ibid., 9 November 1850.
69. *Parl. Deb.*, series 3, vol 115, 1851, col.454, (24 March 1851).
70. *Tablet* 11 January 1851.
71. Ibid., 9 November 1850.
72. Lucas later castigated Dungarvan voters who returned a Conservative candidate in a by-election of March 1851 as the 'rotten, shabby, dirty, muddy, base, vile whig Catholics of Dungarvan' – *Tablet* 29 March 1851.
73. Ibid.,7 December 1850.
74. Letter 14 January 1851 in ibid., 25 January 1851.
75. It was published in sections in ibid., 4, 11, 18, 25 January 1851.
76. See ibid., 1 February 1851.
77. The meeting forwarded an address of congratulations to Wiseman – text in *Irish Catholic Directory* ,1852, pp 121-122 . See ibid., p. 123 for Wiseman's reply 4 February 1851.
78. *Tablet* 1 February 1851.
79. Ibid., 8 February 1851.
80. His speech quoted in ibid., 15 February 1851.
81. For insight into the Act see Kerr, *A Nation of Beggars* , pp 261 – 281.
82. See D.D.A., C.P., Carton 47/1. *A Bill to prevent the assumption of certain ecclesiastical titles in respect of places in the United Kingdom.*
83. Sadleir's reference in *Parl. Deb.*, series 3, vol.115, 1851, col.455, (24 March 1851).
84. Ibid., vol.116, 1851, col.787, (9 May 1851).
85. Quoted in *Tablet* 15 February 1851.
86. Letter in *Times* 11 February 1851.
87. Charles Langdale born in 1787, was third son of Lord Stourton by a sister of Lord Langdale, a Catholic. He was a leading English agitator for Catholic rights and took his seat for Beverley following the Relief Act. He took a special interest in the education of poor Catholic children. He was the biographer of Mrs Fitzherbert, later wife of King George IV. He became a temporal coadjutor of the Society of Jesus immediately prior to his death in 1868. *D.N.B.*, e.v.
88. *Tablet* 15 February 1851.
89. *Times* 11 March 1851, *F.J.* 12 March 1851, *Tablet* 15 March 1851.
90. p. 218 n. 25 below.
91. *Times* 10 March 1851. This editorial contextualised the Ecclesiastical Titles Bill from the perspective of political ethics by which governments were obliged to reflect the majority view of the public.
92. *Parl. Deb.*, Series 3, vol.114, 1851, col.699, (14 February 1851) and vol.115, 1851, col.618, (25 March 1851).
93. N.L.I., Moore Papers, MS. 891, Moore to McHale 17 February 1851, (letter 259).
94. *A.S.* 12 March 1851 (from *Freeman's Journal*).
95. *D.E.P.* 8 January 1853.
96. *Times* 7 February 1851. Sadleir's report recommended a dividend of 6% tax free from the previous half year's net profits of £10,000. The guarantee fund was increased to a respectable £35,000. His report also revealed that the company had exploited the failure of Nash and Neale's bank by opening a new branch in Reigate.

97. His statement in *Parl. Deb.*, Series 3, vol.114, 1851, cols. 667-675, (14 February 1851).

98. *Tablet.* 1 and 8 March 1851 for details.

99. For the interesting debate on the ministerial crisis see *Parl. Deb.*, series 3, vol.114, 1851, cols. 892-896, (24 February 1851), cols. 1029 et. seq., (13 March 1851). The House of Lords debate containing the statements of Aberdeen and Stanley in cols. 887-890, (24 February 1851), cols. 995 et. seq., (28 February 1851). This interesting debate details the efforts of the Queen to have an administration formed either by Stanley or Aberdeen assisted by Sir James Graham and Russell. During the debate both Aberdeen and Graham expressed genuine personal friendship for Russell. While both would not support Russell because of his promotion of the Ecclesiastical Titles Bill against what they considered the legal right of the Pope, they expressed their resentment at the 'haughty' and 'arrogant' tone of both the Pope and Wiseman in the restructuring of the Catholic Church.

100. *Parl. Deb.*, Series 3, vol.114, 1851, cols. 1084-1085, (4 March 1851).

101. *Tablet* 15 March 1851.

102. Ibid. Some constituents reacted swiftly and called upon their representatives to resign. Maurice O'Connell was forced to publish a letter to his Tralee constituents explaining that he could not vote for protection, but that other areas, such as the budget vote, income tax vote, and the vote on Irish Stamp Act would afford the opportunity of showing opposition and would not compromise his anti-protection principles – his letter 27 February 1851 in *Tablet* 15 March 1851.

103. *Parl. Deb.*, Series 3, vol.115, 1851, col.108, (17 March 1851).

104. Ibid., vol. 115, 1851, cols.116-120, (18 March 1851) and *Tablet* 22 March 1851.

105. Drummond's speech in *Parl. Deb.*, vol.23 5, 85 cols 261-280 (20 March 1851).

106. This was known as a *Bill to Prevent the Forcible Detention of Females in Religious Houses.* It was defeated by a majority of thirty two in May 1851 – *Tablet* 17 May 1851. For public meetings in Ireland to protest against the Convents Bill and Drummonds remarks see ibid., 22,29 arch 1851. There was more widespread public reaction in Ireland to another convent Bill which was drafted in May 1653 entitled a *Bill to facilitate the recovery of personal liberty in certain cases* – see *W. T.* 11 June 1853, *Tablet* 25 March 1854, 8 April 1854, 27 May 1854. D.D.A., Cullen papers, Carton 332/3 contains many letters on the bill.

107. Graham's statements in *Par. Deb.*, series 3, vol 115, 1851, cols 280-309, (20 March 1851).

108. Ibid., cols. 454-464, (24 March 1851).

109. For Russell's paranoia about Tractarianism see Kerr, *A Nation of Beggars*, pp 248 – 250,254. 262,264.

110. *Parl. Deb.*, Series 3, vol. 115, 1851, col. 465, (24 March 1851).

111. Kerr, *Peel*, p. 57.

112. *Parl. Deb.*, series 3, vol.115, 1851, col.451, (24 March 1851).

113. see e.g. Whyte, *Independent Irish Party*, p. 111, Kerr, *Peel*, p. 63.

114. See *Decreta Synodi plenariae episcoporum Hiberniae habitae anno 1850* for details of synodical reform.

Chapter 5

The politics of religion and land, March-July 1851

Sadleir's speech of 24 March referred to an analysis of the Ecclesiastical Titles Bill by Thomas O'Hagan, a respected Irish Queen's Counsel. This was commissioned by the Irish hierarchy following a two day conference in the Presbytery, Marlborough Street, under Cullen.[1] It was published as an appendix to their address to the Catholics of Ireland early in March 1851.[2] O'Hagan's brief was concise and specific. He was instructed to advise about the Bill's impact on the Catholic religion, the free observance of the Church's discipline and the continuance of existing trusts and charities as well as the creation of new ones. His response depicted a potentially serious situation if the bill became law, because it would

> prevent the voluntary endowment of Roman Catholic Archbishoprics and Bishoprics, it will render the assumption of *any* local ecclesiastical title by a Roman Catholic prelate illegal, and void all writings and assurances executed by him or to him under such title

The entire bill, he advised, directly conflicted with established Catholic discipline. It would mean the virtual abolition of the Irish hierarchy; and perhaps even invalidate the bishop's written appointments to parishes. This was examined in more detail by taking each clause including the preamble, which contained unfounded statements and facts of law in relation to the Emancipation Act. He did not see it as amending or clarifying that Act but as a new penal law. He condemned section four as not only repressive but unconstitutional. This section obliged prelates to reveal on oath any acts they had carried out which were in breach of the provisions of the proposed bill. Such self-incrimination ran contrary to the practice of every court in the empire.

Charitable bequests were an important source of income to the Catholic Church and a large portion of O'Hagan's opinion dealt with this. Despite the bill's prospective intention he believed that it could have a retrospective impact and seriously interfere with the conveyance of property to Catholic trusts or charities. This was partly because of the great variety of methods used for conveying property to ecclesiastical trustees, normally the bishops and their successors. The amount of property conveyed to the Catholic church over the previous twenty years was significant. O'Hagan counselled that those provisions of the Bill ran contrary not only to the disabling clause of the Emancipation Act but also to the Bequests Act which facilitated the transfer of property from a prelate to his successor. Succeeding bishops would fail in their efforts to claim trusteeships in the Court of Chancery thus thwarting the intentions of the benefactors. He thought that in many cases existing trusts might pass from the control of the bishops and be administered by the Court of Equity. Section three of the bill was particularly serious, because it would confiscate to the Crown any voluntary endowments for the maintenance of Catholic dioceses or deaneries, and could possibly affect religious institutions which might be seen in law as being connected with the maintenance of such units. O'Hagan concluded that the hierarchy would have to relinquish all expectation of endowment from their people, a fact which would run contrary to the Bequests' Act.[3] Sadleir, when referring to O'Hagan's views in Parliament, explained that they were upheld by his cousin, Vincent Scully,[4] who was later asked by the hierarchy for his opinion.[5]

Such a candid verdict helps to explain the emotive language of the hierarchy's address depicting the bill as a penal measure fettering the freedom of the Catholic church. It opened by calling Catholics to receive with Christian docility and patience 'the last and bitter ingredient which is now about to be poured into the cup of your afflictions', and it continued with quotations from Saints Peter and Paul on sharing in the sufferings of Christ. They were reminded that the purpose of the bill was to 'annoy, disorganise and crush' the Catholic hierarchy, which would in turn impede the imparting of religion. The possible destruction of charitable institutions and its consequences for the laity was graphically illustrated,

> The blighting effects of this penal law, if adopted, will be felt by the orphan that is now sheltered in the bosom of Catholic benevolence, and by the destitute sufferer on his death bed, whose pangs are so often soothed by the devoted daughter of charity, whilst they are consoled by the Christian ministry that has called those institutions into existence – by the power of that kindling and creative word which it has been commissioned to preach.

The new English hierarchy was set in the historical context of the the establishment of episcopal sees in England by St Augustine, who had been sent by Pope Gregory the Great, and in Ireland by St Patrick, sent by Pope Celestine. In other words the British Isles owed their Christianity to papal initiatives and in the words of St Irenaeus 'every church, and all the faithful, should have recourse to the Roman Church, on account of her greater principality'.

In defending the status of the Catholic Church the bishops also distinguished between the relative importance of its clergy and that of the clergy of other Christian churches. They developed the idea that the laity was closely bound to its clergy, a common theme in nineteenth century writing, and that any injury to the clergy would affect the people – 'if the branches of the vine were torn from the parent trunk, would they not necessarily wither? If separated from its head would not the mystical body immediately languish and decay?'. The bishops showed no compunction in stating that such was not the case with other Christian religions 'which stript of a sacrifice, and almost of sacraments, and giving an unbounded liberty to the interpretation of doctrine, demand little more than a nominal exercise of the ministerial functions'.

Catholics were urged to pray as a means of defending their church as in psalm 79 by not allowing 'the boar out of the wood to lay it waste, nor the wild beast to destroy it'. There was a triumphant declaration in the address that the Church had survived eighteen centuries of persecution at various times and would continue to do so on the promise of Christ that 'the gates of Hell shall never prevail against it'.

Considering their belittling of the Protestant religion the bishops did not appreciate the irony of immediately issuing an address of loyalty to the Queen, the head of the Protestant Church.[6] They assured her that the Irish Catholic clergy had at all times, even in the most difficult circumstances, inculcated such loyalty. The irony was reciprocated by the reply of the Home Secretary, who wrote on the Queen's behalf to 'The Most Rev. Archbishop Daniel Murray,' and began and concluded his letter with the customary title of 'My Lord'. With some ingenuity Grey would later defend such deference to Irish Bishops. But, he would equally explain that this did not entitle them to use such titles when communicating with the Government, nor, he maintained, did they ever breach the 1829 Act by doing so.[7]

Murray informed his priests in a circular of 20 February that his title and that of his fellow bishops were 'registered in Heaven' and conferred spiritual jurisdiction only. He asked them 'from the bitterness of my heart' to pray with their parishoners that the Government would have the wisdom to legislate for the welfare of all the people. He instructed them to add the collect *Pro Praelatis et Congregationibus Eis*

Commissis to the other collects in every Mass that would be celebrated as long 'as this persecuting bill shall be under the consideration of Parliament'.[8]

Murray's feelings were sharply stated for a prelate of a mild disposition, but such language was the usual preserve of McHale, the most outspoken of the hierarchy against the government's proposal, whose public challenge to Russell consisted of two long letters dated 9 February and 20 February.[9] In the first he sarcastically inquired if the material conditions of the Irish people, which were the responsibility of the Prime Minister, were so satisfactory that he could afford the leisure of turning the 'House of Commons into a stall of theological debate, displaying but little of its light, and much of its noisy strife, while warring against the shadowy phantom of Papal aggression'. His answer was that Russell had failed to provide for the material interests of the people as evidenced by 'depopulated villages, flourishing churchyards, poorhouses springing up, as the mansions of the gentry are falling down'.

Continuing in this vein the Archbishop painted Russell as the unwitting architect of a growing Catholic population in England, due to the influx of Irish Catholics. The Prime Minister was accused of a hidden agenda, stemming not from the rescript, but from his pique at 'Ireland's noble repudiation of the Infidel colleges; the consoling exhibition of the majesty of its ancient and unbroken Hierarchy in the Synod of Thurles; its firm and unconquerable resolve to erect a Catholic University'. McHale resented the synod being discussed in a hostile fashion in Westminster, and concluded that Russell was not satisfied with Caesar's portion alone but wanted a monopoly of the people's 'entire and servile devotion'. He predicted that the ministry would ignominiously fall because of its insistence in pursuing anti-Catholic legislation.

When the draft terms of this legislation were published the Archbishop was prompted to write his second public letter which was more trenchant and contained a strong personal attack upon Russell and his antecedents in Woburn Abbey as persecutors of the Catholic Church,

> Now, my lord, you appear in your genuine colours – the true and legitimate heir of the house of Russell, running the accustomed career of your sires in the hatred of the Catholic Church, by which it has been uniformly distinguished since the memorable epoch of Sir John Russell, who turned a dissolved abbey into a dwelling house and the Church into a stable. It is in the sober records of history that we can discover the true type of your persecuting policy, rather than in those fanciful effusions by

which you were early flattered, exhibiting less of the inspirations of the seer than of the poet, since you have realised the contrary of those partial predictions.

McHale put the Reformation in England in the more ancient context of state persecution of the early Church as proof that no temporal power could subdue or destroy it. He proposed that all law should be consistent with reason, liberty and conscience and the titles Bill contravened all three. In a more jocose tone he reminded the Prime Minister that in view of all the acts performed on a daily basis by the bishops using their titles, the financial penalties incurred 'would soon relieve the nation from all its financial embarrassments' and 'not all California itself would liquidate the pecuniary forfeits' which a bishop would incur 'during a moderate term of Episcopacy'. His apparent opposition to the Government was so fierce that a Conservative alternative would be more acceptable, and he regretted that Irish Catholic M.P.s failed on one occasion to join the Conservatives in a vote which would have brought the Whig Government down.

The Archbishop's Lenten Pastoral of 13 February made only a passing reference to the Bill by calling for petitions against it.[10] A similar plea was inserted into the hierarchy's March address which contained the assurance that Irish Catholic M.P.s would assert the freedom and independence of their Church and would insist that Catholics should be on an equal footing with all other subjects of the Crown.

Petitions began to pour into Parliament from both England and Ireland, not all of which, however, were against the measure. By 24 February 600 petitions signed by 130,000 English people had been forwarded in its favour and 500 signed by 150,000 people living in England were received against it.[11] Irish M.P.s presented a large number from their constituents.[12] Sadleir lodged some from Bagenalstown, Graigue, Portarlington, Cork and from the clergy of Kildare and Leighlin.[13] By May the *Freeman's Journal* reported that the number of petitions from Ireland was so great that Irish members took two hours to present them in the Commons.[14] The *Tablet* was filled with letters from prelates and priests giving details of parish meetings in various dioceses.[15]

The petitions emanated from such meetings at which the Bill was denounced especially by the Catholic priests, many of whom were also members of the Tenant League. Some were held in churches to give added emphasis to their status. One such meeting took place in the church of Saints Peter and Paul, Clonmel, in February under the chairmanship of the Mayor.[16] Michael Burke attacked the Whigs as pandering to religious bigotry in order to retain office. He signalled his strong political indictment with a promise that 'no man shall ever obtain my vote or interest in this borough or county unless he previously repudiate all connection with the unprincipled whigs'. John Baldwin, the Parish Priest of neighbouring St. Mary's, proposed a resolution calling on Tipperary M.P.s to oppose the Whigs in parliament. At a similar meeting in the church in Queenstown, Cork, Dr Power, the county member, was reprimanded for supporting the Ministry,[17] while a Donnybrook meeting protested at the 'audacious measure threatened by the Whigs for the revival of religious persecution'.[18]

A meeting of parishoners from a number of Dublin parishes, which was held in the Rotundo on Thursday 20 February,[19] differed from the others because it was organised by the laity. The Protestant Lord Miltown was the most distinguished individual present. The Leaguers John McNamara Cantwell and A.R. Stritch were also there. A series of resolutions followed, which labelled the Bill a 'mischievous, impolitic, unjust, unmerited and uncalled for persecution'. Government Ministers were charged with falsifying all the previous professions of their lives and casting doubt upon their integrity for the future. One resolution condemned the insult to Murray in particular, whose archiepiscopal title had been recognised in official documents appointing him to two royal commissions.

Lord Miltown proclaimed that he had come as a Protestant to protest against an act which was detrimental to religious liberty. His protest, however, was against the legislation being extended to Ireland, and he was more reticent about its validity in relation to England. Like other speakers he urged that their members of Parliament should 'oppose Lord John Russell, oppose Lord Stanley, oppose any Minister who might possess the power of governing, as long as he did not make the wants and wishes of Ireland his guiding principle'.

As Tenant Leaguers, both Cantwell and Stritch feared that the Bill and the controversy surrounding it would sow discord between the different religious persuasions in the League. To Stritch the 'best guarantee for the happiness and prosperity of Ireland is the union of all her sons, without distinction of class or creed.' Cantwell gave the unrealistic assurance that Catholics would defend their faith without giving offence to their Protestant countrymen. In this temper a resolution of 'warm gratitude' was drafted to the conduct of Protestants and Dissenters in Ireland, who abstained from joining in the 'furious cry of fanaticism against their Catholic fellow-countrymen'.

The meetings which took place did not result in the establishment of a network as in the case of the League, but the movement was eventually formalised. Attempts had been made in 1846 and 1849 to set up a Catholic association but had proved abortive. Rules, however, had been formulated and objectives outlined. W.J. Battersby, publisher of the *Irish Catholic Directory*, had been one of those involved and at the end of February 1851 a group consisting of members of various Dublin Christian doctrine confraternities, with Battersby as secretary, met in the Presbytery at Exchange Street and revived the idea. They published the rules and aims of the earlier still-born project as a basis for the new body.[20]

Battersby published an address on 25 February, to the 'Catholics of Ireland, England, Scotland and the colonies', tracing the history of the previous attempts to form a Catholic association, including the opposition of some bishops, because they felt that the time 'had not yet arrived for such a complete organisation'. His motto was unity of prelate, priest and people a theme he took verbatim from Wiseman's letter of 10 February

> If at any period of our history UNION has been necessary for us, it is more so than ever NOW. Let our decisions be well-matured and our actions firm and combined. Let us BE AS ONE MAN, in resisting, by every means, any new encroachments over the rights of conscience – Let us be true to each other, and steadily keep out of our counsels those who would gladly betray us to the enemies of our Faith, of our Church and of our order.[21]

A second address, this time to the hierarchy and clergy, was published by him, which recognised the importance of episcopal and clerical support to the proposed association,

> How has trodden-down Ireland maintained the clergy, built churches, asylums, schools, supported orphans and widows, and erected institutions rivalling those of the most favoured countries, even when she was frowned upon by the most wicked persecution, and discouraged by apathy equal to any that we now deplore? Because the clergy resolved that it should be so, some of the greatest movements that ever agitated a nation have succeeded with ourselves, owing to the hearty co-operation of the clergy.[22]

Battersby envisaged more than mere co-operation, and included a request for their instruction and correction, which would effectively put the organisation under the control of the bishops. The details of how it would be established laid out a hierarchy of command,

> first and mainly by the special patronage and inspection of the Catholic prelates of Ireland; next of the second order of the clergy, including the

regulars; and lastly and subordinately of the laity, acting with, and in obedience to their prelates and pastors.

The proposed association had ten aims including the defence of Catholicism abroad as well as at home.[23] It envisaged the unity of 'all classes' of Catholics and contemplated the foundation of the Guilds of St Joseph or St Patrick for the 'humbler classes' and the Wykeham and Camden Societies for the 'more favoured sons of fortune'. It would promote the foundation of libraries to cultivate literature arts and science and render them subservient to religion. In the event of emigration it promised to identify locations faraway where the facilities of the Catholic church were readily available. On an immediate level the objective was to use petitions, appeals 'and every possible means' to have grievances affecting Catholics removed and to watch and condemn any legislation 'as may affect the purity or independence of the church and its clergy'.

By coincidence on the same date that Battersby published his address, John O'Connell, in an effort to flog that dead horse further, advocated that the Loyal National Repeal Association would be a fitting organisation to resist the Ecclesiastical Titles Bill at a national level.[24] He hurriedly renamed his organisation the Loyal National Catholic and Repeal Association and asked those who were contemplating the formation of a new body to pause and consider the merits of his movement, 'which only needs general support to become almost on the instant again as powerful as it was in 1843, or as its predecessor, the old Catholic Association in 1829'. But, there was never any likelihood that O'Connell's idea would find favour, partly because repeal was unsupported as a realistic option and partly because of his own personality. Within a few weeks he was bewailing the fact that the Association was without funds and in a letter of 4 March complained that

> three years of a bitter experience of apathy, distrust, suspicion, taunt and wanton imputation, have had their climax capped by recent evidences of abandonment; in the face of which it would be the wildest absurdity, as well as the most unbecoming obstinacy, for me to attempt to continue the struggle.

Battersby's group was not faring any better and there is no evidence that Irish M.P.s had any contact with it, but they were influenced by the mass articulation of popular feeling in Ireland against the titles bill. On 28 March, following its second reading, over forty of them met to discuss the forging of a link with this extra-parliamentary agitation. They appointed a small committee consisting of Sadleir, Keogh, John

O'Connell, Torrens McCullough, and William Monsell, Limerick County, to communicate with the hierarchies of Ireland and England and to prepare amendments to render the bill harmless.[25] Sadleir was selected secretary to the Committee and lost no time in contacting the four Archbishops. His letter to Murray, written from the Albany Club on 29 March, explained the proposed *modus operandi* of the committee.[26] One objective was to hold a series of legal conferences with counsel during the coming week to analyse the impact of the bill on endowments and the spiritual functions of the clergy, and to examine every proviso and amendment which the Irish Members hoped to raise at the committee stage. Sadleir told the Archbishop that the group favoured an address by legal counsel at the bar of the House, provided that this was feasible and agreeable to the bishops.

He promised to keep Murray fully informed and asked for any suggestions the Archbishop might have. Murray's answer has not survived, but in a letter to G.H. Moore on 3 April the more abrasive McHale discussed the reply he had sent to Sadleir.[27] He approved of counsel putting the Catholic case at the bar of the House,

> deeming it calculated, if acquiesced in by the Government, to excite a strong feeling of opposition to the measure, and should it not be suffered, through the ministers' influence, which I think likely from my vague recollection of such parliamentary proposals, I thought the refusal might inspire with new life and energy, some of those, who, alas, are the ready dupes of the ministers persuasive powers.

McHale dwelt upon the importance of Irish Members obstructing the bill by all legal means, and then proceeded to ask Sadleir's assistance regarding some charities under consideration by the Lords of the Treasury. He guarded himself against the accusation of seeking political favours with the proviso that this was 'grounds of a public nature', and he signified that he would not compromise the freedom of any M.P., 'to oppose the Government on every question until they abandon their penal policy'. As a further safeguard he added a *post scriptum* warning that 'if the Irish members, especially the Catholic portion content themselves in Committee with nibbling at the bill without waging a vigorous war on the Government by every obstruction which the forms of Parliament warrant ... they will deserve the reproach of their contemporaries'.

McHale was in constant contact with Moore, who fuelled his suspicion that the resolve of Irish M.P.s was not as strong as it should be. Writing from Belgrave Square on 27 March, Moore's confidence that the bill would be well diluted by the time it became law[28] was made in the knowledge that Irish M.P.s considered obstructive opposition undesirable and would alienate the support of others. Their aim he explained in exasperation was to 'produce as respectable a minority ...as it was possible to muster'. He had yielded to this view on the understanding that following the second reading, the bill would be opposed by every means that the House would condone. He admitted that this was unpalatable to many Irish M.P.s, who would suffer 'great loss of what is called position in the House'. While not underestimating this sacrifice, he was convinced that such opposition was vital. He targeted Torrens McCullagh, Dundalk, a supporter of the Tenant League, as one of the members in favour of a 'mild and gentlemanly opposition'. Moore asked McHale for a letter supporting his stand, which he could show to 'the timid and the hesitating – at once to excite their fears and recruit their courage'.

Four days later Moore wrote to the Archbishop in a testier vein, calling McCullagh a 'Government spy', Keogh an 'expectant of office' and Sadleir 'an unscrupulous attorney looking out for place'.[29] He had no confidence in the committee of which Sadleir was a member seeing them as 'four or five quasi-lawyers', who were drawing up amendments merely to 'make a show of opposition after the deed was done'. The meeting of Irish members, who had set up the committee, had 'expressed a strong resolution against the adoption of what they were pleased to call factions opposition to the Government. In other words they renounced the intention of offering obstructive opposition....' As far as he was concerned the amendments prepared by the committee would be 'swept away like chaff before the wind', and were no more than 'flimsy amendments' prepared by a 'crew of mere fiddling pettifogging lawyers'. Part of Moore's hostility came from his exclusion from this group, and he set about establishing his own nucleus of like-minded colleagues. Earlier in March he had chaired a meeting of M.P.s and issued an address on their behalf alerting constituencies to the failure of some representatives to attend parliamentary divisions.[30]

During April opposition to the bill continued to intensify in Ireland. A group of ten Catholic M.P.s calling themselves the Catholic committee circularised the hierarchy on 19 April to sign an enclosed requisition for an aggregate meeting in Dublin. The circular gave notice of the committee's intention 'to recommend that simultaneous meetings for the same purpose should be held in all the chapels throughout Ireland on Sunday 3rd May'.[31] The representatives who signed included Sadleir, Keating and Scully.[32] The push for a conference was well advanced by then and the *Tablet* of 26 April published a demand signed by hundreds of people including twenty bishops, Members of Parliament, gentry, clergy, Poor law Guardians and Town Commissioners. Murray refused to sign on the basis that he could not attend the meeting because of his advanced age, but he applauded the plan.[33]

Reynolds, Keogh and Thomas O'Hagan were the principal organisers of this meeting and they sent petitions for signature to every part of the country.[34] At such short notice requisitions endorsing the meeting were signed by over 3,000 people, including the entire hierarchy, eleven of the leading Irish gentry, twenty-two M.P.s and all but two of the Catholic Queens Counsels. It was held on Tuesday 29 April and the *Tablet* described the atmosphere,

> The meeting was held in the Great Room of the Rotundo, which was densely crowded in every part long before the hour named for taking the chair. The extensive platform was thronged with most respectable and influential gentlemen from all parts of the country, representing the clergy, professions, mercantile and trading classes, the municipalities, magistrates, landowners etc. The Catholic portion of the bar was especially well represented by its leading and most distinguished members. Not only were the platform and reserved seats crowded to excess, but the body of the Great Room was so filled as not to leave a standing place unoccupied, and large numbers had to remain outside, not being able to obtain admission. A great many elegantly dressed ladies were accommodated in the reserve seats. Altogether, the meeting was one of the most numerous, important and influential that has ever been held in Ireland.[35]

Sadleir's business commitments prevented him from attending, but several M.P.s were there including Keogh, Reynolds and Moore. Charles Preston, son of Lord Gormanstown, was chairman, and James Burke, a Catholic barrister, one of the secretaries. Although they pledged their support in letters, which were read to the assembled crowd, not one bishop attended, but offered various excuses such as shortness of notice, illness, prior diocesan engagements, distance and old age. These may have been valid, but it is difficult to avoid the conclusion that the hierarchy as a body was reluctant to become so closely involved with the agitation.

The opening resolution was the stereotypical expression of Catholic loyalty to the Crown, but outlined their corresponding right to unrestricted religious liberty. Keogh considered the idea of Catholics insulting the Queen as preposterous – 'he should have thought that the person who offered the real insult to the sovereign of the empire was the minister who had the effrontery to propose the passing of a bill through Parliament which was calculated to insult nine million of her subjects'.

Cullens letter of 27 April, which was greeted with prolonged applause, put this more defiantly,

> We render to Caesar that which is of Caesar, and we do so through a conscientious sense of duty. The Catholics of every other country unite with us in holding the same doctrines on this point, and they are everywhere the best and firmest supporters of order and authority. But, we are not prepared to carry our respect for temporal authority so far as to commit to the ministers of any government the direction of the spiritual affairs of our consciences.

Other speakers categorised the Bill as a Cromwellian-like persecution and treated with scorn Russel's amendments lessening its severity. The measured language of Thomas O'Hagan described it as containing the 'seminal principle of a new code of exclusion'. The Young Irelander, Maurice Leyne, asked if those who professed loyalty to the so-called English constitution were satisfied with the state's reciprocation of such loyalty. If they were they should

> stigmatise as demagogues and communists the Prelates of the people, and strike the pastoral staff from their anointed hands. If you be, become bloodhounds of the Whigs and hunt the priest from the altar, the confessional, the deathbed. If you be stigmatise the mother of the crucified, and violate the consecrated abodes where her chosen ministry in virginal purity and holiness, purchase mercy for the world and its sinners. If you be, be hypocrites no more, join the brutal fanatics of England, and abjure the Faith in which you were born. Begone from amongst us.

In such an emotive atmosphere the Bill was described as the thin end of the wedge opening the way for further repressive measures. The Religious Houses Bill, supported by the much censured Drummond, was quoted as an example. It was formally condemned in a resolution by Moore and was included in the petition to parliament agreed at the meeting. Keogh was angered that the Whig administration had not immediately repudiated the bringing in of this Conservative measure.

While Russel was the main object of censure, Clarendon was singled out for criticism by Keogh. The Lord Lieutenant had been soured by the opposition of both Cullen and McHale to the Queen's Colleges, and his reference to McHale as 'an ill-disposed demagogue' and to Cullen's pastoral as containing more 'rank communism than the whole book of Professor de Vericour', was denounced by Keogh. Conversely, Graham and Aberdeen were formally thanked at the meeting. Aberdeen was a statesman with a European reputation who would 'not bow to the prejudice of the hour at the expense of the permanent interests of freedom and humanity'. He was asked to present the petition to the House of Lords,[36] and in a letter of 7 May readily agreed to do so.[37]

The petition was a tangible outcome of the debate, but several speakers were under no illusion about the successful passage of the bill through parliament. Even so the continued resistance by Irish M.P.s was seen as fundamental. Cullen's letter expressed regret that Irish M.P.s had not adopted a uniform policy and hoped that the meeting would inspire unity. Keogh endorsed this and told the delegates that 'there were men in Ireland and in England, too, who were lukewarm in their friendship and who for the sake of the newly acquired friendship of the Whig administration, were ready to forget their old friends, the people of Ireland'. It was felt that Irish M.P.s who did not oppose the Whigs should resign, and a letter was read from Denis Murphy, the Parish Priest of Kinsale, showing that Hawes, the borough member, had been asked to stand down.

Irish M.P.s were called upon to actively oppose not only the current Government but any administration which proposed or supported any anti-Catholic measure. J.D. Fitzgerald Q.C., who was to become Irish Attorney General, left no doubt that this resolution implied a severe threat to M.P.s who failed to follow it,

> They derived all their power from the people; they were bound to obey their commands. It was for that purpose they had been sent to Parliament; and they told them there that day that the greatness of the occasion superceded all other obligations, dissolved every other tie...'

While Fitzgerald was aware that Conservative support for the Bill would nullify the power of the Irish Members, there were other issues where their vote would be crucial, and he denied the opinion of some that this type of independent opposition was unconstitutional. He was supported by Moore, who considered the policy almost as a moral obligation. Moore saw this as moulding a distinct Irish party and he repeated the cliche that Irish M.P.s would 'not again be allowed to return like dogs to the vomit'. He refused to entertain the qualms of some about voting with the Conservatives. Lucas went further still, and to loud applause, read a list of M.P.s, which included Sadleir, who had on one occasion supported Tories. Nevertheless, not all were amenable to him reading a list of those who had abstained, and considerable disruption arose involving a brief altercation between himself and John O'Connell, one such absentee.

Both Lucas and Moore seriously doubted the determination of all

Irish M.P.s to pursue an independent course. Moore vigorously confronted this possibility,

> There is the voluntary servility of the soul, the appraised slavery of the menial heart, that sells itself for hire – the popular prostration, the social venality that eats into the national heart like the moth into a garment, and which in its eager, shameless, desperate and dastardly beggary, makes bondage seem honourable by its side. I protest that I regard the state of prostration into which the representation and the constitution of Ireland have fallen of late as more fatal to the national interest, and more discreditable to the national character, than our national bondage in the days of Grattan".

Inevitably the spirit of O'Connell was evoked as the exemplar of Irish political leadership and achievement. O'Hagan, although professing to differ from O'Connell in 'much and many things', acknowledged a debt of gratitude at the removal of sectarian ascendancy as a governing principle in Ireland. Keogh was more lyrical in his comments on O'Connell,

> He was gone – deeply did they deplore that he no longer led them in that great struggle for religious liberty. He was passed away from the scenes of his struggles and his triumphs; his dust reposed in the receptacle of the dead near this city, the metropolis of Ireland, *sed non in parva manes jacuere favilla nec cinis exiguus tantam compescuit umbram.*[38] Although he reposed in his tomb his spirit still animated them. Emulating his example, the Catholic people of Ireland would not submit to any oppression.

One element of this example was the formation of a Catholic Association. Leyne referred to it as 'the creation of a Titan Tribune's genius and the sceptre of his power ... which inspired life and energy into the cringing, crawling slave in whom hope had died, whom manhood had detested'. A decision was formally made to follow O'Connell's example by establishing a body similar to that suggested by Battersby, who had failed to secure episcopal backing. Cullen's letter to the meeting, however, pledged support for an association confined purely to Catholics. This was an important motivating factor, and the secretaries of the meeting were appointed to a committee, which held regular meetings at 45 Lower Sackville Street, to plan the new organisation and process the petitions coming from all over Ireland. Most of the correspondence was addressed to James Burke.

While these preparations were in progress[39] the Titles Bill moved towards the committee stage. On 9 May Sadleir seconded a motion by

Urquhart, which effectively was a vote of censure upon the Government for introducing a measure which some felt would be persecution if implemented and others a nullity because it could not be implemented.[40] The resolution was one of ridicule of the Government for allegedly encouraging the Pope to establish a diocesan structure in England and at the same time introducing a weak bill against it, which was an inadequate response to Protestant anger. The debate inevitably strayed to the Government's *de facto* recognition of Irish episcopal titles both in its correspondence and in the Bequest's Act. The Conservative Lord John Manners took this a stage further in citing the Government's inconsistency of recognising Catholic titles in the colonies and Australasian communities.[41] He took the case of Archbishop Polding of Sydney as one example. He was no doubt aware that Catholics in other parts of the British Empire knew of the controversy and sympathised with Wiseman.[42]

The harassed Home Secretary did not see official deference to titles in Ireland as transgressing any law, but merely as a manifestation of respect for the majority of Irish people.[43] He held that the passing of Urquhart's motion would negate all the proceedings so far. Sadleir denied this. He repeated his earlier claim that Russell knew very well the value of a regular hierarchy as a stronger protection of priests and people from undue Papal influence, which would be to the Government's advantage.[44] As a lawyer he thought that the Bill was 'injudicious and unwise', because it would bring the law into contempt,

> Let no man who supported the measure endeavour to solve his conscience by the plea that the Bill was of too persecuting a character to allow of ministers enforcing it. Some of the Parliamentary camp followers of the Government were whispering that the Bill, if passed, is to be allowed to remain a dead letter; and the new member for Cork had announced that it was merely a *brutum fulmen*. Such a course of proceeding was only calculated to bring legislation into contempt, especially in Ireland, where, above all places, it was desirable to inspire the people with respect for the law.

He raised a potential dilemma for the Government when he asked if the Attorney General was prepared to prosecute the Archbishop of Cashel for using his title, thereby incurring what he called official disrepute. Sadleir was also realistic in his assessment that the Government's course was foolish, because it would alienate the Catholic clergy, who were strong upholders of law and order in Ireland. He drew attention to archival material in Dublin and to reports of stipendiary magistrates, which confirmed the clergy as opponents of violence and disturbance. Sadleir challenged Grey to state what acts the hierarchy could do without incurring the £100 penalty and he appealed to 'English Gentlemen' not to deny their Roman Catholic fellow subjects the spiritual advantages that would follow from the establishment of a hierarchy. To deny them was a contradiction considering the necessity of having a similar structure for the Protestant Church. He saw another contradiction in Russell's promotion of 'Jewish Emancipation', while now denying the principles of the Catholic Emancipation Act.

Three days later on 12 May Sadleir made a brief intervention in the debate to deal with the spiritualities of the Catholic Church. He feigned surprise that the Solicitor General was unaware that ordination in the Catholic Church depended upon title and local jurisdiction. Moreover, bishops did not have the power to ordain or confirm outside the limits of their own sees,[45] while on the other hand Vicars-Apostolic ordained only as the delegates of the Pope, and not in respect of their own office. Sadleir's real intent was to raise the Government's breach of precedent by failing to refer a Bill with a religious dimension to a select committee. He hoped to use this as a legitimate way to delay its progress, but Russell was alive to his motive and used it as proof that Irish Members were pursuing a course of factious opposition.[46]

A more sophisticated dimension of such delaying tactics was the presentation of a legal opinion on the bill before the House. Later that evening the opinion of three important English lawyers – Fitzroy Kelly, who would soon be Solicitor General, P.B. Brodie and Edward Baddeley – was read.[47] This held that the assumption of titles by the English prelates was consistent with the statute of 10 George IV cap 7 sec. 24, mentioned in the preamble of the titles' Bill as being breached. The opinion was also clear that both the spiritual functions of the hierarchy and their acceptance of any emoluments or endowments in their official capacities would be rendered illegal under the first four clauses.

Russell, however, could not afford to be intimidated by such a formidable presentation and, by a large majority, the bill moved to the Committee stage. Only one Catholic M.P. from an Irish constituency supported it. This was an Englishman, Chisolm Anstey, representative for Youghal, who considered the first clause as advancing rather than retarding civil and religious liberty and reflecting the spirit in the statutes of Richard II and Edward III.[48] Much to Frank Scully's amusement, Anstey, who was not prepared to support an extension of the legislation to Ireland, declared he was representing the sentiments of thousands of English Catholics, who lacked the courage to come forward and support the statements he made in their name.

Conscious of the presence of Cardinal John Hughes, New York, in the House, Sadleir rebutted Anstey's declaration with an extract from a statement signed by a number of English Catholics, including the Earls of Shrewsbury and Newburgh, which rejected

> With the utmost scorn and indignation the imputation that we wish for any interference between our revered prelates and ourselves, or require any protection of our rights and property against them and the powers conferred by the hierarchy. We regard every attempt made to represent a penal law against our bishops as a measure passed for our benefit and at our request, as an attack upon our honour.[49]

Sadleir then moved an amendment to the first clause which would protect the spiritualities of the Catholic Church and render void Papal bills and rescripts issued for temporal purposes only. He quoted Russell's 1846 assertion that it was neither possible nor desirable to prevent the introduction of papal bills, which were absolutely necessary for the appointment of bishops and pastors. Sadleir envisaged that serious points of law would arise from the bill as it stood, which would deny justice to the Catholic Church and he reiterated the arguments of other members that even the rights of parish prints would be endangered in some basic ways. He was supported by Scully in this.

The debate continued on 26 May with some members speaking for more than an hour in their determination to slow the Bills progress.[50] In that debate Sadleir showed his awareness of official displeasure at such delaying tactics. He pointed out that, while Catholic M.P.s were a small minority of the House, they were representing the views of millions of people and 'he therefore trusted that they would hear no more of those wretched taunts in reference to that course of opposition which they had felt it their duty to take'.[51] He had again to listen to Anstey's display of anti-clericalism in his belief that the diocesan system being proposed for England was

> one of the vilest and most contemptible offshoot of Gallicanism that could be conceived. The church of Rome was a Papal and not an episcopal church, and all the recent interferences with the rights of the clergy and the laity had originated, not from the Pope, but from those about him, who desired to set up a. bastardised episcopacy in this country. If this Bill did not pass, there would be no protection for catholic bequests for charitable purposes, and the Catholic clergy and laity of this country would be exposed to the absolute control of Cardinal Wiseman, from whose tyranny they had already suffered so much and so grievously.[52]

This was a different perspective on the contrast Sadleir had drawn between bishops and vicars apostolic, but he chose not to be drawn on it concentrating instead on the legal dimension, which offered greater possibilities of delaying the Bill's progress. He challenged the Attorney General to clarify his statement that some Papal Bills were lawful and others were not, and he accused the Government of avoiding a clear statement of the law. The context here was ministerial explanations that the Bill left the law 'as it found it'. But for Sadleir this law was unclear. He supported an amendment that nothing in the Act should affect any Catholic clergymen carrying out his duties according to the usages and discipline of the Roman Catholic church as they existed prior to 29 September 1850. He rejected Government assurances that the spiritual functions of the Catholic Church would not be affected and took an example of a priest, who was prosecuted for solemnising a marriage between a Protestant and a Catholic in Ireland in spite of legislation allowing mixed marriages. He was supported by James Oswald, Glasgow, who explained that an Act of 33 George III, which abrogated the penalties of former acts against Catholics, failed to include a sixteenth century statute making the celebration of Mass in Scotland penal.[53]

The amendment was lost by a large majority,[54] but the Catholic Members, supported by some Protestants, continued to drag 'explanation after explanation, contradiction after contradiction..' from the Government benches.[55] It took until early June to pass the first clause of the Bill when one Member exclaimed in exasperation that 'in the course of a long experience he had never seen a more patient majority than the present, nor a more factious minority'.[56] But, by the third week of June the second clause passed and Sadleir's final contribution of any length was made on 20 June, when the discussion was on an amendment by William Monsell, which again tried to protect the spiritual functions of the Catholic Church.[57] Patiently William Page Wood, the Solicitor General, showed that the functions of a bishop depended neither on his title nor his ordination, but upon his consecration.[58] The object of the Bill was nothing more than to apply the principles of the Act of 1829 to a 'new description of circumstances'. He made the interesting distinction between the different interpretations of spiritual purposes, spiritual functions and spiritual jurisdictions in the Catholic Church as against the Protestant Church, where some of these were considered to be 'essentially temporal'.[59] Sadleir demurred and sought specific examples. The remainder of his contribution was no more than a reiteration of previous arguments he had put forward. This type of constant repetition and hairsplitting was a characteristic of the entire debate which by then had gone on for almost five months, causing considerable disruption to the business of the House. The Bill was finally passed by a majority of 217 votes on Friday 4 July[60] and at the end of the month was read a third time in the House of Lords.[61]

The most noteworthy feature of the Lords' debate was a lengthy criticism of the bill by Aberdeen, who, the following year, was to have a major influence on the promotion of Sadleir's political ambitions.[62] Aberdeen confirmed his refusal to take office during the ministerial crisis because of his feelings towards an illogical and intolerant measure. He reminded the Lords that as far back as 1812 William Pitt negotiated indirectly with Rome through Sir John Hippesley on the establishment of a regular hierarchy. Aberdeen also noted that successive English Governments had tolerated the Catholic religion, knowing that Catholic bishops could only be appointed by Rome. The existence of the Catholic church in England automatically implied communication with Rome and such communication could only properly be made through the recognised channels of a hierarchy. To him the titles conferred by the Pope merely facilitated this, were purely internal to the Catholic church, did not have the effect of law and could have no impact upon the country's interests.

Nevertheless, he appreciated reaction against the rescript as a demonstration of sound Protestant feeling, which had promising implications for the preservation of the Established Church and religion. But he had no sympathy with the no-Popery element of that reaction. He was in no doubt that a majority of Protestants were opposed to the 1829 Act and were equally hostile to the rescript of 1850, but 'nevertheless, in matters of this kind numbers are not infallible'. This was a remarkable effort to achieve a balanced viewpoint in the presence of the assembled Protestant bishops.

He did not, however, allow their presence to deflect him from labelling the Government's reaction both to the rescript and to the Protestant backlash against it as one of persecution. He quoted from Hallam's *Constitutional History* that there was no middle course 'between the persecution that exterminates and the toleration that satisfies'. Aberdeen saw the Titles bill as a revival of Praemunire, an obsolete statute from the reign of Richard 1, which was hardly relevant to the action of Pius, who could not be expected to acknowledge the spiritual supremacy of the Queen,

> My Lords, I desire to know how this supremacy of the Queen has been invaded. You surely cannot expect the Pope to acknowledge the Ecclesiastical supremacy of the Queen, any more than you can expect him to acknowledge your reformation. He, of course, acknowledges the temporal sovereignty of the Queen, but can, it is clear, know nothing of

her Ecclesiastical supremacy, and accordingly acts upon his own as regards the Roman Catholics of this realm. I desire, however, my lords, to know what this supremacy of the Queen is? What is it? I know, my lords, that formerly it was death to deny it. But fortunately the supremacy of the Queen is not the supremacy of Henry the Eight – the sanguinary creature who made himself pope, and assumed the whole power of the keys – that is not the supremacy of the Queen.

For the benefit of his peers, Aberdeen struggled to find a correct definition of the Queen's supremacy. He mused on the dilemma of the Protestant bishops in trying to do so when they were compiling their address to Victoria condemning the rescript. Three versions of the address were composed before they were satisfied by using the phrase 'an unwarrantable insult has been offered to the Church of Your Majesty, to whom pertaineth the chief government of all estates of this realm, whether they be Ecclesiastical or spiritual'. Another reality was the rejection of the Queen's supremacy by the Church of Scotland with the result that the the Pope could not interfere with her supremacy there, 'seeing that there is none to interfere with'.

Aberdeen was conscious of the widespread anger that the language of the rescript had kindled at all levels and displayed a balanced perception of such language,

> I must say that to complain of the arrogance of the Pope is to complain of the existence of the Pope. It is inherent in the character of the office he holds. The person who tells you he is the "Vice Regent of God upon earth" – why there can be no talk of humility in such a case, even though he calls himself *"Servus servorum Dei"*. But to those at all accustomed to the language of the Roman Catholic Court, there does not appear anything very wonderful in those expressions. The terms are made use of on all similar occasions; and as to any intention to insult the Queen or nation, it is really too preposterous to be thought of for a moment. They are the terms employed in all such instruments, on all such occasions, in all countries of Europe. In Prussia, for instance, your Lordships will find a similar expression used on a similar exercise of Papal authority; but as it is only spiritual authority, it is not considered to interfere in the least with any temporal prerogative. These terms *Gubernare et regere* are the stereotype words in all such documents.

Even, however, if the Pope offended either by such language or by the setting up a hierarchy, Aberdeen would not accept that Catholics should suffer as a result. It was illogical to persecute others for the offence of one person and there were diplomatic channels to deal with such a matter. Diplomatic relations were established with Rome in 1848 and the absence of a Papal Nuncio did not prevent communication with the Pope. He concluded a comprehensive sweep of the debate by highlighting another dimension of the Government's dilemma on the operation of the bill in Ireland. Logically it must apply there, because 'the evil of admitting that the Queen stands in a different relation to the Church of England to which she holds in Ireland would be to sign the destruction of the church in Ireland'.

His speech, while well received, did not convince his peers and the bill passed its third reading in Lords. It received the royal assent in August and the *Tablet* promised

> The expressed determination – that determination to be rigorously fulfilled – of all Ecclesiastics and of all laymen, publicly and ostentatiously to give no obedience to the law; to resist it by every peaceful and constitutional means; to go to prison, and to rot in prison, rather than bestow upon it one particle of compliance, and in the meantime, to give the legislature as little as possible of either peace to its eyes, or slumber to its eyelids, until this penal law shall be repealed; to pursue with unrelenting hostility every government that tolerates the penal law; and to make it and other cognate questions the leading and unsavoury topics of Parliamentary discussion – no matter what other business is impeded – until this foul enactment be unequivocally repealed.[63]

Despite such strong words, the editorial also contained a degree of pessimism because of the conflicting views about what action should be taken. Some felt that the bill was a dead letter and should be left as such. Lucas, however, deplored such views and contended that, it was as much a question of civil as of religious liberty. The proposed Catholic Defence Association was promoted as crucial in removing from the statute book, and from the practice and administration of law, everything that interfered with the independence of the Church and the Catholic citizen.

There was extensive public support from both the clergy and the laity for the association. This had been building since May, when letters from bishops and priests to the committee were a regular feature in the newspapers.[64] Twenty two M.P.s, Sadleir included, requested the establishment of an organisation.[65] McHale envisaged it not only organising resistance to the titles Bill, but also combating 'the enormous evils of the Established Church – evils that have too active a malignity to be demoninated a mere nuisance...'[66] Another role was the 'grave and authoritative censorship' of Irish Catholic representatives, lest they supported 'an avowedly persecuting ministry'. Michael Slattery of Cashel was the only Irish prelate who expressed some hesitation about the association, and refused to publicly identify himself with it until 'I am better acquainted with its construction and plan of action'.[67] The committee appealed for the support of Wiseman, who displayed, probably to their surprise, the same sense of caution,

> I must, however, observe, that if the association be of a political character, and aims at obtaining its object by political means, I must naturally leave it entirely in the hands of those who better understand such matters than I can do. I have rigidly adhered through life to the rule of confining my small share of activity to my Ecclesiastical and spiritual duties, which are more than sufficient to exhaust my time and strength.[68]

Early in June Irish M.P.s were contacted to attend the launch of the Association, but Frank Scully explained that the recess was too short to allow time to travel to Dublin.[69] Then a dispute arose between Lucas and Duffy concerning the wisdom of a public meeting for the launch. Duffy never favoured the proposed organisation and disliked any major show of support. Lucas retaliated with his customary sarcasm contrasting his own presence at the committee meetings with Duffy's absence.[70] Accusing the *Nation* of espousing the philosophy of the tailors of Tooley Street, was not a serious insult, but it did not augur well for harmony within either the association or the league.

Any doubt about the feasibility of holding an aggregate meeting, however, was dispelled by a letter of 30 June from Cullen offering to assist at the meeting.[71] In mid July Lucas published a list of those requesting the launch. This ran to three pages and included the hierarchy, Members of Parliament, nobility, magistrates, gentry, clergy and leading laity.[72] It was clear proof of massive support for a Catholic association.

Intent on further increasing this support and arousing opposition to the Whigs in the next general election, Lucas tried to convince his lay readers that the new bill would have as great an impact upon them as upon their clergy. Despite the loud hints of Sir George Grey that the measure was little more than a cosmetic exercise, Lucas applied it to the material prospects of the laity, using as emotive a vocabulary as he could summon,

> Their children will marry and be married, but the marriage will be null before a Catholic priest. The children of such marriage will be bastards in law, and the 'next Protestant heir' will step in and possess himself of another's inheritance by favour of the Whigs. This bill concerns the laity more than it does the Bishops and their Priests. The Bishops may go to prison, but the lay people, who are now married throughout England, Ireland, and Scotland have, according to this bill, become the parents, not of heirs and legitimate offspring, but of bastards, who may be

dispossessed, and turned into the world penniless and homeless, as memorials of Whig affection for the Church.[73]

Lucas was hardly convinced that this would arise, but such statements were typical of the angry rhetoric of the religious debate. This rhetoric diverted attention from the agrarian movement, which, however, had an network that extended to sixteen counties, although the spread within each county was patchy. While the religious question dominated attention the League continued to organise this network and promote the relative importance of its policies and aims. Meetings of local societies were regularly reported and periodic public conferences were held to keep the issue before the Irish people.[74] An important one was held in January 1851 at the racecourse in Downpatrick.[75] A large contingent of southern leaguers, both lay and clerical, travelled to meet their northern Presbyterian counterparts in a show of unity, which contrasted with the animosities aroused by the religious issue. Thomas O'Shea, O'Keeffee's fellow curate in Callan, and Archdeacon Fitzgerald, Rathkeale, county Limerick, a leading tenant righter, came to show their solidarity.

One purpose of this assembly was to demonstrate the strength of the League and the Presbyterian minister J. McCready of Saintfield, County Down, portrayed it as 'a triumphant answer to those who had predicted that the tenant right agitation was over – that the league was completely dissolved'.

The League responded with a general meeting in the Music Hall, Lower Abbey Street, towards the end of the month, which in turn was attended by Northern Leaguers, most of whom had been at Downpatrick.[76] This time speakers did comment on the danger of division in League ranks, especially between the Presbyterian North and the Catholic South, because of the religious controversy. William Cahill, the curate of Mullinahone, County Tipperary, depicted Lord John Russell as trying to kill the infant league in its cradle by introducing religious discord in the form of the Ecclesiastical Titles Bill, 'a fetid abortion dropped from a prying mind'. Cahill was confident however that unity would be preserved in spite of the fact that

> English statesmen have always attached a wonderful efficacy to those firm words 'Down with the Pope'. Like Holloway's pills, they have considered them a panacea for all the complaints, both social and political, which afflict poor Ireland. Lord John, too, has tried his hand, like some quacks who went before him. He heard us complain of our misery and distress, and to cure our disease he treated us to his pills called 'Down with the Pope'. They did not go down so meekly as of old; we split them up in the North and South; he may put them in his pocket

and burn his pill box... yes down with the Pope, but will that revive the six hundred victims that were flung stark and putrid into one monster grave in Skibbereen? Yes down with the Pope, but will that bring back the hundreds of thousands which famine and pestilence have swept into the tomb? Yes down with the Pope, but will that raise up from their crumbled ruins the 17,865 houses, which the extermination in two short years has levelled to the dust? Yes down with the Pope, but will that give suck to the withered breast which hunger has dried up and which the starving infant draws in vain?

Cahill was supported by the Reverend B. Meyler, a Presbyterian Minister, who, in less metaphorical terms, pledged that nothing would interrupt 'the long designed union of creeds and classes', which characterised the land movement. McCready backed this emphasis on unity of creeds and determination to succeed by quoting the words of 'a nigger poet' to 'go on, go on, go on, go on'. Another northern delegate, the Reverend McCullough, conceded, however, that there was some opposition there to Presbyterian Ministers joining forces with Catholic priests. This he categorised as mistaken, because such collaboration did not endanger the religion of any church, being part of a universal Christian ministry to defend right against oppression. This was endorsed by Thomas O'Keeffe as a duty of charity. The priests saw their own role as crucial. Archdeacon Fitzgerald was almost biblical in his emphasis upon it, and drew an unfortunate analogy between himself and Bartholomew Las Cases, who had ministered to the natives of Hispaniola, exploited by the Spanish in the Sixteenth century. He was confident that every parish in Ireland would soon have a Las Cases. There was an interesting irony in his ignorance of the fact that Las Cases had suggested the bringing of African Negroes to Hispaniola on the basis that they were better capable of withstanding the rigours of the Spanish regime. In this way he hoped to save the indigenous people there, but was an unwitting exponent of black slavery. This irony was further compounded by the revelation of McCullough that he intended going to America where he hoped to 'have the honour of advocating the right of the black slave to freedom'.

But, these images of slavery and starvation were important as an emotional alternative to the titles Act. Famine and eviction themes were developed by drawing on personal experiences. The Reverend John Renteul told the audience that he had travelled from the north to see the evidence for himself. While in the west of Ireland he witnessed houses burned, and people sitting on the roadside 'in the dark cold nights of winter'. Archdeacon Fitzgerald recalled poignant examples among his own parishoners,

He could tell them that he saw as beautiful and modest a woman as ever lived, the wife of a respectable farmer, hunted from her farm, and obliged to take refuge in the mud-built village of Ballingarry, where she lay in a room occupied by twenty persons labouring under diarrhoea; he could tell them of persons who died with nothing but rags to cover them, and of a dozen inquests in a few weeks, one of which, where a man died from starvation was so bad as regarded the conduct of those by whom he should have been relieved, that he caused the inquest to be adjourned – a hunt passed by at the time, and everyone present, except the Coroner and himself, went after the hunt, and left the corpse of the famished man, as if his death was not an incident at which humanity should have recoiled.

Famine rhetoric was all very well for publicity purposes, but the real task was to prepare for the approaching general election. The first principle was to secure a commitment from candidates to give the land question priority in Westminster, A suitable climate of opinion could not be created by publicity alone, but by concrete preparations on the ground. McCready recommended that every elector should be visited by local Leaguers 'and exhorted to do his duty by his country and by his children'. O'Keeffe was harder in his certainty that no candidate in County Kilkenny would dare offer himself except on the principles of the Tenant League.

But, as preparations to establish the Catholic Defence Association progressed some Leaguers felt threatened that the new organisation might undermine the League and monopolise the election platform. Lucas, as the owner of a Catholic newspaper, had to thread warily, but he sought to reassure them that 'the two movements are there before you, both founded in justice, both demanding your support, and both pressing their claims upon you with a strength which cannot be denied or evaded'.[77]

Nevertheless, by mid-May he admitted that the 'interests of the tenant farmers of Ireland have suffered in some degree by the agitation in defence of religious liberty'.[78] But he was pleased that the League was unaffected by religious discord. Moreover, he agreed with the priorities that had emerged – 'Christian men first defend their altars, and then strike for their homes'. He saw, nonetheless, that both were closely related, since the preservation of the Catholic flock was central to the well-being of the Church. For the moment the agrarian struggle was merely put in abeyance until the religious one had concluded. The other league leaders did not share this view. The Council decided that a more energetic approach was appropriate and increased its profile by holding weekly rather than monthly meetings. It also made a decision to establish a monthly publication called The *Irish Tenant League* which would explain details of policy and aims, report progress and discuss land tenures. In May Lucas and McKnight went to London to meet Sharman Crawford and consider the promotion of the land question in Westminster.

Despite the fact that discussions had to be temporarily suspended when Crawford's son Frederick died suddenly on 17 May, considerable progress was made and broad, but not final, agreement was reached on the League's proposals for a land bill. This proposal was based on an amendment of Crawford's bill. It contained five sections dealing with compensation for improvements, consequential damages in case of eviction, and leases either in perpetuity or of moderate length.

Lucas gave details of this at a public meeting of the League in the Mechanics' institute, Lower Abbey Street on 2 June.[79] He admitted that while in London the argument had been put to him that legislation could not bring about a settlement of landlord tenant difficulties. But, precedents in other countries proved otherwise and he cited Prussia, Silesia, Bohemia, Germany and France as examples. The Reverend David Bell praised the progress of the negotiations with Crawford which strengthened the latter's bill, which, however, Bell saw as but an instalment. He proposed the motion that ultimately only legislation containing the full principles of the League would satisfactorily solve the land question. At the same time he stressed that serious differences of opinion did not exist between the Leagues policies and those of Crawford.

During the early weeks of July Irish representatives joined Crawford and the Leaguers, and agreement was reached that the bill would be supported by them at the next session.[80] The newspapers were optimistic that the Government would process some measure favourable to the Irish tenantry. The *Tablet* heralded the existence of 'three things, which we never had before ... a Bill, a party, and an organised support to this Bill and the party in the four provinces of Ireland'.[81]

The optimism of Lucas was increased by a more academic event in July 1851. This was a book on the land question by Vincent Scully, which was reviewed in the *Tablet*.[82] To Lucas it was a hopeful sign that another landlord besides Crawford should recognise that 'conventional rights ... must yield to the altered position of affairs, while the right that those who cultivate the soil shall live on it, and by it, is indestructible'. Both Lucas and Duffy saw Scully's defence of landlord and tenant rights as compatible with the League's aims and described him as an ally of the League. Scully, like Crawford and the Leaguers, advocated legislation to bring about perpetuity of tenure and fair rent. He outlined a scheme of land reform which included a system of land certificates regulated by a land tribunal which would facilitate the eventual purchase of his farm by the occupier. This contrasted with Sadleir's dislike of peasant proprietorship. Like his cousin, however, Scully considered the legal complexity of land tenure as one of the greatest scourges of Irish society.

Crawford shared this view and his proposal did not envisage adding to such complexity. In a letter of 11 July to the organisers of a tenant right rally near the Boyne, he pledged his commitment to pushing a measure as early as possible in the next session, adding that he would keep the bill as simple as possible to maximise its chances of success.[83] The organisers of the Boyne meeting forwarded a petition to parliament on the serious depopulation of Ireland and the need for legislation to protect tenants against unjust evictions and unfair rents. Patrick Quaid, the Parish Priest of O'Callaghan's Mills, County Clare, had heard a rumour that Lord John Russell had serious doubts about bringing in a landlord and tenant bill, but was convinced that a united front would force Russell, 'a living inconsistency', to concede some measure.

Unity was the dominant theme on the Boyne. The location was seen as highly symbolic and the gathering a reversal of 1690 when Irishmen had faced each other in battle. Thomas Montgomery of Aughnacloy in County Tyrone was conscious of this when

> he had left his home that morning in the very heart of Tyrone, some seventy or eighty miles distant, to be present at the union of North and South on the banks of the Boyne. On the 12th of July they used to have demonstrations in the North, to celebrate the battle of the Boyne; but he was happy to say that no such thing took place on Saturday. In fact the whole province was prepared to join heart and soul with the other three provinces for the achievement of the great object all had in view.

But, behind the rhetoric there was dissatisfaction at the League's progress. Patrick Bannon, the parish priest of Louth, expressed regret that it had not received more support in that parish. Comparable sentiments were aired the following day at the weekly meeting of the Tenant League, which reviewed the importance of the Boyne meeting in keeping the land question at the top of the socio-political agenda in Ireland. Archdeacon Fitzgerald questioned the commitment of the priests and seemed genuinely astonished that they were not more alive to 'the wholesale destruction and misery of the people'.[84] In the context of the titles Bill, he had no difficulty in airing his priorities,

> A Catholic University and a Defence Association are no doubt lofty and praiseworthy objects of pursuit, but more lofty and more noble still the

aim to rescue a people from destruction, and a national Church from utter exclusion by the death, and banishment, and horrible emaciation of Catholic millions – the exclusive victims of landlord power for evil in Ireland.

This was a significant public marker coming from a formal Council meeting, and a declaration that henceforth dedicated Leaguers should show no ambivalence in voicing political priorities. It reflected the realistic implication that the Ecclesiastical Titles Act was no more than a statute which would never be invoked in Ireland, where emigration was affecting the Church in a more concrete sense.

References

1. *Tablet* 1 March 1851.
2. D.D.A. Murray Papers, Carton 32/6. *The address of the Catholic Archbishops and Bishops of Ireland to their beloved flocks on the Penal Enactment to which is added an appendix containing the opinions of Thomas O'Hagan, Q.C.*, (Dublin, 1851), (O'Hagan's analysis was also published in the *Tablet* 8 March 1851 and the *Irish Catholic Directory*, 1852, pp 153-155).
3. William Keogh later succeeded in removing this threat from the Bill.
4. *Parl. Deb.*, series 3, vol.115, 1851, cols. 462-463, (24 March 1851).
5. Scully's opinion in Irish *Catholic Catholic Directory* ,1852, pp 131-132.
6. Address 1 March 1851 in *F.J.* 12 March 1851, *Tablet* 8 March 1851.
7. *Tablet* 15 March 1851.
8. Pastoral in *Tablet* 22 February 1851, *Irish Catholic Directory,* 1852, pp 125-126.
9. *Tablet* 1, 15 March 1851.
10. Text in ibid., 22 February 1851.
11. Statement of John Reynolds in *Parl. Deb.*, series 3, vol.114, 1851, cols.1079-1080, (3 March 1851).
12. The *Tablet* of January, February, March 1851 reported these.
13. Ibid., 8, 22 and 29 March 1851.
14. *F.J.* 17 May 1851.
15. e.g. *Tablet* 17 May 1851, letters from Bishop Kelly, Bishop McGettigan, Raphoe; Bishop Derry, Clonfert; Bishop Keane, Ross, Daniel Vaughan, Vicar-Capitular, Killaloe; the same edition had letters from Drumshambo, Athboy, Ferns, Gorey, Templemore, Shillelagh, Castlepollard, Kinnegad, Cashel, Dunboyne. Ibid., also reported meetings in Lisburn, Ballina, Lismore, Dunmanway, Wexford. Ibid., 24 May 1851 listed meetings in 115 parishes.
16. *Tablet* 1 March 1851 *T.F.P.* 19 February 1851.
17. Ibid. .
18. Ibid., For other meetings see *Tablet* 22 February 1851 (Dundalk, Mullingar); ibid., 1 March 1851 (Sligo, Roscommon, Tuam, Tralee, Drogheda (quoted a long letter from Archbishop Cullen); ibid., 8 March 1851(Limerick, Belfast, Rathmines, Douglas, Cork, Urlingford, Co. Kilkenny, Tralee), ibid.,15 March 1851 (Waterford, Galway, Iniskeen, Co. Monaghan).
19. Ibid., 22 February 1851.
20. D.D.A., C.P., Carton 33/. *The Addresses, and Rules of the Catholic Defence Association (solely for Catholic purposes) as unanimously proposed and formed at*

meetings of clergymen and laymen held in Dublin, April and May 1849 and February 21st and 25th 1851, (Dublin, 1851).

21. Ibid., p. 5.
22. Ibid., p. 9.
23. Ibid,. pp 14-15.
24. Letter 25 February 1851 in *Tablet* 1 March 1851.
25. Ibid., 29 March 1851.
26. D.D.A. Murray Papers, letter 33/1, 29 March 1851.
27. N.L.I., Moore Papers, MS. 891, McHale to Moore 3 April 1851.
28. Ibid., Moore to McHale 27 March 1851.
29. Ibid., Moore to McHale 31 March 1851.
30. *Tablet* 8 March 1851.
31. Circular in K.D.A., H.P., FH/1851/04, carton Bp 11.
32. The others were Keogh, Reynolds, Maher, O'Flaherty, O'Brien (Limerick), Higgins and James Fagan (Wexford).
33. Letter 25 April 1851 in *Tablet* 26 April 1851.
34. e.g. ibid., 26 April 1851 – letters from the Mayor of Wexford, Thomas O'Shea, the Callan curate, The Mayor of Waterford, Chairman of Kells Town Commissioners. The Mayor of Clonmel, the Mayor of Kilkenny etc.
35. Ibid., 3 May 1851. (The *Tablet* had a four page supplement on the meeting).
36. Reynolds was chosen to present it to the House of Commons.
37. *Tablet* 10 May 1851. This edition also carried a letter from Graham acknowledging the meeting's vote of thanks to him.
38. 'But the spirit has not resided in a little ember nor has meagre ash contained so great a shade'.
39. e.g. *Tablet* 17 May 1851.
40. *Parl. Deb.*, series 3, vol.116 1851, col.787, (9 May 1851).
41. Ibid., col.795, (9 May 1851).
42. *Tablet* 7 June 1851.
43. *Parl. Deb.*, series 3, vol.116, 1851, col.790, (9 May 1851).
44. His statement in ibid., cols. 799-803.
45. Ibid., col. 885, (12 May 1851).
46. Ibid., col. 889.
47. Quoted in full in *Tablet* 17 May 1851.
48. *Parl. Deb.*, series 3, vol.116, 1851, cols. 1372-1373, (23 May 1851).
49. His speeches in ibid., cols. 1374-1375 and 1381-1383.
50. See Russell's statement to this effect in ibid., col.1452.
51. His statement in ibid., cols. 1455-1457.
52. Ibid., col.1451.
53. Ibid., cols. 1457-1458.
54. *Tablet* 31 May 1851.
55. Ibid., 7 June 1851.
56. Ibid., 14 June 1851.
57. Sadleir's speech in *Parl. Deb.*, series 3, vol.117, 1851, cols. 1014-1015, (20 June 1851).
58. Ibid., col.1012.
59. col. 1013.
60. *Tablet* 12 July 1851.
61. Ibid., 2 August 1851.
62. Aberdeen's speech reported in *Parl. Deb.*, series 3, vol. 118, cols. 1072 et.seq., (21 July 1851).

63. Ibid., 2 August 1851.
64. e.g. *Tablet* 31 May 1851 – letters from Archbishop McHale; Daniel Vaughan Vicar Capitular Killaloe; Bishops Cantwell Meath; O'Higgins Ardagh; Keane, Ross; Tablet 7 June 1851 – Bishops Derry, Clonfert; Kelly, Derry; Ibid., 28 June 1851, Bishops Blake, Dromore, Feeney; Delaney Cork; see also *F.J.* 17 and 18 June 1851 – Bishops Foran, Waterford; McGettigan, Raphoe; McNally, Clogher; Egan, Kerry; The *Tablet* and *Freeman's Journal* for July contained lists of names in almost every edition.
65. Names in the *Tablet* 21 June 1851.
66. Ibid., 31 May 1851.
67. Ibid.
68. Ibid., 7 June 1851.
69. Letter in ibid. This edition also carried letters from John Reynolds, Anthony O'Flaherty and Nicholas V. Maher.
70. *Tablet* 21 and 28 June 1851. Apart from disagreement over the public meeting, Duffy in an editorial of 14 June 1851 was skeptical of the relevance of a defence association at a time when the bill had progressed a considerable distance through parliament. To him the best defence was the total abandonment of all relations with the government. He traced Irish ills to the allegedly close relationship between Irish leaders, lay and clerical, with the Whigs. Duffy placed little heed in the oratory of denunciation of the Whigs – 'speeches are rumbling wind, but the deliberate acts of the Catholic orators travelled quite another road; and in the very tempest and whirlwind of passion, we have no doubt many of them were longing for the happy time when all this unfortunate hubbub would be over, and they and their Whig friends close cronies again'. Duffy's examination of the list of members promoting the Association convinced him that it would be an ineffective organisation.
71. Ibid., 5 July 1851.
72. Ibid., 19 July 1851. See also *F.J.* 19 July 1851.
73. *Tablet* 12 July 1851.
74. Ibid. 25 January 1851.
75. Ibid 11 January 1851.
76. *F.J.* 24 January 1851, *Tablet* 25 January 1851. Among those present were Lucas, Duffy, Archdeacon Fitzgerald, A.R. Stritch, Maurice Leyne, W.J. Battersby, John Hackett, Clonmel. The Northern delegation consisted of Samuel S. Greer, John J. Hughes, Ballybay, David Bell P. M., Ballybay, Fr. Good c.c. Ballybay, Dr. McKnight, John Rogers P. M. Saintfield, Rev. Kinnear P. M. Letterkenny, J.M. McCullagh P. M., Newtownardes, Thomas McCullagh P. M. Ballysillam, William Girdwood, solicitor, Lurgan. J. Godkin, editor of the *Londonderry Standard*, J.J.Hughes, Ballybay.
77. Ibid., 8 March 1851.
78. Ibid., 17 May 1851.
79. Ibid., 7 June 1851.
80. Ibid., 19 July 1851.
81. Ibid.
82. Vincent Scully, *The Irish Land Question, with practical plans for an improved land tenure and a new land system*, (Dublin, 1851), was reviewed in the *Nation* 28 June 1851 in which Duffy devoted his editorial space to the review. It was reviewed in the *Tablet* 5, 12 July 1851. (Scully later published another work entitled *Free Trade in Land Explained* – See N.L.I., Scully Papers, MSS. 27,562 for folders of letters from such individuals as Russell, Graham and Clarendon briefly

acknowledging receipt of copies and diplomatically praising the contents). (Ironically some weeks prior to the publication of the first work a public controversy was going on between a Young Irelander, Joseph O'Grady, and Vincent Scully's brother Rodolph who had evicted several tenants on his Ballyneale estate near Carrick-on-Suir. The *Nation* 7 June 1851 carried one of O'Grady's letters denouncing Scully and describing the aftermath of the evictions,

> I proceeded to Ballyneale on Sunday last to collect the necessary evidence. The scene of the evictions affords a melancholy illustration of the overwhelming quota which landlord power in Ireland may contribute to the aggregate of human woe. Whilst standing in the rude sheds, and trembling with sympathy and with indignation as I listened to the passionate wailing of the widowed mother, softened by the tender and soothing condolence of her intelligent and interesting children, I felt painfully impressed with a conviction of the criminal injustice of the laws which crowns the wholesale exterminator with all the advantage and all the eclat of success, whilst they consign his avenging victim to the gallows.

This was in response to Scully's letter in the previous edition at the end of May which in turn had denied the assertions of O'Grady's first letter on the issue. The files of the *Nation* in Colindale, however, do not contain this earlier correspondence).

83.   *Tablet* 19 July 1851. This reported the Boyne meeting. See also *Nation* 28 June 1851.

84.   *Tablet* 19 July 1851.

Presentation of address against papal aggession (*Illustrated London News*, Dec. 28 (1850)).

Chapter 6

The Catholic Defence Association and the Tenant League, an uneasy relationship – August 1851-January 1852

The Parliamentary recess signalled the return to Ireland of the Brigadiers in the Summer of 1851. Sadleir took up residence in Great Denmark Street and joined a small group of M.P.s who immediately became the focus of the campaign to establish the Catholic Defence Association. In August a sub-committee of Sadleir, Keogh and Reynolds was appointed to prepare resolutions for the launch and draw up an address to 'the friends of religious freedom' for consideration by the General Committee.[1] Sadleir was also appointed one of three joint-treasurers to manage the subscriptions for the Association.[2] This became known as the Catholic Rent.

The conference to launch the Association was scheduled for 19 August and a major Tenant League conference was planned for 21 August. But, prior to this a public disagreement once more surfaced between Lucas and Duffy, which threw light on prevailing priorities and tensions within the leadership of the League. Evidence of widespread public approval of the Association combined with support for it among the Irish and English hierarchies forced Duffy to couch his reservations in more subdued and logical arguments. A *Nation* editorial early in August expressed approval of the Association as a means of guarding Catholic interests and protecting any prelate in the event of prosecution under the new legislation.[3] Ideally, therefore, the organisation should be no more than a reactive mechanism rather than an 'organised and habitual agitation' meeting on a regular basis. What Duffy feared was an organisation which competed with the Tenant League for funds and personnel. To him the religious question had run its course and more urgent needs such as evictions should be addressed. His thesis was that 'a people cannot be impregnated with two ideas at a time; they cannot follow two agitations'. The best guarantee for preserving religious liberty was to preserve the people.

He was also worried that frequent meetings of a Catholic Association might provide a platform for 'the bigotry of shallow spouters', which would damage relations between the Catholic and Presbyterian elements in the League. The union of north and south was 'a more formidable fact to England than the coronation of Cardinal Wiseman'. Ignoring the instinct of investors to make profit, he concluded his editorial with the argument that expressions of bigotry would also alienate Irish Conservatives, who were promoting manufacture and 'other social projects'. In brief, the Council of the Defence Association should only meet occasionally and for specific business. Lucas could hardly disagree with much of this reasoning and conceded that many in the religious movement saw the sense in Duffy's theory, but he felt that their cause was the urgent one.[4] More divisive, however, was Lucas's point that the most serious obstacle to the agrarian movement was the Young Ireland element in the Council, which aroused the suspicion of many would be members and alienated a large body of priests,

> throughout the rest of the three provinces the great obstacle to the success of the League has been the remembrance of the events of 1848, dangers anticipated from local societies from the remembrance of the clubs; the unforgotten policy of the *Nation* in past years on questions connected with religion; the dread that any support given to a widespread organisation, in which Young Irelandism appears to have a predominance, will ultimately tend to the strengthening of Young Ireland principles in Church, and State, and Society; and, finally all these things, deep-rooted aversion for the men who appear as the representatives of those by-gone acts, and (as it is dreaded), of those yet living principles.

Lucas did not think that the spirit of Young Irelandism was extinct. He felt that the *Nation*, as the organ of this political outlook, was being true to form and wrote that many people believed it to be but a 'lukewarm friend' of the Church in its hour of danger. As a leading Leaguer it did not seem to strike him that his public identification of Young Irelandism with the League would sharpen clerical suspicion of it even more. This was unquestionably true of the bishops, who were increasingly involved with the move to set up a Catholic Association. They gave public testimony to this by their presence at its launch in the Round Room of the Rotundo on Tuesday 19 August.[5]

The *Tablet* regarded the occasion as 'perhaps the most extraordinary demonstration of public feeling and sentiment that ever was elicited, or that possibly could be conceived'. Crowds gathered in the surrounding streets from eight o'clock in the morning to get a glimpse of the dignitaries, who were to arrive several hours later. Hundreds of police were in evidence. They were assisted by several thousand quay men or porters, who lined the sides of Sackville Street.

The *Freeman's Journal* described the scene in the Round Room,

> Long before the hour appointed for taking the chair, the platform became crowded with the gentry and clergy from every part of the United Kingdom, and the body of the Room with many of our fellow-citizens and of the Catholics, who had assembled from every part of Ireland to be present at the meeting, while the reserved seats were occupied to a great extent with ladies, whose anxiety to be present at the meeting made them disregard the inconvenience to which they were unavoidably subjected. Although the Round Room was crowded in every part to excess, the vast assembly was as decorous and orderly as the meeting of any private committee. The platform was elevated at a considerable height; in front were arranged arm chairs for the Prelates, and at the head of the table prepared for the secretaries was the gilded chair for the Lord Primate.

Cullen and McHale led the procession of bishops, who included Michael Slattery of Cashel, Charles McNally, Clogher, G.J. Browne, Elphin, Daniel Vaughan, Killaloe, John Derry,Clonfert, Timothy Murphy, Cloyne, Ullathorne, Birmingham, the coadjutor Bishop of the Eastern District of Scotland, the Bishops of Hyderabad and Saldes, Savannah, Georgia, in the United. States. Hundreds of priests were present including T.W. Croke, parish priest of Charleville, and Patrick Leahy, President of St Patrick's College, Thurles, both destined to become Archbishops of Cashel, Archdeacon Fitzgerald, Dean Coll, Limerick, Tobias Kirby, President of the Irish College, Rome, Dr Magee, Parish Priest, Westminster, the Abbe Crevin, Paris, and J. Duggan, St Louis, Missouri. Among the laity were Lord Gormanstown, Sir Piers Mostyn, Charles Bianconi, Sergeant Shee, the mayors of Waterford and Limerick and thirteen M.P.s including Scully and Keating.[6] Also present were Vincent Scully and Leonard Morrogh. Sadleir was one of the three joint secretaries.

Cullen set the tone of the meeting and put down a marker on his perception of the Association's role. Although the movement was permeated by politicians, he chose not to see it as a political one, but as 'a great manifestation of Catholic feeling in favour of the liberty of our holy Church – a manifestation that has the strongest claim to be guided by the voice, and sanctified by the prayers and blessings of the priests of the Most High.' He disliked political involvement by priests and was correspondingly careful to define his own role as non-political, but as part of his 'ecclesiastical duty'.

While he made the usual observations about the titles Act, Cullen was more intent on using the platform to refocus the public debate upon 'a more subtle form of subversion', the education system. He wanted this to be a central part of the Association's agenda,

Our poor are to be protected from a heartless proselytism – the Faith of the children of the soldier and the sailor is to be preserved – the state of our workhouses is to be examined – a Catholic education is to be obtained for our people. In a Catholic country like this there is a great and perfectly organised system of Protestant instruction. Hundreds of thousands are expended in promoting a purely Protestant education, whilst the sums given to Catholic schools (with one exception) are given only on the condition that the system of the schools, which are filled with Catholic children, shall be suited to the education of children of every sect who do not frequent such schools, and we are left without any Catholic University.

In a pragmatic conclusion Cullen urged that the Association should 'have recourse to the press, and send forth clear expositions of our wrongs and a powerful defence of our just claims'. While downplaying the political nature of the organisation, he nonetheless saw its function as endeavouring to have Catholic interests properly represented in Parliament, and cited Count Montalembert and Viscount De Falloux as French examples of Catholic politicians *par excellence.*

Since Cullen and the hierarchy had sought Vincent Scully's opinion on the Bill, he was given the platform to make a brief statement, and, despite their private differences on the management of the Tipperary bank, did not forget to mention Sadleir's zeal in Westminster in opposing the bill. Speaking as a lawyer who had studied the bill Scully condemned it as the 'most atrocious invasion of their rights and privileges as Catholics that had ever been framed since the time of Henry VIII'. Like Cullen, he defended the presence of the bishops because the Bill was 'peculiarly directed to attack, invade and abolish' their jurisdiction.

McHale, who received a standing ovation, felt no need to explain his presence at the meeting. He proposed the distinctly political motion that the current ministry had forfeited the confidence of the Catholics of the United Kingdom. He was almost medieval in his assertion of the superiority of episcopal titles over secular ones, which were as 'transient as they are dazzling'. He told his audience that the Prime Minister little understood

the deep-seated reverence of the faithful for their hierarchy, when he foretold, in his capacity of a deluded seer, that the people would witness without emotions the operation of this bill of divorce which attempted to separate the Bishops from their wedded Sees, leaving those sees in a state of perpetual widowhood, and their flocks in a state of spiritual orphanage, and the Bishops themselves despoiled of the prescriptive honour of eighteen centuries, doomed to go on a roving commission for the discovery of new settlements – the companions of the countless thousands of their exiled countrymen whom his cruel policy has expatriated far beyond the pale of his delegated power.

McHale's penchant for the dramatic was shared by Keogh, who had been made a Queen's Counsel in 1849, and was liable 'to be stripped of my gown, because I gave to the Bishop of my Church a title, which no act of Parliament can destroy'. He held up a copy of the Ecclesiastical Titles Bill and ostentatiously accorded 'to this most Reverend Prelate the title of Lord Archbishop of Armagh'.

In view of his future political career, Keogh's emphasis on a united Irish party was the most significant element of his statement. Despite Moore's fears, Keogh was specific that this party of thirty or forty representatives should be

> determined to stand together as one man and to say to the Minister of the day, we require such and such measures for the people of Ireland, and we require above all and before all, the Repeal of this penal measure – if your representatives say, we will have no terms with any Minister, no matter who he may be, until he repeals that act of Parliament, and every other which places the Roman Catholic lower on a platform than his Protestant fellow subjects....

Reynolds and Moore were the other principal lay speakers. Reynolds was sensitive to the strong Protestant sector in his Dublin constituency, and attempted to square the sectarian circle on this Catholic platform. As an O'Connellite he recalled Protestant support for Catholic Emancipation as proof that many Protestants would not approve of the titles Act. He informed the assembly that Sadleir and himself had secured the legal opinions of Edward Badeley,[7] an ecclesiastical lawyer, and Vincent Scully on the Act, both of whom concurred that bishops could not legally discharge their ecclesiastical duties without fine. Sadleir, Keogh, Anthony O'Flaherty and himself had decided to visit the various constituencies throughout the country during the Autumn to encourage voter insistence that their representatives would unite and 'send the present political hacks and slaves about their business'.

A noteworthy aspect of Moore's presentation was the two clashes between himself and Cullen during its delivery. The Archbishop was provoked by the Mayo M.P.'s illustration of the contradiction between the approval by the British press of the 1844 rescript condemning political involvement by priests[8] and its denunciation of the 1850 rescript establishing the English hierarchy. Moore was simply explaining the recognition of Papal authority in one case and its denial in the other, but the sensitive Cullen only saw the insinuation that the

Pope might be 'inimical to civil liberty'. Moore refused to be intimidated and proceeded to warn of the danger of insurrection at some stage if England's current policy continued. As he cited examples of European rebellion the Archbishop again rebuked him with the assertion that

> even if it was in their power, the Irish people were so attached to their sovereign, that instead of violating their allegiance, they would do everything they could to protect her on the throne. They were sincerely attached to their sovereign, and they had been always so, and they were ready to manifest that respect even when persecuting laws were enacted against them.

Moore's explanation that similar words by him were not censured in the House of Commons was brushed aside by Cullen, who objected to statements contrary to Catholic doctrine being made to a Catholic meeting. Moore, by no means an advocate of revolution, did not give ground and persisted with his example that 'Catholic Belgium did rise in insurrection. Catholic Belgium succeeded and religious liberty was established'.

As one of the secretaries, Sadleir was unable to join in the discussion and was confined to reading some of the correspondence, which included a letter from Wiseman supporting the establishment of the Association under the 'superintendence' of Cullen. He was, however, elected to a committee to define the Association's aims and frame its rules and constitution for approval at the next meeting. This was a cumbersome body of twenty-nine prelates, English and Irish, and seventeen members of Parliament,[9] whose meetings were to coincide with those of the hierarchy in Dublin, a system not entirely conducive to decision making.

While Sadleir worked behind the scenes in the planning process, he also assumed a higher public profile. The day after the launch of the Association he presided over a banquet in the Theatre Royal, Hawkins Street, to honour Reynolds as one of the prominent brigadiers.[10] Five hundred people were present, including Scully, Keating, Crawford, Keogh, Higgins, O'Flaherty and Maher. Priests, Towns Commissioners, High Sheriffs and lawyers came in significant numbers.

The theme of a united Irish party emerged in more detail at this function and henceforth became more prominent in the public arena. Reynolds had his own unique means of addressing this. He denounced specific representatives by name. Sir William Somerville was accused of betraying his Drogheda constituents. Richard Montesquieu, Louth, 'another slave a little below him – a Catholic slave – a Catholic Lord of the Treasury', did not vote for the titles Bill, 'but like a slave, he went out when the votes were being taken, and eat his pudding in silence'. Reynolds next turned to Roscommon and asked the Catholic voters if they would 'allow themselves to be victims of a political trick of the loop? Will they subject themselves to petticoat government representation? Mrs Fitzstephen French is married to a cousin of the bigoted and intolerant Premier; and I must *know*, will the Catholics of Roscommon allow themselves to be deluded any longer'. In a similar manner he attacked Tennyson and Clements who represented Leitrim, and Somers of Sligo.

Sadleir did not indulge in such treatment of individual members, but he supported the policy of an Irish party and condemned Irish representatives, who sustained a 'hostile ministry in office on occasions when a few well-directed votes would have hurled them from power...' He agreed with Reynolds that the constituencies should react strongly against those who misrepresented them in Westminster,

> He would tell that assemblage of Irish men that the neck should be broken in the existence of this system. An end should be put to those acts of those scoffers and sneerers at the faith of their fathers. Their days of political misdeeds were now numbered. This great Catholic country had pronounced against them. The great mass of the people were now cognisant of the fact, that when the opportunity presented itself the Liberal constituencies of Ireland were determined to get rid of the members of this system of political hypocrisy, which had too long lived on the gains, and profited by the immunities of a position acquired more by accident than desert.

Sadleir saw it as fundamental that the Irish representatives be convinced of their strength as a party. The formation of such a party was a 'sensible and intelligent policy, because it protected individual Members from being approached by the Minister or his representative. Another source of strength was the bond between the Irish people and the priests. Any suggestion of disunity was only a ploy by the Government to weaken their resolve. He made sure to defend Cullen and in the process denigrate Clarendon,

> Who amongst them had been so dull as not to have observed the insidious spirit which animated the representative and political correspondent of that government in this country with his unmanly efforts to ensnare within the meshes of the law that dignitary because, in a conscientious spirit, he discharged the functions of his high office. Who forgot the admission of Lord John Russell that Lord Clarendon had taken advice with Her Majesty's Counsel in this country as to whether it

was competent to Her Majesty's Government to prosecute his Grace, the Primate, and other bishops for the conscientious part which they had firstly taken in those proceedings which comprised the Synod of Thurles.

This judicious defence of the Archbishop was accompanied by an avowal of his 'perfect toleration' of his Protestant fellow-countrymen. The Protestant members of the Lords and Commons were complimented in his toast to the Duke of Newcastle, Aberdeen, Graham, Gladstone and Crawford. The latter, who in earlier years was a consistent supporter of Catholic emancipation, briefly responded. He saw his own loyalty to Protestantism as compatible with helping Catholic M.P.s to defend their religious liberty. To do this successfully parliamentary independence was vital and he 'was of opinion that there was no hope for Ireland so long as political subserviency was found to exist amongst her representatives'. To him the 'great source of evil' to Ireland was the support of Irish Members for the measures of the Whig Government.

Crawford had met the Irish M.P.s earlier that day in the Imperial Hotel to discuss the tenant conference, which would be held the following day. Sadleir was present at this meeting along with eleven other M.P.s and leading Tenant Leaguers such as Shee, Fitzgerald, Quaid, Renteul, McCullough and John Francis Maguire, the proprietor of the *Cork Examiner*.[11] Final agreement was reached between Crawford, the M.P.s and the Council of the League on the landlord and tenant bill which Crawford would submit to Parliament next session. This was more fully discussed at the conference next day, which was held in the once famous Music Hall in Fishamble Street[12] and chaired by Crawford. Sadleir was among the eight M.P.s there.[13]

Because of his position as a reforming landlord, Crawford's opinion carried considerable weight. He developed the theme that landlord and tenant interests were synonymous and tenant right had to be consistent with the just rights of landlords. But, an imbalance existed in the relationship between ownership and tenancy, whereby the landlords possessed 'irresponsible power'. Justice dictated that by his very industry the tenant created an interest in the land which should be protected. He did not see legislation on the issues of fixity of tenure or a fair rent as an infringement on the principle of free trade. Like Sadleir he believed that 'the state had a right to interfere in the administration of that property when the circumstances of the country required its interference'. He shared the view expounded on many local platforms that the prosperity of the farming community had a direct influence on the economic well-being of rural dwellers.

Reynolds, as the representative of an urban constituency, broadened such a perspective by equating the rights of urban tenants with those of the farmers. He explained that many tenants in Dublin city had seen the houses built by their fathers or grandfathers pass to fee simple proprietors without receiving any compensation for expenditure on improving them. He quoted the example of houses near Merrion Square purchased by Sidney Herbert.

There was unanimity among the speakers upon the question of arrears of rent. Keogh did not envisage their total abolition, but saw no reason why the statute of limitations should not apply, which would considerably reduce them. Tenants were afraid to improve their holdings and reclaim poor land because they 'would see the landlord's agent waiting at the end of a furrow ready to snatch under the name of arrears the surplus sheaves with which a bounteous providence had rewarded his industry'. Maguire bemoaned the fact that tenants were not given the opportunity of developing the land. The industry of Irish emigrants was evident in America, and bank lodgements at home testified to qualities of thrift among Irish farmers. The Kerry Savings Bank, with lodgements of £100,000, and the Cork Savings Bank, with almost half a million pounds, were examples of such thrift and industry.

In common with the theme at the launch of the Catholic Defence Association, there was also agreement on the necessity of a unified Irish party. Maguire looked to the coming election and urged that only men of integrity be elected,

> Why was this metropolis degraded – why did grass grow in its squares – why was there squalor in its streets? Because there was corruption in the lobby – corruption on the house top – corruption in the closet – corruption in the heart.

His words prompted Reynolds to renew his litany of condemnation. Commenting about Anstey's Tasmanian roots, he declared that 'a more perfect personification of a human kangaroo he had never witnessed'. Morgan John O'Connell, Kerry, nephew of the Liberator, was 'a political renegade and the bully of an intolerant and audacious Minister'. Maguire, however, could not stomach Reynold's attack on Dr Power, Cork, and interrupted the Dublin M.P.

A more serious source of discord at the conference was the embryonic conflict between those who saw the religious issue as the main priority and those who saw the land question as such. Maguire felt it necessary to say that the religious controversy had not damaged the League or its policy of tenant-right, which 'concerned the life and death of the people'. The settlement of the land question was the main priority. Renteul concurred, but Reynolds rated both questions equally and insisted that 'unless the principles of civil and religious liberty were, with those of tenant right, inscribed on their banner, he would not be there that night'. O'Flaherty, on the other hand, felt that they should not be mixed while Scully worried that religious discord might mar the unity of the land movement.

Some of the leading members of the Brigade, however, had no hesitation in giving priority to the religious question. Keogh, as their spokesman, felt that

> he owed it to those honorary gentlemen not to commit them to hasty allegations, for they were engaged in another political cause which he believed to be indispensable to even the tenant-right movement. He and his honorary friends were committed to the great cause of freedom of conscience. He for one believed that cause to be one of the greatest importance, and he would not compromise it by any reckless assertion that might by possibility place it in danger.

Keogh's skill in presenting his case with some humour, and his subsequent endorsement of the land question, prevented audible discord, but the Leaguers were aghast at the tenor of Sadleir's remarks. They were ultra-sensitive to the importance of the northerners to the movement and Sadleir made an uncharacteristic error of judgement in his comments. His brief was to speak on the issue of rent arrears but he began 'in a most friendly and conciliatory manner' to ask 'what portion of the imperial legislature had his countrymen the Presbyterian ministers at their back'. They were, he answered, represented by Catholic M.P.s whose religion had been stigmatised by the Government as one 'calculated to enslave the intellect'. His own defence of the Presbyterians in the Duncan Chisolm case was proof of this. He went on to reveal his own political priority,

> The Catholic representatives of Catholic constituencies believed that the first object of their political exertions must be to secure religious liberty for all. The proper way to put the question was, whether tenant right or any other right was to be conferred on a people at the expense or by the forfeiture of religious freedom. That was the way to put the matter ... Catholic representatives of Catholic constituencies were not prepared to postpone for a moment, for this or for any other cause, the exercise of their parliamentary power to repeal that enactment, and never to rest from their endeavours til they swept from the imperial statute book every link of the chain that had been only partially broken.

When Sadleir made it clear that it was wrong to imagine that progress could be made on the tenant right issue while the titles Act remained unrepealed, Patrick Lalor of Tennakill rose to order and was supported by a clergyman. An unrepentant Sadleir, however, stood his ground,

> Good God! did his Protestant and Presbyterian countrymen imagine that their Catholic fellow subjects could have any political influence to use for the promotion of tenant right, so long as this deep and damnable oppression was fixed upon them. He would be deluding his Protestant and Presbyterian friends, if he did not state openly that he would be governed by the policy enunciated by his honourable friend, the member for Athlone. He and those of his honourable friends who stood with him, would make all their acts subservient to that parliamentary policy, which they considered essential to the establishment of the immutable, just and fundamental principle of religious liberty.

When he eventually addressed and supported the motion on rent arrears, he prefaced his remarks with sympathy for landlords who were 'surrounded with difficulty and trial'. Many of them could be compared with landowners in any part of the world for 'generosity and tolerance'. He emphasised, however, that he recognised tenants' difficulties, and he referred to a paper presented by him to Clarendon on the 'gross injustice which was worked on the tenant' by the current system of landlord and tenant law in Ireland. This paper was later passed to the Attorney General who incorporated the section on arrears into the Security for Advances Bill empowering the Incumbered Estates Commissioners to deal with arrears on the estates that came up for sale in their court. The poor rate and the tithe rent substantially added to the tenants' burden and such arrears in turn increased this burden by preventing tenants from applying for some alleviation of the poor rate.

Only a small part of his speech concerned land, and this was indicative of the emphasis placed by leading Brigadiers on the religious question which had preoccupied them for much of 1851. This emphasis was reinforced from September to November by a series of banquets held throughout Ireland to honour their stand against the titles Act.

On 22 September he chaired the Cashel banquet to honour Scully and Maher.[14] The initial preparation was marked by controversy when the Liberal club, which organised it, did not include Maher because of his poor attendance at Westminster. Several prominent individuals including Sadleir and Patrick Leahy, St Patrick's College, Thurles, strongly urged that Maher as well as Scully be honoured. It was important that Conservatives should not discern any split in the Liberal camp with the election looming[15] One ingredient of unity was hostility to Russell, and the Cashel curate, John Ryan, a master of invective, took the opportunity in his letter supporting Maher to call the Premier a 'miserable little puny, forsworn wretch'.[16]

The banquet was attended by the Honourable Cecil Lawless M.P., Clonmel, and Sir Timothy O'Brien M.P., Cashel, both of whom were poor attenders at Westminster. Other representatives present were Reynolds, Keogh, Higgins and O'Flaherty. Sadleir was accompanied by his brothers James and Clement, several of his Scully relatives and Anthony Norris. Supporters of the Tenant League such as Lucas, William Mullally P.P., Cappawhite, and John O'Dwyer C.C., Doon, were there. Joseph Kenny, the Mayor of Clonmel, and Charles Bianconi attended as did a large number of clergy including James McDonnell and Michael Laffan, respectively Dean and Archdeacon of Cashel and Emly.

The prominence of the League in Tipperary was reflected in the addresses. Sadleir, who may have wished to redeem himself for his Dublin blunder, proposed a toast to the 'cause of the Irish tenant' and attacked the Government's failure to adequately deal with it. He denounced the 'atrocious clause' in the Civil Bills Bill enabling the eviction of tenants, a year in arrears, and pledged his support for Crawford's Bill, which he saw as fair and just. Such justice was a prerequisite to his approval of any land law, and he would never

> be a party to any legislation which would be contrary to the first principles of justice, or inconsistent with the sound practical principles of political economy. He believed it was also pretty well known that no amount of political clamour would induce him to lend his humble aid to the introduction of any measure which he thought was calculated to do injustice to the landlords or any other class in the state.

It took courage to mention landlords in a favourable light in Tipperary, where landlordism was consistently denounced on League platforms. Mullally, who also responded to the toast, had frequently denounced the landlords, while Sadleir blamed the legal system of tenure. Mullally was profoundly influenced by his experience of Famine suffering and recited the particular case of

> Dwyer of Coolacussane, lying on his wad of ferns, seeking a cold boiled turnip to moisten his lips after selling the entire produce of his garden to pay the rent to keep the house over him – the tale after tale and cruel wrongs and foul play – the scalding recital which I had so often to listen to from the quivering lips of the ground-down, broken-hearted tenant himself – of how the landlord treated him..

Mullally's lack of personal experience of emigrant ships did not prevent him depicting the plight of 'Erin's virtuous daughters' descending into 'those brothels called berths' on those ships. He did, however, have experience of 'some of the horrors of the workhouse prisons'. Such horror made Legislation on the land question more imperative than repeal of the Ecclesiastical Titles Act,

> What use is it to repeal the atrocious penal bill when in the next session a worse bill may be forged? First emancipate the tenant sector from tyrant subjugation – make the constituencies independent, and thereby honest, and you will have a strong independent and honest party in parliament and thereby will have secured our ancient holy faith from all future aggression.

No political platform in Tipperary was complete without the presence of Dr Michael Burke, who was asked to address the religious issue. His sense of the dramatic was heightened by the burning of a copy of the Act outside the town hall. This symbolic act was reinforced by his vow of total disobedience to it,

> As the heroism of our fathers in the faith has in former times defied and trampled on more severe penal laws, so the same virtue in those who inherited from them that faith will trample to the dust and defeat this modern penal law, and teach the statesmen and legislators who passed it this lesson, that omnipotent as they may think their Parliament the Catholic people of Ireland will disobey its laws and set them at defiance when these laws are opposed to the rights of conscience, and when they are aimed against the very existence of their church and its hierarchy.

The weapons used to resist this law would not be the 'broad claymores' of the Scots but those of 'religious heroism, passive resistance and the elective franchise'. Burke's tenets were strictly O'Connellite and the clergy were a potent force in preserving the civil and religious rights of the Irish people. The priests of Tipperary would 'take the crucifix' in their hands and lead their people against the Whigs in the election campaign. The criteria for eligibility as a candidate would not be based upon his religious persuasion, but upon a pledge to oppose 'any ministry of which the perfidious and calamitous Russell is the head, or the tail, or the middle'.

This non-sectarian addendum was agreeable to Sadleir, who reiterated for the benefit of Tipperary people that sectarianism was not part of the agenda. Toleration of Protestantism and defence of Catholicism were quite compatible. To those who stated otherwise he would say that he had peculiar opportunities of judging of the spirit of his Protestant fellow-subjects in every portion of the British empire, and from his knowledge of their spirit, he could say that such a suggestion was a libel upon his Protestant fellow countrymen. He believed that the Protestants of the empire would look with well merited contempt upon their Catholic fellow countrymen if at any time, and especially at the present, they did not band together to defend their religion and to sustain their venerated hierarchy.

He used the platform to promote membership of the Defence Association, and prior to visiting Athlone for Keogh's banquet at the end of October became involved in the final preparations for its establishment. He was a member of the preparatory sub-committee, which framed its rules and constitution. The other members were Cullen, as chairman, McHale, Slattery, Keogh, Moore and O'Flaherty.[17] Following the Rotundo conference they forwarded draft copies to the hierarchies of England Ireland and Scotland for their recommendation which would be considered by the full general committee on 25 and 26 September.

Cullen chaired both these meetings, which also endorsed a public address to the Irish people, that had been drafted by the sub-committee.[18] The address outlined the Association's aims, which were further refined at a sub-committee meeting of 16 October and published at a general meeting of the Association the following day. The sub-committee met on a frequent basis under Cullen to ensure that all would be ready for the public conference.[19] Sadleir had gained the Primate's confidence by that stage and at the meeting of 16 October, which finalised the objectives and rules of the new Association, he was appointed one of its temporary honorary secretaries along with Keogh and Reynolds. They were to hold office until a permanent official was recruited.

They were also secretaries to the general meeting next day, which was held in the Hall of the Mechanics' Institute in Lower Abbey Street.[20] It was chaired by Lord Viscount Gormanstown. The conference was a practical affair and the number in attendance was small but included two Tipperary representatives, O'Brien and Maher, and Martin Joseph Blake, Galway Borough. McHale and four bishops arrived later in the proceedings.[21] The new association had twenty one rules and fourteen aims, which concerned religion, education and social issues.[22] Its principal aim was the repeal of the titles Act and any other statutes impinging upon the religious and civil liberties of Catholics in the British Empire. The issues of proselytism both at parish level and in prisons, endowments of Catholic institutions, Catholic education, the 'free exercise of their religion' for soldiers whether at home or abroad, Catholic chaplains in all vessels in the British navy and convict ships, the provision of religious education for the children of Catholic soldiers and sailors, the publication and distribution of religious books 'approved of by the prelates', were all incorporated. Other aims were to use the public press to defend Catholic doctrines and principles and to improve the social conditions of the people. The disestablishment of the Protestant Church was not omitted, but this was accompanied by a pledge to inculcate 'strict allegiance' to the throne and maintain peace among the Queen's subjects. It was recognised that some of these could only be achieved through political means, and section thirteen of the aims laid down as a 'strict and religious obligation' the task of selecting parliamentary representatives, 'whose known integrity and talents' fitted them best to pursue religious rights in Westminster and 'to carry out the objects of this Association'.

The General Committee named at the conference was extensive. It contained the hierarchies of Ireland, England and Scotland as ex-officio members, a number of nobility and gentry such as Gormanstown, Shrewsbury, Kenmare, French, Arundel and Surrey, Arundel of Wardour and Charles Langdale, many priests and eighteen Members of Parliament. Some of Sadleir's relatives were named, including Frank Scully, James Scully, Athassel Abbey, Thomas Scully J.P., Vincent Scully and Anthony Norris.

Apart from the bishops, only those who had paid a subscription of a pound and upwards were eligible for election to this committee. Such subscribers were entitled to attend, speak and vote at meetings, while those who paid less than a pound and not under a shilling could be present but were not entitled to speak. The General Committee was instructed to meet once a month in Dublin and had the power to select from its members a sub-committee. The Association's funds were lodged in an account in the Hibernian Bank to the credit of Cullen, McHale, Bishop John Cantwell, Meath, the Earl of Arundel and Surrey, the Honourable E. Preston, John Clarke and John Reynolds.

Much of the conference was taken up with reading out long lists of subscribers, many of whom were English. A number of nobility and gentry contributed significant individual sums such as the ten pounds from Shrewsbury. Sadleir read a letter from Richard Swift, the High Sheriff of London, enclosing five pounds from himself and one from his chaplain, Thomas O'Connor of Loughglen.[23] He also handed in a two pounds contribution from Thomas Eyre.

Some of those present had links with O'Connell's Catholic Association and inevitably comparisons were made between it and the more auspicious launch of the new organisation. Nicholas Maher recollected that 'when the old Catholic Association was formed in a small room in Capel Street, we could scarcely muster for the first or second day more than fourteen or fifteen individuals'. John Reynolds had been the fifth member enrolled in O'Connell's Association and said that they had 'struggled day after day, and with all the talent and power of Daniel O'Connell we were struggling for more than a year before we occupied so proud a position as we occupy today'. On the surface that position was impressive. More than 600 members were already formally enrolled, and hundreds more had sent their subscriptions. Not only did this represent an initial satisfactory financial state, but the prominent support of the hierarchy and the membership of a large number of influential laity gave the Association a status not held by the Tenant League, although the latter's network made it potentially much more effective.[24]

The Association differed from the League in two other ways. Its membership was confined to Catholics, a stricture which was anathema to the League's philosophy, and, unlike the League, it did not specifically promote a policy of independent opposition on all issues to a Government which refused to concede its principal aims. Considering the extent of these aims, such a policy would not have been feasible. Nevertheless, those differences did not augur well for the mutual understanding and co-operation necessary to secure a separate Irish party. But the presence of some League supporters was at least an outward show of approval.

William Shee, who eventually became the League's parliamentary champion, was one of these. Shee, whose father came from Thomastown in Kilkenny, was a cousin of Wiseman and a barrister of some repute. He was destined to become the first Catholic promoted to the bench since the Revolution in England[25] and his speech to this first public meeting of the Association brought a note of realism and legal clarity, which had sometimes been obscured by the emotive content of the long debate. He also brought the perspective of an English resident, when he pointed out that it would be impossible for an Irish party to secure the repeal of the titles Act unless the support of a significant portion of the English electorate was secured, recalling that the great majority of the Commons had supported the Act and only twenty of the English peerage had opposed it. To him the prohibition of titles, while insulting, was not the worst part of the bill, but rather the Tory clause declaring the constitution of the hierarchy and sees within the realm by Papal Bulls illegal. In a concise sketch of religious legislation to Henrician times, he was convinced that the Catholic episcopacy in Ireland, while not recognised in law, had 'a perfectly legal existence'. This was especially true from 1781 when, to secure the support of Catholics during the American War of Independence, the Irish Parliament had passed the 21 and 22 George III Act declaring that 'Popish Ecclesiastics of every rank should be entitled to be considered good and loyal subjects of the King'. Shee concluded that the alleged legal misinterpretations of the Solicitor General underlying the Act offered the best hope of having it reviewed.

The conference closed on this optimistic note and Reynolds promised that Keogh, Sadleir and himself would devote a portion of their time every day working in the Association's offices in 45 Lower Sackville Street. This unanimity and optimism, however, did not conceal the dissatisfaction of Lucas that the sub-committee meeting of 16 October had finalised the aims and rules of the Association, and presented them as *fait accompli* to the conference.[26] He was more irritated that the General Committee, 'who are to have the absolute management of the Association' had also been decided beforehand. As the self-confessed lay champion of Catholic affairs, his own membership would have been anticipated. He was disappointed in this and his exclusion may have been a tangible indication of his poor standing with Cullen. The enthusiasm with which he had previously promoted the Association waned as he found himself excluded from its counsels. Immediately following the official launch he was lukewarm about its success,

> It would be impossible to deny ... that the disposition of the public mind in Ireland is very much changed, both in regard to its hopes of great results from political struggles, and to the amount of confidence which it is disposed to place in public men, in Parliamentary parties and political organisations. Not merely do the calamities of the hour press upon the minds of men and damp their expectations, but the ill-success of former agitations, and the complete disappointment of all the glowing hopes by which they were attended, have strongly reacted upon the present time.

Lucas was worried that the bishops would not take an active part in the Association and insisted that they and not the politicians 'must be its real leaders and guides as well as founders'. Without such leadership the organisation would not even be able to raise the necessary funds for its operation. He feared that, far from being a conduit of opinion between public and parliament, the organisation would become the tool of some Irish politicians, 'a certain small knot or family circle of Members of Parliament'.[27] The exclusion of the press from committee meetings was one symptom of such control. He blamed Sadleir, Keogh and Reynolds for this policy. He was convinced that the clerical members opposed this policy, but it is hardly likely that it would stand if Cullen had opposed it. Neither Lucas nor Duffy would accept the argument of the three secretaries that O'Connell had set a precedent by excluding newspaper proprietors from meetings of the Repeal Association. The editors rejected any comparison between an organisation devoted to religious matters and one containing a revolutionary element.[28]

Lucas's hostility to the three also focused on their temporary secretaryship of the Association. He was intensely suspicious of their future political ambitions, because of their key role in promoting the organisation's aims at parliamentary level. He did not trust Sadleir and his colleagues to remain independent, especially under a new ministry after the general election. He was accurate in his prediction of 25 October that the Conservatives under Derby would probably hold power for a short time, and would be replaced by a fusion of other elements of the Liberal party consisting of old Whigs, English Liberals, Radicals and Free Traders. He included the

> Graham and Gladstone party, of which it cannot be denied that they have played their cards extremely well, and that through a two sided policy, very skilfully extemporised by Mr Gladstone in Naples, they have earned the enthusiastic, undying and uncalculating gratitude of the Catholic inhabitants of those realms by their speeches on the Aggression Bill.

The *Tablet* editor feared the negotiation of a new Lichfield House compact with Irish representatives in which some objectives of the Catholic Defence Association would be conceded in return for political promotion. Apart from an uncanny accuracy, he was expressing no more than the League policy of undiluted independent opposition and condemnation of place taking, which mid-Victorian businessmen like Sadleir viewed as desirable and well-deserved patronage. Sadleir did not respond to Lucas's warnings, and three days later went to Galway to act as steward at the Ballygar race meeting.[29] He travelled to Athlone that evening for a banquet in Keogh's honour.[30] This was one of the most prestigious of the Autumn banquets and the presence of Archbishop McHale, Bishops John Cantwell, Meath, G.J.Browne, Elphin and John Derry, Clonfert, was testimony to the hierarchy's approval of Keogh's leadership among the Brigadiers and his role as joint secretary of the Defence Association. Eleven M.P's came to share in the celebration under the auspices of Archdeacon Martin O'Reilly, parish priest of Athlone.[31] A large number of priests attended from as far away as Sligo.[32] The Tenant League was represented by A.R. Stritch.

Cullen was unable to come, but wrote praising Keogh's contribution in Westminster and 'his zeal and perseverance in establishing and organising the Defence Association'. His statement on well chosen representatives acting with 'prudence and moderation' to achieve religious equality, was not an endorsement of independent opposition. Cullen also sought to rectify any impression that he was over-preoccupied with spiritual matters to the neglect of his flock's temporal welfare,

> whilst she teaches patience and resignation, including obedience to superiors and respect for the rights of property, she disapproves of every act of oppression and despotism, and is ever ready to raise her voice in favour of those who suffer persecution for justice sake. As a Bishop of such a Church I need scarcely express the gratification I feel when I learn that those who are defending our rights of conscience are not forgetful of temporal interests of our country, but are determined to labour incessantly until they shall have obtained from the legislature some permanent enactment to preserve our people from utter destruction, and to secure to the industrious and meritorious cultivators of the soil just rights in the land of their birth.

This introduced the scene for the main themes of the evening, religion and land, the twin planks of the forthcoming election platform, which would see the Catholic Defence Association and the Tenant League mounting a joint campaign to return a group of M.P.s committed to both issues. Keogh was explicit in his promise that he would not support any party 'which does not make it part of its political creed to do full justice to the tenant in Ireland'. He condemned landlord control over the law, the magistracy, the juries and the police for their own ends – 'and what have they made of Ireland – a garden or a desert, a pleasant place to live in or a howling wilderness?'. The Whigs had ignored the land question for so long and betrayed Irish Liberal politicians, their consistent supporters against the protectionist Tories. He professed to be baffled by such failure, considering the great resources at the government's command and the large majority enjoyed by it when supported by the Irish members.

Carried by the force of his oratory Keogh made a powerful pledge of his parliamentary independence, which would haunt him the following year. He declared that Whigs, Tories, Peelites and Protectionists were 'all the same' to him and

> Here in the presence of my constituents and of my country – and I hope I am not so base a man as to make a declaration which could be contradicted to-morrow – if I was capable of doing that which is insinuated against me – if there was a Peelite administration in office

tomorrow it would be nothing to me. No man ever knew me to disingenuously conceal my inmost thoughts, and I here avow that I did admire that great statesman, and we did feel in the last session of parliament the absence of his avenging sword and of his protecting shield... He has passed away and if all the Peelites in the House joined the Whig administration, I would be their unmitigated, their untiring, their indefatigable opponent til we got that justice.

This justice was the repeal of the Ecclesiastical Titles Act, but in theory Keogh was prepared in the next session to support Russell's reform bill on the franchise, provided that it was not an instalment measure. In practice, he announced, this measure was too restrictive and would be opposed by him, but his ambivalence showed that his principle of opposition did not pertain to measures beneficial to Ireland.

Reynolds, who envisaged Keogh as the leader of an Irish party, spoke on the question of patronage, a concept which aroused the contempt of individuals like Lucas and Duffy. The Dublin M.P., however, did not see any incompatibity between the acceptance of patronage and opposing a Government on issues which were injurious to Irish or Catholic interests. His statement clarified one dimension of Irish mid-Victorianism,

> In the distribution of places and pensions the Government seldom gave any to the man who had stood by the colours of the people. He was not one of those men who declared the representative to be a traitor that exercised patronage, or that it was a crime to seek for patronage for those who were in communion with them. He believed it to be not only not a crime to do so, but if principle was not sacrificed, a duty. For centuries they had been complaining that in the land of their birth they were prevented from sharing in the honours and emoluments of the state, and yet he was to be told they were traitors for endeavouring now to promote the people. But the truth should be told. They were twenty years emancipated and they had not received any state patronage. A few Catholics had certainly been promoted, but had any Catholic nobleman or gentleman ever obtained a seat in the cabinet?

This fully accorded with Sadleir's outlook, but, when his turn to speak came, he chiefly confined his remarks to a condemnation of the Whigs. There could be no 'solid and extended reform' for Ireland under the current government. He did not fear a Tory Government because he felt that any successor to Russell's ministry could only retain office by speedily recognising Irish claims. Retaining office would depend upon its Irish policy. The Whig contribution to Ireland had been a catalogue of disaster and local government was a good example,

> What has the local government of Ireland been under the Whigs? It has been a system of government conducted by military force, by intrigue, by nepotism and by a clique – by suspension of the constitution, by coercion acts, by corruption of the press and the purchase of votes, by defiling the very fountains of justice and packing the jury box. Catholics of Athlone do not forget the jury packing of the Whigs in Dublin, denounced by your representative. Do not forget the jury packing in Mayo, exposed by Mr Higgins. Do not forget the insults heaped upon your Catholic brethren in Tipperary in the case of *Callanan and Cameron.*

For once he named individual representatives, whom he felt had betrayed their constituents. He chose his names from Reynold's pet list, and hoped that, despite the patronage he had showered on the borough of Drogheda, Sir William Somerville would be rejected in the general election. Bellew, a Catholic Government supporter,was an 'unfit personage' to represent 'the Catholic electors' of Louth. Self-help and optimism was the key to success – 'To help ourselves shall be the living and active principle of our political action; to despair would be to betray the country'. In words which unintentionally mirrored Young Ireland parlance he announced that their task was to revive 'the national recollections of those events which give renown to this ancient island'. In less rhetorical terms he portrayed the Defence Association as an influential body reviled by the English press, but whose non-sectarian principles were supported by Aberdeen, 'the greatest living Protestant statesman in Europe'. It was a powerful political instrument which would 'place clearly before the people their power, and they will not hesitate to expose the organised hypocrisy of Downing Street wherever it shall raise its head'.

In a veiled reference to the stance of Lucas, Sadleir rejected 'the bitter falsehoods of our concealed enemies' and the 'sneers and defections of hypocritical friends'. In his report on the banquet, Lucas was forced to admit that McHale and the other bishops at Athlone disapproved of his articles on the secretaryship and the press.[33] McHale was fulsome in his praise of Keogh and Lucas felt it expedient to deny any dissension over the Association and to concede that 'the proceedings at Athlone and particularly Keogh's statement had erased' any 'misunderstandings' about the integrity of some Brigadiers. He also admitted that only one of the three secretaries had advocated the exclusion of the press, one had opposed it and one had suggested legal opinion on the matter.

Soon Lucas and Duffy had to worry about a more serious problem than exclusion from committee meetings. This was the impending arrival of the *Telegraph*, a new paper financed by Sadleir, who had previously tried to buy the *Freeman's Journal*.[37] Frank and Vincent Scully were also involved, but to what extent is not known.[35] James B. Kennedy was the paper's solicitor and registered proprietor,[36] an obvious front to conceal Sadleir's ownership. The resentment of Duffy and Lucas was aroused by the initial claim in its prospectus that the *Telegraph* was being established by the founders of the Association and would by implication be its official organ.[47] Duffy was troubled that the Association was about to be turned into a 'huge advertising van for the private speculation' of Sadleir and his friends.[38] According to him the situation was unprecedented because the *Nation* had never been circulated by the Repeal Association no more than the *Tablet* had been by the Tenant League.

A revised prospectus omitting any reference to the Association eased their minds. A committee meeting under Cullen on 13 November including Slattery, McHale, Vaughan, Browne and Cantwell and nine M.P's arrived at this decision.[39] Significantly, Sadleir seconded McHale's resolution distancing the Association from any connection with 'the opinions of any individual journal as its organ'.[40] The three M.P's were asked to continue as secretaries for a further month until a permanent secretary with a salary of £300 was appointed on 17 December. A resolution appreciating 'the disinterested zeal and efficiency' of the three was moved by Cantwell and supported by McHale.

This momentarily allayed the controversy, and on 18 November Sadleir went to Wexford where the Lord Mayor, Robert Stafford, presided over a public dinner to honour John Thomas Devereux, Member for the borough.[41] Six of his parliamentary colleagues, including Keogh and Scully, attended.[42] As in Athlone the mottoes 'Tenant Right' and 'Civil and Religious Liberty' were inscribed on the wall above the chair and these became the dominant theme of the banquets, which by that stage were part of an election campaign. The speeches largely repeated what had been said in Cashel, Dublin and Athlone. Keogh, however, seemed driven to make an emphatic rejection of patronage as a political option,

> Did they think a representative of the people could go one day to the Minister and in his private closet ask him for a small condescension and then go openly into the House of Commons and vote against the same Minister?... He would say that the representative who sought from the Minister a place – be it ever so small or unimportant – either for his relatives or friends, he should vote in favour of that Minister and against

the people .. A member of Parliament could not serve two masters. He could not serve a Minister who was opposed to the people and 'at the same time do the business of the people who were opposed to' the Minister. He could not, without forfeiting his own personal honour, accept the smallest gift from the Minister unless he gave in exchange that which was not honestly his to give – the confidence of the people.

Keogh's logic was sound but unrealistic in a country where many people depended upon patronage to secure employment. But, Sadleir, one of the strongest proponents of patronage, was prepared to make an exception in the case of the Russell Ministry,

> it was confidently predicted that the Irish Brigade would not resist the influence of the Treasury. They had a few mean and sneaking supporters, but he would challenge this sneaking government to produce one Irish representative who would avow himself the sincere and uncompromising supporter of the Ministry.

His business contacts gave him an understanding of the English middle-class outlook, and he was convinced that these now looked with disfavour on the government's reaction to the establishment of the Catholic hierarchy. Neither, contrary to rumour, did they interpret the spate of banquets as demonstrations 'calculated to outrage the feelings of Protestants'. They all shared the common aspirations of vote by ballot, triennial parliaments and a 'broad and genuine' extension of the franchise. Sectarianism was not a feature of middle-class business transactions and Sadleir was keen to deny that the Defence Association was a sectarian organisation, an allegation which he condemned as a 'stupid slander'. The Brigade supported the Association as a Catholic combination, 'but on broad and practical measures of legislation their efforts were directed to combine Irishmen without distinction of creed or class, in one common effort to preserve the honour and the interests of their native land'.

Land was one of these interests, and Frank Scully was assigned the task of dealing with it. His early Repeal connections convinced him that matters would be different if Ireland was ruled by Irishmen. J.H. Talbot, who represented New Ross, could not resist interrupting with a cry of 'Repeal! Repeal! to which Scully jokingly (replied) – 'I wish with my friend, Mr. Talbot, who manifests all the enthusiasm of youth on the subject of Repeal, that we had it now'. Sadleir was privately less enamoured with the Repeal interjection. He wrote to Moore from Great Denmark Street the following night that 'Keogh and I have just returned from Wexford where everything went off well tho' some efforts were made to whitewash the Repeal hacks'.[43] He had promised

Moore that he would attend another banquet in Ballina on 25 November, but a busy schedule prevented him from going. He explained that he was due in Manchester two days hence, London on the 23 and 24 November and back in Ireland on 25 November as receiver for the sale of the the Kingston estates.

His London visit originated from an invitation to a freehold land conference in the Kings Arms Hotel, Palace Yard, Westminster, and was later followed by a public meeting in St. Martin's Hall, Long-acre.[44] The conference consisted of delegates from English land societies which had been established over the previous three years. Its purpose was to discuss their progress. Sadleir and Richard Cobden, Yorkshire West Riding, well know for his leading role in the Anti-Cornlaw League,were the main speakers. His prominence on the platform was a further illustration of his public standing as a major investor in land. By then it seemed that he had changed his mind about the creation of small proprietors. Re-echoing some of his sentiments at the Devereux banquet, he proclaimed his confidence in the English middle classes as the back-bone of the land societies and of commercial development, and as an example to an under-developed Irish agricultural economy,

> He himself had what he would always consider a great advantage – the opportunity of mixing for the last seven or eight years with the English middle-classes. That he believed to be a great advantage to an Irishman. It would be a great advantage in the same way to have the opportunity of mixing with the people of Ireland. Were international communication more complete, international prejudices would soon disappear. Ireland needed familiarity with the commercial spirit of England; and he was satisfied that Ireland would derive an immense advantage from having a practical course for dealing with the land question shown to her by these societies.

The freehold societies held out an example and a hope to Ireland to raise the people up 'from their present unfortunate and anomalous position'. He had no fear that the system would encourage 'a dangerous and vicious system of subdivision' of land ownership as had happened in other countries, where division among all the children was mandatory upon the death of the owner. Such a system was a 'monstrous error'. Real property law was the principal impediment to the creation of a middle-class of land freeholders. At the earlier private meeting Sadleir had succeeded in passing a resolution for a committee to examine the effect of the law on real property and land societies and 'to take steps for its improvement'. Drawing on his business experience he pointed to the detrimental impact of real estate law on the progress of railway companies.

Cobden was pleased at Sadleir's plan to extend the principle of such societies to Ireland, where land was readily available in the Incumbered Estates Court. He might have been less pleased, however, at the methods used by the Carlow M.P. to get control of an Irish freehold society, which had been Duffy's brainchild.[45] In March Duffy had approached some friends about the feasibility of extending the English system to Ireland. Prompted by their positive response he had travelled to London for practical advice. He was encouraged by James Taylor, founder of the English Societies, John Stuart Mill, John Bright, a close friend of Cobden, Sir Joshua Walmsley M.P., President of the National Freehold Land Society, and W.T. Thornton, author of *A Plea for a Peasant Proprietary*. On returning to Ireland he wrote his *Proposal For Establishing a Small Proprietors' Society of Ireland*, which was published anonymously.[46]

Sadleir may have unintentionally voiced the Young Ireland concept of self-help in his earlier eagerness to castigate Bellew, but his interest in land was mainly speculative. Duffy, on the other hand, genuinely believed in the self-help concept of using the farmers' own industry and capital to acquire ownership. The ideal of Arthur Young, 'give a man possession of a rock and he will turn it into a garden' appealed to him. The target population was savings banks' investors and would-be emigrants. His research into the works of Sismondix De Beaumont, Thier Mill Laing, and evidence in the *Devon Commission* convinced him that a peasant proprietary was the best answer to Ireland's problems. The opportunities provided by the Incumbered Estates' Court were too good to be overlooked by the farming population, and the English freehold land societies had proven that corporate purchasing facilitated the acquisition of estates which could then be divided among their members. This was the only method feasible in the Incumbered Estates Court, which did not deal in small lots making it impossible for individual farmers to buy there. Members of Duffy's proposed society could purchase either half or full shares, £50 or £100 respectively, and the inducement offered for this investment was a higher rate of interest than that of the banks. There was no onus, however, to buy land and from that point of view the organisation resembled friendly societies. While unencumbered land came within the scope of the Society its objective was to purchase an encumbered estate each month. This would then be divided out in different sized allotments according to the number of shares each purchaser held. The distribution of the property would be regulated by ballot and existing tenants could become members eligible for mortgages at 6% if they could not pay the full purchase price of their farms. Duffy felt that a proprietor, unlike a tenant, could thrive on a very modest holding. He considered eight acres adequate, a theory not shared by the more realistic Sadleir.

Following the publication of his *Proposal* Duffy formed a preparatory committee to move the project a stage further. He excluded politicians and called on others with particular expertise such as 'bank directors, land owners and agents, eminent lawyers, opulent Dublin traders, men of practical or scientific experience in the value of property and small proprietors who tilled their own fee simple land'. But, such was Sadleir's reputation that the committee prevailed upon Duffy to include him. Sadleir read the details of Duffy's scheme and was not entirely favourable to it, although he did not give any reasons for his objection. Duffy met him in London in July and found him more entrenched against the project. He brought several prominent members of the English Societies to visit Sadleir, and this, together with the offer of the solicitorship of the Irish society to Sadleir's legal firm, smoothed any remaining difficulties. From them on Sadleir became 'by far the most active promoter of the society'.

But, he was determined to gain control of it, and on returning to Dublin in August he met Duffy on an almost daily basis for a month to draw up its rules and prospectus. These meetings took place in Great Denmark Street, which, without Duffy's knowledge or agreement, became the registered office of the new company. Unruffled by Duffy's indignation Sadleir proceeded to register himself, his partner and one of his clerks as the members of the society and by this legal coup he effectively took initial control of Duffy's brainchild. This was accompanied by a public identification of himself rather than Duffy with the initiative. He used the columns of the *Dublin Evening Post* for this purpose, when he wrote to refute the arguments of a correspondent in favour of the Scottish system of tenure, whereby landlords effected all permanent improvements and erected all the buildings on farms.[47] He reminded the objector to the peasant proprietary project that

> nineteen-twentieths of the Irish landlords cannot erect the necessary farm buildings, make the requisite expenditure in permanent improvements, or execute valid leases, and that many of them cannot even reside in Ireland; and I ask what is the position of the tenants' of estates in Chancery, of estates belonging to owners unable to expend one shilling on their properties, and who are equally unable, however well disposed they may be to grant an industrious tenant the security of a valid lease for a fixed term of years, or to give the improving tenant a valid guarantee that he shall enjoy the fruits of his own enterprising industry? I ask what is the position of the tenant who finds his landlord owning a life interest in the soil, and that life interest overwhelmed with mortgages and other debts?

Ultimate control depended upon the directorate, and Sadleir again upstaged Duffy with an easy confidence that helps to explain his rise in London business circles. He scotched Duffy's plans to include Patrick Lalor on the board. This was a relatively minor tactic, however, when compared with his manipulation of the office of managing director. As the originator of the scheme Duffy had reserved this portfolio for himself. As such he hoped to organise branches throughout the country and so bring to fruition something that was very dear to him. His astonishment turned to fury when he received the list of directors, prepared by Sadleir, and found that not only was he not Managing Director but was omitted altogether.

The calculating politician outmanoeuvred the idealistic editor, and in the process displayed a ruthlessness which he generally managed to conceal. He succeeded in having his own friends appointed as directors. This ensured complete success in his manoeuvres, which had to be completed during the parliamentary recess. He explained to the astounded Duffy that some of these, including More O'Ferrall, M.P. for Longford, had objected that Duffy's reputation as an 1848 rebel would damage the venture. In November Sadleir offered to appoint him a 'masked director'. Duffy immediately resigned and Sadlier effectively destroyed the project which never surfaced again.

Sadleir's victory may have secured him control of the land company, but it cost him the respect of Vincent Scully[48] and also added to the mutual suspicion between the Sadleirite faction of the Brigade and the three Dublin newspaper proprietors. This in itself was damaging to co-operation between the League and the Defence Association. But, in the winter of 1851 the latter was rocked by internal dissension over the appointment of a permanent secretary. Surprisingly, this arose within the General Committee itself. Sixteen applications were received for the position. Both W.J. Battersby and James Burke published impressive testimonials[49] and their previous record gave them an edge over the other applicants. Burke seemed most likely to succeed. The lack of support for Battersby's early proposal for a Catholic association showed that he was not favoured by Cullen. Burke, however, had been secretary of the earlier preparatory meetings before the appointment of Sadleir, Keogh and Reynolds. His testimonials were from Bishops William Keane, Ross, Edmund French, Kilmacduagh and Kilfenora, Timothy Murphy, Cloyne, Michael Blake, Dromore, Charles McNally, Clogher and John Kilduff, Ardagh. He also received testimonials from Sir Colman O'Loghlen and Thomas O'Hagan. Nevertheless, when the three M.P.s took over the secretaryship, Burke had effectively been removed from any further involvement. Writing to Moore as early as 23 September he bemoaned that there had been a 'studied exclusion of your humble servant from the machinery of the committee'.[50] He also revealed that he was refused an invitation to the Cashel banquet. It is almost certain that Sadleir was responsible for this. Burke informed Moore in an undated letter that Sadleir had advised him to retire, but 'I thought it due to myself to consult the Primate, who told me that a personal matter would arise and I therefore retired'.[51] He was further aggrieved that Leonard Morrogh had opened a letter addressed to him and had not forwarded it. Burke's restrained response to this was not one of complaint 'of the Hon. Secs. opening letters addressed to me at '45', but to keep them is not fair'. His prospects were also blighted by the support of the Tenant League and especially Cantwell, one of Sadleir's most tenacious critics.[52]

The permanent secretary was finally appointed on 17 December at a meeting of the Committee chaired by McHale, Cullen being ill and unable to attend.[53] Sadleir was in London on business,[54] but Keogh, Scully, Maher, Reynolds, Moore, O'Brien, O'Flaherty, Higgins, Blake and Sir Percy Nugent, Westmeath, were there. Bishops Browne, McNally, Cantwell and Derry ensured an adequate input from the hierarchy. Although Cullen was absent he was permitted to vote by letter and opted for Henry William Wilberforce, who was elected. The forty seven year old Wilberforce was a convert from Protestantism since September 1850 and had previously been the Vicar of East Farleigh in the Diocese of Canterbury.[55]

He was elected by a large majority and this should have been a satisfactory conclusion to the affair, but an unexpected sequel followed. Seven of the ten M.P.s present took it upon themselves to immediately issue a public letter to protest 'to the people of Ireland' against the appointment.[56] Keogh, who favoured Burke and privately regarded Wilberforce as 'a perfect imbecile',[57] headed the list of signatories, who were Moore, O'Flaherty, Scully, Higgins, Maher, O'Brien. The central theme of the letter was based upon the conclusion that the prime focus of Association was the Irish people. This was clearly a misinterpretation but by circumscribing the new body with national parameters the M.P.s were able to characterise the appointment of an Englishman as weakening 'that noble nationality', which was 'the most important purpose' of the Association. To them it was 'an act of ignoble folly and national degradation'

> in opposition to the wishes of all the prelates assembled – in direct antagonism to the all but unanimous opinion of the representatives of the people, who had fought the Catholic cause, night and day, during the past session, an utter stranger to this country – a gentleman no doubt of very high personal character and position, but wholly ignorant of the feelings, habits and politics of the Irish people.

The letter ended with an invitation to the Irish people to protest by every possible means, through the newspapers, the clergy and communication with the Association. But this did not happen and press reaction revealed a difference of opinion between Gray and Lucas. The editor of the *Freeman's* praised the letter as coming from some of the 'most able, most active and most earnest members of the Irish Brigade'.[58] He was also influenced by the signatories' statement that the five prelates present disagreed with the appointment. Gray supported the thesis that the rooting of the Association in Ireland was the best means of identifying the cause of English Catholics with 'the national enthusiasm of the Irish people', and he also agreed that the Catholic body in England was 'too small and too feeble' to effect any changes in Government policy.

Lucas, on the other hand, interpreted the letter as an insult to the Primate, who had voted for Wilberforce. He rightly queried the reinterpretation of the Association's aims in a national context. Its proper title was The Catholic Defence Association of Great Britain and Ireland, most of whose subscriptions came from England and Scotland.[59] The position of secretary had been advertised by the Committee in seven English and Scottish newspapers. Lucas also knew that the signatories had, at different stages of the voting, supported Wilberforce. He saw Keogh's stand as hypocritical and quoted from an 1849 pamphlet by the Athlone M.P. entitled *Ireland Imperialised*, which decried a national focus as too narrow a basis for the advancement of Irish interests in general and condemned the slogan 'Ireland for the Irish' as a 'narrow and wretched idea – the slang of the cliques who had learned their political creed in the purlieus of the Corn Exchange.'

Keogh and his associates were well accustomed to the sharp edge of Lucas's pen and chose to ignore it, but they were forced to retract their position in the face of criticism from more influential quarters.[60] Cullen was taken aback by the action of the M.P.s. His letter of 19 December to the three honorary secretaries was diplomatic in praising their endeavours, but expressed his 'deep disappointment and surprise at the dispute'.[61] He corrected their re-definition of the Association's parameters,

> from the first formation of the Society, I understood the feeling to be universally entertained that all Catholics of the United Kingdom were to constitute one body, and to be in all respects upon a perfect equality, without distinction of province or country. This, as far as I could judge, was deemed a vital principle, and the one best calculated to advance the interests of our holy religion. I was not prepared for the exception which has been taken to the selection of so distinguished a person as Mr. Wilberforce ... were the association founded for local or merely political

purposes, I would subscribe to the justness of the exception. When, however, it is borne in mind that it's objects are religious and Catholic every question arising should be decided upon religious and Catholic grounds.[62]

His uncle, James Maher, was less tactful in a public letter to Keogh.[63] He was aware that the latter had opposed the adjournment of the the secretary's election because the meeting which made the decision was representative of the Committee as a whole. Keogh's action was, therefore, undemocratic,

> You should in all fairness, have told us before the election that if the majority chanced to dissent from you, you would endeavour, by agitating the country, to overthrow the majority, whose decision we, on our part, felt ourselves bound in honour to respect, even were it contrary to our own private views. Sir, the admission of your principle of conduct must inevitably dissolve any association that was ever formed. Harmonious co-operation among men for any useful purpose becomes perfectly impossible unless the fair decision of the majority governs the body.

Like Lucas, Maher questioned the narrowing of the Association's aims to Irish interests. Wilberforce, 'who has eradicated the heresy which he has drunk in with his mother's milk', was the type of distinguished writer whose talents and 'extensive reading' qualified him to defend Catholic interests and doctrines. Consequently a salary of £300 was decided upon to attract someone of that stature. Maher suggested that if the M.P.s did not adhere to the principles of majority decision they should withdraw from the Association, which was 'a Catholic association, and not an Irish political club'.

James Redmond agreed with Maher's sentiments. He feared that the controversy would damage the internal unity of the Association and co-operation with the League,

> I was never a party to mixing up the tenant farmer's question with the affairs of the Defence Association, for the simple reason of there being many influential men willing to take part in the one and not in the other and vice versa. The two grievances being quite distinct, very reasonably admitted of distinct remedies, and these were admirably supplied by the Tenant League and the Defence Association. I have heartily wished that our revered Prelates would countenance the one as well as the other, and urge their clergy strenuously to sustain both.[64]

Keogh did not publicly respond. He was afraid to challenge Maher because 'he speaks under the protection of the Primate',[65] and following the publication of the controversial address he joined Sadleir in London to attend a press dinner to the railway entrepreneur, Cusack Roney. Sadleir was given the unfamiliar task of speaking on the theme 'Literature and Drama', not, according to the *Liverpool Journal*

> because he is particularly literary or theatrical .. but .. because the promoters were perfectly aware that he was one of those glib possessors of the gift, fairly divided among all well-educated Irishmen who can talk about anything at any time. He has the art of a professed talker; and on matters specially within his own sphere, his business like genius invariably secures him a success. He was very well received; and though not so warmly cheered as the Brigade-General Keogh, he got quite sufficient applause to reward him for his friendly journey, and to send him home again content with having made his offering, the offering of forty-eight hours (no joke to a man occupied as he is) to the altar of Rooney.[66]

Sadleir's absence in London distanced him from the controversial letter of his colleagues. It is unlikely in any event that he would have committed himself to a clearly rash document and might even have prevented its publication.[67] He was a far more cautious individual than those involved and preferred to work behind the scenes to achieve his objects.

References

1. *Tablet* 16 August 1851. (Later George Ouseley Higgins M.P., Anthony O'Flaherty M.P., G.H. Moore M.P., and Thomas Meagher M.P., were added.
2. e.g. *Tablet* 16 August 1851 published lists showing that subscriptions were sent from England from individuals such as the Earl of Shrewsbury, Lord Arundel and Wardour and Lord Lovat of Beaufort Castle.
3. *Nation* 9 August 1851.
4. *Tablet* 16 August 1851.
5. Meeting reported in *F.J.* 20 August 1851, *Tablet* 23 August 1851. *Nation* 23 August 1851, The *Freeman's* carried a supplement to record the lengthy speeches of clergy and laity.
6. Moore, Reynolds, Sadleir, Keogh, O'Flaherty, Scully, Keating, Magan, Higgins, Blake, Nicholas V. Maher, Sir Timothy O'Brien (M.P. for Cashel), Devereux.
7. Edward Lowth Badeley (1823-1868). Graduated from Oxford in 1823, specialised in ecclesiastical law and promoted the spread of Tractarian principles. Became a Roman Catholic and a close friend of Newman. *D.N.B.*, e.v. under Badeley, Edward Lowth.
8. See Kerr, *Peel* , pp 155-156, 173 on the 1844 Rescript which was published in 1845.
9. The Archbishop of Westminster, the Bishops of Birmingham, Nottingham, Hexham, Southwark, Plymouth, Liverpool, Beverley, Salford, Northampton in England, the Archbishops of Armagh, Tuam, Cashel, the Bishops of Ardagh, Achonry, Meath, Cork, Waterford, and Lismore, Clonfert, Killaloe, Cloyne,

Kilmacduagh, Raphoe, Ross, Clogher, Kerry, Killaloe, Elphin, Derry; the following M.P.s John Reynolds (Dublin), William Keogh (Athlone), G.H. Moore (Mayo), John Sadleir (Carlow). George O. Higgins (Mayo), Martin Joseph Blake (Galway), Anthony O'Flaherty (Galway), Oliver D. Grace (Roscommon), William D. Magan (Westmeath), Nicholas Valentine Maher (Tipperary), Francis Scully (Tipperary), Thomas Devereux (Wexford), Sir Timothy O'Brien (Cashel), J.O'Brien (Limerick), Michael Sullivan (Kilkenny).

10.   *F.J.* 21 August 1851, *Tablet* 23 August 1851.

11.   *F.J.* 21 August 1851, *Tablet* 23 August 1851. M.P.s present were M.J. Blake, Galway; Anthony O'Flaherty, Galway; George Ouseley Higgins, Mayo County; G.H. Moore, Mayo; William Keogh, Athlone; Frank Scully, Tipperary County, John Reynolds, Dublin City; W.H. Magan, Westmeath; N.V. Maher, Tipperary; J.T. Devereux, Wexford; Sir Timothy O'Brien, Cashel. Northern Protestant clergymen present were Rev. John Rogers Comber, Co. Down, Rev. W. Dobbin, Banbridge, Rev. Black, Donaghadee, Rev. Rentoul, Co. Antrim, Rev. Bell, Ballybay; Julius McCullagh, Newtownards, Co. Down; Other Tenant Leaguers were Archdeacon Fitzgerald, Thomas O'Shea, Callan, William Mullally p.p. Donohill, John O'Dwyer c.c. Doon, Co. Limerick. James Redmond p.p. Arklow, Co. Wicklow, Thomas Montgomery, Aughnacloy, John Cashel Hoey, Sergeant Shee, Charles Bianconi, Dr. McKnight and John Grey of the *Freeman's Journal.*

12.   *F.J.* 22 August 1851, *Tablet* 23 and 30 August 1851.

13.   Sadleir, Higgins, Reynolds, Keogh, Moore, Scully, Nicholas V. Maher, O'Flaherty.

14.   Banquet proceedings reported in *F.J.* 24 September 1851, *Tablet* 27 September 1851, *T.F.P.* 24 September 1851, *N.G.* 24 September 1851. This was in the *Nation* 23 February 1856.

15.   *T.F.P.* 30 August 1851.

16.   Ibid.

17.   *Tablet* 27 September 1851 (Reynolds speech).

18.   Ibid.

19.   See Reynolds statement in *F.J.* 18 October 1851.

20.   Meeting reported in *F.J.* 18 October 1851, *Tablet* 18 October 1851.

21.   The Bishops of Meath, Clogher, Waterford and Clonfert.

22.   Listed in *Tablet* 18 October 1851 and *Irish Catholic Directory 1852*, pp 138 -141.

23.   See *Tablet* 25 October 1851 for other letters enclosing subscriptions.

24.   A letter 16 October 1851 from B. Ivers, Birmingham in *Tablet* 25 October 1851 stated that Ullathorne intended establishing a local association in Birmingham which would communicate with 'The Parent Association in Dublin'.

25.   See *F.J.* 5 December 1851 for a two column letter from Shee to Joseph Napier challenging him on points contained in Napier's recently published pamphlet *England or Rome – which shall govern Ireland.* Shee (1804-1868) was born in Finchley Middlesex, eldest son of Joseph Shee of Thomastown, Co. Kilkenny and of Laurence Pountney Place in London, a merchant. Attended a French school at Somers town at an early age. In 1818 attended St. Cuthbert's college Ushaw near Durham where his cousin Nicholas (later Cardinal) Wiseman was then a student. Admitted to Lincoln's Inn in 1823; called to the bar in 1828 and acquired an extensive practice. Took the degree of sergeant-at-law in 1840 and appointed queen's sergeant in 1857. In 1852 was elected M.P. for Kilkenny County. In 1860 he refused the chief-justiceship of Madras. In 1863 appointed a judge of the court of queen's bench and was knighted in 1864. He married Mary, the second daughter of Sir James Gordon of Gordonstown and Letter Source, Banffshire. *D.N.B.*, e.v.

26. *Tablet* editorial 18 October 1851.

27. Ibid., 25 October 1851.

28. Duffy in a leading article in the *Nation,* November 1851 considered the decision by the three M.P.s. 'a fatal blunder'. He admitted that one crucial difference between the Repeal Association and the Catholic Defence Association was the actual distribution of the *Nation* by the former. He admitted that some 'newspaper politicians' had attracted suspicion by their personal conduct and their 'slander of each other', but he objected to a blanket ostracisation of all members of the Press from the deliberations of the Association. He defended the integrity of current Irish papers in general and also listed eminent M.P.s. connected with the Press in England.

29. *Nation* 1 November 1851. Lorenzo Alexander, a relative of John Alexander the Conservative candidate who would ultimately unseat Sadleir was a fellow steward.

30. Banquet proceedings in *F.J.* 30 October 1851, *Tablet* 1 November 1851, *Nation* 1 November 1851.

31. Sadleir, Moore, O'Flaherty, O.D.J. Grace (Roscommon), J.T.Devereux (Wexford), M. Sullivan (Kilkenny borough), Reynolds, Frank Scully, Sir Timothy O'Brien, James Fagan.

32. Thomas Phillips p.p. Sligo, Dominick Noone p.p. Kilmacthomas, Co. Sligo.

33. *Tablet* 1 November 1851.

34. Atkinson V. Gray in *Tablet* 16 September 1854. The *Telegraph* was published three times a week but at the end of 1852 it became the *Weekly Telegraph*.

35. *Tablet* 6 March 1852. Onseley Higgins appears to have been a shareholder (reference of G.H. Moore in *Tablet* 3 February 1855). Keogh was also involved, but hardly in a financial sense due to his own money problems – see N.L.I., Moore papers, MS. 892, Keogh to Moore December 1851, (letter 354), do to do 5 January 1852, (letter 353), and do to do January 1852, (letter 357).

36. *T.L.* 24 November 1855.

37. *Tablet* 1 November 1851.

38. *Nation* 15 November 1851.

39. *F.J.* 14 November 1851 – *Nation* 15 November 1851. The M.P.s. were Sadleir, Higgins, Keogh, Thomas Meagher (Waterford City), Sir Timothy O'Brien, Nicholas V. Maher, M.E. Corbally (Meath), Reynolds, Frank Scully. Some of the laity listed were The Hon Edward Preston, The Hon. Charles Preston, The Hon. Thomas Preston. The High Sheriff of Drogheda, the Mayor of Clonmel, the Mayor of Waterford, Myles O'Reilly of Knock Abbey, and John McNamara Cantwell.

40. *The Nation* of 15 November 1851 and the *F.J.* 14 November 1851 expressed approval of this resolution.

41. *Tablet* 22 November 1851.

42. Sadleir, Keogh, Scully, T. Meagher (Waterford City), H.K. Grogan Morgan (Wexford County), J.A. Talbot (New Ross borough).

43. N.L.I., Moore papers, MS 892, Sadleir to Moore 19 November 1851.

44. Meeting reported in *F.J.* 26 November 1851.

45. Details of the project from March to November 1851 and of Sadleir's involvement as outlined above were sketched in Duffy's long letter of 10 March 1852 in *F.J.* 12 March 1852, *Tablet* 13 March 1852. See Sadleir's letter 13 March 1852 and Duffy's reply 17 March 1852 in ibid., 22 March 1852.

46. *Proposal for Establishing a Small Proprietors' Society*, (Dublin, n.d.) in R.I.A., Halliday pamphlet collection vol.2095 (8). See also *Nation* 15 November 1851.

47. Letter in *D.E.P.* 4 October 1851. See ibid., 7 October 1851 supporting Sadleir.

48. See *Nation* 15 November 1851 for Scully's letter 6 November 1851 expressing unease that he had been credited by some newspapers with originating the project. He wished to give Duffy credit for this at an earlier date but had been forbidden by Duffy to do so.

49. Their testimonials in *F.J.* 16 October 1851.

50. N.L.I., Moore papers, MS. 892, Burke to Moore, 23 September 1851.

51. Ibid., Burke to Moore N.D.

52. Cantwell's testimonial to Burke in *F.J.* 16 October 1851.

53. Details in *Tablet* 20 December 1851.

54. *F.J.* 18 December 1851.

55. *F.J.* 29 December 1851; see also H.W. Wilberforce, *Reasons for submitting to the Catholic Church, a farewell letter to his parishoners from a clergyman of the Established Church,* (London, 1851).

56. Letter in *F.J.* 20 December 1851, *Tablet* 20 December 1851.

57. N.L.I., Moore Papers, MS. 892, Keogh to Moore 27 December 1851.

58. *F.J.* 20 December 1851.

59. *Tablet* 27 December 1851.

60. Ibid.

61. Letter 19 December 1851 in *F.J.* 20 December 1851.

62. This letter and the editorial of Lucas placed Gray in an embarrassing position and he hastened to issue a further editorial on 22 December denying that the letter of the seven M.P.s was an appeal against the Primate. He refused, nonetheless, to compromise on his support for their stand, and, while careful to enlarge upon Cullen's status 'in the respect and affections' of Irish Catholics, he explained that Cullen as a cleric viewed the association from the religious standpoint but its constitution and its machinery were political. It's ends could only be effectively accomplished through political action. This political action came from an Irish party which operated on the basis of independence from the English government and the refusal to accept office or favours from this government.

63. Letter 22 December 1851 in *F.J.* 23 December 1851.

64. Redmond's letter 22 December 1851 in *Tablet* 27 December 1851.

65. N.L.I., Moore Papers, MS. 892, Keogh to Moore 27 December 1851.

66. Quoted in *Tablet* 3 January 1852.

67. See N.L.I., Moore Papers, MS. 892, letter 355, Keogh to Moore 5 January 1852 advising that 'we did not think it prudent in a new paper to take up the Wilberforce affair'. It is unlikely that Sadleir would have allowed the protesters to use the *Telegraph*, although Keogh was initially one of its staple writers – see N.L.I., Moore Papers, MS. 892 for several references to this role.

Chapter 7

Towards a General Election – January-March 1852

It is difficult to assess the damage done to the Association by the Wilberforce controversy, but some Leaguers would not have been unduly worried at its possible destabilisation. Lucas's first editorial in the new year was mildly pessimistic.[1] Little had been achieved since its foundation, but the appointment of the new secretary would bring about at least the 'possibility of work'. Wilberforce was challenged to justify his appointment by setting out a clear agenda for the Irish representatives on the Protestant Establishment, proselytism, education, emigrants and 'workhouse Immorality'.

The new secretary ignored the press criticism and over the next two years worked with Cullen, who became closely involved in the Association to the extent of chairing meetings of the general committee. The Archbishop demonstrated his personal interest by chairing the first meeting of 1852, which was also attended by Bishop Daniel Vaughan, Killaloe, who was a valuable link between the Association and the League and helped to smooth relations between the two.[2] Scully, Reynolds, O'Brien and Matthew Corbally, Meath, were at this meeting, which decided to appoint an assistant secretary with a salary of £150 a year. A public conference was arranged for 29 January and Wilberforce prepared an address to the 'Catholic world', which would be published with its proceedings.

The date was carefully chosen to immediately follow a banquet to Arundel and Surrey, member for Limerick County since the previous August, who had resigned his English seat in protest at the Ecclesiastical Titles Bill. It was hoped that many of the guests at the banquet would also attend the Association's meeting. A depressed Keogh wrote to Moore in December that he had no desire to go to the banquet but had promised to do so. He noted that Sadleir, too, wished to go and 'give expression to our views'.[3] Keogh did attend but Sadleir remained in London. Ironically Arundel himself was ill and could not travel from London.[4]

Bishop John Briggs of Beverley, a friend of Arundel, came to the celebration, which was designed not only to honour the Earl but to highlight the Association's mission and its philosophy of strengthening the union between the Catholics of the Empire. Apart from this, the banquet speeches tended to reiterate many of the parliamentary debates on the Titles Bill and lambasted the government while praising the Pope as the most enlightened of all pontiffs and an exemplar of good practice in terms of religious liberty. The Russell ministry was seen as the promoter of religious intolerance not only in legislative terms but almost in tacitly condoning proselytism in Ireland during the Famine.

Proselytism emerged as a dominant theme at the public conference of the Association held in its rooms in Rutland Square two days later.[5] The organisers were disappointed that only five M.P.s (Reynolds, Maher, Blake, O'Brien, and Devereux) present at the Limerick celebration travelled to Dublin. Cullen, as chairman, devoted his keynote address to this theme, and, while his language was part of defensive Catholicism, his portrayal of Protestantism in general as a disease was offensive and did little to heal the bitterness of the religious controversy. In his attack upon particular proselytising organisations he almost congratulated the Catholic Church on purging itself of such infected members

> whose God was their belly, or who were a prey to their pride, their concupiscence or their avaricious spirit, have immolated themselves and their children to Moloch. The drunkard, the unjust, the extortioner, the profligate – men or women who had previously no religion in practice, have occasionally strayed away, and are the prophets of the zeal of our modern pharisees, who, like their prototypes of the gospel compass sea and earth to make one proselyte, and when they have found him, make him a child of Hell tenfold worse than themselves.

The Archbishop also managed to link proselytism to the education issue, and in a wide-ranging indictment of an education system which failed to cater for the needs of Catholic children he underlined the Association's value as a vehicle for reform in that area. He also referred to the difficulties faced by Catholic children in England and overtly gave the appointment of Wilberforce his stamp of approval.

Nicholas Maher was the only signatory of the anti-Wilberforce address present and he publicly apologised 'for having allowed an impression to be made upon my mind that no Englishman could be found to discharge properly the duties of secretary of this association'. He was moved to make such an apology because he was impressed by the address of the Association to Catholics of the United Kingdom drafted by Wilberforce. It covered a wide range of issues and considered how the Association should deal with them. It was, in a sense, an official manifesto, but its details, while highlighting the issues, tended to reveal more weaknesses than strengths in the organisation. One of the main aims outlined was that of information gathering to discover the 'actual state of Catholics in every part of the empire' and to periodically publish reports on this. The question of funding was seen as a problem and it was obvious that the Association would not have a network like the Tenant League, but would rely upon prominent individuals, generally priests, at local level.

The permanence of such a centrally structured movement was seriously in question, but priestly electioneering influence at least guaranteed some substance to its promotion of an independent Irish party. The address began in this spirit,

> The Committee have already been actively employed...in endeavouring to organise and marshal the elective power of each constituent body, so as to secure a right direction being given to every available vote, with the object of creating and sustaining a parliamentary party ready to defend at all hazards and with an independent spirit our civil and religious liberties. With this view they have endeavoured to ascertain in the first place the actual strength of Catholics among the constituencies of each county, city and borough in Ireland, and, while the information thus acquired is very encouraging, it has convinced them that our strength may be much augmented by watchful care over the future registration.

The address also urged leading Catholics in every English and Scottish constituency to discover their actual voting strength on the registry and to impress upon voters the duty of using their franchise 'for the defence of their religion'. It specified the targets for the independent party as the titles Act, the Established Church and equity in public education grants. But its most immediate objective was the removal from office of the Russell administration. Opposition must be offered on all matters in a situation where the two main parties were evenly balanced. It was 'an unpleasant necessity'.

Lucas was present at this meeting and his ensuing editorial congratulated the Association on the opening of its campaign. His suspicion of the *bona fides* of the leading brigadiers, however, was deepened by the publication of Sadleir's newspaper in January.

Whether Sadleir considered the acquisition of a newspaper as a sound business proposition or as a means of securing favourable political publicity is not known, but in 1851 he had discussions with Gray about the possibility of buying the *Freeman's Journal*.[6] When these failed he considered Lucas as a prospective partner in a new venture, but was unable to agree terms, broke off negotiations and acquired a premises in 7 to 8 Lower Abbey Street for the *Telegraph*.[7]

The editor of the new paper, William Bernard McCabe, was an accomplished individual, who was more than a match for his three rivals and defended Sadleir and his associates with considerable skill. Always careful to publicise his editorial freedom[8] he made it clear, nonetheless, that Sadleir's ownership of the *Telegraph* was crucial in prompting him to accept the position of editor – 'the name that decided us to accede to the proposition made was that of John Sadleir – and that solely because of the character which he seemed to have established with the Irish people, as represented by the Irish newspapers'.[9]

In the early 1830s McCabe had been editor of *The Dublin Morning Register* and several provincial papers before going to London to work for the *Morning Chronicle*.[10] He knew several foreign languages and worked for a time as foreign correspondent of the *Chronicle*. He was the author of historical novels, some of which were translated into German, Italian and French. McCabe was also a historian of some note and published a three volume work entitled A *Catholic History of England*. This was presented to Pius IX and in return he received the pontifical blessing through Wiseman.

From its arrival on the market in January the hallmark of the new paper was its Catholicity. Appropriately it took its motto, which appeared over the editorial column, from Denys Scully's pamphlet on the Penal Laws – *The expectation of being useful to our country is our sole support and incitement.* The opening paragraph of its prospectus was a quotation from a lecture by Newman – 'the Catholics are treated with scorn and injustice simply because, though they have a good deal to say in their defence, they have never patiently been heard'.[11] The prospectus described the Association as a great power, but in danger of losing its potency if it lacked 'an earnest advocate' of its principles and policy. It pointed to the Protestant papers as a powerful influence in spreading the sentiments of the Durham letter, but conveniently ignored the role of the Irish papers, particularly the *Tablet* as the defenders of Catholic interests. By implication, too, the *Freeman's Journal*, published on a daily basis, was not considered an effective advocate of Catholic interests,

> It is strange and startling, but not the less true, that whilst every morning and evening, every day and week, every month and quarter, the Protestant Press sends forth hundreds of journals, metropolitan and provincial, all teeming with attacks upon Catholicism, perverting our

annals, libelling the living dignitaries of our Church, even assailing the weak and unobtrusive inmates of our religious houses – *the Catholics of this country do not possess a single morning or evening or even thrice a week paper, the property of Catholics, to advocate, to defend, to maintain the cause of truth and justice.*

It was to end this 'discreditable' situation that the *Telegraph* was established. It saw itself as influential with the Catholic representatives, having been 'called into existence with the authority, aid and full approval of the leading Catholic members of Parliament ..' This in itself did not endear it to Lucas, but he had a more commercial motive for hostility, and vowed that he would not 'for love or money' print its prospectus.[12] The fact was that the new paper considerably undercut its rivals. It sold at threepence a copy as against sixpence for its three competitors,[13] who were forced to lower their prices, but were unable to reach the *Telegraph's* price level.[14] The *Tablet* and the *Nation* suffered heavy losses as a result of the competition.[15] A combination of low price and good quality output meant that the *Telegraph* reached a circulation of over one million copies in 1852 as against a combined total of three quarters of a million for the daily, weekly and evening *Freeman's*.[16] The circulation of the *Tablet* was 215,000 while the *Nation* was only 191,000.

At the time of the *Telegraph's* launch Lucas was already in financial difficulties due to a successful libel suit. He was forced to raise subscriptions to meet the debt. Lists of contributors appeared in every issue of the *Tablet* during January and February. One of these was James Maher, who, although a supporter of Sadleir, named the *Tablet* and not the *Telegraph* as 'the cheapest, because the best Catholic paper in the Kingdom'.[17] Many of those who supported Lucas were priests and the majority were affiliated to the Tenant League.[18]

The League was given a boost by the prospect of the parliamentary campaign in support of Crawford's Bill, and in the early months of 1852 the land question gained in publicity at the expense of the religious one. Both organisations were competing for the purses of the Irish public and the League's organ, the *Irish Tenant League* was pleased at the ' general feeling' in favour of tenant right, but concerned that it had not translated into an expansion of the League whose agitation was 'languid and desultry'.[19]

While the existing tenant societies met on a regular basis,[20] the General Council convened on 13, 14 and 15 January to look at mechanisms for extending the network and promoting Crawford's Bill.[21] Bishop Vaughan took charge of the first session and advised that prominent leaguers should be selected by the Council to visit people in their homes to enrol members and collect money. He saw the towns as neglected and suggested that a beginning could be made in his own diocese. Assuming a degree of civil authority, he said that 'not only would he give them his entire sanction to proceed through his diocese in the manner he had pointed out, but he would also countenance them in every way and support them as far as he possibly could'.

The promotion of Crawford's Bill also demanded a practical strategy which included petitioning parliament and instructing local societies to keep in touch with their parliamentary representatives lest they accept a mutilated version of the bill. The 14 January session reinforced the necessity of supporting only tenant right candidates in the forthcoming election campaign.

An unexpected outcome of the three day conference, representing a departure from the usual theme of unity between the sectarian divides, was the decision to issue a memorial from the Catholic members of the League to the Irish hierarchy. It was a public recognition by the League of the episcopal power which underpinned the Defence Association. It was not published until mid-February[22] and its litany of evils – emigration, the workhouse system and high rents – was hardly new information to the bishops who were urged to motivate their clergy in the recruitment drive for new members. The memorial also sought to reassure all those priests who were suspicious of the League. John Cantwell of Meath and William Keane of Ross were the only bishops to respond with assurances of clerical support.[23]

The memorial was accompanied by an emotive address to the Irish people stating that tenant right was not a question of annual motions and reviews 'but the cry of the hungry for bread and of the weary for justice'.[24] It sought to stir the national conscience by a quotation from the *Times* which was shocking in its sentiments and the clarity of its prophecy,

> We resign ourselves without reserve, though not entirely without misgiving, to her continued depopulation, until only a half or a third of the nine millions claimed for her by O'Connell remain. We may, possibly, live to see the day when her chief produce will be cattle and English and Scotch the majority in her population. The nine or ten millions who by that time will have settled in the United States, cannot well be much less friendly, and will certainly be much better customers than they are now. When the Celt has crossed the Atlantic, he begins, for the first time in his life, to consume the manufactures of this country, and indirectly to contribute to its customs. Unquestionably there is much that is consolatory in that, and even comfortable, in the extraordinary turn that we witness in Irish affairs.

The memorial was clear that the fundamental solution to such potential depopulation lay in a unified Irish party in Westminster rather than 'an indiscriminate herd of members.' But, the unpalatable fact was that League candidates had so far been defeated in by-elections and the general election was the final hope of success. The people were therefore warned against secret enemies representing the popular cause in a 'hideous farce'. Sadleir was certainly considered one of these secret enemies and Lucas further explored the question of parliamentary representation in an editorial of 17 January which reviewed the state of the English parties in Westminster. He knew that representatives like Sadleir favoured the Peelites. Not only had the latter opposed the titles act, but Peel's successful handling of the initial stages of the Famine until his fall in 1846 contrasted strongly with the subsequent Whig failure to provide adequate relief measures. Lucas would not entertain any gratitude for this and warned his readers about putting any trust in them as possible friends of Ireland. He saw no difference in principle between Whigs and Peelites. The opposition of Gladstone and Graham to the Ecclesiastical Titles Bill was no more than serving their purpose to denounce an impractical and foolish policy. He recalled Graham's support for the 'godless colleges' as indicative of his real attitude to the Catholic Church. As far as the land question was concerned he reviewed Graham's response to the League's deputation – 'none was so frank in his opposition to their views as Sir James Graham, none so lofty in the determination he expressed to oppose the legislation of tenant right, and to look at this question of Irish land and Irish life from an English point of view'.

Sadleir's paper disagreed, insisting that it knew 'on the best authority' that Graham, if in power, would repeal the Ecclesiastical Titles Act.[25] His policy was

> the embodying of all that is real in the principle of civil and religious liberty. It proposes to base our civil institutions upon the widest measure of popular support, and to guarantee our religious freedom by placing all sects upon a footing of the most perfect equality. Embarrassed by no oligarchical clique, and incumbered by no prejudice, it will rally to its support the mental energy and practical resources of the leading representatives of the people of England who have been heretofore snubbed and insulted by the lordling faction.

The *Telegraph* also turned its attention to Gray, who had written a leader about Sadleir's alleged canvass of County Galway on behalf of Anthony Norris.[26] McCabe interpreted this as a 'gross, rude and monstrous' effort to injure Sadleir by associating him with an English candidate. Sadleir was hardly pleased at this description of his relative, but he denied the story and labelled it as one of many reports 'calculated with motives not very difficult to discover, and well adapted to prejudice the Irish members of Parliament ... a course of conduct natural enough, perhaps, at the hands of Tory writers, but not to be expected from Catholic or Liberal journalists'.[27]

He attended the commencement of Parliament on 3 February where the opening speeches made little reference to Ireland apart from Derby's thrust at the government's inaction in putting the Titles Act into operation and a brief reference by the Queen to violence in some northern areas.[28] Russell was absorbed by the dismissal of Palmerston as Foreign Secretary. The first motion on Ireland was by Crawford on his land bill and that afternoon nine Irish M.P.s – Sadleir, Keogh, Scully, Devereux, Higgins, Henry Grattan, Meath, O.D.J. Grace, Roscommon, Thomas Meagher, Waterford and John Greene, Kilkenny County – met in the King's Arms to discuss tactics on this.[29] They were concerned at the omission of any reference to the land question by the Queen, but decided against proposing any amendment to her speech because it would not receive the support of any party in the House. Keogh was for continuing the policy of exploiting the balance between the two main parties and it was agreed that the Brigade should all sit together below the gangway on the opposition side of the House. They met Crawford two days later in Sadleir's apartment to consider the introduction of his bill,[30] but the *Telegraph* was unwilling to reveal the tactics devised to support Crawford.[31] It reported, however, that the group had personally canvassed their other Irish colleagues to be present and 'baffle the low pettifoggery of the Whig ministerial clique and to secure for Mr. Crawford an ample and attentive auditory'.

On the same day Sadleir chaired the half yearly meeting of the London and County bank whose continued growth meant that a one per cent bonus was added to the six per cent dividend declared.[32] This expansion had been facilitated by the demise of yet another bank, the Berks Union Banking Company, which transferred the business of all its branches to the London and County. A new branch was opened at Paddington and the existing structure was rationalised by closing six of the smaller unprofitable branches.

Despite the chairman's optimistic report one shareholder was dissatisfied, but did not succeed in getting information about an alleged advance of £10,000 on the property of an Irish nobleman. The same shareholder also failed to get support for a resolution to obtain a charter of incorporation and the appointment of a government auditor to carry out an annual inspection of the accounts.

With the half yearly meeting safely behind him Sadleir could concentrate on the main Irish political agenda. Within a week Crawford opened the debate to bring in the bill 'to provide for the better securing and regulating of the custom of Tenant Right as practised in the province of Ulster, and to secure compensation to improving tenants who may not make claim under the said custom, and to limit the power of eviction in certain cases'.[33] He went through all his previous arguments on compensation for improvements, but after so many failures in the past he tried a more varied approach and made the case that statutory interference in landlord tenant relations was not only justified but was a popular demand by the Irish electorate at public meetings. While his bill aimed to protect the rights of landlords he explained that these were now endangered by agrarian combinations because unsatisfactory tenurial and rent situation provoked tenants to oppose even the just rights of proprietors. Government failure to legislate on the land issue was a major contribution to distrust of the government itself, disdain for the law and an incitement to violence. Landlords were forced to evict 'in a certain degree in their own defence' because tenants were unable to pay their rents.

These were novel arguments made possible because of the threat presented by the League, but the Home Secretary would not accept their validity.[34] Grey was convinced that the Government could not safely legislate on rent and he posed the dilemma of leaving rents unchanged for land whose value had been increased by improvements. He denied that sporadic outrages were caused by a demand for compensation. They were, he said, connected with a demand for rent reduction. Compensation would not solve a problem that was due to subdivision and the failure of the potato.

Neither did Crawford receive any comfort from the Peelites. Sir John Young, the future Irish Chief Secretary, also saw it as a delusion to imagine that legislation could solve the land problem.[35] It was unacceptable to legislate for the transfer of part of a landlord's property to the tenant. Money paid to the outgoing tenant through the Ulster Custom was lost to the land, because part of it was used to pay arrears and the remainder the fare to America. He conceded, however, that there was scope to legislate for compensation for improvements, because it would encourage investment.

Although the Bill was foredoomed, Russell's reason for allowing debate was to identify clauses that might be used in future legislation.[36] Like Young, he opposed giving statutory basis to the Ulster custom, which would constitute a form of legal confiscation. Unlike Young, he had no objection to the custom as a private arrangement between landlord and tenant. The root of the problem was a lack of confidence in the landlord and tenant relationship and no law would establish such confidence. Because of extensive subdivision he was not amenable to the proposal of compensation for improvements. No landlord could be expected to compensate for improvements on five small farms, which could justifiably be merged into one large holding.

Sadleir was one of the most prominent supporters of the Bill, thereby earning the gratitude and respect of Crawford.[37] But, mindful of the hostile comments by cabinet members, the Carlow M.P. felt that instant rejection would be better than a protracted debate ending in defeat. Since the tenants had every right to anticipate legislation their expectations would be heightened by such a debate and the crushing of these expectations could result in agrarian crime. Irish tenants had a genuine interest in the land, which, unlike their English counterparts, was unrecognised,

> In Ireland it is the tenant occupier who risks his money and means, and incurs all the expense, anxiety, and inconvenience of making permanent improvements. This state of things creates in the breasts of the people a passion for the land they have so improved, and creates the notion that the tenant is really a partner in the proprietorship of the land. But the tenant has no security that he may not be turned out to-morrow, and lose all the benefit of his exertions. It is, therefore, very desirable that some alteration should take place which would leave unchecked the enterprise and industry of the tenant occupier who has the spirit to make those improvements, which his landlord is unwilling to undertake.

The Incumbered Estates' Act did not remedy the legislative defects on compensation for improvements. Sadleir, who was by then fully *au fait* with the workings of the Act, claimed to know of many tenants who had invested heavily in drainage and farm buildings, and were then evicted by the new proprietors. Such insecurity was a basic flaw in Irish land tenure and he did not think that Crawford's bill went far enough in addressing it. Like the Leaguers he saw it as a step to a more comprehensive measure.

The second reading took place at the end of the month, but he made no contribution other than presenting petitions in its favour.[38] Two weeks earlier the Russell government had fallen and had been replaced by a Derby administration with Disraeli as leader of the House of Commons.[39] The new Attorney General, Joseph Napier, signalled his intention of dealing with the land question in due course, but Crawford's bill continued to be an opportunity for discussing and clarifying the problems besetting Irish land tenure, pending the tabling of Napier's measures. Further discussion was deferred until after the Easter recess and Derby was committed to dissolving parliament when the essential business had been dealt with.

From that moment the general election campaign effectively commenced and despite their common objective of an independent Irish party considerable disagreement still existed between the League leaders and members of the parliamentary committee of the Defence Association, in particular Sadleir and Keogh.[40] Towards the end of February Lucas and Gray attacked the silence of some Brigadiers during the debate on a motion by Naas condemning Clarendon's use of a Dublin newspaper to malign his political opponents.[41] With the exception of Moore they were accused of trying to 'whitewash Lord Clarendon's personal character', and were listed as 'present and dumb'. Sadleir was portrayed as reserving himself 'for another and more silent course of action', but did not respond to this criticism. Keogh, Higgins, Scully and Reynolds, however, retaliated with letters to the *Freeman's Journal*, which were reproduced in the columns of the *Telegraph*.[42] Keogh explained that the tactic of silence was a deliberate one because the vocal support of Catholic M.P.s might prompt some Protestant members not to support the Naas motion.[43] The crucial act was the casting of votes by the Irish members against the Whigs and the Athlone M.P. accused Gray of an ongoing attempt to discredit the Brigadiers,

> we were made to feel during the last session of parliament how you could run us up or let us down to suit the political thermometer of an individual with whom you are connected... The public has witnessed with disgust the system of petty conspiracy which you and others have joined in, with a view to weakening the influence which my friend, Mr. Sadleir, the member for Carlow, so justly holds throughout the Country. You have endeavoured to sustain this plot by every device. Paragraphs communicated to country journals, innocent of your designs, in order that after a provincial noviciate they might appear in more assured form in your metropolitan columns.

Reynolds sarcastically enquired who had appointed the Protestant Gray as defender of the Catholic faith, while Scully and Higgins curtly dismissed his right to dictate their conduct in Parliament.

Politics was not the sole cause of friction between the leaders at this time. Commercial rivalry flared up again early in March adding to this pre-election rancour. It originated in a series of resolutions by the priests of the Tuam Deanery sympathising with Lucas and praising the *Freeman's Journal*.[44] The priests upheld the benefits of competition, but deplored

> the want of foresight in our countrymen if, in order to procure a cheaper article, they should be so duped as to sacrifice the honest, vigilant, and

long-tried sentinel of their rights to a commercial combination, which after ruining the public censor, could soon be indemnified for its pecuniary losses by a free trade in political corruption.

Gray and Lucas used an article from the *Catholic Standard* praising the resolutions and attacking the *Telegraph* as the political tool of Sadleir, its paymaster,

> the *Tablet* must be muzzled, and the *Freeman's Journal* manacled, or the thousands of pounds expended in starting the *Telegraph* would be absolutely wasted. Whether these thousands came out of English banks, or insurance offices, or mining speculations, it would be a waste of time to enquire. All we want to know as bearing upon the influence of the press is, that the money has been had – that it is in course of expenditure – that the parties who lay it out have no character, no antecedents to screen them from the suspicion of having sinister, selfish objects in view – that they cannot afford to waste a fortune on patriotism or philantropy – and they are accused of bartering seats in parliament either for patronage or influence – that they have not succeeded in vindicating themselves from these heavy accusations.[45]

The article in the *Catholic Standard* had also censured Sadleir and Keogh for their apparent support of Naas in the Kildare by-election to ratify his appointment as Chief Secretary in the new Tory administration. In reality the *Telegraph* had published the manifesto of Naas's Liberal rival, William Cogan, and supported his candidature. But its praise of Naas in one editorial sent out mixed signals, which were gladly interpreted by the *Tablet* and the *Freeman* as support for the Tory candidate.[46] The *Telegraph* of 3 March, however, clarified its support of Cogan and denied that it had been instructed by Sadleir or Keogh to support Naas. Subsequently the parliamentary committee of the Defence Association issued an address to the electors of Kildare to reject Naas as a supporter of the Titles Act.[47] Naas lost the election, but was soon successful in Coleraine at the expense of Sadleir's friend, the Presbyterian Wilson Kennedy, who was supported by the League.[48]

Such a defeat for a certain Sadleirite adherent was a reminder of unpleasant political realities with the general election on the horizon. Sadleir felt that he could no longer ignore the frequent accusations of Gray and Lucas. He replied to the latter on 13 March that it was 'easy to invent and publish calumnies. It is easy and safe for you in one point of view to state that I have been guilty of all the political crimes and personal offences which you allege I have committed'. He challenged Lucas to substantiate any of the allegations made against him.[49]

It was not lost on Lucas that Sadleir's letter, although addressed to him, was sent to the *Cork Southern Reporter*, rather than the *Tablet*. He saw Sadleir's invitation to prove his case as a trap and was wary of restating his accusations,

> we have laid before our readers a complex case, made up out of many facts, most of them notorious, some of the most important of them actually confessed and admitted by those against whom our charges have been made; and if we were to restate them for Mr. Sadleir's convenience, we should either reprint what we have already published, or substitute for it a weaker and more ineffective statement, upon which no doubt Mr. Sadleir would very much prefer to join issue.

While the anti-Sadleir writings of Lucas sometimes contained more rhetoric than substance, Duffy had more damning evidence. At that precise moment he published an account of Sadleir's machinations in the Small Proprietors' Society[50] forcing the Carlow M.P. to respond in a letter also dated 13 March.[51] Sadleir could not refute many details in Duffy's letter, and resorted to the blanket denial of the politician,

> his letter is an apt corollary to the several slanders recently manufactured and circulated for reasons which the public thoroughly understand and which I can afford to despise. I dare say his labours to create ill-feeling between me and the gentlemen whose names he has most unwarrantably introduced into his letter, will not prove more effective than the organised system of calumny by which he and the clique he is attached to, are foolishly attempting to write down to the political party to which I belong.

When Sadleir asserted that the demise of the Society was due to Duffy's refusal to stand down as managing director, the *Nation* editor clarified, in a letter of 17 March, that he had immediately resigned when Sadleir had objected to him playing a managerial role.[52] The latter was blamed for 'strangling' the project, apparently because there were more attorney's costs to be made in purchasing small allotments for English clients.

Sadleir's letters were written from the Imperial Hotel, Cork, where he was involved in the three week by-election campaign of Vincent Scully following the resignation of the sitting M.P., Dr. Maurice Power, who was appointed colonial governor of St. Lucia. Prior to this Scully did not have any plans to enter politics, but when the Cork seat became vacant Sadleir pressed him to run.[53] At that time Scully rightly considered himself the legal owner of Castlehyde, since he had not made any conveyance to Ingram.[54] Sadleir, however, was adamant that

Ingram had purchased the estate although in reality he had not yet been approached by the Carlow M.P. Sadleir soothed Scully with the assurance that Ingram would re-sell so that Scully would have a Cork address to strengthen his claim as a candidate for the constituency. In a letter of 1 March he further assured Scully that Ingram 'understands our game and agreed to say or do as I tell him'.

Scully had no reservations about using Castlehyde as his election address, which he felt gave him as good a claim as the local candidates to appeal to the electorate. These were William Fagan and Alexander McCarthy. Fagan had represented Cork City until June 1850 when he resigned in chagrin following constituency criticism of one of his votes in September. He was supported by Maguire in the *Cork Examiner*, who looked on his return as 'an accomplished fact' because of his strong support base throughout the county.[55] Fagan had commenced his canvass by the end of February and the most conspicuous evidence of support came from an election rally at the horse fair in Millstreet on 1 March, which was attended by several priests.[56]

McCarthy was an individual of considerable means and less sensitivity than Fagan. According to the *Examiner* he had entered the contest too late and was endangering unity within the Liberal camp.[57] Both McCarthy and Fagan stood for civil and religious liberty and for agrarian reform as contained in Crawford's bill.[58]

Scully entered the contest on 3 March having secured the support of Bishop Murphy and the Cloyne priests. They met in Mallow chapel early in March to consider the merits of various candidates[59] and were impressed by Scully's views on the Queen's Colleges, an issue which Maguire considered politically divisive, because opinion in Ireland was equally divided on it.[60] Scully brought his legal ingenuity into operation by favouring the colleges in principle but condemning their constitution as excluding Catholic Church control. This satisfied the Bishop and a majority of the priests. The minority was bound to majority decision and a united front in favour of Scully was presented to the constituency.

He published a detailed address on 3 March listing his political priorities, which placed agrarian reform as the most important and favoured what he called free trade in land, whereby the landlords rights were preserved and the tenant was compensated for improvements.[61] Despite his free trade beliefs in general, Scully saw the uninhibited importation of corn and cattle into Ireland as a burden which, however, could be offset by cancelling repayment of the Famine advances. On the religious side he pledged his continuous support for the repeal of the Ecclesiastical Titles Act, the abolition of tithes and opposition to any system of education, which would 'withdraw from their spiritual fathers the full control of all matters appertaining to faith and religion'.

In an electioneering move, similar to the Carlow tactics of James Maher, Sadleir published an address from Mallow on 5 March supporting his cousin.[62] Most of this concerned the importance of an Irish Party as the only hope of achieving agrarian and religious objectives. Scully was portrayed as a strong supporter of such a party and the voters were exhorted to

> follow up the triumph which Kildare has already secured, and, in your combined power and fixed resolution, give fresh heart and blood, and increased strength to the *Irish Parliamentary Party*, whose policy, decision and energy the Catholics of the Empire have recognised and honoured.

Despite the fact that Scully was supported by the Bishop of Cloyne, Lucas was alarmed at the prospect of another parliamentary addition to the Sadleirites. He impugned Sadleir's intervention as an attempt to dictate to the Cork electors 'to induce them to strengthen his evil confederacy',[63] and satirised him as an Irish Coppock[64] 'hot from the disposal of Kildare to the orangemen'. The *Telegraph* easily parried this less than truthful editorial thrust and published a letter of support for Scully from Moore.[65] McCabe portrayed Scully as an expert on the land question, who understood all the clauses of Crawford's bill.[66]

Scully was not assured of success. Traditionally the Liberal endorsement of any candidate for Cork was made at a county meeting. P. Fitzpatrick, the parish priest of Millstreet, headed a group of priests and electors in demanding such a meeting,[67] which convened at the Chamber of Commerce in Cork city on 8 March.[68] Sadleir did not attend, but Keogh was there and James Morrogh of Fermoy, a relative of Scully, arrived.[69]

A small deputation of Cloyne priests came to propose Scully, and the meeting revealed a deep divide between these and the priests of Cork and Ross who opted for McCarthy.[70] Several of the speakers, including E.B. Roche, the other member for Cork County, who did not support the Brigade, saw Sadleir's interference as detrimental to Scully's chances. Maguire in the *Examiner* pronounced that Sadleir, unlike O'Connell, did not have the stature to make such interference.[71] A proposal to adopt Scully was met with disapproval and had to be withdrawn. A counter proposal binding the meeting to support the favoured candidate was passed. In a major break with tradition both Scully and the Cloyne priests refused to accept this decision. He insisted on putting his case and was frequently interrupted by hecklers who demanded more decisive answers on the Queen's Colleges. His apparent evasiveness was an excuse to reject him and McCarthy was adopted by thirty three votes to ten.

This represented a minority portion of the entire electorate, however, and the Cloyne priests, who represented two thirds of the clerical body in the constituency, had the support of a correspondingly greater number of voters.[72] Bishop Murphy subsequently refused to see McCarthy, who decided to withdraw, ostensibly to avoid splitting the Liberal vote.[73] Scully now only faced a Conservative opponent, Moreton John Edward Frewen, who because of illness on nomination day was represented by his cousin Edward Frewen M.P. for East Essex

The nomination convention was held on 15 March in the County Criminal Court and was presided over by the High Sheriff, John Courtney of Ballyedmond.[74] Frewen was nominated by Lord Bernard of Bandon and Scully by Cornelius Corcoran, the parish priest of Tracton. Sir Colmen O'Loghlen[75] was present to support Scully whose following was reinforced by his relatives. Leonard Morrogh came from Dublin[76] and was joined by Cork city relatives, Henry Morrogh J.P. and Bryan Gallwey.[77] Sadleir arrived with his cousin, Nicholas. Chastened by the previous reaction to his written address, he did not speak, but as the meeting degenerated into a rowdy affair he lost his temper and was involved in a fracas. Speakers found it difficult to state their policies as personal invective punctuated the proceedings. Edward Frewen was accused of moving a clause in the Commons threatening transportation on any priest who appeared on the hustings. Sadleir intervened to verify that this occurred. Scully, on the other hand, was shown as a stringent landlord,whose leases empowered him to seize a tenant's property within three days of defaulting on rent. He was unable to refute this and became increasingly irritated under cross-examination.[78] Most of McCarthy's adherents, however, felt no option but to support him and a show of hands was in his favour.

The Sadleirs accompanied Scully on his canvass throughout the following week. James B. Kennedy was his conducting agent. The poll books for the various booths were opened in the grand Jury room on 22 March and at the end of a two hour count Scully won by 3,956 votes to 3,105. This was not a significant margin and indicated considerable electoral support for the Conservative party and its policy of protection.[79] A breakdown of polling areas showed that Frewen received a majority in the western part of the constituency. The Liberal vote was also smaller than usual because of the resentment at Scully's candidature. Maguire was satisfied at the Liberal victory, but reserved judgement on Scully.[80]

Following the declaration of the poll Scully and his supporters adjourned to the Circus in Mary Street, where post-election addresses were presided over by P. D. O'Regan, the parish priest of Kanturk. Scully was guaranteed support at the forthcoming general election and Cornelius Corcoran, his leading clerical supporter, voiced his indignation at how he had been interrupted and hooted during the campaign. Both Corcoran and Scully pointed to Kinsale and Bandon, where tenants had been intimidated by landlord agents. Scully detailed individual acts of intimidation and quoted from circulars to tenants warning them to support Frewen.

In this more amenable setting Sadleir was applauded for his role in the campaign, but admitted that his address to the Cork electors had caused offence to some, of 'whose exquisite and delicate sensitiveness he confessed he was not then aware'. This mild irony was tempered by explaining that the offence was not intentional. He had felt entitled to involve himself because of his property in Cork and he feared that the Conservatives might triumph , because 'all the English gold and Carlton Club intrigue, conjoined with Bernard Valour, could achieve, would be attempted to crush and strike down the voice of the independence of the county'. Landlord tactics during the election rankled with him, and he made his strongest condemnation of landlordism to date,

> what a pretty document it would be to furnish to the world a statistical account of the thousands of pounds sterling, which in their overweening confidence the tenant farmers of Ireland had deposited with their faithless and dishonourable landlords.

The Liberal press, which should have supported Scully was set on a par with Tory intimidation. 'Vilest slanders' had been made upon the Irish representatives by these papers, but he 'again repeated that he would not succumb to the attacks' made upon himself. Unity among Liberal ranks was essential to a strong Irish party as the solution to Ireland's problems. Sadleir's definition of independent opposition, however, greatly differed from that of Lucas, Duffy and Gray and was consistent with his future course in parliament. The Irish party was one

> determined never to lend themselves to mean, low, paltry or factious opposition, for the purposes of party, or dogging any administration, call it by what name they would – so long as the government was sincerely and honestly engaged in promoting some sound measures for this country they would support them. Some excellent Protestants and some respectable Catholics complained and asked why should the Irish party wear that sectarian hue – why do they not cast aside those sectarian colours and distinctions, and then we would be delighted to join them. But he would ask these men to put their finger on the occasion when

this party flinched from the performance of their duty, or allowed sectarian feelings to prevent them from working side by side with the most rampant and fervent Tory, or the most constitutional Whig, whenever that rampant Tory or habitual Whig was fortunate enough to propose in Parliament those measures which were deserving the support of that Irish party.

That definition was well received indicating that the policy of total opposition to all parties, who did not signal their intention of repealing the titles Act or promote Crawford's measure, was not held by all liberal sectors in Ireland. He further clarified his views at a dinner in honour of Scully in the Imperial Hotel that evening, when he said that any government refusing to espouse these could not have the confidence of the Irish party, which would be disgraced if it did not pressurise the government on them.[81] Such an opinion was far from independent opposition, however, and he did not bear any ill-will towards M.P.s, who seceded from the party, 'some from conscientious motives'.

He made a similar response to a toast proposed by Nicholas Sadleir, who officiated at the dinner. A large number of priests were there and Nicholas praised their role in defending the tenants against landlord threats. He boiled the election down to a priest versus landlord conflict, the priests acting for the national interest, the landlords for their own. Scully also acknowledged clerical support. He had personally explained his policies, especially that on the Queen's Colleges, to the satisfaction of the three Bishops of Cork, Ross and Cloyne, whose support was a guarantee of unity among the clergy during the approaching general election. He realised that unity among the Liberal electors was of fundamental importance when that time arrived and he admitted that such unity had yet to be achieved.

References

1. *Tablet* 3 January 1852.
2. Reported in ibid., 17 January 1852.
3. N.L.I., Moore Papers, MS. 892, Keogh to Moore 31 December 1851.
4. Reported in a supplement to the *Tablet* 31 January 1852. Letters of apology from Cardinal Wiseman, Archbishops Cullen, McHale, Murray and Slattery, Bishops O'Higgins, Blake, McNally, Derry, French, Brown, Feeny, Murphy, O'Donnell, Gillis, Hogarth, Errington and Murdoch.
5. Meeting reported in *Tablet* 31 January 1852.
6. *Tablet* 16 September 1854, evidence in the Atkinson V Gray case.
7. *W.T.* 12 April 1856. See B.N. 10 January 1853 for the assertion that the Telegraph was established 'almost exclusively' with Sadleir's money.
8. *Telegraph* 6 September 1852, *W.T.* 24 December 1852, *C.T.* 21 June 1856. See *F.J.* 26 February 1853 for reference to McCabe's 'servile imbecility'.

9.   *Telegraph* 15 January 1853.

10. See D.N.B., e.v. under McCabe. See also *W.T.* 18 August 1855 and D. Griffiths (ed.), *The Encyclopaedia of the British Press 1422– 1992*, (London, 1992), p. 385.

11. *Telegraph* 5 January 1852.

12. Quoted in *W.T.* 8 January 1853.

13. C. Mitchel, *The Newspaper Press Directory 1857*, (London,1857), esp. pp 86-88.

14. For details of prices and satirical exchanges between the papers see *Telegraph* 10 March 1852, *Tablet* 15 January 1853, *W.T.* 12 March, 16 April, 30 June, 24 December 1853.

15. N.L.I., Moore Papers, MS. 892, John Cashel Hoey, (then proprietor of the *Nation*) to Moore 12 March 1856. When the *Telegraph* was launched Lucas, too, was in such financial difficulties that he was even unable to cover his election expenses of £300, having to rely on Gray for assistance, D.D.A., Cullen Papers, Lucas to Cullen 6 April 1852.

16. See *N.L.I.*, Moore Papers, MS. 892, Keogh to Moore 14 January 1852 expressing satisfaction at the *Telegraph's* performance. See *W.T.* 27 May 1854 for a tabular comparison between the circulation of the *Telegraph* and the other papers, see also *A return of the names of all newspapers in the United Kingdom to which Halfpenny stamps were issued during the year 1852; stating the number of such stamps issued to each newspaper, and the amount paid to the stamp office by each on account of such stamps.* H.C. 1852-55 (432) XXX.509, H.C. 1854-55 (83) XXX.509, H.C. 1859 (230-Sess 2) XV 495.

17. Letter 11 January 1852 in *Tablet* 17 January 1852.

18. e.g. The *Tablet* 31 January 1852. Letter from William McCarton p. p. (Rasharkin Tenant Society), letter from Thomas Mullaney p.p., Drom, Co. Tipperary. Ibid., 7 February 1852 letter from Wm. Keane Bishop of Ross (a collection of £6 made in the diocese; letter from Francis Kelly, Bishop of Derry £2); Ibid., 13 March 1852 letter 8 March 1852 from ten Mayo priests, subscription from Manchester, ibid., 27 march 1852 subscription from Peter Kennedy c.c. Kells, Co. Meath and C. Buckley c.c. Buttevant, Co. Cork; Ibid., 8 May 1852 Daniel O'Keeffe c.c. Hammersmith. Ibid 19 June 1852 list from Manchester. Ibid., 14 February 1852 letter from McHale enclosing one donation for the Tablet Indemnity fund and another for the Tenant League. Ibid., 21 February 1852 Letter 19 February 1852 from Bishop Murphy, Cloyne enclosing £20 for the fund and £100 for the League.

19. Quoted in *Tablet* 3 January 1852.

20. e.g. *Tablet* 17 January 1852 – Meetings in Ballinrobe, Co. Mayo and Duleek, Co. Meath, ibid., 7 February 1852 for monthly meeting of the Kells Society, meetings in Belfast and Sixmilebridge, Co. Clare; ibid., 21 February 1852, meetings in Killaloe, Co. Clare, Castlebar, Co. Mayo; ibid., 13 March 1852 meetings in Banbridge, Wexford and Tipperary.

21. Reported in *Tablet* 17 January 1852.

22. Text in *Tablet* 14 February 1852.

23. Letters in ibid.

24. Published in ibid., 7 February 1852.

25. *Telegraph* 6 February 1852.

26. *F.J.* 2 February 1852.

27. Letter 4 February 1852 in *Telegraph* 6 February 1852.

28. Reported in *Tablet* 7 February 1852.

29. *Telegraph* 4 February 1852.

30. Brief reference to the two hour meeting in *Telegraph* 6 February 1852.

31. *Telegraph* 6 February 1852 reported that the meeting was held at the private residence of 'one of their most active members'. See reference of Henry Grattan M.P. in *Telegraph* 4 June 1852 that the meeting was held in Sadleir's rooms.

32. Ibid., 6 February 1852.

33. *Parl. Deb.*, series 3, vol 119, 1852, col.333, (10 February 1852). Crawford's full speech in cols. 333-340.

34. Ibid., cols. 340-342.

35. Ibid., cols. 351-353.

36. Ibid., cols. 358-361.

37. Sadleir's speech in ibid., cols. 353-356.

38. *Tablet* 3 April 1852.

39. See ibid., 21 February 1852 for details of the office holders in Derby's administration.

40. This committee had twenty two members of whom nine were M.P.s. Vincent Scully and Nicholas V. Maher were members.

41. *Tablet* 21 February 1852. For debate see *Parl. Deb.*, series 3, vol. 119, 1852, cols. 764-856, 19 and 20 February 1856.

42. *Telegraph* 27 February 1852.

43. See editorial in ibid., 16 February 1852 stressing the importance of voting against the Ministry on the Clarendon motion.

44. Quoted in *Tablet* 6 March 1852.

44. *F.J.* 16 March 1852, *Tablet* 20 March 1852.

46. *F.J.* 4 March 1852, *Tablet* 6 March 1852, *Telegraph* 27 February, 1, 3, 12 March,19 May 1852 McCabe may have been influenced by the fact that some Brigadiers felt that Naas might be more valuable to their cause since the Conservatives had just come to power.

47. *Tablet* 13 March 1852.

48. Ibid., 20, 27 March 1852.

49. Letter in *Cork Southern Reporter* quoted by the *Tablet* 20 March 1852.

50. Duffy's letter 10 March 1852 in *F.J.* 12 March 1852.

51. Letter in ibid., 16 March 1852.

52. Duffy's letter 17 March 1852 in ibid., 18 March 1852.

53. *F.J.* 10 December 1856, (Scully's evidence).

54. See p. above.

55. *C.E.* 25 February 1852.

56. Ibid., 3 March 1852.

57. McCarthy finally succeeded when he was elected for Cork County in 1857.

58. Their addresses are in *C.E.* 3 March 1852. Another candidate, William Drew, published an address but was not considered a serious contender.

59. *C.E.* 5 March 1852.

60. Ibid., Maguire's fears of a split in Liberal ranks also increased with Scully's arrival, although he looked favourably on Scully's avowal of the policy of creating a strong Irish party.

61. *C.E.* 5 March 1852, *Telegraph* 12 March 1852.

62. *Telegraph* 8 March 1852.

63. *Tablet* 6 March 1852.

64. James Coppock 1798-1857. Born in Stockport, the eldest son of William Coppock, a textile dealer. Served an apprenticeship in his father's business and was placed as a clerk with a wholesale haberdasher in London. Lost all in capital in a small silk firm and in 1829 articled himself to a solicitor. He was admitted an attorney in 1836 and (like Sadleir) became a parliamentary agent. Was one of the

founders of the London Reform Club. *D.N.B.*, e.v..

65. *Telegraph* 8 March 1852.

66. Ibid., 10 March 1852.

67. *C.E.* 8 March 1852.

68. Meeting reported in *C.E.* 8 March 1852 (see also *Tablet* 13 March 1852).

69. He was probably Leonard Morrogh's father, who was married to Catherine Keating, sister of Robert Keating and granddaughter of old James Scully of Kilfeacle. Morrogh was a member of Scully's election committee, (*C.E.* 15 March 1852).

70. Fagan withdrew because of clerical opposition to his stance on the Queen's Colleges. Fagan always maintained his approval of these.

71. *C.E.* 10 March 1852. Roche argued that Scully was an outsider and 'coming from a party unconnected with this county was not only indecorous to the Liberal Party here', but such a precedent, i.e. selecting Scully, would undermine the 'usefulness' of the candidate ultimately chosen. Roche maintained that Scully's influence in parliament would be damaged if it became known that he was the 'nominee of any party or of any individual'. Roche himself was clear that he would not vote with any party, but on the merits of each individual question. The Brigade was tied to certain individuals and was not a broad party. Cork should be represented by a Cork man and not by someone put forward by a clique. He proposed a resolution condemning the dictation of any person outside the county, but was forced to withdraw it when it was objected to as being divisive. Justin McCarthy, the parish priest of Mallow, denied that the Cloyne clergy were dictating to the constituency and rejected the implication that they had acted 'under the direction of Mr. Sadleir'. McCarthy had been secretary to the meeting of Cloyne clergy which issued its declaration of support for Scully. P. Fitzpatrick, parish priest of Millstreet, strongly objected to the action of the Cloyne priests and felt that the rest of the county had been disfranchised by them. Scully defended Sadleir's right to publish his letter and bring to the constituency the benefit of his parliamentary experience as a member of the Irish party.

72. *Telegraph* 10 March 1852.

73. *Tablet* 13 March 1852. See *C.E.* 12 March 1852 for subsequent addresses by McCarthy and Scully. McCarthy's address pinpointed the power of the priests in electioneering at that time. He complained that the clergy of one diocese undertook to 'dispose of the representation of the county'. Scully's brief address urged unity. The editorial of the *Examiner* called for a united Liberal front from then on.

74. *C.E.* 15 March 1852. *Telegraph* 17 March 1852, *Tablet* 21 March 1852.

75. He was the eldest son of Sir Michael O'Loghlen and was born in 1819. He graduated from Dublin University in 1840 and was called to the Irish bar that year. He took Silk in 1852. In 1863 he became M.P. for Clare. In 1868 he was appointed judge-advocate-general in Gladstone's Ministry and a member of the privy council. He introduced and carried the bill enabling Catholics to hold the position of Lord Chancellor of Ireland. He died suddenly on 22 July 1877 on board the mail boat while crossing from Holyhead to Kingstown (Dun Laoghaire). *D.N.B.* ,e.v.

76. Morrogh brought his legal partner James B. Kennedy.

77. Gallwey was a solicitor. For the Scully Gallwey connection see MacDermot, *I.G*, vol 6, pp 65, 68 et. seq.

78. He later denied that he had such leases – *Tablet* 27 March 1852.

79. Proceedings at the declaration of the poll in *Telegraph* 24 March 1852, *C.E.* 19,22 March 1852.

80. 'We verily believe there are not many men in this County who from their hearts congratulate the electors upon a 'glorious triumph' in the return of Vincent Scully to parliament. If they do, then we can only say they are either great enthusiasts or they are easily pleased ... we saw and heard the man on two public occasion ... and we must confess we were thoroughly disenchanted, if not much more'? *C.E.* 22 March 1852.

81. *Telegraph* 26 March 1852.

Chapter 8

A most contentious General Election

Disunity in the Liberal camp during the Cork by-election did not obscure the value of Scully's victory as an indication that the Irish party would be strengthened in the general election. The Sadleirites could draw satisfaction from an increase in their numbers and the Dublin Liberal press could hardly condemn success over the Conservatives. With the common aim of an independent Irish party to promote their respective policies the Defence Association and the League intensified efforts to secure suitable candidates as the election drew nearer.

Much of the business of the League's monthly meeting on 20 April 1852 was given to reports on preparations for the election in various counties where Leaguers worked with the local election clubs.[1] The meeting published the address of sixty two tenant righters from different parts of Ireland, advocating that support for Crawford's bill should be the central pledge of all candidates,

> our advice, therefore, which we most earnestly desire to impress on all friends of tenant right is, that in every constituency where two hundred, or one hundred, or even fifty voters can be brought together, who are staunch friends of Sharman Crawford's bill, that they should give fair notice to whatever club or committee may be making arrangements for the elections, of their intention either to vote against or, at least to withold their votes from any candidate who shall not heartily and honestly adopt Sharman Crawford's bill.

Thomas O'Shea, Callan, was absent because of illness, but wrote offering his advice on how to approach the election.[2] He proposed prominent leaguers like Duffy, Gray, Lucas, Maguire and Lalor as candidates and asked that their names be forwarded to various constituencies. He suggested a collection for a fund of two hundred pounds to meet the cost of League deputations to canvass those constituencies. The adoption by candidates of Crawford's bill in its entirety was particularly crucial,

> The Council should above all things beware of those shams who talk

about supporting the principle of Crawford's bill, or about compensation, or unexhausted improvements etc; these are the greatest swindlers going. We must have the bill, the whole bill and nothing but the bill, have only what is better than the bill. Let no one be countenanced, but the man who pledges himself to the detail, as well as the principles of the bill. Principles are too spiritual, ethereal, and metaphysical entities to bind those who talk about them. Let us have the plain palpable substance as embodied in our bill.

The substance of Crawford's bill, however, proved unpalatable to Westminster and within two weeks it was refused a second reading.[3] League commitment to promoting tenant right candidates did not waver, but was strengthened by the decision of Lucas, Duffy and Gray to contest the election. Gray ran for Monaghan and Duffy accompanied him to a meeting with the Carrickmacross Tenant Right Association in April.[4] He received the support of a large number of priests and Presbyterian ministers.[5] Duffy opted for New Ross, where his opponent was Sir Thomas Redington, who hoped to retain the seat vacated by his father-in-law, John Hyacinth Talbot of Talbot Hall, Wexford. He was a Catholic, and, like Vincent Scully, an alumnus of Oscott College. The backing of James Walsh, the parish priest, for his candidature was not enough to restrain Lucas from pillorying him in a leading article as a 'thorough political prostitute', who 'held the garments of the executioners when they stripped themselves to the skin to scourge the Redeemer of mankind in the person of His Church'.[6] This exploitation of the religious issue gave a foretaste of what was to come in the election on a national level.

Duffy was joined on his canvass at the end of March by Lalor and O'Shea.[7] The local curate, Thomas Doyle, disagreed with his parish priest and spoke strongly in favour of him as a candidate of integrity. This endorsement, however, was accompanied by a denial that he himself had ever espoused Young Irelandism. Likewise, James Redmond also supported Duffy, while believing him 'to have been mistaken in his former course'.[8] Redmond's sentiments were in a letter read to a meeting at the Tholsel in New Ross on 12 April. O'Shea and Gray were at this rally, which also attracted a deputation of Leaguers from Waterford and priests from several Wexford parishes.[9] While the principal theme was tenant right, the religious issue was used mainly as a weapon against Redington. O'Shea recited a litany of complaints against the ex-Under-Secretary as an emissary of the Whigs during the famine years and wound up on the religious note,

who sought to bastardise the children of Catholic parents by making all the acts of their pastors invalid in the eye of the law? The Whigs, and their Secretary in Ireland was Thomas Redington, and who for all his services obtained as his reward his red ribbon and the letters 'K.C.B.' He was allowed to put these letters after his name, and so well he might, standing as they did for 'Killer of Catholic Bishops'.

Duffy was unable to meet the expenses of an election, but the League Council set up a committee to raise a fund for him, which attracted subscriptions from many areas.[10] Lucas, who was in worse financial straits, told Cullen in a lengthy letter of 6 April that Gray had offered to share election expenses with him and was willing to put down £300, 'what I could not afford'.[11] His letter, which was an attempt to answer some of the Archbishop's reservations about Gray and Duffy,[12] began by congratulating Cullen on his appointment to Dublin and ended with a 'supplication for forgiveness' because he had to join forces with his two newspaper rivals due to the hostility by the Parliamentary Committee of the Defence Association to all their journals. Nonetheless, Lucas defended Duffy as worthy of an Irish constituency and assured the Archbishop that he would be 'kept in order' by the New Ross priests and 'would not play the fool in parliament on the Church question if in his heart he were otherwise disposed'. He also explained that he was prepared to go constituency hunting with Gray, 'a Protestant rival', because their private interest and the public interest were identical. Lucas's own desire for a seat was acute. He reached for Cullen's sympathy with the spectre of success by Gray, Duffy and Maguire, while he himself was in danger of being 'pushed out of every semblance of confidence, popular and personal, a mere foreigner whom nobody cares to trust and who, if he does not look about him, will soon have to make a second migration to Australia or America'. His wish for a seat, however, did not stretch to a joint venture with Keogh, even 'if I were paid for it'.

He could not hide his dislike of the Parliamentary Committee, dominated by the O'Farrells and Prestons and the 'dishonest knot of politicians commonly called the Brigade'. This was incompetent, had excluded him from the Defence Association , and was the 'bitterest and most damaging enemy I have had to my property, my character and my prospects through life'. Unaware of Cullen's good relationship with Sadleir, Lucas said that it was imperative that a group of independent and honest members be returned in the election to counteract 'the Sadleir and Scully firm'.

A fortnight later Lucas was accepted by the Meath constituency, which agreed to meet his election expenses.[13] The sitting member, Henry Grattan, a Brigadier and son of the famous patriot, was rejected by an overwhelmingly clerical selection committee. Despite this favourable turn of events for Lucas and the prospects of electoral success for the other newspapermen, League leaders were worried by the end of May that charges of League promotion of agrarian outrage would damage their prospects in the election. A Crime and Outrage committee, of which Keogh, O'Flaherty and Frank Scully were members, had been established by Parliament to investigate murders, which had occurred in the north. The statement of Maxwell Hamilton, the Crown Solicitor of the North East Circuit,[14] to this committee that the League was the instigator of these crimes, received widespread publicity. The Leaguers drafted a requisition for a meeting, which the Lord Mayor convened in Dublin on 25 May, to refute this. It was attended by the three newspaper editors, Bell, Cantwell, Burke, Battersby, Hoey and other prominent Leaguers.[15] Their position was strengthened by a letter from Bishop Timothy Murphy of Cloyne to treat with 'ineffable scorn the malevolent ravings of this paltry and apparently demented official'. On 22 May Lucas and Samuel Bindon as joint secretaries of the League had written to Joseph Napier, the Irish Attorney General and chairman of the Outrage committee, demanding the opportunity to appear before it.[16] The unrealistic aim of the Dublin meeting was to force the Committee to prolong its sitting beyond the week-end and invite the evidence of League witnesses. Lucas's evidence was clear from his Dublin speech, which proved that the League had been inactive in the counties affected by the murders. His denunciation of Napier in particular and the Derby government in general was one way of ensuring that he would not be called as a witness.

Such an attack was also an election tactic, but it did not receive any support from the Defence Association. Lucas was unhappy at its apparent reluctance to promote the electoral prospects of Leaguers. The previous month he had expressed his dissatisfaction that it had not publicly backed Duffy for New Ross.[17] He wrote that the Association would find itself in an awkward position if it refused to do so considering its support for Vincent Scully. Wilberforce, however, quickly contacted the local election organisers offering the strong opposition of the Association to Redington, as one of the Catholics, who 'professing themselves Liberal in politics, sold themselves to support and serve an administration which was passing a penal law against their own religion'.[18]

Opposition to Redington did not necessarily mean support for Duffy, and the Association made another error of judgment in its policy towards the Meath election. The fault lay not with Wilberforce but with the Parliamentary Committee, which conducted the election campaign insofar as Brigadiers attended election rallies in some constituencies. A meeting of the committee on 2 June passed a resolution that this Association would see with great pain a contested election in the County of Meath, where the patriotic Electors have been so long represented by two men of their own choice, and whose votes have ever been so staunchly recorded in favour of freedom and Catholicity. The present does not seem to be the moment when the Catholics of this country should turn their backs upon Representatives who have served them faithfully. A great battle is now to be fought, and this Association ardently desires to see the whole force of Catholic Ireland, both Electors and Candidates, combined together and acting in unison against the common enemy.[19]

From their point of view support for a member of the Brigade was only logical. Grattan was closely associated with Sadleir and Keogh and had chaired a meeting of the Brigade in London early in May which was attended by Sadleir, Keogh, Reynolds, Vincent Scully, Sir Timothy O'Brien, all members of the Committee.[20] But, their support was politically inexpedient and ignored, deliberately or otherwise, the fact that Bishop and many of his priests were in favour of Lucas. The editor of the *Tablet* used a report from the *Nation* to denounce the committee for opposing the wishes of the clergy.[21] This article referred to one member as an exterminating landlord, another as a salesmaster of constituencies and a third as a semi-aristocrat with brains of sawdust and the airs of a bashaw. It saw the absence of clergy from the committee as significant.

He did not blame the entire parliamentary committee, but rather the Brigadiers as 'the real movers in the secret intrigue which ends in putting the name of poor Mr. Wilberforce to the before-mentioned piece of *Telegraphic* tomfoolery'.[22] Wilberforce, according to Lucas, tried to dissuade the committee from publishing the resolution, but the Brigadier view prevailed over the majority. To Lucas the time had come for it to disband and be re-formed with new members, who would function in a more open way. The controversy opened old wounds on the exclusion of himself, Duffy and Gray from its counsels and on its support for Vincent Scully, who was suspect on the Queens Colleges' question.

Reaction in Meath was swift. Bishop Cantwell wrote reaffirming his support. His reply of 8 June to a letter from Lucas, left no doubt that he expected his priests to explain their own opinions to the electors in their respective parishes and to support the candidates favoured by the majority.[23] He confirmed that a majority of priests and laity saw Lucas as the best candidate, and expressed his own 'cordial concurrence in the estimate they have formed'. Cantwell's most pointed reflection was upon the resolution 'so hastily and so very unwisely published',

It had not my sanction, nor does it convey my sentiments. I regret being compelled to add that it does not, in my opinion, express the sentiments or wishes of the association. It was, I think, eminently calculated to produce the sad evils of discord and dissension which it deprecated, and which I have no doubt the sub-committee were anxious to prevent.

A section of Meath priests and electorate was equally forthright in their views of the resolution. Speakers at a Kells meeting on 4 June passed a motion condemning it as 'unfit to reflect the feelings, or wishes or wants of the Catholic people of Ireland, and is unworthy of our confidence'. The committee was almost exclusively composed of landlords and land agents and their interference in Meath was an offensive attempt to create division among the electorate.[24]

It was not only the Meath clergy who viewed the resolution with dismay. Soon after its publication twenty London priests, who were members of the general committee of the Association, issued a statement of protest.[25] Cullen himself was displeased at the error of judgement, and Wilberforce was later forced to apologise, and explain that the parliamentary committee was unaware of the widespread support for Lucas among the clergy.[26]

It is not easy to accept this. As secretary, Wilberforce was in contact with many constituencies and kept Cullen informed of developments throughout the Spring and early Summer of 1852.[27] The dissension between the Leaguers and the Brigade section of the Parliamentary Committee was a source of worry to him. In a letter to Cullen on 15 March he referred to the 'extreme men' of tenant right, and on 24 April he wrote his concern that if 'the attacks upon the members on the part of the press go on they will grievously weaken and wound us even in the election. Mr. Scully thinks that Your Grace could restore peace by compelling the papers to silence. I am sure Lucas will attend to your advice even much more to your comments'.[28] He was less certain about the *Freeman's* and the *Nation*.

But, as long as the parliamentary committee insisted upon supporting candidates favoured by Sadleir and his colleagues there was bound to be dissension. The committee, however, at all times promoted the view that contests dividing the Liberal interests should be avoided and on the surface at any rate this was the rationale behind the support for Grattan. Sadleir urged this policy upon Cullen. In a letter of 14 April he asked the Archbishop to pressurise More O'Ferrall, the M.P. for Longford, to 'undertake those arrangements by which a contest may be avoided', and he pledged that the committee would act according to O'Ferrall's advice.[29] He also promised to assist by using his influence in London to have O'Ferrall's views prevail among the Brigadiers.

The attacks upon the committee by the *Tablet, Nation* and *Freeman's Journal* did not damage the electoral prospects of its members. Sadleir was approached to represent several constituencies. As early as March he was being considered for Louth. On 21 March, James Patrick Neary of Dunleer wrote to the tenant right priest Patrick Bannon, that he had heard that 'Mr Sadleir would stand for Louth if invited – his having purchased the larger portion of Newtown Termonfeckin would do away with objections to non-connection with the county'.[30] Despite Sadleir's conflict with the Tenant Leaguers, Neary saw him as a sound tenant right candidate who would oust 'our present base and retreat members'. The writer was of some importance as a local organiser and urged Bannon to get up a petition for a county meeting,

> I am certain all (or nearly so) the parish priests would sign it and I think I can promise for those laymen in this quarter who have heretofore taken part with the people. The game is in our hands, if not our own fault, and we have objects to fight for of much greater importance than ever before occupied public attention.

A month later the Louth Tenant Right Independent Club formally invited Sadleir to stand in place of Montesquieu Bellew. Its secretary, Joseph Campbell, curate in Desertcreet, wrote to Sadleir on 27 April assuring him that the club was certain of returning two members with a 'triumphant majority'.[31] The club members had

> the highest confidence in the integrity of John Sadleir, and would gladly avail themselves of the services of such a distinguished patriot as their representative. The present representatives must march, the game of delusion shall be put an end to and whosoever will receive the suffrages of the electors of Louth at the approaching election must adhere steadily to that policy which has already unsettled the Russell government, and promises at no distant day, to make the proud Stanley bite the dust.

Despite these assurances Sadleir refused the offer. His reply of 30 April from the Albany Club made it clear that he was committed to Carlow.[32] His newspaper, however, highlighted the invitation as a vindication of his integrity and proof that 'all the malignant efforts of his slanderers had been futile'.[33] The *Telegraph* had further cause to rejoice at the news that the electors of Queen's County also wished him to represent them. He was popular as the receiver of Lord Portarlington's estates in Emo, Caron and Morette. The address of 144 tenants to him on 29 March not only referred to his benevolence to them during the Famine[34] but praised him as a landlord who was about to pass the estates back to Portarlington in 1852. Sadleir's reply praised them as representatives of Irish tenants in general and set out his philosophy on landlord tenant relations,

> I have, as your representative in his cause, endeavoured to show how under the most adverse circumstances, an Irish tenantry can be strictly honest, untiringly industrious, unceasingly diligent, unflinchingly scrupulous in their dealings towards those whose land they occupy; and on the other hand, I have in my dealings with you, endeavoured to represent his Lordship, so that whilst providing for the demands of those who had legal claims upon his land, the utmost forbearance, the strictest justice and the most scrupulous honesty, should characterise every dealing on the part of the legalised landlord towards the occupying tenant.[35]

On 10 May a meeting of electors, including thirty four priests, met in McEvoy's Hotel in Maryborough (Portlaoise) and passed a resolution formally requesting him to stand in place of J.W. Fitzpatrick, who had supported the Titles Bill.[36] The invitation was reported by McCabe as a 'signal triumph' for Sadleir personally and for the Irish Party generally,

> The incident is a remarkable one in the career of any public man, however high his attainments, or however great his services. It is a reward for anything he may have done and for everything he may have desired to accomplish; but, in the case of Mr. Sadleir, it cannot fail, we are certain to be felt as peculiarly valuable, because it is a demonstration that Ireland is well worthy of the best exertions of her children; that the toils of him who labours honestly in her cause are not unnoticed, and that the love and respect of the people cannot be diminished, much less destroyed, because slander assails his motives and meanness, malignity and malevolence confederate together to put a false colouring upon his actions.

The meeting was chaired by Michael Dunne, who, when Sadleir declined, agreed to stand and was subsequently elected.[37] Sadleir, who had recently arrived in Ireland for the election campaign and for Clement's marriage to Louisa Lalor of Cregg House, Carrick-on-Suir,[38] went to Maryborough with his brother, James, specifically to endorse Dunne, who was a friend of his. That evening he hosted a dinner for forty guests, many of whom were priests. He felt obliged to underline their electioneering influence and they in turn recognised him as a politician of some importance. Nicholas O'Connor, the local parish priest, who had never taken part in politics before, felt compelled to do so then because of the Titles act. He felt so strongly about this that

Derby was preferable to him than Russell. He praised Sadleir as a politician, who did not confine his services to his own constituency, but had given 'our cause a private impetus which I will not now mention'. Sadleir, who dominated the proceedings with several speeches, drew an interesting distinction between the political roles of Irish and English landlords. In Ireland, tenants' votes were regarded as part of their property by some landlords. His own experience was that Protestant voters in England, Scotland or the North of Ireland would not tolerate such interference, but the English landlord class were psychologically closer to the ordinary people, a position occupied in Ireland by the Catholic clergy. In Ireland the landlords were 'arrayed on one side and the great mass of the Irish people, those who form the bone, the sinew and strength of the progressive Liberal Party – are left without those lay leaders who in other parts of the Kingdom head the movement'.

He knew that the religious issue would be the emotive driving force of the campaign, and proposed that a strong advocacy of principles without 'compromising or vacillating' was a trait admired by others. Such principles, however, should not be compromised by any desires of social advancement. As one of its founders, the Irish Party was the only benefit to come from the Ecclesiastical Titles Bill,

> I aspired to the honourable position of representing a portion of my countrymen, without binding myself to become the partizan of any government, or the factious adherent of any opposition. I know that at first those who united with me in the formation of an independent Irish party were regarded as attempting to do that which was considered to be impracticable and chimerical. We were often warned that our attempts were vain, that previous efforts in the same direction had proved fruitless, and had even been defeated by the machination of powerful parties in England.

The formation of such a party was not an act of disloyalty to the Queen, and his constant contact with people in all parts of the United Kingdom 'induced him to attach more importance to this national sentiment than others perhaps did.'

As the receiver of an estate in the county Sadleir restated the rights of property, which included the duty of motivating tenants to improve their holdings especially if landlords themselves, 'either from want of means or in consequence of being shackled by entails', were unable to carry out improvements. This was an enhancement of the landlords' property. Speaking of himself as an extensive landowner, he knew of 'no greater advantage that could be conferred on myself as a proprietor, than that all those feudal restrictions which still exist ...

should be swept away'. Crawford's bill, beneficial in respect of improvements, was inadequate to solve the complexity of the Irish land question.

In setting out his own position Sadleir told his audience that Dunne's views were similar. He was an opponent of the Ecclesiastical Titles Act, a supporter of Crawford's bill and would be a valuable addition to the Irish party when elected.[39] One of the unusual features of the Queen's County election was a written pledge, to be circulated throughout the county, signed by all the electors at the Maryborough meeting to work for Dunne's return.[40] The *Telegraph* saw this as an enlightened and efficient electioneering device, which could profitably be used in all other constituencies.[41]

There was no question of Sadleir receiving a written pledge from the electors in Carlow borough. His prospects in Queen's County would have been excellent, but it was felt that he was the only Liberal candidate capable of keeping the Conservatives out in Carlow.[42] He had visited the town on 26 March to find a rumour circulating that he intended to stand for a neighbouring constituency. He immediately published a denial, which was also a vague election address promising to 'act freely and independently in support of every measure which I thought calculated to benefit our common enemy'.[43]

The first real salvo in the campaign was the usual address of James Maher, issued on 17 May, which informed the electors that 'your character, your interest, your religious liberties are all at stake in the coming contest'.[44] Maher was not as vehement in his attack upon the Conservative candidate, R. Clayton Browne, a local proprietor and a cousin of Lord Mayo,[45] as he had been towards the Englishman, Layard, in 1847. He expressed his respect for Browne as a private individual but eschewed his politics. Unlike Sadleir, Maher never seemed over concerned about alienating the Protestant sector of the electorate. He showed every intention of utilising the religious plank as an electioneering cudgel. Browne was the candidate of the anti-Catholic Derby party who 'after robbing Maynooth and suppressing our Synods, proposes to deal with the ancient faith and religion of the country as if they were a mere emanation of human policy'. His candidacy was an attempt to restore an Orange ascendancy and abolish the 'paltry' Maynooth grant of £26,000, which contrasted with the 'enormous' endowments of the Established Church. It was a flagrant wrong to endow with national property the belief of the thirty nine Articles held by a small minority, rather than the Dissenters' Catechism or the Catholic creed held by millions. Why should such an individual be returned when there had never been any dissatisfaction with Sadleir's representation of them in Westminster, since his return he has ever been at his post – attended every division – voted upon all important questions, and has never given a vote, I believe, which you do not approve. The ability and business-like habits – the integrity and honour of the man whom you have elected – and I am not his panegyrist, I simply state the facts – have won for him a distinguished place in the Commons House of Parliament, where the most highly gifted find it difficult to make way. His opinions are listened to with respect, because they bear the impress of a sound judgement, and the careful thought of the statesman who has mastered and matured his subject. Is there among the representatives of this part of the empire one of whom, as a public man, his country has greater reason to be proud?

Maher's address briefly touched upon the land question, and it did so in the emotive context of the famine, emigration, the workhouses and graveyards filled with the corpses of the poor. Sadleir was a politician who had striven to solve this issue, whereas Browne was driven by 'ill-regulated ambition', lacking in principles held by 'the vulgar people' – farmers, traders, shopkeepers and professional men. Browne was identified with the supporters of class legislation, those who 'have a strong sense of what is due to the aristocracy, to the landlord, to the Irish born'.

Extracts from the address were published in the *Tablet* which, however, omitted every reference to Sadleir.[46] McCabe in a veiled hint at the omission expressed the hope that every Catholic newspaper in Ireland would publish it.[47] His pious editorial of 19 May interpreted Maher's theme,

> as the warning voice of the Irish Catholic priesthood everywhere, in which a true and faithful representative of the people – in which any member of the Irish Brigade is threatened with an opposition – no matter whether it be by Tory, by Whig or by professing Liberal. If Ireland be true to herself her first and paramount duty is not to permit the members of the Irish Brigade to be disturbed in their seats.

This was the rationale applied to the Meath election, which caused the parliamentary committee of the Defence Association to overlook the political realities in that county. But, McCabe equated an Irish Party with the Brigade nucleus, and his article was unequivocal in advancing the cause of an Irish party which would remain independent and isolated from the main English parties, 'as long as there is a penal law against Catholics on the statute books'. Irish electors had a moral obligation to support candidates, who pledged to follow such a course. Failure to do so by any elector placed in peril 'the salvation of his own soul'.

Boosted by Maher's address and the eulogies of his newspaper, Sadleir arrived in Carlow on the 10 a.m. train on 21 May to begin his canvass.[48] He was met by a number of priests and electors, who accompanied him throughout the borough, followed by a crowd including women and children who applauded as each elector visited pronounced for him. The *Telegraph* reported that many Protestant voters expressed approval of his 'public conduct and respect for him as a private individual'. It had no doubt that a 'clear and invulnerable' majority had promised their votes to him.

That optimism was part of the electioneering process, and Sadleir's return was far from guaranteed. This was clear from the fact that Maher felt it necessary to issue a further and longer address on 2 June.[49] It maintained that Browne's tactics included a threat to withdraw landlord patronage from some electors, and to use other methods 'which it is not prudent at present to name'. Maher felt that the Famine theme was worth a second airing, and portrayed a depressed Irish society in its aftermath.

> we are deeply steeped in misery. There is no use in attempting to describe it. It is seen by all. It is apparent in the rags and filth with which seven-eighths of the people are covered. It is apparent in the lashless brows, the pallid lips, the sunken eyes of the population. It is there before us, it meets us at every turn in broad, palpable, hideous characters. It has seized upon every class and section of the people. The farmers, the shopkeepers, the traders, the professions, Protestants, Catholics and Dissenters are all oppressed, impoverished and borne down.

Such ruin was due to the landlords, who charged high rents and refused tenant right. Browne, the landlord representative, shared their views, and was supported by a section of the electorate 'swayed by bigotry, which has eaten into their very core'. To Maher, it was 'awful infatuation', which made oppressed people support the authors of their misfortune.

A second helping of the religious theme was a necessary electioneering accessory to the Famine, but this time Maher took a more philosophical approach. Ignoring the history of the Catholic Church in Europe, he rejected the idea that Catholicism was in any way political – 'we hold that Parliaments, Kings or Queens, Lords and Commons, have nothing whatever to do with our religion, it descends from an infinitely higher source – it comes from God'. Protestantism, on the other hand, was founded on the Book of Common Prayer, 'one huge act of Parliament'. The history of Protestantism in Ireland was one of bigotry, copperfastened in particular by the Penal Laws. Not only was Catholicism the opposite of such bigotry, but the proof lay in the fact that the four representatives prior to the election of Sadleir were all Protestants. Such representatives were acceptable if they supported remedial measures for the country, something which Browne was not likely to do. Not only would he reject tenant right, but as a Derbyte he was anti-Catholic. He had never contributed towards any of the Catholic educational or benevolent institutions in the town but was a supporter of anti-Catholic societies such as the Priest's Protection Society, of whom 'Mr. Browne's cousin, Lord Mayo, is one of the vice-patrons, and his representative, Colonel Bruen, is another'. An extract from the address of the Society's Committee spoke for itself,

> they tell us that Ireland has become a hissing and an abomination amongst the kingdoms of the earth, and the reason assigned is that the Parliament has endowed Maynooth, and incorporated idolatry. Instead, therefore, of two hundred and fifty priests that have issued annually from her filthy walls, we are henceforward to have an annual crop of five hundred priests to issue to pollute and to fester in the land. This college, Maynooth, is in future to be the headquarters of the Pope's black militia.[50]

This uncompromising approach was unlikely to win the support of Protestant voters for Sadleir and the *Telegraph* made no attempt to soften it. An editorial of 4 June saw the address as one of guidance and instruction for 'those whose spiritual welfare and whose morality as Christians are confined to his care'. Not only that, but its principles were of universal application in all constituencies. It was a mortal sin to vote for a supporter of the Derby administration that had 'pandered to the anti-Catholic bigotry that festers in the hearts of the fanatics and infidels of England and Scotland'.

The *Carlow Sentinel* reacted in a different manner and denounced clerical spiritual intimidation,

> Terror at times obtains the mastery over the human mind – especially when inspired by spiritual influences, – but the cases are few and far between when it has, lately, been exercised with safety; for we affirm that the great mass of our countrymen are not inclined to bow their necks beneath the yoke which is frequently sought to be imposed on them for political purposes. They can draw the distinction between the duty which they owe to God, and that which they are called on to discharge towards their neighbour; and they know from experience that the sacred name of religion is frequently invoked not to advance their spiritual welfare or happiness, but to serve private ends.[51]

The *Sentinel* did not name Maher, but pointed to the *Tablet*, which had made no reference to the Carlow election, as expounding tyrannical maxims. It was relieved that the 'speechification' on the streets had eased', but coercion 'in domestic life' was being 'employed with energy' and exclusive dealing was being used to pressurise voters. The *Sentinel* warned that the Conservative Party was too powerful in Carlow 'to permit any person to suffer wrong for daring to exercise a civil right'. It was a mistake for Sadleir to contest the borough, 'and he may yet learn that he was also, possibly, betrayed'.

Sadleir's stature was sufficiently high to prevent any personal attack on him by the *Sentinel*. He was also friendly with local Conservatives, some of whom he met socially at race meetings, and acknowledged by them as a 'man of character' whose parliamentary actions were largely acceptable to them.[52] But his role in the Titles' Bill debate was held against him by the *Sentinel*, and, as a leading member of the Catholic Defence Association he was accused of sectarian hostility by the majority of the landed proprietary.

Apart from the charge of sectarianism, the *Sentinel* saw the policy of independent opposition as obstruction to the progress of useful legislation. It did not, however, accuse him of espousing the policy of obstruction, an accurate observation of his views. It wondered why he complained of Browne's candidacy when he himself had deprived Layard of the representation in 1847, 'upon no other ground (as both were Liberals) but that the one was an Englishman and the other an Irishman'. The underlying message was that Sadleir could not permanently claim the borough.

The paper also disliked his appeal to the non-electors as departing from his 'usual prudent course'. This appeal was made when he addressed a crowd from the window of his bank in Burren Street, near Beggar's Row, on 14 June.[53] It was a common electioneering tactic in the nineteenth century to use a mob, sometimes hired, to intimidate the supporters of rival candidates. But, Sadleir's open invitation for the 'sympathy and co-operation' of that sector was an indication of his worry about the outcome of the election. The sectarian nature of Maher's letters may have reflected this worry and may have been a signal that Sadleir had lost some Catholic support. This was more clearly shown by a third letter from Maher on 30 June addressed directly to Browne's Catholic supporters.[54] Maher's principal ammunition was a royal proclamation of 16 June, in which the Queen reiterated the contents of the Ecclesiastical Titles Act and warned that Catholic clergy who breached it would be prosecuted.[55] He drew the electors' attention to the fact that Derby had publicly supported the proclamation. The proclamation seems to have been inspired to prevent public disorder arising from Catholic processions near

Protestant places of worship, but to him it was 'coarse and insulting'. The Titles Act was only a 'hairs breadth' from the Penal Law, which forbade the celebration of Mass, and Derby's approval of the proclamation was proof of Conservative chagrin at non-implementation of the Act.[56] Under those circumstances a Catholic voter could not in conscience vote for the Conservatives – 'can he trample on the cross and profane all the sacred rites of holy religion? Can he honestly assist Mr. Browne and Earl Derby to send Catholic bishops to the cells of Newgate?'. Such voters would be 'political prostitutes', who would forfeit personal respect and be forever rejected by the Liberal Party. This threat was bolstered by a further grim vision of active Protestant intolerance,

> Men of no religion it is true, may in this land of boasted freedom have their processions. They are at liberty to burn in effigy the Pope, bishops, priests and nuns, in ecclesiastical costumes, and thus familiarise the public mind to deeds of outrage. They may commit to the flames, as they have done, amid yells and blasphemous execrations, the effigy of the ever Blessed Virgin Mary, the Crucifix, and every other sacred symbol, without the slightest risk that Lord Derby will come out upon them with a royal proclamation. But the practices and ceremonies of the religion introduced by St. Augustine into England will not be tolerated. The habits of the religious orders, the magnificent vestments of the clergy, the uplifted cross, are an abomination to Protestant eyes, a scandal to a Protestant people, and a danger to the public peace.

This letter was the strongest of the three and was as close to spiritual coercion as could be found in nineteenth century electioneering.[57] There was no guarantee, however, that it would sway those who were pledged to Browne. But while it was en route to the printing press an event took place in England which gave substance to its emotive appeal, and was milked by Catholic and Liberal newspapers in Ireland. The proclamation referred to by Maher was blamed for serious rioting between Catholics and Protestants in Stockport, near Manchester, a few days after a procession of Catholic schoolchildren on Sunday 27 June.[58] In its sixteen year history this procession, mainly involving Irish people, had never provoked disturbance.

Because of the hostile climate following the Titles Act and the proclamation, the local priests, Randolph Frith and Robert Foster, were careful not to dress in canonicals, although they breached the proclamation by the use of a cross at the head of the procession. This was sufficient to provoke a drunken row which degenerated into racism and religious bigotry, resulting in the death of an Irishman, injury to two hundred others and widespread destruction of their property. There was also a degree of premeditation involved. The words 'Irish' or 'English' were marked on doors to distinguish the nationality of the inhabitants, and subsequently twenty-four houses in Rock Row and Car-Green inhabited mainly by Irish were wrecked,

> the Irish were attacked in their beds, their houses broken into, their families were dragged out naked and the humanity to be found in the bosom of a savage was outraged by an English rabble in their gratification of their licentious bigotry.[59]

Catholics were further incensed by the vandalising of Frith's house and the Catholic Chapels in Stockport and nearby Edgeley. A bonfire of ecclesiastical furniture, books and papers was lit in front of the house. The consecrated hosts were removed from the chapels in time, although the opposite was believed in the immediate aftermath of the riots.[60] The *Tablet* correspondent described the Stockport church with

> its blackened ruins, its still smoking portal, its calcined fixtures, its altar dashed into fragments, its tabernacle and sacred vessels burned to dust, the sacred vestments partly consumed, its fine library and schoolroom a mass of ruins, all clear evidence to the wild fury of the bigoted fanaticism which applied the torch to the consecrated edifice. Vengeance has been wreaked on a classic piece of architecture; the learned records of history were doomed to annihilation, and those silent but eloquent monuments of the taste, piety and genius of Christianity, which would have ensured the forbearance of the vandal and the goth, fell before the ungovernable and profligate fury of a low English rabble.[61]

Sadleir's paper was not as graphic, but an editorial of 5 July castigated the English legal system as partisan,[62] and the riots provided a splendid electioneering addendum to sway those voters who had turned from Sadleir. These were urged to reject the Conservatives, 'by whom such things have been countenanced and applauded'.[63] Bishop Haly and sixteen priests, Maher included, also grasped this electioneering weapon, and published an address in the *Dublin Evening Post* of 8 July expressing 'horror' at the outrage and urging that the best way to defeat the 'machinations of our enemies' was to return 'zealous and able supporters of civil and religious liberty such as messrs Sadleir, Ball and Higgins'.

Electioneering editorials, speeches and addresses contrasted with Sadleir's more sober approach. His manifesto, published when parliament was dissolved on 29 June, avoided an emotional exposé of religious intolerance and called for an end to sectarian ascendancy, justice for all religions, the abolition of the tithe rents and the removal 'of the evils of the grand jury system'.[64] He had faithfully adhered to the principles laid down by him in 1847 and continued to favour a 'broader and bolder application of free trade' and the elimination of legal obstacles to the rapid sale of land.

The address drew attention to his leading role in the Irish Parliamentary Party whose policies promoted agricultural and manufacturing enterprise, which would create employment and stem emigration. His determination to sustain that party, and increase his influence in it, was clear from his visits to other constituencies in support of relatives and friends. On the Sunday of the Stockport procession he attended an open air demonstration for Keogh at the Scotch Parade in Athlone.[65] Lucas was rightly suspicious that Sadleir was financially aiding Keogh, and a few days later privately wrote to Moore about his misgivings,

> Of Mr. Keogh I will say nothing except that a very tolerable prognostic of his motives and future course could be formed if we knew from what quarter is to come the money, which must be spent to return him to Athlone. I cannot say I know but I have my belief on the point and I draw my conclusions accordingly.[66]

Moore, however, was an old schoolfellow and supporter of Keogh. He accompanied him on the mail train from Dublin on 26 June and next morning was joined by Sadleir, the two Roscommon representatives, Oliver D.J. Grace and Fitzstephen French, and W.H. Morgan, Westmeath.[67] The meeting was chaired by Dr. John Kearney, a strong League supporter and vicar-general of the diocese, and attended by eleven other priests, including Archdeacon Martin O'Reilly, parish priest of St. Peter's, Athlone.

Kearney broadened the scope of the occasion to include the election drive in Westmeath and Roscommon. All was not harmony in Westmeath, and he had earlier seconded a resolution to dissolve the Liberal Club there, which 'no longer represented the feelings of the county, but had descended into a clique'. He attacked the subsequent support of some electors for two candidates, who would not pledge themselves to the Irish party.

Athlone was the focus of Moore's brief and he addressed a motion that it would be disgraced if Keogh was not returned by an overwhelming majority. He praised Keogh as an eloquent defender of the Irish people and the Catholic Church, and condemned his opponent Lawes, a London stockbroker. The question at issue was not Lawes versus Keogh, but oppression versus the people, Protestant ascendancy versus Catholic liberty, extermination versus tenant right, the crowbar brigade versus the Irish Brigade, death and exile versus home and fatherland. His reference to emigration and the Irish abroad was more akin to the language of separation than to Irish Liberalism,

> Hundreds and thousands and millions of your countrymen have gone there before you, but let those who have exiled them take care. It is not in the spirit of an idle braggart, but in deep and solemn warning, I bid them beware that the race they have banished across the Atlantic does not some day come back again. Already the clashing of the bayonets of France is heard on the shores of England, carried to the white cliffs of the English coast by a spell more potent than the electric telegraph – carried by the fears of a panic-stricken people. And I would warn them that there are millions of our countrymen looking on, biding their time. We, the Irish, fought for the English at Waterloo – we beat them at Fontenoy: and let them take care that the burning millions at the other side of the Atlantic do not come to fight once more, not under the lilies of France – not beneath the cross of England, but beneath their green banner – the banner of their fathers – not beneath the cross of England, but beneath that sacred cross, before which all Christian nations have knelt.

Moore branded Derby, 'Scorpion Stanley', as the chief promoter of the Queen's proclamation, whose consequence was that 'anointed priests of your Church have been spit upon by the populace in the streets of London'. Keogh's response was to read the proclamation and associate it with the Conservative candidates for Westmeath and Roscommon. Support for such candidates showed approval for a proclamation, which would prevent a priest from shriving a dying man on the roadside, 'without subjecting himself to a heavy penalty'. He highlighted that a legal threat had been made to Bishop John Derry a few days earlier, because he had carried a cross in a procession to lay the foundation stone of a new chapel in Clonfert.

Keogh appreciated the assistance from members of the Brigade, and singled Sadleir out for particular praise. The latter said that he had travelled a long way from 'a remote part of the country' to support his friend, whose election was a certainty. Keogh was the champion of religious freedom, but Lawes played 'the game of the unscrupulous and cold-blooded enemies of the Irish people'. Sadleir viewed the Athlone meeting as a model, which would inspire other areas such as Cork, Limerick and Tipperary. His interest in Tipperary was increased because his brother, James, was standing with Scully.

The Tipperary election was initially controversial due to the circumstances in which Nicholas Maher retired from the contest to make way for James Sadleir. Walter Cantwell, the Administrator in Thurles and secretary of the local election club, demanded that Maher lodge his share of the £2,000 election expenses at short notice. Maher was unable to do so and sent his letter of resignation to Archbishop Slattery.[68] John O'Dwyer of Doon, a leading League priest, was dissatisfied and raised the rumour that Maher had been forced to pull out because of pressure from Sadleir's Bank. This was denied by Maher.[69] In a letter of 3 July a *Tablet* 'subscriber' in Thurles wondered how the politically inexperienced Sadleir had 'been foisted on the County'.[70] His talents, 'that sort of plodding, money-making cunning', might be appropriate for banking, but not for politics, and 'his feet and not his tongue, will tell his sentiments on the floor of the House of Commons'. He was an exterminating landlord on his Ballyvolode estate in County Limerick, but the writer 'blessed Heaven that James Sadleir does not lord it over as many green acres as his cousin, Vincent Scully M.P., for there is reason to fear that if he did the groans and lamentations from Mantle Hill and Donohill would have been without a parallel in the annals of extermination'.[71]

The writer was certain that the selection committee had been packed by Sadleir's supporters from various baronies while representatives of other baronies had been excluded. Worse still, the priests were kept out and

> were put on a level with the lowest scamp in the street in the selection of the candidate whom they are to recommend their people to support, even at the risk of their landlord's wrath, and who cannot be returned if the priests do not use all their exertions to support him.

The sidelining of the priests in the selection process and the retention of their support for James Sadleir was a remarkable feat. The selection meeting was held in Thurles on 1 July and was chaired by the Clonmel parish priest, Dr. Michael Burke.[72] A great number of priests, many of whom were non-electors attended. Three candidates were present. John Carden, a landlord from Barnane, Templemore, who admitted his reputation as an evicting landlord, had no hope of being chosen. The O'Connellite John Lanigan J.P was a popular individual, but was reluctant to enter political life unless no other candidate could be found. The name of John Ball, a Poor Law Commissioner and son of Judge Ball, was mentioned by Patrick Hickey, the parish priest of Doon, and was instantly rejected by the crowd.

James Sadleir, proposed by Archdeacon Michael Laffan, proclaimed himself an adherent of the Irish Party, and was willing to sign a pledge of support for the Crawford Bill.[73] Burke's keynote address suggested that the assembly should delegate all its powers to a small selection committee, whose decision would be binding. There was no dissension to this and It was obvious that it had already been agreed. James Sadleir, himself, proposed that each barony should be represented on the committee, which took only half an hour to decide that he should join Scully as the selected candidates for County Tipperary.

Following this announcement John Sadleir addressed the crowd in language entirely different from that used by him at Carlow election rallies. The political ethos of Tipperary was more nationalistic, and he responded in kind by representing the contest was one between Cromwellian Protestantism and Celtic Catholicism. There was a sense of pride in Tipperary tradition and its political clientele,

> It is cheering to see the giant power that still abides in the valleys of the Suir, testifying here to-day its determination to preserve the county's independence. It is cheering to see the thousand brave hearts that still throb in the plains of Eliogarty. It is delightful to see this. It is a revival of the triumph of former days. It brings to one's mind afresh the remembrance of victories which Tipperary alone could have achieved. It gives new and incontestable evidence of that spirit of self-reliance which will enable the men of Tipperary to resist with triumphant tone and proud defiance the coercive system of a Tyrant Tory Party.

His condemnation of coercive landlord electioneering was juxtaposed with a denial of a rumour that he was exerting pressure on his own tenants in County Tipperary. There was no distinction between tenants on his own land, those on the estates of absentee friends managed by him, or those on estates for which he was the official receiver. They were all 'as free as air', although he was certain that they would vote 'in the way their own consciences directs them, and for the benefit of the land of their birth'.

Three days later he was at an election rally for County Carlow which Keogh and Michael Dunne attended. John Ball, rejected by Tipperary, and Matthew Higgins were standing against the sitting Conservatives, Bruen and Bunbury.[74] James Maher and the parish priest of Bagenalstown, Dr Lalor, shared the platform with a dozen other priests. An attempt was made to derail the Dublin train carrying Sadleir's friends including his relative, Leonard Morrogh, which may have been because it was carrying two companies of the 27th regiment.

Inevitably the tone of the meeting was set by linking Derby with the Queen's proclamation and the Stockport riots. He was portrayed as attempting to destroy the Catholic Church and Bruen was branded a political apostate.[75] The crowd was treated by Keogh to a vision of Carlow as another Stockport, with its cathedral liable to destruction if the Derby administration was returned. Religious persecution would be rife and the sisters of mercy and charity, who led a life of unostentatious piety, assisting the poor and dropping the balm of comfort on the lips of the dying sinner, seeking nothing for themselves, but delighting in every-day acts, full of charity and sisterly love, they were forbidden to appear in public by the proclamation issued by that Government, which Colonel Bruen and Mr. Bunbury would go into Parliament to support.

Although the meeting was ostensibly in support of Ball and Higgins it soon became apparent that it was equally concerned with Sadleir's return. Keogh promised to 'aid his friend, their late member for the borough of Carlow, and who could doubt that before the expiration of one week he would be re-elected to that distinguished honour'. Conservatives were guilty of 'monstrous audacity' in seeking the borough as well as the county. He bore witness to Sadleir's industry in Parliament 'from twelve in the day until three o'clock the following morning without tasting food or retiring for one instant'. His examination of the voting list showed that Catholic electors in the borough were in a majority of thirty over Protestants, and all would vote for Sadleir irrespective of landlord pressure. But if any Catholic did not do so Keogh was convinced that

if he walked into the country every man who met him would turn from him with loathing and indignation, if he passed out on the high road by day I am sure that the children would scorn him, that the women would not look on him, that men would sicken at his sight, and if he proposed to lie down at night every man would shut his door with indignation and contempt in his face.

Keogh's advocacy of social ostracisation was accompanied by the certainty of eternal damnation for any Catholic who voted against Sadleir. Such rhetoric fully coincided with that of James Maher, who devoted most of his speech to Sadleir's cause, and whose sentiments visibly shocked Dr. Lalor, his Vicar General. Maher told his audience that no Catholic could in conscience vote for Clayton Browne, and at once absolved any, who had pledged themselves, from that obligation. Those Catholics who would refuse such absolution were

very few worthless degraded wretches, who would sell their souls to the Devil, and their liberties for a very small trifle of hard cash. I mention the fact thus publicly in the strong and firm hope that Mr. Browne may give them nothing; for assuredly we will have nothing to do with them. He may have them for the merest trifle. The career of some of them through life has been marked by infamy. They have never been prospered by the God of Heaven, their moral character is forfeited, their prospects in life now growing worse and the final period is coming on; the view into the other world such men must take is far from affording them consolation. Let them go and be damned.

Sadleir distanced himself from this rhetoric. Even his reference to the Stockport riots excused the Derby government from any deliberate intention to persecute Catholics. Nevertheless he saw the Conservative as compromised and dependent upon the votes of 'the fanatics of England'. He admitted that he needed Protestant votes, but understood their predicament. Some of these told him 'that they were threatened with utter ruin in various forms and ways, if they did not come forward to vote for my opponent'. But, despite the pressure by Bruen on his Protestant tenants, Sadleir appealed for their votes and challenged them to quote a single instance in which he was offensive to their religious convictions,

> In private as in public life I have had the honour and the happiness of counting from my childhood among my dearest friends many of the most eminent Protestants of the two countries. Often have I had the happiness and the inexpressible satisfaction of exercising the small influence I possess in private life to advance the interests, to second and countenance the laudable efforts of my Protestant and Presbyterian fellow-subjects – to advance their private fortunes and promote the interests of the religious bodies with which they were connected. There is no effort that I have ever made to secure for my Catholic fellow-subjects full and entire religious liberty which I have not been ever ready to confer the same blessing on the Protestants and Presbyterians.

He pledged his support to the two Liberal candidates, especially his friend, Ball. He said that Ball was a person of large fortune, prepared to spend it in vindication of the principles of religious toleration. Ball's credentials were enhanced as the relative of a nun. This was also very agreeable in political terms, since she was 'one of those distinguished and amiable ladies whose holy retreats the present government would subject to degrading visitation'.

Subsequently Sadleir accompanied Ball on part of his canvass throughout the county where, according to his newspaper, there was 'unmitigated hostility to the chapel burners and altar desecrators'.[76] Maher joined him on the canvass. On 10 July in Tullow, they put the election down as a struggle for religious liberty, but the main practical emphasis was to firm voter resolve against landlord power.[77] Sadleir, the moderate Roman Catholic, told them that several of the leading Protestant families of the county were on the Liberal side. He cited 'authoritatively' the example of Lord Bessborough, whom he knew well. Other Protestant voters were determined 'to emancipate themselves from the tyranny of religious fanaticism' and would not allow themselves any longer 'to be dragged through the mire by any petty little county clique'. He enunciated the polarisation of priestly and landlord electioneering influence, and strove to underscore the independence of Carlow people – 'it has been my lot to meet them in Manchester, Leeds, Liverpool, Wolverhampton, Macclesfield and London; and wherever you find Carlow men they are invariably the first and foremost in the struggle for liberty and freedom'.

Sadleir's lengthy speech was one of many which during the course of the nineteenth century slowly conditioned the minds of the tenantry towards a more independent outlook, eventually weakening the spirit of deference to landlords. He also contributed to shifting this deference in favour of priestly power,

> I would not be here to-day if I thought it probable that the large majority of the Catholic electors of Carlow county would deliberately go forward to the booth, and there deliberately, openly and basely turn on their clergy, their bishop and upon those principles which have ever governed them. I sincerely believe it is utterly impossible for any artifice, for any amount of coercion, or any amount of threats to drive the Catholic voters of Carlow county to perpetrate such disgraceful treachery. I beg of them to remember that they do not possess their votes in order to present them like a dish of new peas to their landlords or their agent. They hold their votes for the good and for the protection of the country; they hold that great constitutional power – the only power they possess, the only power left to them – they hold it to defend their liberties and protect their homes.

He contrasted this power with the presumption of a small group to controvert the will of the majority and 'drive the Catholic electors like slaves and like serfs to the poll'. The illusion had to be destroyed that facilitating the political views of their landlords guaranteed security of tenure to tenants,

> There were formerly Catholic electors in this county, who foolishly imagined that by yielding to that threat, and acting in accordance with the caprice of the Tory faction, and amongst them were to be found many of the wealthy farmers of the county, that they were playing a safe game. But where are they now?.. Into whatever part of the country you go you will find men and women to tell you they are all gone.

One of the characteristics of the evicting landlord was the fostering of a hostile spirit between Catholics and Protestants. Another was the upholding of the 'vicious system' of land law, which failed to secure to enterprising tenants compensation for improvements carried out by them to their holdings.

The next day Sadleir led a delegation to Bagenalstown, for a rally in a small field near the chapel. By that stage he had a severe sore throat brought on by frequent speeches, and confined himself to remind the gathered parishoners 'after Mass that 'a landlord would have just as much right to ask his tenant for the coat off his back or the hat off his head as for the vote which the law gave him to exercise according to the dictates of his conscience'.

He hurried back to Carlow town that evening to prepare for the borough nomination on the following day. His newspaper reported that 'very great excitement prevails and the town is literally alive with constabulary. The barracks accommodation not being nearly sufficient, they are quartered in private lodgings on all sides'.[78] A strong police force was strengthened by a troop of the Fifth Dragoon guards drawn up outside the courthouse, where the nomination proceedings were conducted by the High Sheriff, Sir Clement Wolseley.[79] The *Sentinel* contrasted the demeanour of the supporters of both sides; Browne's followers politely listened to the various speeches, while Sadleir's were 'by no means friends of Father Mathew'.[80] This 'drunken rabble' kept up a most 'uproarious scene' during the nomination.

When Browne came he was flanked by some of the most influential individuals in Carlow, Sir Wheeler Cuffe, Bruen, Bunbury, Colonel Vigors, William Duckett, William Fitzwilliam Burton, J.H. Hamilton, his legal adviser, and Richard Johnston, a barrister. He was also accompanied by the Protestant ministers F.F.J. Trench, Edmund Childs, and James Jameson, a Presbyterian minister, John Powell and a Wesleyan minister, the Reverend Reilly. Sadleir came with Dr. J. Walsh, President of the St. Patrick's College, Carlow, Thaddeus O'Shea, the Catholic curates John Dempsey and Daniel McCarthy, and a number of shopkeepers.

Browne was proposed by Samuel Haughton and seconded by Joseph Lynch, an architect and a Catholic, who had been given various commissions by Browne over a long number of years.[81] The presence of a Catholic on the Conservative platform added to an already volatile situation and armed police entered the courthouse to keep the peace during Haughton's nomination address. Lynch's house was later attacked by a mob.

Walsh proposed Sadleir and appealed to the crowd to conduct themselves. He had never previously taken part in politics, but felt compelled to do so then because of the threat of a new Derby ministry. But, Sadleir also appealed to the Conservatives, and pointed out the opposition to the Titles Act by eminent Protestant statesmen. He reminded them of the 'almost irresistible provocation' to Catholics during that debate, 'the misrepresentation of history, the bitter calumnies, the perversions of truth, the uninterrupted outpourings of fanatical vituperation by which the religious convictions of Catholics were assailed'. In a three hour speech he restated the case that he had promoted the interest of all sections of the community, Catholic, Protestant and Dissenter, even in the face of assassination threats.

He tailored his remarks to suit the tenor of the constituency, and his address differed considerably from those given by him in other constituencies. He was circumspect in his references to the Irish Party, and made his most emphatic disavowal of independent opposition,

> whenever a measure, which in my conscience, and in the opinion of the most intelligent and distinguished of Protestant English statesmen, shall be proposed, rest assured that, encouraged by your applause and confidence, at all events, I shall have the public virtue and political patriotism to rise above the low consideration of party or faction, and to give to the authors of such a measure, be they Whig or Tory, that conscientious and generous and timely support by which alone the best and most perfect statesmen can hope to achieve political justice for this country. So my friends, do not allow any man to deceive you or to do me the great injustice of holding me up to you or my fellow men as one who is disposed to enter public life again, eaten up with the poisonous influence of political or party rancour – do not allow any man here or elsewhere to picture me as a public servant who is a slave to any faction. My wish is to enter parliament and to run the course I always followed, that of rising above the consideration or fortunes of political adventurers and holding forward in that straightforward path of public duty by which I shall be ever competent to give aid in repelling an act of national injustice to my country and promoting one of public advantage to you.

The show of hands at the close of a nomination meeting indicated a majority for him, but this was not always indicative of victory at the polls. Conservative confidence that Browne would be elected was reflected in the *Sentinel*,

> The Borough will be won despite the machination of a faction who have employed numerous agencies to strike down rational liberty by intimidation – to uproot all principle by corrupting the heart. Attempts have been made to turn child against parent – the wife against the husband – and when all failed, the golden bait has been thrown out hoping to allure poor people from the path of honour by the violation of solemn pledges. To describe the scenes to which we allude would require the pen of Gibbon and the pencil of Hogarth.[82]

The 'golden bait' theme was developed in a short letter from an anonymous voter on the bank's role,

> I am credibly informed that parties are going from house to house offering accommodation in the 'kite' department – that is tendering cash on a bill. Let them beware of this trap. The bill accommodation system is like the bird lime by which clever boys decoy and catch silly birds. Let them not forget that the 'bills' will be payable after, not before the election, when the money lender's screw will be applied, and the pound of flesh extorted with interest, as it was in 1847.[83]

This was far from fiction, and was illustrated by the fate of Edward Dowling from Timahoe, Queen's County. He had backed Sadleir in 1847, but joined Browne in 1852. He wrote several letters to the *Sentinel* contradicting a rumour, that he had asked the bank to write off a £900 debt and advance him a further £300 in return for electoral support which was significant because he controlled the votes of three or four sub-tenants. He admitted that he had been 'principally instrumental' in securing Sadleir's return in 1847, but only as a more acceptable stranger than the Englishman in the absence of a local candidate. Dowling portrayed Browne, his own landlord, as a benevolent individual, who invested heavily in the town.

The truth was that Dowling expected the Conservatives to meet his debt as a reward for making available the votes at his disposal, but this was contingent upon a Conservative victory. Dowling was in debt not only to the bank, but also to a friend, Daniel Crotty, who had obliged him by endorsing two bills of exchange for £350, which were cashed by Thaddeus O'Shea. These bills were frequently renewed by the bank. Crotty, however, was concerned that he might be called on to meet them, and he secured from Dowling a bond of indemnity and a warrant of attorney, which would enable him to enter judgement upon the bond if Dowling defaulted. In this event he could more easily have Dowling arrested if he so wished, because the warrant dispensed with legal preliminaries.

Crotty was a Sadleirite, and when he learned of Dowling's political change of heart he went with Sadleir and O'Shea to persuade him otherwise. O'Shea offered £300 in cash and a release from £300 of his bank liability if he supported Sadleir. When this was refused, Sadleir used the curate, John Dempsey, to get possession of Crotty's bond, hurried to Dublin and had it executed, so that Dowling found himself sued for non-payment.

The immediate aim was to remove Dowling from the political scene. To achieve this Sadleir ordered Leonard Morrogh to make out two writs of execution, so that he could be arrested in Timahoe or Carlow. A certificate showing the amount of the debt and signed by an attorney was necessary to have these writs enforceable. It was drawn up in Great Denmark Street and validated by the forged signature of a solicitor named Thomas J. Gibbings, who had frequently undertaken work for Sadleir's law firm. Gibbings was then dying in a Cork hospital and unaware of what was happening. His name was attached to the certificate by one of the clerks on Morrogh's instructions. The certificate stated that £717 was due. The writs were rushed to Carlow from whence Edward Corcoran, Morrogh's brother-in-law, immediately went to Maryborough and requested John W. Miller, the sub-Sheriff, to arrest Dowling in Timahoe. When it was learned that Dowling had departed for the election nomination in Carlow, Miller and two bailiffs positioned themselves to intercept him on Graigue bridge, which bordered the two counties. Dowling, however, had reached town before them, but was arrested by the Sheriff of Carlow and imprisoned. Miller was taken to Sadleir and O'Shea at the bank, where he was given wine and provided with a car for his return to Maryborough.

Dowling's arrest was to have serious consequences for Sadleir when the truth was slowly unravelled in the Dowling *v* Crotty, Dowling *v* Lawler and Dowling *v* Sadleir cases, which were held at various times between August 1852 and June 1854.[84] But for the moment election success was the aim. Sadleir intensified his canvass in the few remaining days before polling which took place on 14 July. Voting began at 8 a.m. and an hour previously a large force of police patrolled the avenue leading to the courthouse.[85] Two companies of the 60th Rifles, a troop of dragoons and some mounted police ensured that the passages to the polling booths were kept open. A barrier was erected between these to prevent contact between the two groups of voters. All votes for Sadleir were recorded before mid-day and it became clear that he would have a majority. By the close of poll he had recorded 117 votes to Browne's 95, which was a great deal narrower than his 1847 success, but was a noteworthy achievement in the face of unprecedented opposition by the Conservative sector. Ironically, too, it meant that Dowling's votes would not have been crucial.

The *Sentinel* indulged in the usual post-electoral recriminations of the vanquished.[86] Allowing for exaggeration its comments revealed that many questionable practices, apart from the Dowling scandal, were used. It began with the nationwide Conservative theme of clerical intimidation. Catholic tenants of Browne, who had pledged their votes to him, were absolved from their pledges or physically threatened. Others were kidnapped, one being dispatched to Mitchelstown Castle. The contest had been presented as one between God and the Devil, money was lavishly spent on hired mobs to keep up the excitement throughout the town during the election period. Sadleir's supporters were traitors relying on rabble 'who insulted from the gallery of the courthouse on Monday last those who fed them for years'. The *Sentinel* felt that the social rift, which had been caused, would take some time to heal. A dejected Clayton Browne gave a calmer summary to his relative, Lord Naas – 'I am defeated here. That unfortunate Stockport business has been very detrimental to me... the priests have made a great handle of it ... the Tipperary Bank has been the means of making even Protestants vote against me'.[87]

It was a case of which side could exert the greatest pressure. The columns of the *Sentinel* on tenant ingratitude was itself a form of intimidation. A willingness to name individuals who voted against landlord wishes was as unscrupulous as any bribery or pressure by the bank. A landowner's letter of 15 July was an instance of this,

> I saw Mr. Robert Davies, late of Carlow, with shivering frame and blanched cheeks, produced on the table to vote against the patron, the generous friend of his family for years, Mr. Clayton Browne. What ingratitude to the benevolent proprietor of Browne's Hill, who fostered him – promoted his interests ... placed him in a position to earn honourable livelihood. A contest severs the chaff from the grain; we now know our friends from our enemies in Carlow. Let us not forget our friends.

The chagrin of the defeated was equalled by the rejoicing of the victors. Sadleir's achievement was seen as important for the Brigade. He was the only Catholic ever to represent the borough of Carlow and his re-election against a well-liked local candidate was a notable victory. It was believed that at last the Conservative grip on Carlow was broken and celebrations continued there for the remainder of the week. On the day after the poll he was chaired through the town, where, according to the *Sentinel*, 'the women were especially uproarious, reminding one of the saturnalia of the Poissardes of Paris in 1793'.[88] The *Tipperary Free Press* reported from Clonmel that the victory was the 'triumph of truth over calumny, of Irish patriotism over the old enemies of Ireland, religious liberty over religious persecution'.[89] It was also correct in its forecast of Sadleir's success as the forerunner of Carlow County, where Ball headed the poll, if only by two votes.[90]

But Sadleir's next concern was the Tipperary contest. He immediately went there to continue his support for his brother and cousin. He was joined at the nomination in the Clonmel courthouse on 20 July by other relatives, his brother, William, brother-in-law, Nicholas Biddulph Greene, his cousin, Nicholas, and his Scully cousins, Vincent,

Rodolph, and James.[91] These were augmented by a body of politically experienced priests such as Michael Burke, Archdeacon Michael Laffan, his brother Patrick, parish priest of Holycross, his cousin Martin Laffan, parish priest of Killenaule, and the outspoken John Ryan, curate in Cashel, whose penchant for invective was rarely equalled among the Tipperary priests.

The Conservative hopeful was Captain Robert Jocelyn Otway, who had an estate in Templederry, where the eccentric Young Ireland parish priest, John Kenyon lived. Otway had given up a navy career to take over the estate inherited from his cousin, Otway Cave, and considered himself a benevolent landlord. Despite the conventional heckling that greeted his nomination address, he managed to say that he would oppose any form of religious discrimination in Parliament. As the noise level increased he shouted that he would only support Derby on fiscal matters and only if these were 'perfectly in the right'. When this failed to mollify the audience Otway declared that he had 'always in the letting of my lands given a preference to Roman Catholics because they are the most numerous class'.

Archdeacon Laffan dismissed the Protestant Otway and advised him to

> go home to Templederry and don't be making a fool of yourself here, go home to your old friend Father Kenyon, go to confession to him, tell him all your sins, and maybe when he gives you absolution, we may then be talking to you'. Martin Laffan, condemned Otway as a supporter of the Derby government, which had 'encouraged the most horrid excesses that you have all heard of.

The land question was marked as the most important political issue of the time by Frank Scully. He declared his support for any future bill modelled on Crawford's which was 'founded on justice and fair play'. If it was passed 'there would be no such thing in this country as rack renting, no such thing as seeking from tenants impossible prices for land and consequently no evictions'.[92]

Scully's wide ranging speech targeted the religious questions, the Ecclesiastical Titles Act, the Inspection of Nunneries Bill, and the Protestant Establishment. He vied with John Sadleir in claiming credit for bringing 'before the public the rapacious robbery, and plunder of a noted character in Dublin Castle, I mean Duncan Chisolm, who has since fled to America'. He gave a measured response to any Conservative M.P advocating a reduction of the Maynooth grant,

> they thought indeed that the doing away of Maynooth would be the extirpation of the Catholic Church, that at its fall the clergy should fall

too, but let me tell them it is a great and sad mistake of theirs, for let Maynooth stand or fall the Catholic clergy will be ever found where they have ever been, at the death bed of the dying sinner. And again let me ask my Protestant friends are they consulting their own interests when they endeavour to do away with Maynooth? Would it not be better for them to have among them priests sprung from the people, educated at home with them, knowing their wants and their feelings, than to have priests from foreign countries, where they are taught revolutionary doctrines, which ought not be very convenient to introduce into this country.

Despite the fact that the policy was not regarded as a serious option in 1852, Scully included Repeal in his political platform and James Sadleir, while not embracing the Repeal, promised to 'use every legal and constitutional means to effect the release of Smith O'Brien'.

Scully saw railway expansion as an important facet of Irish life and explained that he had been 'mainly instrumental in hurrying through your county that very great advantage to it, the Waterford and Limerick Railway'. Finally, he considered the wider franchise 'of paramount importance', but was not satisfied that the qualification was still sufficiently low. A borough qualification of £5 would be more realistic than the prevailing £8 valuation.

James Sadleir, who was proposed by the displaced Maher, brought a more local dimension to the Stockport riots, when he revealed that the individual killed, Michael Moran, was a native of Clerihan in South Tipperary. He, too, highlighted the importance of the land question as part of the Irish party's policies. On a personal level he had carried out the Crawford principles on his own estates long before he considered running for parliament,

> I reduced the rents on my estate ten and twelve shillings an acre, I wiped away all arrears, I gave to my tenants new leases, they paid my rent for which they held in their hands stamped receipts, and the consequence now is that they owe me not one sixpence.

As might be expected, one of Otway's supporters, a barrister named John M. Mulcahy, deemed himself unimpressed by such sentiments. While praising James Sadleir as the brother of 'a man who has done honour to his country', he objected to his influence as a banker with a 'screw', which would be applied to any tenant or freeholder who voted against him. He could not resist following this with the observation that the 'ecclesiastical screw was as stringent as Mr. Sadleir's strongbox'.

Mulcahy's reference about James Sadleir's monied connections through marriage, drew a sharp response from John Sadleir, who rose to defend the honour of his sister-in-law, Emma. Mulcahy rightly regarded this as misrepresentation and Sadleir was later forced to retract in a written apology.[93] In his speech at the meeting Sadleir concentrated principally upon the religious issue, and showed the audience a copy of the by now infamous proclamation, which he said was received by the people of London, Liverpool, Wigam and Stockport 'as an order to spit on the priests and to revile the holy symbols of religion'. He blamed both Whigs and Tories as promoters of religious intolerance.

He did not attend for polling a few days later, when his brother and cousin easily defeated Otway,[94] an achievement largely due to priestly exertions, which were at least as vigorous as those in Carlow and which reflected a national phenomenon. The Conservative organ, the *Clonmel Chronicle*, was not amused and drew a graphic picture of clerical actions,

> If shameless intimidation – if terror, caused by the physical operations of maddened, infuriated and drunken mobs – if altar denunciations and imprecations – if threats of withholding the LAST RITES OF THE CHURCH FROM THE DYING ELECTOR who voted contrary to the wishes, or it may be, against the family or personal interests of his Ecclesiastical master – if tampering with mens' wives – if the most beastly and disgusting harangues, – and, finally if the exhibition of the Cross of Christ at a contested election, be recognised as legitimate by the British Constitution, then we must admit that the gentlemen who have triumphed in Tipperary have been duly elected;

Similar clerical resolve resulted in the withdrawal of the Conservative candidates[95] in the contest for Cork County, and the automatic return of Vincent Scully and E.B. Roche.[96] Scully's uncontested return was ironic, considering serious tensions in his camp at the beginning of the campaign, partly because of Sadleir's failure to resolve the ownership of Castlehyde and partly because of Scully's dissatisfaction with the management of the Tipperary bank. Following his victory in the by-election he met Sadleir in London on several occasions in an effort to have the title of the estate transferred from Ingram. Sadleir repeatedly promised to do so but failed to act. Scully pursued the matter when they returned to Ireland for the general election campaign. He was incensed at Sadleir's evasiveness and gave a resignation address to his conducting agent, James B. Kennedy, but was persuaded to withdraw it because the election campaign machinery was already in action.[97] Their animosity was sharpened because of Sadleir's still unpaid debt to Scully, who was also trying to extricate himself from the bank's shareholding. In a letter of 3 July Sadleir assured Scully that he would try and get 'some good capitalist to take your shares and stand in your place in the bank, if you are determined on not remaining any longer in it'.[98]

The Cork Liberal camp was unaware of this hidden controversy and Maguire in the *Examiner* was pleased that the withdrawal of the Conservatives had avoided rancour. He praised Scully for his parliamentary performance in the interval following the by-election, which had demonstrated fidelity to his pledges and earned the respect of his constituents.

Sadleir did not join in the victory celebrations in Cork nor did he become involved in the election of Keating in Waterford. As in 1847 this was an unusual one. Keating's address to the county was in print for several months,[99] when the electoral strategists decided to run him for the city, where he would partner Thomas Meagher, father of the Young Irelander, Thomas Francis Meagher.[100] No ostensible reason was mooted for the change, but it was either due to a rift between Keating and the county electoral committee, or was seen as the best option to defeat the Conservative candidates for the city, William Christmas and Sir Henry Winston Barron.

The first major meeting for the city election took place in Dungarvan on 29 June, two days before the prorogation of parliament.[101] It attracted sixteen priests and was chaired by Sir Richard Musgrave, who urged support for Keating. The latter did not turn up but soon issued an address to the 'Lord Bishop, clergy and electors' detailing his opposition to anti-Catholic legislation, condemnation of the 'paltry grant to the Royal College of Maynooth', and warning that the system of national education was in danger of being 'altered to suit the proselytising purpose of Lord Derby and his supporters'.[102] It highlighted Westminster's rejection of Crawford's bill, and pledged opposition to any Government headed by Russell and support for an independent Irish party.

At the nomination Keating's Irish pedigree was praised and his directorship of the London and County Bank presented not only as an indication of commercial acumen, but as a guarantee of his presence in London on a regular basis to watch over Irish interests in parliament.[103] The only family presence on this occasion was John Duff Coghlan of Kilcop House, who was married to Eliza Scully, daughter of Sadleir's uncle, James Scully of Shanballymore.[104]

The contest concluded on 14 July with Keating and Meagher defeating the Conservatives by a comfortable margin.[105] This victory meant that in July 1852 five grandsons of old James Scully were about to be installed as members of parliament, and reinforced the suspicion of Tenant Leaguers that a Sadleirite family clique was being formed, which would manipulate the Irish party for their own ends.

References

1. e.g. *Tablet* 24 April 1852 for reports on Wexford, Louth, Westmeath, Monaghan, Cavan, Wicklow; ibid., 15 May 1852 for reports on Waterford City, Monaghan, Cavan, Meath and Wexford County.
2. Letter 18 April 1852 in *Tablet* 24 April 1852.
3. Ibid., 5 May 1852.
4. Ibid., 24 April 1852.
5. See ibid., 1 May and 5 June 1852 for a list.
6. Ibid., 3 April 1852.
7. Ibid.,
8. Letter 8 April 1852 in *Tablet* 17 April 1852.
9. Priests were there from Tintern, Rathgyrogue, Poulpeasty and Taghmon.
10. See *Tablet* 15 May 1852 – subscriptions from Rathkeale, Aughnacloy, Kells, Skibbereen, Cork, Ardclair, London, Manorhamilton, Borrisokane.
11. Lucas to Cullen 6 April 1852. D.D.A., Cullen Papers, Carton 325/2.
12. Lucas's letter mentioned Cullen's letter of 4 April which cannot be traced.
13. See *Tablet* 1 May 1852 for details of an electoral meeting in Navan on 23 April where this decision was announced . See ibid., 8 May 1852 for a letter from Lucas accepting the invitation to stand for Meath and ibid., 15 May 1852 for his address setting out his principles in some detail.
14. Counties Monaghan, Louth, Down, Armagh, Antrim and the towns of Drogheda and Carrickfergus. He resided in Dublin.
15. *Tablet* 29 May 1852.
16. Letter in ibid., 22 May 1852.
17. Ibid., 10 April 1852.
18. Ibid., 17 April 1852.
19. Ibid., 5 June 1852.
20. *Telegraph* 12 May 1852.
21. *Tablet* 5 June 1852.
22. Ibid., 12 June 1852.
23. Letter in ibid., Lucas's letter of 8 June sought reassurances that he had the support of the priests and that the resolutions did not reflect the views of the clerical members of the General Committee of the Association.
24. *Tablet* 12 June 1852.
25. Ibid.,
26. D.D.A., Cullen Papers, Carton 325/2, Wilberforce to Cullen 9 September 1852.
27. D.D.A., Cullen Papers, Carton 325/2 contains letters on the various candidates. Wilberforce attended some electioneering gatherings in Dublin, e.g. see *Tablet* 3 July 1852. See ibid., 19 June 1852 for the address of the Catholic Defence Association to the Catholic electors of Ireland.
28. D.D.A., Cullen Papers, Carton 325/2.
29. Ibid., Sadleir to Cullen 14 April 1852.
30. Ibid., Neary to Bannon 21 March 1852.
31. Letter in *Telegraph* 3 May 1852.
32. Ibid.
33. Ibid., 12 May 1852.
34. Ibid., 19 April 1852. (see p. above).
35. Ibid.
36. Ibid., 12 May 1852.
37. Ibid., 26 May 1852.
38. See R.D., 1852, Vol. 17, abs.26, Deed of Marriage settlement. Louisa was the third

daughter of the deceased Thomas Edmund Lalor of Cregg House, under whose will her dowry was £2,500. She was given £700 immediately as a gift from her brother, Thomas. All the dowry money was assigned to Lalor, John Walsh of Jenningstown, Sadleir and Robert Keating as trustees to be invested in the purchase of land in fee simple or in leases renewable forever. Pending the purchase of such land the money was to be invested in Government Stock at 3.5% or in mortgages. This deed mentions an insurance policy of £999 belonging to Clement; for details of this see R.D., 1852, Vol. 16, abs. 157, deed of assignment 3 June 1852. In the event of his death the policy would be assigned to Lalor, Walsh, Sadleir and Keating as trustees. For a dispute between Lalor and Clement Sadleir see R.D., 1854, Vol. 11, abs. 254, a judgement of £1000 of 4 March 1854 in favour of Lalor – cited Clement's land at Arnakarky. See R.D., 1854, vol. 23, abs. 156, mortgage 1 August 1854 by Clement assigning lands at Arnakarky and Castleblake to Lalor and for another assignment see R.D., 1855, Vol. 4, abs. 20, Deed dated 3 January 1855. Clement Sadleir was then living in 18 New Bridge Street, London.

39. See *Telegraph* 30 June 1852 for Dunne's brief election manifesto stating his adherence to the party and its policies.
40. Ibid., 28 May 1852.
41. Ibid.,
42. *W.T.* 22 January 1853 for a retrospective comment on this.
43. *C.S.* 10 April 1852.
44. *Telegraph* 19 May 1852.
45. Mayo also held the title Lord Naas.
46. *Tablet* 22 May 1852.
47. *Telegraph* 19 May 1852.
48. Ibid., 24 May 1852.
49. Ibid., 4 June 1852.
50. Colonel Bruen was one of the M.P.s for Carlow County.
51. *C.S.* 12 June 1852.
52. Ibid., 19 June 1852.
53. Ibid., for a brief synopsis of the meeting.
54. *Telegraph* 30 June 1852.
55. Appendix 6. The proclamation was initially published in the *London Gazette*. The *Sentinel* of 19 June accused the 'ultramontane party' in England of violating the Act and thus provoking the Queen to issue the proclamation.
56. e.g. reference of Lord Winchilsea.
57. Maher was included by the *Dublin University Magazine* as one of a number of priests who had used strong language during the election campaign – *Dublin University Magazine*, vol 40, July – December, CCXXXV111, p. 253.
58. Details of the riots and the subsequent trials in Chester Crown Court in *Tablet* 3, 10 July and 14, 21 August 1852, *Telegraph* 2 July 1852.
59. *Tablet* 3 July 1852.
60. Ibid., Pointed out that the report in the *Manchester Guardian* was untrue.
61. Ibid. This edition also published a letter from a Fr. Collins describing the destruction of Edgeley Church and the attack on the parochial house.
62. The trials showed a determination to gather all the evidence and prosecute the culprits. At the Chester assizes on 9 August 1852 Judge Crompton stressed the duty of protecting the religious and civil rights of the Irish – *Tablet* 14 August 1852.
63. Text in *Telegraph* 30 June 1852.

64. Ibid., 5 July 1852.
65. Report of this meeting in ibid., 28 June 1852.
66. N.L.I. Moore Papers MS. 892, Lucas to Moore 4 July 1852 (letter no.365). The reality was that Sadleir and Sir William Redington were trustees of an election fund for Keogh. Sadleir and Vincent Scully contributed £100 and £50 respectively to this. Lucas produced a private letter at the Corruption Committee hearing to confirm this – *Tablet* 25 March 1854.
67. Reynolds was unable to attend a meeting of his own constituents that week-end, but he wrote his approval of Keogh. His letter 26 June 1852 from Esker House, Rathmines in *Telegraph* 28 June 1852. See *AS.* 9 June 1852 for Keogh's address to the borough.
68. Letter from Nicholas V. Maher in *Tablet* 15 October 1853 referring to the 1852 election. See also *T.F.P.* 26, 30 June 1852.
69. See *F.J.* 11 October 1853 and *Tablet* 15 October 1853.
70. *Tablet* 10 July 1852.
71. Scully's estates.
72. Report in *Telegraph* 2 July 1852.
73. Sadleir's written address of 1 July was dominated by emotive religious issues such as the Ecclesiastical Titles Act, the failed Nunneries Bill which would have subjected 'to a degrading visitation the consecrated homes of those pious ladies', the Maynooth grant and the Derby proclamation – *C.C.* 7 July 1852.
74. *C.S.* 10 July 1852, *Telegraph* 5 July 1852.
75. Bruen had voted for Catholic emancipation.
76. *Telegraph* 12 July 1852.
77. Ibid., see *C.S.* 17 July 1852 for an ironic account of the Tullow meeting by a hostile observer who styled himself 'A Looker on'.
78. *Telegraph* 12 July 1852.
79. *C.S.* 17 July 1852, *Telegraph* 14 July 1852.
80. *C.S.* 17 July 1852.
81. Ibid.
82. Ibid., 10 July 1852.
83. Ibid.
84. p. 269 below.
85. *C.S.* 17 July 1852.
86. Ibid.,
87 N.L.I., Mayo Papers, MS. 11018(11), Browne to Naas, n.d.
88. *C.S.* 17 July 1852.
89. *T.F.P.* 21 July 1852.
90. The Conservative, Bruen, was elected. Ball's running mate, Higgins, had retired from the contest and his replacement came last, although only eighteen votes behind Ball in a closely fought election – see *Tablet* 31 July 1852.
91. *T.F.P.* 21, 24 July 1852.
92. The Conservative *Clonmel Chronicle* viewed Scully's sincerity on the land question with skepticism. Its reporter was aware of the reputation some members of the Scully family had as stringent landlords. He was unwilling or unable to portray Frank Scully as such, but chose instead to label the family in general by quoting from a tenant that 'the Scullys would skin you, I know them well – they may talk as they like about tenant right, but they dont understand it either theoretically or practically', – *C.C.* 7 July 1852.
93. Their exchange of letters in *C.C.* 28 July 1852.
94. Ibid., Scully polled 3512 votes, Sadleir 3467 and Otway 789.

95. These were Edmund Shuldham and George Hudson. The *Cork Examiner* expressed incredulity that Hudson should have been chosen in the first place because he was the son of the Englishman George Hudson, styled the 'Railway King'. The latter was born near York in 1800 and following an apprenticeship as a draper became a partner in the business of Bell and Nicholson. He received a bequest of £30,000 from a relative and by 1833 was head of the Conservative party in York. He founded the York Banking Company. He became heavily involved in railway ventures and was appointed Chairman of the Midland Railway Company, a network with a capital of £5,000,000. As his railway operations extended he indulged in fraudulent practices and with the depreciation of railway shares in 1847 he was forced to resign as chairman of various companies. In 1865 he was committed to prison for contempt of the Court of Exchequer for not paying a debt. He died in 1871. D.N.B. , e.v.

96. C.E. 19 July 1852. For Scully's election address see ibid., 7 July 1852.

97. On 11 February Scully went to Ingram's country home in Rickmansworth, Hertfordshire. Ingram, however, tried to exact a higher price from Scully, who refused to pay for his property a second time. Scully also had the good sense to cancel a memorandum of transfer made out by Sadleir, in which the estate would be vested in himself. When the matter was finally resolved in Scully's favour in 1858, Ingram was exonerated from any fraudulent intent – *F.J.* 10 December 1858.

98. Correspondence in *L.E.* 3 May 1856, *W.T.* 3 May 1856.

99 See *W.N.* 14 May 1852 for the address which covered support for an independent Irish party, Sharman Crawford's bill, civil and religious liberty, the 'complete obliteration of that monstrous fraud, the Irish Church Establishment', the extension of the franchise, the ballot, and the 'utter annihilation' of the Whigs.

100. Keating's place was taken by the young barrister, John Esmonde as candidate for Waterford County.

101. Meeting in *W.N.* 2 July 1852.

102. Address in ibid., 9 July 1852.

103. Ibid., 16 July 1852.

104 The papers upon which MacDermot's articles in the *Irish Genealogist* vol.6, are based were discovered following the partial destruction of Kilcop House in 1863. The John Duff Coghlan who attended the nomination meeting died in 1854 aged twenty-eight – *I.G.* vol.6 op.cit p. 59.

105. *W.N.* 16 July 1852. Keating polled 445 votes, Meagher 463, Christmas 355 and Barron 309.

Sadleir's Family Tree (Abridged)

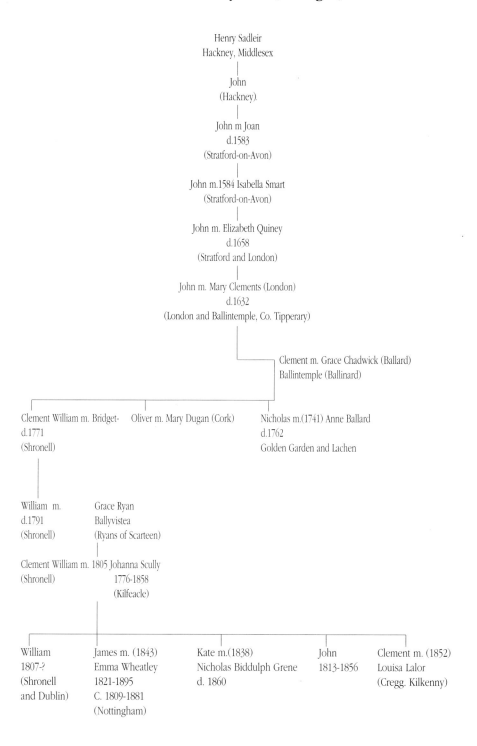

Henry Sadleir
Hackney, Middlesex

John
(Hackney).

John m Joan
d.1583
(Stratford-on-Avon)

John m.1584 Isabella Smart
(Stratford-on-Avon)

John m. Elizabeth Quiney
d.1658
(Stratford and London)

John m. Mary Clements (London)
d.1632
(London and Ballintemple, Co. Tipperary)

Clement m. Grace Chadwick (Ballard)
Ballintemple (Ballinard)

Clement William m. Bridget-   Oliver m. Mary Dugan (Cork)   Nicholas m.(1741) Anne Ballard
d.1771   d.1762
(Shronell)   Golden Garden and Lachen

William m.   Grace Ryan
d.1791   Ballyvistea
(Shronell)   (Ryans of Scarteen)

Clement William m. 1805 Johanna Scully
(Shronell)   1776-1858
                                (Kilfeacle)

William   James m. (1843)   Kate m.(1838)   John   Clement m. (1852)
1807-?   Emma Wheatley   Nicholas Biddulph Grene   1813-1856   Louisa Lalor
(Shronell   1821-1895   d. 1860   (Cregg. Kilkenny)
and Dublin)   C. 1809-1881
                  (Nottingham)

Shronell House – John Sadlier's birthplace.

Kilnahalagh Castle.

Sopwell Hall.

Old James Scully of Kilfeacle, 1737-1816, Sadlier's grandfather.

James Scully II of Shanballymore, 1777-1846.

James Scully III of Athassel, 1807-1878.

Frank Scully, M.P., 1816-1864.

Entrance, Clongowes College.

Clongowes College.

That he has but one apprentice and
is desirous to take ~~the~~ John Sadlier to be an apprentice
if the Benchers shall approve thereof.

Nicholas Sadlier

And the Petition of the said John Sadlier
                                    though
Sheweth That he is the son of Clement Wm Sadlier
of Thomville in the County of Tipperary Esquire and Frances Sadlier
otherwise Scully his wife That he is of the full age of sixteen
years as by the annexed affidavit may appear That he was
educated at the School of Clongows in the County of Kildare
and was instructed in following Latin Books viz. Virgil
and Sallust Petitioner therefore prays that the above named
Nicholas Sadlier may be permitted to take him as an
apprentice,

John Sadlier

Extract from the memorial of Nicholas Sadlier Gent to be permitted to take John Sadlier as an apprentice.

Great Denmark Street, Dublin, location of John Sadlier's Dublin office.

Emo Court, seat of the Earl of Portarlington, one of Sadlier's purchases under the Encumbered Estates Act.

Mitchelstown Castle, one of John Sadlier's purchases under the Encumbered Estates Act (Lawrence Collection).

Parliament of 1847 in which John Sadlier sat as M.P. for Carlow (*Illustrated London News*, vol. ii, July-Dec. 1847).

Jack Straw's Castle, Hampstead Heath, behind which John Sadlier was found dead, 17 Feb. 1856.

Chapter 9

Shaping parliamentary tactics –
August 1852-January 1853

Following the rigours of a difficult election campaign and canvassing
on behalf of family and friends, Sadleir went on vacation to Salthill
where he visited the Galway cattle show on 17 August, which was also
attended by the Lord Lieutenant, the Earl of Eglinton. His first cousin,
John Scully, Resident Magistrate in Oughterard, was there with his wife
Maria MacDermot.[1] Sadleir stayed at the exclusive County Club where
Lord Dunsandle, Lord Claremorris, Lord Clonmel and Lord Talbot de
Malahide lodged. T.A. Bellew, member for Galway County, and a
lukewarm adherent of the Irish Party also stayed there. Other
Brigadiers who arrived for the cattle show were Anthony O'Flaherty
and Martin J. Blake, members for Galway's Borough.

But the pleasure of his vacation was soon marred by the
repercussions from Dowling's imprisonment. As yet Sadleir's role in this
was unknown on a national level nor did he expect it to be uncovered.
Shortly after his imprisonment Dowling sued Crotty for false arrest on
the basis that the bills of exchange covering the debt were not then
due for payment. A court order was issued by Judge Philip Crampton
on 19 August that Dowling be discharged from the custody of the
Sheriff of Carlow, and that the costs of the case be paid by Crotty. This
was immediately appealed to the Court of Queen's Bench on 23
August, again presided over by Crampton.[2] Crotty's attorney was
Thomas Mulhall, who had been Sadleir's election agent, and his
counsel was J.D. Fitzgerald, M.P. for Ennis, an adherent of the Irish
party.[3]

Fitzgerald's first task was to distance Sadleir from any involvement in
the arrest and deny that he ever had possession of Crotty's bond. He
had to admit that the amount entered on the bond was over-stated at
£700, but pleaded that one bill for £221 under it was due at the time of
the arrest. His key argument was that the real purpose of the bond was
to 'perpetrate a gross fraud against the bank' to prevent it seizing
Dowling's assets. In such a case the rule of law established that the
court would not interfere, and he cited several legal precedents in

support. Francis McDonough, Dowling's counsel responded that the arrest was for a sinister purpose. Because the bond was little more than an agreement between friends to protect Dowling's property it should not have been executed. The over-stating of the amount die was a ploy to ensure that Dowling would be unable to meet it. McDonough refused to accept that Sadleir was not the main instigator of the events which led to the arrest. In proof he read an affidavit from a Carlow printer deposing that Crotty was confident of Sadleir's intention to indemnify him for all damages arising from the imprisonment. The affidavit also stated that some days prior to the arrest Sadleir had visited Crotty's house in Browne Street and taken away the bond.

In summing up the evidence, Crampton characterised the circumstances of the case as 'of a novel and singular character'. He judged that there was not any debt legally due at the time of the arrest and that an 'oppressive use' was made of the bond. More significantly he accepted the veracity of the printer's affidavit, which mentioned Sadleir. He condemned the interference with electoral freedom as a 'monstrous proceeding', and 'one of the most unconstitutional and oppressive that had come under his cognizance since he had the honour of sitting in that court'. He ordered the immediate release of Dowling and made Crotty liable for the entire costs of the case.

Sadleir was not called upon to give evidence in the case, but publicity in England made a statement imperative. In a short letter of 26 August to the *Standard* he denied that Crotty had given the bond to anybody, least of all to himself. He accused the Conservatives in Carlow of attempting to connect him with the affair.[4]

The controversy did not hinder plans to celebrate his victory. A banquet was held in Carlow in his honour the day after the verdict, and he interrupted his holiday in Salthill to be present.[5] This was a lavish affair in a pavilion adjoining Cullen's Hotel. His newspaper lauded the decorative efforts of the ladies committee,

> The approach to the dining hall was adorned with triumphal arches, formed of evergreens and beautifully studded with flowers; but the apartment itself excited the admiration of all who saw it. At the head was the Chairman's table; and three others ran lengthwise down the room. The ladies gallery was erected in front of the President's seat. Evergreens, interwoven with the choicest productions of the garden and hot-houses, formed an artificial ceiling immediately within the roof of the building... In the courtyard of the hotel, under canopy and immediately adjoining the grand entrance to the pavilion, was stationed an excellent amateur band, which performed during the evening a well-selected programme of national music and popular *morceaux* from the production of the most gifted Italian composers. The courtyard itself was

studded with evergreens and the rarest flowers, culled from neighbouring gardens, while a monster letter "S", dazzling with the illumination of some hundred gas jets gave the *coup d'aeil* an enlivening character.

Fr James Maher presided over the 150 guests gathered in Sadleir's honour. Even Lucas, who had successfully contested Meath, was among the ten M.P.'s who came for the occasion. On Maher's right sat Sadleir, Frank Scully, Loftus Bland, Kings County, Michael Dunne, Queens County,[6] Thomas Meagher, Waterford City, J.J. Devereux, Maguire, Dungarvan, on his left were Ball, James Sadleir, Keogh, Lucas and Reynolds, who had lost his seat in Dublin. Twenty six M.P.'s, including Keating and Vincent Scully, sent their apologies.[7] His principal supporters in the election campaign were also invited.[8]

Maher's introductory toast to the health of the Queen was ambivalent. The Irish people were loyal to her, not out of any conviction that their rights and liberties were protected, but rather from a sense of duty. They prayed for the Queen and all in high stations, because it was 'recommended by the apostles and recommended on grounds of a personal nature that they might lead a quiet and peaceable life in all piety and charity'.

Unaware of the Dowling details he turned to Sadleir and assured him that he had the full confidence of his constituents, which was inspired by a thorough examination of his political career so far – 'they read his speeches, inquired from their friends whether he was at all times at his post – they criticised his votes with rigour – nothing escaped his lips that they did not canvass diligently and carefully...'. Sadleir was an individual whose opinions were valued 'because they bore the stamp of a sound practical mind and because they showed a mastery of the subject in question'. He was a person of tact and resourcefulness who earned the pride and deserved the gratitude of his constituents. Maher's most significant remark was the expectation that Sadleir would be to the fore in forming 'one great Irish party' to work for the good of the country.

Sadleir responded with the stock pledge to labour for the public good and declared his awareness of the sacrifices made to secure his election. He was aware of the bitterness and division aroused by the election on a national level, and urged moderation and healing. He decried the attacks upon the priests by Tory newspapers following the election, and was unhappy that English Liberals and Free Traders accepted such a portrayal. For their benefit he repeated his unusual theory that the Irish priests were instrumental in maintaining the principles of commercial freedom and enterprise.[9] In England such freedom and progress was due to the leadership of the Liberal aristocracy, but the Irish aristocracy of landlords 'was banded together to resist the progress of the people'. It would be a mockery to enfranchise the Irish people 'if they disenfranchised the national clergy as citizens'.

The Carlow M.P. applauded the statement of Eglinton at a banquet in Galway, when he had exhorted landlords to promote political harmony in Ireland. He had used railway expansion as one example of their leadership role in developing Irish resources. But Eglinton's vision did not soften his antipathy towards the Viceroyalty itself. He always found

> that the Irish Viceroy was entangled in a web of nepotism, and, from the observation of many years he could say that the Irish Viceroy, be he Whig or Tory, was nothing more or less than the political correspondent of Downing Street, rather than the representative of the Crown.[10]

Maher's reference to the Irish party gave Sadleir the chance to articulate his proposals for its policy over the duration of the new parliament. His principles remained unchanged since 1847 and he wished to scotch rumours from Conservative quarters about possible future dissension in the Irish Liberal camp. He specifically refuted the probability of any tension henceforth between the League and the Defence Association,

> The opponents of land reform in Ireland had of late, by artful and furtive insinuations, been endeavouring to create a schism in the great Liberal Irish Party – they had alleged that the Irish Brigade would be found banded together in favour of one theory of landlord and tenant settlement, and that the Tenant League would be found united in support of another and a different theory. Now all these surmises would be laughed to scorn by the friends of the tenant. It struck him that all those who had been returned to Parliament by the sacrifices and by the virtue of the people of Ireland would feel it their first obligation to unite on one broad, intelligible, just and practical basis – to combine together as one great political force, holding itself aloof from Whig or Tory machinations, and bearing always in view the fortunes and the condition of the great elective body of the people of this country.

This was for the benefit of Lucas and Maguire, but he was careful to restate his dislike of indiscriminate opposition. There was a prevailing conspiracy to portray the Irish Liberal

> as some creature sent forward to obstruct all legislative proceedings in the British senate, and accordingly such representatives were held up to the people of England as persons of no character, whose sole purposes

in representing constituencies was to frustrate the intentions of every government, and to put one administration out after the other.

The Irish party, on the contrary, would support all measures beneficial to Ireland irrespective of their origin. Napier's land measures were included, although Sadleir could not bring himself to say anything positive about the Derby administration, and doubted if it was capable of a decent gesture towards Ireland.

Lucas listened carefully, and when his turn came to speak on the land question he abandoned his brief, and explored Sadleir's ideas. Conscious of the pro-Sadleir atmosphere in the pavilion, he carefully built up his case, re-echoing the theme of harmony,

> he was speaking in support of what Mr. Sadleir had said – he was speaking in confirmation of that hon. gentleman's opinion, that their enemies were mistaken, if they thought that between the members of the Irish Brigade and the members of the Tenant League there were any differences. He said this with the most perfect sincerity; and his proof of that sincerity was his presence there that day. He had expressed that sentiment in his letter to the secretary, and he was there that day to carry out the sentiment already given utterance to by the Rev. Chairman and Mr. Sadleir, that if any individual differences existed, they should be sacrificed – that every past dissension should be trampled under foot – that every effort should be made to bind together in one firm, coherent body those Irish members who had been returned to Parliament on tenant right and Liberal principles.

He agreed that, while the Irish party should remain aloof from the Tories and the Whigs, it would be 'the most absurd proposition that could be propounded in politics to throw out every government one after another'. In practice, however, he did not envisage any support for either of the major parties, and, more controversially, was equally strong in his dislike of any Grahamite Ministry, which might come to power. He retraced his earlier condemnation of Graham as the promoter of the Queens Colleges, who had also snubbed a northern delegation of Tenant Leaguers, showing that 'he was no friend of tenant right, but on his own estate a promoter of extermination, the great evil of this country'.[11] Gladstone fared no better. He was arraigned for bowing to English public opinion, and withdrawing his statement on the desirability of dealing with the Church Establishment. The hostility of the *Morning Chronicle* , 'the organ of the Grahamite Party', to 'ultramontane principles' in Ireland was to be deplored, as was its 'delight' at the defeat of Gray and Crawford in the general election. While he agreed with Sadleir that support should be forthcoming for beneficial measures by any government, including a Grahamite one, Lucas 'considered it impossible that a government to which the Irish party could give its support could be formed in England'.

Although aware of Lucas's hostility to Graham and Gladstone, Sadleir was taken aback by its introduction at his victory celebration. He quickly rose to deal with it in a statement which aroused much controversy during the following months. It was, however, an honest personal appraisal of the role of Irish representatives if the political scenario changed in Westminster. It also left no doubt about his own political ambitions, which he saw as perfectly in accord with the national good. Lucas's definition of his views was rejected as an inadvertent misrepresentation. Sadleir considered it poor parliamentary tactics to antagonise essential Peelite allies for the future toppling of the Derby administration, and he also felt genuine gratitude to Peelites like Graham and Gladstone, with whom both he and Keogh had been in constant contact during the debates on the Titles Bill. He continued to make the clearest statement of political intent yet, which signalled a future for Ireland only within the Imperial family,

> I shall not be content till I see within the circle of the cabinet, to whom the destinies of the British empire may be particularly delegated, a fair and due proportion of the Roman Catholic subjects of our sovereign ... I am more sanguine than Mr. Lucas, for I will not take the desponding view he does of the fight – and I do not think it impossible, nay more, I do not think it improbable, that if those men who have been returned by the Liberal constituencies of Ireland are but united, are but honest, are but true to themselves, to their country, to their constituencies, I do think they possess within themselves sufficient natural ability, eloquence, and parliamentary tact, and parliamentary experience, to furnish men, who might with great advantage to Ireland and the British empire at large, take a direct and main part in the government and legislation of these realms.

The participation of Irish Liberal M.P.s in cabinet was necessary in the interests of national justice and the welfare of the country. There was nothing in the principles of Catholicism which precluded such participation, but Sadleir did not envisage Catholics remaining in a government which legislated unfairly against Ireland. Sir Thomas Redington was one example of those Catholic representatives, who 'had not the political virtue or manliness enough to withdraw, as they were bound to do, from the Government, when that Government betrayed the confidence of the country'.

Keogh endorsed this. For five years Irish members had battled against the administration 'unrecompensed as far as government patronage, government consideration or ministerial largesse was concerned'. This was a worthwhile sacrifice under the circumstances, but was not indicative of any lack of future ambition, – 'the man whose craven spirit did not ambition popular applause and parliamentary honour, perhaps ambitioned something a thousand times more to be dreaded'. He reminded Lucas of Cullen's public gratitude to Graham and Gladstone for their outspoken opposition to the Bill.

Lucas silently digested these political confessions, feeling it inappropriate to become involved in a wrangle on such an occasion. Back in Dublin he felt no such restraint, and confronted them in a detailed leader of 28 August. Sadleir and Keogh were left in no doubt that that the post 1852 Irish party differed from the old Brigade, because it contained five Leaguers, which gave the land movement a more focussed voice in Westminster and served as a watchdog of the Sadleirite faction. Turning first to Keogh he quoted a large chunk of the latter's speech at the Athlone banquet the previous October, almost vowing opposition to all future governments, including the Peelites-cum- Grahamites.

Sadleir, on the other hand, always carefully weighed his words and Lucas could not accuse him of hypocrisy. He wrote that he did not differ at all from Sadleir 'on some abstract opinion touching the advantage of having Catholics in the cabinet', provided that in joining cabinet the integrity of policies endorsed by the electorate was not compromised for personal advancement. Lucas chose to see the only difference between them as their respective opinions of the Grahamite party, which in itself was crucial, and had the potential to damage the Irish party. Agreement on abstract principles was of little relevance to the political realities after the general election, when there was a real prospect of an alternative government acceptable to many Irish M.P.s. The fact that neither the Conservatives nor their opponents had a majority was further scope for division, since the Irish party would hold the balance of power, and any involvement in government would be seen as weakening rather than strengthening its influence.

Because of the potentially powerful position of a united Irish party, the Carlow speeches attracted more than usual attention throughout the country. Lucas published extracts from a cross-section of papers from Galway to Louth, all of which cautioned against joining any future administration.[12] Maguire wrote that the taking of office was the antithesis of independence, and would not yield beneficial results. With much justification he could not see how a few people in junior positions could influence cabinet policy, and he cited the case of Richard Lalor Sheil.[13] Other local newspapers agreed, and interpreted Sadleir's praise of Graham as a clever means of smoothing the way for either a personal or a party coalition with the Peelites. The *Freeman's Journal* was so taken by Lucas's article of 28 August that it reprinted it in a leader of 30 August. Urging a low key discussion of the whole controversy, Gray, nevertheless, warned about the constituency retribution which would fall on any representative with ministerial ambitions,

> With regard to the ambition to have Irish representatives treated to seats in the cabinet, it is no doubt a very laudable ambition for the men who desiderate the seats. But we should like to see the reception that would be given on an Irish hustings to the 'popular' candidate who had addressed the constituency, stating that his ambition was to acquire a place for himself in order that, abandoning the popular questions of the day, he might at once advance himself and his country!

The concern of the Liberal press was paralleled by the scorn of Conservative writers at the idea of members of the Pope's Brass Band desiring a place in cabinet. The *Carlow Sentinel* editorialised on the inconsistency of electioneering statements and Sadleir's aspirations,

> There was a batch of 'eleven' – (no less) – at the Carlow dinner, and they cheered to the echo, the wise maxim laid down by Mr. Sadleir – that a patriot out of place was like a fish out of water, floundering out of his native element. It was prudent and useful to abuse the Saxon government before the election – to tell the bewildered populace that their chapels would be pulled down as sure as the sun shines in the firmament, if they did not assist in returning 'Brigadiers' to parliament. What after all is the result of a conflict which has all but shaken the social edifice to its centre? Are the members going to 'die on the floor of the House'. Are all their promises to be realised? By no means: eleven members declare that the sweets of office are charming ... and that nothing can be done for Ireland until the members of the Brigade are snugly seated in the Cabinet to legislate for it.[14]

Like the *Tablet*, the *Sentinel* counter-quoted from a selection of other newspapers, all of which greeted Sadleir's announcement with a mixture of ridicule and anxiety that the inconceivable could happen, a British cabinet containing 'the nominees of the Irish priests'.[15] But the skeptical *Morning Herald* gave Sadleir's ambition more weight, because of his status as 'a hardheaded man of business, that can neither be driven out of his prudence or common sense by the shouts of a Carlow mob or the strength of Carlow whiskey'.

The *Telegraph* in its first editorial following the banquet, did its duty and eulogised him, but did not analyse the implications of what he had said. McCabe admitted that there was a change of policy, but added that this change preserved the original aims of the Irish party to secure full justice for Ireland.[16] This was an understatement in the face of extensive disquiet, which was shared by senior Catholic ecclesiastics such as Bishop Murphy of Cloyne. Answering an invitation to a public dinner in honour of the defeated Crawford, Murphy wrote that he detected 'the germ of unhallowed discord', arising from the Carlow banquet.[17] His principle was one of consultation by Irish representatives on the future course of action, and following such consultation the majority view should prevail. He was perturbed at any hint of Irish Catholics joining the cabinet, irrespective of who took power,

> Is it not a cruel mockery to be talking just now of the formation or composition of cabinets or government parties, or to attempt to amuse with such transparent theories a whole people who are literally being flayed alive, and are flying in wild despair from out of this stricken, though still loved land? What care we, in our present prostrate condition, whether Whigs, Tories, or Liberal Catholics occupy places in the cabinet, as all past analogies sorely convince us that with such folk, no matter how varying the complexion of their religious or political creeds, self-aggrandisement, the emoluments of office, and not the honest advocacy of popular rights, will ever form the dearest objects of pursuit.

As far as Murphy was concerned the old aphorism that in Ireland there was one law for the rich and one for the poor was still alive and well.

Sadleir was more shaken by this public censure from a prominent episcopal figure, who had ensured the election of his cousin, than he was by the many articles in the press. On 6 September he wrote a reply of over 5,500 words from Great Denmark Street.[18] Despite its length, however, it failed to adequately address the central issue of the Irish party's future course. Instead he accused his opponents of being driven by 'malice and hatred' which 'transforms the most innocuous substance into the most deadly poison'. Such malice was inspired by commercial rivalry and the success of the *Telegraph,* which he had established, 'although he had nothing to do with its management as an organ of public opinion'. He went on to accuse Lucas of misinterpretation, and publishing three different versions of his Carlow statement. The almost incestuous combination of some national and provincial papers did not reflect public opinion in Ireland, nor could it be created 'by the half dozen in the country copying from the three Dublin papers any slanders that may be invented there; and then the three Dublin copying back again the approval of their notions by the half-dozen provincials.'

The articles in the rival Liberal newspapers were hypocritical advocating harmony but effectively promoting discord among Irish representatives, – 'they seek to promote cordiality by calumny, union by unjust accusations and harmony by the most base imputations upon the motives and the conduct of the very men they invite to co-operate with them'. He deplored the controversy at a time when unity was essential, and complained 'that an attempt should be made to distract the public attention by vain speculations as to whether or not Sir James Graham would make a Prime Minister', when the reality was that a Derby administration was seeking to gain power 'by an anti-Catholic policy, and is calculating upon obtaining popularity in England by proposing a penal law which will disfranchise our electors and degrade our clergy'.

Sadleir relied upon his reputation to convince the Bishop of his integrity and asked him to

> look to the antecedents of my assailants and my own – to consider our position and our character, to see on which side rests the temptation to do an act, which may bring with it a pecuniary benefit or a personal advantage. I invite the country to this consideration, not for the sake of individuals, but for the sake of those great principles of civil and religious liberty which are placed in peril by an odious controversy that has been forced upon its attention at the present moment. I ask to be judged by my acts, by my votes, not by the misdescription of my sentiments, nor the misrepresentations of my motives, by those who have made themselves known as my enemies.

The *Freeman* quickly exposed the weakness of relying upon past service and sidelining future policy.[19] Gray dismissed the length of Sadleir's letter, when 'ten lines of explanation, of clear, frank, open, manly explanation as to his future policy would have done much to set the controversy at rest'. The editor of the *Freeman* had been defeated in the general election but he was determined to support Lucas and Duffy, successful in Meath and New Ross respectively, in keeping Irish M.P.s to a pledge of opposition, and planned to use a September land conference as the best forum to do so.

This two day conference was scheduled for Wednesday and Thursday 8 and 9 September, and had first been mooted at a meeting of the League Council under Tristram Kennedy, Louth, on 2 August.[20] A fortnight later Gray took charge of a Council meeting, which issued an address outlining the rationale for the conference of breathing new life into the League by discussing machinery for organising petitions, protecting tenant right voters in future, periodically analysing registry rolls, and establishing a line of communication between farmers, voters, the council and the Irish party.[21] The address emphasised that all representatives returned on the Crawford principles were expected to conform, and the conference would provide a platform for setting out the exact details of an acceptable bill to ensure consistency among these representatives. More controversially, It would also try to ensure unity of action so that the M.P.s could not exercise individual responses to legislation,

> The Council is also of opinion that it would not be safe for the cause, or just to the representatives, that the onus of forming a plan of parliamentary action should be thrown together upon them. It is the duty of all who are capable of aiding by their counsel, to assist in framing an effective plan of action; and it is equally their duty to share in the responsibility. Much, of course, must be left to be decided according to circumstances, and as events may develop themselves in parliament. But fixed principles of action – a general rule to serve as a guide on all such occasions – should be considered by a general conference of the whole party.

Sadleir, his brother James, and Frank Scully were among the thirty six M.P.s who publicly endorsed holding a conference. Writing from Galway on 18 August, he signified his intention of being present.[22] Vincent Scully was more circumspect, and wrote from nearby Clifden that he could not attend, but would 'carefully consider all suggestions' coming from the conference.[23]

It was held in the City Assembly House, William Street, and was chaired by Sharman Crawford.[24] Forty one M.P.s including the two Sadleirs and Frank Scully were there. Leading lay Leaguers such as Gray, Lalor and McKnight, were joined by clerical members like Quaid, O'Keeffe, O'Shea, Dowling, Bell, Rogers, and Rentoul. Fr James Maher's presence was an indication of his interest in the formation of a unified party.

The organising committee's desire to exclude members of the press was overruled by the conference and the rancour marring the early stages was reported. Dissension arose from the disquiet felt by several M.P.s, some strongly committed to land reform, at the attempt by an extra-parliamentary organisation to limit their freedom of action in Westminster. Tempers flared before the policy discussions began, when Moore insisted that he was speaking on behalf of a majority of M.P.s who, although deferential to what might be said, 'would not consider themselves party to every proposition that might emanate from the meeting. They would be bound by them only so far as they should consider their duty to their constituents called for'. Crawford sought to impose order by agreeing with Moore that no member should go to parliament pledged to a course of conduct proposed by any body out of the house ... for it might happen that circumstances would arise when the subject came up for discussion in parliament, that would compel members to take a course somewhat different from a resolution to which he might even have been a party.

It was finally accepted that M.P.s who did not agree with any particular resolution should openly say so, to ensure that the public understood their position. Lucas made sure to interject that silence would indicate acquiescence to a proposition.

Part of the problem that caused such chaos was the failure to circulate the agenda beforehand. M.P.s felt excluded and were worried about what might arise during the debate. Time was required to consider proposals beforehand, so that measured responses could be prepared. This was seen in particular when a version of Crawford's bill, divested of legal terminology, was read out. Moore, who supported the bill, was unable to accept this as a proper interpretation, because he had not time to read it. Crawford assured him that it contained 'in a popular way', the general principles of his bill and Shee, who was entrusted with bringing it before parliament, repeated this assurance.

But, several M.P.s, including John Ball, refused to support a resolution binding them to support all its details. They saw it as unreasonable, because it was unlikely that any government would accept every clause. A compromise was suggested that only a bill containing the Crawford principles would be acceptable. The Presbyterians considered this too general, but it was, nonetheless, passed. Many M.P.s were lawyers and had the expertise to compare government legislation with Crawford's. The Leaguers, however, were determined to prevent them from accepting or rejecting any such legislation without referring back, and secured a resolution that

> in the event of the introduction of any measure or proposition, not previously known to and pronounced upon by the conference or by the country, the tenant right representatives take means to have the country informed of, and its opinion elicited on, the probable operation and effect of the proposed measures before they, or any of them, commit themselves to any course in reference thereto.

They also succeeded in putting through a motion that a tenant right office be opened in London during the parliamentary session, to liaise with a parliamentary sub-committee drawn from those present at the conference. Another attempt to tighten the League's grip on M.P.s. was contained in a resolution that tenant right representatives were expected to attend League meetings in Dublin, unless this interfered with their parliamentary duties. This annoyed Moore, who 'did not think that at this time of day he required to be lectured upon the duty which he owed to his constituents'. Lucas stood firm and insisted that the resolution was vital. He cleverly interpreted it as an attempt not to load the M.P.s with more work but to lighten their burden. Keogh, however, appealed to the logic in Lucas's statement and Moore relented. The motion was passed.

The tenacity and determination of Lucas, in particular, succeeded in having all the resolutions passed without any major amendments. The greatest victory was secured in the resolution of opposition that

> In the unanimous opinion of this conference, it is essential to the proper management of this cause that the members of parliament who have been returned on tenant right principles should hold themselves perfectly independent of, and in opposition to, all governments which do not make it a part of their policy and a cabinet question to give to the tenantry of Ireland the full measure of justice provided for by Sharman Crawford's bill.

The earlier principle of Lucas that silence signified assent, meant that all the M.P.s present were now tied to a policy of independent opposition as a means of achieving the full measure of Crawford's bill. This was interpreted by Leaguers as a pledge, even if it lacked the credentials of a written promise on the part of all M.P.s, or verbal affirmation by most.

Sadleir, whose views on opposition were well known, said very little, probably to avoid conflict. Ironically, he was selected to propose the motion which would force M.P.s to refer any government land legislation back to local level, presumably League meetings, prior to making any decisions on it themselves. He had no option but to comply but made the proposal without enthusiasm or comment, on the grounds that O'Shea had said sufficient about it in his introduction. Sadleir had arrived late amid rumours of dissension inside, and opined that he could not see any fundamental differences between speakers. His brief hope was

> that those who were banded together to force on the consideration of the empire matters most important to those interests which the people had confided to their guardianship, would, by their future conduct in that conference, and by their course of action both in and out of Parliament, bring home to the hearts of the people the endearing conviction that each and all of their representatives would be ever actuated by that spirit of united patriotism which would alone obtain what Ireland now sought.

This vague aspiration contained the semblance of an opposition policy, and earned the approval of the assembly.

He attended a banquet in the Rotundo to honour Sharman Crawford on the final evening of the conference, but was not invited to speak.[25] The occasion was used by Lucas to re-emphasise the commitment, forced or otherwise, of the Irish M.P.s to the land question, – 'they had forty-nine members of parliament pledged not merely to the general scope and purpose of the bill, but pledged to every general principle and object which the bill contained – clause, line and word of that bill'. Members of parliament were not free agents but must be closely monitored in their Westminster duties.

Keogh, fortified by a liberal quantity of wine, and perhaps annoyed at Sadleir's exclusion from the list of speakers, stood up and berated Lucas for faulty arrangements in the proposing of toasts. He continued with a disavowal of personal political advancement,

> In 1850 he told them that the accession of parties to power was a matter of perfect indifference to him, and that so long as he enjoyed the confidence of the people of Ireland ... he would rather be in their service than holding the highest office that the government could confer. Let these persons talk of the gew-gaws of office to whom offers never had been made; the man who had been twice offered and had twice refused could afford to despise insinuations. He met such calumnies in the midst of his friends and of the members of parliament with whom he had been associated for six long years.

He was speaking on civil and religious liberty, a theme which had been relegated from centre stage by the land movement, following the general election. With the Irish representatives shackled by pledges on Crawford's bill and independent opposition, the Leaguers were now determined either to oust or control the Defence Association as the vehicle of religious agitation. Although the Association continued to hold monthly meetings,[26] it quickly declined to the status of a grant-dispensing body and would soon be described by Wilberforce as being 'in a state of suspended animation'.[27] This was not immediately apparent, however, and Wilberforce represented it at a meeting in the Northumberland Hotel the day after the land conference, to consider the summoning of a conference on the religious question prior to the convening of parliament.[28] He played no part in the meeting, however, which was presided over by Moore. Lucas and Gray were the secretaries, and Duffy proposed the setting up of a committee to consult with Catholics in England and Ireland on how to promote the question in parliament. A report would then be submitted to the conference which was to be organised by the same committee. The two Sadleirs and Frank Scully joined fifteen other M.P.s in the Northumberland Hotel.[29] James Maher was there as well as other leading political priests like O'Keeffe, O'Shea, and Quaid. Randolph Frith of Stockport, who had also attended the land conference, was present to give a first hand account of bigotry in his locality.

The committee selected had sixty-seven members, forty-seven being M.P.s, and included the two Sadleirs and the two Scullys. Wilberforce, Reynolds, Crawford, Maher and Gray were among the non-parliamentary members. It was subsequently divided into sub-committees that met on a regular basis to prepare for the conference, which eventually was settled for 28 October a week before Parliament assembled. Frank Scully and James Sadleir were active at these meetings.[30] Moore continued to act as chairman with Lucas and Gray as secretaries, but Sadleir did not participate. Sometime in September he returned to London, where his business interests were growing. Within the previous year he had played a leading role in the establishment of two companies becoming chairman of both. These were the Carson's Creek (Californian) Consolidated Mining Company and the Royal Swedish Railway Company.

The 140 kilometre railway line was mooted in 1851 to integrate with the planned mainline network between Gothenberg and Stockholm.[31] Initially the promoters found it difficult to raise funds, but a five year state guarantee by the Swedish Government added confidence to what was apparently a sound undertaking. It was imperative that the line be completed within the five year period and the chief engineer, Sir John Rennie,[32] who was later to receive the order of Gustavus Vasa for laying out a national railway system in Sweden, was optimistic that the line would be in operation by 1854. The involvement of Rennie, famous for the construction of London Bridge, was another intimation that the undertaking would be successful. Sadleir was also a key figure in inspiring confidence, and in 1852 took 48,000 shares at five pounds each, a significant proportion of the £416,000 capital of the Company.

The Carson's Creek company was a less promising prospect, and in February 1852 Vincent Scully had resisted Sadleir's attempts to get him involved.[33] Nonetheless, he soon managed to persuade a group of English businessmen to combine with an American consortium and purchase the goldmine, which was situated on Carson's Hill, near the Stanislaus River in California. He chaired the first public meeting of the company in the London Tavern, where two of the U.S. proprietors were present to hear his report and future plans.[34] He proposed that a working capital of £77,000 be appropriated from the £154,000 English shareholding to purchase machinery and develop the mines, which had been abandoned by a group in illegal possession.

Always conscious of the complexity of the laws of title in England, Sadleir reassured the assembled directors and shareholders that Californian law was more straightforward, being based on squatters title and 'a certain form of registration'. Confirming that the Californian courts had validated their title, he was less precise about the quantity of ore, but pointed to the extravagant lifestyle of the illegal prospectors, who had worked the mines, as some proof of rich deposits. This was hardly a sufficient presentation, but Sadleir was convincing in his declaration that

> all accounts official and otherwise, agreed that there had been an enormous amount of wealth extracted from Carson's Hill. It was acknowledged throughout the whole of America, that that hill was a mass of gold bearing quartz, though undoubtedly its relative value must depend on the successful application of science and machinery to the operations of reducing and crushing the quartz and separating the gold, and also on the advances which the State itself might make and the facilities for obtaining labour. The estimation in which the property was held was proved by the efforts of certain marauding parties to obtain possession of it.

Sadleir strengthened his case with the astute threat of assuring the English shareholders that the Americans present would be willing to purchase their shares, if they wished to dispose of them. He warned that profits would not emerge in the immediate future, but would come with patience, energy and perseverance. A U.S. attorney named Walker, who had advised Sadleir on the law of title in California, was present and supported his optimistic prognosis quoting letters from a Californian senator and a congressman on the mine's 'extraordinary richness'. Walker also gave the opinions of several U.S. lawyers and senators on the validity of the title based on mining customs, and a declaration from the President and Secretary to the Treasury that there would not be any recommendation to Congress to interfere with such customs or to demand any royalty. As proof of his conviction, Walker announced his intention of taking up £30,000 worth of the company's stock, 'if he could obtain it'. The meeting was accordingly convinced, and Sadleir's report adopted.

While Sadleir was engaged in these speculations his cousins in Ireland were equally diligent in finalising arrangements for the October conference on the religious issues. Signalling a shift from defence to equality, the movement was formalised under the title Friends of Religious Equality, and set up offices in 45 Sackville Street. Unlike the Catholic Defence Association its membership was open to Liberal Protestants, and, as the name implied, its principal target was the Established Church.

During preparations for the conference, McHale created a storm in the English press towards the end of September by a public letter to Derby describing the decimation of the 'Parliamentary Establishment' in the Irish general election as a forerunner to the fall of the Protestant Establishment.[35] The election outcome was a rejection of Protestantism, and the policy of independent opposition a signal that the Irish Party would not rest until the Protestant Establishment was ended. Some English journals, including the Liberal *Globe*, were provoked by his suggestion that the Ecclesiastical fund of the Established Church should revert back to the Catholic Church.[36] This was interpreted as an aspiration on McHale's part for a dominant Catholic establishment, an interpretation strengthened by the Archbishop's confident opinion that English Protestants in general were inferior to Irish Catholics,

> Your Lordship, I trust, will readily believe with the *Times* that the Celtic people are tenacious of antiquity, and above all the antiquity of their Faith, and its pure morality, and therefore the English people should be slow in believing that the Irish, notwithstanding their long acquaintance with the Saxon race, have not fallen in love with that brutal system of social demoralisation, which, like a foul cancer, has eaten up all domestic virtue and morality in England, as is unhappily exemplified by so many recent trials for infanticide by unmarried females, all which practices, if we are to believe the panegyrists of this moral, people are the spontaneous fruits of that Protestant system which they are labouring, but, thank God, in vain, to propagate in Ireland.

Neither the theme nor the tone of this letter appealed to the Committee of the Friends of Religious equality. Moore, who had already sent out a circular and agenda requesting the views of supporters in England and Ireland,[37] issued another on 12 October disclaiming 'the remotest intention of seeking for any religious creed in this country civil power or ascendancy over any other'.[38] The demand of the new movement was that any public resources appropriated for religious worship would be divided as equally as possible to all, 'according to the religion in which they are born, or which their consciences may lead them to profess'.

Vincent Scully's reply to the first circular expressed his pleasure that Liberal Protestants could join the new organisation.[39] Their absence would only provoke further anti-Catholic discrimination. Crawford's letter of 18 October to Moore put the question in another light.[40] The injustice of one church having to support another was clear enough, but he favoured the abolition of grants to all religious bodies, including the *Regium Donum* and the Maynooth grant. Only by going down that road, could a complete argument in favour of the disestablishment of the Protestant Church be defended. All funds appropriated should be applied in the national interest and not for religious purposes.

A large number of opinions poured into the preparatory committee in response to Moore's circulars,[41] ensuring that the religious conference passed without incident. It was chaired by Moore and held in the Concert Room of the Rotundo.[42] One of the significant factors, however, was the absence of any prelates from the conference and from the new movement, in contrast to their involvement in the Catholic Defence Association, whose monthly meetings Cullen continued to attend.[43] Nevertheless, twenty-five members of parliament came to the conference and these included the most influential leaders of the land movement, Duffy, Lucas, Shee and Lalor. The Sadleirite faction was represented by James Sadleir, Frank Scully, Dunne and Keogh. Other well known figures there were James Maher, O'Shea, Quaid, Dowling, Croke, and Wilberforce. Lucas and Gray acted as secretaries.

Most of the resolutions passed were contained in one form or another in the report of the preparatory committee and concentrated upon four issues – the Church Establishment, the legal penalties and prohibitions on Catholic ecclesiastics, the legal disqualification of Catholics and Dissenters from holding certain public offices, and 'practical oppressions' not enshrined in law but, 'connived at by the executive'. Of those the Protestant Establishment had moved to the fore, although the Titles Bill was still seen as an insult to Catholics. Unlike the Protestant Establishment, however, it did not have any practical effects upon Catholics, particularly upon their material well-being.

The committee report showed only one area of respondent disagreement, centring on the distribution of appropriated funds. Some respondents felt that they should be divided among the various churches, others preferred a general purpose use, like the relief of grand jury and poor law rates. Many priests disliked the idea of receiving such money, preferring the voluntary system as it existed. Some would even rather see the Maynooth grant abolished, if this safeguarded voluntary maintenance. Ultimately the meeting endorsed the view that any funds from appropriated property on revenue should be used for secular purposes.

The report was invaluable in concentrating the discussion, and facilitating the clear enunciation of resolutions for the M.P.s, who would soon be returning to Westminster. They would not be allowed to depart without accepting the same policy of independent opposition as was agreed at the land conference. Accordingly, a motion was passed that they should remain independent of and opposed to every government, which refused to make the issues contained in the resolutions part of its policy.

Sadleir did not return from London for the conference, but his letter of 26 October to Moore outlined his usual anti-sectarian sentiments. He hoped that its official statement would repudiate any wish for the ascendancy of one creed over another, or the confiscation of one church's revenues to enrich another. The rhetoric of the debate was also important to him, so that nothing would be said 'which can justly excite the fears or wound the sensibilities of those who conscientiously differ from Catholics in their religious convictions'.

Unlike the other respondents to Moore's circular, however, Sadleir, devoted little space to the religious issues involved. The controversy following his Carlow statement had fixed his mind upon the policy of opposition, and he anticipated that the members of parliament would receive similar instructions to those of the land conference. Much of his letter dealt with this and called for 'a cordial union' between the Irish M.P.s and the English Liberal Party. The great evil would be the continuing in power of the Tories, the enemies of Ireland, who hoped for disunion in Irish parliamentary ranks. Tories would portray the Irish M.P.s as an isolated body that would neither work with others nor allow others to work with it, 'unless submitting to its terms and sacrificing their opinions, prejudices or their predilections at its dictation'. He drew his own conclusions from the state of the parties in Westminster,

> It is not necessary to tell you how little the Irish members, unaided by the English Liberal members can effect in parliament. They cannot even obtain leave to bring in Mr. Sharman Crawford's Bill. In our present position, I believe what we shall require most in the House will be, not elaborate debates, but a practical policy. The present state of the parties must be kept in view. The Derby Ministry as opposed to a combined party of Liberals is in a minority. The Derby Ministry is, however, if pitted against the Irish Party alone in a majority – as against the Peel party in a majority – as against the Finance Reformers in a majority. But all these being Free Traders – all being favourable to a Liberal policy – all being opposed to a renewal of penal laws against the Catholics – all being disposed to a fair settlement of Irish questions – are, as compared with the Derby Ministry, in a majority.

Lucas asked his readers to make up their own minds if Sadleir's sentiments were in accord with those of the meeting.[44] The Carlow M.P. had failed to speak out at the land conference, and might have found it equally difficult to do so at the religious one. This was hardly the reason he remained in London, however, but probably because of business pressure. He did not attend a free trade meeting in Manchester on 2 November,[45] although he had previously said he would go.[46] James Sadleir and Frank Scully were there, however, and Keogh spoke on behalf of the Irish M.P.s. Lucas also attended, and reported Cobden's recollection that free trade was conceded by Sir Robert Peel in 1846 only because free trade members of parliament held aloof from either Whigs or Tories. But he wondered why Irish industrial affairs or Crawford's bill were omitted from the main speeches in a similar context. He drew the conclusion that Irish interests were seen even by such free traders as Bright or Cobden as being dealt with, not by an Irish Party *per se*, but by a union of Irish and English Liberals.

Lucas was not prepared to join the Liberals on free trade or any other issue merely to oust the Tories. When Parliament opened on 11 November the Queen's speech asked that any injury to particular sectors because of free trade should be mitigated.[47] This gave rise to the possibility of an amendment by Liberals that free trade had not injured any section of the British economy. Lucas, whose articles were much more sober in tone since his arrival in London, countered that Crawford's bill contained a specific demand for relief because Irish farmers were hit by falling prices due to free trade. Hence the party could not vote for an amendment, which contradicted the bill they were pledged to support. In the event the debate on the Queen's speech closed without amendment, and avoided what might have been a serious split in the party. The Irish M.P.s could now concentrate upon their principal concern, Crawford's bill.

Following the Queen's speech they met and instructed Shee to immediately place on the books notice of a motion for 25 November for leave to bring in the bill. On 22 November, the Irish Attorney General, Joseph Napier, introduced no less than four bills, three of which were not of major concern to the Irish party.[48] One was a bill empowering tenants with a life interest to improve their farms, another to allow the granting of shorter leases facilitating improvements and compensation for such improvements. A third was to simplify and consolidate some aspects of existing land law. The fourth, the Tenants' Improvements Compensation Bill, was of central importance to Irish demands. This went further than the proposals of any previous government, because it was retrospective on the question of improvements. It covered five types of improvements, buildings, reclamation of waste land, main-draining and irrigation, clearing of rock and erection of boundary fencing around ten acres and upwards.

The second reading began on 7 and 15 December. Shee rejected it as being 'scarcely consistent' with the Crawford compensation principles.

Napier's compensation was a 'legal fiction', because the landlord could respond to improvements by raising the rent to meet the claim for such compensation. He saw the omission of the Ulster custom as disastrous and one which could be fatal to the custom itself. His three and a half hour speech was skilful and detailed. It traced the problems arising from Irish land tenure from the Act of Settlement of 1645, and was as much a recommendation of Crawford's bill as a rejection of Napier's.

By that stage it was near midnight, and many M.P.s were becoming restive. Lucas stood to make his brief maiden speech, and showed that he had quickly adopted to the realities of parliamentary life.[49] He was sensitive to

> an assembly so extremely different from any that I have ever addressed before, so critical in its judgement of public speaking, so intelligent in its character of an audience, so intolerant of anything that it deems inconsistent with good taste, good sense or propriety.[50]

He told the House that he opposed the bill because of its inadequacies and not because it came from a Conservative government, who 'were throwing off so many old notions and were abandoning desolate politics'. This was a fair acknowledgment that Derby's ministry was anxious to bring in agrarian reform, even if it did not meet Irish expectations.

Sadleir said very little, but informed the ministers that the Irish members would oppose the bill. He objected to the intention of adjourning the debate until after the recess, feeling that an early and detailed discussion was necessary before the bill's details were referred back to Ireland for judgement. With the budget debate approaching the government was under pressure not to antagonise the Irish party, but it would not relent in its determination to adjourn. It did, however, allow Crawford's bill a second reading without debate, and referred it to the same select committee as Napier's.

This was seen as a victory, and led to the unusual circumstance of a frequently denounced Conservative ministry earning the praise of the *Tablet*, which felt

> some reason to thank them for the fair and candid manner in which they have treated the management of the question before the House. With a little pressure, no doubt, and mainly with the pressure of circumstances very strong upon them ... they have facilitated a discussion on the whole subject; they have given us an early opportunity to submit to the House, through the lips of Sergeant Shee, one of the most powerful statements of our case that has ever been made; they have allowed our bill to be read a second time; and at our request they have consented that all the

bills bearing on this subject shall be referred to a select committee, and shall receive, so far, the same treatment as their own – that is – opportunity for the fullest examination.[51]

Lucas even chided Keogh for a mild enough pass at Napier during the debate, which was to be regretted, because inadequate as his bill was, its terms were 'very much better than any the tenant farmers of Ireland ever received from any former government'.[52] His readers were correctly assured that the government had met all the Irish demands so far in the face of opposition from some of its own party. He concluded that unless the Irish party made it clear that it would meet all fair treatment in a friendly and conciliatory spirit, it would be impossible for any government to deal with it. The responsibility of the Irish Party was to be in opposition to any government that would not do justice to Ireland 'but it is not our business to oppose them in every possible way reasonable or unreasonable'.

Such a Sadleirite outlook on Lucas's part was constrained, however, by his dread of any possibility of a liaison between Peelites and Sadleirites. In the same editorial he could not resist a corresponding swipe at some of the Peelites, who had objected to the land bills being referred to a select committee. At the same time he had a firm grasp of political realities, and did not wish Derby to lose office when a promising path was being taken on the land question. It was evident, too, that the government needed the support of some Irish members to secure the budget, and Lucas was keen to exploit its dilemma. Shee consulted him and Duffy about a private approach in December by Horatio Walpole, the Home Secretary, on the price of such support.[53] The Government's response to a written reply by Lucas, Duffy and Shee was sufficiently encouraging to secure their agreement to bring as many of the Irish party as possible with them in support of the budget. Lucas in his weekly report from London in the *Tablet* of 11 December, prepared the way for such support by praising the budget.

This would have been anathema to members like Sadleir, who had consistently denounced the Tories, and whose political ambitions were pinned to the Liberals, and especially to the Peelites. His newspaper did not give Napier much credit. It published a sarcastic comparison between the Government and Crawford bills.[54] One of its concerns was the irrelevancy of Napier's bill to a large number of small farmers, many of whose improvements were outside its scope. The complex application procedures, too, would be daunting for most farmers, involving a '*chevaux-de-frise* of notices, specifications and objections'. It was deficient in terms of exorbitant rents or the Ulster Custom, and it placed the burden of proof for improvements on the tenant rather than requiring the landlord to disprove them. The compensation offered to evicted tenants was derisory.

But, Derby was under pressure from some of his own followers, who felt that the Government had gone too far in sending the Crawford Bill to the select committee. His need to placate these was seen from his admission to one of them in the House that the referral of Crawford's bill was only a tactic, and did not signify government support for its principles.[55] Lucas then felt no compunction in tearing Napier's measure apart at the conclusion of the second reading on 15 December. He might have done so in any event, and his speech was regarded as an outstanding one for a new member.[56] The entire Irish Party, alienated by Derby's obvious deception on Crawford's bill, joined the Peelites, Whigs and Radicals in opposition to the budget, and brought down the government by nineteen votes at four o'clock in the morning of Friday 17 December 1852.[57]

After this events moved rapidly. Derby held a cabinet meeting that afternoon and travelled to see Queen Victoria at Osborne House on the Isle of Wight that evening to tender his resignation.[58] The following day the Queen invited the Marquis of Lansdowne and Aberdeen to see her. Only Aberdeen could travel and he accepted the responsibility of forming an administration.[59] He spent Christmas week meeting Peelites and Whigs in an effort to form a cabinet and fix appointments to more junior positions. By the end of the week the cabinet was nominated and contained Russell as Foreign Secretary and Leader of the House of Commons, with Palmerston as Home Secretary and Gladstone as Chancellor of the Exchequer. The *Telegraph*, although voicing reservations about Russell, applauded the new ministry, but pointedly regretted the omission of Irishmen from the cabinet.[60] Some junior positions were reserved for Irish M.P.s, however, and Sadleir was earmarked for one. Writing to Aberdeen on 23 December Russell enclosed a note from Lord Bessborough that Irish Liberals wished a place to be offered to Sadleir, and suggested that he 'should have an offer to be Irish Lord of the Treasury'.[61] Aberdeen was happy with this, and Sadleir's reply of 27 December to his invitation indicated that he had the support of some Irish M.P.s, but made it clear that his continuing in office was not unconditional,

I beg to thank you for the kind manner in which you have given me the opportunity of consulting some of my friends in the House of Commons before I accepted or declined the office which your Lordship has been good enough to offer me. With their assent I now accept office. I believe it is unusual for the person filling the office assigned to me to take any part in debate. If circumstances should arise which I thought compelled

301

me to speak on particular questions I presume you will not object to my resigning my office in order that I may be at perfect liberty to speak on certain questions.

Aberdeen's immediate response from Argyll House put Sadleir in his place,

> I apprehend that a sense of propriety would prevent any gentleman from speaking against a government of which he was a member; but I am not otherwise aware of any reason for silence on the part of those holding office. At the same time it must be obvious that any person, who contemplates the probability of being obliged to oppose the government, had better not take office, as the occurrence must be painful to himself and injurious to them.[62]

He did not anticipate any such problem in Sadleir's case and would move the appointment unless otherwise advised by him. The Carlow M.P. accepted, and on 28 December became Irish Lord of the Treasury. He had only recently celebrated his thirty ninth birthday, and while the office was a junior ministry, it was seen as a stepping stone to higher positions. Some M.P.s saw the next stage as promotion to the Secretaryship of the Treasury or even Chancellorship of the Exchequer at some future date.

Keogh was appointed Irish Solicitor General, and a short time later Monsell became Clerk of the Ordnance. All members of Parliament, who took office, were obliged to have their decision ratified by their constituents in a new election. The writ for Carlow was moved by W. G. Hayter at the parliamentary sitting of 29 December.[63]

Three days later Aberdeen was in contact with Sadleir again.[64] The Prime Minister had received a printed letter signed by J. Holmes Hopkins, which censured the appointment as 'injudicious and improper'. It outlined Sadleir's 'antecedents', especially in reference to the Dowling case, and appealed for the removal of 'this unfortunate blot from your young administration'. Aberdeen forwarded the letter to Sadleir as an 'act of friendship' to 'receive such notice from you as it may deserve'. He diplomatically assured Sadleir that copies had not been received by any of his colleagues, and he was uncertain if the signature was genuine.

References
1. *G.V.* 18 August 1852, see also *G.V.* 21 August 1852.
2. Details of the Court case in *C.S.* 28 August 1852.
3. J.D. Fitzgerald, Lord Fitzgerald, 1816-1889 became Solicitor General for Ireland in the Palmerston Administration in 1855, Attorney General for Ireland in 1856. In

1860 he was appointed a Judge of the Queen's Bench in Ireland where he tried such well known figures as the Fenian leader O'Donovan Rossa and Charles Stewart Parnell. In 1882 he was granted a life peerage and was the first Irish judge to be appointed a Lord of Appeal. He first accepted and then declined the Lord Chancellorship of Ireland in 1885. He had thirteen children, three of whom became King's Counsel. D.N.B., e.v..

4. Letter from Salthill 26 August 1852 later quoted in *Tablet* 28 January 1854 as the Dowling saga continued.

5. *Telegraph* 25 August 1852, *Tablet* 28 August 1852.

6. Now County Offaly.

7. Tristram Kennedy (Louth), J.D. Fitzgerald (Ennis), W.P. Urquhart (Westmeath), P. O'Brien (Kings County), Dr. John Brady (Leitrim), Sir Thomas Burke (Galway County), Fulke Greville (Longford), E.B. Roche (Cork County), Hon. C.S. Fortesque (Louth), Ouseley Higgins (Mayo), William Monsell (Limerick County) W.H.F. Cogan (Kildare). M.E. Corbally (Meath), William Fagan (Cork City), M.J. Blake (Galway City), Cornelius O'Brien (Clare), John Greene (Kilkenny County), Timothy O'Brien (Cashel), O.D.J. Grace (Roscommon), D. O'Connor Henchy (Kildare), Charles Towneley (Sligo Borough) P. McMahon (Wexford County), Richard Swift (Sligo County), W.H. Magan (Westmeath), J. McCann (Drogheda), Robert Potter (Limerick City)

8. Fr. John Dempsey, Thaddeus O'Shea, Anthony Coffey, Thomas Coffey, Patrick Kinsella, J.H. Doyle, Edward Flood, William H. Collier, Matthew Byrne, Daniel Crotty, Michael Walsh, Jeremiah Kavanagh, John Vigors, Richard Dunne, Robert Lalor, Edward Lalor, Thomas Price, Daniel Carey, Edward Corcoran, J.P. Cullen, Thomas Corcoran, James Saunders, Martin Mangan, Thomas Mulhall, Andrew Gormly, William Caulfield, Christopher Mulhall.

9. Maher's letter 1 September 1852 in *Telegraph* 6 September 1852.

10. Sadleir's dismissal of the viceregal system of government was consistent with his views aired during the parliamentary debate of June 1850 when Lord John Russell proposed its abolition to bring Ireland under the control of a fourth Secretary of State operating from London. Many Irish M.P.s including Repealers like Frank Scully opposed the proposal as harmful to the Dublin economy and reminiscent of the damage done by the abolition of the Irish parliament. When news of Russell's intentions became known as early as April 1850 public meetings were held in Dublin to protest. These were attended by members of the Irish aristocracy and Repealers alike. During the parliamentary debates in 1850 Sadleir condemned the viceregal structure as an 'empty pageant', which hindered rather than promoted the Dublin trade. As a political system it was an 'insulting and disgraceful' way of governing a Country. The Viceroy himself was 'no more than a correspondent or scout to Downing Street. He was the representative of the Sovereign at a flower show or a race-course; but in his political capacity he was only looked upon or corresponded with as the agent of the English Government'. For details of Sadleir's speech see *Parl.Deb.*, series 3, vol 111, 1850, cols. 1427-1430, (17 June 1850), for other speeches and meetings see *Tablet* 6 April 1850, *Nation*, 6 April, 13 April, 25 May 1850, *F.J.* 4 January 1851, *Tablet* 1 February 1851. For details of the bill see *Bill to provide for the abolition of the office of Lord Lieutenant of Ireland and for the appointment of a third Secretary of State.* H.C. 1850 (359) III.617.

11. He relied upon a recent pamphlet by a Meath landlord, Naper, which quoted statistics of consolidation upon Graham's Netherby estate.

12. *Tablet* 4,11 September 1852 for extracts from the *Kilkenny Journal, Newry*

Examiner, Catholic Standard, Cork Examiner, Galway Mercury, Dundalk Democrat, Tuam Herald, Leinster Express.

13.   Quoted by *Tablet* 4 September 1852.

14.   *C.S.* 11 September 1852.

15.   Ibid., 4, 11 September 1852, extracts from the *Morning Chronicle, Evening Mail, Warder, Morning Herald* and *Leinster Express.*

16.   *Telegraph* 25 August 1852.

17.   Ibid., 6 September 1852.

18.   *F.J.* 7 September 1852, *Telegraph* 11 September 1852.

19.   Editorial in ibid.

20.   *Tablet* 21 August 1852. See Colm Kennedy, *Tristram Kennedy and the Revival of Irish Legal Training (1835– 1885)*, (Dublin, 1996), passim.

21.   Address 14 August 1852 in *Tablet* 21 August 1852.

22.   Ibid.

23.   Letter in *Telegraph* 6 September 1852.

24.   *Tablet* 11 September 1852, *Telegraph* 8 September 1852. *F.J.* 9,10 September 1852.

25.   *F.J.* 10 September 1852.

26.   See e.g. *Tablet* 11 December 1852.

27.   Wilberforce to Cullen 8 June 1853 and 15 July 1853, D.D.A., Cullen Papers. Both these letters refer to the funds of the Association. The letter of 8 June referred to a request from John O'Dwyer, the curate in Doon, Co. Limerick, requesting money to fund legal proceedings in the eviction of a woman who had rejoined the Catholic Church having been a souper. The July letter mentioned funds for anti-proselytising and the mission.

28.   *Tablet* 11 September 1852, *F.J.* 11 September 1852.

29.   Anthony O'Flaherty (Galway Borough), Ouseley Higgins (Mayo),Richard Swift (Sligo County), Patrick McMahon (Wexford County), William Cogan (Kildare), Captain Thomas Bellow (Galway County), Sergeant Shee (Kilkenny County), R. Potter (Limerick City), Tristram Kennedy (Louth), T.W. Devereux (Wexford Borough), Dr. J. Brady (Leitrim), Sir Timothy O'Brien (Cashel), Moore, Duffy, Lucas.

30.   Meetings reported in *Tablet* 18 September 1852.

31.   For reference to the Royal Swedish in 1852 see *R.T.* 4 December 1852, 1,8 March 1956, *B.H.* 1 March 1856, *T.L.* 1 March 1856, *Gentleman's Magazine* 1 May 1856, p. 530, D. Morier Evans, *Facts, Failures and Frauds,* (London, 1859), p. 297, *I.C.R. 1858 and 1859,* vol 9, p. 68.

32.   Rennie Sir John 1794-1874, a civil engineer was born at Stamford Street, London and was educated at Isleworth and Greenwich. He spent some years in his fathers engineering business in Holland Street and in 1813 was placed under Hollingsworth, the resident engineer of Waterloo Bridge then under construction. He went to Europe to study engineering work there and on his fathers death in 1821 he became a partner in his firm. Rennie supervised the construction of London Bridge which had been designed by his father. He was knighted in 1831 when the bridge was opened. he also succeeded his father as engineer to the Admiralty and was involved in Railway engineering from the mid 1820s as well as harbour work. He retired in 1862 and died at Bengeo near Hertford. *D.N.B.,* e.v.

33.   *F.J.* 10 December 1858.

34.   *Telegraph* 6 October 1852.

35.   Letter in ibid., 25 September 1852.

36. Quoted in ibid., See the *Times* 27 September 1852 for a sardonic analysis of McHale's letter.

37. See *Dublin Evening Mail* 27 September 1852 for text of the first circular which was marked private and confidential and dated 15 September 1852. This sought opinions, suggestions and advice on how the religious equality issue should be approached at the next session of parliament. The preparatory committee put forward several ideas including a submission to parliament to review the entire range of legislation on religious issues. This legislation was divided into four categories – 1. The original appropriation of ecclesiastical revenues for secular purposes, i.e. the Church Establishment – 2. The penalties currently attached to the performance of certain spiritual functions – 3. The disqualification from holding certain offices of state on the basis of religion – 4. The connivance between legislative and executive to pervert the 'most benevolent institutions' into 'instruments of persecution'. The Committee were referring to schools, workhouses, the navy and the army in this. The *Evening Mail* saw the contents of this circular as compatible with that of McHale's letter.

38. *Tablet* 16 October 1852, *F.J.* 15 October 1852. The *Freeman's Journal* also published two other circulars from Moore, one to the clergy and one to members of parliament. *F.J.* 15 October 1852 also quotes a lengthy reply from James Maher to the circular. Maher's letter quoted the text of resolution drawn up by a body of English reformers on the Church Establishment, which he hoped would assist the Friends of Religious Equality of which he was a member.

39. *F.J.* 15 October 1852.

40. Letter from Crawfordsburn in ibid., 23 October 1852.

41. See ibid. for several meetings of the committee and reference to the 'large mass of correspondence from all parts of the country'.

42. *F.J.* 29 October 1852, *Tablet* 30 October 1852.

43. *Tablet* 11 December 1852.

44. Ibid., 30 October 1852.

45. See *M.G.* 27 October 1851 for a list of invited guests to the banquet to be held in the Free Trade Hall Manchester on 2 November. The list included 75 M.P.s. Both Sadleirs, Frank Scully, Keogh, Duffy, Lucas and John Esmonde were among the Irish M.P.s invited. See ibid. 3 November 1852 for extensive coverage of the banquet.

46. *Tablet* 30 October, 1852.

47. Ibid., 13 November 1852.

48. Napiers detailed explanation of the four bills in *Parl. Deb.*, series 3, vol 123, 1852, col.s 305-341, (22 November 1852).

49. Speech in *Tablet* 11 December 1852. Lucas also made what was acknowledged as an excellent contribution at the conclusion of the second reading on 15 December 1852 – see *Parl. Deb.*, series 3, vol. 123, 1853, cols. 1545 – 1559, (15 Dec. 1853).

50. Editorial comment in *Tablet* 11 December 1852.

51. Ibid.,

52. Ibid.,

53. See Duffy, *The League* , p. 233 and C.G. Duffy, *My Life in Two Hemispheres*, (London 1898),vol.2. p. 60.

54 *Telegraph* 17 December 1852.

55. *Parl. Deb.*, series 3, vol.123, 1852, cols.1207 et. seq., (10 December 1852).

56. His speech fully reported in *Tablet* 18 December 1852. For reference to the excellence of Lucas's maiden speeches see E.M. Whitty, *St. Stephen's in the*

Fifties. The Session 1852 – 53. A Parliamentary retrospect, (London, 1906), p. 88.

57. Ibid.
58. Details from the *Times, Daily News, Observer, Morning Chronicle, Standard* and *Sun* in *Tablet* 25 December 1852.
59. *Tablet* 25 December 1852.
60. *Telegraph* 27 December 1852.
61. British Museum, Aberdeen Papers, Add. MSS. 43066, Russell to Aberdeen 23 December 1852 and Aberdeen to Russell on the same date with the comment 'I keep Lord Bessborough's memorandum'.
62. British Museum, Aberdeen Papers, Add. MSS. 43248, Aberdeen to Sadleir 27 December 1852.
63. *Tablet* 1 January 1853.
64. British Museum, Aberdeen Papers, Add. MSS. 43248, Aberdeen to Sadleir 1 January 1853. (f.193).

Chapter 10

Defeat at the Hustings – January 1853

Sadleir's appointment as Irish Lord of the Treasury intensified disagreement over the policy of independent opposition and aired the whole question of patronage which was also a controversial issue. Apart from the benefit of having Irishmen close to cabinet, the defectors saw office as the natural progression of their careers. Sadleir had never concealed his approval of official patronage and the opening up of career opportunities for the Irish. Any doubts about his ambition were dispelled by his declaration at the Carlow banquet.

If political patronage was important to wealthy politicians like Sadleir, the non-political type was an integral part of Irish life, and was considered essential in an era of serious unemployment and a relatively narrow-based economy.[1] Cullen, tacitly endorsed this by requesting Sadleir to make representations on behalf of an acquaintance for a post office job.[2] This type of patronage was well illustrated by Matthew O'Keeffe in September 1852 at a meeting of the Callan Tenant Protection Society, when he pleaded with Irish people to resist the temptation of using such influence,

> How are the Irish members to occupy this independent position if they be teased by their constituents for places in the customs, the excise, the post office, the poor law office, and all other offices, where the independence of a country is bought and sold for the emoluments of government patronage. For the sake of this poor old land; for the sake of this last struggle, that it may not be blotted out of the map of civilised nations, do not interfere with your members of parliament, do not cramp their energies, do not diminish their usefulness, do not make them sell that independence, which is the property of a whole country, that one individual may be provided for.[3]

Those who accepted these values greeted the new appointments with fury. Leading Brigadiers had defected to join a ministry containing Russell, the author of the Durham letter and the Ecclesiastical Titles Act. What were seen as solemn pledges of independent opposition passed at the two conventions of September and October 1852 were broken.

In the eyes of many it was nothing short of treachery. For those who lived in the more barren areas of Ireland it was a moral issue in another sense. In the aftermath of the Famine and extensive mid-century evictions it was seen as the abandoning of an effective policy and vehicle to protect the rights of the poor.[4] The Irish party, whose position after Derby's fall had been even stronger when combined in opposition with the Conservatives against a hastily cobbled if talented government of Peelites, Whigs and Radicals, was now weakened both numerically and psychologically. The government consisted of 320 members as against 292 Conservatives, giving the fifty Irish M.P.s the balance of power.

Denunciation came from all sides, the press, politicians, clergy, and the land and religion organisations. The *Freeman's Journal, Tablet* and *Nation* were most strident, and used equally strong selections from the provincial press to prove that anger was nationwide.[5] The most extensive condemnation took place in the early weeks of January 1853. Sadleir was generally deemed the most culpable, and seems to have aroused a degree of personal dislike among some of his antagonists, whose aim was to show that the new government was unworthy of support, not to mention entry to its ranks. The *Freeman's* refused to seriously consider the probability that it would incorporate League proposals in its legislation, and Aberdeen's decision to have the Crawford and Napier bills examined by the committee sanctioned by the previous government was not regarded as *bona fide* by Gray. As proof, an editorial of 10 January used a hostile reference to Crawford's bill by Lord St. Germans, the new Irish Viceroy, when he had been in opposition.

Gray's skepticism on this was nothing to his scorn of the notion that the new office holders could influence such men, or government thinking in general. He ridiculed the Lordship of the Treasury as a high sounding title, with Sadleir, or his predecessor Montesquieu Bellow, as the understrappers of W.G. Hayter, the Joint Secretary of the Treasury,

> now let any of our readers just fancy Mr. Montesquieu Bellow "making terms" with Lord Aberdeen, the Duke of Newcastle, Lord John Russell, Sir James Graham, Earl St. Germans, Lord Palmerston and their colleagues, and reducing the whole cabinet to his sway! *Pantaloon* in the Pantomime never propounded a proposition so mirthfully absurd as that of a Montesquieu Bellow, or his successor in office "making terms" for the government of the country with the whole British cabinet! We hope Mr. *Pantaloon* will accept our apology for the comparison. That personage really is an important individual, and influences largely the fate of his audience for the evening of his power, but an Irish Lord of the Treasury! Pshaw![6]

Gray relished the estimate of the *Cork Examiner* that when the defectors took 'the shilling they must submit to have their hair cut, their persons scoured, and their clothes made for them like all other raw recruits'.[7] A leader in the *Nation* on New Year's Day indicted the characters of Sadleir and Keogh, who 'were not worth a respective tide waitership'.[8] They were guilty of the 'most flagrant dereliction of duty ever beheld' in Westminster. Duffy agreed with Gray that it was absurd to pretend that they had received any promises from Aberdeen on the land or religious questions as a condition for taking office. He flayed Keogh with a narrative of his repeated pledges of opposition at various dinners and assemblies as 'audacious hypocrisy'.

Sadleir could not be accused of hypocrisy, but this did not shield him from the chagrin of Duffy, whose unflattering portrait of the Carlow M.P. displayed a fear of his influence to sway at least seven others, which according to London circles prompted Aberdeen to promote him,[9]

> That Mr. John Sadleir should go straight over to any party conducive to his own personal interests does not surprise us very much. That he should pave his way to this open and avowed treachery, by avoiding many explicit pledges, and by throwing out intimations so suggestive as that given at Carlow, is what any person who has an idea of his intricate and plotting intellect might expect. That the office to which he has been nominated should be the very one charged with the task of intriguing among and attempting to corrupt the Irish members, is a fact that reflects a rather questionable credit on the discriminations of the new Minister. We are anxious to see how many of a tail Mr. John Sadleir will be able to bring after him to the Treasury benches. Mr. John Sadleir is a clever man. Inside that sallow and wrinkled face of his ever play schemes and intrigues by the score. French railroads, English and Irish banks, joint-stock companies, law suits, estate agencies, the Farmers' Society, and the *Telegraph* newspaper all claim superintendence from that busy brain. But he has got one intrigue upon hands that he will find his master. He undertook the most daring of all his speculations when he proposed to bring over an Irish Party to the support of Russell, Palmerston and Graham. We know how the voice of the country will denounce such a compact.[10]

Although Lucas had a well deserved reputation for caustic journalism, his treatment of the defectors was more dignified and equally well reasoned. Yet there was a difference of approach in how he dealt with Keogh, who was treated with far more understanding than Sadleir. His open letter to Keogh, occupying a page of the *Tablet* on 1 January, praised him for the consistency of his work with the Irish party, but demanded an explanation because all parliamentary representatives were on trial following the defection, how stands it with the rest of us? Can we all, with unstained honour, accept its wages? Have the purposes for which the party was originally formed been fully carried out? Has the end of our creation been answered? Are we at liberty from this time forward to disband? to range ourselves under the ranks of the Durham epistle? and to lick the hand of the Secretary of the Treasury when he beckons us into the Ministerial lobby?

Lucas contradicted the reports that the Irish Party had been consulted before the taking of office. They had no knowledge of the new government's policies towards Ireland, and must remain in opposition until more was known. There was a greater onus on the founders of the party, such as Keogh, to sustain such opposition and keep the party to its pledges. On a personal level he was pleased for Keogh in terms of his ability and the sincerity of his wishes to advance Irish interests. In an accompanying editorial Lucas went further and said that Keogh's action was 'partially excusable', because he had no other income except from his profession, and the solicitor-generalship was promotion within that profession. Keogh's political career had swallowed up his professional income and 'a place of some sort may, for aught I know, have been a matter of necessity to him'.[11]

Lucas was also susceptible to Keogh's personal charm,[12] which contrasted with Sadleir's more distant personality. He also felt that Sadleir's desertion was 'the matter of real permanent importance'.[13] There was no apparent financial incentive for Sadleir to seek promotion, and Lucas accepted the stereotype image of him as an underhand schemer, plotting for years to spread his influence throughout Ireland. The Treasury was deemed the best vehicle to extend the tentacles of power, and the *Telegraph's* declaration[14] that Sadleir had refused the Vice-Presidency of the Board of Trade in favour of the Treasury, was pounced on as proof that he intended to cover the country 'with a network of corruption', controlling a 'drilled and compacted clerical influence through the Defence Association', stifling free discussion of the press, and systematically managing official Irish patronage. Power at the Treasury combined with banking, commercial, land and legal interests plus a financial hold on some M.P.s would result in a 'Dundasdespotism' throughout Ireland.[15] Lucas published a column from the *Munster News*, which was convinced that Sadleir wished to erect a 'family government' in Ireland.[16] It could find no other explanation for investing in a newspaper so priced that it could not support itself, and which by January 1853 had changed from a daily to a weekly. It calculated that £7,000 had been lost in that venture alone. Allied to this were large sums spent in the Tipperary, Cork, Carlow, Athlone and Waterford elections, which drew the sarcastic conclusion that 'the head of the family must be overburthened with the poetry of patriotism to be a party in all that scheme for patriotism alone'.

Lucas's public letter to Sadleir on 8 January concentrated on independent opposition.[17] It contained a clear critique of the policy, and upheld its usefulness only as an expedient at particular times. His argument was ingenious if apparently naive. Supporting the Liberals at all times would embitter the Tories, who, instead of legislating for the good of Ireland, would be confirmed in their hostility to Irish interests and motivated to obstruct beneficial legislation. Consequently, joining the Peelite government made the Irish issues a party question, which would always be opposed by a powerful opposition. Lucas, however, did not rule out the taking of place in a government, which legislated fairly for Ireland, nor did he support a general policy which disowned such patronage. But this was largely academic, because he had already made his case against the Aberdeen Government as inimical to Irish interests.

The *Telegraph* countered with an equally vigorous defence of Sadleir, Keogh and Monsell.[18] Provoked by suggestions that he was shackled by proprietorial opinions, McCabe protested his editorial and personal independence.[19] He admitted that he had spoken to Sadleir since taking office, but denied that the latter either wished to know, 'much less suggest, what course the Telegraph was likely to take in the discussion of those questions'.[20]

McCabe, whose paper's circulation was targeted in at least one town,[21] revived the charge of commercial sour grapes against the three Dublin papers and the provincial press which fed into them, with the added accusation of begrudgery at the success of the Irish politicians. He drew a parallel with the destruction of O'Connell,

> Never was there a more melancholy – never a more awful example of the evil consequences of this readiness to make unjust charges, and this promptness to believe them, than what we have witnessed in our own day. We have seen the greatest man that Ireland ever produced, slain by calumny – and that too, as calumny precisely the same type, which is now revived against the three Irish Catholic members. The head that had been filled but with one thought, the good of Ireland, was crowned with sorrows, the heart that had beaten but with one absorbing affection, the love of Ireland, was at last broken; because the patriot found credence given to the accusations that were made against him, that for the sake of an English Ministry, he had abandoned those principles which had animated him from youth to age... He was stabbed to death by the poisoned dagger of insinuation; he was murdered by the accusation that he had been guilty of treason.

The character of Sadleir and his fellow defectors was defended, and that of the rival newspapers, except the *Tablet,* impugned. The *Freeman's Journal* was singled out as 'one of the most malignant and mischievous of newspapers that ever sought to delude a people by the profession of popular principles'.[22] McCabe refused to enter into any controversy with the *Nation* , 'deformed by personalities' and written in unworthy language. He was, however, impressed both by the tone and the contents of Lucas's letter to Keogh, which contained a logic more amenable to a measured response. His most obvious reflection was a sense of relief that the 'priest-persecuting and tenant-right denouncing Administration of Lord Derby' was ended,[23] and was replaced by 'an anti-Ecclesiastical Titles Bill Government'.[24] But, he was candid in his reservations about the *bona fides* of some Ministers towards Ireland, although he did not see any reason for undue worry. There was the possibility that Russell, as Foreign Secretary, would negotiate a concordat with Rome by which Catholics would be 'conciliated into slavery'. Yet despite Russell's bad press in Ireland as the promoter of the titles Act, McCabe was more critical of Palmerston as Home Secretary, an office closely related to the government of Ireland. There was an 'apparent inconsistency' in his Liberal professions and the promotion of Conservative candidates by the agents on his Irish estates. McCabe reconciled this by drawing a distinction between Irish liberalism and that on the continent espoused by Palmerston as Foreign Secretary in the Russell Administration,

> *Continental Liberals* are, in point of fact, *Continental Orangemen* who, like our Orangemen, cry out "Civil and religious liberty" while they are oppressing the poor, persecuting priests, and robbing the Church. Whether Lord Palmerston will act upon his Continental principles of "Liberalism" or display the domestic virtue of "Liberality," as it is understood and practised by the true and sincere "Liberal Protestants of Ireland" time alone can show, and what his Lordship believes to be his own personal and political interests decide.

The important factor was that Aberdeen, 'who sat at the same council table with Metternich and Talleyrand and who proved himself the equal of both in sagacity and foresight', would ensure a favourable policy towards Ireland, and limit the scope of Russell and Palmerston. Other supporters of the Titles Act, like Cranworth, Grenville and Argyll would be neutralised by Gladstone, Graham, Newcastle and Molesworth, who would guard against any anti-Catholic legislation.

If the change of government was for the better, the exclusion of Irishmen from the cabinet was a matter of regret. But, McCabe did not accept that the defectors would be without influence. They would carry greater weight as members of the government than in opposition. Their inclusion was the best guarantee of civil and religious liberty, with Keogh preparing an 'enlarged measure of land reform' early in the session. As Catholics they could 'give practical attestation of their determination to supply the omission of their predecessors in office... by repudiating the bigot doctrine that the Catholic religion should debar any man from participating to the fullest extent in the rights and emoluments of the state'.[25]

McKnight's *Banner of Ulster* shared McCabe's optimism, albeit in a more moderate tone. Its editorial of 4 January reviewing League achievements was immediately followed by an assertion that the defectors, particularly Keogh as Solicitor General, were in a better position to influence government thinking on the land question. It rejected the stand taken by Gray, Lucas and Duffy against Sadleir and his associates 'without any previous enquiry whether they had violated their engagements or not'. The *Banner* did not interpret the defection as treachery because the new administration had not yet been able to demonstrate its policies on agrarian reform.

This stance by a League organ did not augur well for future harmony between the northern Leaguers and their southern counterparts. The seeds of disunity were also contained in an address of 1 January from Sharman Crawford to the tenant farmers of County Down.[26] While most of this was on the land question, it concluded with an affirmation of the power wielded by the Irish Brigade, which would

> continue and increase if the same bond of action shall hold that body together – and still more so when two of its most distinguished members have accepted office; and we cannot doubt that such acceptance of office by them is accompanied by an expected power to advance this particular question to which they are so strongly pledged.

Other politicians, Catholic priests and laity also supported the taking of office,[27] but those who opposed it were more vocal and more active. Moore, like Lucas, had a personal sympathy for Keogh, but was offended that the public letter of Lucas to him had tarred all the members of the 'Old Brigade' with the same brush. In a letter of 3 January he disassociated himself from Keogh and the 'eager extravagance of his pledges at Athlone'.[28] He stressed his own independence of Sadleir and Keogh, but did not consider the breaking of pledges, especially that of the land conference which was 'so comprehensive as to be incomprehensible', as the crucial issue. The impact of the defection on the Irish party was critical, and he was not so much concerned about the loss of the four members as about the future intention of the remaining ones,

> How many Irish representatives are prepared to cross the house with the deserters – how many are prepared with us to close our ranks and still struggle with the people? On this question I have fearful misgivings; and on this question it is of vital necessity that every constituency in Ireland should obtain from its representatives a complete and explicit reply. Whatever may be the fate of the Irish question at this crisis – at all events, let every honest man show his colours. Truth and honour need no disguise; and whatever hope there may be in a wrong-headed politician, there is none in a liar or a craven.

He felt it necessary to reassure his own constituents in a public address on New Years Day,[29] in which he advised that he saw nothing 'in the constitution or the promise of the present government' to attract his support.

If a leading Irish politician was concerned about the political impact of the defection, a leading churchman focussed upon its morality. To McHale everything else was open to interpretation, but the moral issue was explicit and incontrovertible. He wrote to Moore on 15 January about the religious obligation of fidelity to covenants, an obligation the more sacred and the more binding, the greater the numbers involved.[30] The bonds of society depended upon the binding power of such contracts and the inconvenience of a contract was no excuse for breaching it. Any contract was open to acceptance or rejection at the time of treaty, but only at that time. His letter contained the message that fidelity to pledges was part of gospel values,

> If then it is displeasing to God not to perform the things promised, we cannot be parties to the violation of such promises, on the obvious principle of the Apostle, who tells us that those sin not only who do the evil, but they, too, who consent to its infliction. This is the clear and simple doctrine taught to every Catholic child in his infancy, which grows and expands with his maturer years, if his mind be not perverted by false political maxims. It is this simplicity of the Gospel, so much opposed to the cunning and crafty wisdom of the world, that makes the Catholic people of Ireland be filled with astonishment at those violations of promises and breaches of solemn contracts, which the votaries of political expediency treat with levity and derision.

Letters and articles on moral and political perspectives had informed the public of the pros and cons of joining the Aberdeen government, but the real test was the response at local level. There were no meetings in favour of Sadleir and his fellow defectors. But the League, the Friends of Religious Equality and local political organisations mounted a campaign of protest in the early weeks of 1853. Lucas and Gray were at meetings of the Burgesses of the North City and Inns-Quay wards in Dublin on 11 and 18 January, respectively.[31] These were convened to discuss religious equality, Crawford's Bill and the extension of the franchise, but focussed on the defection. Reynolds, who sympathised with the defectors, was heckled during his speech on religious equality and left the Inns-Quay ward meeting. The Skibbereen Liberal Club held a special meeting under Henry Leader, parish priest of Rath and the Islands, which passed a resolution of sorrow by 'the Catholic heart of Ireland' at the alliance with Russell who had 'politically degraded their prelates', and hoped that the 'insulted constituencies' of Carlow and Athlone would reject Sadleir and Keogh.[32] A New Ross gathering on 4 January felt likewise, and issued an address to the electors of both constituencies that the return of a Conservative would be preferable,

> In the name of the Irish farmers, whose rights these men swore to defend, and basely sold in the name of religious equality, which they have sacrificed to the enemies of the Church – in the name of public honour and public decency, which they have bartered for English gold, we implore you to reject them with indignation, that they have the audacity to appear once more on your hustings ...Let every honest voter fold his arms and look calmly on at the struggle between tyranny on the one hand, and corruption on the other; and if you must be misrepresented in parliament, let it be by men of whom you know the worst, and from whom you can expect no good, and not by men who swear to defend that they may the more securely betray.[33]

When Kilkenny Corporation met for the installation of the new Mayor, one Alderman abandoned his prepared speech on the mayoralty to condemn the defection.[34] He had as little time for Aberdeen as for Derby, who were 'English and Scotch to the hearts core and they had no sympathy with Ireland'. Another moved a resolution that Sadleir and Keogh had forfeited the confidence of the Corporation.

As the only organisation with a countrywide network, the Tenant League played a prominent role in the anti-defection cry. Its weekly branch meetings were a ready forum for discussion; e.g. extracts from the *Nation*, *Tablet*, *Freeman's* and *Cork Examiner* were read at the Callan branch, where members had 'a long conversation on the desertion and perfidy' of Sadleir and Keogh.[35] O'Shea impeached the Brigade, 'that counterfeit thing of yesterday', who deserved the title Brass Band because of its 'brazen effrontery'. He had contacted William

Cahill in neighbouring Mullinahone on the need for a county meeting to haul in its Sadleirite representatives. Cahill, a prominent figure in the Mullinahone branch, who, according to the O'Carroll diary, could 'swallow copious draughts of flattery', doubted that such a meeting would be prudent or effective in keeping doubtful members on the right path. The best approach would be an official League deputation to influence electors in the by-elections.

The Carlow election campaign was then beginning. Sadleir had gambled that he would not be opposed, but he faced greater odds than ever before with the Independent Oppositionists and Tories sharing a common desire to defeat him. For the disciples of independent opposition it was the acid test of support for the policy. To the Conservatives it offered an early opportunity of regaining the seat and exacting revenge for the general election defeat, which had resulted in a petition against Sadleir's return.[37]

Conservatives examined various options in the limited time involved, and even sounded the Liberals on the possibility of running their own candidate to split the Liberal vote and ensure Conservative victory. Naas was working behind the scenes, and William Long, one of his Carlow contacts, wrote to him on 1 January that this was 'not on the cards' even for a *quid pro quo* in another constituency.[38] The Liberals were only prepared to run a candidate on tenant right and anti-Ecclesiastical Titles Act principles, who would omit all references to the Established Church, to enable Conservatives, 'if any can be found', to vote against Sadleir. In a second letter on 1 January Long revealed that he had a candidate in mind, who would go forward on this basis. This may have been Dr. Cullen, a local medical practitioner and previously one of Sadleir's strongest supporters.[39]

This scheme did not prove feasible and the Conservatives again turned to Clayton Browne, who, however, was unwilling to risk a second humiliation.[40] They finally found a candidate in John Alexander, a wealthy landed proprietor from nearby Milford. He also had extensive estates in County Antrim, owned the Belfast Flour Mills,[41] and leased property in Barrack Street, the Shankhill and Falls Roads.[42] His campaign was actively supported by William Auchinleck Dane, a Deputy Grand Master of the Orange order in Enniskillen.

The orange label would have repelled even lukewarm Liberal voters, but the *Sentinel* held him up as an independent candidate and a native of Carlow, unmoved by 'place, pension or emolument'.[43] It had no affinity with the *Nation*, *Freeman's* or *Tablet*, but saw the electioneering value of their material, and took every opportunity to air their theme of betrayal, even quoting them in an effort to blacken Sadleir.[44] He was pictured not only as a renegade to his own party but as 'an ultra politician' holding office in 'an unprincipled government', opposed to all Conservative principles.[45]

Sadleir reacted swiftly to this unexpected threat. The petition against his 1852 election on the grounds of bribery was declared not relevant,[46] and when Alexander's candidature was announced he unsuccessfully challenged him before the London Recorder[47] on the legal technicality that he had been improperly designated.[48] He published his brief election address on New Year's Day, which portrayed his acceptance of office as a patriotic sacrifice to assist a government whose character was a guarantee that Irish interests would be safeguarded.[49] His increased influence in office would help 'dispel the prejudices which so injuriously affect our common country'. The electors were assured that he had 'in no way whatever' compromised his political opinions by taking office,

> You know, that from my first entry into public life, I have been the constant and consistent advocate of Religious Equality, Parliamentary Reform, and complete free trade; and in office as well as out of office, I shall always be found the warm supporter of the just claims of the cultivator of the soil, to the fruits of his honest labour.

He set out for Carlow at once and his election campaign began on 4 January with a meeting at the Liberal News Room in Burrin Street.[50] He admitted there that he had not reached any understanding with Aberdeen on Crawford's Bill, but repeated that taking office was consistent with all his public statements. He did not feel bound by the pledge passed at the September land conference and denied that his silence on that occasion indicated support for it.

Lucas and O'Shea were in Carlow since the previous day to assess the political climate.[51] Sadleir sent a note to Lucas in Cullen's Hotel inviting him to attend the meeting and hear his explanation about accepting office.[52] Lucas agreed to go as an observer only, declaring that he had 'no intention to mix myself up with the Carlow election, in which, so far as it is a local contest, I have no concern'. True to his word he did not interrupt the meeting, but returned to Dublin and confronted Sadleir with an open letter in the *Tablet* of 8 January ridiculing the Burrin Street affair as a 'hole and corner' meeting, and his explanation as 'a web of invention and sophistry'. He concluded that Sadleir's cause in Carlow was

> as rotten as your policy and your return is extremely doubtful; that it depends on a very few votes; and that if you are returned at all – which I sincerely deprecate – it will be by the unwilling votes of men who thoroughly condemn your conduct.

Sadleir would have agreed with Lucas's assessment on the tightness of the margin, and the day after the Burrin Street meeting he began a comprehensive canvass of the borough. The Conservatives had hoped that the priests would remain aloof, but Browne informed Naas on 5 January that Sadleir was accompanied that day by a 'leading priest'.[53] He felt that the influence of the priests would be crucial, and confided that despite their difference of opinion on the defection, 'they will, as they have always done, unite against the common enemy'. He might have added that overt opposition to Sadleir by any priest would have incurred the displeasure of Bishop Haly.[54] Some years later Moore privately told Lucas how influential the bishop had been. Haly did some informal canvassing for Sadleir and requested Dr. Cullen's vote in his favour. Cullen recorded his reply,

> My Lord, you know it is scarcely possible for me to refuse any request of yours. I think it my duty, however, to tell you that if I vote for Mr. Sadleir, I shall be voting against my conscience and violating what I think to be my public duty. If you still urge your request I will obey you, but on condition that you give me your solemn promise never again to control my political action.[55]

Haly insisted, gave the promise and Cullen voted for Sadleir. Despite such powerful endorsement, the latter feared not only the propaganda of his three newspaper rivals, but their resolve to use the League and the Friends of Religious Equality to undermine him. The Council of the League prepared for an organised offensive against him.[56] He tried to counteract its statements by issuing a more detailed election address, published on 11 January to coincide with a meeting called to finalise its offensive.[57] The address was totally concerned with the ethics of taking office and offered a complex argument which, on the one hand, questioned the validity of the September opposition resolution and on the other accepted its substance and spirit. Sadleir queried above all the coercive nature of the resolution, which signified his own failure and the corresponding success of his three newspaper rivals in the power struggle preceding the September conference,

> I consented to attend the Conference in September last on condition that a declaration would be publicly made, before any resolution was proposed at the Conference, whereby other members of parliament and myself should be considered as bound by the resolutions of the conference, so far only as we may deem such resolutions in accordance with our conscientious opinions as representatives of the popular cause; and I have never regarded the seventh resolution as a declaration by which I was to be considered as pledged to act otherwise than in strict accordance with my own convictions.

Nevertheless, the address conceded that he had 'substantially assented' to the resolution. Aberdeen's accession, however, had changed the political landscape, and Sadleir attacked the assumption of a recent League statement that he had 'consented to become a member of a Government who decline to give to the Irish tenantry a measure of justice such as that referred to by the seventh resolution'. His principles were consistent within or without government, and his constituents were assured 'of the anxious wish of Lord Aberdeen to respect the honourable consistency of each member of the government'. He believed that government policy would be in accordance with his principles and justify his taking office.

The main thrust of this address was supported by Crawford's reply to his letter of 7 January complaining about League accusations of treachery and desertion. The *Telegraph* published Crawford's letter with the address as an endorsement by the chairman of the September conference. Crawford disliked League tactics of damaging Sadleir's personal reputation, and its assumption of government intentions. He upheld Sadleir's first address to the electors as embodying the basic principle of his bill, and his taking office as compatible with the September pledge. Crawford's letter, nevertheless, signified that Sadleir had acquiesced in the resolution and was honour bound to carry out its spirit,

> I understand you to mean that you expect the government will agree to propose a substantial measure of justice on this subject; and I honestly state to you I would hold you bound by your pledges not to continue to hold office in connection with any government who would refuse it. Let it not be supposed however, that I hold you bound to the precise words or details of my bill. I have always declared the contrary, and for this reason I have lately put forward what I hold to be the essential principle which that bill demands, in order to secure that which you say you will endeavour to obtain – namely, the establishment of the just claims of the cultivator of the soil to the fruits of his honest labour.

Far from seeing the defection as destructive of the Irish Party, Crawford viewed it as a triumph in forcing the government to recognise its power. Unity among its members would strengthen the hands of their colleagues in office. The prompt resignation of the latter in the event of government failure to adequately legislate on the land question would increase the power of the party. Crawford's thesis was that Sadleir and his associates were on trial, and 'by their future conduct in office they ought to be judged, and either honoured or degraded as they shall prove themselves true or faithless servants in their country's cause'.

Crawford's position placed the League in a quandary since the leaders wished to preserve a unified front. The *Telegraph* accused them of ignoring both his letter and Sadleir's address at the 11 January meeting. Nine members of parliament attended this meeting, and most of the session was spent discussing a resolution condemning the defectors.[58] The M.P.s present were Duffy, Lucas, Moore, Devereux, Kennedy, Dunne, Patrick O'Brien, King's County, Patrick McMahon, Wexford County and the chairman, Robert Potter, Limerick City. McKnight, Rogers and Renteul came from Ulster, and Kearney, Dowling, Redmond, O'Shea, Quaid, and William Mullally were the leading League priests there. James McDonnell, Dean of Cashel, who never attended League meetings, was also present. Other prominent individuals there were Gray, Hoey and Leyne.

The discussion exposed a serious difference of opinion in League ranks, mainly between the northerners and southerners. Some of the Ulster delegates had the first opportunity to articulate their outlook in person, and McKnight, whose paper was becoming increasingly strident against his southern colleagues,[59] was vexed that a minority on the Committee had already taken a decision that the defectors had broken their pledges. This was evident from the convening circular, which McKnight felt reduced the delegates' terms of reference to merely deciding on a fitting punishment. To him this was 'very like Jedburgh-justice – namely to hang a man first and try him afterwards'. Even hardliners like Lucas might have accepted this, but McKnight proceeded to praise the M.P.s for taking office; in fact, 'the great evil in his opinion was not that two members had obtained this official addition to their powers, but that twenty members had not been placed in the same position'. He backed Sadleir's sentiments that hostility should be directed against the Tories and not the Aberdeen administration.[60]

The Presbyterian ministers adopted a wait and see policy, although Renteul was in favour of censuring the defectors. Nevertheless, he admitted that many in Ulster believed that they had secured a *quid-pro-quo* from the new government on the land question. Rogers advised that 'the minds of the people of the north generally' would be carried if the League agreed to delay any vote of censure. Pledges should be honoured, but it was not yet clear if Sadleir and Keogh had broken any. He proposed an amendment that it was premature to condemn the defectors until government policy on the land question was known, and until Sadleir and Keogh had explained the terms of their taking office. Government intentions on the Crawford principles could be discovered by means of a League deputation to London. Failure to embody them in its policy would unleash a campaign of condemnation and agitation.

This approach was less likely than McKnight's to aggravate committed Leaguers, but his passing reference to a rumour in Ulster that some in the anti-defection camp themselves coveted office caused a rumpus. Rogers mentioned no names, but Moore was aware of a story linking him with a request for the Chief-Secretaryship, and took the remark as a personal insult.[61] Lucas joined in the angry exchanges between the two, and reduced the Ulsterman to a huffed silence. This deterioration in personal relations between the leaders widened the rift with the northerners, and eventually they seceded from the League.

McKnight and Rogers also reflected the views of the absent Crawford, whose letter to the Down tenant farmers had already spelled approval for a parallel course of action, with some Irish M.P.s working within the Government and the remainder exerting external pressure. His note of apology for not attending contained the same sentiments as those in his letter to Sadleir, and asked delegates not to make unfounded allegations which would damage the defectors' election prospects.[62] He held to his conviction that the government should be given sufficient time to consider the land bills when they emerged from committee. Although Crawford's letter was read to the meeting, its early publication was suppressed by Lucas, Gray and Duffy, and he was forced to send it to the *Dublin Evening Post* and *the Banner of Ulster*.[63]

There was more unanimity among the southern leadership favouring condemnation of the defectors. Surprisingly, however, Patrick Lalor opposed this. Both himself and, less unexpectedly, Michael Dunne argued that such a response would injure the League and alienate those favouring a wait and see policy. They were supported by William Fitzpatrick, a poor law valuator from Maryborough, and a friend of Sadleir, who irritated some delegates by condemning those Leaguers who had publicly attacked the defectors.

The difficulty for such Leaguers was the imminence of the by-elections, where the return of Sadleir and Keogh would be an endorsement of what was seen as betrayal. There was no time to defer judgement and members like Lucas were intent on registering formal condemnation,

> They wished for delay – till when? Till Mr. Sadleir was re-elected for Carlow. Till violated pledges had received their approbation by a corrupt constituency, and till the government and people of England had been told by the wretched and miserable verdict which they hoped to secure, that there was no honesty in Ireland, and that they did not care about the violation of the most solemn engagements.

To Duffy, who got a standing ovation, it was essential that a public example be made of Sadleir and Keogh 'to deter other evil doers from similar offences'. He drew upon his own knowledge of the Repeal campaign and saw a lesson to be learned from the destruction of the Repeal parties of 1832 and 1847 by the venality of some members. He asked how voters could be expected to make sacrifices for the personal advancement of politicians. Duffy acknowledged, with some exaggeration, the blandishments that awaited Irish representatives in London which encouraged such advancement,

> When Irish members got to London a thousand temptations beset them; the power and opulence of that great city overawed them; Downing Street stood open night and day to buy the venal, ... admission to the great English clubs and to London society was supposed to depend upon their pliability; they must leave Ireland outside the door if they entered. Here were temptations enough for poor humanity, without writing it a free pardon beforehand for all breaches of fidelity to Ireland.

The determination of Duffy, Lucas, Quaid and O'Shea that such a free pardon would not be written carried the day. A resolution of unequivocal condemnation was passed, and a decision to send a deputation to Carlow and Athlone was proposed by William Mullally, who had nominated James Sadleir at the Tipperary general election, and was an overt signal to the Tipperary members. The deputation consisted of Kearney, Dowling, O'Shea, and Lucas, all of whom attended a meeting of the Friends of Religious Equality the next day to co-ordinate the plans of both organisations.[64]

Moore presided over it, and with the exception of Duffy, all the M.P.s who were at the League meeting were in attendance.[65] At a committee meeting earlier in the day Moore had proposed a formula, which was accepted by the conference and consisted of a condemnation of Sadleir and Keogh, a resolution calling on the Irish Party to remain in opposition to any ministry refusing to make religious equality a cabinet question, and a proposal to send a deputation to Carlow and Athlone.

Vincent Scully sent his apologies to Moore in a letter of 11 January, and, despite his private reservations about his cousin's business interests, he opposed any condemnation of the defectors. He suggested postponing the meeting until the next parliamentary session, when they would be better informed about what course to take. He made it clear that the taking of office would not be his own choice, but all Irish M.P.s had 'the same object in view'.

Devereux was the only M.P. present who refused to condone a censure or deputation, and withdrew from the meeting. This was a polite rebuff compared with the tactics of Peter Sharkey, a friend of

Keogh's, who came from Athlone to defy Moore and his colleagues. He assured all present that he had dined with Bishop Browne in Athlone the previous day, where they 'drank the health of the able Solicitor General for Ireland'.[66] He promised the deputation a hot reception there, and ridiculed the conference as a 'relic of a meeting' convened to attack able and talented representatives. He moved an amendment that the conduct of Sadleir and Keogh had met the approval of constituencies, bishops and clergy. The mood of the meeting degenerated when Sharkey, provoked by the frequent jeers of the audience, asked Cantwell if he had recently looked for a place, and called Duffy 'the murderer of O'Connell'.

Moore and Gray managed to restore order and all the resolutions were passed. Moore was given the task of visiting the boroughs, and immediately wrote to Sadleir of his intention.[67] Although he accused Sadleir of breaking up the Irish Party, he avoided the type of aggravating language used by Lucas, and assured the Carlow M.P. that his motives were not personal, but were those of public duty.

Sadleir was not mollified by the civility of Moore's declaration to destroy him politically and responded by attacking the Mayo M.P. for allying himself with Lucas, Gray and Duffy.[68] He reminded Moore of the favourable opinions of Crawford and others on the defection, and condemned his opponents for trying to disrupt the Liberal front against the Conservatives in the borough,

> To talk of coming here now, on the pretext of aiding in a course of frank discussion upon a question which you have not scrupled to prejudge, is too absurd to obtain credence in this town. Let your object and intentions be whatever you please, if your mission to Carlow makes any progress it could only tend to defeat the Liberal party, and hand over the representation of the borough to a bitter faction. It has not been considered sufficient to slander me – no, the Liberal electors who have always supported, and who support me at the cost of fearful sacrifices on their part, must be also attacked, and accordingly they are held up to the public as a venal and corrupted constituency, secured by bribes and sustained by bludgeon-men. If you can form an idea of the feelings which such conduct can excite in the breasts of men prepared for any sacrifice rather than forfeit their independence, you can imagine the indignation which this scurrilous system of wholesale calumny has evoked in this town.

Sadleir's blunt refusal to meet Moore was purely a warning to the deputations and avoided any attempt to justify the defection. Moore was stung by its tone, and sent a sharp reply asserting his independence of the other accusers. He recalled Sadleir's close co-operation with him in forming the Irish Party, and could only interpret the taking of office as a betrayal of the principles which Sadleir had so often pronounced in his presence over the previous two years. Sadleir's initial vision of the Party appeared to have shrunk

> to the meagre and narrow conclusion of defeating a Whig government, to establish a Whig and Peelite administration in its place, to transplanting Lord John Russell's anti-Catholic policy from this country to foreign parts, and Lord Palmerston's anti-Catholic policy from foreign parts to this country.

The defection was a blow from within, which opened up a system of 'corruption and venality' that would destroy 'political morality' in Ireland. The enemy from within was more dangerous than the enemy from without, but Moore would not accept Sadleir's accusation that he was promoting the interests of the Tories,

> You presume to insinuate to me that I am endeavouring insidiously to support the Orange faction by returning Mr. Alexander. Was it from you or from me that that faction received the heaviest blow and the greatest discouragement that has been dealt them in modern times? Is it to you or to me that it is owing that Lord Roden was stripped of his honour – that the Beers no longer disgrace the magisterial bench – that the blood that was shed on Dolly's Brae[69] no longer cries to Heaven for vengeance; and that the Orangemen of the north have learned that there is an eye that watches, and an arm that has not struck in vain.

Moore thought it peculiar that Sadleir refused to avail of the opportunity to vindicate his actions by public debate. He attributed this to fear that

> the fancy portrait of your own political career, painted by yourself for presentation to your revered friend, the Bishop, might have lost something of its charming resemblance to the original if confronted with the frightful fidelity of the photograph which the light of public discussion would have drawn.

He refused to accept Sadleir's statement of a united Liberal phalanx in Carlow and maintained that the support of the priests was 'constrained, hesitant and reluctant'. There was some truth in this assertion, although five priests attended the final election rally in the Liberal News Rooms on 12 January.[70] James Maher, however, was not present and largely remained aloof from the campaign. He did not issue his customary address, and possibly was opposed to Sadleir's re-election until he consulted Archbishop Cullen who had not condemned the defection.[71] The meeting was carefully stage managed and one voter, Matthew Byrne, asked Sadleir two questions, did he support Crawford's Bill and would he resign if the government failed to bring in legislation containing its principles. Sadleir answered in the affirmative to both, and assured Byrne that he had the promise of Sir Richard Bethell, the Solicitor General, that the land question before the committee would receive 'bona fide and honest treatment' from the government. He re-iterated, that he would not 'chain himself to any particular machinery', but to the Crawford principles only. The important consideration was that any bill emerging would have a reasonable chance of success, otherwise the entire process was pointless. Land legislation was overdue, and the Incumbered Estates Court 'supplied only a trifling instalment of the justice and relief which was required'. In contrast to his destruction of the Small Proprietors' Society, he advocated that 'the man of small capital ought to have legal facilities to go into the land market, and become, if he wished it, the free and unshackled owner of land'.

Sadleir told Byrne that Crawford's views coincided with his own, and he used Crawford's attitude to the defection itself as a main plank in his platform. Crawford's opinion was 'the strongest proof of the prudence and propriety of the step he had taken'. He had also received a private letter from Crawford, which he could not publish, but which 'expressed the deepest sympathy for him and anxiety for the result of the election'. He did, however, read a letter from Bell to the *Banner of Ulster* protesting that his name had been signed to the circular convening the League meeting of 11 January. As one of its secretaries, the League had permission to use his signature, but in this case he objected to having it on a circular condemning the defection, a charge which he felt showed a lack of sound discretion.[72] Sadleir accused the Leaguers of ignoring the views of such influential figures. He also charged the *Freeman's Journal* with trying to manipulate public opinion by editing some of the more abrasive comments.

If he used the Ulster Leaguers' stance as a means of influencing the electorate, Sadleir also strongly played the anti-Tory card. His portrayal of them as a malign influence in many areas of Irish life was an honest conviction,

> While Derbyism was predominant how were the Catholic and Liberal magistracy treated? Were not our national clergy prosecuted on every possible pretext? In what instance was the franchise permitted to be freely exercised by Liberals possessing it? Were there not missives sent to every person holding a public employment, calling on him to sustain the Government candidate? They knew how the Liberals and Catholics holding the commission of the peace were tyrannised over and teased,

and harassed by the representative of Lord Derby; and with what an air
of triumph their clergy were assailed..

He was careful to add that he would never act in such a way as to
enable the Conservatives regain power, although this was the intention
of the deputations. He may have suspected the early collusion between
the Conservatives and the anti-Sadleirites who

> had no hope of returning Dr. Gray, but were sufficiently in the
> confidence of the Tory Party to know, that if they can confuse or
> confound a very few of the Liberal electors, so far as to induce them to
> abstain from voting, they can fulfil their intention of returning Mr.
> Alexander. They have openly and audaciously announced that anything
> is better than that the Liberal electors should succeed in returning the
> man whom these men have set their hearts on running down.[73]

Sadleir was justifiably worried that the deputations might deprive
him of a few precious votes, and he was incensed that they had the
presumption to physically intrude in the contest. To him they were
'men who had long reviled and blackguarded each other and now
come forward to blacken him'. He told the meeting that they had
already visited Athlone, where they had been 'met by the Bishop and
his clergy' and 'had the discretion to beat a hasty retreat'. He was intent
on ensuring similar treatment in Carlow and made profitable political
capital out of Lucas's accusation that the Carlow borough electors were
'capable of being bought and sold'. He intervened in the debate on
several occasions to expand on this by quoting Lucas's description of
one meeting as 'the assembled electors and bludgeon-men of Carlow',
or his indictment of the 'enormous system of bribery in the borough
election'.

Some of the speakers professed themselves satisfied with Sadleir's
stand. One resolution pledged support for him 'with increased energy
and determination', and another inveighed against Lucas's 'gross,
malicious and false libel against Mr. Sadleir and the Liberal electors of
this borough'. Part of this energy was spent in meeting the League
deputation which arrived two days later. They were greeted by
placards quoting Lucas's worst comments on Carlow. When they tried
to address the crowd from the windows of Cullen's Hotel, Kearney and
O'Shea were hissed, hooted and shouted down by a hired mob under
the direction of a local bell-ringer.[74] The latter had previously picketed
the lodgings of the deputation accompanied by a pig, and shouting
'strayed from the City of Dublin a black pig with a white tail of the
Quaker breed answering to the name of Lucas'. James Maher and some
of the electors negotiated with Lucas and his companions, and

persuaded them in the interests of public order and their own safety to leave Carlow as soon as possible. Another demonstration was staged on the platform fronting Sadleir's election headquarters, where the crowd was addressed by a pro-Sadleirite deputation from Queens County. Maher also addressed them not as Sadleir's supporter, however, but to assure them that the Leaguers would not persist. They departed the following day accompanied by Moore, who had arrived a few hours previously.

Maher accompanied Sadleir on nomination day, but remained silent during the speeches. James and Nicholas Sadleir were also present, and so great was the interest in the election that thirteen reporters took up vantage points.[75] They were not disappointed at the bedlam that interrupted the nomination, which was presided over by the High Sheriff, F.B.B. Brady of Myshall House. Both Sadleir and Alexander were constantly interrupted by shouts augmented by a crow-clapper. A stone was thrown at the Conservative gallery and Alexander was struck in the forehead by a lump of mortar, resulting in the arrest and imprisonment of the culprit. Maher tried to calm the proceedings several times and pointed to a 'fury of a woman' as one of the main delinquents. He eventually insisted that some of those creating a disturbance be removed.[76]

Sadleir managed to deliver his address amid continuous heckling. He branded Toryism as 'obsolete politics', and declared himself a believer in Liberal principles because of their inclusivity. A purely Catholic or purely Protestant party, if such were possible, was anathema to him. He would only join a party embracing all religions and based upon a philosophy of sectarian toleration. Only by the combination of individuals of all creeds could the fruits of the Emancipation Act be realised. By implication the Aberdeen ministry was the epitome of all that was sound in terms of Irish Liberal principles, but Sadleir was challenged by a Conservative supporter to defend his joining a Government containing the author of the Ecclesiastical Titles Act. His response, depicting a chastened Russell humbly and publicly acknowledging his mistake, was ill-judged, if immediately politically expedient,

> I think that on reflection, the gentleman will yield to those generous impulses which suggest to us all the virtue of forgiveness, and although I, a very humble man in public life, have never felt obliged to retract any proposition that I have advanced as a public man, still it seldom occurs that a man passes through the long and distinguished course over which Lord John Russell has passed without having at some time or another retracted an error or acknowledged that fallibility, which is common to our nature ... I would be unworthy of the name of Irishman if I were not

prepared to receive from Lord John Russell a practical guarantee that the course which he took upon the Ecclesiastical Titles Bill, is not the course of policy by which the government of Lord Aberdeen will abide... It is monstrous to lay down a principle that we shall refuse to accept from a public man a public acknowledgement of his public errors; and that we shall deny to the nation the advantages naturally resulting from his personal ability and official experience.

For the first time Sadleir, influenced by his own experience of electoral violence, examined the question of voting by ballot. He proposed that the introduction of the ballot should be a corollary of the extension of the franchise. A wider franchise was a mockery if it could not be properly exercised. There was a connection between these and the settlement of the land question, because they would help to reduce the 'vices of party and the prejudices of faction'. The land question itself demanded urgent action, which would entail the overturning of existing ownership-tenancy principles. Whether the landlords wanted it or not, their emancipation from 'the feudal thraldom that encumbers the ownership of land in this country' was necessary.

Whatever about his interesting association of electoral and agrarian reform, his views on the desirability of the ballot were proven that evening when a fracas broke out between the opposing factions, and one of Alexander's supporters stabbed and seriously wounded an opponent. Sadleir's followers were not slow to use the incident to their advantage, and placed placards all over the town with the untruth that 'two of your fellow-townsmen have been brutally murdered in your streets by the Orangemen.'[77] These were removed by the police, and the Sadleirites had to suffer the erection of other placards containing the text of a letter from McHale to Moore condemning the defection.

An increased police presence ensured a calm period in the run up to the polling two days later. As had been predicted the contest was close and at mid-day both candidates had polled equally. But by five o'clock it was clear that Alexander would win by a small margin, and according to the *Sentinel* Sadleir looked 'careworn and dispirited'.[78] When the poll closed the Liberal vote was ninety-one and the Conservative ninety-seven.[79] Sadleir was so disappointed that he did not attend the courthouse following the close of the poll, but departed for Dublin before the official declaration next morning.[80]

Alexander and his followers were correspondingly jubilant. In Belfast his victory was feted by his employees on the Falls Road,

Flags were seen flying, loud cheering made the welkin ring, and every one in the locality was talking to his neighbour on the exciting subject, cannons were heard booming throughout the day, and little work was done by any person in the region; and when night came bonfires were lighted and the demonstration concluded by a festive meeting at which the loyal electors of Carlow were gaily toasted in flowing bumpers.[81]

At the official declaration he expressed his victory as that of a local person over an import. It was well merited by 'my efforts to advance the trade, commerce and prospects of our country' in general and Carlow in particular. Dane, whose Orangeism had been well publicised by the Sadleirites, savoured the occasion and exacted some revenge by a condescending portrayal of Sadleir's rural background vis-a-vis that of the more socially polished Alexander. He sarcastically wondered 'what the opinion of the representatives of England must be of Carlow when they heard for the first time Mr. Sadleir stand up in the House of Commons to address them with his Tipperary brogue'.

Sadleir's status as an outsider possibly cost him some votes, although this had not prevented his election in 1847 and 1852. The efforts of the deputation may have diverted a few votes from him,[82] but sustained adverse publicity on the themes of betrayal and pledge-breaking was crucial in defeating him. Constant references to his political supping with the demonised Russell made a deep impact on some priests, especially Maher, who was a respected figure and whose lukewarm involvement in the election required little interpretation by the voters. McHale's letter placarded throughout the town, was evidence of clerical disapproval at a high level. The scandal of Dowling's imprisonment, still fresh in the public mind, was another consideration which tainted Sadleir's political cause. Bribery was a widespread practice, as indicated by petitions presented in 1853 against the return of 138 M.P.s.[83] Violence and intimidation was part and parcel of electioneering, but the false imprisonment of a voter was a step too far. The determined Conservative electoral drive was also relevant. It was estimated that a previous Liberal candidate in Carlow had to spend £2,000 to merit some hope of success, and in 1853 the Conservatives were determined to spend at least as much as the Sadleirites. They drew from a fund originally collected to support the petition against Sadleir's previous return. Some voters were paid to abstain or to temporarily leave the borough, one going as far as Belfast.

Sadleir wrote to Aberdeen on 22 January about such tactics,

> The Tory Party did not hesitate to resort to open treating and scarcely less open bribery and thus their efforts were potent with a few who had gone as far as to give my agent written assurances of their determination to vote for me, but who on Wednesday last came up and voted against me. This surprise coupled with the conduct of the Paymaster of Pensioners and the Barrack-Master made it quite impossible for me to

obtain a majority. Mr. Frizell, the Barrack-Master, has his vote out of the appointments used by him in the barracks, and he had stated in a letter to the Solicitor General that he was determined not to vote against me, however, he and the Paymaster of Pensioners did afterwards record their votes against me.[84]

While the Conservatives only increased their 1852 vote by one, such tactics were successful in reducing the Liberal vote. It was estimated that between ten and fifteen Catholics abstained, which with a downward revision of the electoral register from 237 to 208 by 1853, proved fatal to Sadleir.[85] This resulted from a Poor Law revaluation disfranchising a significant number of Liberals. Comparatively speaking Sadleir's vote fell by 45% and 19% over 1847 and 1852, respectively.

His opponents did not attribute his downfall to the adjustment of the register. The *Sentinel* shared the views of Duffy, Lucas and Gray that this decline was a moral victory over 'political corruption'.[86] Unlike them, however, the *Sentinel* greeted Alexander's victory as a blow at the Aberdeen Ministry, and derived all the greater pleasure from it because of Sadleir's publicly stated satisfaction at the Derbyte defeat of 1852. It was also pleased that the 'foreign priesthood' and the 'agents of Rome' had been thwarted from availing of the services of such Catholics as Sadleir in office.

The *Belfast Newsletter* brought its own slant to the post-election analysis. Its satisfaction at a 'genuine Conservative' triumph was increased by Alexander's status as a Belfast merchant and a 'true Protestant'.[87] The victory was hailed as a signal that the 'once popish borough of Carlow' was making way to Protestantism due to the existence of a sound Conservative aristocracy and the support of a Conservative press. To the editor Alexander was

> a true exemplar to the Southern constituency among which so large a portion of his labours are spent, and so large a portion of his property situate, of that sterling worth and honourable enterprise which have made Protestant Ulster what she is, and which are at length becoming duly appreciated even in the former strongholds of Popish bigotry and blind ignorance.

Sadleir's three Dublin opponents refused to be embarrassed by their role in the victory which prompted such triumphalist anti-Catholic statements. The *Tablet* rejoiced that Carlow had been saved the political degradation of being represented by a 'stained and blotted reputation'.[88] The *Freeman's* took the view that the result was a warning to others, and was glad that popular 'vengeance' had followed so quickly upon 'popular betrayal'.[89] Sadleir would be unable to head a 'corps of deserters' in Westminster, 'the theatre of his treason'. Gray tried to reconcile his criticism of the defection with the popularity of Aberdeen, Graham and Gladstone. The election was a lesson to the Prime Minister that good policies rather than the purchase of votes was the proper way to remain in power.[90] The association of the Aberdeen Government with corruption did not augur well for its future.

Only the *Nation* failed to view Sadleir's defeat as an unqualified success for the Irish party. The margin should have been greater, and it was a 'sad spectacle' that so many had voted for Sadleir. Carlow was a traditionally easy prey to political adventurers – Maule, the English lawyer, Raphael, the English Jew, Layard, the English donkey, and Sadleir, the Irish traitor. Duffy was resentful of Maher 'whose name has heretofore meant something in Irish politics'.[91] He was not content with Maher's muted involvement in the election, and felt that he should have denounced Sadleir rather than supporting 'the greedy pack of place hunters who composed his bodyguard, from Mr. Thaddeus O'Shea, Manager of Mr. Sadleir's Bank, to Dr. O'Meara, the government physician to the District Lunatic Asylum'. Duffy could only conclude that Maher's support had been prompted by the 'Castle Bishop'.

These anti-clerical overtones were quickly picked up by the *Telegraph*, which used a letter from a Carlow priest, 'Vicarius' as a reply.[92] This may have been John Dempsey. He contrasted the tolerance of Bishop Haly with the 'brazen effrontery' of the 'would-be dictator of '48'. Some of the probable sources of Duffy's hostility to the Carlow priests were laid out,

> we took no part in fomenting the cabbage-garden rebellion of 48. Neither did we hurry our flocks, broken down by famine and pestilence, to destruction, that on their utter ruin the ambition of a few hairbrained politicians might be gratified, by having their names recorded in history's page as the arch-patriots of the nineteenth century.
>
> We took no part in the proceedings of the packed jury who "burked" honest Crawford's letter, hissed and hooted the independent members of "the League" who dared to express a candid opinion ... There was not from amongst us one to swell the number of the thirty-two "equality" men of Thrash Gregg O'Moore, or hound on that insolent Montebank to exhibit himself on the stage of political controversy in Carlow. The chief accomplishment of that lad appears to consist in declining the little pronoun "ego", running it through its various numbers and cases, but emphasising it particularly in the singular ... we are not going about our different parishes with the begging box, soliciting donations from a struggling people to support the vanity and ambition of a pauper M.P., the scribbler of the *Nation* – God bless the mark!

The *Telegraph* blamed its three rivals for Sadleir's defeat and complained that they had preferred an Orange candidate to a Catholic, who had the support of the local bishop. In a withering article, McCabe drew the obvious conclusion that the election of Alexander was a certain vote against Crawford's bill.[93] He accused Gray of concealing letters, including Crawford's, favourable to Sadleir, while having space for 'anonymous scribblers' and the 'vituperative assertions of such redoubtable organs of public opinion as the *Nore Ignoramus,* the *Ballygawley Blunderbuss,* the *Tyrawley Tractarian,* the *Mayo Proselytiser* or the *Blarney Blatherumskite.*

McCabe's vexation at the outcome of the election was understandable, and politically it was no more than another episode in the long feud between the newspapermen. The defeat itself, however, added to the bitterness within the ranks of the Irish party, although, as modern opinion has maintained, post-defection rancour was not fatal to it.[94] Yet there is little doubt that the personal resentment of the Sadleirites was a serious blow, and the newspaper controversy drove a wedge between the northern and southern elements of the League. Sadleir's defeat significantly widened this rift. Unlike McCabe, McKnight had no compunction in directing his ire at Catholic clerics. He blamed McHale and his 'jesuitical manifesto' to Moore as a prime cause in dissuading a section of Liberal voters from supporting Sadleir.[95] The *Banner* pronounced Alexander's return as a victory for the 'unholy coalition' of 'Toryism, Dr. McHale and the Dublin Cabal'.

This controversy in Sadleir's political life coincided with a more limited criticism about one of his business ventures. Sometime around his appointment to the Treasury he became heavily involved with the East Kent Railway Company, which had been mooted twenty years earlier to construct a line from Strood to Canterbury. In December 1852 meetings were held in separate parts of Kent to raise additional share capital for the completion of the initial project and the extension of lines to Faversham Quays and Chilham.[96] Sir Charles Fox,[97] the well known railway engineer and main contractor, turned to the city for funding, and Sadleir responded by sinking £50,000 into the enterprise.[98]

The company incurred the wrath of the *Railway Times* on a regular basis, chiefly because it had secured parliamentary approval, which had previously been denied to the well established South Eastern Railway, to develop a line in the area. This newspaper suspected the political influence of investors like Sadleir, and called attention to the importance of his status as a Lord of the Treasury. It was also critical of the imbalance in the shareholding by which eighteen investors held the majority of shares. These 'agitators' who had 'disturbed' the County of Kent for some time were listed by the *Railway Times,* and showed that

Sadleir's shareholding was one of the largest.[99] He also persuaded some of his colleagues in the London and County to join him. James Rhodes one of the directors and J.C. Coleman, its accountant, invested £20,000 and £12,500 respectively. Lord Sondes, the railway's chairman, later parried criticism of such heavy contributions by explaining that city investors were required because sufficient money could not be raised in a rural district like East Kent.[100]

References

1. A significant proportion of the Irish labour force worked in some type of industrial enterprise, many agricultural based and cottage industries. See Ó Gráda, *Ireland before and after the Famine*, p. 36, and Ó Gráda, *Ireland A New Economic History*, pp 274,278, 287, 293, 318,

2. D.D.A., Cullen Papers, Sadleir to Cullen 12 September 1853 informing him that he had made representations to Lord Canning, and do. to do. 23 November 1853 assuring Cullen of his success. See do. to do. 16 November 1853 showing that Sadleir did other favours for the Archbishop.

3. *Tablet* 18 September 1852.

4. See *Tablet* 3 February 1855 for the recollection of Patrick Malone, the parish priest of Belmullet.

5. Ibid., 8 January 1853 quoted from the *Tuam Herald, Galway Mercury, Newry Examiner, Dundalk Democrat, Ulsterman, Kilkenny Journal, Drogheda Argus, Galway Vindicator, Waterford News, Cork Examiner, Munster News, Roscommon Messenger.*

6. *F.J.* 10 January 1853. For an earlier attack see editorial 3 January 1853 headed 'saddled and bridled. The Irish Hacks'.

7. Ibid.,

8. *Nation* 1 January 1853.

9. *Tablet* 1 January 1853.

10. *Nation* 1 January 1853.

11. The *Waterford News,* which was hostile to the defection, in an editorial of 31 December 1852 also concluded that Keogh was 'in needy circumstances; and like the poor apothecary, perhaps it was his poverty, not his will, that caused him to accept it'. Nonetheless, the editor hoped that Keogh would be rejected by the Athlone electors.

12. See *Tablet* 18 December 1852 for Lucas's acknowledgement of Keogh's vocal support during his own second speech in Westminster.

13. Ibid., 1 January 1853.

14. *W.T.* 29 December 1853.

15. *Tablet* 22 January 1853.

16. Ibid., 15 January 1853.

17. In ibid., 8 January 1853.

18. O'Flaherty had not yet been appointed.

19. *W.T.* 1 January 1853.

20. Ibid., 8 January 1853.

21. Richard Kelch, the curate in Navan, demanded that McCabe withdraw the *Telegraph's* circulation in Meath. He associated it with anti-Catholic journals as the 'organ of perjurers, pledge-breakers, and apostates for truth – this foul

mouth-piece of the vile herd, whose names will be synonymous to our children for treachery, corruption and dishonour'. His anti-*Telegraph* campaign continued into 1867 when he intimidated the agent in Wilkinstown who, following an interview with him, demanded a public apology from the *Telegraph* to herself and Kelch for allegedly misinterpreting his actions as intimidation of her. Kelch himself sent a solicitors letter to the publisher demanding an apology. This occurred when Kelch learned that Bishop Cantwell had been contacted by the *Telegraph*. The existence of newspaper correspondence on the quotation in Cullen's papers indicates that the Archbishop was also made aware of the dispute – D.D.A.,C.P., carton 339/3.

22 *W.T.* 1 January 1853.
23. Ibid.,
24. Ibid., 8 January 1853.
25. The *Athlone Sentinel* was equally determined to defend Keogh. Its editorial of 5 January 1853 pronounced that Keogh's 'great forensic ability and undisputed parliamentary talent admirably qualify for the office and his appointment, while recognising the abilities of a popular Irishman, gives promise of the intention of the government to legislate for Ireland in a generous and kindly spirit'. It was convinced that Keogh accepted office not for personal gain but for the welfare of Ireland and was 'intuitively persuaded' that he would not disappoint the hopes of the Irish people.
26. *B.U.* 7 January 1853.
27. See O'Shea, *Priest, Politics*, pp 181-182 on the split in the Tipperary priesthood.
28. *Tablet* 8 January 1853, *C.S.* 8 January 1853.
29. *Tablet* 8 January 1853. (The *Dublin Evening Post*, a consistent supporter of Liberal governments and one which did not reckon itself among the enemies of the Irish Party, took issue with Moore on his assertion that he was the leader of the Party and condemned his hostility to the defectors – see *D.E.P.* 8 January 1853).
30. *Tablet* 15 January 1853.
31. Ibid., 15, 22 January 1853.
32. Ibid., 22 January 1853.
33. Ibid., 15 January 1853.
34. *C.S.* 8 January 1853.
35. Report in *Tablet* 8 January 1853.
36. J. Feehan p.p. (Ed), *The O'Carroll Diaries, Diary for the year 1846 of Rev. Thomas O'Carroll, Profiles of Priests by Rev. Thomas O'Carroll, Diary for the year 1862-64 of Rev. James O'Carroll (c.c. Clonoulty)*, (Boherlahan 1997), pp 52-53 for an unflattering portrait of Cahill by James O'Carroll. O'Carroll's portrait of most priests was at least as unflattering. The original diaries are preserved in the Cashel Diocesan Archives.
37. This petition lay on the table of the House of Commons, but was negated by the new writ for the by-election.
38. W. Long to Naas 1 January 1853. N.L.I., Mayo Papers, MS. 11017 (8).
39. Ibid., Long to Naas 1 January 1853.
40. *C.S.* 8 January 1853.
41. Biographical information on Alexander in ibid., 22, 29 January 1853.
42. For reference to some of Alexander's property in Belfast see the following in the Public Record Office of Northern Ireland – Rental tenements in Smithfield Ward, Belfast, of mill lands and miller's pasture in Falls Road, (ref. D1641/2), Map of mill and lands of Belfast Manor Mill, (ref. T2211/1&2), lease of Rathbeg farm

from Marquis of Donegall, (ref. PRO 466 1 Nov. 1823), lease of Barrack St. premises from Marquis of Donegall, (ref. DOD 509/2834, 18 June 1842), leases of premises in the North side of Barrack St., near the Falls Road, Belfast, and near Shankill Road, 18 June 1842, (refs. DOD 509/2835, 36 and 37, respectively), renewal of lease from Donegall of mills and lands near Belfast, (ref. DOD 509/2972), copy of agreement between James Ewart, merchant, and Alexander and others relating to Ewart's property at Malone, (ref. D1954/4/358 Sept. 1844).

43. *C.S.* 8 January 1853.
44. Ibid., 8, 15 January 1853.
45. Ibid., 8 January 1853.
46. Ibid., 22 January 1853 for a notice served on the Carlow returning officer protesting at Sadleir's candidature because of the existence of the petition.
47. A Recorder was a judge of a city or Borough Court of Quarter session.
48. *C.S.* 22 January 1853.
49. Address in ibid., 1 January 1853 and in *F.J.* 3 January 1853.
50. Ibid., 8 January 1853.
51. *Tablet* 8 January 1853.
52. Sadleir's letter 4 January 1853.
53. Browne to Naas 5 January 1853. N.L.I., Mayo Papers, MS. 11017(4).
54. See *D.E.P.* 6 January 1853 referring to the Burren Street meeting at which a letter from Bishop Haly was read.
55. Moore to Lucas (n.d., letter no.487 among the 1855 correspondence), N.L.I. Moore Papers MS. 893. Dr. Cullen (M.D.) told the story to Moore when he was in Carlow.
56. See *F.J.* 7 January 1853 for an attack on Sadleir by the Council of the League.
57. Address dated 7 January in *W.T.* 15 January 1853. This stated that the address had been published in Dublin on 11 January 1853.
58. *Tablet* 15 January 1853, *W.T.* 15 January 1853. (for an amusing and brief account of the meeting for the benefit of its Belfast Conservative readers see *Belfast News Letter* 12 January 1853).
59. See *B.U.* 11 January 1853 for one broadside. Its editorial referred to the special meeting of the League to be held that day and went on to regret, beyond measure, the unreasonably violent spirit in which this question has been prejudged, both by the press and by other organs of political censorship, while the charges put forward are of such a nature as almost to drive the gentlemen mentioned into the ranks of the adversary, without the slightest hope of any subsequent reconciliation being effected between them and the accusing parties. It is affirmed, for example, that Messrs. Sadleir and Keogh have been guilty of a 'violation of their pledge', that one of them has actually committed perjury, or, at all events, a moral offence hardly distinguishable from that crime, and that both are thoroughly destitute of fixed principle. The writers, too, who prefer such accusations as these are, at the same time, guilty of the inconceivable folly of adding a concurrent declaration, that these men of no principle have been long known to them as such, even when they were caressed as bosom companions, feasted as champions of popular rights, and blessed as the anointed guardians of ecclesiastical privileges and of religious sanctity-in fact, that while all the parties alluded to outwardly appeared before men to be a 'holy brotherhood', more than one half of them knew and believed the remainder to be a set of the most arrant knaves on the face of the earth! It considered the stance of the three Dublin papers as 'radically self-destructive' and 'essentially unjust' and condemned Moore in particular.

60. Ten days after this meeting McKnight editorialised similar thoughts in the *Banner of Ulster*. He defended the League in the South, but attacked the Dublin executive for exhibiting 'the most strange phenomena that have ever been witnessed in the proceedings of any regularly constituted body'. The editorial repeated the accusation that the Council had pre-empted the impartial judgement of the general meeting and had acted in an unconstitutional manner in pronouncing authoritatively upon a matter yet to be discussed by the general body. It painted the Council's action as a disregard of all the laws of political uprightness. It condemned the involvement of the League in personal quarrels and local contests as a gross infringement of constitutional propriety which reduced the League to a machine in the hands of five or six individuals. Because of personal animosity, a misreading of political realities and newspaper competition public men who had done signal service for their country were handed over to political and moral execution without trial – *B.U.* 21 January 1853. See ibid., 25 January 1853 for a further editorial broadside on the 'insane policy' of the League executive which also referred to a provocative rumour that Moore was on intimate terms with Disraeli and a conduit between the Conservative Party and the Brigadiers favourable to the Executive. See ibid., 1 February 1853 for a strong attack on the *Nation's* mild editorial on Rogers, Bell and McKnight, (*Nation* 29 January 1853).

61. See ibid., for reference to this rumour which 'of course cannot be true'.

62. Letter in *W.T.* 22 January 1853.

63. His letter of 16 January 1853 to *D.E.P.* was published in The *W.T.* 22 January 1853. The *Telegraph* accused the League of deliberately concealing its contents. The *Tablet* 22 January 1853 published it. The *Telegraph* of 29 January carried a letter 24 January 1853 from Samuel Bindon, the League's secretary, explaining that the letter had been sent to the *Freeman's Journal*, but Gray did not have space to publish it. The same edition carried a letter 9 January 1853 to the meeting from William Fagan, M.P. for Cork city expressing confidence in the Aberdeen Ministry which had not been published either. Fagan's letter was also printed in the *Dublin Evening Post* of 25 January 1853. The *Post*, too, accused the 'newspaper clique' of withholding it. The *Tablet* 22 January 1853 carried a letter from Cecil Lawless M.P., Clonmel, which also pleaded that it was premature to condemn Sadleir and Keogh.

64. This was confirmed by the *A.S.* 12 January 1853.

65. See *F.J.* 13 January 1853.

66. *Tablet* 15 January 1853, *W.T.* 15 January 1853.

67. Letter 13 January 1853 from Morrison's Hotel, Dublin in *Tablet* 22 January 1853, *C.S.* 22 January 1853.

68. Ibid.

69. This referred to a riot in Dolly's Brae, a Catholic area near Castlewellan, County Down on 12 July 1849. A number of Catholics obstructed the passage of a group of Orangemen returning from a celebration on the estate of Lord Roden, the Grand Master of the Orange Order. Catholics were killed and their houses burned. When Roden refused to examine Orangemen during an enquiry ordered by Clarendon he was dismissed from the magistracy. See Kerr, *A Nation of Beggars*, p. 200, Davis, *The Young Ireland Movement*, pp 228 – 229.

70. *W.T.* 15 January 1853.

71. The *Belfast Newsletter*, which kept in touch with events in Carlow because of the candidature of Alexander, reported that Maher had visited his nephew in Dublin and learned that he approved of Sadleir taking office – *B.N.* 19 January 1853.

72. The *Banner of Ulster* later condemned the deputation and repeated rumours about Moore's ambitions which provoked the *Nation* ,whose chagrin was in turn published in the *Tablet* 5 February 1853.

73. See N.L.I., Moore Papers, MS. 891, letter 5 January 1853 from Hugh Connolly, 45 Lr. Sackville Street, (headquarters of the Friends of Religious Equality), to Moore stating that if the Tories worked hard they would defeat Sadleir.

74. *F.J.* 17 January 1853, *C.S.* 15, 22 January 1853, *W.T.* 29 January 1853.

75. Reports in *F.J.* 18 January 1853, *C.S.* 22 January 1853, *W.T.* 22 January 1853, *Tablet* 22 January 1853.

76. The police reported to Dublin Castle that the peace had been preserved at the nomination meeting, indicating a certain acceptable level of bedlam on such occasions – N.A.,C.S.O.,R.P. 1853 444, police reports, 17 January 1853.

77. *F.J.* 19 January 1853.

78. *C.S.* 22 January 1853.

79. *F.J.* 20 January 1853

80. Ibid.

81. *B.N.* 21 January 1853.

82. Lord Sligo agreed with Moore that the deputation had changed the minds of a few voters – N.L.I., Moore Papers, MS. 892, Sligo to Moore 29 January 1853.

83. *Tablet* 23 April 1853.

84. British Museum, Aberdeen Papers, Add. MSS. 43248, ff324-326.

85. Statistics and the reasons underlining them in *C.S.* 22, 29 January 1853, *W.T.* 22, 29 January 1853.

86. *C.S.* 22 January 1853.

87. *B.N.* 21 January 1853.

88. *Tablet* 22 January 1853.

89. *F.J.* 29 January 1853.

90. Ibid., 21 January 1853.

91. *Nation* 22 January 1853.

92. Letter 25 January 1853 in *W.T.* 29 January 1853.

93. Ibid.,

94. See Whyte, *Independent Irish Party*, pp 107 et.seq.

95. *B.U.* 21 January 1853.

96. *R.T.* 25 December 1852. See ibid., 15 January 1853.

97. Sir Charles Fox 1810-1874 was born in Derby and by the age of nineteen was involved in designing railway engines. He was appointed by Robert Stephenson as one of the constructing engineers of the London and Bermingham railway. He designed the Watford tunnel and carried out the rail extension from Camden Town to Euston Square. He became a partner in the firm Fox Henderson and Company which became the first firm to manufacture railway plant in a major and systematic way. Many technical and engineering innovations were due to Fox who was also involved in other projects; for example he built the complex in Hyde Park for the Great Exhibition of 1851. He was also involved in overseas enterprises and constructed the first narrow-guage line in India. He was the engineer to the Queensland Railways, the Cape Town Railways, and the Toronto Railway. He designed many bridges including the Swing Bridge over the Shannon – *D.N.B.*, e.v.

98. *R.T.* 15 January 1853.

99. Ibid.,

100. Ibid., 4 March 1854.

11 Gloster Square
Hyde Park June 15th

My dear Lord Chandos.

I saw Mr Williams yesterday & from
what he stated it seems to me
that the Wotton sale is on the point
of being completed. You know how interested
I am in seeing the further
sales effected with as little
delay as possible & I hope
you agree with me in thinking
that immediate steps ought
to be taken by Mr Williams to
bring forward the Stowe Property
for sale this year, for
if there is any delay in doing
so now, I very much
fear no considerable sales

Extract from Sadlier letter to the Marquis of Chandos (The Grenville Collection, The Huntington Library, San Marino, California).

Chapter 11

Sligo Borough election and subsequent tribulations – February 1853 - November 1854

Sadleir pursued his business interests following his Carlow defeat, but also viewed the political landscape for a suitable vacancy. Neither had he ruled out an overturning of the Carlow result. He had lodged an objection against Alexander's return and was perturbed to learn that Ball, who faced a petition against his own election, was probing Haly on the possibility of a compromise proposed by the Conservatives to withdraw all petitions and secure at least his seat for the Liberal party.[1] An anxious Sadleir wrote to Haly in somewhat contradictory terms on 9 March that the proposal taken as a whole was 'very serious and in my opinion it can not and ought not to be entertained for one moment unless sanctioned by Your Lordship and the clergy'.[2] The concluding section of his letter, however, made a realistic assessment of the county and borough constituencies where Conservative success in fresh elections seemed certain. In this light he saw merit in their proposal but considered it 'a galling thing to see two seats passing into the grasp of the Orange faction, but we must consider and act as political generals in the matter'.

None of the petitions was proceeded with and speculation about Sadleir's future course were rife from January onwards. The press announced that some of his friends or relatives would make way for him in their constituencies. Stories spread that Frank Scully would be offered the Under Secretaryship,[3] or that either Cecil Lawless or Keating might step down in Clonmel and Waterford, respectively. It was even suggested that Maurice O'Connell, who supported the defectors, intended giving up his Tralee seat.[4] The most persistent report was that Michael Dunne, allegedly under an obligation to Sadleir for funding his election campaign, would take the Chiltern Hundreds.[5]

Sadleir did not specifically mention any of these possibilities in his correspondence with Aberdeen after the Carlow defeat. He knew, however, that Irish reforms by the Government would help justify his taking office and enhance his chance of success in another constituency. His letter of 22 January to Aberdeen timidly suggested that a 'number of small measures' would improve the prosperity of Ireland, and 'viewed afterwards as a whole, they would at the close of the session furnish cogent proofs why the Irish Liberals ought to support the government'.[6] He hoped for a seat as soon as Parliament met, and was 'anxious to know your Lordship's wishes'.

The Prime Minister noted on the back of Sadleir's letter that arrangements should be made to find him another seat, and in a brief reply of 24 January encouraged Sadleir by a wish to see his return to Westminster.[7] He refused to be drawn on specific intentions towards Ireland, and vaguely promised that there was 'certainly no reason to suppose that measures for the improvement of Ireland will be neglected'. Such a non-committal response was of little consolation to Sadleir who was to be disappointed in his expectation of an immediate return to active politics. By March he was sufficiently desperate to approach Dunne and call in his political debt, despite the latter's earlier public denial of any intention to give way.[8] In a letter to Haly on 10 March he explained the nature of his meeting with Dunne the previous week.[9] Dunne was in an awkward position and felt obliged to assure him of his willingness to stand down. He intimated, however, that Sadleir would have 'a large host of opponents among the clergy', a view rejected by Sadleir although he asked Haly to

> learn the opinions of the clergy, and if they are, as Mr Dunne gave me to fancy, strongly opposed to me I would at once give up all idea of retaining my office and I would release the Liberal landlords who are now bound by their promise to support me if I should come forward in lieu of Mr Dunne.

Conscious of clerical power he assured the bishop that he would make no move 'except in obedience to the wishes of yourself and the majority of the clergy and Liberal electors'. Haly's reply is not extant, but Sadleir's intention of replacing his friend in Queen's County came to nought, and he was forced to remain in the political wilderness for another three months. This, however, did not signal the end of the place-taking controversy, which continued to damage both the League and the Irish Party.[10] His opponents sustained their public attacks, and were determined to unnerve other M.P.s by the threat of a similar defeat, if they failed to follow the independent opposition line.

Those mainly responsible for sustaining the onslaught were the leading members, lay and clerical, of the League[11] and the Friends of Religion Equality. The latter was in a semi-dormant state, and generally confined itself to collecting petitions against religious inequality, but it organised a meeting in Kells on 1 March which focussed on the defection. Other meetings, not all specifically League ones, but always attended by Leaguers, were held to discuss the crisis. These, for example, took place in Castlebar on 7 February, Callan on 13 February, the Mechanics Institute on 1 March, and a Dublin League meeting on 31 March.[12]

The Castlebar meeting attracted ten other priests and was chaired by Archdeacon McHale. Moore was the principal speaker, and branded the defectors as 'a flock of carrion-crows in their pursuit of their miserable instincts'. He concentrated his attention more on Keogh because the Athlone by-election was still unfought, but he paused to remark that the two Scullys, James Sadleir and Keating were returned on the basis of an independent opposition pledge. A declaration of adherence to the policy was demanded of Moore's fellow Mayo representative, Ouseley Higgins, whose letter to the secretary refused to condemn the defectors and called for a fair trial for the government.

The local tenant right association convened the Callan meeting, which was attended by O'Shea, O'Keeffe, Cahill and four other priests. Corr, the chairman, said that Russell had proposed Sadleir and Keogh for the government positions, an obviously correct opinion in Sadleir's case and one which could be very damaging to him, although it may not have been believed by many. The group delivered an 'unqualified condemnation' of 'the renegades', a theme that also attracted a high level of vilification at the meeting in the Mechanics Institute, where a shopkeeper, Christopher Kelly, announced that 'the devil out of Hell' would receive his vote sooner than Sadleir.[13] Moore, Gray and Cantwell were at this gathering which ridiculed Sadleir's addresses to 'the simpletons of Carlow'. James Plunkett, a Town Commissioner, made the observation that Ireland could never trust England 'from the day Strongbow landed in Wexford to the day Sadleir was kicked out of Carlow'.

The Kells meeting, held earlier that day, and attended by Lucas and Gray, was a more substantial one. While the organising of a petition to parliament on religious equality was its prime object, the convening circular also indicated that time would be devoted to condemning the defection. To achieve maximum publicity the circular requested the permission of invited non-attenders to publish their approval of such condemnation. In his reply of 28 January written from the Erectheum Club in London, Robert Keating not only refused his permission, but unreservedly endorsed the taking of office by his cousin and his parliamentary colleagues.[14] Keating explained his consistency in this by making it clear that he had informed his Waterford constituents from the hustings of the desirability to have 'Irish practical ability infused into the government of the country'. Moreover, the exclusion hitherto of such talent was a 'great national insult'.

Keating's support for his relative was to be anticipated, and it was clearly more pronounced than that of Vincent Scully. Keating's fellow Waterford representative, Thomas Meagher, also defended the defectors and his letter of apology, written from Waterford, refused to be a party to any resolution of condemnation.[15] While endorsing the pledge of opposition in principle, his experience of the defectors' impressive parliamentary performance and the apparent government amenability to Irish reform was sufficient grounds to postpone disapproval until its policy 'shall appear to be inimical to Irish interests'.

But, most letters of apology to Nicholas McEvoy, parish priest of Kells and secretary to the meeting, recommended a statement of censure. These included replies from bishops, the most trenchant of which came from Thomas Feeney, Killala,

> sordid avarice tempted Judas to betray his Divine Master with that token of the most sincere friendship and attachment, but we do not find that he had the audacity to seal the false and perfidious profession of his loyalty with the solemnity of an oath. To allow such depravity to escape unreproved, nay unpunished, would be to countenance, nay, to sanction a profligacy subversive of religion and morality, pernicious to public good faith.

Such clerical concern at pledge breaking was evident by the presence of twenty-five priests at the rally. The resolution hailing the 'great popular victory' in Carlow as a vindication of national honour was proposed by Richard Ennis, the parish priest of Rathmolion. James Dowling, the parish priest of Clonmellon, betrayed a type of biblical anglophobia in his assertion that no man could serve two masters, the Minister and the country. He drew on Byron's words that the union of Ireland and England was 'the union of the shark and its prey'.

Priests like these played a significant role in shaping public opinion against Sadleir and Keogh. One edition of the *Tablet* alone had letters of condemnation from eight priests.[16] They also used clerical meetings exclusively as platforms to condemn the defection and demand assurances from their own M.P.s. The priests of the Midleton Deanery, for example, reminded Vincent Scully and E.B. Roche of their pledges,[17] and the priests of the Ballinrobe Deanery passed a resolution condemning Higgins for voting with the government on the extension of the income tax to Ireland.[18]

Two of the most noteworthy meetings were held by the priests of Killaloe and Cashel in April.[19] Twenty two Killaloe priests met under

Bishop Vaughan, and passed a motion expressing 'chagrin and disappointment at the change of political opinion which has taken place in the minds of some members'. They warned the members for Clare that failure in their duty would result in a demand for their resignation. On 5 April sixty Cashel priests expressed 'painful doubts' about the parliamentary conduct of James Sadleir and Frank Scully, who were invited to explain their positions. Both replied defending their conduct and denying adherence to the Government.[20] Scully was incensed at being publicly reprimanded without any private consultation, and informed his clerical critics that he was not prepared to sit with the 'Spooners, Newdegates, Walpoles, Napiers, *et hoc genus omne*.

The views of the Tipperary representatives on where the Irish Party should sit in the Commons were shared by a majority of that Party. Seating arrangements were seen as symbolically important by the League M.P.s, and proved to be a divisive issue as these sought to impose their will upon their colleagues. Two party meetings in early March to discuss tactics ended in acrimony. Maurice O'Connell chaired the first group of thirty seven M.P.s on 3 March. The two Scullys, Keating, James Sadleir, Ball and Dunne were among the Sadleirites there.[21] Factious opposition was ruled out, but agreement was reached that they would adopt a general opposition to the Aberdeen Government at that time. Lucas admitted 'very considerable differences of opinion' among the members and 'a great desire' by some to sit on the ministerial side of the House in the 'semi-independent' spot below the gangway. He wrote that James Sadleir, Frank Scully, Keating, Ball and Dunne were among the Irish M.P.s who habitually sat on the Government side of the House. A committee of seven was appointed to draw up a policy 'for the regulation of our future course'. The meeting then adjourned for two days.

The adjourned meeting, attended by twenty two M.P.s, was an angry six hour one that deepened division within the party.[22] The press was excluded in an attempt to conceal the extent of the acrimony, but the scathing reports of the *Freeman's Journal, Nation* and *Tablet* defeated this purpose. McCabe, who would have been informed of the details by James Sadleir, described the *Freeman's* report as 'an unmitigated fabrication and a perversion'.[23] Lucas, Gray and Duffy were bitterly disappointed by its thirteen votes to nine decision that individual members should sit and vote as they wished. Nevertheless, Vincent Scully was defeated when he proposed a policy of opposition combined with giving a fair trial to the government. This was amended to read that the party would hold itself independent of the government and act in union irrespective of where individual members sat. In practice the party often split at voting time with some members opposing and some supporting the Government, generally on issues which were not connected with Ireland.[24] A serious row developed in early May when some Irish M.P.s voted for the extension of the income tax to Ireland, and Duffy described them in his parliamentary speech as corrupt.[25] He was challenged by Vincent Scully and John Ball and the incident was widely reported, with Duffy getting due praise from the Dublin newspapers.

Disagreement within the party was reflected at grass roots level, and increased the split between the Ulster Leaguers and their southern counterparts. Representatives from Ulster still attended Council meetings in Dublin in March 1853. McKnight was at one of these on 30 March, but sent a 'formal and decided protest' to a general meeting the following day at the policy of opposition to a government still awaiting the report of the land committee. Until then the southern leaders had been muted in their public comments on the Ulster members. But Lucas could no longer restrain himself, and his leader upon the latest controversy dubbed McKnight a rat, and rebuked the northerners for their lack of financial input to the League.[26] They had allowed 'the interests of wealthy Ulster to be supported out of the beggared purses of the south'. While the frequent 'anti-cabal' editorial blasts from the *Banner of Ulster* festered in Lucas's mind, what really bothered him was the action of the northerners in sending a deputation to London in a fruitless attempt to gain access to the land committee.[27] Such a course was a major vote of no confidence in the southern Leaguers who were ably represented on the committee by Lucas, Duffy and Shee.

The deputation, included McKnight and Rogers, and had been agreed at a tenant right meeting in Belfast on 15 February, because of disquiet that Napier's bills were being given precedence over Crawford's bill, which would not be discussed until after the Easter recess.[28] They met Bright and Cobden as well as some of the Irish M.P.s, and succeeded in getting an interview with Palmerston at the Home Office – to them a major coup since he was the only cabinet Minister on the Committee. Their deferential attitude was not appreciated in the south.

James Sadleir was a member of the land committee, and, considering his recognised expertise on land law, John would have been included had he been an M.P. at that stage. The latter remained aloof from the continuing debate, but with such varied business interests he can hardly have been idle. Nonetheless his prime concern was re-election to take up his duties at the Treasury. Despite the extensive and prolonged adverse publicity, there was sufficient support for his taking office to keep his hopes alive that a suitable constituency would arise early in 1853. He received a setback in February directly as a result of his Carlow assurances on Russell's supposed recantation of the Titles Act. It can only be assumed that Sadleir did not envisage this reaching Westminster ears, but at the 11 February sitting Spooner raised it. He accused Russell of abandoning the principle of the Act, and asked if he still felt that the Pope's action was 'insolent and insidious'.[29] Russell replied that Sadleir had recently informed him that he had been misrepresented in the newspapers, and had merely meant that Russell's participation in a Government led by opponents of the Act was a guarantee that it would not be used to injure Catholics in the U.K. The Foreign Secretary had found this acceptable, and added that in any case the Act was never meant to limit the religious liberty of Catholics.

Some realities were blurred by this response and would not have harmed Sadleir, although the real issue was the continued existence of the Act on the statute books. But Russell's accompanying confirmation that he had not changed his mind about the Papal rescript placed Sadleir in an awkward position, and endangered his immediate election prospects. The Dublin papers seized upon this, and exposed Sadleir's Carlow assertion of the so-called *volte-face* as a lie to justify taking office. The *Freeman's*, copied by the *Tablet* and *Nation*, reported Russell's statement as a re-affirmation of the Durham principles.[30] The *Carlow Sentinel* also used the *Freeman's* and added its own editorial juxtaposing extracts from the Durham letter with Sadleir's speech.[31] In the short term the controversy undermined Sadleir's political credibility, if not his personal integrity which had been under scrutiny for so long. But he remained aloof, and his newspaper diverted attention from the debate with a longwinded attack on Gray for a slight by the *Freeman's* on McCabe's status and editorial independence.[32]

Sadleir was further embarrassed some days later by Russell's honest response to a leading question by Moore on the Church Establishment.[33] The Mayo M.P. challenged him to confirm the government's intention of legislating on religious equality as part of a secret bargain with Sadleir and Keogh for accepting office. Moore was hardly surprised by Russell's explicit denial of any assurances to the defectors, or by his equally clear assertion that it 'had no intention to introduce any measure having reference to the Established Church with the exception of a bill relating to Ministers' money'.

Moore's question had been on the table for some time, and the Sadleirites chose Anthony O'Flaherty, Galway Borough, to reply on their behalf. O'Flaherty dismissed the question as injudicious and 'perfect moonshine' in the current climate of English opinion, which was hostile to any such legislation. Lucas in turn responded on behalf of the Independent oppositionists with a statement that only their policy would force any government to concede religious equality to Ireland.[34]

Despite such parliamentary harassment Sadleir was encouraged by Keogh's success in the Athlone by-election, which had been held up until April pending the outcome of an official investigation following a petition against his return in 1852. A candidate was required to have an income of £300 over and above all encumbrances, but Keogh had twenty-eight outstanding judgement debts against him at various times. A notice of defective qualification was served and he was arrested in London for debt.[35] At the hearing he admitted owing money to at least fourteen individuals, but the committee found in his favour and the 1853 by-election was allowed proceed.[36] His arrest aroused sympathy, and even the *Tablet* found such a course distasteful.[37] On a political level, however, the Leaguers feared his success and Patrick McMahon, the newly elected tenant right representative for Wexford County, privately wrote to Duffy that if he was returned 'to lead the recreants, we will have a hard game to play'.[38] Such a possibility was raised at a League meeting in Dublin on 31 March, but it was decided not to send a deputation to Athlone,[39] causing McCabe to amuse himself with the observation that 'having escaped from being dipped in the Barrow, they will not expose themselves to an immersion in the Shannon'.[40] The Leaguers knew that Keogh was strongly supported by the Athlone clergy and Bishop Browne, who was reminded by the *Freeman's* that the defection had been condemned by his fellow prelates, McHale, Murphy, Vaughan and Feeney.[41] At the nomination on 20 April in Boswell's Brewery Yard, Northgate Street, Keogh, in the presence of Archdeacon Martin O'Reilly and thirteen other priests, made much of Browne's support.[42] Two days later he was returned by a large majority.[43]

Sadleir was then the only defector unsuccessful in his re-election attempts. This 'put the public attitude to the defection in its proper perspective, but his continuing re-election expectations received a setback at the end of May, when, during a parliamentary debate on the Irish Ecclesiastical revenues, Russell alluded to the divided loyalties of Catholics to both Crown and Pope.[44] It was only a brief addendum to a long inoffensive speech, but was insulting to Irish representatives, and the defectors had little option but to resign. Had Sadleir not done so his re-election prospects would have been fatally damaged. His apologetic letter of 2 June to Aberdeen explained the dilemma of remaining in a government which apparently condoned anti-Catholic sentiments,[45]

> I have felt it a high honour to serve in a government presided over by your Lordship and composed chiefly of those in whose liberal and

moderate views I have been long accustomed to coincide, but having carefully reflected on the speech made by Lord John Russell on last Tuesday night I am bound to state to your Lordship that the opinion then expressed by the Leader of the House of Commons differs so much from my well-known convictions that if after his speech I remained a member of the government, my continuance in office would place me in a false position and would be construed as an admission by me that the views stated by Lord John Russell were just and well-founded.

The *Telegraph* quickly used the resignations as a vindication of the defectors who had taken office as defenders of the people and their Church, and were now abandoning power and patronage in the same cause.[46] The resignations represented the determination of the Irish Party to withdraw all support from the government unless there was a cabinet repudiation of Russell's sentiments. McCabe concluded that 'the sooner his fangs are drawn the better'. Even Gray was impressed by the resignations as 'most creditable to the gentlemen, who have thus severed their connections with a government with which they should never have associated themselves'.[47]

Aberdeen was shocked by the crisis, which received widespread press coverage in Ireland and England.[48] He called Russell to a meeting at Argyll House to make known his displeasure,[49] and immediately wrote to Monsell assuring him that

the sentiments of which you complain, are not shared by me nor by many of my colleagues. I wish this to be distinctly understood, as I might otherwise be justly charged with a departure from those feelings which both in and out of office, I have held and still hold with regard to the Roman Catholic body, and the open avowal of which had appeared to several Roman Catholic gentlemen to justify them in accepting office under the government.[50]

The publication of this letter in the *Times*,[51] and subsequently copied in the Irish press, was correctly seen as an official repudiation of Russell's statement. Aberdeen sent a copy to Sadleir hoping 'that the explanation contained in it will induce you to abstain from persevering in the intention you have communicated to me of resigning the office you now hold under the government'.[52]

Sadleir, Keogh and Monsell were satisfied that the public rebuke was a proper reassurance of the government's attitude towards religious equality and withdrew their resignations. McCabe promptly highlighted the public nature of this humiliation as a sign of Irish influence in the government,

The three Catholic members have placed Lord John Russell in a position that is degrading to him: they forced him *either to accept that degradation,* or – *to resign!* It was for Lord John Russell to choose which position he preferred, and no one could have calculated from his previous career, that he would have preferred disgrace to resignation. He has, however, thought proper to do so; and, therefore, we now find the author of the Ecclesiastical Titles Bill, the man who has insulted Ireland and its clergy voluntarily occupying in the face of the world a situation in which he is an object of pity to his friends, of scorn and contempt to his enemies... *We have no hesitation in pronouncing the letter of the Earl of Aberdeen as great a piece of insult by implication as ever Minister levelled against a colleague.*[53]

The eulogies in the *Telegraph* were met by a strong counter-attack from its three competitors, who denounced the M.P.s for 'returning to their vomit' following the 'sham resignations'.[54] By then Cullen was greatly irritated by the prolonged public wrangling. His sympathy lay with the defectors, and he conveyed his irritation to Lucas who wrote a defence of his stand in a letter of 10 June,

I fear what I have written this week over the resignations will hardly please your Grace. My excuse must be that it expressed my honest conviction and was written before the receipt of Your Grace's letter. I have not I think found a single person, Catholic or Protestant who does not feel that the three resigners have lowered their standards by the whole transaction, that they had and have no business to hold office under a cabinet, a considerable section of which is anti-Catholic, and that they go back to their places pledged to approve the policy of keeping up the Established Church and to aid its maintenance.

I do assure Your Grace, as I have always done that there is no question whatever about putting out the present Ministry by any external pressure. There is nobody to take their places. The Tory Party of last December is broken up and has no longer any real existence.[55]

Lucas digressed to condemn Dr. Thomas Phillips, the parish priest of Sligo, for being connected with the 'Steelboys', and for once replying to a remonstrating fellow priest 'my dear sir, you must put your conscience in your pocket until after the retreat'. An equally serious crime to Lucas's was that Phillips had 'made over the borough just now to John Sadleir, and the sham resignations are to be put forward as one ground for giving him support'. Lucas was referring to a vacancy in Sligo borough which had arisen a week earlier and coincided with the resignation crisis.[56] On 3 June a House of Commons committee upheld the petition of John Patrick Somers against the sitting member, Charles Towneley.[57] The petition had been financed by Palmerston, who had property in Sligo.[58] Towneley's agents were found guilty of bribery and treating in the 1852 election. One of the main findings was that the local priests had exercised an influence 'in a manner inconsistent with their duties as ministers of religion and destructive of freedom of choice on the part of the voters'. They were a particularly experienced electioneering group, and the greatest offenders were Phillips and his curate, Patrick White. On the Sunday before polling day Phillips' altar denunciation of Somers was so severe that the latter was forced to leave the chapel to avoid the anger of the congregation. White was found guilty of holding an elector in the priests' house on the night before the election and marching him to the booths the following morning to vote for Towneley. P. O'Gara, the parish priest of Drumcliffe, who was in London for the hearing, had to be removed from the room because of intimidating gestures towards witnesses.

Other electors who had travelled with O'Gara met Sadleir and pledged their support to him. Sadleir had already received a letter from Phillips stating that a meeting of ninety four electors in Sligo were favourable to him standing for the borough.[59] Philips had called this meeting, and Sadleir immediately issued his election address.[60] Half of his short statement was devoted to praising Towneley's wealth and benevolence, a theme which afforded Gray much amusement.[61] Sadleir expected the backing of those who had voted for Towneley, and this was taken as an indirect hint of his own intended benevolence. His principles were identical with those of Towneley, and were based upon civil and religious liberty and 'a full measure of justice' for the tenant farmers.

He remained in London for the moment, however, because parliament refused to ratify the election writ. Members were so concerned at the catalogue of intimidation that they requested a delay of several weeks, until they had an opportunity to examine the details of the yet unpublished report.[62] They were thinking in terms of disfranchising the borough, which by then had acquired a reputation for corruption, but the writ was issued on 23 June and Sadleir arrived in Sligo four days later.[63] He was met by Phillips, who, with O'Gara and White, canvassed with him throughout the following week.

Sadleir had little political capital to show from his membership of the government. The Ecclesiastical Titles Act was still extant, and the land committee had rejected the most important clause of Crawford's Bill. On the other hand his temporary resignation, whether *bona fide* or not, at least enabled him to declare that he was not prepared to abandon his principles. Phillips' endorsement of his election bid was of greatest importance. He was the Sligo equivalent of James Maher, and little wonder that Sadleir was to donate fifty pounds later in the year to a testimonial raised in recognition of his political role in the borough.[64] Phillips secured the support of other priests, but unlike Carlow, Sadleir was actively opposed by eight priests led by Owen Feeney, the Vicar-Forane and ex-parish priest of Sligo. The eight included parish priests of the diocese and some Sligo Dominicans. Following a meeting of 4 July in the Hibernian Hotel they published a set of resolutions condemning Sadleir as the paid servant of an administration hostile to Irish interests.[65] But, their support for Sadleir's opponent, John Patrick Somers, was met with a well organised show of disapproval. One of them, Peter O'Connor, curate in Croghan, County Roscommon, later described the reception they received as they emerged from their meeting in the hotel,

> When we descended from the hotel into the street, Hell let loose could hardly exceed the scene that soon met us. An immense mob suddenly gathered, surrounded us, preceded and followed us ... three prominent followers of John Sadleir were the first to hiss and to hoot, with their tongues out, eight anointed Ministers of the living God; they bellowed at us like brutes.
>
> Upon this signal the mob began. Suddenly reason seemed to be utterly extinct, or utterly changed into a rabid instinct in them. Their yellings and their howlings baffle description – Execrations and blasphemies thickened round us. Language which would pain a pagan's ears was abundantly uttered. They looked not like men but like fiends. A ruffian rushing up to the Very Rev. Dr. Feeney, who was leaning on my arm exclaimed, "you old scoundrel, I'll smash your skull." And in that mob, in John Sadleir's mob, were hundreds on whose heads Dr. Feeney bestowed inappreciable blessings and benefits... it makes my heart bleed more and more to reflect that all this hideous immorality was employed to honour and exalt a traitor who carries the price of his apostasy in his pocket.[66]

The Liberal *Sligo Chronicle* chose to sidetrack the split in clerical ranks. Instead its leader of 6 June blamed Somers for dragging the Sligo priests to London and having them held up to odium in the election committee report,

> And now about the forthcoming struggle. The matter is in the hands of the people themselves. If they be content to let their clergy be insulted and indecently assailed – if it be their good will to have the town misrepresented we cannot help it. But, we believe the resolutions of the House of Commons – the brutal attack upon the Sligo Catholic clergy contained in them – will create a storm of indignation, which will overwhelm by its weight, the power of Mr. John Patrick Somers and his new Tory allies.

The anti-clerical and pro-Conservative catch-cry was re-echoed by Sadleir in his own addresses.[67] The fact that Somers was a Liberal, who had on many occasions enjoyed the support of the priests mattered little. He could, however, expect some of the Conservative vote in 1853. Sadleir had learned a painful lesson in Carlow, and the existence of a hostile clerical block increased his concern at a possible defeat if the Conservatives combined with a sector of the Liberal voters. Accordingly he introduced a new tactic into his campaign in the guise of a stalking horse to split the Conservative vote. This was John Hanly, a native of Sligo and a correspondent with the *Morning Post*, which had first published news of Sadleir's Sligo ambitions. Hanly did not have the financial resources to run a campaign, yet he was able to pay for the distribution of placards, circulars and advertisements, hire a mob and engage a 'carriage and pair' to visit constituents.[68] The Conservative *Sligo Chronicle* published its conviction that Sadleir had financed all of this.[69] But, Hanly was unable to pay for his stay in Nelson's Hotel, the most expensive in Sligo, was prosecuted by the proprietor and briefly committed to jail. The *Chronicle* interpreted this as part of the plot to fool people into believing that there was not any connection between Hanly and Sadleir.[70]

The bogus candidature was a clumsy device, and so overdone as to border on the ludicrous. He presented himself under the strange label of Liberal-Conservative and his address resembled a sixteenth century Lutheran denunciation of the Catholic Church.[71] He praised the Protestant Establishment, and rejoiced that he had abandoned the Catholic Church in his youth as 'not only a monstrous corruption of Christianity, but in its nature and essence inconsistent with it'. Civil and religious liberty was re-defined as freedom from the ecclesiastical ligatures by which Rome fettered and degraded the conscience. He would oppose any measure promoting in any way the 'pretensions of that apostate Church'. Maynooth was a 'fortress of iniquity... a nest for hatching sedition, privy, conspiracy and rebellion... an instrument for producing envy, hatred, malice'. The Pope was a wolf in sheep's clothing, a horrible blasphemer, the antichrist, and priests were the special instruments of the Devil. It did not go unnoticed that his blasphemies were never condemned, even by Sadleir's clerical supporters, and the Sligo Conservatives were not deceived by what the *Chronicle* called this 'suspicious document'. They knew nothing about Hanly, but on 20 June agreed to attend a meeting to be addressed by his 'representative',[72] who was unanimously rejected. The Conservatives passed a resolution repudiating all connection with him and pledging their support to Somers. Hanly arrived in Sligo at the end of June, canvassed for a week and withdrew from the contest shortly before polling.[73]

In exposing the spurious nature of his candidacy the *Chronicle* also turned on Sadleir, and drew upon the greater vituperative content of a *Nation* article,

> Mr. John Sadleir is up for Sligo. The Irish traitor succeeds the English briber. By his election commerce with Carlow he made the electoral body of that town so demoralised and profligate, that its name is abomination in Ireland.
>
> Is not this good news for Sligo? It sucked poor Jack Somers, the model Repeal member, till the marrow left his bones. It swallowed Towneley's cash last time, and flung Somers aside for the sake of the bleeding English Catholic with the long purse; and now its stars send it a member of the British government whose bank for the occasion is the British Treasury. At him Sligo. Pluck him; fleece him; drain him. He is an Irish traitor but he has English gold to any figure. He is false to his country; but, boys, he has places to bestow.[74]

Lucas was not to be outdone. He placed Sligo in the same category as Athlone and Carlow, the latter being 'renowned throughout the habitable globe for the Prostitute venality' of its electorate.[75] Sadleir was an appropriate candidate for Sligo, being 'fitted for it by personal corruption'. McCabe professed that there had never been in the annals of the press anything like the campaign of the three Dublin papers against Sadleir, the 'calumniated layman' supported by the 'calumniated priesthood of Sligo'.[76]

But despite their ranting Lucas, Grey and Duffy were reluctant to commit the League to active intervention in Sligo. A Council meeting of 5 July, whose main business was a discussion of the Tenant Compensation Bill then before the land committee, devoted some time to the election.[77] A Dublin Leaguer, Martin A. O'Brennan, who had been secretary of the Inns Quay Ward meeting, was chosen to deliver the League's views. The fact that he had relatives in Sligo was considered a sufficient defence against the possible charge of outside dictation. He treated a receptive audience to a sweep of Irish history from the time of Brian Boru to when 'the Judas pet of the murderous Whigs' approached Sligo,

> The women of Sligo will teach their children to curse the name of Sadleir – generations yet unborn will execrate his memory as more hated than a Parsons or a Borlass, as the deadliest foe of nationality ... Let Sligo, let Ireland punish Mr. Sadleir how best they can by not allowing him a resting place amongst them...how dared he, the vomit of Carlow venture to solicit the honour of representing Sligo ... the ancestors of the men of Sligo in days of yore fought and bled for their altars and for Erin.

Let them be up now – they need not fight again, but scout the deserter, the English lacquey-hack, the jackall of John Bull, the minister of disunion, the tool of the fanatical Russell, from their town ... let them scout him, rout him, denounce and shun him as an emissary of British rule.

This Council meeting coincided with the nomination of candidates.[78] It was noteworthy for two reasons, the presence of two blocks of priests in opposing camps, and the brawling in the courthouse which was worse than that at Carlow. Sadleir was escorted by four priests, including Phillips and Francis McMahon, parish priest of Kinnitty, Co. Offaly. Seven priests came with Somers. Six of these had actively canvassed against Sadleir and were among the signatories of the resolutions condemning his defection. They took part in a courtroom nomination scene described as the most stormy ever witnessed at an Irish election. The mayhem was so great that Sadleir was unable to make any speech, Somers declined to do so and Hanly entertained the crowd by lying on the judge's bench with a handkerchief tied around his head as if asleep.

Phillips, as Sadleir's proposer, was the only one who managed to say anything, an indication of his influence in the borough. He defended his role in the previous election and said that his altar sermon, referred to in the election committee's report, reflected the views of his bishop, G.J. Browne. He had also read a letter from Bishop Haly to James Madden, one of the Sligo gentry, 'expressing his Lordship's great esteem for Mr. Sadleir and his approbation of his conduct'. He made the interesting revelation that Palmerston, as a local property owner, had disapproved of Sadleir's decision to contest Sligo, and had made his views known to Aberdeen who in turn tried to dissuade him from standing.

Sadleir's clerical opponents, Feeney and O'Connor, were not afforded the same opportunity to air their views. Their speeches were reported in the *Freeman's Journal*, but there is no reason to disbelieve a letter from Phillips and others that they had never actually been delivered at the nomination meeting.[79] Feeney stood his ground for three quarters of an hour in an effort to propose McNamara Cantwell. When the audience grew hoarse from shouting he managed to make a short speech deploring Sadleir's association with Hanly,

Your association with the foulmouthed antichrist, who, forgetful of his obscured and dishonoured origin presumes to vomit forth his abominable blasphemies of God's own Church, proves the reality of your pretended indignation at the offensive language of that leader whom you are paid for following, and while it holds out the prospect of disarming some of your Conservative opponents, will no doubt be advanced as a proof that he is not your paid tool. But thanks to the Conservatives, who, forgetting their prejudices, have repudiated him as well as you.

While his colleague, Peter O'Connor, was trying to convince the unreceptive audience that Sadleir's character stank in the nostrils of Ireland, he was struck with a stone in the back of the head and leaped upon by Hanly, who in turn was kicked and beaten. This led to a riot in the courthouse. Stones were flung from the gallery and some spectators were arrested for carrying loaded pistols. O'Connor was removed from the scene for his retaliation and the Mayor ordered the court to be cleared. The violence of the occasion prompted O'Connor's brother, also involved in the fracas, to write to the *Telegraph* labelling Sligo as the dung pit of Ireland and the repository of every other county's offal.[80]

Polling took place three days later and Sadleir scraped home by eight votes.[81] He promised to resign his office if ever his official obligations interfered with his duty as a public representative. His defence of the Aberdeen government was confined to praising its Irish appointments, specifically that of Lord St. Germans as Lord Lieutenant,[82] which he portrayed as a tribute to Catholics because the Protestant St. Germans had been an opponent of the Ecclesiastical Titles Bill. The Conservatives, on the other hand, were guilty of hypocrisy by supporting Somers who was of a different political persuasion. They were motivated by sectarianism and their dislike of Phillips. The Sligo election was almost a redemption of the electorate; it prevented Sligo inhabitants from becoming a 'press-ridden' people as had happened in Carlow. This was paralleled by McCabe who interpreted the election as significant in demonstrating that the newspaper triumvirate did not have the power to influence parliamentary representation in Ireland. The Irish people were not like the French at the time of the Revolution, and would 'not be dictated to in the choice of their representation by a Doctor Marat in any *ami du peuple* newspaper'.[83]

To the Leaguers the 'temporary return' of Sadleir was one of 'deep shame and bitter sorrow'.[84] This was the verdict of McNamara Cantwell at a Council meeting of 12 July. Sadleir's return could be reversed at another time, but the memory of the 'extraordinary scenes by which that occasion was at once distinguished and degraded' could not be so easily erased. Cantwell and other Council members attributed Sadleir's success to Phillips' support. But, such support was *de facto* responsible for the violent nature of the election and the attack upon the priests. Cantwell accused Phillips of making no effort to defend Feeney and

O'Connor. O'Brennan made the correct observation of clerical political influence that in the 'arena of politics all men, cleric and lay are on an equal footing – superior talent, superior prudence and superior wisdom alone giving distinction'. He also unsheathed a new weapon against Sadleir of an anti-clerical nature, because his money had hired the bludgeon men who attacked God's anointed.

The gloom in League ranks contrasted with the scenes in Sligo where tar barrels blazed throughout the town.[85] Six were defiantly lit on the summit of Sligo Abbey, the property of Palmerston, whose tenants had supported Somers. A *Telegraph* reporter accompanied a group of electors to the Ursuline Convent to announce Sadleir's success, and were told by the Reverend Mother that nuns and boarders had prayed for his return. The bells of the convent tolled to hail the victory which was, according to the reporter, a symbolic act to proclaim his Catholicity. But, unlike the Carlow triumph of 1852 there was no celebratory banquet. From then on Sadleir's political career was menaced by litigation and investigation. He was soon faced by two petitions against his return. The first, by a medical doctor, John H. Wood, was lodged at the end of July and pleaded that some of Sadleir's attorneys, agents, poll clerks and even the Town Clerk should have been disqualified from voting because they had received bribes of money or job promises.[86] It was also alleged that some voters were bribed or treated, and had in turn bribed others. Even the returning officers were accused of corruption by recording votes for Somers in favour of Sadleir. Personation was another charge, with votes allegedly recorded for the absent and even the dead.

Petitioners were legally obliged to have two sureties as a guarantee that the enquiry expenses would be met. Sadleir met the Wood petition with the challenge that one of the sponsors had insufficient means to support his surety.[87] This was heard before the Examiner of Recognizances in the Commons on 19 August, when the surety was considered insufficient pending further investigation. On the same day Isaac Butt gave notice of a petition by Somers.[88] Not only did this second petition complain of the usual bribery, treating and personation but focussed on the issue of interference with the sureties. It made the serious allegation that an agent of Sadleir had endangered the petition itself by trying to bribe one of the sureties to withdraw. Sadleir's response was a denial and a request that a 'public and deliberate enquiry before a properly constituted tribunal' be established to investigate the allegations.[89] He only had the opportunity of contacting one of those accused in the petition, and was assured 'in the most distinct and positive manner that he had no knowledge whatever of the alleged transactions'. He went so far as to deplore the inevitable delay in setting up a tribunal due to the proximity of the parliamentary recess.

Parliament went into recess the following day and the hearings were postponed. Two months later, however, a case was heard in the Revision Court implicating Patrick McNiff, one of Sadleir's electioneering agents, in a particular type of bribery.[90] He was accused of paying rates' arrears to establish the status of some townspeople as voters. He admitted receiving fifty pounds from Phillips, but successfully argued that this was for charitable purposes, and the charge was dropped.

Scarcely a month elapsed when the Dowling case re-emerged in a more complex form, its tentacles reaching closer to Sadleir. The second Dowling *versus* Crotty case was heard on 21 November 1853 by David Richard Pigot, the Chief Baron of the Exchequer.[91] It stemmed from the re-arrest of Dowling on 27 October 1852, when he had been again prosecuted by Crotty for non-payment of the two bills then legitimately due. The following month the bank had successfully issued a second prosecution for other bills due by Dowling, who remained in the Marshalsea debtors prison in Dublin awaiting the hearing by the Chief Baron twelve months later.

Francis McDonough again represented Dowling in November 1853. He sought his release because he had been oppressively dealt with for political gain, and because certain other financial transactions between Crotty and the bank were a sham. McDonough read an affidavit from Dowling containing more detail than that of August 1852, implicating Dempsey, Sadleir and Edward Lawler, a friend of O'Shea. It now became public news that Dempsey had got the bond from Crotty and given it to Sadleir, who went to Dublin to obtain a writ of execution.

According to the affidavit Crotty had become increasingly nervous on learning of Dowling's intention to sue him. Sadleir himself had promised that he should never be liable for the bills held as security against some of Dowling's debts. But, in September 1852 Crotty had threatened to expose the plot unless the bank formally released him from liability. Faced with this threat O'Shea concocted a false paper trail to conceal the original fraud. He instructed Lawler to draw a further bill upon Crotty's impoverished clerk, William Lyng, to cover Crotty's bills. Lyng was given the money to meet the bill, and in turn handed the money to Crotty to redeem the bills from the bank. In effect the bank's own money was used to repay a bogus debt to itself. To complete the fraud Crotty had given Lawler an I.O.U. for the amount of the bill. This ensured that Dowling continued to legally owe Crotty the money, which would justify his second arrest.

This complicated financial scam was compounded by Crotty's death some months before the 1853 trial. Faced with new facts and with Dowling's avowed intention of suing Sadleir himself, counsel for Crotty's executors asked for further time to prepare their briefs, since Sadleir was then in London and might wish to make an affidavit. The Chief Baron agreed, and in his review of the case on 3 December made Edward Lawler the defendant in a new trial before a special jury at a Nisi Prius sitting of Exchequer. It commenced on 19 December, lasted for six days and cost Dowling more than £500. It aroused such widespread interest that details were published in pamphlet form.[92] Whiteside, McDonough and Brereton were counsel for Dowling. Henry Martley, J.D. Fitzgerald and O'Hagan appeared for Lawler and their expenses were undoubtedly met by Sadleir. Political enmities were present in the courtroom with Sadleir's attorney, Mulhall, representing Lawler and the Tenant Leaguer, John McNamara Cantwell acting for Dowling. The courtroom was crowded each day by barristers and others interested in the case.

The issue for trial was whether the web of transactions, resulting in Dowling's two terms of imprisonment, was fraudulent. Four key areas were identified. Two centred upon a possible agreement between Crotty and Sadleir, or anyone on his behalf, releasing Crotty from liability, and if so whether the bank discounted Lawler's bill on Lyng. The third concerned whether the bank genuinely intended holding Lawler liable for this bill, and the fourth whether Crotty had been a *bona fide* trustee for Lawler or the bank in issuing the execution leading to Dowling's second arrest.

Counsel for the prosecution built up a formidable case. It became evident from Whiteside's opening broadside on 19 December that Sadleir was the primary target. Whiteside, who was Conservative M.P. for Enniskillen and later Lord Chief Justice of Ireland,[93] introduced the jury to his law firm in Great Denmark Street where 'five or six able attorneys were employed by him in conducting the weighty and multifarious business in which that gentleman was constantly engaged; and almost every one of them had something more or less to do with this nefarious business'. While naming Morrogh and Kennedy as two of the leading members of this firm, Sadleir was the 'great actor in the drama' and the jury would have to make up their minds if he had 'transgressed the law of the land and the immutable law of justice'.[94]

Sadleir blankly denied any association with the circumstances of Dowling's arrest, although he could scarcely swear that he had not taken Crotty's bond to Dublin to obtain writs for the arrest. In a long prepared defence on 21 December he brazenly explained this action as almost a favour to Crotty to help recover his money.[95] The extent and nature of his denial was not impressive from a jury's point of view,

I never authorised Mr. O'Shea, or any other party on my behalf, to apply to Crotty, or ask him to give up the bond, or to give me control over it; I never at any time agreed with Daniel Crotty that he should be released from all liability on foot of two bills of exchange for £150 and £200 respectively then in the Tipperary Joint Stock Bank;... I got that bond on one occasion when going from Carlow to Dublin; I knew nothing of the bond or the judgement entered upon it; on that occasion I was met by the Rev. Mr. Dempsey, Mr. Edward Lawler and Mr. Daniel Crotty, and I received the bond either from the Rev. Mr. Dempsey or Mr. Lawler; I never saw the bond before that day; ...When the bond was given to me, the Rev. Mr. Dempsey said that it was the wish of Daniel Crotty that it should be put in force against Dowling; Mr. Edward Lawler also spoke to me on the subject and the substance of what he said was that Mr. Daniel Crotty was anxious that an execution should issue against Edward Dowling on foot of his bond debt, and that he had to request I would take charge of the paper and have it entrusted to some Dublin attorney to have it put in force... at the time Edward Lawler spoke to me on that subject, Daniel Crotty was conversing with some people of the town, at some distance on the platform of the railway station; but after I had entered the railway carriage my recollection is, that then for the first time Daniel Crotty came to the window and said to me, "Mr. Sadleir, you will have Mr. Morrogh to attend to my business, and have Dowling arrested," the train was about to move away, and I merely replied that I should take care that Mr. Morrogh should attend to his business, or have it attended to; at the time the bond was given to me I was not aware of the circumstances under which it had been passed...

He placed the responsibility for executing the bond on Morrogh who had temporarily left Ireland, possibly to avoid being called in evidence. Sadleir explained that he had retired as an attorney and handed over his legal business to Morrogh, but admitted that he occasionally financed its operation. Under cross examination by McDonough he tried to distance himself from the events in Great Denmark Street where the final steps were taken to trap Dowling,

I will now explain what I said to Mr. Morrogh when I handed him the bond; it was this – "Daniel Crotty, who is an elector of Carlow, and a great friend and supporter of mine, has a judgement on this bond for the penal sum of £1400, on which there is due to him the sum of £700, and as I was coming to Dublin to-day he handed it to me, requesting of me that I would have you attend to this business for him. His anxiety and wish is that execution should be issued against the body of Dowling, and that he should be arrested. The course for you to take is to place this security in the hands of some intelligent attorney, who will examine the roll, see in what condition the security is, and whether Mr. Crotty is really, as he supposes he is, entitled to issue execution against Dowling;

and in case, according to the condition of the judgement call, Crotty should be entitled to issue execution against Dowling, there ought to be two executions issued, one to the Queen's County and the other to the County of Carlow, because it may be quite uncertain whether he will be in the portion of the town which is in the Queen's County or in that portion of it which is in Carlow.

Pressed by McDonough Sadleir was forced to admit that he wanted to prevent Dowling 'by every proper means' from voting against him. This did not tally very well with his previous assertion that he had no wish to injure Dowling or see him arrested. But in view of this assertion McDonough demanded to know why Sadleir had made no effort to have him released when it became clear that the arrest was illegal in July 1852. Sadleir Lamely replied that on realising that he was being painted as 'the sole criminal' he felt that any interference by him might be interpreted as an attempt to avoid the consequences of any future legal action. It might also be seen as remorse of conscience and a tacit admission of guilt.

Sadleir's statements, combined with the evidence of other witnesses over five days, provided ample ammunition for McDonough's summation on Christmas Eve. Central to this was the imagery of a powerful Lord of the Treasury victimising a weak denizen of Carlow and even undermining the judicial system itself. He dismissed Sadleir's litany of denial as 'an insult to common sense', made most of the forging of Gibbings' signature, and concluded that

> from the days when the celebrated but despicable Bishop of Lincoln invented for Charles the First the new doctrine that there was a public and private conscience there never had been so great a casuist as John Sadleir.

It was difficult for Martley and Fitzgerald to mount a defence sufficiently strong to counteract the emotional appeal to the jury by McDonough and Whiteside. Their argument rested upon the absence of proof, and Martley reminded the jury that they were not an election tribunal and should ignore accounts of distasteful electioneering tactics. The Chief Baron agreed that 'impropriety of conduct did not establish the allegations the plaintiff relied on'.[96] He cautioned that in some of the issues before the court there was no direct evidence of conspiracy and the arguments of both sides should be carefully sifted. Pigot explained that in a civil rights case like Dowling's the court could not try the motives or intentions of anyone pursuing their legal rights. The case on some of the issues was one of inference met by sworn denials on the part of the defence. But his efforts at impartiality were clouded by his moral indignation, which was aimed at Dempsey rather than Sadleir,

> that a Minister of Religion, whose duty was to instruct persons on those rights that depend on the dictates of justice, and to raise his voice against conduct that would be unjust and oppressive, should have suffered himself to be induced to aid in such proceedings, was a thing that he could not merely lament, but which he should also condemn. He hoped that since the Rev. gentleman had time to reflect upon the matter, he repented of the conduct of which he had been guilty, and of the scandal which that conduct must of necessity have given. He hoped and believed that few – he would not use a stronger expression – would tarnish their own order, as well as violate their own duty, by acting in such a manner.

In the wake of such an outburst Pigot's cautioning of jurors to impartially consider the facts was not over convincing. They had, however, long made up their minds, their foreman having made the unusual plea on 23 December for counsel to shorten their presentations because of the proximity of Christmas. Within ten minutes they found for Dowling on all four counts and left Sadleir's political ambitions in ruins.

The hostile press quickly moved to exploit his disgrace.[97] Lucas's editorial of 31 December promised comprehensive trial analysis, and for that week selected 'the ecclesiastical portion of the entertainment'. He was annoyed by Dempsey's shielding of Sadleir, and placed the Sligo curate in the wider context of government disquiet at extensive priestly activity during the controversial 1852 election, prompting some M.P.s to call for a curbing of political involvement of priests. He suspected that some priests, particularly those in his own Meath constituency, had been reported to Rome while those of Carlow, Sligo and Athlone, 'those dens of iniquity', had escaped official censure by Rome.

Dempsey was incensed by the article and its portrayal of him as a perjurer and Sadleirite tool. In a reply of more than two and a half thousand words he trawled through an impressive armoury of vitriol to denounce the 'lay Pope of the Irish people' and the 'unconscientious and unscrupulous reviler' for his 'logical gibbeting' of a 'humble, defenceless, and slandered priest'. The charge of perjury was especially 'hard for flesh and bone' to bear,

> You, the convert to Rome – you who parade your holiness as a pedlar does his bag, and live on the interest of such profession, you accuse me of perjury, and this without the shadow of foundation in fact, and in the

teeth of the declaration of an entire court. Shame, shame upon you! The lowest ruffian in the land, the most characteristic reviler, would hardly descend to iniquity so base.[98]

He made no apologies for supporting Sadleir, who in 1852 had no connection with the government, but was 'an idol of the people' and a 'favourite of the prelates'. The act of bringing the bond to Sadleir was not of major import, and the prospect of Dowling's arrest gave him much satisfaction by preventing a vote in 'direct violation of religion and conscience'. All this was on the understanding that the debt was then legally due and he re-iterated his ignorance of the fact that such was not the case at the time of the arrest.

As might be expected the letter disapproved of the Chief-Baron's departure from courtroom etiquette in issuing a moral condemnation. Lucas saw this from another perspective and noted that Sadleir's role, which had been central to the evidence, was totally ignored in Pigot's address. This was put down to political sympathy by 'an ex-Whig Attorney General' for Sadleir. Had the evidence pointed to his innocence the judge would have had no hesitation in 'trumpeting forth to the world the injured merits of the Whig Lord of the Treasury'.[99]

But, the Chief Baron's silence on Sadleir was partly due to the absence of proof on the issues being tried. He had also admitted at the beginning of the hearing that the complexity of the case required the fullest presentation by counsel and decided that this was sufficient for the jurors to make up their minds without the benefit of a lengthy summation by himself. All this, however, was of little consequence to Sadleir's political fate. While the actual illegal arrest of Dowling was not central to this particular case, Sadleir's role in securing it was clear. It is difficult to see how the government could defend him during the parliamentary interrogation which was sure to follow. He wrote to Keogh for advice, and the Solicitor General in turn contacted Sir John Young, the Chief-Secretary, who informed Aberdeen on 4 January 1854 of the outcome.[100] Sadleir suggested to Keogh that the onus be put on Aberdeen to ask for his resignation as Lord of the Treasury,[101] but Young rejected such a course. He felt that since both Sadleir and Keogh realised the difficulty of defending the case in parliament, 'if they thought of resignation or talked of it at all, the resignation should be explicit and unconditional'. Keogh had no option but to agree and informed Sadleir of Young's opinion.

Sadleir did not delay in submitting his resignation. In his letter of 4 January to Aberdeen he repudiated any complicity in Dowling's illegal arrest, but put the greater good of the government before his own interests,

So much I cannot avoid saying on my own behalf, but whatever my personal feelings may be, there is one which predominates over all others – a determination that as the matters referred to were antecedent to my acceptance of office – so nothing which has subsequently occurred respecting them shall in any way facilitate the designs of those who seek to embarrass Your Lordship and the members of your government, whom it has been my pride to call my colleagues and friends.[102]

Aberdeen could not quite conceal his relief in a courteous and euphemistic reply of 7 January.[103] He acknowledged Sadleir's consideration in sparing the government from 'any unnecessary embarrassment', and admitted that the reports of the trial had produced 'sensations of uneasiness in my head'. He regretted the resignation but agreed that it was the wisest course.

The Leaguers-cum-oppositionists were exultant at Sadleir's political demotion and McNamara Cantwell was determined to bring about his total political destruction.[104] His colleagues, however, were less inclined to pursue him so relentlessly. Lucas was unsure about what course should be taken. Writing to Moore on 3 January he felt that the leading oppositionists should not raise the Dowling issue in Parliament, but 'ought to let other people do that work for us'.[105] He may have wished to protect the oppositionists from an accusation of vindictiveness, but he did not want to be personally involved in Sadleir's downfall or to pursue the Dowling case in parliament or otherwise. According to him Duffy and Maguire shared this view, and he took it for granted that 'Shee will not meddle with it'. He was aware of Cantwell's resolve to destroy Sadleir and his refusal of a monetary offer to withdraw from the Dowling case,

Cantwell, who has literally made the case by his own extraordinary exertions and courage, the outlay of several hundred pounds and the refusal of £750 for his share of a compromise – is most anxious to have the case brought on by our party and has been pressing me to undertake it, promising all the help in his power and the particulars of the suppressed evidence which Pigot[106] refused to admit, with copies of documents not published. I have no wish personally to be very prominent in it, and I told Cantwell last night that your position in the party and the House gave you a sort of right to the management of the case, if you were inclined to take it up.

Moore's reply is not extant, but another letter from Lucas following news of Sadleir's resignation indicated that Moore had intended raising the Dowling case.[107] Lucas was still undecided on what should be done;

he had no wish to 'trample on a man who is down, or anything of that appearance', but felt that the delinquency was 'sufficient ground for public exposure and solemn investigation'. The matter was not raised in parliament subsequently, although at a later stage Carlow Conservatives were anxious to use it for political purposes.[108]

Apart from the political dimension the Dowling scandal may have had limited repercussions for his business career. While he was discussing his options with Keogh and other friends he had to prepare the report for the half yearly meeting of the London and County. It was held on 2 January at the London Tavern, and was momentarily interrupted when a shareholder demanded 'an explanation of the conduct of the hon-Chairman on a late occasion'.[109] It was not clear, however, if this referred to Sadleir's political actions or to his indebtedness to the bank.[110] The interruption was not entertained by the other shareholders, who received his report with satisfaction. Under his chairmanship the bank showed a net profit of £33,256 for the previous half year enabling him to declare a dividend of six per cent plus a four per cent bonus, both tax free. He explained that the healthy state of the balance sheet resulted not from any financial windfall but from ordinary trading operations. The meeting accepted his proposal to double the existing share capital of £1,000,000 by issuing 20,000 new shares to meet expansion requirements. There was also good news for directors and staff. The former were awarded an increase of £2,000 on their salaries and one per cent of the dividend was transferred to the Provident Fund, which provided pensions for the families of deceased staff members. This fund was the brain-child of Sadleir established some years earlier with a personal donation of £4,500,[111] and may have been inspired by the staff welfare provisions operated by the Bank of Ireland.[112]

But, it was his resignation, not his benevolence, that attracted the notice of the press in Ireland. His career as an office holder was ended, but his tenure as Sligo borough representative undisturbed, and so he remained a target. His reputation was by now badly tainted and the *Tablet* published a letter of 6 February from Nicholas McEvoy, the parish priest of Kells, praising McNamara Cantwell for helping to unmask the Carlow scandal, 'the most unheard-of and satan-like plot against the political virtue of Catholic Ireland, which could possibly enter the mind of man, even the most depraved to conceive'. Sadleir was the 'Cataline of this nefarious plot, the Pandarus of Irish political life'.[113] This contrasted with the private request of a Carlow priest that Sadleir, 'now settled in his proper place', would secure an appointment for a parishioner in the Excise Department.[114]

The early months of 1854 did not bring much respite for the beleaguered Sligo M.P. in other respects. Because of legal technicalities and the legitimacy of the second arrest Dowling was not yet released,[115] and his action against Sadleir himself was due for hearing in March. With the re-assembly of Parliament the enquiry into his election for Sligo was about to be initiated and he was also embroiled in what became known as the Stoner case as well as being implicated in an enquiry concerning the Crown lands on the Kilconcouse estate in County Offaly. All of these events took place against the backdrop of an official witchhunt into dubious practices at Irish elections which was carried out by what was popularly known as the Corruption Committee. It was set up following a Commons debate on a *Times* article of 6 February about comments made by Gray and Christopher Kelly on the trafficking in places in Ireland.[116] Butt was appointed chairman, and Moore and Keogh were on the committee, which met intermittently between 2 February and early Summer.[117]

Though Gray and Lucas were called as witnesses, and closely questioned by Keogh, they failed to substantiate any instances of the sale of places. Lucas was forced to interpret pledge-breaking as a species of corruption, and he relied upon extracts from speeches and articles in the *Tablet* as evidence.[118] Gray followed the same line in general and declared that W.G. Hayter continuously pressurised Irish M.P.s indebted to the ministry for places, to vote accordingly.[119] He identified Frank Scully as one compromised because his brother had secured a position through influence. He accused Scully of being reluctant to vote against the ministry on a particular occasion because of this, and testified that Sadleir had confirmed as much. Scully had in fact voted against the government on that occasion, and angrily refuted Gray's evidence as 'a wilful calumny'.[120] He could not deny his brother's appointment, but disclaimed any involvement in it. Sadleir corroborated his cousin's statement.

Nonetheless, even if Lucas and Gray failed to produce worthwhile evidence, other witnesses agreed that the dispensation of patronage was part of the social order and the prerogative of the prevailing ministry. Napier had no doubt about this in relation to legal appointments.[121] He outlined the opinion in legal circles that promotion on merit was non-existent. Political affiliation and a long purse were the crucial factors.

Moore alone had limited experience of the distribution of patronage. On one occasion he had the disposal of an appointment to the post office in Ballina, and was inundated with applications.[122] Apart from this single instance, Moore because of his political independence, had never succeeded in securing an appointment for any of his constituents. But he did learn from an applicant that the normal price of an appointment was one year's salary.

The committee concluded that there was a general impression in Ireland that the sale of places was confined to a small circle of M.P.s. There was, however, insufficient evidence to sustain charges of corruption, and the report condemned the groundless allegations and 'reprehensible conduct' of some witnesses,[123] a result not only disappointing to leading Oppositionists like Lucas, but also embarrassing because the only allegations of any substance were against Sadleir's opponent, Somers. Even Gray had to admit to the committee that Sligo discontent with Somers stemmed from his allocation of patronage there. Evidence also showed that Somers borrowed money from those indebted to him for places, and its repayment was not always forthcoming. One witness, James Walker, a Sligo solicitor, referred to the great number of positions secured by Somers for his constituents because of his influence with Clarendon, Somerville and Hayter.[124] Walker's own family had greatly benefited from Sligo M.Ps., including Sadleir, for whom he had acted as election agent. Four of his brothers had been placed in jobs by such means.

Leaguers were aware of Somer's reputation, and when the appointment of the Corruption Committee was first mooted the London correspondent of the *Tablet* feared that it might be used to discredit him and undermine the two petitions against Sadleir's return.[125] The investigation into his alleged interference with the sureties was conducted by the Recognizance Committee, whose appointment was moved on 6 February by Butt.[126] He was aware that Sadleir intended seconding the motion and, therefore, did not make any statement except to point out that, if proven, the allegations would be tantamount to a contempt of court, 'and would be punished as such'. Sadleir in seconding the motion again denied all knowledge of these allegations.

The committee met on 17 February and concluded on 7 March.[127] Its members were Henry Ker Seymour, Edwin Lascelles, Robert Ingram, John A. Roebuck and William T. Egerton.[128] The basic facts of the case were straightforward. James Walker in his capacity as Sadleir's agent had instructed a Sligo solicitor, Michael Gethin, to investigate the solvency of the two sureties, William Cullen and William Ormsby Rutledge.[129] This was legal in itself, but the evidence showed a willingness by the Sadleirites to go beyond the call of duty in their exertions. The principal culprits were James Simpson and his brother Henry, who was also the agent for John Hanly.[130] These received their instructions from Gethin.[131] They first approached Cullen and then Rutledge and offered bribes to withdraw their securities by signing affidavits understating the extent of their property to render them ineligible as sureties. Gethin had drawn up one of the false affidavits for Cullen as well as a bogus I.O.U. which would exceed and, therefore, negate his security. Henry Simpson, a farmer and shopkeeper with no legal knowledge, admitted drawing up an equally fraudulent affidavit for Rutledge.

The evidence suggested that Cullen was amenable to bribery, but his demand for £100 was considered excessive by Gethin and the Simpsons. After several meetings he was offered £50 and a promise that 'you will either get a good situation or as much money as will satisfy you; and who is better able to do so than Mr. Sadleir, a Lord of the Treasury, and who had got several brothers-in-law in Parliament'.[132] Cullen refused and at no stage did Rutledge entertain any meddling with his recognizance. The latter's evidence was crucial because it included the fraudulent affidavit, which incriminated Gethin and the Simpsons.

The committee found the main allegations of the petition proven, and condemned the evidence of the three Sadleirites as disgraceful 'by its inconsistency and evasiveness'.[133] Subsequently a motion was moved by Seymour and passed by the House instructing the Attorney General to prosecute Gethin and the Simpsons.[134] This was particularly serious for Gethin as a solicitor, who was sacrificed for Sadleir's cause. One of the interesting facets of the case was the determination of all three to shield him. Sadleir had perfected the technique of insulation by using others in such a way that it was difficult to trace any course of events directly to himself. Gethin was adamant that he was not Sadleir's agent or attorney, although he had given 'every assistance in my power to Mr. Sadleir at the election by way of canvassing friends of Mr. Towneley on his behalf'. He insisted that his use of the Simpsons on Sadleir's behalf had not been prompted by the Sligo M.P. He was also careful to state that he had not sent any bill of costs to Sadleir for such assistance. Walker corroborated this, and despite the committee's best efforts he maintained that Gethin had obliged him as a friend and received no remuneration.[135]

Sadleir was ready to be called, but the committee did not consider it necessary and wearily concluded that he did 'not appear from the evidence to have been personally involved'. This acquittal, though welcome, hardly absolved him in the public mind, but his basic objective of holding his seat was achieved. He experienced more good news while the Recognizance Committee was still in session when, following an appeal by Lawler, the decision in the Dowling *versus* Lawler case was set aside. The appeal was heard by the Barons of Exchequer[136] for five days before they pronounced on 21 February.[137] They were unanimous in their conclusion that there was not any evidence to warrant the jury's finding that Sadleir had been involved in a conspiracy of fraudulent financial transactions to release Crotty from liability from the bills for which he was security. They rejected the legal validity of the circumstantial evidence which had been accepted by the jury, and decided that the jurors' judgement had been clouded by their feelings about the illegal arrest, which itself was not pertinent to the four issues being tried. Baron John Richards excused their confusion because of the complexity of the case and the great amount of 'irrelevant matter' introduced. Chief Baron Pigot, however, ordered that the case should be reheard before another jury using evidence not admissible under the previous hearing. The Barons added two further issues to the existing four, one of which was Dowling's use of Crotty's bond as a means of protecting his own property from the bank. This did not augur well for his early release.

But, a fortnight later the focus was on Sadleir himself when Dowling's case against him for alleged complicity in the first arrest was heard before a special jury at the Record Court of the Carlow Assizes.[138] This was presided over by Chief Justice James Henry Monahan, who had been Irish Attorney General in the 1848 prosecution of the Young Ireland revolutionaries.[139] The illegality of the arrest was not contested by Sadleir's counsel, Henry Martley. In his address to the jury, comprised of Conservative electors, he dwelt on the possibility that the case had been taken against Sadleir for political motives. He cited the incongruity of Dowling's straitened financial circumstances with his ability to pursue expensive litigation. This was more than a hint that he was receiving financial backing from the Conservative party in Carlow. Martley practically conceded that damages would be awarded and asked the jury to ensure that these should be fair and reasonable.

Monahan concurred, and briefed the jury on 13 March that a difference in political affiliation between themselves and Sadleir should not have any bearing upon the size of damages, if awarded. Sadleir's involvement in having the bond executed to prevent Dowling voting was beyond doubt, but it was equally important to decide if he had been aware that the bond was not then legally enforceable. The jury took several hours to reach a decision that Sadleir was culpable. They awarded Dowling £1,100 compensation and sixpence costs. This did not, however, form a legal basis for his release since the second arrest had been legally justified.

The cumulative effects of investigations and court cases meant that by March 1854 Sadleir was badly tarnished by the whiff of scandal, but the relentless legal and quasi-legal merry-go-round had not yet run its course. The day after the Dowling verdict the committee to investigate the Wood election petition was formed. This consisted of Sir Francis T. Baring, Sir James Buller East, Edward Ellice Junior, Locke King and John H. Philips.[140] Evidence was heard on 18 March, when Sadleir admitted giving his agent, James Walker, £400 to cover all election expenses, but he denied all knowledge of how this was spent.[141] Some of it was used for bribery and the committee found that three cases were proven, but the evidence presented did not directly implicate Sadleir, and his return was ratified.

No sooner had this decision been issued than Sadleir was indirectly connected to another scandal, which, however, proved more embarrassing to the government than to him. This was the Stonor case which made headlines throughout the U. K. from the end of March until early Summer. Henry Stonor, a member of the General Committee of the Catholic Defence Association and well known to Sadleir, had been found guilty of bribery by the committee investigating Towneley's 1852 election.[142] He was subsequently an active supporter of Sadleir during the 1853 by-election campaign, when, according to Lawrence MacTernan, Somer's agent, he distributed ten pound notes to purchase Towneleyte votes.[143] Five months after the by-election the Duke of Newcastle, the Colonial Secretary, recommended Stonor, whose brother had been Solicitor General in Van Diemen's Land, to a temporary judgeship in Melbourne. Newcastle was unaware of the Sligo investigation and in mid-March G.H. Moore called on parliament to appoint a special committee to investigate the appointment.[144] He identified it with the contemporary debate on political corruption and as a reward for services rendered, in this case the securing of Towneley's supporters for Sadleir,

> ..if Mr. Stonor's testimonials had not been examined, the public had a right to know on what grounds, if not upon those grounds, and upon what recommendations,if not upon those recommendations, Mr.Stonor was appointed. He had reason to believe that this gentleman had been appointed by an influence which had the ear of the Duke of Newcastle, and not in ignorance of Mr. Stonor's corrupt practices, but because of his corrupt practices. He believed Mr. Stonor was appointed to this office because he had handed over to the hon. gentleman now the member for Sligo, and then a Junior Lord of the Treasury, any influence that he had obtained in Sligo by corrupt practices during the election of 1853.

Although the main charge was directed at Newcastle, Sadleir was so upset by Moore's inference that he was twice reprimanded by the Speaker for accusing the Mayo M.P. of slander and libel on him personally.[145] Moore denied that such was his intention, and his tenacity in pursuing the affair succeeded in embarrassing the government into cancelling the appointment of Stonor, who was en route to Australia unaware of the fate that awaited him.[146] Moore was not mollified by the sacrificing of Stonor, persisted in his motion for an investigating committee to highlight alleged corruption in high places,[147] and the government conceded in an effort to extricate itself from the charge, resulting in the unusual sight of Gladstone, the Chancellor of the Exchequer, seconding Moore's motion. Gladstone rejected Moore's accusation that the appointment was in any way due to Sadleir's influence or that Sadleir had ever made any representations on Stonor's behalf.[148]

Despite considerable sympathy for Stonor's plight,[149] the committee duly met and displayed a total lack of knowledge about the affair. Moore, refused to assist unless he was appointed to the committee, where he would have the opportunity to grill the Duke and his associates. He was eventually included as a non-voting member[150] and questioned Newcastle, his private secretary, and the two Colonial Under-Secretaries. As the only actors in the drama they were unlikely to incriminate themselves. Moore was especially interested in any alleged involvement by Newcastle in the Sligo election.[151] The Duke denied any knowledge of it and was positive that neither Sadleir nor any other M.P. had approached the colonial office on Stonor's behalf. Who was to contradict him? Inevitably Moore failed to convince the committee of any deliberate intention by Newcastle and his staff to recommend the appointment of a tainted lawyer to the bench in Victoria. Its report of 1 June was appropriately sharp and regretted 'that upon grounds so insufficient as those which appear to have led to this enquiry, so serious an accusation should have been proposed'.[152]

The final issue concerning Sadleir's use of political influence on behalf of an ally involved a tenancy on the Crown Estate of Kilconcouse in County Offaly. This occurred during his brief tenure at the Treasury but only reached the public arena in March 1854.

Francis McMahon, the parish priest of Kinnitty, brought the good will of an emigrating tenant to a twenty-five acre farm in 1843 when it was detached from a joint tenancy of fifty acres. An 1851 investigation into the affairs of the estate by Patrick F. Kennedy, the newly appointed Chief Commissioner of the Crown estates in Ireland, discovered that Kilconcouse was poorly managed, yielded little financial return and was 'overrun with a pauper population'.[153] Since McMahon's lease had expired in 1850 the Commissioner decided to re-unite the two farms under the other tenant as part of an overall rationalisation plan.

McMahon was served with a notice to quit, and when he baulked he was prosecuted in Chancery. His reluctance stemmed from dissatisfaction at the compensation offered for considerable improvements carried out by him. On a broader level he was aggrieved because the farms of Catholic sub-tenants like himself were subject to rationalisation while Protestant subtenants were undisturbed.[154]

McMahon's luck changed for the better with the arrival of the Aberdeen Government. He wrote to Sadleir who used his influence with Gladstone, the Chancellor of the Exchequer, to bring about the Commissioner's dismissal.

Kennedy in turn appealed to the Earl of Donoughmore, who raised the matter in the House of Lords on 23 June 1854, and, despite Aberdeen's reservations, succeeded in persuading Lords to set up a select Committee to investigate the complaint.[155] Its report vindicated Kennedy's integrity, but much to the satisfaction of the *Telegraph* did not result in his re-instatement. McCabe politicised the controversy by justifiably portraying McMahon as being victimised because he opposed a Conservative candidate, related to Donoughmore, in the 1852 election campaign. On a more current political level he used the case to justify the taking of office by Sadleir, by contrasting the prosecution of the priest during the Derby administration 'from which all Catholics were excluded' to his rehabilitation under the Aberdeen ministry 'in which Catholics have been permitted to hold office'.[156]

Sadleir was not called to give evidence at the enquiry, but was forewarned that the subject would become public knowledge when he received a letter from Donoughmore in May. He forwarded this to Aberdeen on 23 May, and defended his stance on the basis that McMahon's eviction would have been 'most oppressive and unjust, and he was confident that a full investigation would prove the wisdom of the Treasury in dismissing Kennedy.[157] Sadleir also interpreted the resurrection of the issue at this time as a pretext for yet another attack by those who have 'long laboured to represent me as one who was required by Your Lordship to retire form office in January last '. His resignation was almost a sacrifice to protect the Ministry from the attacks of his enemies who would use the Dowling verdict as a political weapon,

> I felt certain that if I remained in office after that verdict was had, a great effort would have been made to use the fact in order to embarrass the Ministry and I therefore at once determined to do all in my power to defeat that effort and accordingly without consultation or communication with anyone I resolved to ask Your Lordship to accept my resignation and this resolution I immediately carried into effect, and though the verdict in question has been since set aside I continue to think I was justified in retiring from office so that whatever might be the ultimate fate of that verdict, the Government could not become in any way affected by it.

Aberdeen's reply exonerated Sadleir from any wrong doing in the Kilconcouse case,[158] but did not mention the Dowling case, which continued to excite public comment since Dowling was still imprisoned while the various investigations impinging upon Sadleir were in progress. The newspapers were unwilling to condone the apparent legal incongruity between his continued incarceration and the findings of two courts in his favour. The *Daily Express,* quoted in the *Sligo Chronicle* of 20 May, condemned the legal system which allowed such a situation, and wondered if Dowling would eventually petition parliament to have Sadleir unseated. The Barons of the Exchequer again deliberated on the matter on 26 May and condemned Sadleir as the root of the unpleasant saga.[159] Nevertheless, they rejected counsel's motion for Dowling's discharge. This rested on a clear point of law. Any attempt to use the plot by Sadleir for Dowling's false imprisonment in July 1852 was inadmissable as a means of securing his release for non-payment of a debt. Dowling's dilemma was financial. He did not have any money and did not have the means of raising some. This was partly solved in November 1854 when Judge Crampton at a sitting of the Court of Queens Bench ordered the payment of the £1,100 awarded at the Carlow Assizes in March. Dowling received £700 and the remainder was paid to his attorney, McNamara Cantwell.[160]

While Sadleir was embroiled in political scandals there were signs that the Tipperary bank was beginning to unravel at shareholder level. This was evident towards the close of 1853 when important shareholders began to offload their shares. In November James B. Kennedy sold to William Austen who in turn sold to James Sadleir the following year.[161] Some months earlier Vincent Scully finally determined to get rid of his shares and confronted Sadleir in a letter of 13 September,

> As you are now in Dublin you can, I presume, make the necessary arrangements for definitely winding up all dealings between us. I am particularly anxious to leave the Tipperary Bank, being entirely ignorant of its affairs and having lost all confidence in its management.[162]

Sadleir parried with a promise that a wealthy capitalist named Goldsmid was willing to buy the shares, but by January 1854 had taken no steps to sell, which prompted Scully to require a postponement of the annual meeting to give him the opportunity of being present. His letter of 31 January demanded that his name be withdrawn as a nominal director, and revealed that other shareholders also wished to break this link with the bank, because of dissatisfaction with the Sadleirs' lack of accountability. He sent a similar letter to Wilson Kennedy as Public Officer. Kennedy refused to involve himself in the squabble but conceded that the dispute over the Kingston estate had been 'a serious injury to the Bank'.

James Sadleir's denial of Scully's accusation and his refusal to postpone the annual meeting provoked Scully to visit Sadleir in Gloucester Square. Under such pressure Sadleir signed an agreement on 8 August to purchase the 700 shares for £7000, payable on 1 July 1857.[163] These were transferred to Keating on 20 December 1854 to hold in trust for Sadleir until he had the money to pay for them. The transfer was not registered until 4 April 1855 which drew several letters from Scully complaining that it was 'monstrous to have to write so repeatedly about a single matter' and wondering 'how on earth do you get on at all with others if this is your way of managing serious business'.[164]

References

1. John Ball to Haly 24 February 1853. K.D.A., H.P., FH/1853/04, carton Bp 11.
2. Sadleir to Haly 9 March 1853, K.D.A., H.P., FH/1853/06, carton Bp 11.
3. *F.J.* 20,22, January 1853, *C.S.* 29 January 1853, *Tablet* 22, 29 January 1853.
4. See *Tablet* 5 March 1853 for his address to the Tralee electorate and ibid., 19 March 1853 for O'Connell's letter 15 February 1853 denying the Rumour.
5. The term used for an M.P. resigning his seat. It was a district in Buckinghamshire whose stewardship was a nominal office of the Crown, the temporary acceptance of which enabled an M.P. to vacate his seat.
6. p. 329 above.
7. British Museum, Aberdeen Papers, Add. MSS. 43248 – Aberdeen to Sadleir 24 January 1853 (f334).
8. See *F.J.* 22 January 1853 for Dunne's denial that he would step down.
9. Sadleir to Haly 10 March 1853, K.D.A., H.P.,FH/1853/07, carton Bp 11.
10. Whyte, *Independent Irish Party*, pp 107 *et. seq.* holds that the party was not badly damaged, but his statistics do not reflect the deep divisions among M.P.s.
11. Lucas, who corresponded frequently with Cullen, wrote on 1 March 1853 that the 'only hope' was to treat English parties according to their merits and keep them "bidding" for Irish support – D.D.A, Cullen Papers, Lucas to Cullen 1 March 1853.
12. *Tablet* 12, 19 February, I 5 March, 2 April 1853.
13. This gave rise to a sarcastic response from the *Telegraph* in the form of two letters from 'Old Nick' to 'Kit Kelly' – see e.g. *W.T.* 12 March 1853.
14. Keating's letter in *W.N.* 11 February 1853. The *Waterford News* was the only paper to carry the letter. This paper, however, was hostile to the defection – see *W.N.* 21 January 1853 which applauded the defeat of Sadleir and hoped that Keogh would suffer a similar fate.
15. *W.N.* 11 February 1853.
16. *Tablet* 5 February 1853 – E. Aylward p.p. Castlecomer, Co. Kilkenny, P. McLoughlin p.p. Kiltullagh, Co. Galway, B. Meyler p.p. Ferns, Co. Wexford, William Cahill c.c. Mullinahone, Co. Tipperary, John Brennan p.p. Warrenpoint, Co.Down, Thomas Byrne Oldcastle, Co. Meath, James Bermingham p.p. Borrisokane, Co. Tipperary, Walter Curran c.c. Portlaw, Co. Waterford.
17. Ibid., 21 May 1853. See also ibid., 2 July 1853 for a letter from P. Greene p.p. Kilavullen to Scully and Roche on pledges and ibid., 30 July 1853 for reference to a resolution by the priests of Coachford Deanery on the principles by which Scully was elected.

18. Ibid., 21 May 1853. Sadleir himself was unhappy about the substitution of income tax for the Irish consolidated annuities. He led a deputation of Irish M.P.s. to see Gladstone, the Chancellor of the Exchequer and succeeded in persuading him to apply the Income Tax to the immediate lessors, rather than the tenants, in rural areas. All farms paying an annual rent below £300 would be exempt. *W.T.* 4 June 1853.

19. Killaloe meeting in *Tablet* 9 April 1853, Cashel meeting in ibid., 16 April 1853, *W.T.* 16 April 1853.

20. *Tablet* 23 April 1853 for Scully's letter 18 April 1853 from the Reform Club and Sadleir"s letter 14 April 1853 from the Reform Club. See also *W.T.* 16 April 1853.

21. *Tablet* 5 March 1853.

22. *W.T.* 12 March 1853, *Tablet* 12 March 1853.

23. *W.T.* 12 March 1853, see also *Tablet* 19 March 1853 quoting a strong article from the *Nation.*

24. See e.g. *Tablet* 26 March 1853.

25. Ibid., 14 May 1853.

26. Ibid., 2 April 1853.

27. Ibid., 12 February 1853. The members were listed in ibid., 26 February 1853 and included contrasting figures like Palmerston, Naas, Walpole, Napier and Bright.

28. Report from the *Banner of Ulster* in *Tablet* 26 March 1853. The Committee eventually rejected Crawford's Bill, in particular the first clause which concerned tenant improvements, (*Tablet* 7 May 1853).

29. *Parl.Deb.*, series 3, vol.124, 1853, cols.38-40, (11 February 1853) for this exchange. See also *Tablet* 19 February 1853.

30. *Freeman's Journal* quoted in *Tablet* 19 February 1853, which also carried an extract from the *Cork Examiner* on similar lines. See also *Nation* 19 February 1853 for extracts from other papers.

31. *C.S.* 19 February 1853

32. Ibid., 26 February 1853.

33. *Parl. Deb.*, series 3, vol.124, 1853, cols.352-355 for Moore's question, col.355 for Russell's response, (21 February 1853).

34. Ibid., cols.356-357.

35. See T.D. Sullivan, *A record of Traitorism, or the Political Life and adventures of Mr Justice Keogh*, (Dublin,1891), pp15 et. seq. This work is an uncritical rehash of material published in the *Nation* in the 1850s.

36. Details of the evidence and Keogh's financial difficulties in *Minutes of Evidence taken before the Select Committee on the Athlone Election Petition*, H.C. 1852-53(383)V111, *passim,* (henceforth *Athlone Election Petition*). See also *Report from the Select Committee on the Athlone Election Petition with the Minutes of the Proceedings*, H.C. 1852-53(321)V111 passim, (henceforth *Athlone Election Petition Report*), see *Tablet* 16 April 1853, *W.T.* 16 April 1853.

37. *Tablet* 16 April 1853.

38. McMahon to Duffy 5 March 1853. N.L.I., Duffy Papers, MS. 5737.

39. *Tablet* 2 April 1853.

40. *W.T* . 16 April 1853. See *A.S.* 12 January 1853 for anger in the borough at the League's initial discussion of sending a deputation there. One meeting of electors was held (according to the notice calling it) to repel the 'foul, lying and slanderous assertions of Messrs. Gray, Lucas and Co. against the Athlone constituency'. This meeting was attended by several priests. By that stage Keogh, the local priests and some electors had been entertained by the Bishop at dinner. The League did, however send a deputation, consisting of Lucas, Gray, Duffy

and Moore, to Clonmel for the 1853 by-election when John O'Connell the candidate, was unwilling to support the policy of Independent opposition. For details of this see *Tablet* 12, 26 November 1853, *W.T.* 12, 26 November 1853.

41. Quoted in *Tablet* 16 April 1853.
42. Nomination proceedings in ibid., 23 April 1853.
43. Ibid.,
44. *Parl. Deb.*, series 3, vol.127, col.945, (31 May 1853). *Tablet* 4 June 1853.
45. British Museum, Aberdeen Papers, Add. MSS 43520, ff 131-140, for letters of resignation, 2 June 1853 from Monsell, Keogh and Sadleir.
46. *W.T.* 4 June 1853.
47. *F.J.* 4 June 1853.
48. e.g. *Sligo Champion* 11 June 1853 carried reports from the *Morning Herald* which in turn had quoted the *Observer.*
49. *W.T.* 4 June 1853.
50. British Museum, Aberdeen Papers, MS 43250, ff 131-134, Aberdeen to Monsell 3 June 1853.
51. see e.g. *Tablet* 11 June 1853, *W.T.* 11 June 1853, *Sligo Champion* 11 June 1853, for text.
52. British Museum, Aberdeen Papers, Add. MSS 43250, f 146, Aberdeen to Sadleir 3 June 1856. (This file also contains a similar letter to Keogh.
53. *W.T.* 11 June 1853.
54. *Tablet* 11 June 1853. The reference made by Lucas was to an editorial in the *Freeman's Journal* 7 June 1853 headed 'returning to their vomit'. In this Gray pointed out that prior to the taking of office by Sadleir and Keogh it was common knowledge that Aberdeen and Russell did not agree on the religious questions so that their government was in effect based upon a compromise regarding such issues.
55. Lucas to Cullen 10 June 1853, D.D.A., Cullen Papers. (Lucas mistakenly dated his letter Friday 10 May, but the reference to the resignation indicates that the date should be Friday 10 June. See *Tablet* 9 July 1853 for further condemnation of Phillips by Lucas.
56. A vacancy had also arisen for the borough of Tralee at which, according to the *Freeman's Journal*, Sadleir looked 'most wistfully'. Gray was definite that Sadleir was a candidate, as yet unrevealed, for Tralee.
57. For details see *Sligo Borough Petition, Petition of John Patrick Somers*, H.C. 1852-53 (600) XVIII passim, (henceforth *Sligo Borough Petition*). See also *S.J.* 3 June 1853, *S.C.* 4 June 1853, Sligo News 6 June 1853. Abstracts of police reports to Dublin Castle show a high level of intimidation in Sligo during the general election of 1852, a pattern also found in other counties – see N.L.I., Mayo (Naas) Papers, abstracts of police reports, MS. 11037(28), see also MS. 11034 for an incident in the Reform Club, London, between Keogh and Somers.
58. *Sligo Champion* 20 June 1853.
59. Phillips' nomination speech in *W.T.* 19 July 1853. John Gray was also nominated at this meeting but failed to get a seconder – *Sligo Champion* 13 June 1853.
60. *Sligo Champion* 6 June 1853, *Tablet* 11 June 1853.
61. Editorial in *F.J.* 10 June 1853. Gray used Sadleir's address as proof that not only was he similar to Towneley in terms of using his wealth to bribe electors but that his political principles were, like Towneley's, those of a Whig. Gray sought to use the 'mock resignations' against Sadleir's aspirations of success in Sligo – 'Let the Bishop, the clergy, the people of Sligo then have him if they will, but let it be known what they are doing. Mr. Sadleir has no longer a mask to wear. Lord

Aberdeen has removed the last shred of it'.

62.	Ibid., 18 June 1853.
63.	*S.J.* 1 July 1853, *Sligo Champion* 27 June 1853, *S.C.* 2 July 1853.
64.	Sadleir's letter in *Sligo Champion* 5 September 1853. See ibid., 12 September 1853 for an article on this and for a list of contributors. Towneley also contributed fifty pounds.
65.	*F.J.* 7 July 1853, *Tablet* 9 July 1853 for their meeting in the Hibernian Hotel. The priests involved were Owen Feeney p.p. v.f.. Riverstown, Thomas Hibbitts O.S.D., Dominick Noone p.p. Geevagh, Michael D. McEvoy O.S.D., George Gearty p.p. Killinumerry, Bernard J. Goodman O.S.D., Edward Henry p.p. Aughana, Peter Lee c.c. Killinumerry.
66.	Letter 20 July 1853 in *Tablet* 30 July 1853. See *F.J.* 7 July 1853 for an unusually severe editorial from Gray on the 'hideous iniquity of electing Sadleir'.
67.	*S.J.* 8 July 1853. (The election rallies were poorly reported in the newspapers).
68.	*S.J.* 24 June 1853.
69.	Ibid., 2 July 1853.
70.	*S.C.* 30 July 1853.
71.	Address in *Sligo Champion* 17 June 1853, *S.C.* 18 June 1853.
72.	*S.J.* 24 June 1853.
73.	*W.T.* 9 July 1853, *S.J.* 1 July 1853.
74.	Extract from the *Nation* in *Sligo Champion* 11 June 1853. It also quoted from the *Freeman's Journal* . See also *Tablet* 11 June 1853 for another extract from the *Freeman's*.
75.	*Tablet* 11 June 1853.
76.	*W.T.* 11 June 1853.
77.	*Tablet* 9 July 1853.
78.	*W.T.* 9 July 1853, *S.C* . 9 July 1853, *Sligo Champion* 11 July 1853.
79.	Phillips's letter in *W.T.* 16 July 1853. This letter was signed by fifteen others including John Gore Jones, Barrister, later Resident Magistrate in County Tipperary and a strong supporter of Sadleir. J.B. Kennedy signed as did Thomas Strickland. See ibid., for a letter 11 July 1853 from A.B. Kelly, the *Telegraph's* reporter confirming that the speeches reported in the *Freeman's* were never made.
80.	Letter 10 July 1853 from Patrick Henry O'Connor in *W.T* . 16 July 1853.
81.	The poll results were 150 votes for Sadleir and 142 for Somers. A list of those who voted for both candidates was given in *S.C.* 9 July 1853.
82.	Speech in *W.T.* 9 July 1853.
83.	Ibid.,
84.	Ibid., 16 July 1853.
85.	Ibid., 9 July 1853.
86.	*S.J.* 29 July 1853.
87.	*Sligo Champion* 22 August 1853.
88.	*Parl. Deb.*, series 3, vol.129, 1853, col.1818, (19 August 1853).
89.	His response in ibid., cols. 1818-1819.
90.	*Tablet* 29 October 1853.
91.	Court proceedings in ibid., 26 November 1853, *F.J.* 17 December 1853 gave a clear resume of the saga from the general election of 1852.
92.	See p. above. See also *Tablet* 24, 31 December 1853.
93.	Whiteside was a formidable advocate and orator. He was born in 1804 at Delgany, Co. Wicklow, where his father was a curate. He was a graduate of Trinity College and was called to the bar in 1830. He became a queen's counsel

in 1842 and defended O'Connell at the state trials in 1843 and William Smith O'Brien in 1848. He was elected for Enniskillen in 1851 and Trinity in 1859. In 1852 he was appointed Irish Solicitor General under the Derby administration when his brother-in-law, Joseph Napier was Attorney General. In 1866 he succeeded Thomas F. Lefroy as Irish Chief Justice of the Queen's Bench. He died at Brighton in 1876, *D.N.B.*, ev.

94. *Dowling* , p. 7.
95. Ibid., pp 60-67 for Sadleir's evidence.
96. Ibid., pp.115 et. seq.
97. See *Tablet* 7 January 1854 for comments from the *Press, Wexford People, Munster News, Limerick Examiner, Wexford Guardian, Sligo Chronicle*.
98. Dempsey's letter in *S.C.* 14 January 1854 and *Tablet* 7 January 1854.
99. See *Tablet's* comment 7 January and 4 February 1854. The article of 7 January was a lengthy defence of his stand by Lucas and a denial that he had accused Dempsey of perjury.
100. British Museum, Aberdeen Papers, Add. MSS. 43521, ff 326-330, Young to Aberdeen 4 January 1854.
101. Sadleir would continue to represent Sligo.
102. British Museum, Aberdeen Papers, Add MSS. 43521, f322, Sadleir to Aberdeen 4 January 1854.
103. British Museum, Aberdeen Papers, Add. MSS. 43252, f35, Aberdeen to Sadleir 7 January 1854.
104. The leading Leaguers had been planning a parliamentary onslaught on Sadleir with a view to forcing his resignation. Moore had been chosen to manage a motion.
105. Lucas to Moore 3 January 1854 in N.L.I., Moore papers, MS 892, letter 434.
106. Chief Baron Pigot.
107. Lucas to Moore 8 January 1854 in N.L.I., Moore Papers, MS 892, letter 435.
108. J.C. to Naas, Christmas Day 1853 in N.L.I., Naas papers, MS. 11017(8). This individual urged Naas to choose an M.P. to raise the matter in Parliament and to 'get the press to thunder forth and work the topic'.
109. *W.T.* 4, 11 February 1854.
110. pp 386-9 below.
111. *W.T.* 16 February 1856.
112. See MacDonagh, *The Victorian Bank*, p. 41 on the Bank of Ireland scheme.
113. Letter 6 February 1854 in *Tablet* 11 February 1854. (Cantwell had taken over the case following Dowling's arrest).
114. Fr. J. Kinsella, Killegin, to Haly 18 October 1853, K.D.A., H.P., carton Bp 11. Kinsella asked Haly to contact Sadleir and assured him that when it became known 'that this deserving young man shall have been provided for it will, I think, be acknowledged that a member of Parliament has never acted more prudently than in taking the suggestion of a Bishop in this regard, and rest assured that gratitude will not be less desirable than the general approval of the appointment'.
115. See ibid., 14 January 1854.
116. See ibid., 11, 18 February 1854.
117. Its report was published in June 1854. See *Minutes of Evidence taken before the Select Committee on Complaint, together with the Proceedings of the Committee and Minutes of Evidence*, H.C. 1854(314)VIII, passim. (Henceforth *Corruption Committee*). See also *Tablet* 11, 18, 25 March and 1 April 1854.
118. *Tablet* 11, 18, March 1854.

119. *Corruption Committee*, pp 195 et.seq.
120. Ibid., pp 216-217 for Scully's evidence.
121. *Tablet* 18 March 1854.
122. *Corruption Committee* , p. 286.
123. Ibid., p. 453.
124. *Tablet* 18 March 1854.
125. Ibid., 25 February 1854.
126. *Parl. Deb.*, series 3, vol.130, 1854, cols. 289 et. seq., (6 February 1854), *Tablet* 11 February 1854.
127. See *Report from the Select Committee on the Sligo Borough Petition, together with the proceedings of the Committee and Minutes of Evidence*, H.C.1854(78)VIII.625 passim. (Henceforth *Sligo Borough Election Committee*).
128. Lascelles was replaced by William Deedes, Conservative member for East Kent. (Seymour, Conservative, Dorsett; Lascelles, Conservative, Ripon, Ingham Liberal for South Shields; Roebuck Reform Sheffield; Egerton Conservative North Cheshire).
129. Their evidence in *Sligo Borough Election Committee*, pp 637-641 and 646-648. Evidence of Cullen's father on pp 631-637 and of Rutledge's father-in-law on pp 641-644.
130. Henry Simpson's evidence in ibid., pp 648-661 and James Simpson's evidence on pp 661-668.
131. Gethin's evidence in ibid pp 668-677.
132. Ibid., p. 638.
133. Ibid., pp 627-628.
134. *Tablet* 1 April 1854.
135. Walker's evidence in *Sligo Borough Election Committee*, pp 677-679.
136. Pigott, Greene and Richards.
137. *W.T.* 25 February 1854.
138. The case was heard on 10, 13 March – see *Dowling*, pp 125-130, *W.T.* 18 March 1854, *Tablet* 18 March 1854.
139. James Henry Monahan 1804-1878. Born in Portumna, County Galway. Became a Q.C. in 1840 and a leading counsel in Chancery cases. Appointed Irish Solicitor General in 1846 under the Russell administration and was elected M.P. for Galway Borough in 1847. Appointed Irish Attorney General in 1847. Became Chief Justice of the Common Pleas in 1850, a position he held until 1876. In 1867 he presided over a special commission for the trial of Fenian prisoners in Cork and Limerick. *D.N.B.*, e.v.. under Monahan James Henry, also F.E. Ball, *The Judges in Ireland 1221 – 1921*, (New York, 1927), p. 290.
140. Baring, Liberal Portsmouth; East, Conservative, Winchester; Ellice, Liberal, St. Andrews; King, Conservative, East Surrey; Phillips, Independent Conservative, Haverfordwest.
141. See *Tablet* 25 March 1854.
142. *Sligo Borough Petition*, pp 615,687,723, *S.J.* 3rd June 1853, *Sligo Champion* 18 June 1853.
143. MacTernan to Moore, n.d. (letter 441.), N.L.I., Moore Papers, MS. 892.
144. Moore's statements in *Parl. Deb.*, series 3, vol.131 cols.688-689, 692 and cols.973-955, (13 and 17 March 1854).
145. Ibid., cols.985-986, (17 March 1854) for the exchange between Sadleir and the speaker.
146. See ibid., cols.689-691,856-857, 976, (13, 16, 17 March 1854).
147. *Parl. Deb.*, series 3, cols. 527-534. (Lucas's speech in cols.555-558).

148. Gladstone's statement in ibid., cols. 534-540.
149. The Committee was made up of members from different parties. Sotherton, Conservative, North Wiltshire; Carter, Liberal, Winchester; Gaskell, Conservative, Wenlock Borough, Horsman was independent Liberal for Stroud, Duckworth, Conservative, Exeter.
150. *Parl. Deb.*, series 3, vol.133, 1854, cols. 165-169, (11 May 1854).
151. *Report of the Select Committee on Henry Stonor, together with the Proceedings of the Committee, Minutes of Evidence and Appendix.* H.C. 1854(278)VIII passim, (henceforth *Stonor Committee*), see also *W.T.* 28 October 1854 for a letter 30 June 1854 from Stonor to the *Sydney Argus* outlining the affair and defending himself.
152. *Stonor Committee*, p. 686.
153. Evidence of the Earl of Donoughmore in the House of Lords – *Parl. Deb.*, series 3, vol.134, 1854, cols.599-603, (23 June 1854).
154. McMahon's evidence in *W.T.* 20 January 1855. For a comprehensive insight into the Kilconcouse affair see *Report from the Select Committee of the House of Lords appointed to inquire into the Management of the Crown Estates of Kilconcouse in the King's County, and into the circumstances attending the occupation of a portion thereof by the Rev. Francis McMahon P.P. of Kinnitty; together with the proceedings of the Committee, and Minutes of Evidence.* H.C. 1854 XXII.3 (192). (Henceforth *Kilconcouse*).
155. i.e. *Kilconcouse* above, see *Parl. Deb.*, series 3, vol. 134, (23 June 1854), cols. 603-604 for Aberdeen's response.
156. *W.T.* 1 July 1854.
157. Sadleir to Aberdeen 23 May 1854 in Aberdeen Papers, British Museum, Add. MSS. 43253, ff140-142.
158. Aberdeen to Sadleir 25 May 1854 in ibid., f151.
159. *Tablet* 3 June 1854.
160. Ibid., 18 November 1854.
161. *C.T.* 5 July 1856.
162. *L.E.* 3 May 1856, *W.T.* 3 May 1856, see also *I.C.R. 1856 and 1857*, vol 6, p. 72 et. seq. for some of Scully's correspondence between 1853 and 1855.
163. *I.C.R. 1856 and 1857*, vol 6, p. 73.
164. Scully's letters and Sadleir's replies in *L.E.* 3 May 1856, *W.T.* 3 May 1856.

Chapter 12

Prince of swindlers –
November 1854-February 1856

Sadleir was a tough-minded individual and it is unlikely that the tribunal investigations of 1854 made a deep impact upon him. The ruin of his political ambitions because of the Dowling scandal, however, was a different matter. His opponents celebrated his downfall as the timely undermining of an elaborate scheme to set up a network of political corruption with its roots in the Treasury itself. But the assertion of the journalist David Morier Evans[1] that his resignation was forced because of irregularities at the Treasury[2] is not supported by the Aberdeen correspondence. Had he not been forced to resign it is likely that he would have held his position when Aberdeen left office in February 1855. Sadleir may have defeated Palmerston's protege in the Sligo by-election of 1853, but when Palmerston succeeded as Premier only the Peelite section resigned. Keogh was not asked to step down as Solicitor General, but was promoted to Irish Attorney General on the resignation of Abraham Brewester.[3] His promotion was endorsed by the Athlone electorate in March and Bishop Browne demonstrated the strongest possible approval of office taking by proposing him on nomination day.

Sadleir can only have been pleased at his friend's progress towards the bench,[4] and attention was diverted from his predicament by a remarkable conflict that developed between the leading Leaguers[5] and a powerful section of the Catholic Church at the end of 1854. This originated in the suspension of O'Keeffe and O'Shea by Bishop Edmund Walsh of Ossory, and a move to curb the political activity of priests especially in the Archdiocese of Dublin. At a Callan meeting in late October Lucas announced his intention of going to the Vatican with a petition against these restrictions.[6] From there the movement gathered momentum and anger at Cullen and Walsh was publicly aired in Thurles the following month, when Lucas, Moore, Duffy and Richard Swift, Sligo County, attended a meeting which attracted twenty-four priests from the Archdiocese of Cashel and Emly.[7] Ostensibly it was called to discuss the land question, but the threat to priestly political involvement was the main theme.

Moore dominated with an outspoken attack upon the two prelates. He drew an amusing biblical analogy between the role of priests in politics and the political interference of the angel 'who warned the Holy Family of their danger' from 'that model Lord Lieutenant – Herod of Judea'. He had no doubt that 'the High priest of the day, if he had been able, would have suspended him in the performance of his angelic functions'. The priests' role in the struggle for tenant right was part of their ministry of defending the poor. This conviction was accompanied by an equally strong castigation of any bishop who sought to limit that pastoral role. While he did not openly name Cullen, Moore's inference of foreign influences at work in the Irish Church was clear enough, and was a powerful if indiscreet attack made in the episcopal seat of Cashel and Emly,

> What then are we to think of those who forbid the clergy to do their duty to the people – who make it a crime in a priest to watch over and warn his flock – who, to use the language of Richard Sheil, would place a padlock upon his lips, although they cannot stop the throbbings of his big and indignant heart? What are we to think of those who would sever the priest from his flock, and who seek to put asunder those whom God and country, and common struggles, and mutual faith, and love have bound for ages together? I will not undertake to answer that question just as yet – the more so, as the question lies deeper and darker than any of us yet have been able to fathom. But it is well known that a dark and fatal influence is creeping at this moment through the Church of our fathers in a shape and attitude which is strange to us, and which we have long believed that the founder of our Church had banished for ever from our soil – which walks not as we walk, but "creeps on its belly all the days of its life" – which speaks not in our tongue, but whispers in foreign phrase, in the ears of our sleeping Church, things of which she is naked.

Sadleir did not comment on this controversy but his newspaper saw it as a means of upholding its own Catholicity and denouncing its opponents as anti-Church and anti-hierarchy.[8] McCabe traced the movement's progression from Callan, 'an out of the way town of the County Kilkenny' to Thurles 'the seat of the venerable and universally beloved Archbishop of Cashel'.[9] Both Lucas and Swift had sat on the Corruption Committee, and McCabe used their presence in Thurles to denigrate both the Committee and the League.[10] He was also aware of Cullen's antipathy towards Young Irelandism, and devoted an article of 23 December to the Young Ireland element in the dispute.[11] He drew a parallel between this and a controversy in the United States between Mitchel Doheny and a section of the priests. With some ingenuity he continued to link all of this with the penal days and Archbishop Oliver Plunkett,

> Under the mask of politics an attack is made, as we conceive, on Catholicity in Ireland, in the assaults now especially aimed at the good Bishop of Ossory, and the pious Archbishop of Dublin. It is a renewal under another form of the attacks made upon the last martyr to the Penal Laws, the saintly Archbishop Plunkett; and it is strange how like in many particulars are the persecutors of the two Archbishops. The witnesses against Archbishop Plunkett, like the accusers of our Archbishop and Bishops, were in their day "flaming patriots!" "Independent Opposition" gentlemen – ballad mongers of the Shan Van Voght school – nay, they even had a Ballingarry of their own.

The *Telegraph* was rewarded for its defence of the hierarchy by a letter from Bishop Walsh of 21 December. McCabe was well pleased that the bishop had used the paper to make a public stand against 'an insolent and unscrupulous cabal, composed of nominal Catholics, undisguised heretics, semi-infidels, or infuriated partisans'. The bishop was finally provoked, not so much by the public meetings as by the contents of the petitions to Rome which were 'hawked about for signatures'. Two memorials were forwarded via Lucas, one from a group of M.P.s and one from the Irish clergy representing little more than 5% of their total body.[12] The former was signed only by seven representatives – Lucas, Moore, Duffy, Swift, McMahon, Maguire and John Brady, Leitrim. The majority of priests were from Cashel and Emly, Meath, Tuam and Achonry. The memorials were similar in content, and elaborated upon the importance of independent opposition and the support of some 'Whig' bishops for the defection of Sadleir and Keogh. Both Cullen and Walsh were cited as belonging to this Whig episcopal school.[13]

Walsh smarted at this label. He repudiated the 'false and calumnious statements' of the memorials and condemned the press for defaming him. Far from being a Whig bishop he always abstained from political involvement or seeking the favours of any political party. He denied that this in any way indicated lack of sympathy with his flock, but was an indication that his pastoral duty was not a political one. On the other hand he did not seek to interfere with the civil rights of his priests, but only to curb the abuse of such rights by the two politically intemperate priests.

Cullen was not so meek. He perfectly understood the Pope's mind. Pius was hardly interested in the meaning of independent opposition, but he appreciated the contents of Cullen's memorandum in Italian linking Duffy with revolution.[14] Cullen portrayed the *Nation* as the supporter of Mazzini and Kossuth. Lucas could not be identified with Young Irelandism, but was presented as one who wished to undermine episcopal authority.

Cullen was in Rome when Lucas arrived, and had already briefed Cardinal Barnabo, the Secretary of Propaganda, on the affair. The courteous reception of Lucas by Barnabo and by the Pope himself was no more than common diplomacy and the memorials met with no response. The dispute, however, sapped the energy of the leading Leaguers and diverted their attention from the land question. Improving economic conditions in the mid 1850's also weakened the League. Shee, whose relationship with the organisation deteriorated, was the main promoter of land legislation in 1855. The Tenants' Compensation Bill, debated from May until July, was a considerably watered down version of Crawford's bill, and various amendments rendered it almost valueless, so that even Irish M.P.s were relieved when it was withdrawn.

It went through thirty divisions and Sadleir was present for twenty-six of these.[15] But, apart from voting he took little part in the debates. His only real involvement was on the deletion of clause 14, which proposed compensating evicted tenants for improvements carried out during their tenancy. This clause was opposed by several cabinet members who abstained in the vote.[16] In an unprecedented move eighteen Irish M.P.s, including the two Sadleirs and the two Scullys, went to Palmerston in August requesting its re-instatement.[17] Some of the English M.P.s were scandalised by this breach of protocol in seeking to have a clause restored which had been defeated by the democratic parliamentary process. One categorised it as disgraceful and disgusting,[18] and was immediately reprimanded by Sadleir on the irrelevant grounds that the deputation did not represent any party, but was a group of individuals 'influenced only by a wish to have restored to the bill a clause which they considered of the utmost importance to the interests of Ireland'.[19] Independent oppositionists had no qualms about protocol, but condemned the deputation for a different reason. Maguire predictably argued that an independent course in the House was the only way to gain concessions.[20] Vincent Scully reacted with some cynicism to this because independent opposition leaders had been absent from the division on the disputed clause.

Sadleir's paper elaborated in considerable detail upon Scully's observation. It published a table showing how Irish members had voted on each of the thirty divisions.[21] This was accompanied by an article drawing attention to particular M.P.s including, not surprisingly, Duffy, Lucas and Moore,

Among those absent from the division on the fourteenth clause, we may particularise no fewer than six out of the "Seven pseudo-Champions of Christendom,"namely-

1. Mr. C.G. Duffy, who was occupied in giving himself a "ticket-of-leave" at his Dublin Tenant League;

2. Mr. George Henry Moore, who was occupied in processing his tenantry at Partree;

3. Mr. Patrick McMahon, absent at his petty sessions at Brentford;

4 Mr. Fitzstephen French, coloneling it in Roscommon;

5. Mr. Martin Joseph Blake, vegetating at Ballygluine; and, last but not least,

6. Mr. Frederick Lucas, who was indisposed to be present.

The reader of these Tables cannot fail to remark, as a very curious illustration of how unprincipled was the agitation carried on in Ireland during the last winter, under the pretence of "Tenant Right," that the very men who made use of "Tenant Right" as a pretext for exciting clergy and people against their bishops – not one of them attended in his place in Parliament to vote for the clause (the 14th) involving Tenant Right. Mr. Duffy, Mr. Lucas, and Mr. G.H. Moore were absent from that division. Mr. Duffy, Mr. Lucas and Mr. Moore – who were at Callan, or Thurles, or Wexford, making speeches about Bishops under the name of Tenant Right – did not, when they could have voted for it.

While his newspaper continued to engage in such controversies with his adversaries, Sadleir practically abandoned political life except to promote in parliament the cause of the East Kent line.[22] The construction of a bridge over the Medway at Rochester was proving more expensive than anticipated, a problem compounded by the interruption of investment by the Crimean War, and the directors found it difficult to raise further funds.[23] Late in 1854 Sir David Salomons, who had invested immense personal energy into the project, resigned as Deputy Chairman.[24] The *Railway Times* greeted his resignation with satisfaction, but refrained from comment on the appointment of Sadleir as his successor.[25]

Sadleir however, tacitly endorsed its view that directors should shoulder the blame for the slow progress of the line. He chaired the half-yearly meeting in the London Tavern in February 1855, and encouraged a more energetic approach on their part.[26] His own dynamism was reflected in his rejection of negative overtones among the directorate because of the problem, and in a threat to withdraw from the company if full co-operation was not forthcoming,

He could only say for himself that if he should find those efforts which he thought they were bound to make to proceed with the undertaking in a broader and bolder spirit than heretofore – if he should find those efforts were unavailing to secure the arrangements essential for that end, he felt to remain a member of that board would be to continue in a false position, and they must consider him, as under such circumstances, withdrawing from any control with reference to this undertaking. Having stated the readiness of the board to supply any information that might be required by the shareholders, the hon. gentleman went on to remark that he was sure they were animated with but one spirit with regard to his undertaking, and that they would not hastily broach any subject which might temporarily affect the position or calibre of the company as a commercial undertaking. There were companies in this country in which gentlemen holding only a small stake were too much in the habit of addressing questions which, for any practical purposes, were pointless, and too frequently it had no other effect than to throw a momentary shade over the operations of the undertaking with which they were identified.

While Salomons denied that the directors had been remiss, Sadleir received the support of the influential Sir John Tylden, who not only endorsed the viewpoint of the new Deputy Chairman, but praised his willingness to invest heavily in the line and to promote its progress.[27] His promotion intensified in mid-1855, when, partly due to Sadleir's efforts, parliament released the original guarantee deposit of £50,000 specifically to complete the Medway Bridge.[28] A bill facilitating the extension to Dover received its third reading in June.[29] That month Sadleir travelled as part of a deputation to Dover to raise finance there.[30] A public meeting chaired by the Mayor endorsed the project, and at the end of the month Sadleir was the principal speaker at a special shareholders' meeting in London to promote support for the bill before Parliament. He was optimistic of ultimate success because the government, and allegedly the public, realised that the line was as much a military as a commercial advantage.[31] He was dismissive of the South Eastern's opposition as 'very feeble', and chided the *Railway Times* for its cynicism. By August, however, he was condemning the 'fierce if not unmitigated hostility of the South Eastern', which had tried to thwart parliament's decision to release the £50,000 deposit.[32]

He could have added that the *Railway Times* was equally unmitigating in its criticism. An editorial of 24 November was skeptical of the venture's success,

Encouraged by the aid it has already received from Government, flattered perhaps by the pecuniary prospects of making a line into Dover citadel, the directors of the East Kent wax fat and rich. They have forgotten the condition of their subscription list : they appear to despise the responsibilities that are already incurred. They stretch out their feelers in fourteen directions, and insanely imagine that in none of them shall they receive any hurt. It is not always good, certainly, to have friends in court, who proverbially like not to be relied on overmuch.

At that stage Sadleir favoured the formation of a strong consortium to ensure the rapid completion of the line, but by then he was increasingly engrossed by other more pressing financial difficulties of his own. The years 1854 and especially 1855 were ruinous to him, and passed in a merry-go-round of disastrous speculations accompanied by dubious methods of meeting his financial problems.

He had borrowed a large sum of money from the Carson's Creek Gold Mining Company, which was due for repayment in January 1855. Unable to do so he offered his Ballylanders estate in Co. Limerick as security and lodged the deed of conveyance in the London and County, where he had easy access to it. He removed it without the permission or knowledge of the directors and used it as security to raise money elsewhere.[33] Such assignment of property was frequently used by him, and by 1854 a large proportion of his lands was heavily encumbered. In July 1854, for example, he transferred lands to his cousin William Francis Eyre, Paris, in return for a loan of £7,000.[34] This was urgently required to help pay for the Glengall estate, officially known as the Kilcommon estate, which Sadleir had purchased from the Incumbered Estates Court at the end of 1853. The estate included Cahir House, Cahir Castle, and a demesne of 779 acres.[35] The sale was vigorously resisted by the Glengalls, and by bidding against Sadleir Lady Glengall drove the price to £67,970 which he found difficult to raise.[36] The Incumbered Estates Commission refused to grant him extra time, and he was forced to borrow not only from William Francis Eyre, but raised a mortgage through the Albion Insurance Company.[37]

The conveyance of the estate was finally registered in May,[38] but in October 1854 Sadleir was forced to assign 14,000 acres to Thomas J. Eyre who by then had loaned him a total of £52,000.[39] While he was the individual to whom Sadleir was most heavily indebted the two main sources of borrowing were the Tipperary and the London and County. At the close of 1854 his overdraft in the Tipperary stood at £145,000, although at that time he was trying to persuade investors to put money in German mines.[40] Several months later this increased to almost £200,000 placing the bank in severe danger.[41] In June 1855 Wilson Kennedy, the bank's Public Officer, who protested in vain against further advances, decided to sever his connection with it, and sold all his shares to James Sadleir for £500, which he later claimed was only half their value.[42] James Sadleir agreed to buy them, not because of their value, but because he feared that his brother's overdraft might become public knowledge in the event of a dispute with Kennedy.

By then James was seriously concerned about John's ability to meet the repayments. Sadleir, however, was unrelenting in his demands for advances. On 6 March he extracted a promise from the directors of the London and County to discount a bill of the Tipperary for £20,000, although he had not yet approached James Sadleir about it.[43] The latter was incensed and refused to accept the bill. He replied by return,

> My Dear John – What do you mean? You wrote you lodged £3,000 at Glyn[44] and Co's on Saturday evening, and not one penny to credit, and all you have lodged is £5,000 to pay £15,000 last week; so that the other credits, which you have advice of, must be refused. I would not be burthened with your constant lies any longer. You may provide for the credit or let it alone. Until I see the money ordered lodged I will not accept the £20,000, or move in it. Your constant lying is worse than anything else, and very little would make me send back the £5,000 odd cheques this day, after Keating's. In fact, your doings and impertinence beat anything.[45]

Keating was equally worried and on 8 March called to see Josiah Wilkinson, a partner in the law firm, Wilkinson, Stevens and Gurney of Nicholas Lane, which was solicitor to the London bank and also an agent for many of Sadleir's financial transactions. Keating hoped that Wilkinson might be able to induce Sadleir to sell some of his Irish estates to ease the financial crisis. Whether by accident or design the latter arrived in the office that day, and they succeeded in persuading him to sell and to write a letter empowering Keating to organise the sale.[46]

While these negotiations were in progress James Sadleir sent a further angry letter to his brother reprimanding him for his 'roguish' and 'disgraceful' conduct,

> I consider your ruin, as you call it, of very little consequence. I hear of R. Keating's coming to Dublin, and to-morrow or after coming down the country to look for J.B. Kennedy, who was here this day. I told him what we would now require – the fullest legal authority to Wilson Kennedy and myself to sell all property, as we think proper, to pay your debts to this bank, James B. Kennedy to be our solicitor; and I expect we will require at least one or two more with him, besides two or three clerks – you to sit down and look at us, as I consider you quite incapable and quite unfit. We will have nothing to say to Mr. Keating, for he could not do it; nor does he know how soon he may have to pay money in some cases. I am certain you bungled every property you had to do with. The sooner a legal letter to this effect comes into my hands the better, and I will expect it here on Wednesday morning, the latest, and will then submit it to J.B. Murphy here, if good so far, and to prepare a deed on it

at once. Then we should be put into possession of all debts due, if any, besides the bank, and all assets on hands, &c, and all title deeds handed up to us. This letter should be in a legal form, or I will not accept the bill. The cheque for £10,500 came here. I will hold until Wednesday morning, and if vested by full powers by legal letter on Wednesday morning to dispose of all your property as Mr. Kennedy and I think proper, to pay all debts due to the bank in the first instance, and all moneys got from the bank for your account or in the name of other's, such as Gould's account, Mr. Clintock's account, Kingston, &c. Your debts to the bank are about £170,000.[47]

By the time Sadleir received this letter Keating had arrived in Clonmel to draw up an agreement conveying Sadleir's land as security for this overdraft. On 12 March Keating, William and James Sadleir and James B. Kennedy, drew up a memorandum of agreement which was finalised and checked by counsel on 15 March.[48] This gave Keating and James Sadleir full power to sell Sadleir's land. But, contrary to Kennedy's advice James Sadleir instructed him not to register the agreement lest his brother's credit be injured. His mind now at ease he gave Keating the bill for £20,000 which Sadleir had earlier requested.

Keating, however, was frustrated by the haggling that took place, and on his return to London informed Wilkinson that he would not have any further involvement in Sadleir's affairs. Wilkinson was unaware of the extent of Sadleir's indebtedness to the Tipperary, and presumed that the sale of his lands was for the benefit of the London and County. Keating did not enlighten him. Neither did he fulfil his duty as a director of the London bank by informing its board of the Clonmel agreement. Instead he reassured Farmery John Law, a fellow director, that the lands would be sold to pay Sadleir's debt to the London bank.

In reality Sadleir had little intention of selling his lands. He soon told Wilkinson that the arrangement had been abandoned, because he had other means of raising money. These, however, did not materialise and he again turned to the London bank for assistance. He met the chief accountant in May, and assured him that he intended putting a proposition to the board for the further working of his account.[49] At the June board meeting he told his fellow directors that there was a delay in selling his lands, and successfully sought an advance of £25,000 for three months, £20,000 of which would be repaid from the proceeds of the recent sale of the Kingston estates. The Tipperary would issue a bill of exchange for £25,000 to be cashed by the London bank. He also proposed to deposit with the bank the deeds of the Coolnamuck estate as further security.[50]

The advance was soon swallowed and on 24 July he applied for an extra £15,000. Only then were the directors fully alive to his predicament. They not only refused, but withdrew his cheque book and froze his current account.[51] That day, however, James met the board and managed to get the money on the security of his twenty one day promissory note. The following day he met a special committee of the board to secure a more comprehensive arrangement for Sadleir. He was well aware that the fate of his brother and that of the Tipperary bank were inextricably linked. He requested an advance of £95,000, grossly understated the overdraft in the Tipperary bank as £40,000, and concealed the Clonmel agreement of 15 March laying claim to Sadleir's lands. The directors had no reason to disbelieve him, assuming that he would not damage an institution in which he had so personal and so profitable a stake.

Wilkinson was requested by the committee to prepare a report on Sadleir's lands for a special board meeting of 31 July. This report merely described the securities according to James Sadleir's statement of their nature and value. It made no other comment except to recommend the deal. The committee accepted the recommendation. At first sight this seemed preposterous, but they saw it as an opportunity for the bank to avoid serious losses by securing a grip on the estates. The board adopted its resolution that there was sufficient property to meet the overdraft. Unaware of a rapidly developing financial crisis in the Tipperary they made it guarantor for any losses that might be sustained because of Sadleir's debt,

> Mr. James Sadleir proposes that property of Mr. John Sadleir to the extent of £450,000 and £480,000 shall be assigned to three trustees, of whom he, Mr. James Sadleir shall be one and the other two shall be chosen by and from among the Bank directors. That the trust shall be created with full powers of sale, as speedily as possible, of so much of the property of Mr. John Sadleir as shall liquidate and discharge any advances which may be made by the bank to the trustees, and also the debt now due to the bank. That the bank shall advance to the trustees so much money, not exceeding £100,000, as shall discharge all the outstanding liabilities of Mr. John Sadleir. That the debt of Mr. John Sadleir to the Tipperary Joint Stock Bank, amounting to about £40,000, shall stand over and remain in abeyance until all the liabilities due to the London and County Bank are fully paid and discharged. That the Tipperary Joint Stock Bank shall guarantee the London and County Bank against any ultimate loss for any advances they may in future make to the trustees, as well as in respect of the debt of Mr. John Sadleir, at the expiration of eighteen months at the latest. Mr. James Sadleir represents that there are freehold properties, with the nature and value of which he is perfectly acquainted, to the extent of £174,000, which he can realise before December next, and pay off so much of the Bank debt.[52]

No fewer than twenty deeds were executed on 2 August assigning Sadleir's Irish estates to J.W. Burmester and Law as trustees for the London bank.[53] James Sadleir was included as guarantor for the debt on behalf of the Tipperary bank. The £95,000 was paid in instalments to him, and he averted certain disaster by depositing half of it in Glyn's clearing house to the credit of the Tipperary.[54]

A week later the London and County sent Stevens, Wilkinson's partner, to Dublin to make more thorough enquiries about Sadleir's property, and to register the deeds. Stevens called to Kennedy in Great Denmark Street for assistance. Kennedy remained silent about the Clonmel agreement but not about securities held by Eyre on 443 acres of the Kilcommon, Clonmore, Castlegrace and Shanakill estates. Stevens communicated this to Wilkinson, who advised the London bank to stop the remaining instalment pending release of these securities.

Sadleir had originally assigned this land to Eyre in October 1854 as security on a loan.[55] Now, desperate to get the remaining instalment of the £95,000, he did not hesitate to swindle his trusting relative. The Royal Swedish Railway Company was used to achieve this and in turn was the subject of a major fraud. It needed capital to continue its development and received permission from the Swedish Government to raise £100,000 on debentures and obligations. These required the signatures of two directors, and Sadleir as chairman took charge of them for that purpose. Their nominal value was £346,000 and he sold them on the stock exchange for less than a third of this.[56] He kept the proceeds for his own use and went on to forge a further 20,000 shares.

He decided to offer Eyre these forged shares not only for the release of Kilcommon, but for other lands held as security against loans to Sadleir. They were supposedly worth £5 each and he pretended that the arrangement had been agreed ·by a special resolution of the company.[57] His letter to Eyre on 13 August outlines in detail how he proceeded,

I suppose you have with you the indemnity deed signed by me, in which we both agreed that a proviso should be to the effect that I might substitute for the lands included in the deed other lands, or shares paying £5 per cent. *I am transferring now the lands included in the deed,* in order to enable me to pay up all my shares in the Royal Swedish Railway, which is likely to turn out a very valuable concern, and to provide for other payments, such as calls on the East Kent shares I hold, and other matters; and I want you to instruct J.B. Kennedy to prepare, at my expense, such deed or deeds as may be requisite to carry out our instructions according to the proviso in the indemnity deed. My notion is that, as I have to pay you £3000 a-year, and, as I shall be entitled to £3000 a-year on 12,000 Royal Swedish shares of £5 each, fully paid up (and with coupons for the interest at £5 per cent, payable half-yearly), it is better for you, and also for me, to have this certain means of my paying the £3000 regularly to you, than I should lose the present opportunity of making a general arrangement as to the mortgaged lands, which certainly enables me to have a very large stake in the Railway, which will have its first opening in next month. If you desire to have more property in the indemnity deed than the £60,000 of Railway shares, paying £3000 a-year, I have no objection to have the Wall lands[58] made liable under the indemnity; and, if you would prefer that the yearly payment by me to you should be £5000, and not £3000, I shall be quite prepared to meet your wishes in this particular; for, certainly, by substituting the Railway shares, paying £5 per cent., for the lands, I become enabled to pay £5000 a-year far easier than £3000 without such an arrangement. If I have not sufficiently explained this matter to you in this letter, I shall go to Bath, and explain my position and plans to you more fully. I hope you will be able to write to me a line by Tuesday's post, to No.11 Gloucester-square, for I am rather anxious not to let the present opportunity slip; and, from what I have heard this day, I feel unwilling to delay the affair. You might wish to refer to J.B. Kennedy the task of carrying out the alteration in the indemnity, and the substitution of property according to the proviso in the original deed, in a way which would be just and proper, as regards our respective interests; and, with that view, I think if you sent him this letter, with your own written instructions, the business could be done by him in a satisfactory manner. Of course, before I would expect you to sign any deed of release of lands, I should hand you over the Railway shares, with the coupons for the dividends or interest. I do not know whether you consider it unreasonable to wait for the £1500 I am to pay, until I get my coupons paid at the Royal Swedish next month; but if it is inconvenient to you to give me until then, I believe I can have no difficulty in discounting the coupons now at once, and so be able to pay in the £1500 to your credit.

Sufficiently confident of Eyre's compliance, Sadleir assured Wilkinson of the immediate release of the lands. This was prior to any response from Eyre. The chain of events which followed shows Sadleir's ingenuity in manipulating others, and partly explains how he managed to survive so many questionable transactions. Eyre replied on 14 August that he would comply only on the advice of James B. Kennedy.[59] Sadleir immediately telegraphed Kennedy that he had received a 'favourable letter from Bath, which I send you'. Kennedy forwarded this message to Stevens, who was in Killarney. Simultaneously James Sadleir pressed Wilkinson for the remaining £25,000, but he refused until Eyre's mortgage was satisfactorily sorted out. John Sadleir increased the pressure on Wilkinson by informing him that he had a letter from Eyre undertaking to release the lands from the mortgage. Wilkinson took him at his word and issued the final instalment of the £95,000.

Under the circumstances it was essential to complete the fraud as speedily as possible. Sadleir wrote to Eyre on 15 August, and tried to calm whatever fears his seventy five year old relative may have harboured about the wisdom of accepting them,

> I am quite satisfied that the operation of substituting other security for the lands now included in the indemnity deed should be according to what J.B. Kennedy may consider right and fair as between us two. From the beginning to the end, I have but the one object, and that is, to manage matters so as that, whatever delays or annoyances you may have had to experience e heretofore, no ultimate loss should at all events happen. This change of security will greatly facilitate me in my efforts, without, I trust, at all damaging your position. In fact whatever serves me, in this respect, cannot, I believe, damage you. The lands included in the indemnity deed are worth, I suppose, about £106,000, subject to mortgages to the amount of £46,000. I am looking to recovering losses on foot of lands, by the gain on the Royal Swedish shares; and I think that in proposing to substitute for the indemnity lands 12,000 Royal Swedish shares, producing £3000 a-year, and agreeing to the Wall lands standing also as an indemnity, and increasing the yearly payment to you from £3000 to £5000, I will be carrying out an arrangement which must be of the two more favourable to your interests than the present one. The present arrangement was the best I could offer and make at the time; but I told J.B. Kennedy at the time, that I would want to act on the proviso for liberty to substitute securities, in order to carry out my own plans for covering and protecting myself against loss. You must bear in mind that, after all, it may turn out that I will not have to make good a very serious loss, *in re Kingston*, and that when the policy for £4000, *in re Smith v Dennehy*, falls in, the loss in that case will be lessened too. However, we shall see what view J.B. Kennedy will take of the matter. Mr. William Eyre has not any charge or claim on the Wall lands. He has obtained from me a security on portions of the Cahir

lands, and the other lands not included in the indemnity deed; so that what I propose is, that your indemnity should attach on the Wall lands, subject only to Judge Moore's £15,000, and your own claim thereon.[60]

The reference in the letter to the Kingston estate was an effort by Sadleir to cloak a further swindle on Eyre who was unaware that his £40,000 loan to the Earl had never been passed on or a record kept by James Sadleir of how it had been disbursed.[61] In June the Earl had received a court decree charging Eyre and the bank as mortgagees and rendering them liable to show what rents they had received from the estate since the 1840s. Kingston filed his charge under the decree in August, and was awaiting judgement at the time Sadleir was corresponding with Eyre about the transfer of the railway Shares.[62]

Sadleir was determined to ensure that the transfer was quickly secured, and immediately instructed Kennedy to travel to Bath and negotiate the share substitution. Kennedy proved as trusting as Eyre. Armed with a copy of a share certificate, the prospectus of the railway company and healthy annual reports he arrived in Bath and lodged at the White Hart Hotel.[63] He advised Sadleir that 20,000 shares of £3 each would be necessary to secure Eyre the £5000 a year income mentioned in the letter of 15 August. Since Sadleir had forged these shares, he sent Kennedy several telegrams confidently confirming that this would not present any difficulties. He also reassured him that James Sadleir, if required, could guarantee the £5000 annual income. Such a minor untruth weighed little with Sadleir. To remove any doubts from Kennedy's mind Sadleir also told him that a £12,000 promissory note of William Dargan, the railway engineer, could be given as added security.[64] The promissory note was a forgery.

Unsuspecting that he was the emissary of a swindler, Kennedy met Eyre, who finally agreed to endorse the proposal provided that the value of the shares and the status of the railway company were confirmed. Back in London the following day, he secured written answers from Sadleir to Eyre's queries and immediately posted a recommendation to Eyre, who released the lands three days later. The London and County drew up a deed on 7 September confirming the transfer of Sadleir's lands in trust for its use, and allowing any surplus from their sale to be used for the benefit of the Tipperary.[65] The declaration of trust was forwarded to Clonmel for endorsement by the board of the Tipperary. William Kelly, the manager, returned it to Sadleir, who inserted the names of sham directors on the minutes. There was never any board meeting and James Sadleir concocted the minutes.

The release of Eyre's mortgage was formalised by a deed of 5

October in the offices of the London and County. A week later Eyre formally executed the articles of agreement transferring the forged railway shares.[66] This agreement cited the fictitious resolution of the railway company dated 25 August that the shares carried a five per cent annual interest. It also cited the transfer of the forged promissory note to Eyre and the conveyance of part of the Kilcommon estate to him. Sadly for Eyre this conveyance was also a forgery, and even if genuine, the charges on that portion of the estate exceeded its value.

In November Stevens travelled to Dublin to satisfy himself that Kennedy had registered the release, which then meant that the London bank had clear title to all Sadleir's estates. It immediately began the process of selling some of these, and brought to a conclusion that particular scene from the drama as yet hidden from the public. There were, however, other unsavoury scenes. One of the most fascinating was hatched in April, when Sadleir went to Clonmel to discuss with James a scheme to sell Tipperary bank shares on the English market.[67] Of the 10,000 original shares only 4055 had been taken up at ten pounds each. Sadleir hoped to dispose of the remainder using the London and County branch network. The Sadleirs realised that the sudden arrival of a large number of unappropriated shares on the market would arouse suspicion. It would also render them practically worthless and damage the value of all the bank's shares, since investors would rightly conclude that such a significant increase in the shareholding would halve the dividend. Accordingly, a scheme was adopted to conceal the fact that the shares were new by entering them in the name of Austen Ferrall, an old school companion of Sadleir, whom he occasionally used to transact business.

As far back as 1846 Sadleir had received permission from Ferrall to enter his name as the holder of shares for an imaginary female cousin, who allegedly did not wish her name to appear as a shareholder.[68] Ferrall was still registered as a shareholder in 1855, so that transactions with new investors in these shares would simply be seen as share transfers.

The Tipperary's deed of partnership stipulated that all share transfers should be ratified by the court of directors. There was no such court in 1855, Vincent Scully and Wilson Kennedy having retired. James Sadleir was the only director at that time. Such a serious violation of the partnership deed caused little worry to the by now desperate brothers. William Kelly signed blocks of blank shares which were then entered in Ferrall's name on a phased basis, beginning on 9 May.[69] Kelly, while apparently not suspecting a fraud, noticed that the certificates differed in some respects from those normally used. James Sadleir issued a false certificate of registration to cover some of these, and no attempt was made to register the remainder. Sadleir easily persuaded Ferrall to agree the transfer of shares which he still believed were being held in trust for the fictitious relative. He was unaware that so many had recently been entered in his name ready for transfer to unsuspecting English investors. By April 1855, in any case, he was anxious to have his name removed from the shareholding of the Tipperary,[70] and did not initially enquire too closely when Sadleir visited him on several occasions to sign presumably blank transfer forms.[71] There is little doubt that Ferrall stood in some awe of Sadleir. Their relationship had altered since he had left Ireland to work as a clerk in Young's Wine Merchants in Lime Street, London. When he had resided in Dublin his social standing had been high, but he had lost most of his fortune and was forced to emigrate, while Sadleir had become increasingly more powerful and ostensibly very wealthy.

His main problem was to entice English investors to purchase the shares which were in Ferrall's name. To accomplish this the brothers embarked upon an act of deception later described by a judge as 'unparalleled in the annuals of fraud'.[72] They first enhanced the status of the shares by offering them at twenty five per cent above par. This was a clear indication to investors that the Tipperary was in a thriving condition. They took every precaution to demonstrate this. They issued a bogus prospectus, annual report and balance sheet for 1854, supposedly presented to the annual general meeting of 1 February 1855. The bank's paid-up capital was shown as £100,000. This was an important device of the fraud because the publication of the true figure of £40,550 would have immediately alerted investors that the shares offered were unappropriated, since they alone amounted to £59,450. The fabricated balance sheet put customers' balances at £724,351 instead of the real figure of £424,35. The profit and loss surplus was almost double the true amount. The assets were shown as £842,279, but in reality were only £481,045 and this figure included Sadleir's overdraft. To give added credibility to the accounts the reports showed the directors as James Sadleir, Robert Keating, Frank Scully, John Ryan D.L., J.P., and Matthew R. Sausse Q.C., all of whom were his relatives.

Sadleir gave a large number of the false documents to Farmery John Law, for distribution to the branch managers. Law, who did not suspect any fraud, was promised a commission of a pound for every share sold. The managers were equally gulled. They had no reason to question the integrity of two directors of the bank, one of whom was its chairman. Motivated by a commission of ten shillings per share sold, they enthusiastically canvassed customers highlighting the connection between the Tipperary and the Bank of Ireland. Investors were urged to purchase immediately to avail of the 6% dividend then pending.

Payment of dividends on such shares was an additional fraud upon existing shareholders, since they should be paid only from the date of issue. Between May and September managers in the Chelmsford, Petersborough, Uxbridge, Luton and Leighton Buzzard branches were particularly successful in disposing of batches of useless shares at £12.10.0 each. But, Sadleir was dissatisfied at the number sold and decided to cast a stronger bait. In December he concocted a very favourable balance sheet for the year 1855, and on 31 December wrote to James with precise instructions on the preparation of falsified accounts for the benefit of the English market alone, which would tally with the previous one. His letter deserves scrutiny as a masterpiece of fraud,

My Dear James – The accounts should be made out *treating the paid up capital as* £100,000 on the 31st of December 1854; therefore the requisite number of shares, to make this account square, should be entered as vested in A. Ferrall, Esq., and he should be debited accordingly in an account in respect of the shares.

The 'Reserved Fund' should be treated as £14,072. 0s. 3d, on the 31st of December 1854.

It will not be requisite to print and circulate amongst the Irish shareholders a balance-sheet, but as all the English shareholders are in the habit of getting from every Bank in which they hold shares a printed balance-sheet each half-year, we must give them a printed balance-sheet at least once a-year, and for the year ending 31st of December 1855.

By this means the English shareholders will double their present holdings in the Tipperary Bank, and I dare say the balance sheet of the £100,000 of stock will be quickly taken up.

Now, I know many of the English Joint-stock Banks, in order to give a good appearance to their balance, have constantly trebled the amount of their balances, &c., &c., by making a series of entries, whereby they appeared to have assets and liabilities to four times the amount they really possessed or had. This has been always kept very quiet, and what at first was a kind of fiction became gradually to be bona fide.

I enclose you the figures I gave Law (i.e. Farmery John Law) and some few others; and the balance-sheet for the year ending the 31st of December 1855 should be framed so as to tally with this balance-sheet for the year ending 31st December 1854.

An increase of about £30,000 in the item of customers' balances, &c., &c., should be made to appear. The item trade fixtures should be increased or decreased as you considered best.

The way to shove the customers' balances up to say £759,223. 16s. 2d., or thereabouts, would be of course by crediting certain accounts, deposit or current accounts, or both, and debiting certain other accounts for sums which in the whole would represent the same.

For example, six or seven deposit receipts may be issued to me for such and such sums, amounting in the whole to four or five hundred thousand pounds, and then four or five accounts might be opened, such as:-

1st. The South-Eastern Swiss Railway Company	...	£163,000
2nd. The Prussian Coal Company	...	157,000
3rd. The Rome and Frascati Railway Company	...	36,000
4th. The Grand Junction Railway Company .	..	48,000
5th. The East Kent Railway Company	...	157,000
		£561,000

and each of the foregoing accounts might be debited with advances made to me as representing each of said Companies, to the extent of the sums I set opposite each of the five accounts, and which sums would amount in all to £561,000.

Then the deposit receipts for £21,500 granted to Backhouse might be added, and I should be debited with said sum in an account called 'John Sadleir, trustee in the Backhouse mortgage.'

All the foregoing accounts would be looked on as so many trust accounts obtained by arranging to advance as much as was received; and as the Bank could not be called on to pay any of the deposit receipts so long as one penny was due on any of the accounts, the safety of the Bank was perfect, and the question of interest both ways could be so adjusted as to work out enough of *profit* to enable the Bank to pay the £6 per cent. interest, and £3 per cent. bonus on the £100,000, and to carry to the reserved fund a good sum, say £5000.

I hope you will see this matter in the light I do; perhaps I have not sufficiently explained the case, but I am sure I am right, and that the whole thing can be so managed as to defy any criticism, if such should be started, but of course we should not court any. When I go over I can explain all. The books should be kept open for the requisite entries.

There is nothing to prevent the Tipperary Bank from doing what has been done in the ――――― Bank and the ――――― Bank, and the ――――― Bank, and that is all I advise; namely, to open two accounts for A B, to credit one account as having received from A B £100,000 on deposit, to debit the other account £100,000, as having lent A B so much on the security of his deposit receipt, and his personal security, of course; in every case the Tipperary Bank should receive the deposit receipts, and retain same as security.

F. Law will send you or Mr. Kelly the account of the money got on placing of shares, and not previously accounted for.[73]

James Sadleir later denied that he had complied with these instructions, but had written to his brother 'that the suggestions contained in his letter could not be carried out'.[74] He asked the opinion of William Kelly who allegedly responded that 'it was very foolish of

John Sadleir to put forward such a document'.[75] According to Kelly, James Sadleir agreed and told him that 'the balance sheet in John Sadleir's handwriting was manifestly fraudulent, both as regards the paid-up capital and the assets and liabilities of the bank, and also in the profit and loss account, all of which are overstated by a vast amount'. It is difficult to believe James Sadleir's denial of involvement; the fraudulent documents were printed and Kelly's name signed to them.[76] This may have been done by John Sadleir in London, but his brother could not deny involvement in the ordinary annual report for the Irish shareholders on 1 February 1856, which announced a 6% dividend and 3% bonus for a flourishing concern, when the bank was beyond redemption.

The impressive list of directors appended to the false accounts and report for the English market showed only one change from the previous ones. John Sadleir's name replaced that of John Ryan. This was to cover tracks because Sadleir was shown as a director on the share transfer certificates along with those of James and Keating. Altogether nearly 1300 were purchased for £15,000. About seventy investors were netted, thirty of them from the Leighton Buzzard district. Two-thirds were from the four counties of Essex, Bedfordshire, Hertfordshire and Buckinghamshire.[77] These invested sums ranging from £200 to £500 each.

Even if he had been successful in executing this fraud to the fullest extent it would have been entirely inadequate to meet his accumulating losses. Moreover, sources of credit were drying up as the year progressed. The London and County, having secured most of his property as collateral, was henceforth closed as a means of getting finance, and he resigned as chairman towards the end of 1855.

In desperation he resorted to other measures of raising money. One novel course was proposals of marriage to several wealthy Catholic heiresses, who wisely resisted his advances.[78] He also approached a number of private individuals for advances and offered forged deeds as security. According to Josiah Wilkinson a locked box in his office containing deeds had been tampered with.[79] The extent of these frauds on individuals cannot be traced and contemporary sources suggested that those involved preferred to carry the losses rather than risk their reputations as dupes. One which came to light, however, was his misappropriation of Sir George and Lady Clara Goold's substantial marriage settlement, which he held in trust.[80] There is also evidence, however, that he received £30,000 from Edward Backhouse,[81] but the security offered was later subject to a rival claim from the London and County.[82]

The Backhouse Mortgage was negotiated in October 1855, when an opportunity arose for Sadleir to lay his hands upon more funds. The victim was the Newcastle-Upon-Tyne Commercial Banking Company. It was a small bank founded in 1836 by the Walker family, and when William Walker, it's Managing Director, suffered a stroke in 1853 a decision was made to put it on the market as a going concern.[83] Negotiations with the Royal British Bank for its purchase failed, but Wilkinson recommended it to Sadleir as a valuable acquisition. An agreement was signed on 6 October by which James Sadleir, Law and R.H. Kennedy, a London Alderman, who was a friend of Sadleir, purchased it. They held a majority shareholding of 4,000 shares at £5 each. The new owners nominated five new directors including James Sadleir, Law and Robert Keating. These constituted the London board and existing directors were ousted.[84] The manager was sacked and replaced by Thaddeus O'Shea. By November £59,000 was transferred from Newcastle to the London and County as the nominated agent. Of this, £52,000 was used to bolster the Tipperary, and was covered by six drafts of the latter, which were of no value and were not protected by any securities.[85]

The allocation of the money for the Tipperary rather than Sadleir was an indication of its troubled state. This had seriously deteriorated by the end of 1855 in parallel with Sadleir's own precarious financial position. During that year the bank had advanced him £177,000 bringing his overdraft to £247,000. James Sadleir was guilty of serious dereliction of duty in allowing the overdraft to reach such enormous proportions as to place the bank in jeopardy. His later defence that he believed his brother had sufficient property to cover it does not altogether stand up under scrutiny.[86] He admitted being aware of Sadleir's investments in railway expansion in England, France, Germany, Sweden, Switzerland and Italy. He claimed that he denounced his brother 'in the strongest language I could for having allowed himself, under any circumstances, to be engaged in so many undertakings'. Nevertheless, the statistics he received from Sadleir and the assurances of his friends on the adequacy of these investments to meet his debts mollified him. He was satisfied at the end of 1855 that 'the worst was over and that he was fast getting out of the temporary difficulties he had got into, and that he would have a very considerable surplus after paying all debts that I had any knowledge of'.

But, James Sadleir knew the enormity of his brother's London overdraft, an indication in itself of vast expenditure. He had also connived in ensuring that this bank had at least an equal claim to Sadleir's landed property. His failure to secure it as collateral contrasted with the controls exercised by the Bank of Ireland upon its branches and agents.[87] He knew that the property was very extensive because much of Sadleir's overdraft was used in land purchase.

James Sadleir was also familiar with the expense of parliamentary representatives. They did not receive a salary, and although Sadleir's social life was relatively frugal, living in the West End was expensive. The rent of the apartment in the Albany and later his house in Gloucester Square had to be met. Electioneering costs were also heavy. Usually a single election campaign ran into several thousand pounds. Captain Otway spent £2,500 on the 1852 election in County Tipperary, a small enough sum compared with the £11,000 disbursed by Lord Cahir in the 1818 election there.[88] One source put Sadleir's Carlow and Sligo expenses at from £6,000 to £8,000.[89] It is also likely that he contributed to the election expenses of his relatives and friends.[90]

His electioneering expenses also had an unusual dimension not only in disbursements, but in concessions granted by the Tipperary to some of its customers. A *Nation* writer was not exaggerating when he referred to the 'tremendous screw which the proprietor of a bank can wield among the small traders of a provincial town'.[91] Some electors may have been able to resist the vicious treadmill of bills being renewed in return for votes, but others had no option but to avail of the opportunity to put off the evil day. Votes may have been gained for Sadleir, but at the expense of mismanaging the bank's resources.

Compared with his land purchases Sadleir's accumulated political expenses made only a marginal impact on his overdraft by the close of 1855. This was not so, however, in the case of the Chandos mortgage. It dated back to February 1849 when Sadleir involved himself in a money lending speculation, and became enmeshed in the financial morass of the Duke of Buckingham, the leading landowner in Buckinghamshire, with seats at Stowe and Wotton. By then the Duke's debts amounted to a million pounds, much of his land was in the process of being sold and his less extravagant son, the Marquis of Chandos, was endeavouring to clear his debts.[92] Sadleir considered the Marquis a sound risk and advanced him £90,000 as part of a £134,000 mortgage.[93] The mortgage was considered good security for advances of up to £150,000, and from 1852 the London and County had held it as collateral against his increasing overdraft. In May 1853, however, he removed it from the bank without the prior consent of the board of directors, and succeeded in raising £55,000.[94] The £90,000 debt was still unpaid in 1855, despite the best efforts of the Third Duke of Buckingham and erstwhile Earl of Chandos, to clear his father's liabilities. In June 1855 Sadleir urged the Duke to expedite the sale of Wotton and Stowe,

for if there is any delay in doing so now, I very much fear no considerable sale can be made this year. As I think my interests can only be served by speedy sales I am naturally anxious to see delays avoided as far as possible. Of course, I earnestly hope the course most likely to improve my position as a creditor will be that most conducive to the interests of Your Lordship.[95]

He was unsuccessful in his attempts to pry repayment from the hardpressed Duke. These properties were not sold for several years when the beneficiary was the London and County.[96] Given his record, it is unlikely that Sadleir would have handed over the money if the Duke had been able to make the repayment.

Another enterprise for which James Sadleir might have justifiably chided his brother was the venture into the newspaper world where margins were tight and competition keen. Not only had new plant to be purchased and staff hired, but the low price of the *Telegraph* was achieved at a cost which was hardly offset by its high sales.[97] Its reduction from a tri-weekly to a weekly in 1853 points to a failing enterprise, which by December 1855 was part of his accumulated losses.

Newspaper outlay, land purchase, the Chandos mortgage and political costs account for about one third of Sadleir's total expenditure and losses, which stood at £1,500,000 by January 1856. It is impossible to precisely trace the £1,000,000, but it is certain that it was lost in speculation. Not all of this was obviously risky, however, and Sadleir was unfortunate to lose money on the Westminster Improvement Bonds' scheme. These had been floated to finance improvement between Buckingham Palace and the Houses of Parliament, which included the construction of a new street. But, because of poor financial management by the commissioners the bonds depreciated and many investors were ruined.[98]

The bulk of Sadleir's losses came, however, from far more risky ventures through the stock exchange. He was a frequent visitor there and it was not difficult in those years to lose, and occasionally to gain, vast amounts of money.[99] The *Times* saw this type of speculation as one of the evils of the time,

> It is impossible to be mixed up with society in London – and the provincial capitals, it appears, are not behind us in this respect – without becoming painfully aware of the range of illegitimate speculation. The men who engage in this unfortunate career never seem to consider that they are playing against loaded dice. One succeeds in the desperate game, and a thousand perish – the success of one is magnified and proclaimed with admiration and envy from month to month; the ruin of the thousand passes without notice and without comment. The art of converting airy nothings into solid coin is far too much in vogue for public security or public happiness.[100]

Allowing for exaggeration, one normally reliable source remarked that 'there were few men outside the house of Rothschild who speculated to such an extent in foreign, continental railways and mining undertakings'.[101] It was alleged that in a single day in the Autumn of 1855 he lost £120,000 on a sugar speculation. On other occasions he lost £35,000 on a 'hemp transaction' and £50,000 on an iron venture.[102] In January 1856 his speculations were equally enormous and equally disastrous, and James Sadleir was forced to advance him a further £41,000 bringing his overdraft to £288,000.[103] James sought to conceal the bank's predicament by purchasing shares when they came on the market. In January 1856 he was by far the largest shareholder with 1,838 shares, of which 756 had been bought in 1854 and 1855.[104] He hardly considered these a sound investment but their purchase was a signal of confidence that the bank was in a healthy state.

This facade of wealth was upheld on all fronts. In January the Sadleir brothers attended the marriage of Frank Scully to Marie Virginie Clotilde Moorat, the daughter of the wealthy John Samuel Moorat, Sadleir's neighbour in Gloucester Square.[105] Their high social status was confirmed by the presence of Cardinal Wiseman to officiate at the ceremony. Anthony Norris and M.R. Sausse were guests.

After the wedding James Sadleir returned to Ireland to present the annual report of the Tipperary for the previous year. This did not contain any hint of difficulty, but reported a very satisfactory state of affairs,

> The directors were happy to have it in their power to report to the shareholders that the course of the bank continued satisfactory, and that the improving aspect of the affairs of the country induced them to feel confident that the business of the bank would go on extending, that the annual profits would thus be steadily increased, and that the directors had the honour to lay before the meeting the usual detailed statement of the accounts of the bank, with the assets and liabilities, for the information of the shareholders.[106]

This optimistic account was supported by the declaration of a 6% dividend and 3% bonus. In reality there was not any meeting of shareholders. James Sadleir was the only individual involved in this fraudulent report, which no doubt prompted farmers and other investors to confidently deposit greater amounts in the bank.

Some weeks later the directors of the London and County were guilty of a much more minor act of deception by inviting Sadleir, who had already resigned as Chairman, to preside at the annual general meeting on 7 February.[107] This may have been a gesture of good will for the expansion of the bank during his tenure, but more likely it was a move to allay the suspicion of shareholders following his enforced resignation.

In his address Sadleir reviewed progress over the previous ten years which saw the paid up capital increasing from £200,000 to £500,000, deposits and balances from £1.4 million to £5 million and the value of shares increase from £17.10.0 to £43. New branches had been opened in the Borough and Oxford Street, and the Chatham branch had captured Government business for its catchment area. In declaring a dividend of 9%, Sadleir coolly announced that the prosperity of joint-stock banks 'depended on the ability and efficiency of their officers and the integrity of their directors'.

Edward Johnstone, the Vicar of Hampton, responded by praising Sadleir's courage for once recommending an increase in the bank's capital and guaranteeing to purchase any shares not taken up. The bank officials received a 10% increase on their salaries and the General Manager was appreciative of the £500 allocated to the Sadleir Provident Fund, which then stood at £17,000.

Sadleir's paper took the opportunity to praise this fund as testimony of Sadleir's care for the working class, and asked 'the assailants of Mr. John Sadleir to look to these proceedings – to reflect upon them – to act if they had the power, as he has done; and when they have done so, then ask of their own consciences this question – can he who so acts be aught else but an honest man?'.[108]

This question soon received a dramatic answer. Within a week rumours began to spread about the perilous condition of the Tipperary. The *Times* of 12 February reported that Glyn's clearing house, the bank's London agent, had refused its drafts.[109] Morrogh and Kennedy immediately moved to qualify the report by a letter of 13 February, telegraphed to the Dublin papers to counteract alarm in Irish circles,

> should you refer in your paper of to-morrow to a statement which appears in the City article of the *Times* to-day, and telegraphed to the Chamber of Commerce, to the effect that the drafts of the Tipperary Joint Stock Bank were returned by their agents, Messrs. Glynn and Co., you will have the goodness to add the fact, which has just reached us by telegraph, that the drafts alluded to have been this day paid – that their non-payment on yesterday arose from accident and that the bank's payments go on as usual.[110]

This damage limitation exercise was not fully successful and a run began on several branches. One of the Tipperary curates, Michael O'Brien, who was in Dublin on 13 February brought the news home.[111] O'Brien was thwarted from withdrawing the £2,500 church building fund lest it ignite a major rush. The branch, however, was besieged but managed to survive until closure time on Saturday 16 February. The Roscrea branch experienced a similar situation beginning on 14 February but also managed to meet all demands until it closed at the week-end.[112]

Saturday 16 February, however, was a fateful day in the history of the bank and in the life of Sadleir. Throughout that week the Bank of Ireland tried to bolster the Tipperary by accepting its useless drafts, but on Saturday it yielded to the inevitable and refused to take any more. Sadleir's options for saving it and himself had also run out. His acceptances were by then running at an untenable twenty-five per cent discount. He realised that the extent of his financial ruin, the methods used to prevent it, and the consequences for others would soon be public knowledge. Norris was alarmed at his demeanour throughout the week, especially on that Saturday,

> Latterly he seemed rather haggard. During the last week particularly I had noticed a great change in his appearance... He appeared to be quite borne down by the extent of his business, and particularly by some occurrences which took place to his affairs last week. They were losses and pecuniary embarrassments which had lately come upon him, and it was about these that he talked to me during an interview on Saturday night. During the interview I noticed a peculiarity in his manner. His eyes were bloodshot. He was very restless, and evidently not in his usual temperament when I saw him. I had not seen him in such a state before... He was always cool and collected until within the last few days. From Wednesday last, inclusively I had seen him every day.[113]

Even at that late stage James Sadleir continued to place his confidence in the apparent financial wizardry of his brother. He could not believe that the collapse of the bank was imminent because its drafts would not be met the following Monday at Glyn's. That Saturday he optimistically telegraphed Sadleir about the bank's survival of the run, and assured him that everything was 'all right at the branches – only a few small things refused there. If from twenty to thirty thousand over here on Monday morning all is safe'.[114]

Sadleir had poor prospects of raising such a sum. He visited Wilkinson, however, and sought a substantial loan to save the bank. He proposed several schemes which were rejected by Wilkinson, who later said that he

> became very excited, put his hand to his head and said "Good God, if the Tipperary Bank should fail the fault will be entirely mine, and I shall have been the ruin of hundreds and thousands." He walked about the office in a very excited state and urged me to try and help him, because

he said he could not live to see the pain and ruin inflicted on others by the cessation of the bank.

He grew even more agitated when informed that Stevens, was going to Dublin that evening to register one of his deeds given as security against a loan from Wilkinson.[115] The security was a forgery, but Sadleir had attached to it a seal from the Incumbered Estates Court. This was a wafer taken from a genuine deed.

He remained in the City throughout the remainder of the day trying to raise money from other sources. He met both Norris and Keating, and towards evening spoke with a fellow speculator named MacKenzie. His parting words to this individual were ominous, 'good bye; I am going to make a long journey and we may not meet for some time'. When he reached home he sent his butler, Joseph Elwin, to Maitland's Chemist in Chester Place for a bottle of Essential Oil of Bitter Almonds, commonly known as Prussic Acid. Meticulous to the last, he had studied Alfred S. Taylor's book, *On Poisons in Relation to Medical Jurisprudence and Medicine*, published some years earlier.[116] This was as much a treatise on the effectiveness of various poisons as a means of suicide, as it was a chemical analysis of them. Prussic Acid was given a high rating by Taylor, who also obligingly described it as a popular method of suicide. Maitland's assistant assumed that it was to be used as a hairwash. Nevertheless he sent Sadleir a note cautioning him not to allow it to fall into the hands of 'inexperienced persons who may perchance be unaware of the danger of using it'.[117]

Sadleir went to his club as usual that evening and did not return until 10.30, when he ordered coffee and wrote four letters, one to Emma Sadleir, one to Norris, and two to Keating in Clapham.[118] His letter to Norris signalled his intention to take his own life. He accepted full responsibility for his actions and forecast the shame that they would bring upon his family. His letter to Emma exonerated her husband from all blame, and asked that she would 'be to him at this moment all the support you can'. One of his letters to Keating stated that if the Tipperary Bank was to be saved £10,700 would have to be paid to Glyn's Clearing House by Monday morning. The other deserves to be quoted for its coherent, if emotional, declaration of remorse, and its revelation that unwise speculation was the main cause of his ruin,

Dear Robert,
To what infamy have I come step by step – heaping crime upon crime – and now I find myself the author of numberless crimes of a diabolical character and the cause of ruin and misery and disgrace to thousands – aye to tens of thousands.

Oh how I feel for those on whom all this ruin must fall – I could bear all punishments but I could never bear to witness the sufferings of those on whom I have brought such ruin. It must be better that I should not live.

No one has been privy to my crimes – they sprang from my own cursed brain alone – I have swindled and deceived without the knowledge of anyone – Stevens and Norris are both innocent and have no knowledge of the fabrication of deeds and forgeries by and by which I have sought to go on in the horrid hope of retrieving.

It was a sad day for all when I came to London. I can give but little aid to unravel accounts and transactions.

There are serious questions as to my interest in the Grand Junction and other undertakings.

Much will be lost to the creditors if these cases are not fairly treated.

The Grand Junction, the East Kent and the Swiss railways, the Rome line, the coal company are all liable to be entirely lost now – so far as my assets are concerned.

I authorise you to take possession of all my letters, papers, property etc. etc. in this house and at Wilkinson's and 18 Cannon Street.

Return my brother his letters to me and all other papers. The prayers of one so wicked could not avail or I would seek to pray for those I leave after me, and who will have to suffer such agony, and all owing to my criminal acts.

Oh that I had never quitted Ireland – Oh that I had resisted the first attempts to launch me into speculations.

If I had had less talents of a worthless kind and more firmness I might have remained as I once was, honest and truthful – and I would have lived to see my dear father and mother in their old age – I weep and weep now but what can that avail.

Sadleir left his house around midnight, walked through Hampstead Heath and lay on the grass at the rear of Jack Straw's Castle, an inn where he sometimes lodged. He consumed the Prussic acid mixed with sugar and opium, and kept his razor close by in the unlikely event of the poison failing to work. His sense of style did not desert him in those final hours. Contemporary sources described his dress – a black hat from Christy's of Bond Street, 'frock coat, raised silk plush waistcoat, fancy tweed trousers, grey lamb's wool socks, walking shoes, buckskin gloves, black silk neckerchief and a fancy shirt'.[119] He consumed the poison from a silver cream jug.

The following morning a local labourer came upon the corpse of the forty-three year old M.P. and called the police. It was taken to the workhouse slab in Hampstead, and was quickly identified because Sadleir had taken the precaution of putting a slip of paper in his pocket showing his name and address. William and Clement formally identified the remains which was left in the workhouse for three days during which an autopsy was carried out by Robert Nicol, a surgeon from Hampstead. This showed a considerable quantity of opium pellets and Prussic acid in his stomach.

Late on the night of 19 February the body was removed to 11 Gloucester Square, and William arranged for the burial to take place in the early hours of 21 February.[120] Canon law declared a suicide excommunicated[121] and Sadleir was not allowed the rites of a Christian burial, but was interred in unconsecrated ground in Highgate Cemetery.[122] A priest, however, was present at the interment.

In the meantime the inquest[123] on Sadleir's death was opened by Dr. Thomas Wakley, Coroner for West Middlesex.[124] As M.P. for West Finsbury until 1852 he knew Sadleir and was destined to share his fate as a suicide.[125] William and Clement, both Scullys, Keating, Morrogh and Norris were present at the inquest. Frank Scully had only returned from his honeymoon that fateful Saturday. Wakley's first objective was to assess Sadleir's mental state immediately prior to his suicide, and he sought the letters of 16 February as a means of doing so. The inquest which opened on 19 February was adjourned for a week so that they could be produced. When it resumed on 26 February the Sadleir family instructed William Manning, Coroner of the Queen's Household, who attended on their behalf, to release them. Wakley felt that their lucidity indicated mental stability, but there was the possibility that Sadleir's claims of causing widespread ruin were exaggerated and might, therefore, constitute evidence of mental imbalance. Accordingly, he adjourned for a second time to assess the emerging catalogue of delinquency.

He resumed on 11 March, and Keating was the only close relative present.[126] The magnanimous Wilkinson declared his belief that Sadleir was greatly overstating the extent of his offences. He based this on the numerous bona fide transactions that Sadleir had with him over a long period. He also felt that the reports of frauds on the Incumbered Estates Court were exaggerated, if not unfounded. He was more definite in his assertion that the London and County had not been defrauded by its chairman.

Manning supported this line of argument and produced a letter from the London bank testifying to the genuineness of the many deeds held as security. He put this forward as proof of exaggeration in the letters, and pleaded that the case should rest upon the evidence of Sadleir's friends about his unbalanced state of mind. Manning was less credible when he interpreted the autopsy finding of opium as possible proof that Sadleir was a habitual 'opium eater'. This would explain his calm disposition despite a heavy daily work load and might indicate a state of depression following a heavy dosage in his final hours, thus absolving him from responsibility for his actions.

The efforts of Wilkinson and Manning to secure a verdict of insanity were also prompted by the perception that a contrary verdict would result in the forfeiture of Sadleir's property. Manning produced a translation of a charter of Edward VI to Sir Thomas Wroth and his heirs in the manors of Northal, Downbarnes and Hampstead, which declared that a verdict of *felo de se*,[127] or wilful self-murder, entitled the Lord of the Manor to the criminal's property, which would then be lost to his creditors. But, this was a spurious argument since only the Crown could seize property, and then only 'goods, chattels and credits' in the immediate possession of the deceased, and not landed property.[128]

Wakley was not persuaded either by Wilkinson or Manning. Pressed by the Coroner, Manning was forced to concede that he was not aware of the charter ever being enforced. In his summing up, Wakley, an experienced medical writer, researcher and practitioner, advised the jury that while there was no legal definition of insanity, it was not depression, mental agony or remorse. He also reminded them that justice and humanity were as much due to society as to an individual. Their verdict on Sadleir's state of mind must come from a careful examination not only of the evidence, but also of the letters written on the night of 16 February. He again read these for their benefit and gave them clear directions,

> There was no confusion of ideas, apparently no disturbance of mind. These letters were not in any way inconsistent with a perfect retention of his reasoning and reflective powers, or with the maintenance of an accurate memory. At the same time it was impossible not to know and feel, from the manner in which the letters were expressed, that the writer must have been suffering from intense mental agony; indeed the circumstances of the suicide itself must prove the mental suffering, which drove him to such an act of desperation. But, then again rose the question – was he in such a state of mind that made him irresponsible – was he driven to the act by an uncontrollable impulse that weighed down his reasoning and reflective powers or was he aware of what he was doing and had he the power of controlling his action to such an extent as to make him responsible? If the jury had any doubt upon the matter he recommended them to give Mr. Sadleir's memory the benefit of the doubt, but at the same time it was his duty to tell them that they must not for a moment take into consideration the consequences of their verdict.

It took the jury only twenty-five minutes to return a verdict of wilful self murder, and Wakley agreed that, considering the evidence, no other conclusion was possible.

References

1. Evans was a financial journalist who worked at various times for the *Morning Herald*, the *Standard*, the *Times*, the *Banker's Magazine*. He published several books. He was born in 1819 in Llanidloes, Montgomeryshire and died in 1874. – *D.N.B.*, e.v. under Morier Evans.

2. Evans, *Facts, Failures and Frauds*, p. 232. M. Dillon, *The History and Development of Banking in Ireland*, (Dublin, 1889) p. 84 is quite definite that Sadleir resigned because he had used some of the Treasury funds to finance his business schemes.

3. Abraham Brewester was born in Ballinulta in 1796, received his early education at Kilkenny College and took his B.A. in Trinity in 1817. He was called to the Irish bar in 1819 and took silk in 1835. He was Solicitor General of Ireland in 1846 and Attorney General in the Aberdeen government. Derby appointed him Lord Justice of Appeal in Ireland in 1866 and Irish Lord Chancellor the following year. He died on 26 July 1874. *D.N.B.*, e.v.

4. Keogh became a judge the following year.

5. John Gray remained aloof from this.

6. *Tablet* 4 November 1854. (N.L.I. microfilm p. 5524 contains a great deal of material on the 'Roman Mission'.The original file is in Propaganda Archives, Rome, S.C. Irlanda, vol.158.

7. *W.T.* 2 December 1854. See also *Tablet* 18,25 November 1854.

8. *W.T.* 2 December 1854.

9. i.e. Michael Slattery.

10. i.e. the Tenant League.

11. McCabe was then in the process of finalising several volumes of his *Catholic History of England* and requested Cullen to present them to the Pope. This request was accompanied by examples of attacks made on him by the anti-Sadleirites – D.D.A., Cullen Papers, Carton 332/6, McCabe to Cullen 27 February 1855.

12. See N..L.I., MS. 1587 for the original memorials and signatures. A third appeal was forwarded on behalf of O'Keeffe and O'Shea.

13. See O'Shea, *Priest, Politics*, pp 188 *et.seq.* See Whyte, *The Independent Irish Party*, pp.118 *et. seq.* for a good explanation of the various appeals.

14. Propaganda Archives Rome, S.C. Irlanda, vol.158.

15. *W.T.* 18 August 1855.

16. Lord John Russell was one of those who opposed the clause.

17. List in *W.T.* 18 August 1855. See also *Parl. Deb.*, series 3, vol.139, 1859 cols. 842-843, (12 July 1855) for Vincent Scully's remarks on the deputation.

18. *Parl. Deb.*, series 3, vol.139, 1859 col.848 (12 July 1855).

19. Ibid.

20. Ibid., cols. 845-846, (12 July 1855).

21. *W.T.* 18 August 1855.

22. See *R.T.* 26 May 1855 for reference to his parliamentary promotion of the East Kent.

23. During the course of the Crimean War the *Telegraph* engaged in an interesting controversy with the *New York Citizen* on the question of a rebellion to free Ireland while England was preoccupied with the war. McCabe rejected not only the violence of a rebellion doomed to failure, but saw Republicanism itself as an undesirable philosophy, which would militate in particular against the Catholic Church. He cited the plight of Irish people under Cromwell in England and the 'know nothings' in America as the only experience Irish people had of Republicanism – see *W.T.* 7 April, 28 July 1855.

24. See p. 151 no. 32 above.

25. R.T. 6 January 1855.
26. Ibid., 24 February 1855.
27. Tylden, Sir John Maxwell 1787-1866 was one of the leaders of the Liberal party in East Kent. Eventually a Lieutenant Colonel in the British Army he served in the 1807 expedition to Monte Video and Buenos Aires as brigade major to his uncle Sir Samuel Auchmuty. He joined the 1st battalion of the 43rd in the Peninsula in 1813 and the following year went to America where he took part in the unsuccessful attack on New Orleans. *D.E.B.*, e.v.
28. *R.T.*, vol.XVIII, no. 2, 1855, p. 512.
29. Ibid.,no.22, 1855 p. 570 and ibid., 25 August 1855. Ibid., vol.XVIII,no.25 1855, p. 626 contained the text of the bill. (The bill was given royal assent in August).
30. Ibid., vol.XVIII, no.22, 1855 p. 570.
31. Ibid., 30 June 1855. The Dover extension would connect with the naval arsenals and depots at Woolwich, Chatham, Sheerness, Maidstone, Canterbury and Dover itself.
32. Ibid., 8 September 1855. Sadleir's statement was made at the half yearly meeting in the London Tavern, which was chaired by Lord Sondes.
33. *T.F.P.* 16 November 1855, evidence of H. Nesbitt, Secretary to the then defunct company.
34. R.D., 1858, vol.18, memorial 54, a memorandum of agreement 30 July 1854 citing four deeds of conveyance from the Incumbered Estates Court 21 June 1854. The money was borrowed in the name of Edward Corcoran who was involved in the Dowling scandal, but the security covering it was Sadleir's lands.
35. The town of Cahir with its 3000 inhabitants, military barracks and several flourmills was part of the estate. The demesne lands had 155 acres of woodlands containing 415 oak, 220 ash, and 286 elm, trees as well as beach and fir from twenty-five to sixty years growth. On the demesne there were stalls for 100 head of cattle, extensive stabling, barns, a saw mill, cottages and 1000 feet of farm buildings with two yards, all enclosed by an exterior wall. The mansion house had attachments of considerable out offices, gate lodges, nurserymen's cottages, a pheasantry and dog kennels. The nursery grounds covered ten acres and a deer park with a 'noble herd of deer' was enclosed by a wire fence almost two miles long. The mansion house garden consisted of three acres, was well stocked and enclosed by a brick wall – See *Descriptive particulars of the Kilcommon Demesne, Cahir Castle and other portions of the estates of the late John Sadleir M.P. Situate in the Counties of Tipperary and Limerick*, (Dublin, 1857).
36. *B..M.*, Vol.XVI, 1856, p. 406. For more insight into the Glengall transactions see R.D., 1854, vol.8, memorial 157, Indenture of Conveyance 22 February 1854, R.D., 1854 vol.11 Memorial 172, Indenture of Conveyance, 2 May 1854. For reference to transfer of land to the Globe Insurance Company see R.D., 1854, vol.15, Memorial 207, deed 9 June 1854. See also R.D., 1854, vol.28, Memorial 200, Conveyance 22 November 1854.
37. See *S.N.* 7 March 1856 on the notice from the Albion Insurance Company restraining the removal of timber from the estate.
38. See R.D., 1854, vol.11, Memorial of Conveyance 2 May 1854. See also R.D., 1854, vol.18, Abs. 157, see *W.T.* 11 March 1854. See also *L.R.* 26 September 1856 on the pressure placed by Glengall trustees on Sadleir to pay at a time when he was overextended through purchasing in other areas.
39. R.D., 1854, vol.30, Memorial 261, Indenture 20 October 1854. This cited a long list of townlands and was witnessed by James B. Kennedy.
40. *F.J.* 11 December 1858.

41. *I.C.R. 1855, 1856 and 1857*; vol.5, p. 187.
42. *W.T.* 3 May 1856, *Times* 21 May 1856.
43. *I.C.R. 1858 and 1859*, vol.6, pp 47-48. The transactions of March to December are recorded on pp 41-87.
44. Glyns was the London clearing house for the Tipperary.
45. *T.F.P.*, 9 November 1858.
46. *I.C.R. 1858 and 1859*, vol.9, p. 72 for details of the meeting.
47. *T.F.P.*, 9 November 1858.
48. *I.C.R. 1858 and 1859*, vol.9, p. 49.
49. Ibid., p. 70.
50. Ibid., p. 80.
51. See *T.F.P.* 12 November 1858 for the evidence of Lance, a director of the Landed Estates Court.
52. *I.C.R. 1858 and 1859*, vol.9, pp 80-81.
53. Ibid., p. 50.
54. Ibid., p. 55.
55. See R.D., 1857, vol.34, abstract 67.
56. Details in *R.T.* 26 April 1856, *B.M..*, vol.XVI, 1856 pp 293-299. See also *R.T.2*, 1 March 1856 and *N.G* 1 March 1856. This fraud was not discovered by the Secretary until February 1856. Sadleir was confronted on 15 February and promised to furnish a full report on 18 February – *R.T.* 1 March 1856.
57. *I.C.R. 1860 and 1861*, vol.11, pp 5-7.
58. The Coolnamuck estate.
59. *I.C.R. 1860 and 1861*, vol.11, p. 7.
60. Ibid., p. 8.
61. See *L.R.* 8 July 1856 for details of this.
62. The case did not come to court until after Sadleir's death.
63. The Bath episode in *I.C.R. 1860 and 1861*, vol.11, pp 9-10.
64. William Dargan was born in Carlow in 1799 and educated in England. In the 1820s he was involved in road building in England and Ireland. In 1831 he became the contractor for the construction of the railway from Dublin to Kingstown (Dun Laoghaire), the first line in Ireland. By 1853 he had constructed over 600 miles of railway including the Dublin and Drogheda Railway, the Great Southern and Western and the Midland Great Western lines. He also constructed the Ulster Canal between Lough Erne and Belfast. He became involved in other less successful business ventures and died on 7 February 1867. *D.N.B.*, e.v..
65. *I.C.R. 1858 and 1859*, vol.9, p. 56.
66. Ibid., p. 11.
67. Details of this plot in *I.C.R. 1855, 1856 and 1857*, vol.5, pp 181-206. See also *Times* 31 May, 5 June 1856, *C.T.* 28 June 1856.
68. Letter cited in *Copies of the informations and warrants against Mr. James Sadleir and of the Bills of Indictment, if any, found against him, and of the names of the witnesses and finding of the grand jury thereon*, H.C. 1856(394)L587 ms.p.593. Henceforth *Informations and Warrants (394)*. (The volume contains another paper of the same title but numbered 394-1, (henceforth *Informations and Warrants (394-1)*. Part of the above letter read, 'I want an honest man for a few months to hold a few shares in the Tipperary Bank as a trustee for a cousin of mine. I do not wish any of her family to be the person, and, with your permission, take the liberty of using your name. I will substitute another in a few months as a trustee. I do not think you will incur any responsibility; but lest you may I enclose a guarantee, which is but fair ... will you be ready to ride at three o'clock?'.

69. For details of the fraud in Clonmel see ibid., MS. pp.589-592.
70. His letters 25 and 30 April 1855 in ibid., MS. p. 594.
71. By September 1855 Ferrall was becoming suspicious because of the large number of transactions – ibid., MS. p. 596.
72. Spoken by the Master of the Rolls – *C.T.* 28 June 1856.
73. Letter in *I.C.R. 1855, 1856, and 1856*, vol. 5, pp 198-201.
74. Letter 15 May 1857 from Paris in T.F.P. 22 May 1857.
75. *Informations and Warrants (394)*, ms. p. 591.
76. Kelly only saw the printed balance sheet with his name appended when it was produced as evidence in the litigation following Sadleir's death.
77. *B.H.* in T.L. 8 March 1856. See appendix 7.
78. *T.F.P.* 12 November 1858 for Wilkinson's evidence in the Landed Estates Court.
79. Morier Evans, *Facts Failures.*, p. 239.
80. *C.S.* 9 August 1856.
81. Edward Backhouse was born in Darlington in 1808. He was a partner in banking and collieries enterprises. He did not take an active role in these, however, preferring to travel, study, write and paint. A Quaker, he spent much of his time in philanthropic pursuits. He died in 1879. *D.N.B.*, e.v.
82. See e.g. *C.T.* 7 February 1857 showing Backhouse as a petitioner in the Incumbered Estates Court.
83. Information on the sale of the bank revealed at the 1856 a.g.m. report in *Newcastle Chronicle* 22 August 1856, *Newcastle Messenger and Advertiser* 9 August 1856.
84. William Walker successfully resisted being ousted on the basis that the purchase money of £50,000 had not yet been paid.
85. See *Times* 15 October 1856 and *C.P.* 18 October 1856.
86. His letter 8 May 1857 to the *Dublin Evening Post* in *T.F.P.* 15 May 1857. See *I.C.R. 1858 and 1859*, vol.9, p. 45 for the somewhat sympathetic view of Judge Mountifort Longfield in the Landed Estates Court that James would not have initially expected the bank to founder since its investments were sound, but that his failure to exercise proper controls ultimately placed him in an intolerable position.
87. The board of the Bank of Ireland sanctioned overdrafts and stipulated that any excess over the agreed amounts must be guaranteed by the sureties of the branch agents – see *Instructions to Agents, Sub-agents and Clerks at Bank of Ireland Branches*, (Dublin, 1849), p. 12.
88. Details of election expenses in Tipperary County Library, Thurles.
89. *L.R.* 26 September 1856.
90. See *Athlone Election Petition Report*, pp 2 et.seq.
91. *Nation* 22 January 1853.
92. See E. Walford, *The County Families of the United Kingdom*, Vol 1, (London 1865), p. 543, F.M.L. Thompson, 'The End of a Great Estate' in *Economic History Review*, 2nd series, VIII, No 1, August 1955, pp 36-52, D and E. Spring, 'The Fall of the Grenvilles 1844-1848, *Huntington Library Quarterly*, pp 165-190.
93. See R.D., 1849, vol 15, abstract 142, deed poll 3 February 1849 between the most Honourable Richard Plantagenet Campbell Grenville Nugent Temple, only son and heir to the Duke of Buckingham. See *T.F.P.* 16 November 1858 – Landed Estates Court.
94. He received the money from an individual named Barker. For details of his use of the Chandos mortgage see *I.C.R. 1860 and 1861*, vol 11, p. 3, *T.F.P.* 12 November 1858, *F.J.* 7 December 1858.

95. Sadleir to Chandos, 15 June 1855, Huntington Library, San Marino (California), Grenville Papers, STG, Carton 398(25). (This collection contains 300,000 pieces).

96. *F.J.* 7 December 1858.

97. See *F.J.* 16 March 1852 for a comment on its lack of popularity. Gray circulated a lithographed letter to the effect that the Telegraph was being sold below cost – *Tablet* 15 January 1853, *W.T.* 29 January 1853.

98. The *Times* 27 January 1855 reported a meeting of bondholders on 26 January which set up a committee to investigate the proceedings of the commission under which the bonds were issued and to devise a plan for recovering the amount invested and for placing the property on which they were secured on a more satisfactory footing. The commission had been set up under special acts but the bonds were not government guaranteed. The general liabilities in January 1855 stood at over one million pounds of which the bonds represented £700,000. A further million was required to complete the building work. At that period it was not possible to raise such finance because of the state of the money markets. The committee appointed by the meeting recommended the replacing of the commission by a joint-stock company and the conversion of the bonds to shares. The *Times* 24 February 1855 reported a further meeting at which more information was revealed which showed that the commission had flooded the market with unstamped bonds by using them instead of cash to pay the contractors. Builders received large advances from money lenders on the security of these bonds. See also *Times* 14 March 1855 for another meeting of bondholders which again mooted the conversion of the venture to a joint-stock company. See *B.M.*, vol XVI 1856 p. 293. For the dissatisfaction of the official appointed to investigate the affair see *Report by E. Lawes to First Commissioner of Woods on Westminster Improvement Acts Amending Bill*, H.C. 1850 (396) XXXIII.709

99. e.g. in December 1852 mining shares in California quadrupled from half a crown to ten shillings – *Tablet* 25 December 1852.

100. Quoted in *D.E.P.* 11 March 1856.

101. *Morning Chronicle* 18 February 1856.

102. Ibid.

103. *I.C.R. 1855, 1856 and 1857*, vol.5, p. 187.

104. Appendix 7.

105. *D.E.P.* 12 January 1856, T.L. 19 January 1856. See R.D., 1856, vol.3, abstract 55, (Marriage settlement 26 January 1856).

106. Rolls Court evidence in *Times* 6 March 1856.

107. Report in *W.T.* 16 February 1856, *L.E.* 23 February 1856.

108. *W.T.* 16 February 1856. See ibid., 1 March 1856 condemning the *Nation* for failing to mention Sadleir's role in this in its report on the proceedings.

109. *B.M.*, vol.XVI, 1856, p. 152.

110. *W.T.* 16 February 1856.

111. See Marnane, *Land and Violence*, pp 75-76 for reaction in Tipperary Town.

112. *L.E.* 23 February 1856.

113. Evidence at Sadleir's inquest in *W.T.* 23 February 1856.

114. *Times* 26 February 1856.

115. *C.C.* 23 February 1856. Originally it was thought that Sadleir's forgeries on the Incumbered Estate Court were confined to one or two, but on 7 April a London solicitor arrived at the Registry of Deeds with a carpet bag of conveyances and certificates of registry on lands apparently sold to Sadleir in the Court. It was discovered by the Principal of the Registry office that five of the deeds of Conveyance were forgeries and bore the false signatures of two commissioners.

The purchase price of an estate on a genuine conveyance was changed from £2000 to £5000. All the certificates of Registry were fictitious and bore the forged signature of the First Assistant Registrar. The forged conveyances amounted to £44,000 on which Sadleir had raised £16,000 – *W.T.* 12 April 1856, *Times* 26 February 1856.

116. *B.H.* 1 March 1856. Sadleir's copy is now in Archbishop's House, Thurles. Contemporary sources reported that he had turned down page 644 which began the relevant section. On checking the author found the page still turned down, realistic testimony to his last hours.

117. *Times* 20 February 1856, *W.T.* 23 February 1856.

118. *S.N.* 20 February 1856. Sadleir's last hours were described by Elwin at the inquest and widely reported; see *Times* 20, 26 February 1856. See also *Bucks Herald* 1 March 1856 which carried the texts of the letters and see also *L.E.* 1 March 1856, *Sligo Champion* 1 March. (Interestingly Emma Sadleir forwarded John Sadleir's letter to her as evidence but requested Norris to return it after the inquest.

119. *C.S.* 23 February 1856, *Times* 18,20 February 1856.

120. *B.H.* 1 March 1856. Rumours spread that Sadleir had not committed suicide and that the corpse belonged to another individual. This was discounted by William Manning, Coroner of the Queen's Household who was a friend of the family. See his letter 2 April 1856 in *Times* 3 April 1856.

121. Letter from a priest in *Nation* 8 March 1856.

122. Highgate Cemetery Records show William Sadleir as the owner of the grave (plot number 7158/30). These records confirm the date of internment as 21 February 1856. Some contemporary sources reported that the body was exhumed and shipped to Dublin, but this was no more than sensationalism – *C.S.* 20 September 1856, 4 October 1856.

123. The inquest details were widely reported and contained the narrative of his activities on Saturday 16 February. See e.g. the *Times* 20 February 1856, *W.T.* 23 February 1856, *C.S.* 23 February 1856 for the first sitting.

124. Thomas Wakley 1795-1862. He was a member of the Royal College of Surgeons from 1817. He practised first in Regent Street and later in the Strand. Wakley was the founder of a medical journal called the *Lancet*. A confrontational individual within his own profession, he made a public and sustained attack on nepotism within the ranks of surgeons. He publicly criticised both hospitals and the Royal College of Surgeons. He entered politics to gain a stronger voice in the reform of medical institutions and became M.P. for the Borough of Finsbury in 1835. He played a major role in influencing legislation on medical matters. He was an advocate of Repeal and an opponent of the corn laws. He retired from Parliament in 1852 and is best remembered as Coroner for West Middlesex. Charles Dickens served on one of his juries in 1841. He died in Madeira in May 1862. *D.N.B.*, e.v.

125. It is interesting that William Keogh shared a similar fate. He cut his throat on 30 September 1878 in Bingen-on-Rhine. he was buried in the Alterfriedhof near the Railway Station in Bonn. See the *Times* 2, 7 October 1878.

126. *C.P.* 15 March 1856, *W.T.* 15 March 1856.

127. i.e. Felon of himself.

128. In Sadleir's case the Crown waived its right in favour of the creditors and of Clement William Sadleir his next of kin. The administration of such property was given to Anthony Norris; see P.R.O. Letter of Administration 21 August 1856 ref.PRO B7/70/70.

Number and Description of Grave.	Name and Address of Owner.	Names of Persons interred.	Year.	Depth.
7157 6 6 x 2 6 5 Square Depth 5 **Cons**d. 10/—	Maria Steward Norfolk New Brighton £3. 3 p 21 Feby 1856			
7158 6 6 x 2 6 5 Square Depth 7 New **Cons**d.	William Sadlier Gloucester Sq Hyde Park £3. 3 p 21 Feby 1856	John Sadler	1856	

Register of Highgate Cemetery, London, indicating location of Sadlier's grave and date of internment.

Chapter 13

Bank and business failure – a tale of misery and a lawyers' harvest

Immediate press reaction to Sadleir's death was largely sympathetic. At national level the *Freeman's Journal* reported on the 'deepest sympathy' evident for him and conceded that past hostilities 'seemed to be forgotten' in the wake of the tragedy.[1] Locally the *Carlow Post* expressed its 'heartfelt sympathy and condolence with those to whom ties of consanguinity, friendship or connection in any shape with the deceased must render the sudden and unexpected bereavement more than ordinarily appalling and lamentable'.[2] In England his death was seen by the *Morning Advertiser* as a blow to commercial and banking interests,

> Mr. John Sadleir was greatly respected by the class of capitalists among whom he moved, and in political circles, he was esteemed and admired. His melancholy death leaves a vacancy in the representation of Sligo borough and in the direction of the London and County Bank, over which he presided with tact, ability and signal success. The Royal Swedish Railway, the Grand Junction Railway of France, the Rome and Frascati Railway, and a variety of other foreign enterprises also lose the benefit of his counsel and services.[3]

Duffy had emigrated to Australia the previous October[4] and Lucas had died in the same month,[5] but their absence did not soften the hostility of the *Nation* or the *Tablet* to Sadleir, even in death. Both were more concerned with his political stance than with his frauds. The *Nation*, under the editorship of John Cashel Hoey, led the attacks of the anti-Sadleirite Press. One of its articles, which received widespread coverage in the provincial papers,[6] consigned Sadleir to the company of Judas Iscariot, Luttrell and Castlereagh,[7] and exacted revenge for the less than sympathetic tone of the *Telegraph* on the death of Lucas and the emigration of Duffy.[8] This unforgiving article continued the denunciation of Sadleir's political manoeuvrings which had

reduced Ireland to almost as pitiable a case as that corpse which lies in a workhouse shell at Hampstead ... of all his frauds his political ambition was the deadliest and the most effectual. John Sadleir is dead, indeed; but he has left a goodly stock of Sadleirists behind him. You find them mocking at public virtue, and greedy of government offal in every corner of the country.

The *Tablet* followed much the same line, and compared Sadleir unfavourably with Lucas both in the manner of their deaths, and in the contribution they made during their lives.[9] Lucas was the representative of 'independent purity', Sadleir of 'slavish corruption'. Conscious of Keogh's ambition towards the bench the *Tablet* was not satisfied that one 'great public offender' had been removed, but urged a petition to the Queen to forbid 'the bench of justice' from becoming the reward of 'political profligacy'.

The bitterness between the *Telegraph* and these two papers reached new levels when the loyal McCabe reacted with fury against their attacks. Two editions were devoted to denouncing them.[10] He was careful not to minimise Sadleir's misdemeanours, but took the view that his deliberate choice of suicide was the greatest possible punishment, surpassing the 'vengeance of the law', which would have been transportation or penal servitude for life. He could not understand why his rivals connected Sadleir's frauds with his political career, and reviled the 'two miserable newspapers that are seeking to convert such a death, accompanied by such circumstances into political capital'. In both editions McCabe published the Judas Iscariot article, to expose 'the atrocity of those paragraph-scribbling, grave-grubbing, resurrection men, who would eke a penny profit out of the body of a poor dead Irishman'. He condemned as barbarous any gloating over such a tragedy, and was not averse to introducing a political note himself by railing against what he termed the 'wild inhuman and anti-Christian teaching of the new class of politicians that have risen up of late years in Ireland'.[11]

McCabe's stance did not receive universal favour in Sadleir's native county. The radical *Tipperary Leader*,[12] under Leyne's editorship, adopted the *Nation's* views and also copied the harsh article in its edition of 1 March. An editorial of 15 March,[13] analysing the concept of Sadleirism, was coloured by a Young Ireland perspective of hostility to a section of the Irish priesthood. This was contextualised in a historical sketch of the debt owed by the Catholic Church to the laity for sheltering its priests 'when England hunted them down like wolves'. This debt was betrayed by the Sadleirite priests,

they are causing the ruin of millions by their support of Sadleir's policy

... and how bishops and priests could have been duped into the sustainment of that policy is indeed a mystery. Let the truth be told at all hazards – they have supported it, and through their sanction and co-operation John Sadleir has been able to bring down ruin upon his country and upon thousands of his fellow creatures. There is no denying it, the stigma of Sadleirism rests upon a large portion of the Irish Church, and much of the responsibility of the ruin rests at their door ... they saw their flocks scattered over the wide, wide world, they saw their chapels becoming empty week after week, they saw the virtuous Irish peasant flung upon the roadside with his wife and children by cruel landlordism, and they only helped to break up the party which Ireland sent to the British Parliament to prevent such a calamity; ... they saw the Irish race flying in their thousands from the land of their fathers and instead of putting forth their hands to save them, they sanctioned the wretched policy which drove them to that extremity; they saw them flying to a country where every ruin awaited them – loss of life, loss of morals, loss of faith – and yet instead of saving their poor flocks from such misery, they crushed the faithful priests who nobly flung themselves between the country and ruin to save the lives of their perishing people. Good God, that this should happen in Ireland and in the Irish Church.

It might be thought that even Tenant League priests would have found this indictment of their colleagues too graphic, but at a tenant right meeting in Rathkeale three weeks after Sadleir's death Archdeacon Fitzgerald issued a severe condemnation of Cullen, Haly and Browne as Sadleirite supporters, which earned him the displeasure of his own bishop, John Ryan.[14] The Archdeacon was obliged to issue a written apology to the Vatican and to the three prelates, and a pledge to submit all past, present and future writing by him to the 'just judgement' of the Holy See, the Congregatio de Propaganda Fide and his own bishop. A sample of his statement about the bishops explains the reason for official church displeasure,

> John Sadleir had three godfathers of Irish degree. I trust they did not entrust their 'daltha' with the keeping of their money bags, and that the simplicity of the 'dove'[15] was mixed up with a little of the hardening alloy of the cunning of the serpent. And talking of serpents ... do not they who throw the sanction of their high and holy influences over deeds such as those of Athlone and Sligo inflict a deadly wound and sting to death not only the dearest interests in a temporal sense of wronged and outraged people, but virtually wound morality, truth and honesty... but I ask you what filial affection do you or I owe to the suffragans of Connaught or Leinster?... But what are the Bishops in Connaught to us more than Bishops in Spain or Brazil? ... I respect honest Tom Shee, Heaven forgive me, a thousand times more than his ordinary, and so I

am sure does every one who hears me ... Tom Shee is in the eyes of aristocratic bloated Bishops, a sinner and a publican. To be sure the Bishops of Connaught and Leinster are, as we read in the *Telegraph*, overloaded with virtues of every kind ...Tom O' Shea wrote an unguarded letter lately to the Tenant League. He called the Archbishop of Dublin an arch apostate ... If instead of calling Primate Cullen an apostate, he had said that Primate Cullen was an obstacle, and the great and insuperable obstacle in the way of tenant justice, if he had proclaimed that it would be happy for the Irish masses that Dr. Cullen had spent all his years in the learned researches of the Vatican, so far as relates to their temporal interests ... he would have found some that I knew of to agree with him ...Tom O' Shea's name will be venerated by honest Irishmen when the names of higher dignitaries will be forgotten as ninnies and imbeciles, or remembered as worse.

Apart from such manifestations of division within the clergy, Cullen was also concerned about the damage done to the Irish Party, not, however, by Sadleir's defection or frauds, but by the 'tenant right faction'. In a letter of 14 April to Monsell he identified them as 'generally the editors of newspapers' motivated by personal gain and the increased circulation of their journals.[16] The weakening of the Liberal Party and the gains of the Conservatives were 'the legacy which Duffy and Lucas has left us'.

His uncle, Fr James Maher, did not confine himself to the privacy of confidential correspondence to complain about the Leaguers. Two weeks prior to Cullen's communication with Monsell the Carlow priest launched an attack on Hoey, which in the exaggerated opinion of James Redmond 'dealt a deadly blow' to the paper.[17] Maher's letter of 2 April to the *Freeman* was a response to a condemnation of him by Hoey at a recent League meeting, because at one time he had refused a request for moral and financial support for the movement.[18] The letter severely denounced Hoey as an individual without experience, knowledge, intellect or respect for authority, and considered that it was 'seldom that one of his class, so little distinguished from the general mass of society by intellectual training – without social position, unconnected with any of the professions – succeeds in doing so much harm'. Offended by such a personal insult Hoey retaliated in kind that Maher was a 'brawling firebrand', an unscrupulous, uncharitable person, discreditable to the priesthood, who had 'blackguarded me to his hearts content'.[19] Insults were traded in a further exchange of letters until both had vented their dislike on each other.[20]

Despite such individual feuds and the stance taken by the *Tablet* and *Nation,* public opinion in general was more concerned with the human rather than the political consequences of Sadleir's life. When the extent of these became apparent hitherto sympathetic newspapers turned on him reflecting a hostile public opinion. The *Dublin Evening Post* caught this mood when it cast aside

> false pity for the wretched author of all this sorrow. If the heinousness of crimes be measured by their consequences, the man who carries disaster, if not absolute ruin, into a hundred families, is stained with a deeper guilt than the mere ruffian who attacks life.[21]

The *Carlow Post* also changed direction and quoted from the *Leader* which placed Sadleir's swindles in a wider concept of mid-Victorian hypocrisy and falling values, where being caught was the prime crime,

> We have a right to assert that he is a type. The class is not always so completely developed; but he is only taller than plants of the same bed. Such practical and material contradictions could not exist if it were not for what appears to us to be at this day the ruling vice of society ... It is not the commercial depravity, which is only the ultimate symptoms on the surface, though it threatens to undermine our commercial strength, by taking away nationally that character for the "sterling" which we have lost individually. It consists in the habit which has grown upon us of having a set of morals which we profess to uphold in public and betray in private. The code of society decrees certain laws; the open infraction is punished, the open denial is treated as infamy; yet the veiled avoidance is winked at, and the wholesale infraction is tolerated, so that it be not avowed.[22]

The 'commercial depravity' and 'moral hypocrisy' condemned in this extract was well illustrated in the catalogue of fraud that emerged within weeks of Sadleir's death. With the exception of the London bank, which had secured its loan,[23] most of the institutions connected with him were seriously damaged or destroyed, injuring thousands of investors, including his family, relatives and friends. Some companies were damaged through their connection with the Tipperary bank and others suffered through the direct frauds of Sadleir himself.

One of those damaged was the East Kent whose losses, however, were relatively light at £8,000 deposited in the Tipperary on his advice.[24] Even allowing for the mistaken expectation that this could be recovered from the assets of the bank, the board could afford to be optimistic that expansion would not be checked. The half-yearly meeting of shareholders two weeks after the suicide of their Deputy Chairman confirmed this.[25] £95,000 had been spent on line extension during those six months, and the board was confident that a call of two pounds ten shillings per share would finance the works for these extensions, which included the Rochester line and the purchase of a large tract of land between Chatham and Sittingbourne. The Rochester and Chatham tunnels had commenced, and £33,000 spent on the Dover extension.[26]

The Royal Swedish was not so fortunate because Sadleir's frauds on it were far more substantial. Within a week of his death the company was in chaos. The directors held a meeting with stock exchange jobbers, and issued a general statement on the improper over-issue of shares.[27] Shareholders and bondholders were requested to present their documents at the office for examination and verification. This resulted in an immediate drop in the value of the shares and their suspension from the stock exchange. The *Railway Times* accused the directors of colluding with the jobbers to conceal the true state[28] of the company, which took several months to clarify by a committee appointed by the enraged shareholders, who blamed the directors for allowing Sadleir such scope to defraud them.[29] Shareholders insisted on the resignation of the board and dispatched some of the new directors to Sweden to secure the state guarantee and an extension of time to complete the project.[30] Despite the optimism of King Oscar that the line would be incorporated into a proposed national rail network,[31] the Diet rejected all suggestions for government resuscitation of the Royal Swedish.[32] By February 1859, when £700,000 had been spent on development since construction began under Sadleir's chairmanship, receipts had reached an extremely low level, leaving the railway at the mercy of the Diet, which according to the *Railway Times* enjoyed the discomfiture of both the King and the shareholders.[33] The demise of the Royal Swedish was nicely summed up by this journal,

> The receipts do not meet the working expenses. The whole of the available funds have been expended in completing the line previously described as finished, and consequently no means are available for constructing the remaining nine miles between Arboga and Koping, which require an outlay of £15,000. There is no probability of payment of overdue interest to the bondholders; the directors devote themselves zealously to the undertaking without remuneration; the officials and working staff do the best they can; but bankruptcy, nevertheless, stares the concern out of countenance. Such is the Royal Swedish, and such, we fear, it is destined to remain.

The Carson's Creek Gold Mining Company shared a similar fate, but unlike the Royal Swedish was unable to make any attempt at survival. The management of its affairs had been under Sadleir's total control, and was shrouded in secrecy. There was no board of directors to pursue its claim against his estate, and the secretary was unaware of where its securities had been deposited or that they had long been disposed of by Sadleir.[34]

Neither did the Newcastle Bank survive, but Walker was determined to honour its debts. He called a general meeting six months after Sadleir's suicide, and the *Newcastle Messenger* remarked with understated irony that 'the proceedings were of a somewhat animated character'.[35] The large attendance of shareholders was formally told of how the bank had been gutted. Creditors were then due £18,000 which could not be immediately met and total liabilities were set at £89,000, but shareholders were assured that the bank held securities to meet most of this. It is not clear if these securities included the six drafts of the Tipperary.

Following the meeting Walker issued a circular to creditors requesting time to raise the money.[36] He put the bank's obligations at under £24,000 and gave the assurance that 'the fortune of each shareholder is available for the creditors until every debt is discharged'. This was based upon the knowledge that some of the one hundred shareholders were individuals of considerable means. Walker was also determined to pursue a legal case against the Tipperary.

The collapse of the latter was the most poignant of all, generating alarm throughout the U.K. not only because of the spectacular frauds which destroyed it, but also because it was one of a number of banks to fail around that time.[37] In Ireland the banking repercussions were localised. There were serious runs on the National Bank in Thurles, Tipperary and Nenagh, where some depositors even demanded gold for Bank of Ireland notes, so that 'an immense pile of bullion met the eye of every individual who presented a note for payment'.[38] The run on the National Bank in Tipperary lasted for three days.[39] There was also a less severe run on the National and Provincial banks and the Bank of Ireland in Kilkenny, all of which met the demands of their depositors.[40]

The Tipperary's depositors were not so fortunate. Branches came under pressure on Monday 18 February, when news of Sadleir's suicide reached Ireland. The managers vainly tried to calm the crowds who besieged their offices. Thurles depositors, especially tenant farmers, were in a violent mood and the police were called to guard the doors, a response which drew the ironic remark of one depositor that 'if you don't get gold you'll get lead'.[41]

In Nenagh the manager refused payments that Monday, but kept the door open for several days and did his best to 'appease the numerous disappointed claimants for their money'.[42] The Tipperary manager, Michael Dillon, told customers that the assets of shareholders were sufficient to meet the losses,[43] and they were also re-assured by the arrival of James Scully, who was shocked by the collapse and anxious to uphold the family's integrity as bankers. He endorsed some deposit receipts as a guarantee of future payment.[44] Such depositors were lucky because Dillon was soon forced to demand a week's notice of withdrawal.[45] William Kelly, the manager in Clonmel, required ten days notice.[46]

These manoeuvres were a cosmetic exercise in an institution whose funds were exhausted. The bank officially closed on 20 February with total liabilities of £430,000.[47] Such liabilities varied from branch to branch according to the level of deposits,[48] Clonmel having the highest losses at £108,000 and Nenagh one of the lowest at £20,000. Behind these lay a long train of individual misery, depending on the status of those involved and the amounts lost. Because of the higher than normal rate of interest offered by the bank and its identification with the Bank of Ireland substantial sums, often representing life's savings, were lodged there. Ultimately 1,700 debts were proved, and reflected losses by all classes – farmers, widows, shopkeepers, policemen, merchants, schoolteachers, millers, clergymen and gentry.[49] Richard O'Flaherty, a farmer from Killusty lost £2,180, Michael Carroll, a Roscrea tanner merchant £1,306, and the Earl of Bessborough £3,000. Some clergy also suffered. Thomas Blake, the parish priest of Roscrea, lost £182 while Archdeacon Laffan, Francis McMahon, Peter Nolan, curate in Birr and Andrew James Scanlan, parish priest of Couraganeen were victims. The Tipperary chapel fund for £2,400 was also lost. Several local institutions were damaged, too. The Thurles Savings Bank, which opened once a week to cater for small depositors, was unfortunate in transferring its account from the National to the Tipperary because of the higher rate of interest. It lost £696 as a result, but had sufficient reserves to meet the loss.[50] Some Poor Law Unions were badly hit and acrimonious haggling took place between electoral divisions, because new rates had to be struck to maintain the workhouses.[51] The loss was apportioned according to the cash for each division. Both the Roscrea and Donaghmore Unions lost their respective £1,800 and £1,050 in the Roscrea branch. This caused a conflict between both unions which was eventually referred to the Court of Queen's Bench by the Donaghmore Guardians.[52] The Thurles, Athy, Thomastown, and Nenagh Poor Law Unions lost sums varying from £500 to £1,600. Those who guaranteed union funds were also affected. Simon Armstrong, an old man from Tipperary, unable to pay his security was prosecuted by the Nenagh Board and, it seems, imprisoned as a result.[53] Richard Sadleir of Scalaheen was the other surety pursued by the Nenagh Board, and escaped only because he died.

Initially it was believed by some depositors that individual losses would eventually be small.[54] The altar assurances of several priests reinforced this,[55] and at face value the assets were reckoned to be £443,000,[56] which, however, included Sadleir's £288,000 overdraft.[57] In reality assets were a mere £35,000, later increasing to £50,000.[58]

A small number of creditors sold their deposit receipts to speculators, who hoped to make a profit by claiming any further assets raised through the courts.[59] It was by the process of law, however, that most chose to recover their money. The law of limited liability did not apply to banks in 1856 and shareholders' property was vulnerable to creditors through lawsuits. Such suits entailed a great number of complex cases, many of them merely to decide points of law, and were heard in the Rolls Court, Court of Chancery, Nisi Prius Court of Exchequer and Queens Bench. Some were appealed to the Irish Lord Chancellor and ultimately the Lords.[60] Protracted legal battles ensured that the lawyers were the real beneficiaries of the Tipperary bank crash.[61]

Part of the problem lay in the confusion that existed as to whether the Irish Bankers Act of 1760, the 33 Geo.11 Cap 14 (Irl.), (henceforth referred to as the old Act), had been repealed by the joint stock winding up acts of 1848 and 1849, the 6 Geo IV Act, (henceforth referred to as the new Act). The old Act was bankruptcy legislation, and if applicable to the Tipperary would make the entire property of shareholders liable to be sold for the benefit of creditors. The later Act, however, was a winding up act constituting a different process whereby shareholders were liable only in proportion to their shares. The extent of their liability was determined by calls per share.

A number of creditors were convinced that the Tipperary came under the terms of the old Act and began individual proceedings. The shareholders were alive to the danger of a bankruptcy judgement and, apart from protecting their property, were anxious to avoid a barrage of individual and costly lawsuits. Some of the larger ones moved swiftly and pressurised James Sadleir to balk those creditors pushing for bankruptcy proceedings. Sadleir complied and sought the advice of Morrogh and Kennedy on how to outmanoeuvre them. On 21 February, his bailiff, David Rafferty, presented a petition to the Irish Lord Chancellor for the dissolution and winding up of the bank under the new Act.[62] Rafferty was a person of very modest means who had received his shares in October 1855 when they were of little value.[63] He was clearly a pawn, and was denounced in the press as a 'stalking horse to secure to the chief living author of this wholesale robbery the winding up of his own delinquency'.[64]

The winding up acts were administered under the jurisdiction of Chancery,[65] consisting of the Rolls Court and the Court of Chancery. Despite John Sadleir's often justifiable criticism of its delays, Chancery, as the principal agent of equity, was suited to seeing that justice was done irrespective of the complexity of the issues at stake.[66]

Over 1,500 creditors favoured this avenue, but because of their Sadleirite connections they feared that Morrogh and Kennedy might seek to exercise an influence over the winding up process, and protect the shareholders from just claims. A group of depositors in the Tipperary area were determined to forestall this, and issued a circular calling a meeting in the Market House on 27 February.[67] The Sadleirs' solicitors responded prior to the meeting with a public assurance, which was posted in all the towns where a branch of the bank had existed,

> Our duty, as solicitors for the petitioner, will have been discharged as soon as we shall have obtained an order referring the matter to one of the Masters, who will have the exclusive charge of the winding up, and whose first duty will be to appoint an official Manager, to whom (as a quasi assignee under Bankruptcy) the business of winding up will be entrusted, and who must give ample security for the proper assignment of his duties. To that officer, not to us will be entrusted the winding up, and there can be no doubt, but that the Master, in selecting that officer, will regard the interests of the creditors, and also of the shareholders, and will select none but a competent, trustworthy and independent individual, who shall give ample security for the faithful and impartial discharge of his very responsible duties.[68]

There was no denial in this statement that the purpose of the petition was to protect the shareholders from 'unjust or unequal pressure'. It proposed, however, that the winding up acts were in the best interests of the creditors by providing the quickest and most effective means of redress. There was also the added advantage that the English shareholders would be equally liable under these acts, because the orders of the Irish Court of Chancery were enforceable in English courts. The statement also revealed that two solicitors could be appointed to safeguard the interests of the shareholders and the creditors. This was shown as a precaution to ensure the impartiality of whoever would be appointed official manager.

This at least mollified the creditors who met in Tipperary. Interestingly, their suspicions of Morrogh and Kennedy were shared by some shareholders, and when Rafferty's petition was heard in a crowded Rolls Court on 4 March, James Scully's counsel made clear his client's concern 'that the carriage of the proceedings, if they were to go on, should not be placed in the hands of Mr. Kennedy, Mr. Rafferty, Mr. Morrogh, Mr. James Sadleir, or anybody in connexion with the Sadleir family'.[69] This was the first public statement of the the rift between the

Scullys and the Sadleirs which was to intensify over the following months. Other counsel for depositors and shareholders expressed similar views, and urged that the control of the bank be immediately removed from Sadleir.

The Master of the Rolls, Thomas Berry Cusack Smith,[70] understood their concern. Despite the protestations of Morrogh and Kennedy to the contrary, he rightly surmised that Rafferty's petition was inspired by James Sadleir, and viewed it as a ploy to secure control of the dissolution process. While exonerating them from any culpability in the bank failure, he was determined to exclude their influence in its winding up and was outspoken in his denunciation of James Sadleir,

> Why I believe in the recollection of no living person has there been a case of such gigantic fraud upon the community at large; ... The unfortunate contributors have been defeated and swindled out of their property by a proceeding of this kind, and it is most horrifying to think that anyone's property may be brought into such a state of jeopardy if they happen to subscribe to a bank on the faith and supposition that its proceedings will be carried on with common honesty and integrity ... am I, under these circumstances, to allow the confidential solicitors of the late John Sadleir, and the present confidential solicitors of Mr. James Sadleir, to carry on proceedings in this case, and substantially to exercise the influence which the carriage of proceedings always gives to the appointment of an official manager, who is enabled to raise funds for the purpose of paying creditors, and to exercise control as to who is to be sued and who is not to be sued? And is it possible for me to suppose that to have those proceedings carried on in the office, 5 Great Denmark Street, where Mr. James Sadleir, I dare say, resides, would be just or fair towards the legitimate creditors...? It is one of the most monstrous propositions I have ever heard.

Smith issued a formal order barring the solicitors of James Sadleir, or anyone connected with the fraudulent annual report of 1 February, from any involvement in the legal process. He also advised the creditors to meet in the Bank of Ireland offices in Dublin and agree upon a solicitor, which would avoid squabbling during the winding up proceedings. He dissolved the Tipperary and entrusted the winding up to Jeremiah J. Murphy, the Master of Chancery, whose first task was to appoint an official manager. The latter's function was to realise as high a dividend as possible by having the maximum number of shareholders held as contributories. These would then be liable to periodic calls based upon their respective number of shares, and it was in the manager's interest to show consistent energy in his task since his salary was fixed at 5% of monies raised, out of which he had to pay his staff.

He was also obliged to pledge £20,000 as security and supply the names of guarantors for that amount.[71] Each applicant had to submit the names of three solicitors, one of whom would be chosen to assist him. Another independent solicitor would be agreed upon by shareholders and creditors to act as watchdog over the manager.

Some delay in the appointment was inevitable because applications were invited by press advertisement. When Murphy convened his court some days after the dissolution he discovered the anxiety of some creditors and shareholders over this delay.[72] They pushed for the immediate appointment of an interim official manager to remove the residue of the bank's cash from Kennedy, who had taken the precaution of collecting it at the various branches. The interim manager could also demand payment of the bills due to the bank, which were about to mature. Murphy considered this at a second sitting[73] and agreed to appoint the Bank of Ireland, which had sustained substantial losses in trying to bolster the Tipperary, to take charge of the cash in Kennedy's possession, and to receive any bills falling due.[74]

Applications for the post of official manager were considered by him on 15 March, and the successful candidate was the Belfast-born George McDowell, a barrister and Junior Fellow of Trinity College, whose appointment was supported by the Scully brothers, James, John and Frank. Murphy later admitted that the views of James Scully had strongly influenced him in making the appointment.[75] The firm of Gibson and Adair was given carriage of the proceedings, a choice which did not please some creditors, because Gibson had frequently acted for Sadleir's law firm. The real influence, however, lay with McDowell's solicitor, J.D. Meldon.[76]

With the appointments completed, the scene was set for one of the most interesting legal battles in nineteenth century banking history. In theory the parameters of legal procedures were clear but the practical course was far more complicated. Creditors were required to prove their claims before the Master of Chancery by a specific date, and the official Manager drew up a list of shareholders to meet these claims. McDowell would place the maximum number of contributors on this list, and it was Murphy's duty to examine and ratify or modify it on appeal by those shareholders who wished to be struck off, or have their liabilities reduced.[77] While they may have been liable under the law they, too, saw themselves as victims and were determined to avoid ruin.

The initial shareholding was substantial, but the property of some was encumbered by mortgages, marriage settlements and other provisions.[78] More ominously it included John Sadleir to whose property the London and County had a strong claim. The possibility of holding the English shareholders liable was also in doubt, and the position of any shareholders who had transferred their shares within three years of the crash was not clear cut under the new banking act.[79]

The resolution of these issues would clarify several points of law and ultimately determine the size of the dividend realised for the creditors. It would also dictate the burden to be shouldered by these shareholders remaining on the list. It was in their interest to retain as many as possible and so spread the weight of this burden. John Bennett of Riverstown, Nenagh, who held twenty shares, raised the importance of this before Murphy in March.[80]

By the end of April McDowell had completed his list, which was then examined by Murphy.[81] Within a month he was faced with fifty four appeals,[82] mostly from proprietors who had transferred their shareholding within three years of the failure and who were known as qualified contributors. The initial Chancery and Rolls interpretation was that their liability stretched only to the engagements of the bank at the date the transfer of shares was registered. But, after many legal discussions and delays they were finally released from any liability by the Lord Chancellor early in 1857.

Vincent Scully was one of these, but creditors were confident that he would be retained on the list because he had been a director of the bank. When his case was first argued before Murphy in May 1856 he proclaimed his willingness to meet his liabilities to the last shilling, but pleaded that he should not be listed as a director, since this would implicate him in the scandal.[83] He outlined his protracted attempts to have his shares transferred, and explained that this was not due to any loss of confidence in the bank, but rather to dissatisfaction with its management.

Scully's appeal against Murphy's decision to leave him on the list of contributors was heard with some sympathy by the Master of the Rolls in June.[84] Smith exonerated him from any blame for the frauds, and ruled that he had not been a *bona fide* director, because the necessary deed of trust procedures had been breached when appointing him. Nevertheless, the Master felt that depositors had just reason to complain of Scully's long public identification with the bank, and refused to strike him off. But, the Irish Lord Chancellor, Maziere Brady,[85] reversed this decision in April 1857 and saved Scully from having to respond to McDowell's calls, which would have cost him £203,000.[86]

John Sadleir's Presbyterian friend, Wilson Kennedy, was not treated so sympathetically. Jeremiah Murphy interpreted Kennedy's sale of his shares at half price and the surrender of his salaried position of public officer as evidence that he wished to sever his connection with a failing enterprise.[87] Murphy accused Kennedy of dereliction of duty by leaving the bank's management entirely to James Sadleir. Kennedy received an even more severe rebuff when he appealed to the Rolls Court,[88] where the irascible Smith charged him with being privy to the fraud and while not 'criminally guilty, he is still responsible for a great deal that has occurred'. He accused him of a serious breach of trust in allowing Sadleir's overdraft to continue increasing, and of suffering 'his silence to be purchased by taking £500 for the shares he held'. This moral indictment was accompanied by a refusal of the appeal with costs.

Creditors received some satisfaction from this but they expected little financial return from Kennedy, who was not a rich person. The striking of the qualified contributors, however, was a serious blow to their hopes.[89] Thomas Hone and James Stirling were examples. They were wealthy individuals who held 188 shares.[90] Hone was a Dublin stockbroker who owned tenements and plots in the Strand part of the Newtown Castle Byrne estate in the parish of Monkstown.[91] Their combined wealth was reckoned at £200,000 which would easily have met the two calls of £40 and £250 per share made by McDowell in May 1856 and May 1857 respectively.[92]

What particularly galled the creditors was the morally corrupt but legal method used by Hone to offload his shares and avoid liability, while retaining the profits from them, a method also used by other shareholders such as Hugh Waugh of Dromore, County Down. The system was a transfer of shares to an employee of very limited means, who dutifully handed over the annual dividend.[93] In 1847 Hone had transferred the shares to his clerk, Thomas Edwards, who testified before Murphy that he had never received any dividend on these, and in 1854 had sold them to John Sadleir's clerk.[94] Proceeds from the sale went to Hone who allowed his clerk £22 commission on the transaction.

Such corruption was clearly not applicable to the English shareholders. As the victims of blatant dishonesty, they had most cause to feel aggrieved. Yet the morality of their case might not necessarily translate into legal justice. Although living in England they were liable under the new banker's Act, but not under the old one,[95] and McDowell was as determined to hold them on the list as he was to keep the Irish shareholders. Some of them were not optimistic about the outcome and left the country to avoid possible ruin,[96] but the remainder established a committee to plan strategy, opened a defence fund and engaged the best advice at the Irish bar.

While evidence of gross irregularities against the English shareholders was beyond doubt, Chancery decided to leave their fate to the Rolls Court[97] which deliberated on the case in May and June 1856.[98] At an early stage in the hearing Smith issued what amounted to a public rebuke of the Irish executive, by accusing it of 'very great dereliction of duty for failing to prosecute the authors of the scandal'.[99] He did not name these, but James Sadleir was the individual in mind.[100] Smith's stance was unusual for a judge and prompted J.D. Fitzgerald, Irish Attorney General since early April and counsel for John Sadleir in the Dowling cases, to contact William Kemmis, the Dublin Crown Solicitor.[101] His letter of 6 June presumed that the Master would take the normal course of handing over incriminating documents to Kemmis following his ruling. Fitzgerald instructed Kemmis to contact the official manager, in the meantime, for relevant documentation 'to guide my judgement as to the future course to be pursued'.

Within days the affair began to escalate into a public controversy between the Irish Attorney General and the Master of the Rolls. It was used in the Commons to embarrass Fitzgerald, whose response to the challenge of George Bowyer on 9 June was necessarily evasive.[102] Evidence of a legally criminal nature against James Sadleir had not yet been gathered, and Fitzgerald pleaded ignorance of his misdemeanours 'beyond those rumours which met the public eye from time to time in the newspapers'. He wrongly explained that Murphy had examined Sadleir in private and exonerated him.[103] Nevertheless, Fitzgerald decided to go to Dublin for the Roll's judgement, which he mistakenly thought would be given on 12 June.[104] While there he met Kemmis, who informed him that McDowell would not release any information until that judgement had been delivered. Fitzgerald was unable to wait for this but briefed the Irish Solicitor General and assigned Abraham Brewster, who had been Irish Attorney General in the Aberdeen administration, as counsel to help him. He instructed Kemmis to attend the judgement and returned to London where he personally studied 150 affidavits relevant to the case. This was an unprecedented involvement by an Attorney General, whose functions did not involve pursuing cases of fraud against individuals. But, Fitzgerald was sensitive to the impending political storm following Smith's public utterances. The latter gave his judgement on 20 June and had no difficulty in striking the English shareholders from the list.[105] In doing so Smith re-iterated that James Sadleir should have been prosecuted, a statement which increased pressure on Fitzgerald.

Confronted by this renewed challenge, the Solicitor General, the Crown Solicitor and Brewster met to formulate a response for the Irish Attorney General. The minutes of their meeting indicated that fraud against individuals, however serious, did not fall within the realm of the criminal law. Further, they advised that a successful prosecution of James Sadleir for conspiracy was improbable, since the chief witnesses were part of the plot and unlikely to incriminate themselves. Fitzgerald was also cautioned that if prosecuted they would probably withdraw their co-operation from McDowell and seriously endanger the creditors' prospects. In this they were thinking of William Kelly, manager of the Clonmel branch.

Fitzgerald was still worried about the political consequences of not taking action and consulted with Sir Alexander Cockburn, the English Attorney General, who recommended prosecution, and on 27 June Fitzgerald instructed Kemmis to proceed against Sadleir for conspiracy. Sworn statements from key witnesses were essential and it took until 4 July to persuade Kelly, who was then employed in the offices of McDowell, to provide details of Sadleir's role in the fraud.[106] On 8 July a statement was also obtained from Ferrall which complemented Kelly's and completed the information jigsaw necessary in the legal preliminaries for Sadleir's arrest.[107]

By then the latter had fled the jurisdiction and the opposition knowing this, but unaware of Fitzgerald's behind the scene activities, were intent on extracting maximum political capital from his apparent dilemma. A debate in early July, began by Butt, on whether Sadleir had applied for the Chiltern Hundreds, quickly focussed on government inaction in pursuing him.[108] Whiteside followed Butt by recalling the unusual circumstances of an eminent judge publicly accusing the government of dereliction of duty. Fitzgerald was sufficiently provoked to issue a relatively mild rebuke of the Master which was not to pass unnoticed by the sensitive Smith,

> Now if the Master of the Rolls had adopted the course which became him, he ought either to have made an order directing the evidence to be laid before the Attorney General for Ireland, or in his capacity of a Privy Councillor he ought to have waited upon his Excellency the Lord Lieutenant, and apprised him that materials were before him to enable him to declare that a Member of Parliament had been guilty of a serious breach of faith.

Moore soon tabled a motion on Sadleir's perceived immunity from arrest, and the beleaguered Irish Attorney General responded to the inference that the government, and specifically himself, were somehow implicated in Sadleir's successful evasion of the law.[109] He related that active steps had been taken the previous week, including the issuing of warrants both in England and in Ireland for his arrest. Fitzgerald was unable to resist a stronger barb at Smith by concluding that Sadleir had only absconded following 'the irregular observations of the Master and not through any fault of the law officers of the Crown'.

The opposition pounced upon this injudicious, if accurate, opinion and the controversy grew. Smith took the irregular step of sending Napier documents detailing his complaints against Fitzgerald. On 11 July Napier confronted Fitzgerald with these. He expressed his confidence in Smith and demanded that Fitzgerald either withdraw his accusation 'or insist on a thorough investigation of the case'.[110] Enjoying the thrust, Napier went further and complained that the honour of the House was at stake because the Attorney General stood 'charged with being concerned in a gigantic fraud'. He was supported by both Moore and Whiteside who added that Sadleir's political influence had been a factor in the government's acquiescence in his escape. Fitzgerald was sure of his ground and refused to retreat, but fuelled the row with a further accusation that the Master had 'turned his Court into a political arena'.

This was not altogether untrue. Earlier that day a large crowd crammed into the Rolls Court to hear the retaliation of the hot-tempered Smith, who had once challenged an opposing counsel to a duel. He did not disappoint them and opened the session with a long address, which he announced was nothing less than 'putting the Irish Attorney General on his trial before the public'.[111] He reminded the crowd and the assembled press that he had implicated James Sadleir in the frauds on the depositors as far back as March, when giving judgement on the winding up of the bank. He read extracts from newspaper reports of March and April detailing the misfortunes of depositors, and deduced that 'the Attorney General had no sympathy with the poor people and closed his ears and shut his eyes to everything which was said or written in relation to the Sadleir frauds'. Even the revelations in late May and early June about the swindling of the English shareholders had not brought any response from the Attorney General who

> had fallen asleep from the 4th of March to the 3rd of June, notwithstanding that every newspaper which he took up must have suggested to him the duty which he had to perform, awoke on the last mentioned day in consequence of my observations, and an electric telegraph message was sent from London to the Registrar, or some other person, to know when I should give judgement. Having indicated that I would not give judgement for some time, the Attorney General turned his head upon his pillow and again fell asleep.

Smith had no doubt that from the date of his appointment McDowell had sufficient documentary evidence to indict Sadleir. According to him the only significant document missing was John Sadleir's letter of 31 December 1855, and this had been passed by Meldon to the Crown

Solicitor on 14 June. The previous day the solicitor for the English shareholders had sent a copy of his brief to the Crown Solicitor. The Master concluded his attack with the assurance that 'no sophistry, mystification of misrepresentation can get rid of the plain, unvarnished details of facts which I have put forward, which can neither be gainsayed nor denied'.

The *Times* patronisingly seized upon the quarrel as an example of a 'real genuine Irish row, of the fine old Irish cast', all the more interesting because the disputants were both Privy Councillors.[112] Despite its initial irony, however, the *Times* had little sympathy with Smith's intervention, which it saw as politically motivated, and it questioned his brief as a judge to become embroiled in such controversies, his conduct being worthy of

> the gravest reprobation – of reprobation so grave indeed as to render it more than doubtful whether a judge possessing so little discretion, and so little temper and moderation, and knowing so little what is either due to himself, to his office, or to others, should be permitted even in Ireland, that Alsatia for judicial extravaganzas, to preside in a court of justice ... what shall we say of a judge who states publicly from the bench that he did not give any private information to the government of the crime of James Sadleir, because he believed it would receive no attention from them, for causes publicly known – that is of a judge who uses his position as a dispenser of justice to charge upon a government to which he is politically opposed the stifling and hushing up of crimes from the basest motives of partisanship, or who amid the cheers of an admiring audience, delivers a philippic against a law officer of the crown on a matter arising, indeed out of a cause tried before him, but utterly irrelevant to the discharge of his judicial duties, and transmits that philippic as a brief to his friends in the House of Commons.

Fitzgerald targeted this political motivation of the Master of the Rolls. He directed his fire at Napier, who had been privy to Smith's documents. On 14 July he challenged Napier to formally bring a charge of conspiracy against him.[113] Napier quickly back-pedalled, denying that he had personally accused Fitzgerald of negligence, but felt that a committee of enquiry should be established to investigate Smith's charges. The Irish Attorney General having gained considerable ground, demanded and was given permission to make a full statement the following day, for which the normal business of the House was adjourned.[114]

Fitzgerald was careful not to impugn Smith's integrity as Privy Counsellor, but merely his irregular procedure. He could only assume that Smith had been misinformed and revealed that the Master had not spoken to him of the affair on the several occasions they had met since March. The gross breach of trust committed by Sadleir was not necessarily a criminal offence, and it was not the function of the Attorney General to usurp the rights of Resident Magistrates by personally initiating criminal proceedings. He took obvious satisfaction in detailing his own involvement with the case during June. Napier had little option but to accept Fitzgerald's explanation and agree that a charge of negligence could not be made against him. He felt it prudent, nonetheless, to defend the honour of Smith and excuse his having 'boiled over at what he thought was the neglect of the executive'.

As the political controversy wound down the final legal procedures for Sadleir's arrest were being completed. On 18 July the South Tipperary Assizes in Clonmel indicted him on eight counts of fraud and conspiracy against the English shareholders and the Irish depositors.[115] Many of those who sat on the Grand Jury would have been his friends or acquaintances. The judge of the Assizes immediately issued a warrant for his arrest, although it was widely known that he had left the jurisdiction.

Sadleir's abscondence and failure to defend himself was tantamount to a confession of guilt. His remaining a public representative in such circumstances was deemed a disgrace to parliament, and within days of issuing the warrants a messenger from Commons was sent to Clonacody and Great Denmark Street with an order on him to take his place in the House.[116] The Tipperary M.P. was only given two days to appear, when Roebuck proposed a motion to formally expel him.[117] This was seconded by Napier.[118]

Their arguments were based more on moral sentiments than upon sound legal or parliamentary precedent. To them Sadleir had forfeited the title Honourable Member and had treated the House with contempt by not responding to its order. It was bound to defend not only its own honour, but to uphold the rights of the Tipperary constituency. Both quoted precedents of expulsion and Napier used an 1807 parliamentary report detailing such precedents as far back as the sixteenth century.

Roebuck would brook no delay in freeing the House from contamination. To protract the affair was 'as though a man should lie down by the side of a dead body and attempt to compose himself with the noisomeness thereof'.[119] The majority of M.P.s, however, took a more measured view and the motion was defeated. On the levels of justice and common sense Sadleir had not been given sufficient time to attend the debate, and with prorogation due in a few days his attendance would not be necessary for some time.

The most influential contributors to the debate, Fitzgerald, Cockburn and the Prime Minister, Palmerston, resisted any attempt to expel

Sadleir at that time.[120] Expulsion of a member was a rare and serious occurrence and both Attorney Generals could find no precedent which exactly matched the case. In their minds a hasty decision would only create an unsafe precedent and compromise the principles of justice underlying parliamentary conduct. They both agreed that Sadleir could be safely expelled following either an admission of guilt, an adverse verdict in court, or an investigation by a parliamentary committee. Failure by him to answer the courts' summonses, however, would result in his outlawry, a step which would automatically lead to his expulsion.

Fitzgerald offered a reward of £100 for information leading to his capture and extensive searches were made in Ireland and in London.[121] The Deputy Inspector General assured Kemmis that the 'suspected localities, not only in the County of Tipperary, but elsewhere were watched, patrolled or searched by night as well as day'.[122] All police stations in Ireland were supplied with warrants for his arrest. Repeated searches were made in Cahir, Clonmel, Carrick-on-Suir and Cashel. Cahir House and Clonacody were visited on several occasions, and his father had to suffer the indignity of the police searching his house in Shronell. The home of his relatives in Grennanstown, near Athboy, County Meath, was checked, and police visited a hotel in Bray where he had lodged late in June. A watch was kept on the pier in Kingstown, and the detective division of the London Metropolitan Police sent a member to check his haunts in the city.[123]

By February 1857 political pressure was again mounting for his expulsion although outlawry proceedings were not yet complete and matters substantially stood as they were the previous July, when Roebuck's motion of expulsion was shelved. On 16 February Fitzgerald made a formal proposal and the Conservatives availed of the brief debate to further embarrass him for the protracted delay which was portrayed as political expediency.[124] Whiteside, in particular, relished expanding on the farcical police searches for Sadleir when it was well known that he had fled the jurisdiction, leaving the police to keep 'watch on the pier, to gaze out on the sea, and enjoy the fresh air for as many days as the Attorney General directed the sham to be gone through'.[125]

Despite such political point scoring the House was unanimous that Sadleir be expelled, and on 16 February 1857 he became the first M.P. to suffer this fate in over forty years. Parallel court proceedings moved equally slowly, concluding in April 1857 with a writ making him an outlaw and a criminal.[126] The gratification of creditors at this outcome was increased by the fact that Sadleir had already assigned his property to McDowell, who sold it in the Incumbered Estates Court for their benefit.[127] They were, however, disappointed by the removal of the English shareholding, although not all were depending upon the winding up process of the new banking Act to recover their losses. Seventy five creditors had moved against leading shareholders, such as James and Vincent Scully, in individual suits prior to the appointment of the official manager. This was alarming to the shareholders whose property was now at risk from individual claims under the old banking Act and from McDowell under the new one. The official manager, worried that his prospects of raising dividends would be reduced by these competing claims, was determined to halt their court proceedings.[128] But, having proved their debts in Chancery they were allowed to carry on, although ultimately only twenty-one did so and arrived at settlements with a small number of shareholders.[129]

Only one depositor went ahead without having to prove his debt in Chancery. Michael Carroll of Roscrea was permitted to do so because he began his action within five days of Sadleir's death, and was the first creditor to do so.[130] In May 1856 Chief Baron Pigot in Exchequer had given him permission to sue 'any party he may think proper, who is responsible for the liabilities of the bank without waiting for the termination of Chancery proceedings'.[131] By November Carroll was granted a writ of *scire facias*[132] against James Scully, and some months later successfully sought a mortgage on some of Scully's lands.[133]

Scully pleaded that Carroll's suit was invalid because the Tipperary had been wound up under the new banking Act and was not subject to bankruptcy proceedings.[134] The Chief Baron did not offer an opinion on this apart from expressing the hope that the old act was still in force, otherwise there would be no bankruptcy act for banking institutions.[135] This was a major point of nineteenth century banking law and its clarification was only decided by the O'Flaherty *v* McDowell case, which began in the Rolls Court in June 1856 and concluded a year later in the House of Lords. Because of the consequences for all concerned it was followed with keen interest by shareholders, creditors and banking concerns.

Richard O'Flaherty, who held a substantial farm in Killusty,[136] was joint-petitioner with three other creditors, Southwell Mulcahy of Kenilworth, Ellen Mulcahy of Newlands, and Edmond Power, a Clonmel solicitor.[137] Their 200 page petition, lodged in the Rolls Court on 11 June 1856, was responded to not only by McDowell, but by J.D. Fitzgerald, a sure indication of its importance.[138] It was filed under the old bankers Act,[139] and sought to have a receiver appointed to sell all the property of the shareholders, while restraining McDowell from disposing of any such property.

Despite the expertise of Sir Colmen O'Loghlen on behalf of

O'Flaherty and his fellow creditors Chancery found against them on 19 July 1856,[140] and their appeal to the Irish Lord Chancellor was deferred until November.[141] By the Autumn the other creditors, proceeding under the new banking Act, were becoming alarmed at the realistic prospect of interminable litigation, and support for a compromise was increasing among them as the extent of legal costs was beginning to emerge. Individual fees for small cases were proportionately more substantial than those relating to larger sums; for example a judgement in favour of Patrick Dooley, an Offaly farmer, incurred costs of £15, which was 40% of the total debt.[142] A great deal of expense arose in deciding shareholders' liability, points of law, or authorisation to proceed with further litigation in various courts. Apart, also, from the ordinary process of legal resistance some shareholders used other means to reduce the amount of property available to creditors; for example by executing deeds and leases conveying it to relatives.[143] It was illegal, but the procedures for tracing it were difficult and expensive. All this prompted the *Freeman's Journal* to remark in mid November, prior to the Lord Chancellor's judgement in the O'Flaherty case, that 'the multitude of law proceedings tearing away in various directions is enough to take anyone's breath away'. It acidly remarked on the lawyers having 'rare pickings off the carcass'.[144]

The *Freeman*, with its long experience of reporting bankruptcy cases, had advocated the path of compromise from an early stage.[145] The message from the *Times* was similar, and it also reminded creditors that the shareholders did not have sufficient property to meet all the liabilities.[146] Even in the early months after John Sadleir's death there was not universal creditor antipathy towards the concept of compromise, but a suspicion of the process which could only be facilitated through an act of Parliament. Ordinary depositors saw members of parliament as a wealthy elite automatically favouring the shareholders, and there was also a perception among them that the lingering influence of the Sadleirs and Scullys in Westminster would have clauses detrimental to their interests inserted, and passed *sub-silentio*.[147] Their fears were realised in July 1856 when a bill was drafted without consulting them, which was denounced by the Master of the Rolls as 'an Irish job' and an attempt to rob depositors.[148]

The first practical move at ground level for a compromise emerged only in September 1856, and came through James Howley, parish priest of Tipperary and Vicar-General of the Archdioceses of Cashel and Emly.[149] By then there was a growing willingness among depositors in the Tipperary town area not to ruin the shareholders, especially the Scullys, who were willing to bear a portion of the loss. But a reasonable offer was expected.

On the morning of 2 October McDowell and his solicitors, Meldon, Gibson and Adair, came from Dublin and privately consulted Howley on tactics for a public meeting, later held in the courthouse under Howley's chairmanship.[150] It was hoped to persuade the two hundred depositors present to adopt the principle of compromise, and appoint a committee consisting of members from each branch to negotiate a realistic demand through McDowell.

Howley used his considerable influence to sway some initially doubtful creditors, and displayed impressive pragmatism in his presentation. His own conviction as a depositor that compromise was the only sensible course carried weight, and he strengthened his case with a letter from Bishop Vaughan, who had lost a fund for charitable purposes on deposit in the Nenagh branch. Howley was convinced that the rejection of compromise would strengthen the resolve of shareholders to contest liability, even if it meant consuming much of their assets in legal expenses. On the other hand he believed in the shareholders' willingness to meet their obligations as fully as possible, without incurring total ruin, and quoted a letter from James Scully as proof,

> When one party is indebted to another, the general course is to discover what means there are for payment, whether the sums will be willingly afforded or otherwise. As far as I am concerned I shall willingly afford the sum my property will allow; and I would, therefore, humbly submit to the meeting that a committee of three persons be selected by the creditors, in whom they place confidence, and instruct them to confer with the Official Manager and arrange with him as to the best mode of proceeding, so as to secure to the creditors the largest reliable dividend. It will be a serious loss indeed not merely to the shareholders, but also to the creditors should not some course of this kind be adopted, as if law proceedings are commenced, the entire sum, which is now willingly about to be offered will be lost. It is a most erroneous impression that the shareholders are not willing to come forward and meet the difficulty. Such does not exist as I am aware that the great majority of those possessing means are most anxious to bring the matter to a termination, and have already determined to make large sacrifices of their property, if they should only be afforded the means of doing so by entering on a compromise, which, if successful, will entitle them to a discharge, by which means alone they will be enabled to borrow money to meet the several sums which they propose to pay.

McDowell felt it best to make no comment, but Gibson, as one of the solicitors intimately involved with the legal proceedings, was able to provide authoritative information in support of Howley. He saw the failure to adopt compromise at an earlier date as a missed opportunity. Having already visited London he had learned from their solicitor that the English shareholders had initially been prepared to compromise. They had set aside £10,000 either as a defence or a compromise fund depending on how events progressed. He was convinced that the hoped for negotiations between them and McDowell would have realised £40,000. The Rolls Court decision had ended this possibility. Gibson presented the central question as whether the largest dividend could be raised through litigation or through compromise. Legal costs were a crucial factor in answering this and he gave a breakdown of these, which he reinforced with a warning that shareholders' continued resistance in the courts would increase costs further. The Earl of Bessborough representing Carrick-on-Suir depositors, agreed with Gibson and addressed the issue of litigation costs on the smaller depositors. He calculated that there were 800 individuals with deposits under fifty pounds, and produced a list of these for the Carrick-On-Suir area willing to support the decision of the meeting. Bessborough pledged to call a similar meeting in Carrick, and proposed a resolution to begin the practicalities of reaching a compromise,

> That having heard the statement of the liabilities of the Tipperary Joint Stock Bank and the resources from which a further dividend may be expected, and placing full reliance on the official Manager, and his desire to protect the creditors, that our very Reverend Chairman be requested to put himself into immediate communication with Mr. McDowell, and ascertain if he be in a position to undertake within a short period the collection of funds sufficient to pay the bank's creditors a further dividend on their respective demands, independent of any sum that may hereafter be realised out of the assets of the late John Sadleir and the claim of the bank against the Kingston estates;[151] and, if the same can be accomplished, it is the opinion of this meeting that such compromise should be accepted by the general body of the creditors; and that the very Reverend Chairman and the seconder of this resolution be appointed as a committee for the purpose of carrying out such arrangements as will secure for the creditors the largest practicable dividend and save them from the ruinous consequences of lengthened and expensive litigation; and that the creditors of the several other branches of the bank be visited to select one or more persons to represent them on the committee.

McDowell, anxious to sustain this initial enthusiasm and energise the depositors of other districts to follow suit, met with a positive response for the compromise movement in four other branch areas. Meetings in Nenagh, Athy, Thomastown and Carrick-On-Suir nominated members to a committee, which would negotiate with McDowell at a Dublin venue in late October and early November.[152]

Ironically, the first discordant note in the compromise movement came from the Carrick-On-Suir district in an open letter of 7 October to the creditors from Philip Landy, a depositor who farmed in Ballydine.[153] It was a well-thought out attack on the movement, portraying Gibson as the paid agent of the shareholders and McDowell and Meldon as 'the representatives of an interest diametrically opposed to yours'. The threat of litigation to frighten creditors and failure to produce particulars of the shareholders' property aroused the suspicion of Landy, who was also skeptical of Howley's and Bessborough's ability to unravel such particulars, which were rapidly being enmeshed in a legal tangle by shareholders anxious to put their property out of the creditors' reach. He doubted that either had experienced the same psychological or emotional impact as other depositors, feeling that

> my Lord Bessborough and the Rev. Mr. Howley can afford to treat their losses with indifference and set an example of philosophic resignation. Perhaps if all they possessed in the world were involved in this great ruin, it would have taken a greater effort to reconcile them to the philosophy contained in a resolution pledged to a compromise of an undefined amount, perhaps of ruinous sacrifice.

Landy did not share the apparent sympathy of some creditors with the plight of the shareholders, asking why

> all this maudlin sympathy for a class of men who for years received their interest of six per cent, with a bonus of three per cent, and in whose hands were vested the powers to guide, control, and investigate the affairs of this bank unrivalled in mercantile history for its gigantic frauds and consummate system of swindling? Why should the greater portion of this loss, or any of it, whilst property remains to meet it, be thrown upon you, who never participated in the profits, and who possessed no power to control or regulate the internal management of this mighty swindle?

He was convinced that the shareholders had sufficient property to yield a large if not a full dividend, and was also confident that the judgement of the Lord Chancellor in the O'Flaherty case would bring the Tipperary under the terms of the old bankers Act and expose all this property to forfeiture by the creditors. Landy was more influenced in his thinking by Clonmel, which became the main centre of opposition to compromise publicly articulated at a meeting on 24 October[154] presided over by Archdeacon Laffan and attended by O'Flaherty, who was one of his parishoners. But, the prime mover behind the anti-compromise drive and the O'Flaherty case was the Clonmel solicitor, Edmond Power, who represented depositors with a combined loss of £10,000. He drafted the main resolution which referred to the helplessness of depositors under the winding up acts, and welcomed the failure of the July attempt at compromise. Nevertheless, it conceded the desirability of avoiding further litigation, if possible, and supported the expediency of electing members to the negotiating committee. The resolution, however, pre-empted the aims of this committee by defining its purpose as one of investigating the affairs of the bank, and inspecting the properly certified details of individual shareholders' circumstances, which would enable creditors to determine the optimum course in the recovery of their losses.

Apart from Clonmel, Roscrea also emerged as a centre of antipathy towards the compromise policy. Initially the Roscrea stance was less clear-cut, when Daniel J. Bergin, a local solicitor independently pursuing the claims of twenty-eight depositors, gave a qualified support to the compromise movement. He wrote on 8 October to confirm that 'if an honourable compromise were offered in some defined manner and secured by the names of the principal shareholders, I should, consistent with my duty to my clients, use my humble exertions to follow it'.[155] Bergin, however, was neither as single-minded nor as influential as his Clonmel counterpart. But, Andrew James Scanlan, the volatile pastor of nearby Couraganeen, was virulently opposed to compromise and carried most of the Roscrea depositors with him. Nevertheless, like those in Clonmel, they did not wish to be excluded from the negotiations. At a meeting held towards the end of October a resolution was proposed by Scanlan that the 'only compromise we are disposed to adopt' was a full dividend.[156] His contradictory statement was adopted by the depositors despite the attempt by Gibson to change their minds. The confusion that erupted was so great that the meeting failed to select two members to represent them on the committee.

At an adjourned meeting a few days later Gibson challenged Scanlan to produce evidence that shareholders had sufficient property to meet a full dividend.[157] Scanlan was less motivated by rationality than by his sense of injustice, and held his ground on the alleged ability of shareholders to respond fully to depositor losses. This meeting, however, sanctioned participation in the Dublin discussions, not as an endorsement of the compromise principle but as an opportunity to gauge if it might be the best course forward.

Two meetings were held in Dublin, one on 30 October and the second on 6 November.[158] McDowell refused to invite the Clonmel members to the first because their objection to a compromise had been more stringent, but he relented for the second meeting on the somewhat flimsy excuse that he may have been mistaken in his interpretation of their resolution.[159] The proceedings were private and reporters had to rely on briefings by Meldon. Vincent Scully and other shareholders addressed the committee at this first meeting. A large number of shareholders were present and were accompanied by their solicitors, who presented deeds and other papers relating to their property. They had to endure the humiliation of making individual cases, some of which the creditors accepted and others they rejected. Despite the reservations of the Roscrea delegates a resolution in favour of compromise was issued.

The Clonmel delegates were present at the second meeting when the process was progressed further. A resolution from this formally recognised the principle of compromise, and required the shareholders to take an oath pledging adherence to an agreed compromise. While deprecating individual creditors pursuing their own courses through the courts, it was without prejudice to those pleading under the O'Flaherty case. This was clearly the input of the Clonmel contingent. Finally, it sanctioned the serving of the preliminary notices for securing the act of parliament necessary to underpin the compromise. One of the most important clauses of the resolution was the demand that a draft of the bill should be examined by a meeting of the creditors prior to its introduction in Westminster.

While the compromise bill was being prepared the O'Flaherty case came to judgement, and was decided by the Irish Lord Chancellor on 25 November following five days of argument.[160] In his summation Brady saw the case as an examination of 'the whole statute law regarding the position and liabilities of bankers and banking companies in Ireland'.[161] He ruled that the old banking Act, by confiscating shareholders' property, frustrated the intention of the new Act, and was therefore defunct. Sympathising with the defeated O'Flaherty and his fellow petitioners, he declared that it was 'impossible to exaggerate the character of the proceedings which have led to so much ruin, or to say too much of the importance of staying the vast torrent of litigation that has been let loose by the calamities of those who have been defrauded'.[162]

They immediately sought the opinion of Sir Fitzroy Kelly, and encouraged by him, decided on an appeal to the Lords.[163] This did not ease the fears of the public, whose confidence in banking institutions was momentarily shaken following the Lord Chancellor's ruling. The most extreme reaction, however, was limited to County Tipperary and Kilkenny city, where a run lasting several days was made upon the branches of the National Bank.[164] Branches in Thurles, Clonmel,

Nenagh, Cashel and Tipperary were affected, but the bank had sufficient gold reserves to meet the demand. The run in Tipperary was the most severe where some of the shopkeepers there refused National Bank notes, and depositors queued all night on 15 December withdrawing £50,000 in gold the following day. The correspondent of the *Clonmel Chronicle* visited the scene,

> At an early hour on Tuesday morning, a large crowd assembled outside the Bank door, waiting to have it opened, when immediately a rush was made to see who would reach the counters first. The Manager had to send for the Sub Inspector and a party of Police, (who were immediately on the spot), to keep order, while the depositors were receiving the respective amounts lodged by them. There was a great reduction in the market prices yesterday, in consequence of the run on the Bank, particularly in the article of Butter, many of the Merchants who keep their accounts in the National Bank being unable to get access to the establishment, in order to draw funds for the market.

By the time the banking crisis subsided McDowell had completed work on the draft bill for a compromise, which he sent to members of the creditors' committee on Christmas Eve 1856 for discussion at a meeting in Dobbyn's Hotel, Tipperary, on 29 December.[165] But the bill, scheduled to be lodged in the parliamentary office for private bills on 31 December in readiness for the new session, only served to harden attitudes among the pro and anti compromise groups. Animosity flared at the Tipperary meeting when Power handed Bessborough a written protest against the bill signed by Andrew J. Scanlan. Several amendments were proposed by Power, one of which was a clause to preserve the rights of creditors under the O'Flaherty case, in the event of a reversal of the Lord Chancellor's judgement by the Lords.

The bill, published in January, stipulated that shareholders willing to compromise under its provisions would be required to file a schedule of all their property at the time of the bank failure,[166] to be verified by affidavits and lodged with the Master of Chancery for inspection by the creditors, who would have the right to examine shareholders under oath. The Master would decide if the compromise should be adopted or amended and call a meeting of creditors. It was a requirement that three quarters of these endorse the compromise which would then be binding on all.

Power, relying upon Fitzroy Kelly's opinion on the probable reversal of the Lord Chancellor's judgement, now publicly attacked the bill. In a letter to the creditors of 8 January he denounced it as 'a skilfully contrived plot' instigated by the shareholders and promoted by McDowell, 'the itinerant champion of that body'.[167] He recalled that

McDowell was on intimate terms of friendship with some shareholders, being related to one. Power saw the haste in rushing the bill without adequate time to consider it as part of a plot to help them evade their responsibilities. The Clonmel solicitor continued to forge a stronger union with the Roscrea area and attended a meeting there on 13 January where a resolution was passed sanctioning the drawing up of a petition to parliament against the bill.[168] The process of progressing this petition was continued at a Clonmel meeting soon afterwards. McDowell refused an invitation to attend and upheld the principle of compromise,[169] which had been endorsed by the legal profession and the largest creditors, including the Bank of Ireland and the Newcastle Bank. An examination of the Tipperary's books and schedules and of the shareholders' property convinced the official manger that only a moderate dividend could be realised and this only by avoiding further litigation. Despite this, however, McDowell stated that he was not prepared to promote the bill any further in the face of opposition by Power and his adherents, and sourly stressed his determination to confine himself henceforth to his duties as official manager.

The withdrawal of the bill took the vehemence out of the meeting which was held in the Clonmel courthouse on 27 January.[170] Scanlan brought a contingent from Roscrea representing creditors of £20,000, and a resolution of 'unfeigned satisfaction' at the demise of the compromise movement was passed. Power re-iterated his intention of appealing the O'Flaherty case to Lords, and a decision was made to open subscription lists in the various branch areas to defray the expenses of the appeal, which was heard by the Lords over four days in June 1857.[171] Sir Fitzroy Kelly was counsel for the petitioners and Sir Richard Bethell, the English Attorney General, defended for the respondents. Essentially the same themes were pursued as had been heard in the Irish courts with additional cases cited in support. The Lord Chancellor delivered the unanimous judgement of the Lords on 9 July, which concurred with that of his Irish counterpart[172] and at last settled an important point of banking law, boosting the morale of shareholders. It also brought the prospect of a compromise into a more realistic focus. By August this was accepted by both shareholders and creditors as the only solution, and in early 1859 the matter was put beyond doubt when the final piece in the legal jigsaw was completed with the judgement on the destination of John Sadleir's property.

The board of the London and County was so confident it would be given priority over the Tipperary, that immediately prior to Sadleir's death it had begun to dispose of his estates. J.E. Coleman, the bank's accountant, told the shareholders at their half-yearly meeting in August 1856 that the debt had already been significantly reduced by the ongoing realisation of securities.[173] He was satisfied that it would be entirely discharged within a year, but did not tell them that McDowell was contesting their claim to Sadleir's lands.

McDowell was then beginning his case before Jeremiah Murphy in Chancery,[174] although it took until November 1858 to have this progressed to the Landed Estates Court, where the final schedule of encumbrances on Sadleir's estates was decided.[175] Judge Mountifort Longfield delivered his decision on 6 December 1858. The tone of his judgement was unsympathetic to the directors of the London bank, whom he accused of dereliction of duty. Sadleir's massive overdraft was in violation of its by-laws, of the shareholders' duty and of his own duty as chairman. Longfield rejected the directors' plea that they had obtained adequate securities and had every reason to trust their chairman. Nevertheless, he appreciated how such a situation could have developed, and understood that some of the directors were compromised because they had secured their directorships through Sadleir's influence, while the bank officials were 'in some respect dependent on the chairman for their emoluments and comforts, and perhaps to some extent for the stability of their offices'. This did not, however, excuse director negligence, and he condemned their indulgence and ultimate response to Sadleir's abuse of office as 'very gentle expostulations'.

Despite his rebuke, however, Longfield ruled that legally the London bank had priority over the Tipperary because it had registered the deeds assigning Sadleir's land in August 1855. He considered as reprehensible and illegal the decision of James Sadleir not to register the March 1855 memorandum conveying these lands to the Tipperary, and dismissed the vital argument that the London bank directors were aware of this memorandum and guilty of fraud in drawing up their subsequent agreement with Sadleir.

McDowell appealed Longfield's decision to the newly established Court of Appeal in Chancery,[176] where the Lord Chancellor finally decided the issue on 19 February 1859 after four days of argument.[177] He upheld Longfield's judgement and pronounced that any claim against Sadleir's estate to the detriment of the London bank was against every principle of justice. He concluded that the law left the unregistered deed of the Tipperary bank 'where it found it, a secret claim in the pocket of the sole Managing Director'.

The official manager decided not to appeal this decision, and the loss of the proceeds from the sale of Sadleir's lands was a heavy blow to both shareholders and creditors equalling a dividend of six shillings in the pound, which, when added to the amount devoured in litigation, meant that a major sum was lost to the creditors. By 1858 Gibson's partner, Adair, estimated that the court costs and the fees of eighteen attorneys and forty-three lawyers had reached £70,000 or the equivalent of four shillings in the pound dividend.[178]

Not surprisingly, therefore, from 1858 onwards compromises were finalised and paid over the following two years. Details of these are difficult to trace. At the beginning of 1858 the English shareholders offered £5,000, which McDowell was anxious to accept despite the reluctance of Murphy.[179] Hone and Stirling had originally offered £5,000, but since the O'Flaherty judgement was in their favour Stirling eventually came forward with a mere £1,000 which was rejected by Murphy.[180] John Pepper of Lismore House, Toomevara, County Tipperary was one of the more unfortunate shareholders who not only met his compromise with McDowell, but was also successfully sued by individual creditors such as Andrew J. Scanlan.[181] His twenty shares rendered him liable for £5,800 under the two calls by McDowell. His compromise of £1,400 was accepted by McDowell and paid in 1859.[182] On a smaller scale, £100 was accepted from David Rafferty and £50 from Ellen Quillinan.[183]

Sadleir's legal partner, James B. Kennedy, who had sold his shares in 1853 was one of the lucky ones struck off by the Rolls Court, but he agreed to a modest compromise of £100 to ensure that private prosecutions ceased.[184] Other friends were more seriously affected. It is not clear what the settlement of Wilson Kennedy was, but he emigrated to America following his disgrace.[185] The career of Farmery John Law was also destroyed. Law was one of those specifically mentioned in Sadleir's last letters as liable to ruin. He had worked his way up through the ranks of the London and County first as a branch manager, then a manager in the head office and finally, due to his connection with Sadleir, a paid director. He suffered dearly for this patronage and resigned when the scandals broke forfeiting an annual income of £1000.[186] When he fled to France he was pursued by McDowell's solicitor, who threatened to bankrupt him if he failed to return for a Chancery hearing on his fate as a shareholder.[187] He presented himself in May but left again for Norway assuming that he would share the favourable judgement of the English shareholders. He was, however, excluded and he was forced to plead an individual case before eventually having his name removed from the list.[188]

While not a shareholder, Josiah Wilkinson was also drawn into the litigation ordeal, and brought into conflict with Eyre. One of Sadleirs forgeries was a conveyance of the Coolnamuck property, which he had purchased for Eyre in 1854. Sadleir gave this worthless conveyance to Wilkinson as security for a loan. He pursued the case as far as the Lord Chancellor who validated his claim to the extent that Eyre was the victim. In his desperation to raise money shortly before his death Sadleir had also forged Wilkinson's name on a cheque.

Wilkinson was an usually even tempered individual who held no ill-will towards Sadleir. Similarly William McCabe was restrained in his comments in the *Telegraph* as the frauds unfolded. But, considering his years of loyal support and defence of Sadleir's integrity, his discomfiture may be taken for granted. His immediate objective, however, was to save the newspaper. Its name was changed to the *Catholic Telegraph and Irish Sun* and the motto of Sadleir's Catholic uncle replaced by that of the pagan Cicero – *neither dare to say anything that is false, nor fear to say anything that is true, nor give any just suspicion either of favour or prejudice.* McCabe's proclamation that a new era was dawning for the paper was followed by his resignation within four months of the crash.[189] Ostensibly his reason for leaving was due to editorial interference by the paper's publisher, John William McDonnell.[190] McCabe subsequently went to Brittany and lived there for many years, but eventually returned to Ireland and died in Donnybrook in 1891. The *Telegraph* continued publication until August 1867.

References

1. *N.G.* 20 February 1856, *C.S.* 1 March 1856. (Sadleir's father and sister received the condolence of many people as they drove through Tipperary Town – *B.H.* 1 March 1856).
2. *C.P.* 23 February 1856.
3. *Morning Advertiser* 18 February 1856.
4. Duffy sailed to Australia on 8 October 1855 to practise as a barrister in Melbourne. He was granted property worth £5,000 by a group of admirers and in 1857 was elected to Parliament. In 1871 he became Prime Minister of Victoria. He was knighted in 1873, and became Speaker of the House of Assembly in 1876. He left Australia in 1880 and died in Nice in 1903.
5. Lucas died on 22 October 1855, like Sadleir aged 43. His health collapsed under the strain of his Roman mission. He returned from Rome in May so altered in appearance that when he presented himself at the House of Commons the doorkeeper did not recognise him. On his death McCabe in the *Weekly Telegraph* afforded him dubious praise as a 'truly great man' who had been unable to defend his religion 'unalloyed by the contaminating contact of factious politics,' and of espousing an anti-episcopal polity – *W.T.* 27 October 1855.
6. Quoted in *Waterford Advertiser* 1 March 1856, *C.S.* 1 March 1856. See *Nation* 1 March 1856 for a further editorial by Hoey which saw Sadleir's misdeeds as a vindication of the *Nation's* stand over the years – 'Mr. John Sadleir could hardly have done his work more effectively had he sold himself to Satan. All we have ever said of him, living or dead, has been more than fulfilled.' Such onslaughts were a feature of the *Nation's* editorials for many weeks; for example, an editorial of 15 March 1856 used the theme of Sadleirism to comment upon the by-elections in New Ross and Sligo. Sligo was indicted in severe terms as a

constituency where Catholics had 'sunk deeper and deeper at each successive election into a position of profligacy and disgrace, which almost justifies the allegation of one of our libellers that we were no more fit for self government than the blacks'.

7. Luttrell, Henry Lawes, second Earl of Carhampton 1743-1821, Commander of the British Army in Ireland in 1796. In 1795 he had suppressed the Defenders in Connaught and his impressment of many rebels as sailors provoked widespread antagonism. An assassination attempt on him in May 1797 failed. He was also regarded as a traitor for changing from anti- to pro-union. *D.N.B.*, e.v. Stewart Robert, second Marquis of Londonderry and Viscount Castlereagh 1769-1822. Chief Secretary for Ireland in 1798, his action against the United Irishmen was not forgotten in the popular mind. He was one of the leading supporters of the Act of union. *D.N.B.*, e.v.

8. Notes 4 and 5 above.

9. Quoted in *Waterford Chronicle* 1 March 1856.

10. *W.T.* 1, 8 March 1856.

11. McCabe continued his counter attack in April 1856 when further frauds were uncovered. He rejected the tarnishing of those connected with the *Telegraph* and pointed to Sadleir's innocence in the year 1851 – *W.T.* 12 April 1856.

12. See *T.L.* 3 February 1855 for its prospectus, part of which read that 'in one word, as far as Tipperary is concerned the *Leader* will labour to rid the popular ranks of the base and perjured systems recognised by the loathed names of Whiggery and Sadleirism', (10 February 1855).

13. e.g. *T.L.* 15 March 1856.

14. D.D.A., C.P., Carton 339/2 contains Fitzgerald's statement and written apology.

15. Bishop Browne was known as the Dove of Elphin because of his mild personality.

16. Cullen to Monsell 14 April 1856 in N.L.I., Monsell Papers, ms 8317 (3).

17. Redmond to Cullen 26 April 1856 in D.D.A., C.P., Carton 339/4. Interestingly, in a letter of 17 April Redmond had reviewed the political fall out from the defection of 1852 -53. He interpreted Sadleir's return for Sligo and Keogh's return for Athlone as public endorsement of the policy. In Carlow almost half the electorate including most of the Liberals had voted for Sadlier in the first by-election (these letters are part of a large collection of Redmond's correspondence with Cullen.) A.M. Sullivan, who was on the staff of the *Nation*, saw McCabe and the *Telegraph* as buttressing Maher – Sullivan to Moore, 27 April 1856, in N.L.I., Moore Papers, ms 893.

18. *F.J.* 4 April 1856. This was in contrast to the approach of Cullen in similar circumstances. In spite of his suspicions of the Young Ireland element in the League, Cullen had contributed to its coffers when approached at his Drogheda residence in October 1851 by Lucas and three priests – *Nation* 1 November 1851.

19. *Nation* 5 April 1856.

20. See e.g. ibid., 12 April 1856 for Hoey's reply to a second letter from Maher.

21. *D.E.P.* 28 February 1856.

22. *C.P.* 15 March 1856.

23. Rival claims, however, were unsuccessfully contested in the courts.

24. *W.C.* 1 March 1856. B.H. 1 March 1856.

25. Meeting in *R.T.* 1 March 1856.

26. By August 1856 the *Railway Times* grudgingly admitted that the company's financial situation was not as bad as it had anticipated and that construction was steadily proceeding. See *R.T.* 30 August 1856.

27. Ibid., 23 February 1856.
28. Ibid.
29. See ibid., 8 March 1856 for a letter from an angry shareholder referring to an earlier drop in share prices. He blamed the directors and Secretary for not exercising proper financial control and was skeptical of the value of some of the Company's assets such as bonds and shares of the Netherlands Land Company. See *T.L.* 8 March 1856 and *R.T.* 1 March 1856 for a meeting of shareholders in the London Tavern, and *R.T.* 26 April 1856,*B.M.*, vol.XVI, 1856, pp 293-299 for a report of the committee which included the Swedish Consul, the chairman of the Stock Exchange and the chairman of the South Western Railway Company.
30. See *R.T.* 19 July and 29 November 1856.
31. Ibid., 8 November 1856.
32. Ibid., 24 January 1857 and 10, 17 April 1858.
33. Ibid., 15 May 1858 and 19 February 1859.
34. See *T.F.P.* 16 November 1858 for the evidence of its ex-secretary.
35. *Newcastle Messenger and Advertiser* 9 August 1856.
36. Circular in ibid., 28 August 1856.
37. See e.g. *B.M.*, vol.XVI 1856, pp 231 et.seq. on the collapse of a bank owned by Strachan, Paul and Bates. See ibid., pp 302-303 and *C.S.* 3 May 1856 on the collapse of the Lichfield Bank with a deficit on closure of £62,000.
38. *Times* 28 February 1856, *T.L.* 23 February 1856.
39. *T.F.P.* 29 February 1856. (Marnane, *Land and Violence* p. 76 details its pattern of withdrawals from 13 to 29 February. 22 February was the most intense with only £42 deposited and £12,883 withdrawn. On 29 February, however, £363 was deposited and £280 withdrawn).
40. *L.E.* 28 February 1856.
41. *T.L.* 23 February 1856, 1 March 1856, *C.S.* 1 March 1856, *L.E.* 23 February 1856.
42. *N.G.* 20 March 1856.
43. *C.S.* 23 February 1856.
44. Ibid.
45. *B.H.* 1 March 1856, *Times* 8 March 1856.
46. *W.T.* 23 February 1856.
47 *Times* 27 May 1856, *I.C.R. 1856 and 1857*, vol.6, p. 352.
48. Appendix 8.
49. *C.T.* 22 November 1856. See also *L.R.* 23 May 1856, *Times* 27 May 1856, *I.C.R. 1856 and 1857*, vol.6, p. 352.
50. Appendix 9.
51. Ibid
52. Ibid.
53. *Times* 28 February 1850. See also *L.R.* 26 September 1856, *N.G.* 14 May 1856.
54. *C.P.* 23 February 1856.
55. *B.H.* 1 March 1856.
56. *Times* 27 May 1856.
57. *I.C.R. 1855, 1856 and 1857*, vol.5, p. 704.
58. *L.E.* 15 March 1856, *I.C.R. 1856 and 1857*, vol.6, p. 352.
59. *N.G.* 26 March 1856, *T.L.* 29 March 1856.
60. The Common Law Courts were the Queens Bench, Common Pleas and Court of Exchequer. Courts of Equity were the Rolls Court, the Court of Chancery and the Court of Appeal in Chancery. Chancery issued writs allowing parties to proceed in the Common Law Courts, but such permission did not guarantee success in the Common Law Courts. The Judicature (Ireland) Act 1877 merged the

administration of the Common Law Courts and the Courts of Equity, although the systems of Common Law and Equity continued. Henceforth, however, judges of either courts had the authority to decide both Common Law and equity elements of a case, but the principles of equity prevailed if there was a clash of principle. See J.C.W. Wylie, *Irish Land Law*, (London, 1975), pp 69 et. seq., R. Byrne and J.P. McCutcheon, *The Irish Legal System*, (Dublin, 1996), pp 29 – 33.

61. This figure was given by Adair in 1858 – *T.F.P.* 16 February 1858.
62. Petition in *T.L.* 8 March 1856.
63. See *B.M.*, vol. XVI, 1856, p. 227.
64. *Times* 10 March 1856.
65. The bankruptcy jurisdiction was also transferred from the Bankruptcy Court to the Court of Chancery in 1857 – Wylie, *Irish Land Law*, p. 86.
66. Ibid., pp 69 et.seq.
67. *T.L.* 8 March 1856, *Times* 3 March 1856. This circular was signed by John Massey, Thomas Dwyer and William Chadwick who were 'professionally concerned for a large body of creditors'.
68. Ibid.
69. Report in *Times* 6 March 1856, *C.S.* 8 March 1856, *W.T.* 8 March 1856, *T.L.* 8 March 1856. See also *I.C.R. 1856 and 1857*, vol.6, p. 353 and *B.M.* vol.XVI, 1856, pp 226-229.
70. Thomas Berry Cusack Smith was the second son of Sir William Cusack Smith, an Irish judge from 1801 until 1836. His grandfather was Master of the Rolls in Ireland from 1801 to 1806. Smith was born in 1795 at Newtown County Offaly, and served as Solicitor General and Attorney General in Ireland in 1842 and conducted the prosecution of Daniel O'Connell, who nicknamed him 'Alphabet' Smith and 'the Vinegar Cruet.' In 1846 he was appointed Master of the Rolls a position he held until his death in 1866 – *D.N.B.*, e.v. under Smith.
71. *T.L.* 15 March 1856.
72. *D.E.P.* 8 March 1856 for proceedings in Murphy's office.
73. See *T.L.* 15 March 1856, *D.E.P.* 11 March 1856, *W.T.* 15 March 1856, *Times* 10 March 1856, *L.E.* 15 March 1856.
74. Because the Bank of Ireland continued to discount the Tipperary's bills after Glyns had refused payments it found itself £32,448 out of pocket, but it held government stock of £20,000 as security from the Tipperary – *L.E.* 15 March 1856, *C.T.* 28 June 1856, *I.C.R. 1855, 1856 and 1857*, vol.5 pp 203-204. (The editor of the *Leinster Express* wrote to the *Freeman's* condemning the Bank of Ireland for ignoring the disastrous state of the Tipperary with which it had extensive dealings and consequently early knowledge of its problems – *L.E.* 15 March 1856).
75. *W.T.* 3 May 1856.
76. Meldon was entitled to charge two guineas per claim for processing each depositor's schedule. Normally two schedules were required which would cost approximately £7,000; Meldon, however, only charged for one schedule – *Times* 26 September 1856.
77. *Times* 21 April 1856.
78. *C.T.* 11 October 1856.
79. *Times* 21 April 1856 (Some of these had considerable wealth).
80. *T.L.* 22 March 1856.
81. *L.E.* 3 May 1856.
82. *C.T.* 21 June 1856.
83. *L.E.* 3 May 1856, *W.T.* 3 May 1856. See also *Times* 21 May 1856.
84. *C.T.* 14, 21 June 1856, *I.C.R. 1856 and 1857*, vol.6, pp 72-81.

85. Sir Maziere Brady 1796-1871, graduated with an M.A. from Trinity College in 1819 and was called to the bar that year. In 1837 he was Irish Solicitor General and Attorney General in 1839. He became chief Baron of Exchequer in 1840 and was raised to the bench in Chancery in 1846. He was Irish Lord Chancellor from 1846 to 1852, 1853 to 1858 and from 1859 to 1866. Gladstone made him a baronet in 1869. He died at his residence, Upper Pembroke Street on 13 April 1871. *D.N.B.*, e.v.

86. *C.T.* 2 May 1856, *I.C.R. 1856 and 1857,* vol.6 pp 524-532.

87. *Times* 21 May 1856, *W.T.* 24 May 1856.

88. I.C.R. 1856 and 1857, vol.6, pp 121-123, see also *C.T.* 21 June 1856.

89. i.e. those who had sold their shares within three years of the crash.

90. See appendix 3. (James B. Kennedy was also struck off – *I.C.R. 1856 and 1857,* vol.6, pp 180 et. seq.

91. R.D. 1857, vol.13, abstract 50.

92. *Times* 27,29 May 1856, *T.F.P.* 15 May 1856, *W.T.* 7 June 1856, *C.T.* 14 June 1856. (Calls could be made in instalments. Shareholders disputing their liabilities were excluded pending the outcome of their appeal. Insolvencies and debts due to shareholders could be offset against calls).

93. Waugh had transferred his shares to his governess who had little money – *Times* 5 July 1856.

94. *C.T.* 22 November 1856.

95. *I.C.R., 1856 and 1857,* vol.6, p. 9.

96. *B.M.,* vol.XVI, 1856, p. 335.

97. *Times* 30 April and 24 May 1856, *B.M.,* vol.XVI, 1856, pp 363-366.

98. *I.C.R. 1855, 1856 and 1857,* vol.5, pp 206-218. See also *C.T.* 7 and 14 June 1856.

99. *W.T.* 7 June 1856.

100. As with his brother the initial public reaction to James Sadleir had been sympathetic at a time when his collusion with John on his overdraft and duping of the English shareholders was unknown. The *Times* was especially friendly seeing James as 'the chief victim of his brother's frauds' and being 'in fact a ruined man' – *Times* 3 March 1856. Other papers were less so and were motivated by residual political bitterness. The *Munster News* questioned the 'mesmerisation' of Tipperary in not displaying exasperation against Sadleirism and demanding his resignation as County member. It felt that Tipperary 'may yet rival in merit and peculiar fame, the Borough of Sunderland, by which Hudson was held in loving embrace, whilst the worst of the Tories scorned him, and journals spewed their rheum upon his name' – quoted in *T.L.* 29 March 1856. See *F.J.* 3 April 1856 for an indictment of James Sadleir.

101. Letter quoted in *C.T.* 19 July 1856.

102. *Parl. Deb.*, series 3, vol.142, 1856, col.164 (9 June 1856).

103. Fitzgerald was mistaken; Murphy had merely indicated that he had insufficient evidence. The master's minute of 29 July 1856 stated that the matter of James Sadleir's guilt had never arisen. At the request of McDowell he had privately examined Sadleir on 19 March about a transfer deed and other documents about John Sadleir's transactions with English banks. At that stage James Sadleir had not been officially accused of any involvement in the frauds and Murphy's role was confined to examining the documents. He had, however, feared that Sadleir might abscond and extracted a promise from him to remain in the jurisdiction. This minute published in *T.F.P.* 29 July 1856. See also *D.E.M.* 7 July 1856 reporting the displeasure of the Master of the Rolls that Murphy had not disclosed to him the contents of his examination of Sadleir.

104. Fitzgerald's actions throughout June were detailed in his statement to the House of Commons – *C.T.* 19 July 1856.

105. *I.C.R. 1855, 1856 and 1857*, vol.5, pp 206-218. (Early in 1857 the Irish Lord Chancellor supported the ruling).

106. Kelly's statement quoted in full in *Informations and Warrants (394)*, ms.pp.589-592.

107. Ferrall's statement in ibid., MS. pp 592-596.

108. *Parl. Deb.*, series 3, vol.143, 1856, col.381 (4 July 1856).

109. Ibid., cols. 399-401 (7 July 1856), see also C.T. 12 July 1856.

110. *C.T.* 12 July 1856.

111. *C.P.* 19 July 1856, *C.T.* 12 July 1856.

112. Quoted in *C.P.* 19 July 1856.

113. Parliamentary exchanges in *Parl. Deb.*, series 3, 1856, cols. 736-740, (14 July 1856).

114. Fitzgerald's lengthy statement in *C.T.* 19 July 1856.

115. *Informations and Warrants (394)*, ms.pp.587-589 for copies of warrants and certificate of indictment. For more detailed statement of the eight charges see *Information and Warrants (394-1)*, ms.pp.607-612.

116. *Parl. Deb.*, series 3, vol.143, 1856, col.1399 (24 July 1856).

117. Ibid., cols. 1386-1391.

118. Ibid., cols. 1391-1396.

119. Ibid., cols. 1388-1389.

120. Ibid., cols. 1398-1408.

121. *Copies of the several warrants issued for the apprehension of Mr. James Sadleir, a member of this House, and of the Reports from the Crown Solicitor and Officers of Constabulary of the steps taken for his arrest, and of the several proceedings in the process of outlawry against him*, H.C. 1857 (22 sess – 1) XIV. 363 ms. pp. 365-372, (henceforth *Copies of the Several warrants...James Sadleir 22-Sess 1)* . There is a paper of similar title 37-sess. 1 henceforth referred to as *Copies of the Several Warrants, 37 sess. – 1*.

122. Ibid., MS. p. 365.

123. Now Dun Laoghaire.

124. Fitzgerald's address in *Parl. Deb.*, series 3, vol.144, 1857, cols. 702-710 (16 February 1857).

125. Ibid., col.718.

126. Detailed in *Copies of the several warrants...James Sadleir*, MS. p.364. (Events in County Tipperary moved more rapidly with preparations for a by-election beginning in July 1856, when an Independent Club was formed 'for the purpose of ridding this county of the Sadleirs' – *Tipperary Vindicator* 25 July 1856. For details of the election campaign see e.g.*T.F.P.* 6 March 1857, *Tipperary Vindicator* 27 February and 3 March 1857).

127. R.D., vol.24 abs.136; see also *C.T.* 26 July and 29 November 1856.

128. See *W.T.* 22 March 1856 for the case of Thomas Blake p. p. Roscrea v Wilson Kennedy, see also *D.E.P.* 8 March 1856.

129. See Appendix 10. See also *C.T.* 8 November 1856.

130. *T.L.* 15 March 1856. The Earl of Bessborough began proceedings against James Sadleir at the end of February but later used the Winding Up Act to pursue his claim – *C.S.* 1 March 1856, *C.P.* 15 March 1856, *B.M.*, vol.XVI, 1856, p. 228.

131. *Times* 9 May 1856. See also *W.T.* 21 June 1856.

132. A writ requiring an individual to appear and show cause why a judgement against him should not be enforced.

133. *I.C.L.R. 1856 and 1857*, vol.6, pp 6-15.

134. *I.C.R. 1856, 1857, and 1858*, vol.7, pp 239-241.

135. *I.C.L.R. 1856 and 1857*, vol.7, p. 13.

136. He farmed 242 acres and leased several houses – *Griffiths Valuation* 1850 p. 337.

137. *Times* 13 June 1856.

138. Ibid., and *C.T.* 14 June 1856.

139. *An Act for Repealing 8 Geo 1 and Providing more Effectual Remedies for Securing the Payment of Debts due by Bankers.*

140. Arguments of the case in June and July in *C.T.* 21 June 1856, *Times* 5 July 1856, *C.T.* 19 July 1856, *I.C.R. 1856 and 1857*, vol.6, p. 353.

141. Lord Chancellor's preliminary hearing in *C.T.* 26 July 1856.

142. Appendix 10.

143. *Evening Packet* quoted in *C.T.* 4 October 1856.

144. Quoted in *C.T.* 15 November 1856.

145. Quoted in *T.L.* 29 March 1856.

146. *Times* 31 March 1856.

147.   Ibid., 12 May 1856.

148. *C.T.* 12 July 1856.

149. *L.R.* 26 September 1856. This issue also reported that the Nenagh Board of Guardians would accept a compromise which it would itself negotiate.

150. *F.J.* 3 October 1856, *L.R.* 3 October 1856.

151. In a letter of 11 October 1856 John McNamara Cantwell, Kingston's solicitor, stated that so far from the estates owing the bank anything, the reverse was the case following John Sadleir's maladministration. Over ten years 2,000 tenants had been involved and the accounts were almost three quarters of a million pounds, which would involve a slow process of examination and unravelling in Chancery. Cantwell was confident that when the mess was sorted out the shareholders would owe an enormous sum to the estate – *F.J.* 13 October 1856.

152. See appendix 11. The Nenagh meeting was held on 8 October and presided over by Michael Scanlon, the parish priest of Cloughjordan. The Thomastown meeting met on 10 October and was chaired by Colonel Tighe, who represented the Thomastown Board of Guardians. A private meeting was held in Carlow around the same time but details were not published. Michael Dunne facilitated the Athy meeting, and Archdeacon Cotton was prominent in the Thurles meeting. Cotton was heavily involved in the Trustee Savings Bank. The Earl of Bessborough chaired the meeting in Carrick-On-Suir. For details of these see *Times* 9 October 1856, *F.J.* 10 and 13 October 1856, *C.T.* 1 November 1856. See *C.T.* 10 January 1857 for reference to a private meeting in Carlow. Carlow did not become involved in the compromise movement until November.

153. Letter in *F.J.* 9 October 1856.

154. *T.F.P.* 24 October 1856, *Times* 27 October 1856.

155. *Times* 10 October 1856.

156. *L.R.* 18 October 1856, *Times* 23 October 1856.

157. *C.P.* 1 November 1856, *L.E.* 1 November 1856.

158. Appendix 7 for delegates and sources.

159. Correspondence between McDowell and Power in *C.P.* 8 November 1856 (citing *Saunder's Newsletter*).

160. *I.C.R. 1856 and 1857*, vol.6, pp 350 et.seq. See also E. Frazer, *The Banking Laws of Ireland, a full and accurate Report of the Judgement of the Lord Chancellor of Ireland in the case of O'Flaherty and others v McDowell and others* , (Dublin,

MDCCCLVI), see *C.T.* 22 and 29 November 1856, *T.F.P.* 28 November 1856.

161. Frazer, *The Banking Laws*, p. 9.

162. Ibid., p. 31.

163. *Times* 12 January 1857.

164. See *C.C.* 17, 20 December 1856, *L.E.* 27 December 1856, N.A., C.S.O,.R.P.1856, 2058/2.

165. *L.R.* 30 December 1856, *T.F.P.* 2 January 1857.

166. Full text in *C.T.* 10 January 1857 of a Bill to Facilitate the winding up of the affairs of the Tipperary Joint Stock Banking Company.

167. Text in *T.F.P.* 13 January 1857.

168. *T.F.P.* 16 January 1857. This meeting was followed by another letter from Power on 15 January renewing his accusation of dishonesty on McDowell's part for reneging on the principles hammered out in Dobbyn's Hotel, and failing to comply with the 6 November resolutions in Dublin. He was skeptical that Westminster would promote an *ex-post facto* piece of legislation, which would compromise creditors' rights under the pending appeal of the O'Flaherty case in Lords. See ibid., 20 January 1857 for this letter.

169. His letter in ibid., 30 January 1857. See also McDowell's letter 12 January 1857 to *Freeman's Journal* in *T.F.P.* 16 January 1857 explaining that the omission of the agreed clause on the O'Flaherty case was a result of advice from his counsel that parliament was unlikely to pass a bill which depended upon a Lord's decision that might not be made for several years. Such a clause, however, could be inserted at the committee stage. McDowell denied any ulterior motive for the delay in furnishing particulars of the bill. He explained that he had been involved in other cases concerning the bank and had been subpoenaed to appear in London for the Newcastle Bank case. (In October 1856 the Newcastle Bank received the permission of Chancery to proceed independently with the winding up acts. Its targets were Howe, James Sadleir and James and Vincent Scully. McDowell defended the case and in December 1856 before Thomas Lefroy, the Lord Chief Justice of Queen's Bench, the Bank established £25,000 as the debt owed by the Tipperary Bank. McDowell successfully proved that the remainder of the £51,000 due on the useless Tipperary Bank drafts had been used by John Sadleir for his own personal use. For details of the various cases see *Times* 15 October 1856, 8 November 1856, 11 and 12 December 1856, *Newcastle Messenger and Advertiser* 13 December 1856, *L.R.* 11 November 1856, *C.T.* 24 January 1857, *C.P.* 18 October 1856).

170. Times 29 January 1857, T.F.P. 27 January 1857.

171. *The English Reports, vol. X, House of Lords, Containing House of Lords Cases (Clark's)*,, vols. 3-6, (London, 1901), pp 142-188.

172. Ibid., pp 154 et.seq. See also *F.J.* 11 July 1857. As a result of this judgement Howe was one of those put beyond the creditors' reach. The tenacious O'Flaherty however, continued to pursue him through the courts but failed to follow proper legal procedures and on 17 January 1859 the Irish Lord Chancellor reprimanded him for an abuse of legislation in this. He considered O'Flaherty's conduct 'vexatious and unconscientious in a high degree', gave the costs against him and removed the 'cloud' from Hone's title to his property – see *I.C.R. 1858 and 1859*, vol.9, pp 119-131).

173. Report of the meeting in *T.F.P.* 12 August 1856. For details of lands sold by the London Bank prior to this see e.g. R.D. 1856, vol.5, deed no.84, indenture of 4 February 1856, deed no.95, conveyance 16 February 1856, deed no.248, memorandum of agreement, R.D. 1856 vol.9, deed no.144, indenture of

conveyance 27 February 1856. (At least three directors had been replaced following Sadleir's death).

174. *T.F.P.* 15 August 1856.
175. *I.C.R. 1858 and 1859*, vol.9, pp 42-59, *T.F.P.* 9, 16 November 1858, *F.J.* 7 December 1858.
176. This Court was established in 1856.
177. *I.C.R. 1858 and 1859*, vol.9, pp 64-87. The case was argued on 10, 11 and 14 February 1859.
178. *T.F.P.* 16 February 1858.
179. *T.F.P.* 16 February 1858. (Ibid., 26 February 1858 shows the compromise as £6,500.
180. See *L.E.* 29 November 1856 for the original offer.
181. Appendix 10. See ibid., for details of such settlements by John Bennett of Riverstown, Nenagh, County Tipperary.
182. R.D., Vol.26, 1859, abs.204 and 205. In September 1857 Pepper had assigned lands to McDowell which were re-assigned to him by the official Manager when he met his compromise, presumably by raising a mortgage – see R.D., vol.13, 1857, abs.149, 6 May 1857 and abs.244, 9 September 1857; R.D., vol.26, 1859, abs. 204 and 205.
183. *T.F.P.* 4 May 1858.
184. *W.T.* 25 May 1856.
185. R.D., 1858, vol. 6, abs 156 memorial of an indented deed 30 July 1858.
186. *Times* 17 July 1856.
187. *C.T.* 19 July 1856.
188. Wilkinson's evidence in *T.F.P.* 12 November 1858.
189. *C.T.* 21 June 1856.
190. Presumably McDonnell was the proprietor at that time. There is no evidence of the connection between McDonnell and Sadleir. His parting with McCabe was acrimonious and initially he refused to publish the latter's letter of resignation alleging interference with his editorial freedom. The letter was soon published, however, as a damage limitation exercise when the *Freeman's Journal* carried the story. – see *C.T.* 21 June 1856.

Epilogue

Shame and family dissension

As might be expected it was Sadleir's family and relatives who were the principal targets of McDowell and individual creditors. They also carried the ignominy of being closely associated with him. Some were seriously damaged financially and their political prospects ruined. Not surprisingly the scandal created a legacy of bitterness between several branches of the family.

Sadleir's family suffered the greatest trauma in terms of personal tragedy and an enduring stain on its good name. Sadleir's mother was spared some of this by her death in 1858. His father, while wholly unconnected with the bank, initially found himself on the list of contributors as heir-at-law. Murphy refused to strike him off lest some of Sadleir's property fall into his hands, but he was subsequently released.[1] There is, however, a possibility that he made some attempt at restitution since he disposed of land in the Encumbered Estates Court in 1857.[2]

William Sadleir was not a shareholder and was not subject to litigation, but his career as a barrister cannot have been enhanced by his brother's swindles. Clement, who had been branch manager in Carrick-On-Suir was a secondary contributor, having disposed of his seventy shares to John in December 1854.[3] There is no indication of any settlement on his part, but his property was encumbered by mortgages to his brother, William, and to his in-laws, the Lalors of Cregg House.[4] There is also evidence of conflict with the Lalors two years before the crash, when they resorted to the courts to secure advances already made to him.[5] There does not appear, however, to have been any rift between him and his wife, Louisa. He moved to Kilkenny, and in 1858 the Lalors sought to safeguard their 1852 marriage agreement from the bank's creditors, while Louisa secured title to a brewery and premises in Carrickbeg owned by Clement but mortgaged to John Sadleir.[6] By an order of the Lord Chancellor on 12 February 1858 Clement was replaced as one of Louisa's trustees under the marriage settlement by Emma Sadleir's brother, Frederick Windle Wheatley.[7]

The Wheatleys, were equally determined to secure their rights from their Sadleir connection and preserve as much of James Sadleir's property as possible from McDowell. The latter had secured the Clonacody estate, which he sold in the Incumbered Estates Court,[8] but the Coolnamuck property was not so easily gained because of encumbrances and prior claims upon it, particularly by Thomas J. Eyre. John Sadleir's use of other estates as security for its mortgages was a further complication. Emma's other brother, John Sherwood Wheatley, was a wealthy lace manufacturer in Nottingham and had the money to meet heavy expenses in his conflict with McDowell over Coolnamuck.[9] The official manager was confident that he had followed the correct legal procedures in his claim to the estate, which included not only the Coolnamuck demesne, but the lands of Kilconnell and Curraghtarsna in County Tipperary. His claim resulted from Sadleir's failure to pay McDowell's call of £40 per share in June 1856 amounting to £70,000. An order from Chancery to pay this was served in September, registered in October and on 3 November 1856 McDowell issued an affidavit to register it as a statutable mortgage on the estate.[10] The Wheatley family objected that the Chancery order was not capable of being registered as a statutable mortgage, but Longfield directed McDowell to proceed with an ejectment order. The Wheatleys appealed to the Court of Common Pleas that this order was defective because it failed to show James Sadleir's trade, profession or last place of abode. In May 1858 Chief Justice Monahan reversed the Chancery decision on this legal technicality, and ruled that McDowell had no title to the property.[11]

The Wheatleys were also successful in another case against James Sadleir himself. On his marriage he had received £10,000 which was vested in trustees.[12] In April 1857 his brother-in-law, sought to protect this marriage settlement and secured a judgement for it, which he registered lest it be lost to McDowell.[13] This money was used to sustain Sadleir who had fled the jurisdiction early in June 1856.[14]

Prior to his departure he succeeded in selling some of his cattle and horses in Clonmel, and three drayloads of his furniture were sent to Dublin, where it was traced to Dillon's showrooms.[15] The Master of the Rolls immediately placed an injunction on the sale of any of his property,[16] and Dillon was served with a copy of this order.[17] A large quantity of plate and jewellery could not be traced, but in September more of his furniture, including a mirror worth £130, was discovered in a Clonmel store. The following month additional furniture was found in Littledale's auction rooms on Ormond Quay.[18] According to Daniel J. Bergin this was seized and sold by Richard O'Flaherty.[19]

Following his departure from Ireland Sadleir travelled to Mulmoe near Copenhagen under the name of John Smith.[20] He remained there for less than a week and then left for Paris. He later went to Boulogne and an 1859 affidavit by McDowell described him as 'carrying on no trade or business or exercising no profession' there.[21] He finally settled in Zurich where he lived for many years on the annuity from the Wheatleys.[22] Like his brother he met a tragic end when he was murdered on 4 June 1881 following an attempt to rob him while he took an afternoon walk on the Zurichberg.[23] James Sadleir and his wife did not have any children, but Emma declined to accompany him when he left Ireland. Instead she returned to England and lived with her brother in Calverton Hall, Nottingham.[24] She died there in 1895 aged seventy-four.

If James Sadleir had been intimately associated with his brother's affairs, his cousin Robert Keating was not perceived as blameless either because of his close connection with Sadleir in the London and County and his role in the March 1855 negotiations with the Tipperary. Shortly after Sadleir's death he was forced to resign from the London bank because 'he was a relation of John Sadleir and the board wished to cut off the connection'.[25] His political career also ended, and he did not contest the 1857 general election. He was pursued through the courts by McDowell because he once held 700 shares in trust for Sadleir. In May 1856 he vainly sought to have his name removed from the list of contributors, pleading that he was merely a trustee rather than a *bona fide* shareholder. Murphy refused to strike him off, and condemned him as a weak individual who allowed himself to be made 'the tool of a man who appears to have secured a wonderful ascendancy over the minds of all who came within his reach'.[26] McDowell finally secured a judgement for £4,000 against him,[27] and Keating was forced to sell Garranlea which had been in the family since 1783. He moved to Dublin where he died in 1893 aged ninety-two.[28]

John Ryan of Scarteen did not share the ignominy of Keating but was pursued by the creditors. He was less well off than Keating and held only held thirty five shares. He compromised for £1,500 which was only a quarter of what was due under McDowell's calls. It did, however, cause the family considerable financial difficulties and for the first time the Ryan's lost the mastership of its famous pack of hounds.[29] It was only through the benevolence of a neighbour that they were allowed remain at Scarteen until the family was in a position to resume the mastership.[30]

Although he shared neither the shame nor the reduced circumstances of Keating or Ryan, the wealthy Thomas J. Eyre endured years of complex litigation after Sadleir's death, which ultimately cost him £52,000 loaned on defective mortgages.[31] Not only was he the direct victim of Sadleir's swindle on the Royal Swedish, but he also suffered because of the various land speculations carried out on his behalf by Sadleir, which took years to resolve in the courts. His involvement in the Kingston estate is a good example, although insufficient evidence makes it impossible to properly unravel it. As joint-mortgagee with the Tipperary bank Eyre was pursued by Kingston before and after Sadleir's death for the recovery of rents and profits which he had never received, but which had found their way via the bank into John Sadleir's pocket.[32] Kingston pleaded that his property had been vested in Eyre in trust.

Sadleir's success in convincing the London and County that the Eyre encumbrance on portion of the Kilcommon, Clonmore and Shanakill estates was lifted by the October 1855 agreement was yet another swindle which involved Eyre in several years of legal conflict with that bank. When the Landed Estates Court was considering the final schedule of this property in October 1859, Eyre argued that his mortgage was still an encumbrance on it, which he was entitled to recover from the proceeds of the sale by the London bank. Strangely, however, Longfield ruled that the release of the mortgage in October 1855 was valid, and he dismissed Eyre's claim.[33]

Longfield's ruling was appealed and heard in the Chancery Court of Appeal on 21 and 31 May 1860. The Lord Chancellor and Justices of Appeal upheld Longfield's decision and Eyre went to the House of Lords.[34] It took a further two years for the case to be heard there, but the Lords found in his favour and gave him priority over the London bank to the lands in question.[35] His legal odyssey was not yet ended, however, because Lords ordered that the matter be referred back to the Landed Estates Court for execution. Due to an error by his counsel only part of his mortgage was entered against the estates, and he was forced to appeal once more to the Court of Appeal in Chancery to have the entire mortgage entered as a priority encumbrance.[36] He finally succeeded on 23 June 1862, more than six years after Sadleir's death, but it is unlikely that the proceeds from the sale of the 443 acres met his mortgage.

Eyre was less successful in the Coolnamuck litigation about the 1845 mortgage of £30,000 advanced by him to Sadleir, which had not been registered. Part of the security later given by Sadleir was a £17,000 draft of the Tipperary bank, which was not cashed prior to the crash and was, therefore, valueless. Eyre failed to have this mortgage recorded as an encumbrance on the estate when the case was heard by the Landed Estates Court in December 1858.[37] But, in May 1863 the Irish Lord Chancellor ruled that he was the *bona fide* owner of some portion since Sadleir had purchased it in trust for him, despite conveying it to

James Sadleir.[38] Eyre, however, was allowed only to claim the £17,000 part of the mortgage. The Court of Appeal in Chancery upheld the Lord Chancellor's judgement in its ruling of December 1863.[39]

Despite his heavy losses Eyre's great wealth was not seriously undermined, and in July 1856 he swore that he was still worth £150,000.[40] He was extremely fortunate in not being a shareholder whereby this wealth would have been seen by creditors as a prime source to recover their losses. Such was the case the Scullys, whose reputation for integrity and perceived wealth ensured that they were relentlessly pursued. Vincent was the wealthiest, not only by inheritance from his father, Denys, but from his lucrative law practice. Rightly irate at his prolonged failure to dispose of his shares at an earlier date because of Sadleir's evasive tactics, he was determined to resist all claims. He employed the services of Abraham Brewster, who in the Scully trials fully justified his reputation on the Irish circuit.

Although he succeeded in being struck off the list of contributories in April 1857 Scully was faced with the individual actions of thirteen creditors[41] including the Newcastle Bank.[42] He resisted each of these on the basis that he was not a shareholder. One case was heard by William Keogh who had succeeded Justice Torrens as a judge in the Court of Common Pleas.[43] Scully used legal technicalities to frustrate these cases, most of which were held in the Court of Exchequer.[44] When a small number of creditors succeeded in getting permission to serve writs on him in November he refused to meet the process server when he arrived at his residence in 13 Merrion Square.[45] He also managed to delay Exchequer proceedings in January and February 1857.[46] In February he succeeded in deferring a hearing brought by the Newcastle Bank for an order of *scire facias* to be made absolute.[47] Even when nine creditors registered judgments against him, they were not marked in the Registry of Deeds as ever having been satisfied.[48]

He was, however, anxious to extricate himself with some honour from the scandal, and when freed from liability to McDowell he agreed to take part in the compromise scheme, and settled for a payment of £10,500. To meet this he auctioned 3166 acres with a net rental of £2,109 in the Incumbered Estates Court on 17 November 1857.[49] These included the Kingwilliamstown estate in Cork and the Ballyrobin, Donohill and Ballinahinch lands in County Tipperary. He stated that this sale was specifically to meet the compromise, but might have added that he made a profit of almost £3,000 on the sale of the Kingwilliamstown estate.[50]

While this was a significant settlement it did not make serious inroads into his wealth,[51] and his son later built an impressive monument, known as Scully's cross, beside the tombs of his ancestors on the Rock of Cashel.[52] Unlike his cousins his political career was not ruined either. He did not hesitate to put himself forward for Cork again in 1857, but was forced to withdraw. Nonetheless he was proposed two years later, succeeded and sat for Cork until 1865.[53] He died in London on 4 June 1871.

His cousins John and Frank Scully were considerably less affluent. John lived in Oughterard, County Galway, and had no interest in the Tipperary bank except to draw the dividend on fifty-eight shares inherited from his father, James Scully of Shanballymore. He only returned to Ireland in 1847, the year after the latter's death, following a failed venture into sheep farming in the Swan River settlement in Western Australia.[54] Scully was successfully sued by two creditors, John Bergin and James Kelly, but he never satisfied their judgments against him.[55] McDowell secured a judgement against him for £2,320,[56] but accepted a compromise of £1,000 offered in May 1858,[57] although it took until 1862 to sell the land to meet this.[58] This was 124 acres in Marlhill, County Tipperary, also inherited from his father. He managed to conceal from creditors that he still owned 200 acres in Western Australia.[59] He died on 24 June 1890, one month short of his eightieth birthday.[60]

Frank had a less happy outcome. Like John he did not satisfy the judgments of the same two creditors, but unlike him he was unable or unwilling to compromise. McDowell initially secured a judgement of £7,000 against him on the first call, which was beyond his means to meet.[61] His wealthy Moorat in-laws were not amenable to rescuing him, but in May 1858 his father-in-law gave him £2,200 which was, however, secured by the transfer of his property in Tipperary and Limerick City.[62] Scully used this to flee to Paris where the Moorats had relatives.[63] He had once quoted the aphorism that 'any name is a good name while it is well taken care of',[64] and the disgrace to his family as well as the destruction to his ambitions preyed upon his mind while he lived in Paris. He was eventually confined to an asylum where he died on 17 August 1864.[65] Six years later his widow, Marie, wed Augustus Gallwey, brother of Catherine Gallwey, who was married to his brother James.[66]

James was as conscious of the family's good name as Frank. His actions in endorsing the deposit receipts in Tipperary during the run on the bank is an indication of this. Though not as wealthy as Vincent, he did not oppose either McDowell or individual creditors with the same resolve as his cousin. Having conveyed 311 acres out of the reach of creditors in May 1856 he made preparations to meet some of the demands on him.[67] In November 1856 McDowell registered a judgement for £23,400 against him,[68] and Scully, then in Tramore, requested further time, but assigned lands to the official manager as proof of his *bona fides*.[69] Nevertheless, the strain of possible ruin and the prospect of interminable law suits from individual creditors caused him to flee to Paris for a period of respite in the Hotel Louvre on the Rue de Rivoli. Much to his annoyance he came upon James Sadleir in the city, and so great was his animosity towards him that on 12 February he notified the Irish Attorney General of Sadleir's whereabouts and semi-disguise,

> Sir, – I consider it my duty to inform you that the *notorious* culprit James Sadleir is now in Paris, having seen him last night enter a restaurant in the Palace Royal, where I dined, and having caught my eye, he immediately withdrew. The proprietor, M. Dupuis, afterwards informed me that he dines there every day. If the Government is anxious to arrest him, by sending over persons acquainted with his personal appearance, the object can be attained. His countenance is much altered; having lost his flesh and colour, and also wearing a moustache, a considerable change has taken place. This information shall be kept secret by me until I receive your reply.[70]

Scully had greater reason to be incensed three months later when Sadleir wrote a series of letters to the Irish press portraying himself as the dupe of his brother, and downplaying his role in the swindle on the English shareholders and the ongoing violation of the bank's deed of partnership.[71] Scully was infuriated not only by these excuses, but at the assertion that he had enjoyed very favourable credit terms at the bank while refusing to accept responsibility in its management by becoming a director. His letter of 14 May from the Hotel Louvre captures his sense of outrage,

> I have this moment read a letter in the *Dublin Evening Post* from the notorious culprit James Sadleir ... and were it not for justice to my own character, I would not now notice anything coming from such a tainted source, and from a person who should now ... be undergoing, in some distant colony in irons the punishment he so fully merited, instead of being allowed to parade the public rooms and promenades here, with as much safety and protection as that afforded the most honest person. I stated that I never bought any shares in so rotten and cursed a concern as the Tipperary Bank; the few shares that my father gave me ... were sold to Dr. John Ryan, Tipperary, in 1848 and that the only shares I held were those derived from administration to my father.

He went on to defend his own credit terms and show that he was not in debt to the bank when it closed. He denounced James Sadleir's indulgence of his brother, and scorned his assertion of sound management as well as personal loss through the crash. He was furious that Sadleir's letters had drawn a comparison between their mutual predicaments,

> He had a credit of £5,000, but he does not mention the sums he extracted for salary and from dividends on shares entered in fictitious names amounting to a very considerable sum annually. As to devoting his whole time to the management, such, appears, could have been profitably dispensed with, as there could not possibly be found a more fraudulent and incompetent director. "What is Mr. James Scully's case worse than mine"? What audacity to attempt to institute any comparison – one so heinously guilty, the other so perfectly innocent; but unfortunately, one comparison can be drawn; We are undergoing the same punishment, exiled from the country, far more severe on me when guilty of no crime, and anxious to pay as far as my property allows – I am separated from my wife and children.

It is not known how long James Scully remained separated from his family, but he returned to Ireland when the prospect of a compromise was certain. His offer of £14,000 at the end of 1858 was approved by Murphy in May 1859 and his lands were released back to him.[72] He was forced, however, to raise a mortgage on the Shanballymore estate towards this.[73]

Not alone did Scully meet this compromise but in 1859 he also satisfied judgments against him by twelve depositors.[74] He appears to have been the only member of the Scully family to do so. Under normal circumstances his means would have been sufficient to meet his compromise and maintain his status as an Irish country gentleman. But Scully had married twice and fathered fourteen children.[75] Nonetheless, despite his financial losses he managed to send his sons to Stoneyhurst and his daughters to convents in England.[76]

Still, the combined weight of his losses from the failure and the maintenance of his large family forced him to abandon his Athassal mansion for the more confined lifestyle of 45 Merrion Square, not far from Vincent's residence. Such proximity, however, was of little consolation to him because he harboured a grudge against his cousin,[77] partly, perhaps from a sense of his own voluntary financial martyrdom and exile to the city, and partly because he resented the stout defence of his more wealthy relative against claims. He harboured a deeper animosity towards the Keatings, and ostracised them for the remainder of his life.[78] He also severed relations with his Morrogh cousins because of their close association with the Sadleirs and the Keatings.[79]

When James Scully died aged seventy-one in 1878, relations between the family branches can only have improved, but the connotations of

Sadleirism in terms of financial dishonesty and perceived political apostacy lived on for generations among the wider public.[80] Ordinary depositors were obviously less concerned with political principles than with their own misfortunes. Their losses were exacerbated by law costs, and despite the heroic efforts of McDowell to pursue calls, negotiate compromise and prosecute those indebted to the bank he only managed to raise £140,000 yielding a dividend of seven shillings in the pound, the last of which was paid as late as August 1881 when £3,000 was available to creditors.[81]

Considering the ultimate level of their losses it was fortunate that the Tipperary did not have the power to issue its own notes. It would have been easier to forge bank notes than deeds and such a money producing institution would have afforded Sadleir an irresistible means of swindling an even larger amount. As it was, the overall extent of his swindles was enormous, reaching at least one and a half million pounds.

Even this was probably understated. Morier Evans was convinced that many other victims remained silent because they were more easily able to bear their losses.[82] He might also have legitimately concluded that some were too embarrassed to admit that they had been taken in by John Sadleir who was to become the target of several nineteenth novelists, including Dickens, and earn the well-justified title, Prince of Swindlers.[83]

References

1. *Times* 15 October 1856, *C.P.* 18 October 1856, *C.T.* 22 November 1856, *I.C.R. 1856 and 1857*, vol.6, p. 357.
2. *T.F.P.* 20 November 1857, *C.T.* 21 November 1857. See also R.D., 1858, vol.1, abstract 14, Lease 3 April 1856.
3. Appendix 3.
4. See R.D., 1853, vol.25, abs. 69, Articles of Agreement 8 March 1852. Clement William Sadleir was party to this agreement. The mortgage was on the 351 acre farm in Arnakarky.
5. See R.D., 1854, vol.11, abs.254, judgement from the Court of Queen's Bench 4 March 1854 for Thomas Lalor, Cregg House, Clement Sadleir's brother-in-law, for £1,000. This also cites Clement's land in Arnakarky. See also R.D., 1854, vol.23, abs. 156, mortgage 1 August 1854, assigning Arnakarky (Castleblake) to Lalor. John Sadleir, Robert Keating and Clement William Sadleir were party to this. See also R.D., 1855, vol.4, abs.20, Deed of Assignment 3 January 1855 also citing this property. Clement Sadleir was then living in 18 New Bridge Street, London. See also R.D., 1858, vol.21, abs. 264, deed 13 May 1858 citing Anthony Norris as administrator of John Sadleir's estate.
6. See R.D., 1858, vol. 21, abs.264, deed 13 May 1858 between Anthony Norris, administrator of John Sadleir's estate, Clement Sadleir of Cloncunny, Kilkenny, and Louisa Sadleir etc. citing the marriage deed of settlement of £3,000. This

showed that Clement had mortgaged Arnakarky to John Sadleir. It also showed that Clement had a brewery and premises at Carrickbeg. Louisa paid Norris £100 to purchase John Sadleir's claim on this and Norris agreed to release the brewery to her. For Clement Sadleir's marriage settlement see R.D., 1852, vol.17, abs.26, Deed of settlement 3 June 1852. Louisa was granted £2,500 under her deceased father's will. Her brother Thomas also gave her £700 as a gift. This deed mentions Clement's insurance policy of £999. John Sadleir and Robert Keating were trustees of this settlement. See R.D., 1852, vol.16, abs.157 on this insurance policy.

7. See R.D., 1859, vol. 17, abs. 208, Deed of Conveyance 26 May 1859 between Clement Sadleir, John Sherwood Wheatley, Nottingham, and Frederick Windle Wheatley of 20 Great Marlborough Street London.

8. *Times* 3 September 1856.

9. Details of the case including the background of McDowell's legal proceedings leading to an ejectment order in *I.C.L.R.1856, 1857, and 1858*, vol.7, pp .562-570.

10. A mortgage recognised by statute. See R.D., 1859, vol.24, for the registration of this call. It is shown as £65,000. With the second call Sadleir's liability was increased to £434,000 – R.D., 1859, vol.11, abstract 134.

11. *I.C.L.R. 1856, 1857 and 1858*, vol.7 p. 566.

12. *W.T.* 5 April 1856.

13. R.D., 1857, vol.12, abstract 97. See also R.D., 1866, vol.28, memorial 275, deed dated 14 November 1865 assigning the lands of her trust to Samuel William Baukart, London who had advanced the Calverton dowry.

14. J.D. Fitzgerald's statement in *Parl. Deb.*, Series 3, vol.144, 1857, col.705, (16 February 1857). Fitzgerald revealed that an affidavit of Sadleir dated 9 June was not sworn at the proper office in Dublin but in Kingstown (Port of Dun Laoghaire), an indication that Sadleir was then en route to Europe.

15. *C.P.* 19 July 1856, *C.T.* 19 July 1856.

16. Ibid.

17. *C.T.* 26 July 1856.

18. *F.J.* 10 October 1856.

19. Letter 8 October 1856 from Bergin in *Times* 10 October 1856.

20. *Copies of the Several Warrants...James Sadleir 22-Sess.1*, p. 1. See also Ibid., (*37-Sess. 1*) XIV 375.

21. R.D., 1859, vol.24, abs.136; see also R.D., 1858, vol.35, abs.46, R.D., 1858, vol.36, abs.228, R.D., 1859, vol.4, abs.52.

22 MacDermot, *I.G.*, V.6, p. 360.

23. *Times* 21 June 1881. See also R.D., 1883, vol.5, abs.95 for the date of his death.

24. See R.D., 1883, vol.5, abs.95.

25. Evidence of a Director of the London and County in the Landed Estates Court in 1858 – *T.F.P.* 12 November 1858.

26. *Times* 24 May 1856.

27. MacDermot, *I.G.*, vol 6, p. 361.

28. R.D., 1858, vol.27, abstract 181, (judgement for £4011 and £90 costs).

29. MacDermot, *I.G.*, vol.6, p. 361.

30. See MacEwan,*The Ryan Family,* p. 38. (MacEwan is incorrect in regarding John Ryan as a director of the bank).

31. Ibid., p. 356.

32. Case in *C.T.* 28 June 1856. Evidence of Leonard Morrogh on this in *W.T.* 5 April 1856. See *C.T.* 12 July 1856 for a report of the Rolls Court's refusal to appoint a

Receiver to the Mitchelstown estate and his exoneration of Nicholas Sadleir as agent.

33. *I.C.R. 1860 and 1861*, vol.11, pp .11 et.seq.

34. Ibid., pp .1-19.

35. *I.C.R. 1862, 1863 and 1864*, vol. 14, pp .48-56.

36. Ibid., p. 53.

37. *T.F.P.* 14 December 1858. For one transaction between Sadleir and Eyre involving Coolnamuck Estate see R.D., 1856, vol.17, memorial 32, memorandum of agreement 13 May 1855.

38. *I.C.R. 1862, 1863, and 1864*, vol 14, p. 126.

39. Ibid., vol. 15, pp .1-15.

40. *C.T.* 12 July 1856.

41. p. 435-6 above.

42. *L.R.* 11 November 1856, *C.T.* 8 November 1856.

43. *C.T.* 15 November 1856.

44. e.g. *C.T.* 29 November 1856, *I.C.L.R. 1856 and 1857*, vol 6 pp .274-277. He objected that there was not sufficient evidence on the abstract of a *Nisi Prius* judgement.

45. *L.R.* 11 November 1856.

46. *C.T.* 24 January 1857, 7 February 1857.

47. *Times* 9 February 1857.

48. See appendix 10. Similar judgements against other shareholders were marked as satisfied in the Registry of Deeds Records.

49. See *T.F p.* 28 August 1852 for schedule of lands. (In August 1857 Scully had mortgaged property consisting of nineteen townlands, including Mantle Hill – see R.D., 1857, vol.24, abs.297, indenture 19 August 1857.

50. He had purchased it for £6,750 and it was sold for £9,500 in the Incumbered Estates Court – *F.J.* 10 December 1858.

51. Evidence in the Ingram (Castlehyde) case in *F.J.* 10 December 1858.

52. MacDermot, *I.G.*, vol 6, p. 363 for details. See N.L.I., Scully Papers, MS. 27,558 for various documents on the Ó Scolaidhe memorial monument erected on the Rock in 1867

53. Ibid., p. 362.

54. Ibid., pp .72-73. He had been an army officer prior to his departure for Australia.

55. See Appendix 10. See R.D., 1856, vol 32, abstract 175 for registration of these judgements which were not endorsed as satisfied.

56. R.D., 1856, vol 132, abstract 175.

57. *T.F.P.* 4 May 1858.

58. R.D., 1862, vol.19, abstract 9, (memorial 27 May 1862).

59. MacDermot, *I.G.*, vol 6, pp .72-73.

60. Ibid.

61. R.D., 1856, vol.132, abstract 174, (26 November 1856).

62. R.D., 1858, vol 14, abstract 17, (deed of conveyance 5 May 1856. The lands and property are listed in this deed).

63. The date of his going to Paris is not known. His second son, Francis Edward, was born c.1859 and it is likely, but not certain, that this took place in England.

64. This was in 1853 – MacDermot, *I.G.*, vol.6, op.cit, p. 362.

65. Ibid., pp .75,356.

66. Ibid., p. 70. Augustus Gallwey was the uncle of Blanche, wife of Charles O'Conor, the last Master of the Rolls.

67. R.D., 1856, vol 13, abstract 219, (lease 9 May 1856 to Richard Butler during the

life of his son Francis Scully, Athassel).

68. R.D., 1856, vol 31, abstract 54, (12 November 1856).
69. R.D., 1856; vol 32, abstract 38, (deed of conveyance 14 November 1856).
70. This letter was read by J.D. Fitzgerald to the House of Commons on 16 February 1857 – see *Parl. Deb.*, series 3, vol 144, 1857, cols.708-709.
71. Sadleir's letters and the ensuing correspondence between the two in *T.F.P.* 15, 19, 11 and 26 May 1857.
72. R.D., 1859, vol 17, abstract 116, (deed dated 25 May 1859). This cites details of the 1856 and 1859 agreements.
73. R.D., 1859, vol.17, abstract 117, (Deed of Mortgage 27 May 1859). See ibid., abstract 184 and R.D. 1856, vol 31 abstract 54 which was endorsed by a reference to these. For other details of Scully's efforts to raise money by way of mortgage see R.D., 1856, vol. 31 abstract 120, mortgage 14 November 1856, R.D., 1856, vol.31, abs. 140, mortgage 14 November 1856. R.D., 1859, vol. 17, abstract 184, Deed of Mortgage 27 May 1859.
74. Appendix 6.
75. He had five children by his first wife, Helen Sheridan, and nine by his second wife Catherine Gallwey.
76. MacDermot, *I.G.*, vol 6, p. 75.
77. Ibid.
78. Ibid., p. 361.
79. Ibid.
80. e.g. Reference of David Humphreys c.c. Tipperary Town to the defection during one of his many conflicts during the Land War – *L.R.* 5 May 1891.
81. Dividends calculated from information in *C.T.* 14 June 1856, *T.F.P.* 30 July 1857, 29 June 1858, *I.C.R. 1856 and 1857*, vol 6, p. 356, Dillon, *The History and Development of Banking*, p. 86, Collins, *Law and Practice of Banking*, p. 91.
82. Morier Evans, *Facts Failures and Frauds*, p. 239.
83. Appendix 8.

Bibliography

PRIMARY SOURCES

A. MANUSCRIPTS
Belfast
Public Record Office Northern Ireland
Rental Tenements in Smithfield Ward, Belfast.

California
Huntington Library, San Marino
Grenville Papers

Carlow
Kildare Diocesan Archives
Papers of Bishop Francis Haly

Cashel
Cashel Diocesan Archives – Church of Ireland
Vestry Books

Dublin
Dublin Diocesan Archives
Papers of Archbishop Murray
Papers of Archbishop Cullen

Kings Inns Library
Memorials for admittance as students, solicitors , barristers

National Archives
Registered Papers, Chief Secretary's Office
Outrage Papers
Private Index Papers

National Library of Ireland
Memorials to Pope Pius IX
C.G. Duffy Papers
Mayo Papers
Monsell Papers
G.H. Moore Papers
Scully Papers

Public Record Office Ireland
Tithe Applotment Books

Registry of Deeds
Abstracts for the years 1728 – 1883

Trinity College
Donoughmore Papers

London
British Library
Papers of the Earl of Aberdeen

Public Record Office
Letters of Administration of the estate of John Sadleir.

Highgate Cemetery
Records of grave plots

Thurles
Tipperary County Library
Poor Law Minute Books for County Tipperary
Minute Books of Thurles Savings Bank 11827 – 1871
Miscellaneous election papers

Patrick J. O'Meara, Solicitors
Copies of correspondence of George Bourke on the Tipperary Joint Stock Bank

B. UNPUBLISHED MATERIAL
Martin, John H., 'Aspects of the Social Geography of Dublin City in the Mid nineteenth Century', M.A. Thesis, N.U.I., 1973.

O'Shea, James, The priest and politics in County Tipperary 1850-1891, 2 vols., Ph.D. thesis, N.U.I., 1979.

C. WORKS OF REFERENCE
Annual Register 1856, or a view of the history and politics of the year 1856, London, 1857.

Burke, Sir Bernard, *A genealogical and Heraldic Dictionary of the Landed Gentry of Great Britain and Ireland,* London, 1868 and 1904 editions.

Burke's Irish Family Records, London, 1958 and 1976 editions.

Burke's Genealogical and Heraldic History of the Landed Gentry of Ireland, London, 1958.

Census of Ireland. General alphabetical index to the townlands and towns, parishes and baronies of Ireland, Dublin, 1861.

Dictionary of National Biography.

Dod, Charles R., *Electoral Facts 1846-1856*, London, 1856.

Dod, Charles R., *Electoral Facts from 1832 to 1853*, London, 1853.

Dod, Charles R., *Parliamentary Companion 1846 – 1856*, London, 1856.

Doubleday, H.A. and de Waldon, Lord Howard, *The Complete Peerage*, vol. 3, London, 1929.

Dublin Almanac and General Register 1838 and 1843.

Elmes, R., *Catalogue of Engraved Irish Portraits*, Dublin, 1936.

Farrar, Henry, *Irish Marriages, being an index to the marriages in Walker's Hibernian Magazine 1771-1812, with an index, vol. 2, K – Z..*

Griffiths, Dennis (ed.), *The Encyclopedia of the British Press 1422-1992*, London, 1992.

Hayes,R.J., *Manuscript sources for the history of Irish civilisation.*

Irish Catholic Directory 1847– 1856.

Laffan, Thomas, *Tipperary's families, being the hearth-money records for 1665-6-7*, Dublin, 1911.

Lewis, Samuel S., *A history and Topography of Dublin city and county*, Dublin, 1980, (reprint).

Lewis, Samuel S., *A topographical dictionary of Ireland,* 2 vols., London 1837.

London Directory, 1850.

London Post Office Directory 1850.

Longman's atlas of modern British history. A visual guide to British society and politics 1700– 1970, London, 1978.

Mitchell, Charles, *The Newspaper Press Directory containing full particulars relative to each journal published in the United Kingdom and the British Isles together with a complete guide to a newspaper press of each county 1846 -1856*, London, 1857.

Mozley and Whitley's Law Direct Dictionary, London, 1970.

Palmer, Samuel, *Index to the Times Newspaper*, London, 1887.

Pigott's Directory 1824, London, 1824.

Post Office Annual Directory, Dublin 1838, 1843, 1844.

Thoms Irish Almanac and Official Directory, 1839-1851

The Treble Almanac, Dublin 1835.

Thrift, Gertrude, *Irish record series, indexes to Irish wills*, vol. 3, London, 1913.

Vicars, Arthur, *Index to the prerogative wills of Ireland 1536-1810*, Dublin, 1897.

Walford, E., *The county families of the United Kingdom*, London, 1865.

Watson's commercial and general London directory 1854.

Wilson's Dublin Directory for the year 1830, Dublin, 1830

NEWSPAPERS
Athlone Sentinel
Banner of Ulster
Belfast Newsletter
Buck's Herald
Carlow Post
Carlow Sentinel
Catholic Telegraph and Irish Sun
Champion or Sligo News
Clonmel Chronicle
Dublin Evening Mail
Dublin Evening Post
Freeman's Journal
Galway Vindicator and Connaught Advertiser
Illustrated London News
Leinster Express
Limerick Reporter
Manchester Guardian
Morning Advertiser
Morning Chronicle
Nation
Nenagh Guardian
Newcastle Chronicle
Newcastle Messenger

Railway Times
Saunders Newsletter
Sligo Chronicle
Sligo Journal
Tablet
Telegraph
Times
Tipperary Free Press
Tipperary Leader
Waterford Chronicle
Waterford Mail
Waterford News and General Advertiser
Weekly Telegraph

E. OFFICIAL PUBLICATIONS

Census of Ireland for the year 1851, col. 1, Province of Leinster.

Griffith, R. General valuation of rateable property in Ireland, County Tipperary, S.R., Barony of Clanwilliam. Unions of cashel and Tipperary. Primary Valuation of the several tenements comprising the said barony, Dublin, 1851

Hansard's Parliamentary Debates, series 3, 1847-1858.

The Civil Survey A.D. 1654-1656, County of Tipperary, vols. 1 and 2, reprinted Government Publications Office, Dublin, 1931.

Minutes of evidence before the select committee of Lords appointed to inquire into the state of Ireland, H.C. 1825 (181), IX.

Minutes of evidence before the select committee sess. 1824 on the disturbances in Ireland, H.C. 1825 (20), VII.

First report of the commissioners appointed to inquire into the manner in which railway communication can be most advantageously promoted in Ireland, H.C. 1837 (75), XXXIII.283.

Report of the select committee of the House of Commons to inquire into the operation of the acts permitting the establishment of joint stock banks in England and Ireland in 1837, H.C. 1837 (531), XIV.1

A return of the joint stock banks existing in England and Wales in each of the three years ending with the 5th day of January 1839, specifying the date of the establishment of each bank, the number and situation of its branches and the number of partners in each bank. Similar returns for Scotland and Ireland, H.C. 1839 (530), XXX.

Copy of all resolutions and memorials presented to the Lord Lieutenant of Chief Secretary of Ireland, or to the Chancellor of the Exchequer, respecting railroads in that country, H.C. 1839 (154), XLVI.

Accounts of the number of private and joint stock banks registered in Ireland in each year from 1820 to 1844, H.C. 1844 (232),XXXII.

Evidence taken before her Majesty's Commissioners of Inquiry into the state of the law and practice in respect of the occupation of land in Ireland, part III, H.C. 1845 (657), XXI.

Disease Ireland. Abstracts of the most serious representations made by the several medical Superintendents of public institutions (fever hospitals, infirmaries, dispensaries, etc.) in the provinces of Ulster, Munster, Leinster and Connaught, H.C. 1846 (120), XXXVII.

Copies of the order to the government agent in Ireland, Dr Cooke, to withold the Regium Donum from the congregation of Clonmel in connexion with the general assembly of the Presbyterian church, and of any correspondence between the Irish government and Dr Cooke on the subject, H.C. 1847-48 (448), XLIX.

Accounts and papers 1848. Relief of distress and union workhouses (Ireland), H.C. 1847-48 (955), LVI. (Reproduced by I.U.P. 1970).

Return of the passengers and goods traffic on each railway in Great Britain and Ireland for the two years ending 30 June 1846 and 30 June 1847; together with a summary for each year, showing the number of passengers, divided into classes, the receipts from each class, and from goods, H.C. 1847-48 (937), LXIII.53.

A Bill to continue for a limited time the Act of the last session for empowering the Lord Lieutenant or other chief governor or governors of Ireland to apprehend and detain such persons as he or they shall suspect of conspiring against her Majesty's person and government, H.C. 1849 (9), III.137.

Incumbered estates (Ireland): Bill further to facilitate the sale of incumbered estates in Ireland, H.C. 1849 (235), III.211.

Do. as amended by the committee, H.C. 1849 (284), III.233.

Do. as amended by the committee and on re-commitment, H.C. 1849 (309), III.257.

Do. as amended by the Lords, H.C. 1849 (444), III.283.

A Bill to alter the oaths to be taken by members of the two houses of Parliament not professing the Roman Catholic Religion, H.C. 1849 (65), IV.419.

Return of the number of passengers conveyed on all railways in the United Kingdom during the Year ending 30th June 1848, showing the different classes, the receipts from each class and from goods etc., also the number of miles of railway open on 1st July 1847 and on 30th June 1848, H.C. 1849 (6), L.1.

Return of the number of passengers conveyed on all the railways in the United Kingdom during the half year ending in 31st December 1848, showing the different classes, the receipts from each class and from goods etc., also the number of miles of railway given at the commencement and at the termination of the half year, H.C. 1849 (418), L.1.

Proceedings of the select committee on Poor Laws Ireland, part II, H.C. 1849 (572), XV.

Relief of Distress and union workhouses (Ireland). Papers relating to the proceedings for the relief of the distress and state of unions and workhouses in Ireland, Part II. Distress indicated in the clothing of the peasantry and pawnbrokers returns, H.C. 1849 (1042)XLVIII.221.

A Bill to provide compensation to tenants for improvement effected by them in certain cases, and to amend the law of landlord and tenant in Ireland, H.C. 1850 (64), III.489.

A Bill intituled an Act to amend and improve the relations of landlord and tenant in Ireland, H.C. 1850 (551),III.529.

Report by E. Lawes to First Commissioner of Woods on Westminster Improvements Acts amending bill, H.C. 1850 (396), XXXIII.709.

A Bill to provide for the abolition of the office of Lord Lieutenant of Ireland and for the appointment of a Fourth Secretary of State, H.C. 1850 (359), III.359.

Copy of any correspondence between the Moderator of the general assembly of the Presbyterian church in Ireland and the Irish government relative to the stoppage of the Regium Donum of the minister of Clonmel, on the order of George Mathews, alias Duncan Chisolm, H.C. 1850 (631), LI.

A Bill as amended by the committee and on consideration of a Bill as amended to prevent the assumption of certain ecclesiastical titles in respect of places in the United Kingdom, H.C. 1851 (451), III.73.

Copies of any correspondence between John Sadleir Esq. M.P. and his Excellency, the Lord Lieutenant, relative to a fund of about £4,500 placed under the control of Duncan Chisolm, alias George Mathews, lately absconded from the office of the Chief-Secretary in Ireland, H.C. 1851 (279), L.

Return showing the number of passengers conveyed on all the railways in England and Wales , Scotland and Ireland respectively during the half year ending 30th June 1850 distinguished in different classes, and the receipts from each class of passengers, and from goods etc., compiled from returns made to the Commissioners of Railways, in pursuance of the provisions of the Act 3 & 4 Vict. c.97; also the length of railway open at the commencement and at the termination of the half year, together with a summary comparing the traffic with that in the corresponding period of 1849, H.C. 1851 (12), LI. (Do. for the half year ending 31 December 1850 is H.C. 1851 (313), LI).

Minutes of evidence taken before the select committee in the Athlone election petition, H.C. 1852-53 (383), VIII.

Report from the select committee on the Athlone election petition with the minutes of proceedings, H.C. 1852-53 (321), VIII.

Sligo borough petition, petition of John Patrick Somers, H.C. 1852-53 (600), XVIII.

Return showing the number of passengers conveyed on all the railways in England and Wales, Scotland and Ireland respectively during the half year ended the 30th June 1852, distinguished in different classes, and the receipts from each class of passengers and from goods etc., compiled from returns made in pursuance of the provisions of the Act 3 & 4 Vict. c.97; also the length of railway open at the commencement and at the termination of the half year; together with a summary comparing the traffic with that in the corresponding period in 1851, and a supplement showing the aggregate number of miles travelled by each class of passengers; the number of passenger trains and of goods trains respectively and the number of miles travelled by such trains during the above-mentioned half year, H.C. 1852-53 (252), XCVII.

A return of the names of all the newspapers in the United Kingdom to which halfpenny stamps were issued during the year 1852, stating the number of such stamps issued to each newspaper and the amount paid to the stamp office by each on account of such stamps, H.C. 1852-53 (422),LVII. Similar returns for other years in H.C. 1854 (117), XXXIX, H.C. 1854-55 (83), XXX, H.C. 1854-55 (438), XXX, H.C. 1857-58 (489), XXXIV.

Report from the select committee on the Sligo borough election together with the proceedings of the committee and minutes of evidence, H.C. 1854 (78), VIII.

Report from the select committee on Henry Stonor, H.C. 1854 (278), VIII.

Minutes of evidence taken before the select committee on complaint, together with the proceedings of the committee and minutes of evidence, H.C. 1854 (314),VIII.

Report from the select committee of the House of Lords appointed to inquire into the management of the crown estate of Kilconcouse, in the King's County, and into the circumstances attending the occupation of a portion thereof by the rev. Francis McMahon P.P. of Kinnitty; together with the proceedings of the committee and the minutes of evidence, H.C. 1854 (192), XXI.3.

Copies of the informations and warrant against Mr James Sadleir, and of the bills of indictment, if any, found against him, and of the names of the witnesses and finding of the grand jury therein, H.C. 1856 (394),L and 1856 (394-1), L.

Return showing the names, age, date of appointment and amount of salaries and emoluments of all persons holding office in the Incumbered Estates Court, with the dates of such persons being called to the bar or enrolled as attorneys to practise in any of the Courts of Law in Ireland, H.C. 1856 (70), LIII.427.

Return of the several purchases made in the Incumbered Estates Court by the late John Sadleir, H.C. 1856 (187), LIII.

Copies of the several warrants issued for the apprehension of Mr James Sadleir, a member of this house, and of the reports from the Crown Solicitor and officers of constabulary of the steps taken for his arrest, and of the several proceedings in the process of outlawry against him, H.C. 1857 (22 sess. 1), XIV and 1857 (37 sess.i), XIV.

Returns by provinces and counties (compiled from returns made to the Inspector General, Royal Irish Constabulary) of cases of evictions, which have come to the knowledge of the constabulary in each of the years 1849 to 1880 inclusive, H.C. 1881(185), LXXVII.725.

F. NINETEENTH CENTURY BOOKS, PAMPHLETS, ARTICLES
Addresses, resolutions and rules of the Catholic Defence Association, Dublin, 1854.

Bankers' Magazine, 1845 – 1856.

The Brass Band. A true and succinct account of the rise, progress and character of the celebrated troupe, Dublin, 1853.

Collins, C.M., *Law and practice of banking in Ireland*, London, 1880.

Dillon, M., *The history and development of banking in Ireland*, London, 1889.

Duffy, Charles Gavan, *Proposal for establishing a small proprietors' society of Ireland*, Dublin, 1851.

Duffy, Charles Gavan, *The League of north and south*, London, 1886.

Duffy, Charles Gavan, *My life in two hemispheres*, 2 vols., London, 1898,

English reports, x, House of Lords, containing House of Lord's cases (Clark's), vols. 3-6, London, 1901.

Evans, D. Morier, *Facts, failures and frauds*, London, 1859, (reprinted New York, 1968).

Frazier, E., *The banking laws of Ireland. A full and accurate report of the judgement of the Lord Chancellor of Ireland in the case of O'Flaherty and others v McDowell and others*, Dublin, MDCCCLVI.

Full report of the trial of the issues directed by the Court of Exchequer in Ireland in the case of Edward Dowling v Edward Lawler, Dublin, 1854.

Gilbert, J.T., *A contemporary history of affairs in Ireland from 1641 to 1652*, 3 vols., London, 1880.

Incumbered Estates Court. Descriptive particulars of the Kilcommon demesne, Cahir Castle and other portions of the estates of the late John Sadleir M.P. situate in the counties of Tipperary and Limerick, Dublin, 1857.

Instructions to agents, sub-agents and clerks at the Bank of Ireland branches, Dublin, 1849.

Irish Chancery reports. Cases in the High Court, Rolls Court, Landed Estates Court and Bankruptcy Court ,1850 -1866, 17 vols.

Irish Common Law reports. Cases in the Queen's Bench, Common Pleas, Exchequer, Exchequer Chamber, and Court of Criminal Appeal,1849-1866, 17 vols.

Keogh, William, *Ireland Imperialised, a letter to His Excellency the Earl of Clarendon*, Dublin, 1849.

London as it is to-day, where to go and what to see during the great exhibition, London, 1851.

London at table or how, when, where to dine and order a dinner and where to avoid dining, London, 1851.

Lucas, E., *The life of Frederick Lucas M.P.*, 2 vols., London, 1886.

Malcolmson, R., *The Carlow parliamentary roll*, Dublin, 1872.

Perrand, Adolphus, *Ireland under British rule*, Dublin, 1864.

Prendergast, J.P., *The Cromwellian settlement in Ireland*, Dublin, 1875.

Reid, T.W., *Cabinet portraits, sketches of statesmen*, London, 1872.

Scully, Denys, *A Statement of the Penal Laws which aggrieve the Catholics of Ireland*, 2 vols., Dublin, 1812.

Scully, Denys, *A letter to Daniel O'Connell Esq. occasioned by the petition adopted at the late aggregate meeting of the Catholics of Ireland*, Dublin, 1824, (published under the pseudonym of 'An Irish Farmer').

Scully, Vincent, *The Irish land question*, Dublin, n.d., (R.I.A. pamphlet 2094).

Scully, Vincent, *Notes on Ireland and the land question*, Dublin, n.d., (R.I.A. pamphlet no. 2110).

Scully, Vincent, *Free Trade in land explained*, Dublin, 1854, (R.I.A. pamphlet no.2162).

Sullivan, A.M., *New Ireland*, London, 1882.

Sullivan, T.D., *A record of Traitorism or the political life and adventures of Mr Justice Keogh*, Dublin, 1891.

Taylor, Alfred S., *On poisons in relation to medical jurisprudence and medicine*, London, 1848.

Trollope, Anthony, *An autobiography*, London, 1883.

Walker's Hibernian Magazine, 1806.

Walford's old and new London, vols. 1,4, London, 1881.

Wilberforce, H.W., *Reasons for submitting to the Catholic Church, a farewell letter to his parishoners from a clergyman of the Established Church*, London, 1851.

Wright, G.N., *An Historical guide to the city of Dublin*, Dublin, 1825.

SECONDARY SOURCES

TWENTIETH CENTURY BOOKS, PAMPHLETS, ARTICLES.

Arundel, Dennis, *The story of Sadler's Wells 1683-1977*, London, 1978.

Auchmuty, James J., *Sir Thomas Wyse 1791-1862. The life and career of an educator and diplomat*, London, 1939.

Avery, Gillian, *Victorian people in life and literature*, London, 1970.

Ball, F. Elrington, *The Judges in Ireland 1221-1921*, 2 vols., New York, 1927.

Barrow, G.L., *The emergence of the Irish banking system 1820-45*, Dublin, 1975.

Beckett, J.C., *The making of modern Ireland 1603 -1973*, London, 1966.

Bonaparte-Wyse, Olga, *The spurious brood. Princess Letitia Bonaparte and her children*, London, 1969.

Briggs, Asa, *Victorian cities*, London, 1982.

Burke, W.P., *History of Clonmel*, Waterford, 1907.

Byrne, Raymond and McCutcheon, J.P., *The Irish legal system*, Dublin, 1996.

Clarke, Desmond, *Dublin*, London, 1977.

Connolly, S.J., 'The Great Famine and Irish politics' in Póirtéir Cathal, *The Great Irish Famine*, Dublin, 1995.

Corcoran, T., *The Clongowes Record 1814-1932.*, Dublin, 1932.

Costello, *Clongowes Wood. A history of Clongowes Wood College 1814-1989*, Dublin, 1989.

Craig, Maurice, *Dublin 1660-1860*, Dublin, 1980.

Crotty, R.D., *Irish agricultural production : its volume and structure*, Cork, 1966.

Daly, Mary E., 'The operation of famine relief 1845 -47' in Póirtéir, Cathal, (ed.), *The Great Irish Famine*, Dublin, 1995.

Davis, Richard, *The Young Ireland movement*, Dublin, 1987.

Drummond, Humphrey, *Our man in Scotland. Sir Ralph Sadleir 1507-1587*, London, 1961.

Fitzpatrick, Samuel A.O., *Dublin, a historical and topographical account of the city*, London, 1907.

Gallwey, Hubert, *The Wall family in Ireland 1170-1970*, Naas, 1970.

Gates, Paul, *Landlords and tenants on the prairie frontier : studies in American land policy*, London, 1973.

Gleeson, Dermot G., 'An unpublished Cromwellian document' in *North Munster Antiquarian Journal*, vol. 1, 1936.

Gray, Peter, 'Ideology and the Famine' in Póirtéir, Cathal, (ed.), *The Great Irish Famine*, Dublin, 1995.

Hayes, William J., *Tipperary in the year of rebellion 1798*, Roscrea, 1998.

Hogan, Daire, *The legal profession in Ireland 1789-1922*, Naas, 1986.

Keane, E., Phair, P.B., Sadleir, T.U., (eds.), *King's Inns admission papers 1607-1867*, Dublin, 1982.

Kelleher, D.L., *The Glamour of Dublin*, Dublin, 1929.

Kennedy, Colm, *Tristram Kennedy and the revival of Irish legal training (1835-1885)*, Dublin, 1996.

Kerr, Donal A., *Peel, priests and politics*, Oxford, 1982.

Kerr, Donal A., *'A nation of beggars'? Priests, people and politics in Famine Ireland (1846 – 1852)*, Oxford, 1994.

Kerr, Donal A., *The Catholic Church and the Famine*, Dublin, 1996.

Kinealy, Christine, *The Great Calamity. The Irish Famine 1845-52*, Dublin, 1994.

Lenox-Conyngham, M., *Diaries of Ireland, an anthology 1590-1987*, Dublin, 1998.

Lucas, R., 'Irish provincial directories 1788 – directory of the six towns in Tipperary' in *The Irish Genealogist*, 3 (11), 1966.

Lyons, F.S.L., *Ireland since the Famine*, London, 1974.

Lyons, F.S.L, (ed.), *Bicentenary essays, Bank of Ireland 1783-1983*, Dublin, 1983.

McCarthy, J.F., 'The story of Sadleir's bank' in *Clonmel Historical and Archaeological Society*, vol. 1, no. 3, 1954-55.

MacDermot, Brian C., 'Letters of John Scully to James Duff Coghlan 1923-1927' in *The Irish Genealogist*, vol. 6, no.1, 1980; no.2., 1981; no.3, 1982.

MacDermot, Brian C., (ed.), *The Catholic Question in Ireland and England 1798-1822. The papers of Denys Scully*, Dublin, 1988.

MacDermot, Brian C., (ed.), *The Irish Catholic petition of 1805. The diary of Denys Scully*, Dublin, 1992.

MacDonagh, Oliver, 'The Victorian Bank, 1824-1814, in Lyons, F.S.L., *Bicentenary essays, Bank of Ireland 1783-1983*, Dublin, 1983.

MacEwan, Michael, *The Ryan family and the Scarteen hounds*, Lambourn Press, 1990.

McGrath, Thomas, *Religious renewal and reform in the pastoral ministry of Bishop James Doyle of Kildare and Leighlin, 1786-1834*, Dublin, 1999.

McGrath, Thomas, *Politics, interdenominational relations and education in the public ministry of Bishop James Doyle of Kildare and Leighlin, 1786-1834*, Dublin, 1999.

Marnane, Denis G., *Land and Violence. A history of west Tipperary from 1660*, Tipperary, 1985.

Marnane, Denis G., 'The coming of the railway to County Tipperary in 1848' in *Tipperary Historical Journal*, Thurles, 1998.

Marnane, Denis G., 'South Tipperary on the eve of the Great Famine', (parts 1, 2, 3 and 4) in *Tipperary Historical Journal*, Thurles, 1996, 1997, 1998 and 1999.

Moloney, John N., *A soul came into Ireland. Thomas Davis 1814-1845, a biography*, Dublin, 1995.

Moore, Maurice G., *An Irish Gentleman, George Henry Moore*, London, 1913.

Moran, Gerard, 'William Scully and Ballycohey, a fresh look' in *Tipperary Historical Journal*, Thurles, 1992.

Morrissey, Thomas, *As one sent, Peter Kenney S.J. 1779-1841. His mission in Ireland and North America*, Dublin and Washington, 1996.

Mulligan, Fergus, *One hundred and fifty years of Irish railways*, Belfast, 1983.

Murphy, Nancy, *Guilty of innocent? The Cormack brothers – trial, execution and exhumation*, Nenagh, 1997.

Nolan, William, 'The Irish Confederation in County Tipperary' in *Tipperary Historical Journal*, Thurles, 1998.

O'Brien, John B., 'Sadleir's bank', in *Journal of the Cork Historical and Archaeological Society*, LXXXII, 1977.

O'Connor, John, T*he workhouses of Ireland. The fate of Ireland's poor*, Dublin, 1995.

Ó Fearghail, Fearghus, *St. Kieran's College, Kilkenny 1782-1982*, Kilkenny, 1982.

Ó Foghludha, Risteárd, *Ar bruach na coille muaire, Liam Dall Ó hIfearnáin*, Dublin, 1939.

Ó Gráda, Cormac, *Ireland before and after the Famine. Explorations in economic history 1800-1925*, Manchester, 1988.

Ó Gráda, Cormac, *Ireland a new economic history 1780-1939*, Oxford, 1994.

Ó Gráda Cormac (ed,), *Famine 150, commemorative lecture series*, Dublin, 1997.

O'Mahony, Chris, 'Emigration from Tipperary workhouse 1848-1858 in *Tipperary Historical Journal*, Thurles, 1994.

Ó Néill, Tomás, *Fiontan Ó Leathlobhar*, Áth Cliath, 1962.

O'Shea, James, *Priest, Society and Politics in post-Famine Ireland, a study of County Tipperary 1850-1891*, Dublin, 1983.

O'Shea, James, 'Thurles Savings Bank 1829-71' in Corbett, William and Nolan, William, (eds.), *Thurles. The Cathedral Town*, Dublin, 1989.

Póirtéir, Cathal (ed.), *The Great Irish Famine. The Thomas Davis lecture series*, Dublin, 1995.

Power, S., (ed.), *Census of Ireland c.1659*, Dublin, 1939.

Sadleir, Michael, *Trollope, a commentary*, London, 1933.

Sadleir, Thomas Ulick, *A brief memoir of the Right Hon. Sir Ralph Sadleir, Knight Banneret P.C., M.P.*, Hertford, 1907.

Salbstein, M.C.N., *The emancipation of the Jews in Britain : an essay on preconditions*, Brighton, 1977.

Schoenbaum, S., *William Shakespeare, a documentary life*, Oxford, 1975.

Socolofsky, H.E., *Landlord William Scully*, Kansas, 1979.

Spring, D. and E., 'The fall of the Grenvilles 1844-48 in *Huntington library Quarterly*.

Thompson, F.M.L., 'The end of a great estate' in *Economic History Review*, VIII, no. 1.

Vaughan, William E., *Landlords and tenants in mid-Victorian Ireland*, Clarendon Press, 1994.

Wall, Maureen (O'Brien, Gerard, ed.), *Catholic Ireland in the eighteenth century*, Dublin, 1989.

Wetherall, Rose, *Standon*, Standon, 1988.

Whitaker, T.K., 'Origins and Consolidation' in Lyons F.S.L., *Bicentenary essays, Bank of Ireland 1783-1983*, Dublin, 1983.

White, James (ed.), *My Clonmel scrapbook*, Waterford, 1908.

Whitty, Edward M., *St. Stephen's in the fifties. The session 1852-53. A parliamentary retrospect*, London, 1906.

Whyte, John H., *The independent Irish party 1850-9*, Oxford, 1958.

Woodbridge, George, *The Reform Club 1836-1978, a history from the club's records*, New York, 1978.

Wylie, J.C.W., *Irish land law*, London, 1975.

JOHN SADLEIR IN FICTION
Bradden, Mary E., *The Trail of the Serpent*, London, n.d.
Dickens, Charles, *Little Dorrit*, London, n.d
Hatton, Joseph, John Needham's Double, London, n.d.
Lever, Charles, *Davenport Dunn. A man of our day*, 2 vols., London, 1898.
Trollope, Anthony, *Phineas Finn*, London, 1869.

Appendix 1

(A) BRANCH NETWORK OF THE TIPPERARY JOINT-STOCK BANK

Branch	Address	Manager	Year
ATHY (Co. Kildare)	Premises of Martin Kavanagh near Shrew Lane opposite the Grand Canal	Henry Stevenson George J. Hore 1849-1856	1846
CARLOW	Premises or Mrs Mary Ann Butler in Burren Street, near Beggars Row	Thaddeus O'Shea	1846-1856
CARRICK-ON-SUIR		Clement Sadleir (John's brother) Stanislaus J. Lynch	1845 1854-1856
CLONMEL (head office from 1847)	12 Duncan St (Now 9 Sarsfield Street)	William Kelly (he was manager, secretary, and head-accountant from 1853; other personnel were John B. Sparrow, George O'Connell, Simon R Prossor, David Twomy and Thaddeus Ryan.)	1853
NENAGH	30 Castle and 19 Castle Street	Thaddeus O'Shea William C. Moroney William Healy - Rock	1845 1846 1848-1855 1856
ROSCREA		William C Moroney John Sidney Smith George J Hore James M Dowley	1845 1846 1848 1851-56
THOMASTOWN (CO KILKENNY)		William Clifford	1845
THURLES	Bank Lane (site of present Ursuline Convent)	Patten S Bridge	1845-1856
TIPPERARY	Bank Place	James Scully John Savage Michael Dillon	1845 1848-1855 1856

(B) CLEARING HOUSES FOR THE TIPPERARY JOINT-STOCK BANK

LONDON: Glyn Halifax, Mills and Co.
LIVERPOOL: Bank of Liverpool
MANCHESTER: Union Bank of Manchester
BRISTOL: The West of England and South Wales District Bank
SCOTLAND: The Glasgow Union Banking Co.
PARIS: Charles Laffitte, Blount and Co.
IRELAND: Bank of Ireland

(C) BANK NETWORK IN CATCHMENT AREA OF THE TIPPERARY BANK
(OPENING DATES IN BRACKETS)

ATHY:	London & Dublin (1845), National (1849),Tipperary (1845)
CARLOW:	Bank of Ireland (1834), Tipperary (1845)
CARRICK-ON-SUIR:	National (1835), Tipperary, (1841)
CLONMEL	National Bank (1835), Provincial (1825), Tipperary (1842), Bank of Ireland (1825)
NENAGH:	National (1836), The Agricultural and Commercial, (1834), Tipperary (1839)
ROSCREA:	National Bank (1835), The Agricultural and Commercial (1835), Tipperary (1842)
THOMASTOWN:	The Agricultural and Commercial (1835), Tipperary (1841)
THURLES:	The Agricultural and Commercial Bank of Ireland (1839) The Clonmel National Bank (1839)
TIPPERARY:	National (1835), The Agricultural and Commercial (1835), Tipperary (1838)

Most of these towns also had a savings bank which opened for one hour per week.

SOURCES

R.D., 1856, vol. 16, abstract 283, vol. 26, abstract 157, *W.T.* 22 September 1855, *The Dublin Almanac and General Register, 1843*, p.186, *Thoms Irish Almanac and Official Directory, 1845*, p.426, ibid., 1846, p.422, ibid., 1847, p.394, ibid., 1848, p.396, ibid., 1850, p.402, ibid., 1851, p.473, ibid., 1854, p.551, ibid., 1856, p.695, *London Post Office Directory, 1855*, pp.2474, 2477-8, 2489, 2492, 2494, J. F. McCarthy, 'The story of Sadleir's Bank' in *Clonmel Historical and Archaeological Society*, vol. 1, no. 3, 1954-55, p.4, *A return of the joint stock banks existing in England and Wales in each of the three years ending with the 5th day of January 1839; specifying the date of the establishment of each bank, the number and situation of its branches and the number of partners in each bank during each of the abovementioned years. Similar returns for Scotland and Ireland,* H.C. 1839 (530),XXX.215, pp.14-15, Barrow, *The Emergence of the Irish Banking*, pp.215-219.

Appendix 2

LANDS PURCHASED (OR HELD IN TRUST) BY JOHN SADLEIR FROM THE ENCUMBERED ESTATES COURT

Title of the Estate	Amount of Purchase Money £
JAMES J. WALL	36,000
EARL OF GLENGALL	67,970
EARL OF KINGSTON	18,930
MATHEW COOKE	27,000*
LORENZO CLUTTERBUCK	6.500
TRUSTEES OF SIR GEORGE GOOLD	580
HYACINTH DARCY	14,900
JOHN HYDE	19,425
WILLIAM DE MONTMORENCY	30,100
EARL OF PORTARLINGTON	11,830
Total	233,235

*Sadleir was allowed to retain £21,380 due to him as a mortgagee on the estate in part discharge of the purchase money.

Sadleir had purchased approximately 30,000 acres by 1855, but it is unclear whether this was all bought in the Incumbered Estates Court, He had land in Tipperary, Cork, Waterford, Mayo, Galway, Kerry, Limerick and Roscommon.

SOURCES

Return of the several purchases made in the Incumbered Estates Court by the late John Sadleir or any one in trust for him, specifying the name or title of the estate or matter in which each purchase was made, the names of the solicitors having the carriage of the sale, and the amount of the purchase money, H.C. 1856 (187), LIII.431, pp.6-7; for details of the townlands and acreage of his estates see R.D., 1854, vol.18, abstracts 187, 189; 1855, vol. 28, abstract 160, vol. 33, abstracts, 22,24,25; 1856, vol. 17, abstract 32, vol. 9, memorial no 34, memorandum of agreement, 15 March 1855, vol. 11, memorial no. 149; 1858, col. 18, abstract 15;

Appendix 3

SHAREHOLDERS OF THE TIPPERARY JOINT STOCK BANK

A. IRISH SHAREHOLDERS

Name	Address	Occupation	No. of Shares
SIMON ARMSTRONG	TIPPERARY	MERCHANT	71
WILLIAM AUSTIN	–	–	373
MICHAEL BARRY	GURTACLONA, LIMERICK	FARMER	17
ELLEN BEARY	CORK	SPINSTER	17
JOHN BENNET	RIVERSTOWN, NENAGH, TIPP	FARMER	20
SERGEANT BERWICK	–	SENIOR COUNSEL	UNKNOWN
JOHN CLEARY	CAHIRVILLAHOW, GOLDEN, TIPP	GENTLEMAN	1
PATRICK CLEARY	THOMASTOWN, GOLDEN, TIPP	FARMER)	104)
WILLIAM CLEARY	CAHIRVILLAHOW, GOLDEN, TIPP	FARMER)	)
WILLIAM CONDON	BALLINAMARSOUGH, TIPP	FARMER	9
HENRY DWYER	BALLYQUIRKE CASTLE, BORRISOKANE, TIPP	LANDOWNER	4
CHARLOTTE HALLIDAY	SION HILL, DROMORE, DOWN	SPINSTER	401
JAMES HAMMERSLEY	GRANGE, TIPP	FARMER	9
LEONARD KEATING	GARRANLEA, CASHEL, TIPP	FARMER	10
ROBERT KEATING	DO.	BANKER/M.P.	700
JAMES B. KENNEDY	DUBLIN	SOLICITOR	5
THOMAS J. KENNEDY	DUBLIN	–	21
BERNARD MCKEY	CARRICK-ON-SUIR, TIPP	MERCHANT	50
THOMAS MAHONY	TEMPLEBRADEN, LIMERICK	PRIEST	3
CATHERINE MURNANE	KNOCKARDING, TIPP	WIDOW	9
LEONARD MORROGH	DUBLIN	SOLICITOR	UNKNOWN
WILLIAM D. PALLISON	GEASEHILL, OFFALY	GENTLEMAN	4
JOHN PEPPER	LISMORE HSE., ROSCREA, TIPP	FARMER	20
ELLEN QUILLINAN	BALLYNEALE, TIPP	WIDOW	8
DAVID RAFFERTY	OOLA, TIPP	FARMER	45
JOHN RYAN J.P.	SCARTEEN, BRUFF, LIMERICK	FARMER	35
PATRICK RYAN	KILROSS, TIPP	FARMER	4
PATRICK RYAN	MURROE, LIMERICK	FARMER	UNKNOWN
JAMES SADLEIR	CLONACODY, CLONMEL, TIPP	BANKER/M.P.	1838
JOHN SADLEIR	DUBLIN AND LONDON	SOLICITOR/M.P.	150
ROBERT SAMPSON	CARRICKAROCHE, TIPP	FARMER	18
SIR MATHEW R. SAUSSE	BOMBAY, INDIA	JUDGE	88
FRANCIS SCULLY	ATHASSEL, TIPP	BARRISTER	175
JOHN SCULLY	OUGHTERARD, GALWAY	FARMER	58
RICHARD SCULLY	TIPPERARY TOWN	MERCHANT	8

B. ENGLISH SHAREHOLDERS

Name	Address	Occupation	No. of Shares
WILLIAM FURY BAKER	HILLINGDEN, MIDDLESEX	ARMY CAPTAIN	20
JOHN BARNARD	WALTHAM, ESSEX	FARMER	15
EDWARD BIGGS	LEIGHTON BUZZARD, BEDS.	FARMER	30
HENRY BIRD	CHELMSFORD, ESSEX	MEDICAL DOCTOR	50
WILLIAM JAMES BODGER	TRING, HERTS.	GENTLEMAN	25
WILLIAM BOYES	STONEYSTRATFORD, BUCKS	DRAPER	50
EDWARD BRIGGS	BURCOTT, BEDS.	FARMER	UNKNOWN
CHARLES BUCHMASTER	TOTTENHALL, BEDS.	MILLER	30
GEORGE A. BURRELL	BARKING, ESSEX	MERCHANT	60
THOMAS HENRY CANDY	SIDNEY, SUSSEX COLLEGE CAMBRIDGE	–	77
WILLIAM C. CHILD	HAMPSTEAD, MORINT, ESSEX	GENTLEMAN	2
JOHN COOKE	STEPPINGBY, BEDS.	FARMER	30
SARAH COOKE	HENSBORN, CRAWLEY, BEDS.	SPINSTER	16
RALPH DALBY	9 WATERLOO LANE, LONDON	–	10
EDMOND DOCKER	FOXFIELD, HANTS. –	MINISTER OF RELIGION	40
HENRY JOHN DOYLE	LONDON –	GENTLEMAN (SADLEIR'S CLERK)	44
JOHN ELLIOTT	RICKMANSWORTH, HERTS.	GENTLEMAN	20
JOHN FLEXMAN	WATFORD, HERTS.	MERCHANT	UNKNOWN
MRS FRANK FLINT	LEIGHTON BUZZARD, BEDS.	–	3
CAROLINE GADSEN	WHARFINGER, SLAPTON, BUCKS	SPINSTER	5
WILLIAM GADSEN	DO.	–	10
RICHARD GARDNER	ISLINGTON-VILLA, TORQUAY, DEVON	GENTLEMAN	50
WILLIAM GARDNER	–	–	UNKNOWN
JOHN GINGER	FIELDSEND, HEMEL HEMPSTEAD	FARMER	40
GEORGE L. GIRLING	ST. IVES, HERTS	SURGEON	10
CHARLES GOODE	15 LR. BELGRAVIA, PIMLICO	GENTLEMAN	10
GEORGE GRACE	BUCKS.	FARMER	20
HENRY GREGORY	BUNDYMEAD, HERTS.	FARMER	10
ROBERT GREGORY	TRING, HERTS.	FARMER	23
JAMES HARKNESS	ST. ALBANS, HERTS.	GENTLEMAN	40
JOHN HARVEY	LONDON	COLONEL	UNKNOWN
HENRY HOLLAND	STREETMAR, HERTS	GENTLEMAN	20
JOHN HORN	WYMONDLY PRIORY, HERTS	GENTLEMAN	5
GEORGE HORNE	TILESWORTH, BEDS.	MERCHANT	10
HENRY LACY	PETERSFIELD	BANKER	3
STEPHEN LANGSTON	SOUTHBOROUGH, KENT	MINISTER OF RELIGION	80
FARMERY JOHN LAW	14 MANSFIELD ST., LONDON	BANKER	50
THOMAS LINNELL	MILTOWN BRYANT, BEDS.	FARMER	20
JOHN LINTON	UXBRIDGE	GENTLEMAN	10
CLARISSA A. LIVERMORE	LITTLE BADDIN, ESSEX	SPINSTER	8
THOMAS B. LUDLOW	SLAPTON, BUCKS.	MINISTER OF RELIGION	10

Name	Address	Occupation	No. of Shares
MARK EDWARDS MAJOR	HAMPSTEAD	GENTLEMAN	10
SAMUEL MUMFORD	THAXTED, ESSEX	FARMER	10
JOHN OSBORN	LEIGHTON BUZZARD, BEDS.	MERCHANT	100
STEPHEN PARNELL	HASLEMERE, SURREY	GENTLEMAN	80
WILLIAM PATMORE	QUENDON, ESSEX	FARMER	2
THOMAS, G. PIERSON	HITCHIN, HERTS	SOLICITOR	5
THOMAS PRICE	LINSDALE, BUCKS.	GENTLEMAN	10
JOHN PROCTOR	RICKMANSWORTH, HERTS.	FARMER	50
THOMAS PROCTOR	DO.	GENTLEMAN	40
E.F. REDDER	SANDWICK, KENT	BANKER	40
WILLIAM RODNELL	13 BLENHEIM TCE., LONDON	BANKER	10
ROBERT SEAR	MURTMORE, BUCKS.	FARMER	10
CALEB SMITH	EATON, BRAY, HERTS.	GENTLEMAN	10
HENRY SMITH	HEASBORNE, CRAWLEY, BEDS.	FARMER	20
SOPHIA A. SMITH	BEDS	–	5
THOMAS STORMER	LUTON, BEDS.	TRADER	10
WILLIAM STRANGE	HEATH & REACH, BEDS.	FARMER	8
OWEN SWANNEL	RICKMANSWORTH, HERTS.	GENTLEMAN	20
SAMUEL TAVERNER	LINSDALE, BUCKS	GENTLEMAN	20
CHARLES TIMES	HITCHIN, HERTS	SOLICITOR	20
RICHARD TURNEY	BUCKS.	MERCHANT	5
CHRISTOPHER TYLE	RICKMANSWORTH, HERTS	GENTLEMAN	UNKNOWN
CHRISTOPHER TYLER	ILFORD, ESSEX	COAL MERCHANT	50
STEPHEN WALDRON	HUNGERFORD, BERKS.	GENTLEMAN	20
JOHN WHITE	RICKMANSWORTH, HERTS.	FARMER	10
ELIZABETH WILLIS	SAFFRON WALDEN, ESSEX	SPINSTER	32
STEPHEN A. WILSON	ICKLETON GRANGE, ESSEX	GENTLEMAN	12
THOMAS WILSON	BUCKS.	FARMER	10
SUSAN WOOD	WALTON HALL, KELSO, ROXBOROUGH	SPINSTER	9

C. SHAREHOLDERS WHO SOLD THEIR SHARES WITHIN THREE YEARS OF THE BANK'S CLOSURE (LIABLE AS SECONDARY CONTRIBUTORS)

Shareholder	Address	Occupation	No. of Shares
WILLIAM AUSTEN	DUBLIN	–	373
ANNE BEARY	PALLAS, LIMERICK	WIDOW	17
ELLEN BEARY	CORK	SPINSTER	17
PATRICK CONNELL	TIPPERARY	FARMER	18
THOMAS EDWARDS	DUBLIN	CLERK	44
AUSTIN FARRELL	LONDON	GENTLEMAN	164
FREDERICK GOODYEAR	LONDON	MERCHANT	10
THOMAS HONE	FOSTER PLACE, DUBLIN	STOCKBROKER	44
JAMES KEATING	CASHEL	–	88
JAMES B. KENNEDY	DUBLIN	SOLICITOR	373
WILSON KENNEDY	CLONMEL, TIPP.	BANKER, ETC.	100

Shareholder	Address	Occupation	No. of Shares
EDMUND RAFFERTY	TIPPERARY	FARMER	13
CLEMENT SADLEIR	CARRICK-ON-SUIR, TIPP.	BANKER	70
VINCENT SCULLY	MANTLEHILL, TIPP.	BARRISTER	700
JAMES STIRLING	DUBLIN	–	144
WALTER THORPE	MANCHESTER	MEDICAL DOCTOR	10
HUGH WAUGH	DROMORE	–	401
CHARLES J. WHITLEY	CORK	–	
JOHN B. WHITLEY	ROSCARBERY, CORK	MINISTER OF RELIGION	35

SOURCES

Bankers' Magazine, vol. xvi, 1856, pp. 300-1; *Tipperary Free Press* 18 April 1856, 22 April 1856; *Dublin Evening Post* 17 April 1856; *C.T.* 5 July, 22 November 1856; *Times* (London) 30 April 1856, 21 May 1856; *Tipperary Free Press* 19 May 1857; *Leinster Express* 23 Feb. 1856; *Carlow Post* 2 Feb. 1856; *H.C.* 1856 (394-1) L, p. 12; *Irish Chancery Reports* 1856-1857, vol. 6, p. 351; *Dublin Gazette,* 8 February 1856.

Appendix 4

LIABILITIES PER BRANCH ON CLOSURE OF THE TIPPERARY JOINT STOCK BANK IN FEBRUARY 1856

Branch	Deposit Balance £
ATHY	NO EVIDENCE
CARLOW	NO EVIDENCE
CARRICK-ON-SUIR	70,000
CLONMEL	108,000
NENAGH	20,000
ROSCREA	30,000
THOMASTOWN	56,000
THURLES	NO EVIDENCE
TIPPERARY	75,000

SOURCES

L.E. 23 February 1856, *D.E.P.* 28 February 1856, *C.S.* 23 February, 1 March 1856, *T.L.* 23 February 1856, *N.G.* 20 march 1856, *Times* 19, 26 28 February, 6 March 1856.

Appendix 5

(A). A SAMPLE OF DEPOSITORS IN THE TIPPERARY JOINT STOCK

Name	Address	Occupation	No. of Shares
ATHY BD. OF GUARDIANS	ATHY	N.A.	530
JOHN BAGWELL	CLONMEL	LANDOWNER	UNKNOWN
DANIEL BERGIN	LEAP	FARMER	150
JAMES BERGIN	CAMLIN	FARMER	201
JOHN BERGIN	FARNCROFT MILLS	MILLER	499
MICHAEL BERGIN	CLOUGHAN	FARMER	255
PATRICK BERGIN	MOUNTDUDLEY	–	39
EARL OF BESSBOROUGH	CARRICK-ON-SUIR	LANDOWNER	3,000
- BLACKETT	–	–	2,287
THOMAS BLAKE	ROSCREA	PARISH PRIEST	182
- BOURKE	PALLAS	FARMER	100
- BUTLER	LEIGHLINBRIDGE	BOATMAN	100
MICHAEL CARROLL	ROSEMARY SQ., ROSCREA	TANNER AND LEATHER MERCHANT	1,306
ANDREW CLEARY	CARRICK-ON-SUIR	–	UNKNOWN
CORRY CONNELLAN	–	–	UNKNOWN
DANIEL COSTIGAN	BALLINRALLY	FARMER	41
JAMES COSTIGAN	BALLINRALLY	FARMER	154
THOMAS COSTIGAN	BALLINRALLY	FARMER	81
JEREMIAH COTTER	TIPPERARY	–	UNKNOWN
A.H. CRAWFORD	NENAGH	ENGINEER	UNKNOWN
JAMES DELAHUNT	SHINRONE	SHOPKEEPER	203
DONAGHMORE BOARD OF GUARDIANS	DONAGHMORE	N.A.	1,050
JAMES DOOLEY	BALLINRALLY	FARMER	61
MICHAEL DOOLEY	BALLINRALLY	FARMER	40
PATRICK DOOLEY	BALLYDUFF (OFFALY)	FARMER	37
ANDREW DOWLING	PINTOWN	CATTLEDEALER	471
RICHARD EVERARD	–	–	UNKNOWN
- FEEHAN	MEALIFFE	FARMER	500
CALEB GOING	TRAVERSTOWN	LANDOWNER	UNKNOWN
A. HAMILTON	–	–	UNKNOWN
WILLIAM HANNON	CASTLEROAN	FARMER	20
- HARDIN	–	FARMER	1.500
JAMES HAYES	TIPPERARY	–	UNKNOWN
JAMES HOWLEY (CHURCH) FUND)	TIPPERARY	PARISH PRIEST	2,400
- INNES	THOMASTOWN	–	UNKNOWN
ROBERT KEATING	GARRANLEA	MEMBER OF PARLIAMENT	4,000
JAMES KELLY	ROSCREA	MERCHANT	582
JOHN KIRWAN	BALLINRALLY	FARMER	86
COLONEL KNOW	THURLES	LANDOWNER	400
MICHAEL LAFFAN	FETHARD	CATHOLIC ARCHDEACON	UNKNOWN
THOMAS LALOR	CREGG HOUSE	FARMER	UNKNOWN

Name	Address	Occupation	No. of Shares
PHILLIP LANDY	BALLYDINE	FARMER	UNKNOWN
R.H. LANGRISHE	–	–	UNKNOWN
- MCCARTHY	MEALIFFE	FARMER	600
FRANCIS MCMAHON	KINNITTY	PARISH PRIEST	247
J.R. MINNITT	ANNABEG	LANDOWNER	UNKNOWN
WILLIAM MORRISSEY	CARRICK-ON-SUIR	–	UNKNOWN
SOUTHWELL MULCAHY	KENILWORTH	–	315
ELLEN MULLALLY	NEWLANDS	–	342
- MURNANE	TIPPERARY	–	UNKNOWN
JAMES MURPHY	COOLKERRY	FORMER	47
NENAGH BOARD OF GUARDIANS	NENAGH	N.A.	1,224
PETER NOLAN	BIRR	PRIEST	86
JOHN O'BRIEN	ROSCREA	CLERK	40
EDMUND POWER	CLONMEL	SOLICITOR	110
ROSCREA BOARD OF GUARDIANS	ROSCREA	N.A.	1,800
- RUSSELL	BALLYDUAG	FARMER	900
MARTIN RYAN	CLONBRENNAN	FARMER	20
ANDREW J. SCANLAN	BOURNEY	PARISH PRIEST	98
MICHAEL SCANLAN	CLOUGHJORDAN	PARISH PRIEST	UNKNOWN
PATRICK SLYNE	TIPPERARY TOWN	POLICE CONSTABLE	UNKNOWN
PATRICK STEPHENSON	CARRICK-ON-SUIR	SOLICITOR	UNKNOWN
-STERLING	–	DOCTOR	UNKNOWN
PATRICK SULLIVAN	CARRICK-ON-SUIR	–	UNKNOWN
THOMASTOWN BOARD GUARDIANS	THOMASTOWN	N.A.	1,600
THURLES BOARD OF GUARDIANS	THURLES	N.A.	49
THURLES SAVINGS BANK	THURLES	N.A.	695
THOMAS TOOHER	CLASHMORE	FARMER	72
DANIEL VAUGHAN	NENAGH	CATHOLIC BISHOP	UNKNOWN
JOHN M. WALKER	KNOCKALTON	LANDOWNER?	UNKNOWN
PATRICK WALL	KILMORE	–	UNKNOWN

SOURCES

R.D., 1857, vol.7, abstract. 71; vol. 14, abstracts 289, 291-294, 296-29 vol.16, abstracts 17-21; vol. 22, abstracts 128-137, 195-196, 270; vol. 23, abstracts 51-52, 54-55,118; vol. 24, abstract 253; vol. 25, abstracts 39-41, 43, 132; vol. 33, abstract 85. Irish Common Law Reports 1856 58, col. 7, pp.45 et.seq., *C.P.* 8,15 March, 11 October, 1 November 1856, *C.S.* 1 March 1856, *C.T.* 14, 28 June, 5 July, 1, 15 November 1856, *T.L.* 23 Feb., 1, 8 March 1856, *L.E.* 23 Feb., 15 March, 10 May 1856, *L.R.* 23 May, 26 Sept., 3, 24 Oct. 1856, *B.H.*1 March 1856, *Times* 28 Feb., 21 May, 18 Aug., 23, 27 Oct. 1856, *S.N.* 3 Oct. 1856, *N.G.* 14 May 1856, F.J. 3,9,10,13 Oct. 1856.

(B). A SHORT CALENDAR OF MANUSCRIPT SOURCES RELATING TO DEPOSITORS

1. CORRESPONDENCE OF GEORGE BOURKE, LISCAHILL, TO THOMAS CAHILL

LETTER 18 FEBRUARY : I have been a lucky man to you – John Sadleir is dead – the poor man poisoned himself – the Tipperary Joint Stock Bank is shut up and police guarding it, and not one penny for any of the depositors – when will you come over as i wish to see you?

P.S. Commins and the boys were with me last night. I was sorry we had not you, but I didn't know they were coming until 4 o.c. – they say you should give me £50 at least for saving you from the crash.

LETTER 21 FEBRUARY: I am in recpt. of yours and it gives me the greatest pleasure to have been instrumental in saving you. John Sadleir left his home on Saturday night and on Sunday morning was found dead at Hampstead Heath near London with a bottle of poison by his side and a case of razors in his pocket. The banks are all closed. Phill. Bourke of Pallace lost £100, the Hardins near £1,500, Russell of Ballyduag £900, McCarthy of Mealiffe £600, Feehan from near the same place £500, In fact it would take up this sheet to tell you one tenth of the victims. You must come over on Sunday and hear all the news. I will go back with you on Monday morning. Don't fail to do this. Mrs Mansergh went into the bank on Saturday and got letters of credit for £40 which are all dishonoured so she must pay over again. It was scandalous to take her money when they knew they could not pay. Colonel Knox came to me on Saturday – I advised him to draw – he neglected it and is now stuck for £400. It was a most deliberate suicide – well planned and prepared. You would be horrified to see the farmers in on Monday and Tuesday and not a penny for them – they were met by 15 or 20 police. They were all told they will be paid on the 28th feby, (that is this day week), and indeed it would be worth your while even if you had to walk over, to come into town on that day – I need not say you will have the fullest report of the case in the 'Leader'. Come over here on Sunday.

(This correspondence is in the possession of Mr Patrick J. O'Meara, Solicitor, Thurles).

2. EXTRACTS FROM THE POOR LAW MINUTE BOOKS FOR THE UNIONS OF THURLES, NENAGH AND ROSCREA.

A. THURLES UNION BOOK DECEMBER 1855 TO JULY 1856
16 Feb. 1856 – motion to present a cheque for £49-16-0 at the Tipperary for payment.
1 March 1856 – National appointed treasurer instead of the Tipperary.
31 May 1856 – letter from George McDowell that their claim had been proved before the Master of Chancery. A dividend of 2/- in the £ declared.

B. NENAGH UNION BOOK NO 19, SEPT. 1855 TO MARCH 1856
16 Feb. 1856 – cheque for £1,224 presented at the Tipperary and refused. The Tipperary the treasurer of the union.
1 March 1856 – National appointed treasurer instead of the Tipperary.

BOOK NO. 20, MARCH 1856 TO SEPT. 1856

2 August 1856 – letter from the poor law commissioners on how to apportion the deficiency caused by the failure to the electoral divisions. The Solicitor General of the opinion that the amount in credit at the date of failure was the sum to debit.

C. ROSCREA UNION BOOK NO. 21, NOV. 1855 TO NOV. 1856

16 Feb. 1856 – the withdrawal of £1,800 from the treasurer, the Tipperary bank, was sanctioned. The Provincial appointed treasurer. The manager of the Roscrea branch of the Tipperary refused to cash the union's cheque, but offered a letter of credit on the Bank of Ireland, Dublin, saying that it would be promptly paid. The Bank of Ireland refused to pay. The guardians anxious to strike a new rate because the outstanding rate would only realise £100. The commissioners replied that a new rate should be struck immediately.

8 March 1856 – Letter from the manager of the National in Roscrea offering to accommodate the union until it was in funds again.

22 March 1856 – the Bank of Ireland had opened a branch in Nenagh agreed to honour the union's drafts during 'the present difficulty consequent upon the defalcation of their late treasurer'.

10 May 1856 – The commissioners of inland revenue had been paid £100 out of the Tipperary's assets.

31 May, 7 June, 9 August 1856 – dividend of 2/- declared which would be put to the credit of the electoral divisions.

11 Oct. 1856 – meeting of the Tipperary's creditors. The deputation from the union consisted of James F. Rolleston, John D. Hutchinson and James J. Birch. They were instructed not to enter into any conclusive agreement on compensation without authority from the board.

BOOK NO. 22, 5 DEC. 1856 TO 29 MAY 1857

27 Dec. 1856 – the loss to be apportioned according to the cash for each electoral division. Portion of this to be applied to that section of the union then part of the Donaghmore union.

17 Jan. 1857 – Donaghmore protested to the poor law commissioners, and the commissioners agreed that the loss be borne by the Roscrea union as it then existed. The board of the Roscrea passed a resolution of regret at the decision and referred to a previous opinion of the Solicitor General about a similar matter. They argued that the electoral divisions of the old union were responsible for the funds in their keeping and the new union should not have to suffer for this. The union boundaries had been altered by the date of the bank's failure, but the accounts were still open. The new Roscrea union had to repay the old union the £482 involved.

31 Jan. 1857 – letter from the Donaghmore guardians asking what the Roscrea board intended doing.

7 Feb. 1857 – letter from the commissioners that they would consult the Solicitor General.

28 Feb. 1857 – Decision to form a committee to prepare a case.14 March 1857 – The case to be laid before Sir Colmen O'Loghlen and Charles Rolleston, Queens Counsels, for an opinion.

25 April 1857 – Both agree that the old union should bear the loss. The clerk instructed to send the case and the opinion to the commissioners.

BOOK NO. 23, JUNE 1857 TO MAY 1858

19 Sept. 1857 – Donaghmore pressurise the commissioners to make Roscrea pay the balance to its credit before the bank crash.

10 Oct. 1857 – letter from the commissioners that 'eminent legal authority had differed in opinion as to where the loss should fall, and as no question likely to form a precedent in the administration of the poor law is involved' the commissioners were not prepared to compel the Roscrea board to transfer any money to Donaghmore. The latter free to go to court but the commissioners felt that the ultimate loss would not be considerable.

23 Jan. 1858 – letter from the commissioners on how to charge the loss belonging to the former section of the union. Letter enclosed from the Donaghmore board urging them to take legal action against Roscrea. They refused. Legal proceedings would cost more than the sum involved.

30 Jan., 6 Feb. 1858 – Donaghmore sent a copy of a Queens Counsel's opinion of the case. Roscrea felt no reason to change their minds.

20. Feb. 1858 – letter from Donaghmore suggesting that both boards get a senior counsel to arbitrate. Roscrea refuse, they had no power to levy a further rate to get money for Donaghmore. Advised that Donaghmore recover the loss from the townlands concerned.

17 April 1858 – letter from Roscrea to the commissioners to check a newspaper report that Donaghmore had instructed a solicitor to begin legal action.

1 May 1858 – commissioners confirmed this. Roscrea board pressed the commissioners to intervene and prevent the ratepayers of Roscrea new union being further 'mulcted in one farthing expense in the shape of costs or damages on account of the loss of the former union'.

15 May 1858 – the commissioners refused to intervene.

22 May 1858 – A long list of resolutions saying that the commissioners were responsible for the adjustment of the former union and any disputes arising from it.

BOOK NO. 24, JUNE 1858 TO JUNE 1859

29 May 1858 – Donaghmore served Roscrea with notice to show cause 'within ten days why a *mandamus* should not be issued by the Court of Queen's Bench to compel the Roscrea board to pay to the Donaghmore board the sum charged to townlands now in Donaghmore union..'

20 Nov. 1858 – letter from the solicitor that judgement was delivered by Queen's Bench and the mandamus refused.

11 Dec. 1858 – letter from the commissioners stating that the Donaghmore union requested their intervention to prevent further litigation. Roscrea to consult their legal advisers.

18 Dec. 1858 – the legal advice was that the Queen's Bench court only concerned the question the mandamus. it could not settle the question of the debt. The report in the *Freeman's Journal* was not fully correct.

8 Jan. 1859 – commissioners again refuse to intervene but had suggested to the Donaghmore board to renew the proposal of arbitration.

12 Feb. 1859 – Roscrea refused on the grounds that (a). in equity they did not owe the Donaghmore union the debt, (b). even if they did , they did not have the power to legally raise funds to discharge it.

9 April 1859 – commissioners sent a copy of a letter from Donaghmore requesting one of their officers to settle the row.

30 April 1859 – commissioners' letter to Donaghmore regretting Roscrea's refusal, but they still would not allow their officers to become involved.

2 July 1859 – bill of costs from solicitor for £55.

Appendix 6

A. COURT JUDGEMENTS AGAINST SADLEIR'S RELATIVES WHO WERE SHAREHOLDERS OF THE TIPPERARY JOINT STOCK BANK BY INDIVIDUAL CREDITORS

Shareholder	Amount £	Legal Costs £	Creditor	Year Satisfied
JAMES SADLEIR	1,306	14	MICHAEL CARROLL	N.S.
	10,039	6	HENRY PADWICK	PARTLY IN 1856
	23,064	627	NEWCASTLE BANK	N.S.
FRANK SCULLY	498	15	JOHN BERGIN SNR. & JNR.	N.S.
	1,582	7	JAMES KELLY	N.S.
JAMES SCULLY	150	13	DANIEL BERGIN	1859
	255	13	MICHAEL BERGIN	1859
	40	14	MICHAEL DOOLEY	N.S.
	246	14	FRANCIS MCMAHON P.P.	1859
	40	16	JOHN O'BRIEN	1859
	86	14	PETER NOLAN C.C.	1858
	61	14	JAMES DOOLEY	N.S.
	37	15	PATRICK DOOLEY	N.S.
	1,321	UNKNOWN	MICHAEL CARROLL	1859
	98	13	ANDREW J. SCANLAN P.P.	1859
	1,582	7	JAMES KELLY	1859
	197	18	THOMAS BLAKE P.P.	1859
	39	18	PATRICK BERGIN	1859
	20	14	WILLIAM HANNON	1859
	203	13	JAMES DELAHUNT	1859
JOHN SCULLY	498	15	JOHN BERGIN SNR. & JNR.	N.S.
	1,582	7	JAMES KELLY	N.S.
VINCENT SCULLY	498	15	JOHN BERGIN SNR. & JNR.	N.S.
	1,582	7	JAMES KELLY	N.S.
	1,207	UNKNOWN	MICHAEL CARROLL	N.S.
	110	7	EDMUND POWER	N.S.
	2,180	7	RICHARD O' FLAHERTY	N.S.
	342	7	ELLEN MULLALLY	N.S.
	315	7	SOUTHWELL MULCAHY	N.S.
	23,064	627	NEWCASTLE BANK	N.S.
	471	15	ANDREW DOWLING	N.S.
JOHN RYAN (SCARTEEN)	246	14	FRANCIS MCMAHON P.P.	N.S.
	182	14	THOMAS BLAKE P.P.	N.S.
	72	15	THOMAS TOOHER	N.S.
	98	12	ANDREW J. SCANLAN P.P.	N.S.
	40	15	JOHN O'BRIEN	N.S.
	206	14	JAMES BERGIN	N.S.

Shareholder	Amount £	Legal Costs £	Creditor	Year Satisfied
	259	13	MICHAEL BERGIN	N.S.
	150	13	DANIEL BERGIN	N.S.
	498	15	JOHN BERGIN SNR. & JNR.	N.S.
	206	13	DANIEL BERGIN	N.S.
	20	12	MARTIN RYAN	N.S.
	31	13	DANIEL BERGIN	N.S.
	47	14	JAMES MURPHY	N.S.

B. JUDGEMENTS AGAINST OTHER SHAREHOLDERS

Shareholder	Amount	Legal Costs	Creditor	Year Satisfied
HENRY DWYER	57	UNKNOWN	JAMES MURHPHY	N.S.
JOHN BENNET	98	13	ANDREW J. SCANLAN P.P.	1860
	61	14	JAMES DOOLEY	1860
	201	15	JAMES BERGIN	1860
	150	13	DANIEL BERGIN	1860
	255	13	MICHAEL BERGIN	1860
	37	15	PATRICK DOOLEY	1860
	86	14	PETER NOLAN C.C.	1860
	40	14	MICHAEL DOWLING	1860
	39	15	PATRICK BERGIN	1860
	1,582	7	JAMES KELLY	1860
	154	14	JAMES COSTIGAN	1860
	81	14	THOMAS COSTIGAN	1860
	471	15	ANDREW DOWLING	1860
	86	14	JOHN KIRWAN	1860
	41	13	DANIEL COSTIGAN	1860
JOHN PEPPER	98	13	ANDREW J. SCANLAN P.P.	1859 &1860
	1,582	7	JAMES KELLY	1859
	1,306	14	MICHAEL CARROLL	1859
	471	15	ANDREW DOWLING	1859

NOTES

1. n.s. = not satisfied according to the abstracts in the Registry of Deeds.
2. Henry Padwick was from Berkley Square, London.
3. The three Daniel Bergins were from Leap, Cloghan and Clyduff, respectively.
4. *C.T.* 8 Nov. 1856 claimed that John Ryan, Scarteen, had paid £1,500 in claims, this is unlikely. The Registry of Deeds' records show the judgements against him as unsatisfied. see R.D., 1857, vol. 23, memorial 117 for his lands.
5. The fact that a judgement was recorded as satisfied did not mean that the shareholder in question paid the entire sum.. As the above table shows the same sums appear under more than one shareholder, meaning that the creditor filed against several shareholders to maximise the prospect of recovery. Sometimes a judgement for the same creditor against several shareholders was satisfied by only one.

SOURCES

R.D., 1856, vol. 10, abstract 258; 1857, vol. 7, abstract 71; vol. 12, abstract 97; vol. 13, abstracts 16-21, 137-138; vol. 22, abstracts 26, 127-136, 194-202, 269-270; vol. 23, abstracts 25,28, 51-52,54-55, 117-118; vol. 24, abstracts 118, 253; vol.25, abstracts 39-41, 43, 132-134, 168-169; vol. 33, abstract 85; 1859, vol. 26, abstracts 204-205.

Appendix 7

COMPROMISE NEGOTIATIONS OCTOBER AND NOVEMBER 1856

PART 1

COMMITTEE OF DELEGATES WHO MET THE OFFICIAL MANAGER ON 30 OCTOBER 1856

Name	Branch
DR HOWLEY P.P.	TIPPERARY
MAJOR MASSEY	TIPPERARY
EARL OF BESSBOROUGH	CARRICK-ON-SUIR
P. STEPHENSON	CARRICK-ON-SUIR
ANDREW J. SCANLAN P.P.	ROSCREA
JAMES F. ROLLESTON J.P.	ROSCREA
MICHAEL SCANLAN P.P.	NENAGH
A.H. CRAWFORD	NENAGH
ARCHDEACON COTTON (PROT.)	THURLES
JOHN THOMAS GOING J.P.	THURLES
ROBERT LANGRISHE J.P.	THOMASTOWN
MICHAEL DUNNE M.P.	ATHY

PART 2

COMMITTEE OF DELEGATES WHO MET THE OFFICIAL MANAGER ON 6 NOVEMBER 1856

MAJOR MASSEY	TIPPERARY
EARL OF BESSBOROUGH	CARRICK-ON-SUIR
ANDREW JAMES SCANLAN P.P.	ROSCREA
JAMES F. ROLLESTON J.P.	ROSCREA
MICHAEL SCANLAN P.P.	NENAGH
A.H. CRAWFORD	NENAGH
EDMOND POWER	CLONMEL
RICHARD EVERARD	CLONMEL
ARCHDEACON COTTON (PROT.)	THURLES
JOHN THOMAS GOING J.P.	THURLES
MICHAEL DUNNE M.P.	ATHY
THOMAS CRAWFORD BUTLER	CARLOW

Appendix 8

JOHN SADLEIR IN FICTION

Dickens, Charles Lever, Joseph Hatton, Mary Elizabeth Bradden and possibly Anthony Trollope modelled various dubious characters on John Sadleir – Merdle in Dickens' *Little Dorrit*, John Needham in Hatton's *John Needham's Double*, Davenport Dunne in Levers novel of that name, and Jabez North in Bradden's *The Trail of the Serpent*.[1]

Sir Shane Leslie holds than Phineas Finn[2] in Trollope's Palliser novels is based upon Sadleir, but the amorous, honest, outgoing Finn cannot have been inspired by Sadleir, and is more likely, as one commentator writes, to have represented John Pope Hennessy, an Irish M.P. of the time.[3] There is more merit in the suggestion that Trollope's Melmotte in *The Way We Live*, was modelled on Dickens Merdle, and hence on Sadleir, although Trollope himself denied this.[4]

The novels based on Sadleir have one common characteristic – his virtues are suppressed and his vices highlighted and decorated by the imagination of these writers. Hatton's John Needham is a murderer, who poisons his 'double', Joseph Norbury, deposits the body on Hampstead Heath, escapes to America, is apprehended and dramatically poisons himself while under arrest. The fallacy that the body on Hampstead Heath was not that of Sadleir was not just a figment of the novelists' imagination, however, and was to be found in some newspaper reports shortly after his death.[5]

Dickens' caricature is more predictable and the writer himself acknowledged his 'extravagant conception'. His Merdle is reserved, dull and moody with the 'constitution of a rhinoceros, the digestion of an ostrich and the concentration of an oyster'. He is a melancholy individual courted by society, but uneasy in its presence and ill at ease even in the splendour of his own house and the company of his butler, Merdle is a man who did little real good for anybody but was, according to his stepson, 'a doosed extraordinary phenomenon in buying and banking and that'. His wealth is so legendary that schoolchildren learning to write were given the task of copying the words 'Merdle, millions'.

Dickens builds up Merdle's reputation for honesty, integrity and dispensing patronage; paints him as the eighth wonder of the world with a peerage on the horizon and then explodes him as 'the greatest forger and the greatest thief that has ever cheated the gallows'.[6]

Lever lacks Dickens' irony, but his two volumes are entirely based on Sadleir. Davenport Dunn, a wealthy bachelor, has some of Merdle's characteristics. Like Merdle, Dunn has no real friends, nor does he cultivate any, so immersed is he in his many commercial enterprises, each one bolstering up the other. The pompous Lord Lackington dismisses the idea of inviting him to a social gathering – 'he is quite unsuited to this kind of thing – a mere creature of parchments. The very sight of him would only suggest thoughts of foreclosing mortgages and renewal fines'. But, unlike Merdle, Dunn is not too awkward in the presence of ladies, and has the self-assurance and suavity to mix easily in high society. Moreover, he has aspirations to a peerage and rejects the idea of a mere baronetcy. His entry into the ranks of the peers would be accompanied by his marriage to Lady Augusta, Lord Glengariff's sister.

Beneath the reserve and suavity however, Dunn is haunted by a gnawing shame at his own humble origins and is fired by a relentless silent, pursuit of vengeance for the slights, real or imagined, suffered in boyhood at the hands of the now ruined Kellett family, a ruin he revels in.

He is also a far more dangerous individual than Merdle. He is more Machiavellian and has carefully studied people, learned to exploit their weaknesses and misfortunes. He is a hypocrite who sometimes ingratiates himself with the very people he has helped to ruin, a blackmailer who uses unsavoury family secrets and political power to ruin his enemies. Dunne is ultimately admired by those characters in the novel who live on their wits and who are the parasites of society.

Sadleir suffers the most severe mangling at the hands of Mary Elizabethan Bradden,[7] whose gothic portrayal of him as Jabez North is vivid if nothing else. He progresses 'form the workhouse brat to the Sunday school-teacher, from the Sunday school-teacher to the scrub at Dr Tappenden's Academy, from the scrub to usher of the fourth form, and from fourth form usher to first assistant, pet toady and factotum', all 'so may steps in the ladder of fortune which Jabez mounted as in seven-league boots'.

This ambition is achieved by infanticide, the murder of an old man and a pregnant woman, all ruthlessly executed and accompanied by a potpourri of forged cheques, poisoning, intrigue, marriage into the aristocracy to a wife who loathes him, the establishment of a bank in South America and finally a gruesome death in a prison cell.

1. See also *C.S.* 20 September 1856 for extracts from a short work called *The Joint-Stock Banker* by Dudley Costello. See *C.T.* 21 November 1857 for a review of Levers Book. See J.S. Crone, *A Concise Dictionary of Irish Biography,* (Dublin, 1928), under Sadleir.
2. A. Trollope, *Phineas Finn,,* (Oxford University Press), 1974 ed., P.V.
3. M. Sadleir, *Trollope a commentary,* (London, 1933), pp.398, 416
4. Ibid
5. *C.S.* 4 October 1856 refutes this suggestion. See *T.F.P.* 8 April 1856 for a letter to the *Times* from Sadleir's solicitor also denying it.
6. C Dickens, *Little Dorrit,* (London, n.d.), p.8.
7. M.E. Bradden, *The Trail of the Serpent,* (London, n.d.)

General Index

Gray, John, 30, 102, 108, 215, 231, 243-5, 286, 288, 292-3, 308-9, 341, 343, 345, 349, 365.
Greene, John, 228.
Greene, Nicholas Biddulph, 29.
Greer, Samuel, 108.
Grennanstown, 434.
Grey, Sir George, 65, 68, 72, 145, 157, 169, 176, 229.

Habeus Corpus Act, Suspension of, 66-7.
Hackett, John, 61.
Hall, Sir Benjamin, 104.
Haly, Bishop Francis, 56, 258, 318, 331, 339-40, 417.
Hamilton, J.H. , 266.
Hamilton, Maxwell, 246.
Hampstead Heath, 405.
Hampton, 402.
Hanly, John, 351, 354, 365.
Harney, Charles, 12-3.
Hatchell, John, 128.
Haughton, Samuel, 266.
Hayter, W.G., 138, 308, 364.
Her Majesty's Theatre, 51.
Hertfordshire, 397.
Heywood, James, 131.
Hibernian Hotel, Sligo, 350.
Hickey, Fr Patrick, 261.
Higgins, Ouseley, 228, 231, 341.
Highgate Cemetery, 406.
Hobhouse, Sir, J.C. , 130.
Hoey, John Cashel, 415, 418.
Holycross, 16, 101.
Home, Thomas, 428, 445.
Howley, Fr. James, 436-7, 439.
Huddleston, Mary, 6, 11.
Huddleston, Richard, 10.
Hughes, John Cardinal, 170.

Hume, Joseph, 103, 129.
Hyde, John, 100.

Imperial Hotel, Cork, 238.
Incumbered Estates Court, 211.
Incumbered Estates Acts, 87-92, 98-9, 230.
India, 130.
Ingram, Herbert, 49, 101, 234.
Inverness, 121.
Ireland Imperialised, 215.
Irish Catholic Directory, 161.
Isle of Wight, 300.

Jack Straw's Castle, 405.
Jameson, James, 266.
Jewish Rights, 124-6.
Johnstone, Rev. Edward, 402.
Judgement Debtors Act, 89.
Judgements (Ireland) Bill, 95.
Jury System, 127-8.

Kanturk, 237.
Keane, Bishop William, 226.
Kearney, Fr. John, 259.
Keating, Leonard, 12, 29, 61, 62, 102.
Keating, Lucy, [nee Scully], 12.
Keating, Robert, 60, 164, 189, 274, 339, 341-3, 372, 386-7, 394, 404-6, 457.
Kells, 248, 341-2.
Kelly, Christopher, (Kit), 341, 364.
Kelly Sir Fitzroy, 170, 441, 443.
Kelly, James, 460.
Kelly, William, 393-4, 397, 430.
Kemmis, William, 429-30, 434.
Kenilworth, 435.

Kenmare, Earl of, 92.
Kennedy, James B., 27-8, 49, 208, 236, 273, 357, 371, 386-7, 389, 402, 423-4, 426, 445.
Kennedy, Patrick F., 369-70.
Kennedy, R.H., 398.
Kennedy, Tristram, 288.
Kennedy, Wilson, 28, 120-1, 232, 371, 385, 393, 427-8, 445.
Kennedy, Fr Peter, 16-7.
Kenyon, Fr John, 271.
Keogh, William, 109, 127, 141, 162, 165, 167, 191, 195-6, 198, 200, 204-6, 208-9, 214-7, 228, 231, 235, 246-7, 259-60, 262-3, 284-5, 292, 298, 300-1, 308-9, 342, 346-7, 361, 379, 416, 459.
Kerry, 94.
Kerry Savings Bank, 195.
Kilcommon, 107,
Kilcommon, Estate, 385, 389-90, 393, 458.
Kilconcouse Crown Estate, 364, 369-70.
Kilconnell, 456.
Kildare, 232.
Kildare and Leighlin, 159.
Kilfeacle, 4, 5, 12.
Kilkenny, 2, 3, 72-3, 421, 441, 455.
Kilkenny Academy, 9.
Kilkenny Corporation, 315.
Killala, 342.
Killaloe, 342-3.
Killarney, 92.
Killenaule, 25.
Killusty, 422, 435.
Kilnehalagh, 2.
Kilsaran, 137.
Kilymaenllwyd, 135.
Kingston, Earl of, 26-7, 99, 100, 392, 458.
Kingstown, 434.
Kingswilliamstown Estate, 459.

506